RETHINKING THE RELATIONSHIP BETWEEN INTERNATIONAL, EU AND NATIONAL LAW

The book's interdisciplinary embedding and novel conceptual approach to addressing the relationship between legal orders offers a significant and original contribution to the literature. The first part of the book provides an analytical account of the dominant approaches to explaining this relationship, criticizing theories of Kelsenian monism, dualism, legal pluralism and constitutionalism. In the second part, Kirchmair engages with an innovative idea by applying insights from social contract theory to the relationship between international, EU and Member State law and establishes his theoretical approach: consent-based monism. The book focuses on the main structural features of the external relations law of the EU as well as the primacy of EU law over national constitutional identity, which is demonstrated in the third part.

LANDO KIRCHMAIR specializes in international, European and national public law as well as legal philosophy. He is currently Deputy Professor for National and International Public Law with a Focus on the Protection of Cultural Heritage at the University of the Bundeswehr Munich. His interests include the interplay between the international, EU and national legal orders, the doctrine of sources of (international/EU) law, the law of technology, the protection of cultural heritage and interdisciplinarity.

ASIL Studies in International Legal Theory

The purpose of the ASIL Studies in International Legal Theory series is to clarify and improve the theoretical foundations of international law. Too often the progressive development and implementation of international law has foundered on confusion about first principles. This series raises the level of public and scholarly discussion about the structure and purposes of the world legal order and how best to achieve global justice through law.

This series grows out of the International Legal Theory project of the American Society of International Law. The ASIL Studies in International Legal Theory series deepens this conversation by publishing scholarly monographs and edited volumes of essays considering subjects in international legal theory.

Books in the series

Rethinking the Relationship between International, EU and National Law Lando Kirchmair

Consenting to International Law Edited by Samantha Besson

The Death Penalty's Denial of Fundamental Human Rights John Bessler

Theories of International Responsibility Law Edited by Samantha Besson

Human Dignity in International Law Ginevra Le Moli

Tipping Points in International Law: Commitment and Critique Edited by Jean d'Aspremont and John D. Haskell

Ethical Leadership in International Organizations: Concepts, Narratives, Judgment, and Assessment Edited by Maria Varaki and Guilherme Vasconcelos Vilaça

Whither the West?: Concepts on International Law in Europe and the United States Edited by Chiara Giorgetti and Guglielmo Verdirame

International Law as Behavior Edited by Harlan Grant Cohen and Timothy Meyer

Space and Fates of International Law: Between Leibniz and Hobbes Ekaterina Yahyaoui Krivenko

Why Punish Perpetrators of Mass Atrocities?: Purposes of Punishment in International Criminal Law Edited by Florian Jeßberger and Julia Geneuss

The Challenge of Inter-Legality Edited by Jan Klabbers and Gianluigi Palombella

The Nature of International Law Miodrag A. Jovanović

Reexamining Customary International Law Edited by Brian D. Lepard

Theoretical Boundaries of Armed Conflict and Human Rights Edited by Jens David Ohlin

Human Rights in Emergencies Edited by Evan J. Criddle

The Theory of Self-Determination Edited by Fernando R. Tesón

Negotiating State and Non-State Law: Global and Local Legal Pluralism Edited by Michael A. Helfand

Jus Post Bellum *and Transitional Justice* Edited by Larry May and Elizabeth Edenberg

Normative Pluralism and International Law: Exploring Global Governance Edited by Jan Klabbers and Touko Piipaerinen

The Future of International Law: Global Government Joel P. Trachtman

Morality, Jus Post Bellum, *and International Law* Edited by Larry May and Andrew T. Forcehimes

Global Justice and International Economic Law: Opportunities and Prospects Edited by Chios Carmody, Frank J. Garcia, and John Linarelli

Parochialism, Cosmopolitanism, and the Foundations of International Law Edited by M. N. S. Sellers

The Role of Ethics in International Law Edited by Donald Earl Childress III

The New Global Law Rafael Domingo

Customary International Law: A New Theory with Practical Applications Brian D. Lepard

International Criminal Law and Philosophy Edited by Larry May and Zachary Hoskins

Rethinking the Relationship between International, EU and National Law

CONSENT-BASED MONISM

LANDO KIRCHMAIR
University of the Bundeswehr Munich

CAMBRIDGE
UNIVERSITY PRESS

CAMBRIDGE
UNIVERSITY PRESS

Shaftesbury Road, Cambridge CB2 8EA, United Kingdom

One Liberty Plaza, 20th Floor, New York, NY 10006, USA

477 Williamstown Road, Port Melbourne, VIC 3207, Australia

314–321, 3rd Floor, Plot 3, Splendor Forum, Jasola District Centre, New Delhi – 110025, India

103 Penang Road, #05–06/07, Visioncrest Commercial, Singapore 238467

Cambridge University Press is part of Cambridge University Press & Assessment, a department of the University of Cambridge.

We share the University's mission to contribute to society through the pursuit of education, learning and research at the highest international levels of excellence.

www.cambridge.org
Information on this title: www.cambridge.org/9781009380201

DOI: 10.1017/9781009380171

First published 2024

A catalogue record for this publication is available from the British Library

Library of Congress Cataloging-in-Publication Data
NAMES: Kirchmair, Lando, author.
TITLE: Rethinking the relationship between international, EU, and national law : consent-based monism / Lando Kirchmair.
DESCRIPTION: Cambridge, United Kingdom ; New York, NY : Cambridge University Press, 2024. | Includes bibliographical references and index.
IDENTIFIERS: LCCN 2023035033 (print) | LCCN 2023035034 (ebook) | ISBN 9781009380201 (hardback) | ISBN 9781009380157 (paperback) | ISBN 9781009380171 (ebook)
SUBJECTS: LCSH: International and municipal law–European Union countries. | Court of Justice of the European Communities. | Constitutional courts–European Union countries. | Conflict of laws–European Union countries. | Monism.
CLASSIFICATION: LCC KJE5057 .K55 2024 (print) | LCC KJE5057 (ebook) | DDC 340.9094–dc23/eng/20231003
LC record available at https://lccn.loc.gov/2023035033
LC ebook record available at https://lccn.loc.gov/2023035034

ISBN 978-1-009-38020-1 Hardback

Contents

Figures and Tables

FIGURES

TABLES

Preface

The core idea behind this book engages with an insight which seems to me, by now (after several years of thinking about it), to be surprisingly obvious. Nevertheless, as far as I am aware, nobody has pursued the idea so far. Essentially, this book applies insights from social contract theory to the relationship between international, European Union and national law alike. I consider this patently obvious as the EU, for instance, is based on treaties and public referenda. There is no other organization or legal community as developed and sophisticated as the EU that is actually based on treaties to which individuals had to give their explicit consent (albeit sometimes via representatives of their Member States). Those treaties, hence, are largely legitimized by public referenda held in the Member States. However, in this book I do not engage with the usual goals of social contract theories, which are to legitimize and justify moral duties. Instead, I draw on a somewhat more neutral account of social contract theory with the simple aim of engaging in a structural analysis of the relationship between international, EU and national law. While this area has been largely dominated so far by theories of Kelsenian monism, dualism and, nowadays, global legal pluralism and global constitutionalism, I argue that all those theories are, for various reasons, unable to answer the key question. In order to find out how we can know who has the final say, I suggest engaging with social contract theory and its basic tenet *pacta sunt servanda*. Consent-based monism, so goes the argument, allows us to focus on the most important structural characteristics of the relationship between international and EU law as well as the relationship between EU and Member State law. In a rather straightforward way, I want to offer the insight that this has some important implications for the effect of international law in the EU and national legal orders.

Acknowledgments

I am always disappointed when a book lacks a preface: it is like arriving at someone's house for dinner, and being conducted straight into the dining-room. A preface is personal, the body of the book impersonal: the preface tells you the author's feelings about his book, or some of them. A reader who wishes to remain aloof can skip the preface without loss; but one who wants to be personally introduced has, I feel, the right to be.

Michael Dummett, *Frege: Philosophy of Language*

As the subject of this book is law, it feels wrong to deny the reader what philosopher Michael Dummett called the reader's *right* to a personal introduction. To me, such a personal introduction means expressing my gratitude, for if I had not been lucky enough to get to know several important people, this book would not exist. Without Kirsten Schmalenbach, I probably would never have become part of an academic faculty (but would have become a music band manager). I am grateful to her for her support since my first stumbling steps at university as a PhD candidate and even more so as she continues to care to this day. Gudrun Zagel is responsible for facilitating my somewhat more independent steps at university – without her, very likely, I would have been let loose on the unsuspecting world as a business consultant. Daniel-Erasmus Khan has been a true inspiration ever since I met him for the first time – and will continue to be so. It is his support, encouragement and, above all, his passion for academia that I am most thankful for having received and experienced. I could not imagine a better mentor than him. Likewise, Christina Binder took and still is taking care of my academic adventures – thank you. András Jakab is a true role model of an academic to me. Since our meeting years ago, he has taught me many things about how academia works and how academic works work, and, even more importantly, he enabled me to regain what I call my "juridical creativity" when I had lost it. Michael Thaler saved the world from probably the worst carpenter you can imagine. He is a constant source of the most useful advice, without which

I would have committed many more mistakes in academia than I actually have done. Without Helen Heaney and Joan Dale Lace, this book would probably be much harder to read. Sebastian Ambros was kind enough to review the proofs.

Beyond these wonderful people, I was always extremely lucky to have the best colleagues: Jane Alice Hofbauer, Philipp Janig, Florian Lehne, Donald Riznik and Cornelia Schäffer in the Department of Social Sciences and Public Affairs at the University of the Bundeswehr Munich, as well as Sebastian Krempelmeier, Norbert Paulo, Isabel Staudinger, Teresa Weber and Paul Weismann in the Law Faculty at the University of Salzburg, to name just a few. All of them were important discussion partners and friends during the process of writing this book and without every single one of them this book would be different – in a negative way.

Institutionally, I am very grateful to the Department of Social Sciences and Public Affairs at the University of the Bundeswehr Munich, and its former Deans Stephan Stetter and Kathrin Groh, as well as its current Dean Marc Frey, for providing a perfect environment to teach and carry out research. In particular, the encouragement to use interdisciplinary approaches makes for a pleasant and stimulating research environment. Reinhard Klaushofer is a wonderful head of the Department for Public Law, Public International Law and European Union Law at the University of Salzburg. I also owe appreciation to the former head Benjamin Kneihs. Beyond that, I am grateful for research stays at the Max Planck Institute for Comparative Public Law and International Law and to its Co-Director Armin von Bogdandy for his invitation, as well as the HAS Centre for Social Sciences, Institute for Legal Studies at the Hungarian Academy of Science and its former Director András Jakab.

It is also my pleasure to acknowledge that a previous (longer) version of this book was accepted as a *Habilitationsschrift* by the Department of Social Sciences and Public Affairs at the University of the Bundeswehr Munich. My profound gratitude – despite the risk of repeating myself – goes to the members of the *Fachmentorat*, Daniel-Erasmus Khan, András Jakab and Kirsten Schmalenbach, for their generous support and advice. I am also most grateful for what I experienced as truly stimulating and encouraging expert opinions provided by Theo Öhlinger and Ulrich Fastenrath; now that the process has been accomplished I can say out loud that I admire them both for their elegance and rigor. Sadly, Theo Öhlinger did not live to see this. I hope he knew how much I admired him and how important he was to me and many others. Beyond these individuals, I am thankful to the whole department for entrusting me with the *venia legendi*.

Parts of this book have been presented at various conferences and workshops, among other venues, at the University of the Bundeswehr Munich, the European

University Institute, Florence, the University of Gießen, the University of Hull, the International Academy of Comparative Law's Younger Scholars Forum in Fukuoka, the International Society of Public Law conference in Copenhagen, the V. Tagung für praktische Philosophie, the Internationale Vereinigung für Rechts- und Sozialphilosophie's world congress in Washington, DC, the Institute for Legal Studies at the Hungarian Academy of Science, Budapest, the fourth meeting of the International Network on Transnational Legal and Political Theory at the University of Cartagena and the University of Salzburg. I am furthermore grateful for discussions, comments and helpful critique from Frances Buttelmann, Maksymilian Del Mar, Matthias Goldmann, Klaus Günther, Tamás Hoffmann, Stephan Kirste, Jan Klabbers, Friedrich Lohmann, Dirk Lüddecke, Ralf Michaels, John Mikhail, Sophie Milward, Christoph Möllers, Norbert Paulo, Otto Pfersmann, Csaba Pléh, Thomas Rauter, Donald Riznik, Mortimer N. S. Sellers, Gábor Sulyok, Szilárd Tattay, Michael Tomasello, Vassilis Tzevelekos and Neil Walker, as well as to the editors and anonymous reviewers of the *European Journal of Legal Studies*, the *German Yearbook of International Law*, the *Goettingen Journal of International Law*, the *Journal of Legal Pluralism and Unofficial Law*, the *Journal of Theoretical and Philosophical Psychology* and the *Zeitschrift für praktische Philosophie*, where I published earlier versions of some parts of this book. I am grateful to the publishers of these journals for permission to reprint (reworked) parts of these papers in this book. It remains clear, however, and belongs to the nature of such a book, that any errors that remain are my sole responsibility. Moreover, I am most grateful to Mortimer N. S. Sellers and Mark David Agrast for accepting my book as part of the ASIL Studies in International Legal Theory series. A big thank-you also goes to Tom Randall, Marianne Nield and Shaheer Anwarali at Cambridge University Press and anonymous reviewers for very helpful suggestions.

Last, and by no means least, an enormous portion of gratitude goes to my family and friends. It holds true for everyone mentioned so far that I would be a different person without meeting them. For my family and friends, this is even truer. They know that. So I will pick out only some of them. Without my grandmother, I would have had a much harder time learning what I think by now is essential for a good life. My father taught me many things, as long as I had the chance to be with him. He would not satisfy my curiosity as a child by telling me truisms but would only provide me with clues to how I could find out the answers to my questions on my own. My mum is the most wonderful person I know. Without her, nothing would be as it is – not me, and hence, not this book either. Christina, finally, my love and my wife: Without your joy, kindness and patience I would not be able to do what I do. How grateful I feel by far surpasses what I am capable of expressing with words.

Table of Cases

COURT OF JUSTICE OF THE EUROPEAN UNION

Case 26/62 *Van Gend & Loos v Netherlands* ECLI:EU:C:1963:1.
Case 6/64 *Costa v ENEL* ECLI:EU:C:1964:66.
Case 28/67 *Firma Molkerei-Zentrale Westfalen/Lippe GmbH v Hauptzollamt Paderborn* ECLI:EU:C:1968:17.
Case 29/69 *Erich Stauder v Stadt Ulm – Sozialamt* ECLI:EU:C:1969:57.
Case 11/70 *Internationale Handelsgesellschaft* ECLI:EU:C:1970:114.
Case 22/70 *Commission v Council* ECLI:EU:C:1971:32.
Joined Cases 21/72 to 24/72 *International Fruit Company NV and Others* ECLI:EU:C:1972:115.
Case 9/73 *Carl Schlüter v Hauptzollamt Lörrach* ECLI:EU:C:1973:110.
Case 181/73 *R. & V. Haegeman v Belgium* ECLI:EU:C:1974:41.
Case 87/75 *Conceria Daniele Bresciani v Amministrazione Italiana delle Finanze* ECLI:EU:C:1976:18.
Joined Cases 3, 4 and 6/76 *Cornelis Kramer and Others* ECLI:EU:C:1976:114.
Case 33/76 *Rewe-Zentralfinanz eG and Rewe-Zentral AG v Landwirtschaftskammer für das Saarland* ECLI:EU:C:1976:188.
Case 106/77 *Amministrazione delle Finanze dello Stato v Simmenthal SpA* ECLI:EU:C:1978:49.
Case 138/79 *SA Roquette Frères v Council* ECLI:EU:C:1980:249.
Case 270/80 *Polydor Limited and RSO Records Inc v Harlequin Records Shops Limited and Simons Records Limited* ECLI:EU:C:1982:43.
Case 17/81 *Pabst & Richarz KG v Hauptzollamt Oldenburg* ECLI:EU:C:1982:129.
Case 283/81 *Srl CILFIT and Lanificio di Gavardo SpA v Ministry of Health* ECLI:EU:C:1982:335.

Case 104/81 *Hauptzollamt Mainz v C.A. Kupferberg & Cie KG a.A.* ECLI:EU:C:1982:362.
Case 294/83 *Parti ecologiste "Les Verts" v European Parliament* ECLI:EU:C:1986:166.
Case 12/86 *Meryem Demirel v Stadt Schwäbisch Gmünd* ECLI:EU:C:1987:400.
Case 314/85 *Foto-Frost v Hauptzollamt Lübeck-Ost* ECLI:EU:C: 1987:452.
Case 104/86 *Commission v Italy* ECLI:EU:C:1988:171.
Case 70/87 *Fediol v Commission* ECLI:EU:C:1989:254.
Case 30/88 *Hellenic Republic v Commission* ECLI:EU:C:1989:422.
Case C-192/89 *S. Z. Sevince v Staatssecretaris van Justitie* ECLI:EU:C:1990:322.
Case C-69/89 *Nakajima v Council* ECLI:EU:C:1991:186.
Case C-6/90 and C-9/90 *Francovich v Italy* ECLI:EU:C:1991:428.
Case C-163/90 *Administration des Douanes et Droits Indirects v Léopold Legros and others* ECLI:EU:C:1992:326.
Case C-286/90 *Anklagemindigheden v Poulsen and Diva Navigation* ECLI:EU:C:1992:453.
Case C-207/91 *Eurim-Pharm GmbH v Bundesgesundheitsamt* ECLI:EU:C:1993:278.
Case C-312/91 *Procedural issue relating to a seizure of goods belonging to Metalsa Srl* ECLI:EU:C:1993:279.
Case C-405/92 *Etablissements Armand Mondiet SA v Armement Islais SARL* ECLI:EU:C:1993:906.
Case C-327/91 *France v Commission* ECLI:EU:C:1994:305.
Case C-280/93 *Germany v Council* ECLI:EU:C:1994:367.
Case C-290/94 *Commission v Greece* ECLI:EU:C:1996:265.
Case C-61/94 *Commission v Germany* ECLI:EU:C:1996:313.
Case C-162/96 *Racke v Hauptzollamt Mainz* ECLI:EU:C:1998:293.
Case C-10/97 *IN.CO.GE.'90 and others* ECLI:EU:C:1998:498.
Case C-149/96 *Portugal v Council* ECLI:EU:C:1999:574.
Case C-329/97 *Sezgin Ergat v Stadt Ulm* ECLI:EU:C:2000:133.
Joined Cases C-300/98 and C-392/98 *Parfums Christian Dior SA v TUK Consultancy BV and Assco Gerüste GmbH and Rob van Dijk v Wilhelm Layher GmbH & Co KG and Layher BV* ECLI:EU:C:2000:688.
Case C-162/99 *Commission v Italy* ECLI:EU:C:2001:35.
Case C-307/99 *OGT Fruchthandelsgesellschaft mbH v Hauptzollamt Hamburg–St Annen* ECLI:EU:C:2001:228.
Joined Cases C-27/00 and C-122/00 *The Queen v Secretary of State for the Environment, Transport and the Regions, ex parte Omega Air Ltd (C-27/00)*

and Omega Air Ltd, Aero Engines Ireland Ltd and Omega Aviation Services Ltd v Irish Aviation Authority (C-122/00) ECLI:EU:C:2002:161.

Case C-476/98 *Commission v Germany* ECLI:EU:C:2002:631.

Case C-76/00 P *Petrotub SA and Republica SA v Council of the European Union* ECLI:EU:C:2003:4.

Case C-112/00 *Eugen Schmidberger, Internationale Transporte und Planzüge v Republik Österreich* ECLI:EU:C:2003:333.

Case C-211/01 *Commission v Council* ECLI:EU:C:2003:452.

Case C-93/02 P *Biret International SA v Council of the European Union* ECLI:EU:C:2003:517.

Case C-233/02 *France v Commission* ECLI:EU:C:2004:173.

Case C-286/02 *Bellio F.lli Srl v Prefettura di Treviso* ECLI:EU:C:2004:212.

Case C-377/02 *Léon Van Parys* ECLI:EU:C:2005:121.

Case C-344/04 *The Queen, on the application of International Air Transport Association and European Low Fares Airline Association v Department for Transport* ECLI:EU:C:2006:10.

Case C-311/04 *Algemene Scheeps Agentuur Dordrecht BV v Inspecteur der Belastingdienst – Douanedistrict Rotterdam* ECLI:EU:C:2006:23.

Case C-459/03 *Commission of the European Communities v Ireland* ECLI:EU:C:2006:345.

Joined Cases C-317/04 and C-318/04 *European Parliament v Council and Commission* ECLI:EU:C:2006:346.

Case C-431/05 *Merck Genéricos – Produtos Farmacêuticos Ld^{a} v Merck & Co Inc and Merck Sharp & Dohme Ld^{a}* ECLI:EU:C:2007:496.

Case C-351/04 *Ikea* ECLI:EU:C:2007:547.

Case C-426/05 *Tele2 Telecommunication GmbH v Telekom-Control-Kommission* ECLI:EU:C:2008:103.

Case C-308/06 *The Queen, on the application of International Association of Independent Tanker Owners (Intertanko) and Others v Secretary of State for Transport* ECLI:EU:C:2008:312.

Joined Cases C-402/05 P and C-415/05 P *Kadi and Al Barakaat International Foundation v Council and Commission* ECLI:EU:C:2008:461.

Joined Cases C-120/06 and C-121/06 P *Fabbrica italiana accumulatori motocarri Montecchio SpA (FIAMM) and Fabbrica italiana accumulatori motocarri Montecchio Technologies LLC (C-120/06 P), Giorgio Fedon & Figli SpA and Fedon America, Inc. (C-121/06 P) v Council* ECLI:EU:C:2008:476.

Case C-203/07 P *Greece v Commission* ECLI:EU:C:2008:606.

Case C-228/06 *Mehmet Soysal und Ibrahim Savatli v Germany* ECLI:EU:C:2009:101.

Case C-314/08 *Krzysztof Filipiak v Dyrektor Izby Skarbowej w Poznaniu* ECLI:EU:C:2009:719.
Case C-386/08 *Firma Brita GmbH v Hauptzollamt Hamburg-Hafen* ECLI:EU:C:2010:91.
Case C-533/08 *TNT Express Nederland BV v AXA Versicherung AG* ECLI:EU:C:2010:243.
Case C-428/08 *Monsanto Technology LLC v Cefetra BV* ECLI:EU:C:2010:402.
Case C-409/06 *Winner Wetten GmbH v Bürgermeisterin der Stadt Bergheim* ECLI:EU:C:2010:503.
Joined Cases C-288/09 and C-289/09 *British Sky Broadcasting Group plc (C-288/09) and Pace plc (C-289/09) v The Commissioners for Her Majesty's Revenue & Customs ECLI*:EU:C:2011:248.
Case C-399/09 *Marie Landtová v Česká správa socialního zabezpečení* ECLI:EU:C:2011:415.
Case C-548/09 P *Bank Melli Iran* ECLI:EU:C:2011:735.
Case C-366/10 *Air Transport Association of America and others v Secretary of State for Energy and Climate Change* ECLI:EU:C:2011:864.
Case C-135/10 *Società Consortile Fonografici (SCF) v Marco Del Corso* ECLI:EU:C:2012:140.
Case C-130/10 *Parliament v Council* ECLI:EU:C:2012:472.
Case C-364/10 *Hungary v Slovak Republic* ECLI:EU:C:2012:630.
Case C-286/12 *European Commission v Hungary* ECLI:EU:C:2012:687.
Joined Cases C-320/11, C-330/11, C-382/22 and C-383/11 *Digitalnet OOD and Others v Nachalnik na Mitnicheski punkt – Varna Zapad pri Mitnitsa Varna* ECLI:EU:C:2012:745.
Case C-617/10 *Åkerberg Fransson* ECLI:EU:C:2013:105.
Case C-399/11 *Stefano Melloni v Ministerio Fiscal* ECLI:EU:C:2013:107.
Joined Cases C-335/11 and C-337/11 *HK Danmark, acting on behalf of Jette Ring v Dansk almennyttigt Boligselskab (C-335/11) and HK Danmark, acting on behalf of Lone Skouboe Werge v Dansk Arbejdsgiverforening, acting on behalf of Pro Display A/S (C-337/11)* ECLI:EU:C:2013:222.
Case C-584, C-593, & C-595/10P *Commission v Kadi* ECLI:EU:C:2013:518.
Case C-595/10 P *Commission and others v Kadi* ECLI:EU:C:2013:518.
Case C-414/11 *Daiichi Sankyo Co Ltd and Sanofi-Aventis Deutschland GmbH v DEMO Anonymos Viomichaniki kai Emporiki Etairia Farmakon* ECLI:EU:C:2013:520.
Case C-137/12 *Commission v Council* ECLI:EU:C:2013:675.
Case C-206/13 *Siragusa* ECLI:EU:C:2014:126.

Case C-363/12 *Z. v A Government department and The Board of management of a community school* ECLI:EU:C:2014:159.
Case C-356/12 *Wolfgang Glatzel v Freistaat Bayern* ECLI:EU:C:2014:350.
Case C-377/12 *Commission v Council* ECLI:EU:C:2014:1903.
Case C-658/11 *Parliament v Council* ECLI:EU:C:2014:2025.
Case C-198/13 *Hérnandez ea v Reino de España* ECLI:EU:C:2014:2055.
Case C-114/12 *Commission v Council* ECLI:EU:C:2014:2151.
Case C-399/12 *Germany v Council* ECLI:EU:C:2014:2258.
Joined Cases C-401/12 P to C-403/12 P *Council v Vereniging Milieudefensie and Stichting Stop Luchtverontreiniging Utrecht* ECLI:EU:C:2015:4.
Joined Cases C-464/13 and C-465/13 *Oberto* ECLI:EU:C:2015:163.
Case C-425/13 *Commission v Council* ECLI:EU:C:2015:483.
Case C-105/14 *Criminal proceedings against Ivo Taricco and Others* ECLI:EU:C:2015:555.
Case C-263/14 *European Parliament v Council* ECLI:EU:C:2016:435.
Case C-543/14 *Ordre des barreaux francophones et germanophone and Others* ECLI:EU:C:2016:605.
Case C-687/15 *Commission v Council* ECLI:EU:C:2017:803.
Case C-42/17 *Criminal proceedings against MAS und MB* ECLI:EU:C:2017:936.
Case C-64/16 *Associação Sindical dos Juízes Portugueses v Tribunal de Contas* ECLI:EU:C:2018:117.
Case C-284/16 *Slovak Republic v Achmea BV* ECLI:EU:C:2018:158.
Case C-612/15 *Kolev ea* ECLI:EU:C:2018:392.
Case C-244/17 *Commission v Council* ECLI:EU:C:2018:662.
Case C-416/17 *Commission v France* ECLI:EU:C:2018:811.
Case C-167/17 *Klohn v An Bord Pleanála* ECLI:EU:C:2018:833.
Case C-207/17 *Rotho Blaas Srl v Agenzia delle Dogane e dei Monopoli* ECLI:EU:C:2018:840.
Case C-493/17 *Weiss et al* ECLI:EU:C:2018:1000.
Case C-219/17 *Silvio Berlusconi and Finanziaria d'investimento Fininvest SpA (Fininvest) v Banca d'Italia and Istituto per la Vigilanza Sulle Assicurazioni (IVASS)* ECLI:EU:C:2018:1023.
Case C-202/18 and C-238/18 *Ilmārs Rimšēvičs and European Central Bank v Republic of Latvia* ECLI:EU:C:2019:139.
Case C-896/19 *Repubblika v Il-Prim Ministru* ECLI:EU:C:2021:311.
Case C-487/19 W Ż ECLI:EU:C:2021:798.
Case C-561/19 *Consorzio Italian Management e Catania Multiservizi and Catania Multiservizi* ECLI:EU:C:2021:799.

Joined Cases C-357/19, C-379/19, C-547/19, C-811/19 and C-840/19 *Euro Box Promotion ea* ECLI:EU:C:2021:1034.
Case C-430/21 *RS* ECLI:EU:C:2022:99.
Case C-261/21 *F Hoffmann-La Roche Ltd ea v Autorità Garante della Concorrenza e del Mercato* ECLI:EU:C:2022:534.
Case C-629/21 P(R) *Puigdemont i Casamajó ea v Parliament and Spain* ECLI:EU:C:2022:413.
Infringement action brought by the *Commission against Hungary* Case C-769/22.
Opinion 1/75 *Understanding on a Local Cost Standard* ECLI:EU:C:1975:145.
Opinion 1/76 *Draft Agreement establishing a European laying-up fund for inland waterway vessels* ECLI:EU:C:1977:63.
Opinion 1/78 *International Agreement on Natural Rubber* ECLI:EU:C:1979:224.
Opinion 1/91 *Draft agreement between the Community, on the one hand, and the countries of the European Free Trade Association, on the other, relating to the creation of the European Economic Area* ECLI:EU:C:1991:490.
Opinion 1/92 *Draft agreement between the Community, on the one hand, and the countries of the European Free Trade Association, on the other, relating to the creation of the European Economic Area* ECLI:EU:C:1992:189.
Opinion 1/94 *Competence of the Community to conclude international agreements concerning services and the protection of intellectual property* ECLI:EU:C:1994:384.
Opinion 2/92 *Competence of the Community or one of its institutions to participate in the Third Revised Decision of the OECD on national treatment* ECLI:EU:C:1995:83.
Opinion 3/94 GATT – WTO – *Framework agreement on bananas* ECLI:EU:C:1995:436.
Opinion 2/94 *Accession by the Community to the European Convention for the Protection of Human Rights and Fundamental Freedoms* ECLI:EU:C:1996:140.
Opinion 2/20 *Cartagena Protocol* ECLI:EU:C:2001:664.
Opinion 1/00 *Proposed agreement between the European Community and non-Member States on the establishment of a European Common Aviation Area* ECLI:EU:C:2002:231.
Opinion 1/03 *Competence of the Community to conclude the new Lugano Convention on jurisdiction and the recognition and enforcement of judgments in civil and commercial matters* ECLI:EU:C:2006:81.

Opinion 1/08 *General Agreement on Trade in Services (GATS)* ECLI:EU: C:2009:739.

Opinion 1/09 *Draft Agreement – Creation of a unified patent litigation system* ECLI:EU:C:2011:123.

Opinion 2/13 *Draft international agreement – Accession of the European Union to the European Convention for the Protection of Human Rights and Fundamental Freedoms – Compatibility of the draft agreement with the EU and FEU Treaties* ECLI:EU:C:2014:2454.

Opinion 1/17 *Comprehensive Economic and Trade Agreement between Canada, of the one part, and the European Union and Its Member States, of the other part* (CETA) ECLI:EU:C:2019:341.

Opinion of advocate general Jacobs, C-162/96 *Racke v Hauptzollamt Mainz* ECLI:EU:C:1997:582.

Opinion of advocate general Kokott C-308/06 *The Queen, on the application of International Association of Independent Tanker Owners (Intertanko) and Others v Secretary of State for Transport* ECLI:EU:C:2007:689.

Opinion of advocate general Kokott, C-366/10 *Air Transport Association of America and others v Secretary of State for Energy and Climate Change* ECLI:EU:C:2011:637.

Opinion of advocate general Sharpston of 15 May 2014 in joined Cases C-103/12 and C-165/12, *Parliament and Commission v Council (Venezuelan Fishing Opportunities)* ECLI:EU:C:2014:334.

GENERAL COURT OF THE EUROPEAN UNION

Case T-115/94 *Opel Austria v Council* ECLI:EU:T:1997:3.

Case T-315/01 *Yassin Abdullah Kadi and Al Barakaat International Foundation v Council and Commission* ECLI:EU:T:2005:332.

Case T-231/04 *Greece v Commission* ECLI:EU:T:2007:9.

Case T-85/09 *Kadi v Commission* ECLI:EU:T:2010:418.

Case T-512/12 *Front populaire pour la libération de la saguia-el-hamra et du rio de oro (Front Polisario) v Council of the European Union* ECLI: EU:T:2015:953.

INTERNATIONAL COURT OF JUSTICE

ICJ *Reparation for Injuries Suffered in the Service of the United Nations*, Advisory Opinion of ICJ Reports [1949] 174.

ICJ *Asylum Case (Columbia v Peru)* Judgment ICJ Reports [1950] 266.

ICJ *Fisheries Case (United Kingdom v Norway)* Judgment ICJ Reports [1951] 116.
ICJ *North Sea Continental Shelf Cases (Federal Republic of Germany v Denmark; Federal Republic of Germany v Netherlands)* Judgment ICJ Reports [1969] 3.
ICJ *Military and Paramilitary Activities in and against Nicaragua (Nicaragua v. United States)* Judgment ICJ Reports [1986] 14.
ICJ *Land, Island and Maritime Frontier Dispute (El Salvador/Honduras: Nicaragua intervening)* Judgment ICJ Reports [1992] 3.
ICJ *Kasikili/Sedudu Island (Botswana/Namibia)* Judgment ICJ Reports [1999] 1075.
ICJ *LaGrand (Germany v USA)* Judgment ICJ Reports [2001] 466.
ICJ *Certain Questions of Mutual Assistance in Criminal Matters (Djibouti v France)* Judgment ICJ Reports [2008] 177.
ICJ *Jurisdictional Immunities of the State (Germany v Italy: Greece Intervening)* Judgment ICJ Reports [2012] 99.

NATIONAL CONSTITUTIONAL COURTS

Austria

Austrian Constitutional Court, Verfassungsgerichtshof VfSlg 14.886/1997.
Austrian Constitutional Court, Verfassungsgerichtshof VfSlg 15.427/1999.
Austrian Constitutional Court, Verfassungsgerichtshof VfSlg 15.450/1999.
Austrian Constitutional Court, Verfassungsgerichtshof VfSlg 17.065/2003.
Austrian Constitutional Court, Verfassungsgerichtshof VfSlg 19.632/2012.

Belgium

Belgian Cour d'Arbitrage, Decision of October 16, 1991 – 26/91, printed in (1992) Journal des Tribunaux 6670.
Belgian Constitutional Court, Cour Constitutionnelle Decision of March 15, 2018 No 29/2018.

Czech Republic

Czech Constitutional Court, Decision of February 14, 2012 – Pl Ús 5/12.

Denmark

Danish Supreme Court, Højesteret, Decision of April 6, 1998 – I 361/1997 (*Maastricht*).
Danish Supreme Court, Højesteret, Decision of February 20, 2013 – 199/2012 (*Lisbon*).
Danish Supreme Court, Højesteret, Decision of December 6, 2016 – 15/2014 (*Dansk Industri (DI) on behalf of Ajos A/S v Estate of Karsten Eigil Rasmussen*).

France

French Constitutional Council, Conseil Constitutionnel, Decision of July 26, 2018 No 2018-768 DC.
French State Council, Conseil d'État, Decision of April 21, 2021, No 393099.

Germany

BVerfGE 22, 293 (*EWG Verordnungen*).
BVerfGE 31, 145 (*Lütticke*).
BVerfGE 37, 271 (*Solange I*).
BVerfGE 58, 1 (*Eurocontrol I*).
BVerfGE 73, 339 (*Solange II*).
BVerfGE 75, 223 (*Kloppenburg*).
BVerfGE 89, 155 (*Maastricht*), English translation of the judgment in 1 (1994) Common Market Law Review 57.
BVerfGE 102, 147 (*Bananenmarktordnung*).
BVerfGE, 111, 307 (*Görgülü*).
BVerfGE 113, 273 (*European Arrest Warrant*).
BVerfGE 123, 267 (*Lisbon*), English translation available on the homepage of the German Federal Constitutional Court: www.bundesverfassungsgericht.de/SharedDocs/Entscheidungen/EN/2009/06/es20090630_2bve000208en.html [last accessed February 1, 2023].
BVerfGE 126, 286 (*Honeywell*).
BVerfGE 132, 195 (*ESM einstweiliger Rechtsschutz*).

BVerfGE 134, 366 (*OMT*), English translation available on the homepage of the German Federal Constitutional Court: www.bundesverfassungsgericht.de/SharedDocs/Entscheidungen/EN/2014/01/rs20140114_2bvr272813en.html [last accessed February 1, 2023].
BVerfGE 135, 317 (*ESM*).
BVerfGE, 140, 317 (*Identitätskontrolle*).
BVerfGE 141, 1 (*Völkerrechtsdurchbrechung*).
BVerfGE, 142, 123 (*OMT Decision*).
BVerfGE, 143, 65 (*CETA einstweiliger Rechtsschutz I*).
BVerfGE, 146, 216 (*PSPP Vorlage*).
BVerfGE 151, 202 (*Europäische Bankenunion*).
BVerfGE 152, 216 (*Recht auf Vergessen II*).
BVerfGE 154, 17 (*PSPP*).

Hungary

Hungarian Constitutional Court, Alkotmánybíróság, Decision of December 20, 32/2021 (XII. 20.) AB.

Italy

Italian Constitutional Court, Corte costituzionale, Decision No 183/73 of December 27, 1973 *Frontini* ECLI:IT:COST:1973:183, English translation available in (1974) 2 Common Market Law Review 372.
Italian Constitutional Court, Corte costituzionale, Decision No 170/84 of June 8, 1984 *Granital* ECLI:IT:COST:1984:170, English translation available in (1984) Common Market Law Review 756.
Italian Constitutional Court, Corte costituzionale, Order No 24 of 2017, available at www.giurcost.org/decisioni/2017/00240-17.html [English translation available at www.cortecostituzionale.it/documenti/download/doc/recent_judgments/O_24_2017.pdf] [last accessed February 1, 2023].
Italian Constitutional Court, Corte costituzionale, Decision No 20/2019 of January 23, 2019.

Poland

Polish Constitutional Tribunal, Trybunal Konstytucyjny, Decision of November 24, 2010, K 32/09 (*Lisbon Treaty*), English translation available at www.trybunal.gov.pl/eng/index.htm [last accessed February 1, 2023].

Polish Constitutional Tribunal, Trybunal Konstytucyjny, Decision of November 16, 2011, SK 45/09.

Polish Constitutional Tribunal, Trybunal Konstytucyjny, Decision of October 7, 2021, K 3/21.

Portugal

Portuguese Constitutional Tribunal, Tribunal Constitucional, Decision of July 15, 2020, No 422/2020 (Rapporteur: Justice José António Teles Pereira), English translation available at www.tribunalconstitucional.pt/tc/en/acordaos/20200422.html [last accessed February 1, 2023].

Romania

Rumanian Constitutional Court, Curtea Constituţională a României, Decision of June 8, 2021, No 390, published in the official Gazette No 612 of June 22, 2021, English translation available at www.ccr.ro/wp-content/uploads/2021/07/Decizie_390_2021_EN.pdf [last accessed February 1, 2023].

Spain

Spanish Constitutional Tribunal, Tribunal Constitucional de España, Decision of July 1, 1992, 108/1992, reprinted in (1993) Europäische Grundrechte-Zeitschrift 285.

Abbreviations

ACHR	American Convention on Human Rights
BGBl	Bundesgesetzblatt (Federal Law Gazette)
BVerfG	Bundesverfassungsgericht (German Federal Constitutional Court)
BVerfGE	Entscheidungen des Bundesverfassungsgerichts (Decisions of the German Federal Constitutional Court)
B-VG	Bundes-Verfassungsgesetz (Austrian Constitution)
CFR	Charter of Fundamental Rights of the European Union
CFSP	common foreign and security policy
CIL	customary international law
CJEU	Court of Justice of the European Union
EC	European Commission
ECB	European Central Bank
ECHR	European Convention on Human Rights
ECtHR	European Court of Human Rights
ECLI	European Case Law Identifier
ECC	General Court of the European Union
EP	European Parliament
ErläutRV	Erläuterungen zur Regierungsvorlage (Explanatory remarks to the government bill)
GATT	General Agreement on Tariffs and Trade
GG	Grundgesetz (German Basic Law)
ICJ	International Court of Justice
ICJ Statute	Statute of the International Court of Justice
ILC	International Law Commission
MS	Member States
OMT	Outright Monetary Transactions (ECB)

PSPP	Public Sector Purchase Programme (ECB)
SC	Security Council
TEU	Treaty on European Union
TFEU	Treaty on the Functioning of the European Union
UMG	universal moral grammar
UN	United Nations
UNCLOS	United Nations Convention on the Law of the Sea
VCLT	Vienna Convention on the Law of Treaties
VfGH	Verfassungsgerichtshof (Austrian Constitutional Court)
VfSlg	Verfassungssammlung (Decisions of the Austrian Constitutional Court)
VVDStRL	Veröffentlichungen der Vereinigung der Deutschen Staatsrechtslehrer (Publications of the German Association of Public Law Scholars)
WTO	World Trade Organization

Introduction

Setting the Stage

The relationship between international and national law has been debated for centuries. Generally, the floor has been divided between two approaches: dualism and monism, mostly as advocated by Hans Kelsen. I argue that, in the light of major developments since their inception, such as the establishment of the European Union (EU), these theories can no longer comprehensively explain the relationship between international, EU and national law. While dualism as developed by Heinrich Triepel liberated the international legal order from an overly dominant national perspective some 125 years ago, it is not well equipped to accommodate the massive overlaps between international, EU and Member State legal orders today. In Hans Kelsen's version, monism is an epistemological theory about what the law might be. It does not provide satisfactory guidance for the doctrinal solution of norm conflicts between international, EU and Member State law. Thus, a key focus of this book is to reconceptualize the theoretical relationship between legal orders. Even though some scholars have doubted the relevance of theoretical inquiries such as dualistic or monistic analyses of the relationship between legal orders, I cannot agree with those who trivialize this theoretical discussion by saying it would be "unreal, artificial and strictly beside the point."[1] If we continue reading Fitzmaurice's view, it becomes clear that this is simply a dualistic argument. Yet current developments, fundamental changes and new phenomena such as the massive increase in international institutions, actors, norms and tribunals as well as adjudicators make it imperative to seek new

[1] Gerald G Fitzmaurice, "The General Principles of International Law Considered from the Standpoint of the Rule of Law" (1957) 92 Recueil des Cours de l'Académie de Droit International 1–227 (71).

theoretical concepts. The so-called globalization of law[2] as framed in the famous constitutionalization of international law[3] may be mentioned, among other developments, to elucidate the ever-growing importance of the debate on whether international, EU or national law has the final say.[4]

I start from the assumption that it is essential to have a theoretical concept for the relationship between legal orders because I hold that we cannot discuss this relationship intelligibly in the absence of such a concept. Without a theoretical concept, underlying assumptions often remain implicit and are not addressed clearly.[5] This book is based on the conviction that a common (normative) denominator of international, EU and national law is necessary to solve norm conflicts between overlapping legal orders. Without such a common denominator, we are left with non-normative or unilateral solutions for norm conflicts between overlapping legal orders. Therefore, legal pluralism in whatever shape is no normative option. Global constitutionalism, in contrast, suffers from the shortcoming of presuming too many substantive

2 In relation to this designation, see Jean-Bernard Auby, "Globalisation et droit public" in *Gouverner, administrer, juger. Mélanges en l'honneur de Jean Waline* (Dalloz 2002) 135–157; Anne Peters, "The Globalization of State Constitutions" in Janne Nijman and Andre Nollkaemper (eds) *New Perspectives on the Divide between National and International Law* (Oxford University Press 2007) 251–308; see also David J Bederman, *Globalization and International Law* (Palgrave 2008); Neil Walker, *Intimations of Global Law* (Cambridge University Press 2014).

3 Alfred Verdross, *Die Verfassung der Völkerrechtsgemeinschaft* (Springer 1926); Jan Klabbers, *The Constitutionalization of International Law* (Oxford University Press 2009); Oliver Diggelmann and Tilmann Altwicker, "Is There Something Like a Constitution of International Law? A Critical Analysis of the Debate on World Constitutionalism" (2008) 68 Heidelberg Journal of International Law 623–650.

4 Mattias Kumm, "Who Is the Final Arbiter of Constitutionality in Europe? Three Conceptions of the Relationship between the German Federal Constitutional Court and the European Court of Justice" (1999) 36 Common Market Law Review 351–386 (384), famously held that "*within a pluralist framework, it does not make sense to speak of a final arbiter of constitutionality in Europe*" [emphasis original] and thus he thought that there are "good reasons to stop asking" the question on "the final arbiter of constitutionality in Europe." He did so by "replying" to a discussion between Theodor Schilling, "The Autonomy of the Community Legal Order: An Analysis of Possible Foundations" (1996) 37 (2) Harvard International Law Journal 389–409, and Joseph H H Weiler and Ulrich R Haltern, "The Autonomy of the Community Legal Order – Through the Looking Glass" (1996) 37 (2) Harvard International Law Journal 411–448.

5 Compare also András Jakab, *European Constitutional Language* (Cambridge University Press 2016) 1 quoting John Maynard Keynes, *The General Theory of Employment, Interest and Money* (Palgrave Macmillan 1936) 383 concerning economics: "The ideas of economists and political philosophers, both when they are right and when they are wrong, are more powerful than is commonly understood. Indeed the world is ruled by little else. Practical men, who believe themselves to be quite exempt from any intellectual influence, are usually the slaves of some defunct economist."

values for the envisaged common normative denominator in order to be a helpful concept for the relationship between international, EU and Member State law. Thus, global constitutionalism cannot carry what I term the "burden of universality" and with constitutional pluralism we are likely to end in a "constitutional stalemate."

In this book, I seek to offer new theoretical insights in particular concerning the relationship between international, EU and national law because I hold that the current approaches do not provide satisfactory accounts. Before doing so I will first critically review the current dominant theories (dualism, Kelsenian monism, global legal pluralism and global constitutionalism) on this relationship in Part I. The idea behind this critical reconstruction is to demonstrate the flaws of prominent theoretical explanations of the relationship between legal orders. This is guided by an "evolutionary approach." I am convinced that reconstructing the arguments of dualists, monists, pluralists and constitutionalists will remind us of the historical background of these theories. This will reveal two important insights. First, it highlights which questions were the most important to ask. And, second, we will see how these questions have been answered in the realm of their historical context. This assumes that there is no time-independent theoretical approach to answering pressing questions from different times.[6] We can still learn from earlier theoretical approaches. Yet, due to major developments, we need an up-to-date theoretical approach. This is what I will provide in Part II.

Hence, after rejecting available theories advanced in the first part of the book, I devote the second part to developing my own theoretical account to solve legal norm conflicts of EU law with international law and with Member State law. This is important as this book is guided by the conviction that we need a common denominator for legal norm conflicts if we do not want them to be solved by brute force. In order to find out how we can know which legal order is superior in the case of a norm conflict, I engage with *pacta sunt servanda*, which, arguably, is a foundational legal principle to all three legal orders and can thus serve as a common denominator. When we seek a

6 See Ralf Michaels, "Law and Recognition – Towards a Relational Concept of Law" in Nicole Roughan and Andrew Halpin (eds) *In Pursuit of Pluralist Jurisprudence* (Cambridge University Press 2017) 90–115 (91): "Questions as to the nature of law are never just definitional or ontological questions; they carry with them ideas of legitimacy, they serve a purpose, and they are always colored by the experience of the time and place in which they are proposed." With further reference in n 2 to Hermann Kantorowicz, *The Definition of Law* (Cambridge University Press 1958), and Julie Dickson, "Towards a Theory of European Union Legal Systems" in Julie Dickson and Pavlos Eleftheriadis (eds) *Philosophical Foundations of European Union Law* (Oxford University Press 2012) 25–53 (26–30).

doctrinal solution to conflicts between legal systems then the following need to be taken into account: (1) if we take the point of view of one of the legal orders as being superior to the other two or (2) if we have a measure external to the legal orders concerned or (3) if we can detect a common denominator to all legal orders involved. In order to establish the latter, I use the generic legal principle *pacta sunt servanda*, which, arguably, is a foundational legal principle to all three legal orders, because the other solutions available are either dualistic/pluralistic/monistic (in a Kelsenian version – not offering doctrinal solutions) or constitutionalist (which are value-laden, with too many values not embraced by all the legal orders involved for doctrinal solutions to work). Concerning (1) and (2), we do not have a common solution to the norm conflict, which is very likely to be unacceptable for one legal order involved, where the norm conflict solution is regarded as brute force. That is why this book follows approach number (3).

The practical question I aim to answer is the following: how can we know who has the final say – international, EU or national law? The way I respond to this question does not follow Kelsenian monism or dualism, or legal pluralism or constitutionalism.[7] I answer it by introducing the theoretical concept of consent-based monism (Part II). In short, consent-based monism aims at reconceptualizing the monism–dualism–pluralism–constitutionalism debate. The intention is to establish whether it is up to EU law (when confronted with international law) or national law (when confronted with EU law) to determine the effect and validity of international or EU law within the "domestic" (constitutional) legal order. Answering this question is essential to provide a theoretically sound reply as to how the relationship between legal orders can be conceptualized and to offer a solution to norm conflicts with EU law – be they norm conflicts between international law and EU law or norm conflicts between EU law and Member State law. In more general terms, I wish to provide a theoretical concept to answer the question of how we can know who has the final say.

This, so goes the argument, allows us to focus on the most important structural characteristics of the relationship between international, EU and national law. Concerning the relationship between EU and Member State law, I generally make the point that the division of competences is decisive. Concerning the external relations of the EU, I aim to show in a rather

[7] If you agree with me that current theories cannot offer a convincing account for norm conflict solution regarding the relationship between international, EU and national law, you can skip the critique of current theories (Part I) and proceed directly to Part II, the explication of consent-based monism.

straightforward way in the last two chapters how norm conflicts between international agreements and EU law as well as between customary international law and EU law can be solved. For such norm conflicts, the approach developed in this book arguably provides for a thin but sufficient common denominator.

This book engages with an innovative idea by applying insights from social contract theory to EU law and its relationship with international as well as Member State law. However, instead of engaging with the usual goals of social contract theories, which are to legitimize and justify moral duties, this book draws on a somewhat more neutral account of social contract theory with the simple aim of a structural analysis of the relationship between international and EU law as well as between EU law and Member State law.

Consent-based monism does not provide a general solution that fits any norm conflict stemming from overlapping legal orders. The purpose of this book is to develop a legal theory that facilitates understanding of the interaction between international, EU and national law. Consent-based monism shares its point of departure with most social contract theories: a hypothetical state imagined as a legal vacuum, denoted as the "legal desert." However, in contrast to political philosophy, the hypothesis behind consent-based monism aims solely to elucidate the structural relationship between legal orders, without saying anything about how legal orders in particular or society in general should be organized. The theory is thus based on an abstract definition of law – the necessary common (normative) denominator – as the binding consensus between natural persons. The basis of what constitutes the fundamental principle *pacta sunt servanda* is not, however, simply presupposed but found after an in-depth analysis of the origins of morality. While the most promising approach to an innate "universal moral grammar" (UMG) as advanced by John Mikhail is critically evaluated and rejected, innate intersubjectivity is identified as key to human cooperation. Its origins are highlighted in neurobiology as well as (developmental) psychology. On this basis, an argument will be established for the normative *pacta sunt servanda* principle.

Against the background of this theoretical foundation, I engage with practice (Part III), applying consent-based monism to the relationship between international, EU and national law. I present a doctrinal analysis of relevant provisions at EU level according to consent-based monism. I am convinced that a theory-based argument on the relationship of EU and Member State law will contribute to key questions of EU law, such as the doctrine of direct applicability or the primacy question between EU law and the fundamental constitutional law of its Member States. This theory will provide a convincing argument, solving potential tensions between the constitutional courts of the Member States and the Court of Justice of the EU (CJEU). For instance, arguments embedded in a sound theoretical explanation may help to clarify a potential stress ratio between European integration and the concept of (German) "constitutional identity," which, according to the German Federal Constitutional Court, is resistant to integration.[8]

Part III of this book provides an account of the doctrinal relationship between EU and Member State law. First, we will take a look at what a theoretically informed view of the relationship between EU and Member State law looks like in general. Then the book engages with the relationship between international and EU law by analyzing the effect of international agreements and customary international law, arguably the two most important sources of international law, and their effect on the EU legal order. After a doctrinal analysis of the status quo in case law and literature, I submit a somewhat different interpretation based on theoretical insights provided by consent-based monism. Finally, the major conclusions of this book will be outlined.

In brief, this book proposes a theory for international, EU and constitutional lawyers as well as for legal theorists about the relationship between legal orders. My intention is: (1) to present a critique of currently dominating theories; (2) to show in an intelligible theoretical manner my own answers to solving norm conflicts between legal orders; and (3) to demonstrate the practical relevance of this theoretical approach by presenting concrete examples of its application in a doctrinal fashion involving the relationship between the EU and Member State legal orders, as well as international agreements and customary international law and their effect on the EU legal order.

8 See the case law cited below in Section 7.1.2. For an overview, see Gerhard van der Schyff, "EU Member State Constitutional Identity: A Comparison of Germany and the Netherlands as Polar Opposites" (2016) 76 Heidelberg Journal of International Law 167–191.

PART I

Common Theories on the Relationship of Legal Orders and Their Flaws Concerning the EU Legal Order

Two lawyers have the task of discussing a problem and presenting a solution. After hours of painful negotiations, they come up with three different solutions. Is this just an ironic representation of the way lawyers see themselves? Bearing in mind the judgments of the Court of Justice of the European Union (CJEU) on the relationship between international and EU law and EU law and Member State law, however, this simple joke has much more than a grain of truth to it.

Once the European Community had begun to take shape and its institutional setting became more powerful, the quest started to clarify the relationship of this young institution to the laws of its Member States. The CJEU famously declared in *Costa v ENEL* that the law of the European Communities is itself a legal order. Furthermore, the CJEU stipulated in the *Van Gend en Loos* judgment that this law has a direct effect on the legal orders of the Member States.[1] Hence, the CJEU postulated the autonomy of the Community legal order for many years in order to unify EU and Member State law.[2] Yet, concerning the relationship of EU and international law, the CJEU also found it "important to note at the outset that Security Council

[1] See Case 26/62 *Van Gend & Loos v Netherlands* ECLI:EU:C:1963:1.

[2] See Case 6/64 *Costa v ENEL* ECLI:EU:C:1964:66 p 593: "[T]he EEC treaty has created its own legal system"; the German version has "*Rechtsordnung*"; the French version uses "*ordre juridique*"; see Opinion 1/91 *Draft agreement between the Community, on the one hand, and the countries of the European Free Trade Association, on the other, relating to the creation of the European Economic Area* ECLI:EU:C:1991:490 para 2, which postulated the "autonomy of the Community legal order"; compare the German version "*Autonomie des Rechtssystems der Gemeinschaft*"; see further on this Werner Schroeder, *Das Gemeinschaftsrechtssystem: Eine Untersuchung zu den rechtsdogmatischen, rechtstheoretischen und verfassungsrechtlichen Grundlagen des Systemdenkens im Europäischen Gemeinschaftsrecht* (Mohr Siebeck 2002) 104–105 (with further references in nn 6 and 7). See the more recent Case C-284/16 *Slovak Republic v Achmea BV* ECLI:EU:C:2018:158 para 33.

resolutions and Council common positions and regulations originate from distinct legal orders."[3]

We therefore have one and the same international organization introducing two different opinions. Depending on its own perspective – and not on the differing standpoint of an observer – the CJEU applies a unifying doctrine relating to its Member States and a separating doctrine relating to international law; in other words, two completely diverging doctrines. The relationship between international and national law has been, and probably always will be, a long-running debate in public international law. International organizations and supranational organizations such as the EU are obvious examples of entities based on international and EU law acting within the legal orders of its Member States as much as on the international stage. International organizations with decision-making capacities do have an enormous influence on and within the legal orders of Member States and even non-Member States.

Quite a few commentators were tempted to frame the relationship between EU and Member State law and between EU and international law in terms of two old but very dominant theories: dualism (Section 1.1) and monism (Section 1.2). The theoretical foundation of this relationship always was and still is dominated by the heavily disputed dualistic and monistic doctrines, which will be critically reviewed. The first chapter of this part aims at stress testing whether such an endeavor is promising or not. I will conclude that neither Kelsenian monism nor dualism is an appropriate tool to analyze current complex relationships between multifaceted legal orders.

Yet nor are more recent theories such as global legal pluralism (Section 2.1) or global constitutionalism (Section 2.2) very helpful in terms of analyzing the relationship and possible norm conflicts between the EU and other legal orders. While legal pluralism can provide a very powerful descriptive account of current developments, it lacks a clear prescriptive framework. Constitutionalism, on the other hand, too easily implies value questions from one legal order over another without ensuring the commonality of the values in question in both legal orders. Concerning these two approaches, I hold that neither global legal pluralism nor global constitutionalism is of much help when answering our question as to how we can know who has the final say on

3 See Case C-548/09 P *Bank Melli Iran* ECLI:EU:C:2011:735 para 100; cf Joined Cases C-402/05 P and C-415/05 P *Kadi and Al Barakaat International Foundation v Council and Commission* ECLI:EU:C:2008:461 paras 285 ff and 326–327; see also Bardo Fassbender, "Triepel in Luxemburg: Die dualistische Sicht des Verhältnisses zwischen Europa- und Völkerrecht in der 'Kadi-Rechtssprechung' des EuGH als Problem des Selbstverständnisses der Europäischen Union" (2010) 63 (8) Die öffentliche Verwaltung 333–341 (336 ff).

the relationship between international, EU and national law. Thus, with regard to modern theories on the relationship of legal orders, I conclude that they too lack satisfactory tools. We cannot, therefore, rely on them when we face the challenge of solving conflicts between norms from overlapping but different legal orders.

Discussing these theories leads us to the question of whether the postulated autonomy of the EU legal order might suffice for a proper theoretical approach (Chapter 3). Or rather: Is the CJEU to be criticized for mixing different approaches when confronting norm conflicts between international and Member State law? Or does this example uncover flaws in the doctrines discussed, which fail to explain current developments satisfactorily? One might say: In for a penny, in for a pound. Once a decision has been taken in favor of one doctrine, a stringent application of that one doctrine should be maintained consistently. However, in order to address these complex problems, it is important first to examine these diverging theories. Finally, this part will conclude by stating that the postulated autonomy of the EU legal order is not a self-standing theoretical approach; nor are dualism, Kelsenian monism, legal pluralism or constitutionalism theoretical approaches that are able to provide adequate solutions to norm conflicts between international, EU and Member State law.

1

Dualism and Kelsenian Monism

The relationship between international and national law is a topic of great importance. Generally, the floor has been divided between dualism (Section 1.1), as developed by Heinrich Triepel, and monism (Section 1.2), mainly formulated by Hans Kelsen, both of which need to be reviewed critically from today's perspective. I argue that these theories can no longer comprehensively explain the relationship between international and EU law or EU and national law and that due to their emergence almost a century ago, they must be understood in their historical context. Current challenges posed by international or supranational organizations such as the EU, and the development of international law in general, overburden these outdated theories.

1.1 DUALISM: LIBERATION FROM INTERNATIONAL LAW AS "EXTERNAL STATE LAW" 125 YEARS AGO

The international and national legal orders are "two circles, which possibly touch, but never cross each other."[4] This is the famous statement made by the then only thirty-year-old Heinrich Triepel in 1899, which forms the cornerstone of the dualistic divide of international (or EU) and national law. Dualism's divide of legal orders was primarily based on the view that the law of the international (or EU) and national legal orders emanate from different sources, leading to the supposition that international (or EU) law and national law arise from different legal orders relying on different grounds for validity.[5] Although it still holds true that international, EU and national law emanate

[4] Heinrich Triepel, *Völkerrecht und Landesrecht* (C L Hirschfeld 1899) 111 [emphasis omitted; translation in the text by the author].

[5] Dionisio Anzilotti, *Lehrbuch des Völkerrechts* (W de Gruyter 1929 German translation by Cornelia Bruns and Karl Schmid) 38–39.

from different sources, dualism also assumes that the addressees and content of international and national law cannot be identical.[6] Thus, dualism turns a blind eye to direct interaction between international law and individuals. It does so by stating that international law is purely inter-State law and can only stipulate obligations for States;[7] nor does international law share the same addressees with EU or national law.[8] The division of the legal systems implies that international law may not derogate from national law, and national law may not derogate from international law.[9] In order to give international law an effect within a national legal system, dualism demands a special procedure to transform or incorporate the international norm into a national norm.[10] As a result, the basis of validity of international law within national law rests solely within national law, and the basis of validity of EU law within national law rests, too, solely within national law.

Dualism faces serious difficulties explaining the basis of international or supranational organizations, because, according to dualism, there would be one international and as many *x*-national bases of validity of international or supranational organizations as there are Member States.[11] In other words, the validity of an international organization would have to be divided up over its Member States instead of having a uniform validity. Equally hard to grasp is the concurrent (dualistic) assumption that international, EU and national law

6 Triepel (n 4) 9, 11, 228–229; Anzilotti (n 5) 41–42.

7 Triepel (n 4) 119–120, 228–229, 271; Anzilotti (n 5) 41 ff. Gustav A Walz, *Völkerrecht und staatliches Recht: Untersuchung über die Einwirkungen des Völkerrechts auf das innerstaatliche Recht* (W Kohlhammer 1933) 238–239, was considered to be a moderate dualist, yet he did not postulate the impossibility of international law addressing individuals. He stated in 1933 that the character of international law at the time was "mediatized" through municipal law.

8 This criticism was already expressed by Alfred Verdross, "Die normative Verknüpfung von Völkerrecht und staatlichem Recht" in Max Imboden et al (eds) *Festschrift für Adolf Julius Merkl zum 80. Geburtstag* (Wilhelm Fink 1970) 425–441 (432 ff); Riccardo P Mazzeschi, "The Marginal Role of the Individual in the ILC's Articles on State Responsibility" (2004) 14 Italian Yearbook of International Law 39–51 (42–43) with further references in n 12: "This means that international law now regulates some relationships between States and individuals in a formal manner (and not only in a substantive one)"; ICJ *LaGrand (Germany v USA)* Judgment ICJ Reports [2001] 466, 494 para 77.

9 Triepel (n 4) 257–258; Anzilotti (n 5) 38.

10 Anzilotti (n 5) 41, 45–46.

11 Stefan Griller, "Völkerrecht und Landesrecht" in Robert Walter et al (eds) *Hans Kelsen und das Völkerrecht – Ergebnisse eines Internationalen Symposiums in Wien* (Manz 2005) 83–120 (97); see also the general criticism by Joseph G Starke, "Monism and Dualism in the Theory of International Law" (1936) 17 British Yearbook of International Law 66–81. For an attempt to save dualism, see Gaetano Arangio-Ruiz, "International Law and Interindividual Law" in Janne Nijman and André Nollkaemper (eds) *New Perspectives on the Divide between National and International Law* (Oxford University Press 2007) 15–51 (22).

by default cannot have the same content or addressees.[12] This assumption is flawed as it would make norm conflicts between international, EU and national legal orders impossible, which is not the case. Norms from overlapping legal orders conflict constantly. If, for instance, EU law never conflicted with national law, the primacy of EU law would be meaningless.

While these flaws are obvious for us today, it was not so when dualism was emerging at the turn of the twentieth century. One flaw that is evident today is the dualistic assumption that international law (EU law did not even exist at that time) is purely inter-State law and so can only oblige States but not individuals.[13] While this was certainly true when Heinrich Triepel was shaping dualistic thinking, it can no longer be perceived as an accurate depiction of international law today. International law nowadays also addresses individuals directly and shapes national law in many ways. Moreover, trying to fit EU law and its relationship with international and national law into a dualistic scheme is like attempting to square the circle, as the dualistic assumptions do not match our understanding of EU law, which has at its core primacy and direct effect. EU law is binding on national authorities and the basis of validity of EU law is not dependent on national law. Moreover, if there is a conflict between EU and national law, EU law takes precedence over national law.

Historically, dualism was progress, as the separation of international and national law helped international law become independent. Thus, dualism liberated international law from being understood as "external State law,"[14] and was even referred to as a "cleansing thunderstorm" by the monist Alfred Verdross.[15] In sum, the legal landscape has changed drastically since the turn of the twentieth century, and the core assumptions of dualism are no longer correct. As a consequence, dualism fails to explain the relationship between international, EU and national law today.

1.2 KELSENIAN MONISM: A QUEST FOR PURITY AT THE EXPENSE OF PLAUSIBILITY

The main characteristic of monism is the assumption of a single unified legal system. Monism was developed most prominently by Georges Scelle, Hans

[12] Triepel (n 4) 9, 11, 228–229, 254 ff; Anzilotti (n 5) 41–42.

[13] Triepel (n 4) 9, 11, 228–229, 254 ff; Anzilotti (n 5) 41–42 with further references.

[14] For the term "äußeres Staatsrecht," see Georg W F Hegel, *Grundlinien der Philosophie des Rechts* (Nicolai 1821) §§ 330 ff.

[15] Alfred Verdross, *Die völkerrechtswidrige Kriegshandlung und der Strafanspruch der Staaten* (Engelmann 1920) 34 "[R]einigendes Gewitter."

Kelsen and Alfred Verdross at the beginning of the twentieth century.[16] It is Kelsenian monism – and to some extent this also includes Verdross' conception – that still enjoys substantial popularity and is arguably the most sophisticated account of monist theories. Therefore, I will focus on Kelsenian monism, which must face the criticism of having a highly fictitious understanding of the world: nothing less than the "unity of the legal world order" is proclaimed.[17]

According to Kelsen, a legal order is a multiplicity of general and individual norms that regulate human behavior.[18] This multiplicity constitutes an order if it forms a unity. Unity in turn is established if these norms have the same basis for validity.[19] This understanding is based on the famous Kelsenian chain of validity, because the unity of a legal order is formed by the chain of validity.[20] Therefore, this understanding of a legal order is necessarily connected with the Kelsenian pure theory of law because law has to be perceived from one perspective as an noncontradicting single entity.[21] It is this understanding that undergirds Kelsenian legal monism, stating that if international, EU and national law are valid legal orders, they have to form a unity.[22] Different legal orders can only be considered valid if they have the same basis for validity.[23] The relationship between these legal orders must then be conceived of in either hierarchical or horizontal terms with separated spheres of validity. The latter conception, however, necessitates a higher order that entails a norm being the basis of validity for both legal orders.[24]

[16] Hugo Krabbe, *Die moderne Staatsidee* (Nijhoff 2nd ed 1919); Léon Duguit, *Souveraineté et liberté* (Éditions La Mémoire du Droit 1922); Georges Scelle, *Précis de droit des gens: Principes et systématique Vol I* (Librairie du Recueil Sirey 1932); Hans Kelsen, "Les rapports de système entre le droit interne et le droit international public" (1926) 14 Recueil des Cours de l'Académie de Droit International 227–331 (299); Alfred Verdross, "Le fondement du droit international" (1927) 16 Recueil des Cours de l'Académie de Droit International, 247–324 (287); Paul Gragl, *Legal Monism: Law, Philosophy, and Politics* (Oxford University Press 2018); for an overview see Christine Amrhein-Hofmann, *Monismus und Dualismus in den Völkerrechtslehren* (Duncker & Humblot 2003) 152 ff.

[17] Alfred Verdross, *Die Einheit des rechtlichen Weltbildes auf Grundlage der Völkerrechtsverfassung* (JCB Mohr 1923); Hans Kelsen, *Reine Rechtslehre* (Deuticke 2nd ed 1960) 329; Arangio-Ruiz (n 11) 18, speaking of "the natural unity of human kind … [a]s a matter of pure speculation."

[18] Hans Kelsen, "Der Begriff der Rechtsordnung" (1958) 1 (3) Logique et Analyse 150–167 (150).

[19] Kelsen (n 18) 150.

[20] Kelsen (n 18) 155.

[21] Kelsen (n 18) 161.

[22] Kelsen (n 18) 160.

[23] Kelsen (n 18) 159.

[24] Kelsen (n 18) 159.

This understanding results from Kelsenian adherence to neo-Kantian epistemology, "because it is only this method [the monist concept of law] and its focus on the *manner* of cognizance, not its *objects*, which allows to ascertain *a priori* how positive law is even possible *qua* object of cognizance and *qua* object of the legal science."[25] In Kelsen's own words, "[t]he unity of national law and international law is an epistemological postulate."[26] In a more extensive manner he stated:

> It is . . . true, in the sense of Kant's theory of knowledge, that legal science qua cognition of the law is like all cognition: It is constitutive in character and therefore "creates" its object in so far as it comprehends its object as a meaningful whole. Just as natural science, by means of its ordering cognition, turns the chaos of sensory impressions into a cosmos, that is, into nature as a unified system, so likewise legal science, by means of cognition, turns the multitude of general and individual legal norms issued by legal organs – the material given to legal science – into a unified system free of contradiction, that is, into a legal system.[27]

Moreover, according to him, "[i]t is logically not possible to assume that simultaneously valid norms belong to different, mutually independent systems."[28] Hence, Kelsenian monism is also unthinkable without the Kelsenian quest for purity fueling his pure theory of law. What is appealing about Kelsenian monism is the attempt to understand both international and national law as law with the same conception of law, which allows for a comparison, and a succinct solution to legal norm conflicts. However, it is the quest for purity in the Kelsenian enterprise and the claimed epistemological basis that is understandable considering the historical circumstances under which Kelsen developed his legal theory. Yet it is precisely these elements that expose Kelsenian monism to strong criticism today.

Dualism and monism alike have been heavily criticized. For instance, Armin von Bogdandy holds that "from a scholarly perspective, they are intellectual zombies of another time and should be laid to rest, or

[25] Paul Gragl, "The Pure Theory of Law and Legal Monism – Epistemological Truth and Empirical Plausibility" (2015) 70 (4) Zeitschrift für Öffentliches Recht 665–736 (668–669) [emphasis original; footnotes omitted] with further references.

[26] Hans Kelsen, *General Theory of Law and State* (translated by Anders Wedberg Harvard University Press 1945 [1928]) 373.

[27] Kelsen (n 17) § 16 quoted after (and translated by) Stanley L Paulson, "On the Kelsen–Kant Problematic" in Ernesto Garzón Valdés et al (eds) *Normative Systems in Legal and Moral Theory. Festschrift für Carlos E Alchourrón and Eugenio Bulygin* (Duncker & Humblot 1997) 197–213 (206).

[28] Kelsen (n 26) 363.

'deconstructed.'"[29] Yet monism in particular proves to be a hard-to-kill zombie. Recently, Paul Gragl has advanced a sophisticated account defending Kelsenian – or, as he puts it, legal monism as imagined by the Vienna School of Jurisprudence and the pure theory of law.[30] He defends Viennese legal monism with its "*epistemological* terms of the pure theory of law,"[31] upholds its "descriptive value"[32] and finally even claims its "moral superiority" over other theories on the relationship between legal orders.[33] This deserves further scrutiny, with the goal to deconstruct Kelsenian monism as suggested by Armin von Bogdandy.[34] We will begin by looking at the claim that legal monism as envisaged by the Vienna School of Jurisprudence follows from an epistemological and logical necessity.

1.2.1 *Kantian Epistemology as the Basis for the Pure Theory of Law and Kelsenian Legal Monism*

Gragl correctly points to the Kelsenian claim that his pure theory of law and thus his version of legal monism follow from Kantian or neo-Kantian epistemology.[35] When Immanuel Kant asks "how *subjective conditions of thinking* should have *objective validity*,"[36] Kelsen asks "how to cognize whether a given legal norm is objectively valid or not."[37] We will first revisit

[29] Armin von Bogdandy, "Pluralism, Direct Effect, and the Ultimate Say: On the Relationship between International and Domestic Constitutional Law" (2008) 6 (3–4) International Journal of Constitutional Law 397–413 (400).
[30] Gragl (n 16).
[31] Gragl (n 16) ch 3, 8 [emphasis original].
[32] Gragl (n 16) ch 4.
[33] Gragl (n 16) ch 5.
[34] See von Bogdandy (n 29) 400.
[35] Gragl (n 16) 58 n 10, he does so by following the illustration in Michael S Green, "Hans Kelsen and the Logic of Legal Systems" (2003) 54 (2) Alabama Law Review 365–413. For a description of the Kelsenian position see András Jakab, "Kelsens Völkerrechtslehre zwischen Erkenntnistheorie und Politik" (2004) 64 Heidelberg Journal of International Law 1045–1057 with further references. See Danilo Zolo, "Hans Kelsen: International Peace through International Law" (1998) 9 (2) European Journal of International Law 306–324 (323), pointing to the importance of the neo-Kantian philosophy for legal monism as envisaged by Hans Kelsen when Zolo holds that "[o]n the plane of the epistemology of legal knowledge, Kelsen's monistic assumption stands or falls with the neo-Kantian philosophy from which it derives."
[36] Immanuel Kant, *Critique of Pure Reason* (Cambridge edition of the works of Immanuel Kant translated and edited by Paul Guyer and Allen W Wood Cambridge University Press 1998 [*Kritik der reinen Vernunft* (Johann Friedrich Hartknoch 1781/1787)] A 89–90 / B 122 [emphasis original].
[37] Gragl (n 16) 61.

how Gragl portrays Kant, whose undoubtedly important and influential work dates back to the eighteenth century. Second, we will revisit some of the criticism that was advanced against Kant by other important philosophers in order to, third, examine briefly how the philosophical discipline of epistemology has evolved from the eighteenth century until now. Beyond that we will also look at neo-Kantian philosophy, as this philosophy is claimed to be the touchstone of the Kelsenian pure theory of law and legal monism (Section 1.2.2). This will allow us to evaluate whether this is a solid epistemological basis for making the leap to Kelsenian monism and a sound *legal* epistemology today (Section 1.2.3). In other words, after discussing the (neo-)Kantian epistemological basis, we will deal with the question of whether this is a convincing basis for the law, since the analogy between Kelsenian legal epistemology and Kantian epistemology depends on it. The Kantian enterprise asks "how *subjective conditions of thinking* should have *objective validity*" and thereby engages with the relation between (subjective) thinking and the (objective) world. The Kelsenian goal – in contrast – is to find out "how to cognize whether a given legal norm is objectively valid or not" and, thus, is about the validity of norms. Pointedly, the commonality and therefore the justification of such an analogy is the very same letters, "v a l i d," apart from which both endeavors – questions of what is knowledge (of the external world) and questions of what is law or legal knowledge – are worlds apart. Therefore, we should carefully separate validity claims about scientific theories and validity claims pertaining to norms. Before addressing such a critique focused on the appropriateness of this analogy, however, we will begin with Kantian epistemology as portrayed by Gragl.

Kant famously criticized radical rationalism and radical empiricism. In his *Critique of Pure Reason* Kant famously holds that "[t]houghts without content are empty, intuitions without concepts are blind"[38] and points, in the words of Gragl, to the "opaque concept of the transcendental thinking self."[39] This is because only from the union of thoughts and intuitions "can cognition arise."[40] In brief, "whatever a person is thinking, there always is a subject of thought which can never be made an object."[41] Therefore, "the self which thinks cannot be an object of experience"[42] and, "since the unity of the transcendental self is not experienced, its unification of ideas can be regarded

[38] Kant (n 36) A 51 / B 76.
[39] Gragl (n 16) 61, with reference to Kant (n 36) B 131–134.
[40] Kant (n 36) A 51 / B 76.
[41] Gragl (n 16) 61.
[42] Gragl (n 16) 61.

as objectively valid."[43] "Owing to its nature of being a necessary (and hence not being experienced as a contingent) self, the transcendental self can unite all thoughts in a non-contingent manner, and by doing so, it can represent necessary connections in nature."[44] That is – according to Gragl – the basis for Kant's "Copernican" revolution holding "that it is not our knowledge that must conform to objects, but that objects must conform to our knowledge."[45]

First, Gragl deserves praise for having outlined what, "eventually, influenced the pure theory of law, trying to find a way between metaphysical natural law and empiricist sociology or psychology."[46] All too often, we read about dualism and monism without a neat sketch of the theoretical preconditions of these theories. However, having described the preconditions clearly, further questions are provoked. A first intuition might be that, despite the impressive leap accomplished by Kant back in time, the philosophical discipline of epistemology has not stood still since the eighteenth century. Although

[43] To enforce this point, Gragl (n 16) 62 n 40 quotes Ludwig Wittgenstein, *Tractatus Logico-Philosophicus* (translated by Kevin C Klement alongside both the Ogden/Ramsey and Pears/McGuinness English translations 2015 [original German Kegan Paul 1922]), available at http://people.umass.edu/klement/tlp/tlp.pdf [last accessed February 1, 2023] para 5.633: "[Y]ou do not see the eye. And nothing in the visual field allows you to infer that it is seen by an eye"; however, this is unfortunate. As Wittgenstein elaborates on solipsism in this passage he is inspired by another critic of Kant, Arthur Schopenhauer, *The World as Will and Representation Vol I* (translated by Judith Norman and Alistair Welchman and edited by Christopher Janaway Cambridge University Press 2010 [*Die Welt als Wille und Vorstellung* 1818]) and Schopenhauer's famous "eternal eye of the world" (*Weltauge*) 308–309; Arthur Schopenhauer, *The World as Will and Representation Vol II* (translated by Judith Norman and Alistair Welchman and edited by Christopher Janaway Cambridge University Press 2018 [*Die Welt als Wille und Vorstellung* 1848]) 3rd book ch 29 "On the Cognition of the Ideas." For the link between the two, see Gottfried Gabriel, *Grundprobleme der Erkenntnistheorie. Von Descartes zu Wittgenstein* (utb 3rd ed 2008) 167. Roughly, according to Schopenhauer, Kant's division into phenomenal (as we perceive it) and noumenal (as it is) collapses into one world, with two aspects, namely will and representation, as the title of Schopenhauer's opus magnum says. For the pessimistic Schopenhauer, contemplation such as aesthetic contemplation of music, might provide a means of escape from the meaningless will. Wittgenstein proposed something similar in this passage 5.631 ff where the empirical subject becomes the object. As a result, solipsism and pure realism collapse. See Schopenhauer (5.64): "Here it can be seen that solipsism, when its implications are followed out strictly, coincides with pure realism. The self of solipsism shrinks to a point without extension, and there remains the reality co-ordinated with it." And 5.641: "Thus there really is a sense in which philosophy can talk about the self in a non-psychological way. What brings the self into philosophy is the fact that 'the world is my world.'"

[44] Gragl (n 16) 62 with reference to Kant (n 36) B 141–142.

[45] Again Gragl (n 16) 62 with reference to Kant (n 36) B xvi and A 369–370 / B 519–521.

[46] Gragl (n 16) 62.

this in itself might not be a sufficient criticism,[47] such skepticism might make us wonder, in general, how to figure out what is state of the art in epistemology today and, in particular, which arguments have been advanced against the Kantian concept of "transcendental idealism." Gragl is aware of Hilary Putnam's criticism of this position as solipsistic.[48] He negates that criticism of Kant, however, by holding that "it is impossible to make such judgments about the thinking self."[49] Rather, Gragl states, the transcendental self "is a *condition for*, not an *object of* knowledge."[50] Before we see how this applies to the law, we need to consult further criticism that has been advanced against this position.

To begin with, a caveat is in order. It is clearly impossible within the framework of this book to outline the theory of knowledge as it stands today. Nor is it possible to take a sophisticated look at Kant's elaborated epistemology. What must suffice for the purpose of this book is to show that Kelsenian *legal* monism, with its heavy reliance on (neo-)Kantian epistemology, does not take into account the critique that has been advanced against Kant in this regard and the development of epistemology in general since 1781 and 1787.[51] This, as we will see, is a major mistake.

47 See, however, Hanno Sauer, "The End of History" (2022) Inquiry, doi.org/10.1080/0020174X.2022.2124542, for an intriguing argument holding that "studying the history of philosophy is philosophically unhelpful."

48 Gragl (n 16) 62 with reference to Hilary Putnam, "Why Reason Cannot Be Naturalized" (1982) 52 (1) Synthese 3–23 (10).

49 Gragl (n 16) 62 with reference to Kant (n 36) B 399–432.

50 Gragl (n 16) 62, n 47 with reference to Robert C Solomon, *From Rationalism to Existentialism: The Existentialists and Their Nineteenth-Century Backgrounds* (Rowman & Littlefield 2001) 21, who states clearly: "If the world of which we are conscious is necessarily objective and public, it must be the case that all philosophical theories which suppose that the objects in question are nothing other than mere 'ideas' or 'mental entities' are seriously confused. Accordingly, all the versions of 'idealism' which assert such a thesis must be distinguished from what Kant calls his 'transcendental idealism' and rejected as philosophically absurd. For the transcendental idealist (Kant, and, we shall see later, Husserl), the world is not my idea: the world is the phenomenon which must exist independently of my idea of it." This interpretation of Kant, however, is first far from clear from Kant's writing, and second, as we shall see, runs into unsurmountable problems, see below n 90. The same applies to the book review of Strawson which is quoted by Gragl (n 16) 62, 47 as another source, H E Matthews, "Strawson on Transcendental Idealism" (1969) 19 (76) Philosophical Quarterly 204–220 (216–217).

51 Literally emphasizing great progress in philosophy in the last 200 years in his *philosophical* introduction to a theory of knowledge, see Markus Gabriel, *Die Erkenntnis der Welt – Eine Einführung in die Erkenntnistheorie* (Karl Alber 5th ed 2016); compare also for instance Robert Audit, *Epistemology. A Contemporary Introduction to the Theory of Knowledge* (Routledge 3rd ed 2011) 107, denoting the Kantian position as the "best-known answers . . . and probably the only ones we should call the *classical* answers" to the questions "[h]ow might we understand the justification of our beliefs of self-evident and apparently necessary propositions? And how do we know them?" [emphasis original]. See also Michael Rohlf, "Immanuel Kant"

Yet, to provide sufficient context, we need to understand what drove Kant to write his *Critique of Pure Reason*. According to our intuition, and also for a long time in philosophy, a statement is considered to be true if it describes reality aptly.[52] Conceptions of truth that follow such an account were and still are usually referred to as "correspondence theories of truth" and can be traced back to ancient Greek philosophers. Aristotle, for instance, famously stated that "[t]o say of what is that it is not, or of what is not that it is, is false, while to say of what is that it is, and of what is not that it is not, is true."[53] Thomas Aquinas similarly stated that "[t]ruth is the adequation of things and intellect" and thus "[a] judgment is said to be true when it conforms to the external reality."[54] According to this approach, we can consult a "truthmaker" in order to find out whether a statement is true. A truthmaker is anything that makes a statement true.[55] René Descartes, another prominent advocate of the "correspondence theory of truth," pointed out the obviousness of this approach, which is a considerable strength. In fact, Descartes is said to have brought about a Cartesian revolution in philosophy as he famously identified its foundations. According to Dummett, "the Cartesian revolution consisted in giving this role to the theory of knowledge." Descartes asked, "What do we know, and what justifies our claim to this knowledge?"[56] Cartesian doubt was introduced by Descartes as a methodology to question our knowledge as a route to the point of certain knowledge. This led Descartes to question what

in Edward N Zalta (ed) *Stanford Encyclopedia of Philosophy* (January 25, 2016) available at https://plato.stanford.edu/entries/kant/index.html#ref-11 [last accessed February 1, 2023].

52 Note that talking about true statements is already an intricate issue. According to Marian David, "The Correspondence Theory of Truth" in Edward N Zalta (ed) *Stanford Encyclopedia of Philosophy* (May 28, 2015) available at https://plato.stanford.edu/entries/truth-correspondence/ [last accessed February 1, 2023], "Correspondence theories of truth have been given for beliefs, thoughts, ideas, judgments, statements, assertions, utterances, sentences, and propositions. It has become customary to talk of *truthbearers* whenever one wants to stay neutral between these choices" [emphasis original].

53 Aristotle, *Metaphysics* book 4 section 1011b25, quoted after David (n 52).

54 Thomas Aquinas, *Truth* (translated and edited by R W Schmidt, Robert W Mulligan, James V McGlynn Hackett 1994 [*Quaestiones disputatae de Veritate* 1256–1259]), quoted after David (n 52) Q.1, A.1–3. Generally, Bertrand Russell, "On the Nature of Truth and Falsehood" (1906–1907) 7 Proceedings of the Aristotelian Society 28–49; early Wittgenstein (n 43) 2.1 ff, especially 2.222; George E Moore, *Some Main Problems of Philosophy* (MacMillan 1953) ch 15; as well as Alfred Tarski, "The Concept of Truth in Formalized Languages" in *Logic, Semantics, Metamathematics* (Hackett 2nd ed 1983 [1935]) 152–278; and Karl Popper, "Philosophical Comments on Tarski's Theory of Truth" in *Objective Knowledge: An Evolutionary Approach* (Oxford Clarendon Press 2nd ed 1972) 319–340, can be identified – besides many others – as belonging to this group.

55 David (n 52), which obviously also holds for any other truthbearer.

56 Michael Dummett, *Frege: Philosophy of Language* (Harper & Row 1973) 666.

makes you certain that you are awake and not dreaming. He answered this in retrospect by stating that "when I distinctly see where things come from and where and when they come to me, and when I can connect my perceptions of them with my whole life without a break then I can be certain that when I encounter these things I am not asleep but awake."[57] Moreover, with his "*cogito ergo sum*" he concluded that at least his own existence was proven precisely by himself "thinking *all* [his] thoughts might be mistaken."[58] In a sense concerning the correspondence theory of truth, Descartes was in good company with such important philosophers as Baruch de Spinoza, John Locke, Gottfried Wilhelm Leibniz, and David Hume[59] and Immanuel Kant,[60] in a way.[61] However, can we linguistically portray something external to linguistics? What does it actually mean that a statement matches reality? Is it not the case that this theory presupposes truth, for if it would not do so, how could we validate our truth claims?

57 René Descartes, *The Philosophical Writings of Descartes* (edited by John Cottingham, Robert Stoothoff and Dugald Murdoch Cambridge University Press 1984) 2:61 f quoted after Lex Newman, "Descartes' Epistemology" in Edward N Zalta (ed) *Stanford Encyclopedia of Philosophy* (February 15, 2019) available at https://plato.stanford.edu/entries/descartes-epistemology/ [last accessed February 1, 2023], who also provides an overview of various possible interpretations.

58 For a detailed overview see Newman (n 57) [emphasis original], quoting the entire passage by Descartes (n 57) 2:16 f which reads: "I have convinced myself that there is absolutely nothing in the world, no sky, no earth, no minds, no bodies. Does it now follow that I too do not exist? No: if I convinced myself of something then I certainly existed. But there is a deceiver of supreme power and cunning who is deliberately and constantly deceiving me. In that case I too undoubtedly exist, if he is deceiving me; and let him deceive me as much as he can, he will never bring it about that I am nothing so long as I think that I am something. So after considering everything very thoroughly, I must finally conclude that this proposition, *I am, I exist,* is necessarily true whenever it is put forward by me or conceived in my mind" [emphasis original].

59 See David Hume, *A Treatise of Human Nature. A Critical Edition Vol 1* (edited by David Fate Norton and Mary J Norton Oxford University Press 2007 [1739–1740]) 295: "Reason is the discovery of truth or falshood. Truth or falshood consists in an agreement or disagreement either to the real relations of ideas, or to real existence and matter of fact." However, Hume adds that "[w]hatever, therefore, is not susceptible of this agreement or disagreement, is incapable of being true or false, and can never be an object of our reason. Now 'tis evident our passions, volitions, and actions, are not susceptible of any such agreement or disagreement; being original facts and realities, compleat in themselves, and implying no reference to other passions, volitions, and actions. 'Tis impossible, therefore, they can be pronounc'd either true or false, and be either contrary or conformable to reason."

60 See Kant (n 36) A 58 / B 82: "The nominal definition of truth, namely that it is the agreement of cognition with its object, is here granted and presupposed." However, Kant does not hesitate to add "but one demands to know what is the general and certain criterion of the truth of any cognition."

61 For an overview see David (n 52).

To understand these objections and to relate the Kantian critique to early versions of such an approach we must first consider David Hume, who questioned whether we have direct access to the external world. According to Hume, we can only relate to the external world via our impressions.[62] Hume differentiated between *impressions* (feelings) and *ideas* (thinking) while he held that all ideas are "faint images"[63] – in other words, copies of impressions.[64] Impressions, however, face the problem of induction. According to Hume, we can only explain that we process impressions inductively, but we cannot justify that we do so. In his words, "'[t]is therefore by *experience* only, that we can infer the existence of one object from that of another."[65] So, he goes on, if we remember that when we perceive a flame we have also felt heat, we likely conjugate all past instances of seeing a flame and feeling heat. Hence, "[w]ithout any farther ceremony, we call the one *cause* and the other *effect*, and infer the existence of the one from that of the other."[66] However, this operation is only perceived and remembered by our senses as we make "*constant conjunctions*."[67] He hypothesizes "*that all our reasonings concerning causes and effects are deriv'd from nothing but custom; and that belief is more*

[62] David Hume in turn must actually not be understood as the originator of epistemology. Epistemology as a philosophical discipline with its proper name originating in the seventeenth century. See Jan Woleński, "The History of Epistemology" in Ilkka Niiniluoto, Matti Sintonen and Jan Woleński (eds) *Handbook of Epistemology* (Springer 2004) 3–54. Questions pertaining to the discipline of epistemology, however, have been asked ever since philosophical questions have been asked. See Peter Baumann, *Erkenntnistheorie* (JB Metzler 3rd ed 2015), quoting on the very first page of his introduction an old Chinese story retold by Chuang Tzu, *The Complete Works of Chuang Tzu* (translated by Burton Watson Columbia University Press 1968) 188–189.

[63] Hume (n 59) 7: "All the perceptions of the human mind resolve themselves into two distinct kinds, which I shall call *impressions* and *ideas*. The difference betwixt these consists in the degrees of force and liveliness, with which they strike upon the mind, and make their way into our thought or consciousness. Those perceptions, which enter with most force and violence, we may name impressions; and under this name I comprehend all our sensations, passions and emotions, as they make their first appearance in the soul. By ideas I mean the faint images of these in thinking and reasoning; such as, for instance, are all the perceptions excited by the present discourse, excepting only those which arise from the sight and touch, and excepting the immediate pleasure or uneasiness it may occasion. I believe it will not be very necessary to employ many words in explaining this distinction. Every one of himself will readily perceive the difference betwixt feeling and thinking" [emphasis original].

[64] Hume (n 59) 9: "*that all our simple ideas in their first appearance are deriv'd from simple impressions, which are correspondent to them, and which they exactly represent*" [emphasis original]. Cf 73–74.

[65] Hume (n 59) 61 [emphasis original].

[66] Hume (n 59) 61 [emphasis original].

[67] Hume (n 59) 61 [emphasis original].

properly an act of the sensitive, than of the cogitative part of our natures."[68] This view has been named radical empiricism, for it holds that, ultimately, we cannot access the external world. We are left with the impressions from our senses. In Hume's beautiful prose:

> Reason first appears in possession of the throne, prescribing laws, and imposing maxims, with an absolute sway and authority. Her enemy, therefore, is oblig'd to take shelter under her protection, and by making use of rational arguments to prove the fallaciousness and imbecility of reason, produces, in a manner, a patent under her hand and seal. This patent has at first an authority, proportion'd to the present and immediate authority of reason, from which it is deriv'd. But as it is suppos'd to be contradictory to reason, it gradually diminishes the force of that governing power, and its own at the same time; till at last they both vanish away into nothing, by a regular and just diminution.[69]

It was this powerful finding by Hume that awoke Kant from his self-diagnosed "dogmatic slumber."[70] While, according to Hume, there is no a priori possibility to discover what is out there without our senses and, thus, there is also no a priori causality as a relation between things, Kant famously criticized radical rationalism, but also radical empiricism. In his *Critique of Pure Reason*, Kant

68 Hume (n 59) 123 [emphasis original].

69 Hume (n 59) 125. See also David Hume, *An Enquiry Concerning Human Understanding* (edited with an introduction and notes by Peter Millican Oxford University Press 2007 [1748]) 18 ff, esp 19: "I shall venture to affirm, as a general proposition, which admits of no exception, that the knowledge of this relation is not, in any instance, attained by reasonings *a priori*; but arises entirely from experience, when we find, that any particular objects are constantly conjoined with each other. Let an object be presented to a man of ever so strong natural reason and abilities; if that object be entirely new to him, he will not be able, by the most accurate examination of its sensible qualities, to discover any of its causes or effects" [emphasis original].

70 See Immanuel Kant, *Prolegomena to Any Future Metaphysics That Will Be Able to Come Forward as Science* (translated and edited by Gary Hatfield Cambridge University Press 2nd ed 2004 [*Prolegomena zu einer jeden künftigen Metaphysik, die als Wissenschaft wird auftreten können* 1783]) Preface 10: "I freely admit that the remembrance of *David Hume* was the very thing that many years ago first interrupted my dogmatic slumber and gave a completely different direction to my researches in the field of speculative philosophy" [footnotes omitted; emphasis original]; cf Paul Guyer and Allen W Wood, "Introduction" in Immanuel Kant, *Critique of Pure Reason* (Cambridge edition of the works of Immanuel Kant translated and edited by Paul Guyer and Allen W Wood Cambridge University Press 1998 [*Kritik der reinen Vernunft* (Johann Friedrich Hartknoch 1781/1787)]) 1–80 (23): "it was the recollection of David Hume that many years ago first interrupted my dogmatic slumber and gave an entirely different direction to my investigations in the field of speculative philosophy." Kant was not the only one to be impressed. Also Jeremy Bentham is reported to have said that the writings of David Hume have "caused the scales to fall," see William Edward Morris, "David Hume" in Edward N Zalta (ed) *Stanford Encyclopedia of Philosophy* (April 17, 2019) available at https://plato.stanford.edu/entries/hume/ [last accessed February 1, 2023].

agrees with Hume to a large extent when he states that "[w]hat may be the case with objects in themselves and abstracted from all this receptivity of our sensibility remains entirely unknown to us."[71]

However, Kant, in contrast to Hume, does not think that causality is a relation between things, but an a priori necessary precondition of human beings perceiving things. And, more controversially, that things are also causally constituted. To this end, it is important to note the difference between a priori, which basically means independent of experience, and a posteriori, which means on the basis of experience.[72] Moreover, we can also differentiate between analytical judgments and synthetic judgments. Kant specifies this as follows:

> In all judgments in which the relation of a subject to the predicate is thought (if I consider only affirmative judgments, since the application to negative ones is easy), this relation is possible in two different ways. Either the predicate *B* belongs to the subject A as something that is (covertly) contained in this concept A; or *B* lies entirely outside the concept A, though to be sure it stands in connection with it. In the first case I call the judgment analytic, in the second synthetic.[73]

[71] Kant (n 36) A 42 / B 59. Note, however, that in the previous passage stating that "[w]e have therefore wanted to say that all our intuition is nothing but the representation of appearance; that the things that we intuit are not in themselves what we intuit them to be, nor are their relations so constituted in themselves as they appear to us; and that if we remove our own subject or even only the subjective constitution of the senses in general, then all the constitution, all relations of objects in space and time, indeed space and time themselves would disappear, and as appearances they cannot exist in themselves, but only in us." Kant denies a form of things in themselves except through our appearance. This readily conflicts with Kantian premises as we do not have direct access to things in themselves and, thus, cannot deny or approve their given forms and qualities as they are. See on this M Gabriel (n 51) 262, who insightfully quotes Kleist (Heinrich von Kleist, "An Wilhelmine von Zenge, Berlin, d. 22t März, 1801" [letter to Wilhelmine von Zenge] in Dieter Heimböckel (ed), *Heinrich von Kleist. Sämtliche Briefe* (Reclam 1991) 209–215 (213)), who sums this up by stating that "if all human beings would have green glasses instead of eyes they would consequently have to conclude that all the objects they see through such glasses *are* green. … We cannot decide whether what we call truth is truthfully true or whether it only seems to us." In German: "Wenn alle Menschen statt der Augen grüne Gläser hätten, so würden sie urtheilen müssen, die Gegenstände, welche sie dadurch erblicken, *sind* grün – und nie würden sie entscheiden können, ob ihr Auge ihnen die Dinge zeigt, wie sie sind, oder ob es nicht etwas zu ihnen hinzuthut, was nicht ihnen, sondern dem Auge gehört. So ist es mit dem Verstande. Wir können nicht entscheiden, ob das, was wir Wahrheit nennen, wahrhaft Wahrheit ist, oder ob es uns nur so scheint."

[72] Kant (n 36) A 4 / B 8 holds in this regard, for instance, that "Mathematics gives us a splendid example of how far we can go with *a priori* cognition independently of experience" [emphasis original]. See generally G Gabriel (n 43) 48–53.

[73] Kant (n 36) A 6 / B 10.

Analytical judgments, thus, are in a way given to the subject. Synthetic judgments are not contained in the subject but, nevertheless, are related to it.[74] As an example, Kant mentions that "[a]ll bodies are extended" is an analytic judgment, whereas "[a]ll bodies are heavy" is a synthetic judgment.[75] Having made these distinctions, we can principally illustrate the distinction between Hume and Kant. While for both, all analytical judgments are a priori, it is only Kant who considers the possibility of synthetic judgments being a priori.[76] Figuring out how such a priori synthetic judgments are possible is the task of a "transcendental critique."[77] Causality, to return to the example, is considered by both Hume and Kant to be a synthetic judgment. However, the latter also considers causality an a priori judgment. Causality cannot be justified by custom as we could repeatedly ask for the beginning of the cause. Hence, only "because we subject the sequence of the appearances and thus all alteration to the law of causality that experience itself, i.e., empirical cognition of them, is possible."[78] In other words, the law of causality is a precondition for the possibility of representation, and thus it is a transcendental argument, prior to experience.

Furthermore Kant distinguishes mere illusion, the appearance of objects and things in themselves:

> If I say: in space and time intuition represents both outer objects as well as the self-intuition of the mind as each affects our senses, i.e., as it *appears*, that is not to say that these objects would be a mere *illusion* ["*Schein*"]. For in the appearance the objects[, and] indeed even properties that we attribute to them, are always regarded as something really given, only insofar as this property depends only on the kind of intuition of the subject in the relation of the given object to it then this object as *appearance* is to be distinguished

[74] Kant (n 36) A 7 / B 10 also speaks of analytic judgments as "those in which the connection of the predicate is thought through identity" whereas synthetic judgments are "those in which this connection is thought without identity". Kant (n 36) A 7 / B 11 further clarifies: "One could also call the former judgments of clarification and the latter judgments of amplification ('*Erläuterungs-* und *Erweiterungsurteile*'), since through the predicate the former do not add anything to the concept of the subject, but only break it up by means of analysis into its component concepts, which were already thought in it (though confusedly); while the latter, on the contrary, add to the concept of the subject a predicate that was not thought in it at all, and could not have been extracted from it through any analysis."

[75] Kant (n 36) A 7 / B 11. Cf G Gabriel (n 43) 70–73; Robert Hanna, "Kant's Theory of Judgment" in Edward N Zalta (ed) *Stanford Encyclopedia of Philosophy* (October 23, 2017) available at https://plato.stanford.edu/entries/kant-judgment/ [last accessed February 1, 2023].

[76] Kant (n 36) A 9 / B 13.

[77] Kant (n 36) A 11 / B 25, beyond that Kant "call[s] all cognition transcendental that is occupied not so much with objects but rather with our a priori concepts of objects in general."

[78] Kant (n 36) A 189 / B 234.

> from itself as object *in itself*. Thus I do not say that bodies merely *seem* to exist outside me or that my soul only *seems* to be given if I assert that the quality of space and time – in accordance with which, as [a] condition of their existence, I posit both of these – lies in my kind of intuition and not in these objects in themselves.[79]

What is important here is to highlight that Kant – in a way as a response to the challenge of David Hume's skepticism – was eager "to show that a critique of reason by reason itself, unaided and unrestrained by traditional authorities, establishes a secure and consistent basis for both Newtonian science and traditional morality and religion."[80] Hence, it was Kant's goal to show that physics needs to be a priori because the laws of physics apply to all objects without our needing to analyze whether objects actually follow these laws.[81]

The famous dictum of Kant, namely that "[t]houghts without content are empty, [and] intuitions without concepts are blind,"[82] unfolds as follows:

> Our cognition arises from two fundamental sources in the mind, the first of which is the reception of representations (the receptivity of impressions), the second the faculty for cognizing an object by means of these representations (spontaneity of concepts); through the former an object is *given* to us, through the latter it is *thought* in relation to that representation (as a mere determination of the mind). Intuition and concepts therefore constitute the elements of all our cognition, so that neither concepts without intuition corresponding to them in some way nor intuition without concepts can yield a cognition.[83]

Roughly speaking, this brings together content by intuition and form by thought. By the former, Kant provides for the possibility that we assume we see a tree when we actually face a tree. The latter provides grounds for things appearing to human beings in the same way.[84] However, a powerful criticism of this conception was already advanced by Friedrich Heinrich Jacobi in

[79] Kant (n 36) B 69 [emphasis original; German translations in the text, except for Schein, omitted].

[80] Rohlf (n 51); see also in this vein M Gabriel (n 51) 265.

[81] M Gabriel (n 51) 265 highlights the fact that Kant did not think of the possibility of a historically variable a priori in relation to human history and points to Michel Foucault and Richard Rorty for a thesis of a "historic apriori" sharing Kantian premises, albeit without sharing Kantian transcendental idealism.

[82] Kant (n 36) A 51 / B 76.

[83] Kant (n 36) A50 / B 74 [emphasis original].

[84] M Gabriel (n 51) 267.

1787.[85] If causality is restricted to representations, if causality is a necessary precondition for us to cognize objects, then we cannot assume at the same time that things in themselves exist which affect our receptivity, by which they provoke our impressions. Hence, if causality only belongs to the form of our cognition, the content cannot be brought about by causality as well. We lack force to explain that we see a tree because there is a tree. If we solve this puzzle by ascribing causality to the things in themselves, however, we lack a reason for differentiating things in themselves from our perceptions of them. No matter how we turn, the form–content dualism implodes. Kant needs the thing-in-itself in order to explain the content of representations and to assume receptivity at all. Yet, in order to do so, he has to award properties to the thing-in-itself which do not pertain to it from Kantian premises.[86] In Jacobi's words: "I must admit that I was held up not a little by this difficulty in my study of the Kantian philosophy ... because I was incessantly going astray on this point, viz. that *without* that presupposition I could not enter into the system, but *with* it I could not stay within it."[87] In order to avoid this criticism, we could turn to a passage in the *Critique of Pure Reason* where Kant seems to retreat to a position labelling the thing-in-itself a mere "boundary concept, in order to limit the pretension of sensibility."[88] More expansively, Kant stated:

> If, therefore, we say: The senses represent objects to us *as they appear*, but the understanding, *as they are*, then the latter is not to be taken in a transcendental but in a merely empirical way, signifying, namely, how they must be represented as objects of experience, in the thoroughgoing connection of appearances, and not how they might be outside of the relation to possible experience and consequently to sense in general, thus as objects of pure

85 Friedrich Heinrich Jacobi, "Ueber den transscendentalen Idealismus" in *Werke Vol 2* (edited by F Roth and F Köppen 1976 [1787]) 291–310; see also Friedrich Heinrich Jacobi, "David Hume on Faith or Idealism and Realism: A Dialogue" in George di Giovanni (ed) *The Main Philosophical Writings and the Novel Allwill. Friedrich Heinrich Jacobi* (translated with an introductory study, notes, and bibliography by George di Giovanni McGill-Queen's University Press 1994 [1787]) 253–338 (336)). See in this regard M Gabriel (n 51) 268; G Gabriel (n 43) 115. Cf on Jacobi, George di Giovanni and Paolo Livieri, "Friedrich Heinrich Jacobi" in Edward N Zalta (ed) *Stanford Encyclopedia of Philosophy* (December 6, 2018) available at https://plato.stanford.edu/entries/friedrich-jacobi/ [last accessed February 1, 2023].

86 M Gabriel (n 51) 268–271.

87 Jacobi (n 85) David Hume on Faith or Idealism and Realism 336 [emphasis original]; in German see Jacobi (n 84) Ueber den transscendentalen Idealismus 304: "Ich muß gestehen, daß dieser Anstand mich bey dem Studio der Kantischen Philosophie nicht wenig aufgehalten hat, ... weil ich unaufhörlich darüber irre wurde, daß ich ohne jene Voraussetzungen in das System nicht hineinkomme, und mit jener Voraussetzung darin nicht bleiben konnt."

88 Kant (n 36) A 255 / B 310–311.

> understanding. For this will always remain unknown to us, so that it even remains unknown to us, so that it even remains unknown whether such a transcendental (extraordinary) cognition is possible at all, at least as one that stands under our customary categories. With us *understanding* and *sensibility* can determine an object *only in combination*. If we separate them, then we have intuitions without concepts, or concepts without intuitions, but in either case representations that we cannot relate to any determinate object.[89]

However, if we accepted this interpretation,[90] it would be difficult to sustain speaking of things in themselves in the plural.[91] Finally, while Kant holds that it is synthesis, a process of the cognizing subject, which provides for order and determination, this is hard to sustain because[92] "[a]ll organizational forms immanent to the transcendental consciousness – or within the genome: the logical position of the problem remains strictly identical in the two cases – cannot provide anything if the 'material' they are to 'form' does not already include in itself the 'minimal form' of being form*able*."[93]

This leads straightforwardly to another very well-known Kantian counterpart. Georg Wilhelm Friedrich Hegel is another important "early" critic of Kant. Hegel criticized Kant – among other things – for his concept of a "thing-in-itself," which is found to exist by Kant even though we cannot perceive it.[94] To Hegel – in close agreement with Jacobi[95] – such a thing-in-itself is a "ghost," for we cannot say anything about it since Kant, by holding that this thing-in-itself exists, construes a causal relationship between the appearances

[89] Kant (n 36) A 258 / B 314 [emphasis original].

[90] See in this regard Rohlf (n 51), pointing to the "two-objects interpretation" and the "two-aspects interpretation" of Kantian "transcendental idealism," of which the former was the standard reading during Kant's time and for a long time after, but which runs into the Jacobian problem referred to here. However, the latter interpretation does not help either as we can constantly ask ourselves whether it is things in themselves or representations of them which affect us. See on this M Gabriel (n 51) 279.

[91] See M Gabriel (n 51) 272–280 for a discussion about possible understandings of Kant's form-content dualism and the differentiation between representation and the thing-in-itself. However, Gabriel concludes that the Kantian form–content dualism implies the flawed assumption that things in themselves are under-determined.

[92] M Gabriel (n 51) 279–280.

[93] Cornelius Castoriadis, "The Logic of Magmas and the Question of Autonomy" in *The Castoriadis Reader* (translated and edited by David A Curtis Oxford University Press 1997) 290–318 (306), points to this when asking "could the living being organize an *absolutely chaotic* world?" Answering in the negative, Castoriadis points to this "old problem of Kantian criticism" and he furthermore adds "[l]et it be noted in passing that the idea of an *absolutely* disordered universe is for us unthinkable" [emphasis original].

[94] However, for ambiguities of the Kantian conception of the thing-in-itself, see for instance nn 90–92 above.

[95] See above n 87.

(*Erscheinungen*) and the thing-in-itself.[96] According to Hegel, the thing-in-itself is "itself only the product of thought,"[97] a "*Gedankending*."[98] Hence, if we think, we are thinking; nothing more and nothing less can be proven by that and thus the thing-in-itself is a product of our thinking and not a thing in the external world.[99] To put it differently, it is impossible to claim something would exist in the external world which, nevertheless, cannot be proven. Even more bluntly, how could I ever find out whether your version of the thing-in-itself looks like mine? For Hegel, our understanding of knowledge has a history – a history of the whole human being that includes its physiological competence, its social environment, as much as its religious, political and philosophical convictions.[100] In Hegel's words, an "aspect of spirit's coming-to-be, *history*, is that *knowing* self-*mediating* coming-to-be – the spirit relinquished into time."[101] In very broad strokes, this is the fundamental difference

96 Georg Wilhelm Friedrich Hegel, *The Science of Logic* (translated and edited by George di Giovanni Cambridge University Press 2010 [*Wissenschaft der Logik* 1832]) 40–41, 46: "But to want to clarify the nature of cognition prior to science is to demand that it should be discussed outside science, and outside science this cannot be done, at least not in the scientific manner which alone is the issue here."

97 Hegel (n 96) 41.

98 Hegel (n 96) 16.

99 Georg W F Hegel, *Encyclopedia of the Philosophical Sciences in Basic Outline Part I Science of Logic* (translated and edited by Klaus Brinkmann and Daniel O Dahlstrom Cambridge University Press 2010 [*Enzyklopädie der philosophischen Wissenschaften* I 1830]) § 44 and 124, esp § 60: "In every dualistic system, and especially in the Kantian system, its basic flaw reveals itself through the inconsistency of *combining* [*vereinen*] what a moment ago has been declared to be independent and thus *incompatible* [*unvereinbar*]. While what had been combined was just declared to be true, so now instead it is declared to be true that *the two moments*, whose separate existence on their own has been denied to them in the combination which was to be their truth, possess truth and actuality only insofar as they exist in separation. Such philosophizing as this lacks the simple consciousness that in going back and forth in this way, each of these individual determinations is declared to be unsatisfactory, and the flaw consists in the simple inability to bring together two thoughts (and in point of form there are only two of them present). It is therefore the greatest inconsistency to admit, on the one hand, that understanding acquires knowledge of appearances only while maintaining, on the other, that this kind of knowledge is something *absolute* by saying that knowing *cannot* go further, that this is the *natural*, absolute *barrier* [*Schranke*] for human knowledge [*Wissen*]. Natural things are limited [*beschränkt*], and they are merely natural things, insofar as they *know* [*wissen*] nothing of their universal barrier, insofar as their determinacy is a barrier only *for us*, not *for them*. Something can be known [*gewußt*], even felt to be a *barrier*, a lack only insofar as one has at the same time *gone beyond* it" [emphasis original].

100 See M Gabriel (n 51) 281 with further reference to Georg Wilhelm Friedrich Hegel, *Glauben und Wissen oder Reflexionsphilosophie der Subjektivität in der Vollständigkeit ihrer Formen als Kantische, Jacobische und Fichtesche Philosophie* (1803); Georg Wilhelm Friedrich Hegel, *Die Differenz des Fichteschen und Schellingschen Systems der Philosophie* (1801).

101 Georg Wilhelm Friedrich Hegel, *The Phenomenology of Spirit* (translation by Terry Pinkard Cambridge University Press 2018 from *Phenomenologie des Geistes* 1807) 466 [emphasis original].

between Kantian "subjective idealism" and Hegelian "objective idealism."[102] Hence, our thinking not only captures subjective constructions, or crude empirical facts, but follows the objective structure of being. In Hegel's own words, introducing the *spirit*: "The *I* that is *we* and the *we* that is *I*."[103] It is this switch, departing from a Kantian "I think," that could be called "methodological solipsism," finally arriving at a "We think." This Hegelian unity claims that "analytical unity" can only exist in "synthetic unity."[104] Thinking presupposes complex conceptual faculties that can only be acquired in a community. The existence of a subjective spirit presupposes an objective spirit. And, thus, philosophy as much as epistemology has to dismiss "methodological solipsism."[105]

This is still the very beginning of the nineteenth century. Hence, the "linguistic turn" in philosophy is still to come. Writ large, we can say that whereas Kant aimed at a criticism of pure reason and rational assumptions when thinking about what we can know, after the linguistic turn, the transcendental criticism turned to a critique of language.[106] This so-called linguistic turn in philosophy, brought about, among others, by Ludwig Wittgenstein, further challenges metaphysical assumptions and is thus also of relevance here.[107] Wittgenstein makes the argument – as did Hegel – that it is a

[102] See Vittorio Hösle, *Die Krise der Gegenwart und die Verantwortung der Philosophie. Transzendentalpragmatik, Letztbegründung, Ethik* (C H Beck 3rd ed 1997) 205–208, for an evolutionary classification into "realism/naturalism," "subjective idealism" and "objective idealism," and his own goal of an intersubjective transformation of objective idealism informed by transcendental pragmatism.

[103] Hegel (n 101) 108 [emphasis original]. Cf Terry Pinkard, *Hegel's Phenomenology. The Sociality of Reason* (Cambridge University Press 1994) and the qualification of "sociality of reason" in the subtitle.

[104] M Gabriel (n 51) 249.

[105] See on this issue see Markus Gabriel, *An den Grenzen der Erkenntnistheorie. Die notwendige Endlichkeit des objektiven Wissens als Lektion des Skeptizismus* (Karl Alber 2nd ed 2014) § 10, esp 286, who even goes so far as to claim that not only without a community would we lack truthful convictions, but also without dissent. In this sense Gabriel (286, n 141) quotes David Macarthur, "Naturalism and Skepticism" in Mario De Caro and David Macarthur (eds) *Naturalism in Question* (Harvard University Press 2004) 106–124 (122): "To believe involves a commitment to its being the case that one's truth-taking is regulated by what is in fact true. What performs this regulative function is the answerability of belief to rational criticism. Of course, we sometimes accept something on faith, without any evidence or reasons. But our entitlement to think of any given belief as true, including a belief accepted on faith, depends on its being answerable to rational criticism should we acquire sufficient reason or evidence to suggest it may be false." See also M Gabriel (n 51) 249, where he argues in a similar vein.

[106] See G Gabriel (n 43) 129–130, speaking of a transformation from epistemology to the philosophy of language.

[107] Among others it was Wittgenstein (n 43) who was responsible for the "linguistic turn." While the notion goes back to Gustav Bergmann, *Logic and Reality* (University of Wisconsin Press

contradiction to speak about limits of our knowledge (*Erkenntnis*) because by knowing the limits one has to have transcended the limit already. Without a point of reference external to our knowledge (*Erkenntnis*) (via our senses, experience or consciousness), we do not have a reason to question the limitlessness of our thinking about objects. In Wittgenstein's famous saying:

> *The limits of my language* mean the limits of my world.
>
> Logic fills the world: the limits of the world are also its limits. We cannot therefore say in logic: This and this there is in the world, that there is not. For that would apparently presuppose that we exclude certain possibilities, and this cannot be the case since otherwise logic must get outside the limits of the world: that is, if it could consider these limits from the other side also. What we cannot think, that we cannot think: we cannot therefore say what we cannot think.
>
> This remark provides a key to the question, to what extent solipsism is a truth. In fact what solipsism *means*, is quite correct, only it cannot be *said*, but it shows itself. That the world is *my* world, shows itself in the fact that the limits of the language (*the* language which I understand) mean the limits of *my* world.
>
> The world and life are one.[108]

Without entering into all the intricacies of Wittgensteinian philosophy in particular,[109] and the linguistic turn and the "birth" of analytic philosophy in general,[110] it is nevertheless important for us to understand that a

1964) 177, as evinced by Richard Rorty, "Introduction" in Richard Rorty (ed) *The Linguistic Turn: Essays in Philosophical Method. With Two Retrospective Essays* (University of Chicago Press 1967 reprinted in 1992) 1–39 (9); see also Peter M S Hacker, "The Linguistic Turn in Analytical Philosophy" in Michael Beaney (ed) *The Oxford Handbook of the History of Analytic Philosophy* (Oxford University Press 2013) 926–947 (926), specifying this to Gustav Bergmann, "Strawson's Ontology" (1960) 57 (19) Journal of Philosophy 601–622. Dummett (n 56) 665 ff traces back the origins of the linguistic turn to the work of Gottlob Frege, *The Foundations of Arithmetic. A Logico-Mathematical Enquiry into the Concept of Number* (translated by J L Austin Harper 2nd ed 1953 [*Die Grundlagen der Arithmetik. Eine logisch mathematische Untersuchung über den Begriff der Zahl* Wilhelm Koebner 1884]). For – according to Dummett (n 56) 665–666 – Frege "achieved a revolution as overwhelming as that of Descartes." To Dummett (n 56) 666, "Frege's primary significance consists precisely in the fact that he made this area of philosophy [philosophy of logic] not a specialized branch, but the starting-point for the whole subject." See, however, for a critical assessment of this qualification, Joan Weiner, "Frege and the Linguistic Turn" (1997) 25 (2) Philosophical Topics 265–288.

[108] Wittgenstein (n 43) 5.6–5.621 [emphasis original].

[109] On Wittgenstein and the development in his philosophy see for instance Joachim Schulte, *Wittgenstein. Eine Einführung* (Reclam 2nd ed 2016).

[110] See Michael Dummett, *Origins of Analytical Philosophy* (Harvard University Press 1993) 5, pointing again to "Frege's *Die Grundlagen der Arithmetik*[2] of 1884." Dummett continues by

fundamental skepticism relating to things a priori goes hand in hand with this development. While it can, in a way, be described as a transformation from epistemology to the philosophy of science, it is common ground shared by proponents of logical empiricism, such as Moritz Schlick and Rudolf Carnap, and their adversaries from critical rationalism, such as Karl Raimund Popper, that natural laws are not valid a priori.[111] While the advocates of logical empiricism aim to avoid metaphysics altogether for the sake of science, advocates of critical rationalism accepted metaphysics as being of heuristic value for science.[112] Beyond that, Popper and Carnap alike deny the possibility of a priori synthetic judgments.[113]

Interestingly, however, Wittgenstein famously ends his *Tractatus* with the metaphor of a ladder. "[A]nyone who understands" him, Wittgenstein says, "recognizes" his propositions "as nonsensical, when he has used them – as steps to climb up beyond them."[114] He then suggests that the reader "throw away the ladder" after having "climbed up it"; his propositions must be transcended to "see the world alright."[115] For "[w]hat we cannot speak about we must pass over in silence."[116] Thus, again, we are left with a clear warning against metaphysical claims a priori. This, I think, is fair to conclude from this finding.[117] While this was not the end of philosophy of science and even

saying that "[a]t a crucial point in the book, Frege raises the Kantian question, 'How are numbers given to us, granted that we have no idea or intuition of them?' His answer," so he goes on, "depends upon the celebrated context principle, which he had laid down in the Introduction as one of the fundamental methodological principles to be followed in the book."

111 G Gabriel (n 43) 138.

112 G Gabriel (n 43) 142.

113 G Gabriel (n 43) 143.

114 Wittgenstein (n 43) 6.54.

115 Wittgenstein (n 43) 6.54.

116 Wittgenstein (n 43) 7.

117 However, Wittgenstein's take in the Tractatus that (logical) language can accurately depict facts in the world as assumed by logical atomism (Bertrand Russell, *The Philosophy of Logical Atomism* (Routledge 2010 [Fontana 1972]) sec 1, can also be criticized as an implicit assumption that needs to be justified. See for a discussion G Gabriel (n 43) 151–159. For criticism of logical atomism, see for instance John Henry McDowell, *Having the World in View. Essays on Kant, Hegel, and Sellars* (Harvard University Press 2009) 6, who writes, in examining Wilfrid Sellars', *Empiricism and the Philosophy of Mind* (Harvard University Press 2nd ed 1997) part III: "In an empiricistic foundationalism of the usual kind, it is not just that the credentials of all knowledge are ultimately grounded in knowledge acquired in perception. Beyond that, the grounding perceptual knowledge is atomistically conceived. Traditional empiricists take it that each element of the grounding knowledge can in principle be acquired on its own, independently not only of other elements of the grounding perceptual knowledge, but also of anything in the world view that is grounded on this basic stratum of knowledge."

Wittgenstein himself seemed to have continued climbing,[118] one message appears to be rather clear-cut. Metaphysical assumptions are a daring venture and if we are to advance something of this sort, utmost prudence and reluctance seems to be in order, and a proper justification for any assumption we consider necessary is indispensable and yet must be regarded with suspicion. What is more, since Kant famously pointed to the need for critical metaphysics, science has made huge advancements, which at least suggest that what Kant tried to establish as granted a priori cannot be defended as given.

In this vein, the criticism advanced by Charles Sanders Peirce is pertinent as he states that he "cannot admit the proposition of Kant – that there are certain impassable bounds to human knowledge."[119] This seemed wrong to Peirce because "[t]he history of science affords illustrations enough of the folly of saying that this, that, or the other can never be found out."[120] Yet, despite this critique, the so-called founder of pragmatism was an admirer of Kant and indeed can be labeled as a defender of objective idealism despite his pragmatism.[121]

Being aware of the pragmatist approach of Peirce, Karl-Otto Apel developed transcendental pragmatism (*Transzendentalpragmatik*)[122] and Jürgen Habermas universal pragmatics (*Universalpragmatik*).[123] The former analyzes

118 See, for instance, his later work: Ludwig Wittgenstein, *Philosophical Investigations* (translated by G E M Anscombe Basil Blackwell 2nd ed 1958 reprinted 1986 [*Philosophische Untersuchungen* 1953]); Ludwig Wittgenstein, *On Certainty* (translated by G E M Anscombe and Denis Paul and edited by G E M Anscombe and G H von Wright Harper 1972 [*Über Gewißheit* 1969]). Yet Wittgenstein's work is hotly debated and this is certainly not the place to offer yet another interpretation, except for pointing to the notable difference to his earlier work.

119 Charles Sanders Peirce, "Science Immortality" in Charles Hartshorne and Paul Weiss (eds) *Charles Sanders Peirce. Collected Papers Vol VI: Scientific Metaphysics* (Harvard University Press 1935) sec 6.556.

120 Peirce (n 119) sec 6.556.

121 For a synopsis see Susan Haack, "The Legitimacy of Metaphysics: Kant's Legacy to Peirce, and Peirce's to Philosophy Today" (2008) 36 (1) Philosophical Topics 97–100 (109): "In briefest summary, then: (part of) Kant's legacy to Peirce was a lasting conviction that metaphysics does not have to be the hopelessly 'airy science' Hume had pooh-poohed, but could and should become a legitimate and valuable area of investigation; and (part of) Peirce's legacy to philosophy today is a distinctively plausible post-Kantian reconception of how this might be achieved."

122 Karl-Otto Apel, *Understanding and Explanation: A Transcendental-Pragmatic Perspective* (translated by Georgia Warnke MIT Press 1984 [*Die Erklären-Verstehen-Kontroverse in Transzendental-Pragmatischer Sicht* Suhrkamp 1979]).

123 Jürgen Habermas, "What Is Universal Pragmatics?" in *On the Pragmatics of Communication* (ed Maeve Cooke MIT press 1976 ["Was heißt Universalpragmatik?" in Karl-Otto Apel (ed) *Sprachpragmatik und Philosophie* Suhrkamp (1976) 174–272]) 21–103; Jürgen Habermas, *Communication and the Evolution of Society* (Beacon Press 1979); see also Jürgen Habermas,

transcendental – that is, enabling – conditions for human action. The latter, also called "formal pragmatics" by Habermas when he first wrote about it, is conceptualized as "reconstructive science." The point is to "render theoretically explicit the intuitive, pretheoretical know-how underlying such basic human competences as speaking and understanding, judging and acting."[124] Importantly, and "[u]nlike Kant's transcendental analysis of the conditions of rationality, reconstructive sciences yield knowledge that is not necessary but hypothetical, not a priori but empirical, not certain but fallible."[125] By closely focusing on language and conceptualizing "reconstructive science," Habermas departs in important ways from Kant, which is also relevant to us. For Habermas, philosophy is no longer "the sole judge in normative matters." What is more, nor is philosophy "the methodological authority that assigns the various domains of inquiry to their proper questions." In contrast, according to the approach advanced by Habermas, "philosophy must engage in a fully cooperative relationship with the social sciences and the empirical disciplines in general."[126] "Once we have dropped foundationalist claims, we can no longer expect a hierarchy of sciences."[127] Beyond that, Jürgen Habermas, among others, has also developed a consensus theory of truth.[128] According

The Theory of Communicative Action. Lifeworld and System: A Critique of Functionalist Reason Vol 2 (translated by Thomas McCarthy Polity Press 1987 [*Theorie des kommunikativen Handelns Band 2: Zur Kritik der funktionalistischen Vernunft* Suhrkamp 3rd ed 1985]) 400–404, explaining that universal pragmatics provides for a "non-foundational universalism" for a social and political theory. See, however, for the criticism, that despite not being a representational foundationalism in the sense of Richard Rorty (*Philosophy and the Mirror of Nature* (Princeton University Press 1979)), Habermasian universal pragmatics are nonetheless a "non-representation foundationalism" although not resting on a "representational epistemology" (ie correspondence theory of truth), Hudson Meadwell, "The Foundations of Habermas's Universal Pragmatics" (1994) 23 (5) Theory and Society 711–727.

124 James Bohman and William Rehg, "Jürgen Habermas" in Edward N Zalta (ed) *Stanford Encyclopedia of Philosophy* (August 4, 2014) available at https://plato.stanford.edu/entries/habermas/ [last accessed February 1, 2023]; Habermas (n 123) *The Theory of Communicative Action. Lifeworld and System: A Critique of Functionalist Reason Vol 2* ch 1.

125 Bohman and Rehg (n 124).

126 Bohman and Rehg (n 124).

127 Habermas (n 123) *The Theory of Communicative Action. Lifeworld and System: A Critique of Functionalist Reason Vol 2* 400.

128 See Jürgen Habermas, "Wahrheitstheorien" in Helmut Fahrenbach (ed) *Wirklichkeit und Reflexion. Walter Schulz zum 60. Geburtstag* (Neske 1973) 211–265; Jürgen Habermas, *Truth and Justification* (translated by Barbara Fultner MIT Press 2003 [*Wahrheit und Rechtfertigung. Philosophische Aufsätze* Suhrkamp 1999]). For early criticism see Ansgar Beckermann, "Die realistischen Voraussetzungen der Konsenstheorie von J. Habermas" (1972) 3 (1) Zeitschrift für allgemeine Wissenschaftstheorie 63–80. Cf, for criticism, Nicholas Rescher, *Pluralism: Against the Demand for Consensus* (Oxford Clarendon Press 1993); for criticism of this criticism, see Seamus O'Neill, "Book Review: Nicholas Rescher, Pluralism: Against the

to this view, truth is what can be claimed in a noncoercive general and justified consensus. For participants in a rational discourse, we have to assume pragmatic prerequisites, which are a sort of aspiration; in Habermas' words they are "an unavoidable supposition, reciprocally made in discourse."[129]

A pragmatic theory of truth, in turn, does not accept the consensus theory of truth and takes practical life – instead of consensus – as a yardstick. According to this view, a proposition is true if its consequence helps solve a practical problem or answer a question related to such a problem.[130] As has been spelled out before, this cannot be brought in line with the Kantian assumptions as borrowed by the Kelsenian pure theory of law either. Yet this approach too faces criticism that because something is useful does not mean it must be true. False facts, as is proven over and over again, can be very useful. This, however, does not render lies true.

The coherence theory of truth is another major competitor in the question of what is truth.[131] According to this conception, a proposition is compared to an already established system. Hence, to figure out whether a proposition is true, we need to evaluate whether this proposition can be included in a system without contradiction – in other words, whether this proposition is coherent with the system. This, however, is likely circular or necessitates a preestablished system. Beyond that, coherence is quite a weak criterion for truth. However, importantly for our purpose, it does not support the Kelsenian pure

Demand for Consensus" (1995) 7 (2) Utilitas 340–343. However, see also Jürgen Hagermas, "Kommunikatives Handeln und detranszendentalisierte Vernunft" in *Zwischen Naturalismus und Religion. Philosophische Aufsätze* (Suhrkamp 2005) 27–83; and Jürgen Habermas, "Zur Architektonik Der Diskursdifferenzierung Kleine Replik auf eine große Auseinandersetzung" in *Zwischen Naturalismus und Religion. Philosophische Aufsätze* (Suhrkamp 2005) 84–105.

[129] Habermas (n 128) Wahrheitstheorien 258, quoted in Thomas McCarthy, *The Critical Theory of Juergen Habermas* (MIT Press 1978) 310.

[130] Charles Sanders Peirce, "Truth and Falsity and Error" in James Mark Baldwin (ed) *Dictionary of Philosophy and Psychology Vol 2* (1901) 716–720 (718–720); see also William James, *The Meaning of Truth: A Sequel to "Pragmatism"* in *Pragmatism and The Meaning of Truth* (edited with an introduction by Alfred J Ayer Harvard University Press 1978 [1909]); William James, "Pragmatism's Conception of Truth" in Michael P Lynch (ed) *The Nature of Truth. Classic and Contemporary Perspectives* (MIT Press 2001 [1907]) 211–228. See also John Dewey and Arthur Bentley, *Knowing and the Known* (Beacon Press 1949). For an overview, see John Capps, "The Pragmatic Theory of Truth" in Edward N Zalta (ed) *Stanford Encyclopedia of Philosophy* (March 21, 2019) available at https://plato.stanford.edu/entries/truth-pragmatic/ [last accessed February 1, 2023].

[131] Nicholas Rescher, *The Coherence Theory of Truth* (Oxford University Press 1973); cf James O Young, "The Coherence Theory of Truth" in Edward N Zalta (ed) *Stanford Encyclopedia of Philosophy* (June 26, 2018) available at https://plato.stanford.edu/entries/truth-coherence/ [last accessed February 1, 2023].

theory of law as it does not help restore what has been lost through the critique of the Kantian assumptions of the Kelsenian project.

Finally, in contemporary epistemology it is important to note Donald Davidson, who also argues that thought hinges on language.[132] Yet, according to his deflationary theory of truth, the term truth does not denote a real property of sentences or propositions. To him, it is a "folly" to try to define truth,[133] for it is precisely the point of this theory of truth to prove the irrelevance of its subject matter.[134]

Obviously, this was a strikingly brief overview lacking many important details. However, to return to the reason why we started engaging with epistemology and theories of truth, I think it should have become clear by now that Kantian epistemology, despite its genius, is not a stable foundation for legal epistemology. It is not up to date and has been heavily criticized, and rightly so. Therefore, it is no firm basis for a theory on the relationship between legal orders. For a proper legal epistemology, we cannot but consider the philosophical progress achieved since the eighteenth century.[135] Nevertheless – leaving the criticism just expressed to one side – we will now take a look at some neo-Kantian defense against criticisms aimed at Kant in particular and neo-Kantian philosophy in general. We will do so in order to determine whether the leap from Kantian to neo-Kantian epistemology can provide fruitful grounds for the axioms of the pure theory of law and Kelsenian legal epistemology, which is the basis for Kelsenian legal monism.

[132] See, for example, Donald Davidson, *Inquiries into Truth and Interpretation* (Oxford University Press 1984); cf Donald Davidson, "The Centrality of Truth" in Jaroslav Peregrin (ed) *Truth and Its Nature (if Any)* (Springer 1999) 105–115.

[133] Donald Davidson, "The Folly of Trying to Define Truth" in Michael P Lynch (ed) *The Nature of Truth. Classic and Contemporary Perspectives* (MIT Press 2001) 623–640. See, however, Paul Horwich, "A Defense of Minimalism" in Michael P Lynch (ed) *The Nature of Truth. Classic and Contemporary Perspectives* (MIT Press 2001) 559–578.

[134] See also Ralf Poscher, "Wahrheit und Recht. Die Wahrheitsfragen des Rechts im Lichte der deflationären Wahrheitstheorie" (2003) 89 (2) Archiv für Rechts- und Sozialphilosophie 200–215, who refers to the deflationary theory of truth and in doing so adapts the argument from Paul Horwich holding that the precise point of this theory of truth is to prove the irrelevance of its subject matter for the *law*. For an overview of truth theories and the law, compare Martina Deckert, "Recht und Wahrheit. Zum gegenwärtigen Stand der Diskussion" (1996) 82 (1) Archiv für Rechts- und Sozialphilosophie 43–54; see also Annette Brockmöller, Stephan Kirste and Ulfrid Neumann (eds) *Wert und Wahrheit in der Rechtswissenschaft* ARSP Beiheft 145 (2015).

[135] For a general overview, see Isaak I Doore, *The Epistemological Foundations of Law* (Carolina Academic Press 2007).

1.2.2 *Neo-Kantianism and Its Conception of Epistemology*

"It seems to be obvious that great ideas and insights inevitably become dogmatized."[136] Kant developed his *Critique of Pure Reason* and the arguments expressed therein to enable scientific metaphysics. In his *Metaphysics of Morals* generally and in his *Doctrine of Right* in particular, for instance, Kant did not return to his epistemology in the sense that the Kelsenian pure theory of law does concerning the law.[137] What Kant considered as synthetic a priori judgments on epistemology in general – causality, for instance – is quite different from legal validity. Kelsen, however, simply adopted what he labeled a (neo-)Kantian position with regard to the law. So what Kant considered necessary concerning the cognition of the external world and how we perceive nature, Kelsen postulates – without giving reasons for this intriguing analogy – would apply to the regulation of human behavior as well.[138] Before elaborating on this claim and the problems arising with such an alliance, we will first analyze relevant neo-Kantian positions.

Kantian philosophy was immensely influential and, alongside the criticism partly outlined earlier, some scholars – today commonly referred to as neo-Kantians – answered criticisms of Kant and became well-known for their philosophical battle cry "back to Kant!"[139] Again, a caveat is in order.

[136] Rainer Stollmann, *Groteske Aufklärung. Studien zu Natur und Kultur des Lachens* (M & P 1997) 44. Stollmann further continues this statement by adding that knowledge is power and thus, also victim of misuse of power [translation in the text LK].

[137] See Immanuel Kant, *Metaphysics of Morals: Doctrine of Virtue Vol I* and *Doctrine of Right Vol II* (edited and translated by Mary J Gregor Cambridge University Press 1997 [*Die Metaphysik der Sitten: Tugendlehre und Rechtslehre* 1797]); on this see for example Karl Ameriks and Otfried Höffe (eds) *Kant's Moral and Legal Philosophy* (Cambridge University Press 2009). Interestingly, this is noted by Kelsen, who was quite clear that Kant "can be regarded as the most nearly perfect expression of classical natural law theory as it developed out of Protestant Christianity during the seventeenth and eighteenth centuries." See also Stanley L Paulson, "The Neo-Kantian Dimension of Kelsen's Pure Theory of Law" (1992) 12 (3) Oxford Journal of Legal Studies 311–332 (322, n 39), quoting Hans Kelsen, *Philosophical Foundations of Natural Law Theory and Legal Positivism* (translated by Wolfgang H Kraus as an appendix to Kelsen, *General Theory of Law and State*, translated by Anders Wedberg Harvard University Press 1945 [1928]) 389–445, esp 444–445. Other Kelsenians also hold that "Kelsen's Kant was the Kant of epistemology in the *Critique of Pure Reason*, and not the Kant of moral philosophy in the *Metaphysics of Morals* and the *Critique of Practical Reason*." See Gragl (n 16) 64–65 with further reference to Paulson (n 27) 198.

[138] See the early criticism expressed by Erich Voegelin, *Der autoritäre Staat. Ein Versuch über das österreichische Staatsproblem* (Springer 1997 [1936]) 105–106, 108.

[139] See Christian Krijnen, "'Back to Kant': Neo-Kantianism" in Gary Banham, Dennis Schulting and Nigel Hems (eds) *The Bloomsbury Companion to Kant* (Bloomsbury 2nd ed 2015) 318–324 (320, n 112), who explains that the dictum "back to Kant" was first expressed by Otto Liebmann, *Kant und die Epigonen* (1865) when he "wrote at the end of each chapter: 'Hence,

As neo-Kantianism is better classified as a rather loose philosophical movement than a specific school of thought, it is impossible to outline all positions and arguments attributed to this label.[140] Hence, we will again only refer to those arguments that are related to Kelsenian legal epistemology. In this vein, the neo-Kantianism from Marburg, most prominently represented by Hermann Cohen, is of interest to us.[141] The neo-Kantianism that was located in Baden around Wilhelm Windelband will therefore be left aside here. Yet doubts about the Kelsenian interpretation of Kant might already be supported because he chose not to align with those neo-Kantians who focused on the humanities, namely those located in Baden. Their value-laden approach was actually quite far from what Kelsen was aiming at. This is not in itself a strong argument against the Kelsenian interpretation of Kant. However, it is still interesting that Kelsen claimed to follow those neo-Kantians who were not so much interested in the humanities as in physics and mathematics.[142]

Neo-Kantians did not follow Kantian positions blindly but deviated from Kant in some important respects. This is significant as changes introduced to or criticism expressed of Kantian conceptions by his successors have to be

we must return to Kant [*Also muß auf Kant zurückgegangen werden*]'" [emphasis original]. For a historical overview of the movement, see Thomas A Willey, *Back to Kant. The Revival of Kantianism in German Social and Historical Thought 1860–1914* (Wayne State University Press 1978).

140 For a general overview, see Jeremy Heis, "Neo-Kantianism" in Edward N Zalta (ed) *Stanford Encyclopedia of Philosophy* (May 18, 2018) available at https://plato.stanford.edu/entries/neo-kantianism/index.html#ref-11 [last accessed February 1, 2023]; for an overview with particular emphasis on the origins and evolution of neo-Kantianism, see Klaus Christian Köhnke, *Entstehung und Aufstieg des Neukantianismus. Die deutsche Universitätsphilosophie zwischen Idealismus und Positivismus* (Suhrkamp 1993).

141 For an introduction see Sebastian Luft, "Introduction: Hermann Cohen (1842–1918)" in Sebastian Luft (ed) *The Neo-Kantian Reader* (Routledge 2015) 93–100, 107–116. Cf especially Hermann Cohen, *Kants Theorie der Erfahrung* (Dümmler 2nd ed 1885 [partially translated by David Hyder as "'The Synthetic Principles' from Kant's Theory of Experience (1885)" in Sebastian Luft (ed) *The Neo-Kantian Reader* (Routledge 2015) 107–116]); Hermann Cohen, *Logik der reinen Erkenntnis* (Georg Olms Hermann Cohen Werke Vol 6 I 4th ed 1977 [Bruno Cassirer 2nd ed 1914]); Hermann Cohen, *System der Philosophie, Zweiter Teil: Ethik des reinen Willens* (Georg Olms Hermann Cohen Werke Vol 7 II 5th ed 1981 [Bruno Cassirer 2nd ed 1907]).

142 See Fritz-Joachim von Rintelen, "Philosophical Idealism in Germany: The Way from Kant to Hegel and the Present" (1977) 38 Philosophy and Phenomenological Research 1–32 (24); see also Heis (n 140): "Typically (not exclusively), the Marburg philosophers were concerned with the physics and mathematics of the late nineteenth and early twentieth century, which (they emphasized) differed fundamentally from that of Kant's own day. The Southwest Neo-Kantians, on the other hand, were more concerned with the so-called '*Geisteswissenschaften*' (the 'human sciences'), which had come into their own in the nineteenth century and now deserved (they argued) to be recognized as autonomous and fully scientific" [emphasis original].

followed closely when claiming to adopt either a Kantian or a neo-Kantian approach. To put it bluntly, cherry-picking has to be treated with caution. For Marburg neo-Kantians, for instance, things in themselves were a postulation and the distinction between sensibility and understanding was rejected too.[143]

[143] Heis (n 140); on the rejection or reinterpretation of the things in themselves, see Cohen (n 141) *Kants Theorie der Erfahrung* 503 ff; on the rejection of the distinction between sensibility and understanding, see Cohen (n 141) *Logik der reinen Erkenntnis* ch VII; see also Paul Natorp, "'Kant and the Marburg School' (1912)" in Sebastian Luft (ed) *The Neo-Kantian Reader* (translated by Frances Bottenberg Routledge 2015 ["Kant und die Marburger Schule" (1912) 17 Kant-Studien 193–221]) 180–197 (186): "In the end, 'intuition' no longer remains a cognitive factor which stands across from or is opposed to thinking. It *is* thinking, just not thinking in terms of laws, but thinking in terms of full objects. In its implementation, in its exercise, intuition is to conceptual thought as function is to the law of function. This requires that every one of its states be strictly and unambiguously determined, but they must be determined in respect to the lawful functions of thinking itself: particularity, quantity, quality and causal reciprocality must be determined according to their respective laws. The result is something which *is* 'given' for the first time, but which seemed to *be* given as a fixed sum. This makes quite transparent the following oddly illuminating sentence (which appears in the section concerning the highest principle of synthetic judgments): 'To give an object, if this is not again meant only mediately, but it is rather to be exhibited immediately in intuition, is nothing other than to relate its representation to experience (whether this be actual or still possible)' [Kant (n 36) A 156 / B 195]. Kant is only now in a position to prove the 'possibility' of experience within a system of grounding principles. Givenness has transformed itself into a *postulate* of reality; it adopts purely modal meaning." Importantly, Natorp continues: "This is pure idealism and nothing else. To neither consider nor straightforwardly carry out this radical correction, which at its core is a self-correction already contained in Kant, would entail giving up the most profound dimension of the critique of reason, only for the sake of saving, at any cost, the long-disproven, stale provisions of the Transcendental Aesthetic contained in the inaugural dissertation of 1770 (an at least partially if not wholly dogmatic account)" [footnotes omitted; emphasis original]. Cf Wilhelm Windelband, "Philosophy of Culture and Transcendental Idealism' (1910)" in Sebastian Luft (ed) *The Neo-Kantian Reader* (translated by Alan Duncan Routledge 2015 ["Kulturphilosophie und transzendentaler Idealismus" in Wilhelm Windelband, *Präludien. Aufsätze und Reden zur Philosophie und ihrer Geschichte* Vol II (Mohr 5th ed 1915) 279–294] 317–324 (323): "transcendental idealism has no more need of 'another world,' as Kant originally would have deemed necessary in the concept of the 'thing in itself'; after all, he himself made us at home in this world afterwards through practical reason, and thus tore down the boundary." However, Windelband continues by highlighting that "one thing must be stressed again and again against intentional and unintentional misunderstandings of this doctrine: that the individual must never think of itself as the creative power in the creation of objects; we are involved, inasmuch as genuine cultural values are concerned, never as individuals, nor even as instances of our genus, but act rather as domiciles and hosts of transcendent functions of reason, and therefore functions factually grounded in the essence of things themselves. Only these functions of reason determine the 'objects' that are necessarily and universally valid. This participation in a larger world of rational values that nevertheless make up the sense of all the orders upon which our little worlds of knowledge, will and formation are built up, this insertion of our conscious life of culture into rational orders that far transcend us and our entire empirical existence – this is the inconceivable mystery of all spiritual activity. But the entire process of human culture, the strengthening and expansion to which its valuable achievements are subject in history, repeatedly confirms to us

Yet they nevertheless considered as essential the "existence of substantive a priori concepts and principles that make knowledge possible,"[144] though not necessarily those concepts and principles identified by Kant since the scientific theories he referred to were (partly) considered outdated.[145] What is particular to neo-Kantian philosophy is its proponents' interest in the scientific methodology and the question of how we can know anything about the different branches of science: in their words, "the logic of the sciences."[146]

For Cohen in particular, it was important to distinguish philosophy from psychology.[147] While the former, according to him, aims at objectivity, the latter is utterly subjective.[148] What Cohen aligns closely with Kant, however, is the "transcendental method," which, in Cohen's conception, "begins with a fact – paradigmatically, the fact of science – and investigates the conditions that make that fact possible."[149] Interestingly, the Marburgian transcendental

this upward growth of our life into rational contexts that mean more than ourselves" [footnotes omitted].

[144] Heis (n 140).

[145] See eg Natorp (n 143) 180 when addressing the Kant Society in Halle on April 27, 1912, who started his talk by stating that "[a]nyone wishing to advance in philosophy today considers it his first duty to come to terms with Kantian philosophy." However, Natorp goes on to clarify that "it was never anyone's wish nor intent to cling to Kant's doctrines in an absolute way. Talk of an orthodox Kantianism within the Marburg School was never justified, and it has lost every shred of supposed justification as this school has continued to develop."

[146] Heis (n 140) quoting (and translating) Hermann Cohen, "Biographisches Vorwort und Einleitung mit kritischem Nachtrag" in Friedrich Lange (ed) *Geschichte des Materialismus und Kritik seiner Bedeutung in der Gegenwart* (Baedeker 6th ed 1898) xv–lxxvi (x): "The transcendental method does not research the principles of human reason but rather the foundation of science that conditions scientific validity. Our organization is, insofar as it comes into question in general, a question of psychology; and there is at least no methodological means for procuring secure, scientific, and exact information from the ultimate and simplest parts of our mental essence. But the sciences lie before us in books. What makes them into sciences, wherein their character of generality and necessity rests, from which concepts their epistemological validity within their region can be derived, what tools and ways of knowing explain in its validity those historical facts of knowledge – the sciences – this is a methodological question, this is the question, which the sciences themselves pose, whenever they feel the impulse to think about their own principles – this and nothing else is the transcendental question."

[147] And so Cohen (n 141) 109 interpreted Kant in his *Kant's Theory of Experience*); and in *Logik der reinen Erkenntnis* (Cohen n 141) 44, where he distinguishes the "metaphysical a priori" and the "transcendental a priori." While the former, which can be empirically studied, is irrelevant to the transcendental philosopher, the latter only makes objective validity possible.

[148] Hermann Cohen, *Das Prinzip der Infinitesimal-Methode und seine Geschichte* (Dümmler 1883) § 6. For a partial translation, see Hermann Cohen, "'Introduction' to The Principle of the Infinitesimal Method and Its History (1883)" in Sebastian Luft (ed) *The Neo-Kantian Reader* (partial translation by David Hyder and Lydia Patton Routledge 2015).

[149] Heis (n 140) also with reference to Natorp (n 143); Cohen (n 148) § 7–9; Cohen (n 141) *Kant's Theorie der Erfahrung* § 12; and Alan Richardson, "'The Fact of Science' and Critique

method begins with a "fact" that is historically verifiable – a "fact of science" regarding theoretical philosophy and a fact of "social order" concerning practical philosophy.[150] In a second step, what makes objective validity possible is analyzed from this fact, by identifying the "laws" or "form" of the specific discipline.[151] The "goal of the transcendental method is to provide foundations for culture" that "are not meant to be certain" and, thus, "[t]ranscendental logic, one might say, is a semantic, not a Cartesian project."[152] Beyond that, Marburg neo-Kantians too considered themselves as "idealists," which is expressed in their transcendental method and their belief in substantive a priori principles that make experience possible. The conception of objectivity "grounded in the idea of the unity of knowledge according to laws" and their philosophy of science, which is held to be "radically unlike the features that the world appears to have to untutored, everyday experience," also point in this direction.[153]

What becomes apparent from this brief overview of neo-Kantianism is that neo-Kantian philosophers were actually ready to reconsider Kantian positions

of Knowledge: Exact Science as Problem and Resource in Marburg Neo-Kantianism" in Michael Friedman and Alfred Nordmann (eds) *The Kantian Legacy in Nineteenth-Century Science* (MIT Press 2006) 211–226.

[150] Heis (n 140) also with reference to Natorp (n 143).

[151] Paul Natorp, "'On the Objective and Subjective Grounding of Knowledge' (1887)" in Sebastian Luft (ed) *The Neo-Kantian Reader* (translated by Lois Phillips and David Kolb Routledge 2015 ["Über objective und subjective Begründung der Erkenntniss" (1887) 23 Philosophische Monatshefte 257–286]) 164–179 (esp 165): "If every science inquires after the objective foundation underlying each appearance of its truth, then every science must have some concept of this foundation and of the grounding relationship of the object to the appearance." Natorp goes on (165) by stating that "[a]ll scientific knowledge aims at the law. The relation of the appearance to the law (the relation of the 'manifold' of the appearance to the 'unity' of the law) must therefore explain the original relation to the object in all knowledge. The interpretation of the appearance in accordance with laws is taken as the objectively true interpretation. We may take as impartially established this universal correlation between law and object, ancient as it is in the history of philosophy and the sciences. It has been established not through the whim or the passion for system of this or that philosopher, but rather through the action of science that everywhere constitutes the object in law." Yet Natorp cautiously adds that "[g]iven these fundamentals we can confidently take a stand on the pending problems of logic. Whoever cannot agree with us on this common basis will probably find most of the following said in vain"; cf Cohen (n 141) *Logik der reinen Erkenntnis* § 11.

[152] Heis (n 140). See also Krijnen (n 139) 320: "To understand neo-Kantianism properly, however, it is important that the emphasis on the cultural-philosophical aspect does not lead one to disregard the specific way in which the neo-Kantians put culture on the philosophical agenda. Not just *that* neo-Kantianism can be understood as a philosophy of culture and that it understands itself as such, but also *how* it is to be seen as a philosophy of culture is what explains the peculiar nature and unity of neo-Kantianism as well as its relation to Kant and ultimately its argumentative potential" [emphasis original].

[153] Heis (n 140).

quite extensively.[154] For Kant, roughly speaking, Aristotelian logic, Euclidian geometry and Newtonian mechanics were state of the art and thus the laws constituting and enabling our understanding of these approaches were "postulated as valid."[155] Neo-Kantians were aware that science advances and therefore the a priori needs to be adapted, even to the extent that they tried to understand and capture the evolution of science as well. By now our knowledge in each field has arguably advanced again noticeably, to put it mildly. What we learn is that maybe Kant was right in a sense that experience and our perception of experience preconditions some sort of form or faculty in us.[156] Yet what we might potentially consider as "given" has changed with the development of science since Kant thought about it and very likely will change again with further developments in the future.[157] Hence, it is of utmost importance to be very careful when postulating a given faculty or form as being a precondition for knowledge: "objective validity" in a neo-Kantian sense on the one hand and legal validity on the other. In fact, we should acknowledge that "objective validity" concerning our knowledge of the external world and the legal validity of norms must be kept apart. The law is arguably quite different from any physical object. Therefore, we have to take a

[154] In this regard consider the quote by the Badian neo-Kantian Wilhelm Windelband, *Präludien: Aufsätze und Reden zur Philosophie und ihrer Geschichte Vol I* (Mohr 5th ed 1915) iv, holding that "to understand Kant means to go beyond him." This famous quote also appears on the very first page of Sebastian Luft (ed) *The Neo-Kantian Reader* (Routledge 2015) v. See also Natorp (n 145), as well as Hermann Cohen, *Kants Theorie der Erfahrung* (Georg Olms 1987 *Hermann Cohen Werke Vol 1 I.3* [Dümmler 1st ed 1871]), where he states in the preface that he is about to justify Kant's doctrine of the a priori anew as to him this doctrine did not appear to be right in Kant's writing.

[155] See in this regard Guyer and Wood (n 70) 22: "Kant's bold attempt to resolve with one stroke two of the most pressing problems of modern philosophy has seldom been accepted by his successors without qualification. Some feel that Kant's identification of the basic principles of science with the fundamental principles of human understanding itself betrays too much confidence in the specifically Newtonian mechanistic physics that prevailed at his time, leaving too little room for subsequent scientific developments, such as the theory of general relativity and quantum mechanics."

[156] For a detailed state of the art analysis of a potential innate human faculty for cognizing morality, see Chapter 5.

[157] See Vittorio Hösle, *Hegels System. Der Idealismus der Subjektivität und das Problem der Intersubjektivität Vol 1: Systementwicklung und Logik* (Felix Meiner 1st ed 1987) 22–38, who points to Fichte (Johann Gottlieb Fichte, "Über den Begriff der Wissenschaftslehre" in *Werke Vol 1* (1971 [1834–1846]) 27–81, who already criticized that Kant's categories claim to constitute knowledge, but does not explain why this would be true knowledge. This is why Fichte developed a "doctrine of science" (*Wissenschaftslehre*).

close look at how to establish and argue for conditions necessary for *legal* knowledge.[158]

1.2.3 *Kelsenian Legal Epistemology*

Hans Kelsen claimed that his pure theory of law in the form of its basic norm is a priori necessary in order to cognize any legal order.[159] And so those who follow Kelsen are likely to elaborate on the "transcendental undergirding for legal science."[160] Kelsen asks, "how is positive law *qua* object of cognition, *qua* object of cognitive legal science, possible?"[161] Thereby he aims at establishing a "*legal* a priori" in the sense of Kant's "transcendental a priori."[162]

[158] This, however, is something that arguably needs an in-depth analysis of current state-of-the-art insights in psychology and neurobiology and will thus be postponed to Chapter 5.

[159] Hans Kelsen, *Das Problem der Souveränität und die Theorie des Völkerrechts* (Mohr Siebeck 1920) vi.

[160] Gragl (n 16) 64, quoting Carsten Heidemann, *Die Norm als Tatsache: Zur Normentheorie Hans Kelsens* (Nomos 1997) 43, who nevertheless mentions critically that Kelsen does not bother to give detailed explanations or justification for his transcendental thesis. Rather, he apodictically postulates them and uses their powerful associations for justifying their plausibility instead of arguing properly why they hold. See furthermore Gragl (n 16 19 n 2), claiming (and pointing to further references, such as Horst Dreier, *Rechtslehre, Staatssoziologie und Demokratietheorie bei Hans Kelsen* (Nomos 2nd ed 1990) 33, n 40, speaking of "eclecticism") that a detailed analysis of Kelsenian positions quickly reveals that his concepts and arguments are rather vague and are often insufficiently received sets of pieces of various philosophical directions. This would particularly be the case according to the epistemological basis of his theory. For a comparative overview of Hans Kelsen and other democratic scholars of public law during the Weimar period, see Kathrin Groh, *Demokratische Staatsrechtslehrer in der Weimarer Republik. Von der konstitutionellen Staatslehre zur Theorie des modernen demokratischen Verfassungsstaats* (Mohr Siebeck 2010).

[161] Hans Kelsen, *Natural Law Doctrine and Legal Positivism* (translated by Wolfgang Herbert Kraus as an appendix to Kelsen, *General Theory of Law and State* (Harvard University Press 1945 [1928]) 389–446 (437), quoted (and translated slightly differently by) Stanley L Paulson, "Kelsen's Legal Theory: The Final Round" (1992) 12 (2) Oxford Journal of Legal Studies 265–274. See also Hans Kelsen, *Pure Theory of Law* (University of California Press 2nd ed 1967) 202: "How is it possible to interpret without recourse to meta-legal authorities, like God or nature, the subjective meaning of certain facts as a system of objectively valid legal norms describable in rules of law?" Kelsen does so explicitly following Kant when he (*Pure Theory of Law* 202) quotes "Kant asks: 'How is it possible to interpret without a metaphysical hypothesis, the facts perceived by our sense, in the laws of nature formulated by natural science?'").

[162] Gragl (n 16) 66 with further reference (also to Robert Alexy, "Hans Kelsens Begriff des relativen Apriori" in Robert Alexy et al (eds) *Neukantianismus und Rechtsphilosophie* (Nomos 2002) 179–202 (194), however, comes to the conclusion that the Kelsenian a priori is relativized because of necessity the law must include morality (Gragl n 16 201–202) and that this "construction of the concept of 'ought' hence represents the ambitious attempt to complement Kant's table of categories by one additional category." Cf Claudius Müller, *Die Rechtsphilosophie des Marburger Neukantianismus: Naturrecht und Rechtspositivismus in der*

In this vein, Kelsen's clear vision to uphold the is–ought dichotomy is also of interest.[163] To him, law – the ought – is one thing, and the is – politics, psychology, sociology, morality – is something to be held clearly distinct.[164] In fact, this is the essence of his quest for purity. As describing and prescribing are acts to be held apart,[165] the science of law must be distinguished from natural and other sciences.[166] As with causality, Kelsen claims, legal validity also must find its final source. In his words, the "search for the reason of a norm's validity ... must end with a norm which, as the last and highest, is *presupposed*."[167] And thus "[s]uch a presupposed higher norm is referred to in this book as basic norm."[168] This, importantly, is connected with the claim that the validity of one norm can only derive from another norm.[169] It is of particular interest for our purpose that precisely this feature of the Kelsenian pure theory of law, and thus also of Kelsenian legal monism, is referred to as "Kelsen's reply to the juridico-transcendental question." It is claimed that this stipulation is "[i]n a similar fashion to Kant's 'Copernican revolution' through which he realized that a priori (i.e. necessary) knowledge is not possible by conforming intuition to the nature of objects, but by conforming the object to

Auseinandersetzung zwischen Hermann Cohen, Rudolf Stammler und Paul Natorp (Mohr Siebeck 1994).

163 For the approach on the is–ought dichotomy adopted by this thesis, see below, 69–70.

164 Kelsen (n 161) *Pure Theory* 1; Hans Kelsen, *Allgemeine Staatslehre* (Springer 1925) 62, holding that not the human being but the legal person is the subject of the law.

165 Kelsen (n 161) *Pure Theory* 5–6, where he explicitly states: "The difference between *is* and *ought* cannot be explained further. We are immediately aware of the difference. Nobody can deny that the statement: 'something is' – that is, the statement by which an existent fact is described – is fundamentally different from the statement: 'something ought to be' – which is the statement by which a norm is described. Nobody can assert that from the statement that something is, follows a statement that something ought to be, or vice versa." Yet it is important to acknowledge that Kelsen (n 161 6) also holds that "[t]his dualism of is and ought does not mean, however, that there is no relationship between *is* and *ought*" [emphasis original]. He further explains (6) that the is and the ought "are two different modi" and hence "[o]ne and the same behaviour may be presented in the one or the other of the two modi." Yet he holds that "[t]herefore it is necessary to differentiate the behaviour stipulated by a norm as a behaviour that ought to be from the actual behaviour that corresponds to it."

166 Kelsen (n 161) *Pure Theory* 8–9, introducing the concept of the basic norm which provides for the objective validity of "norms of a moral or legal order."

167 Kelsen (n 161) *Pure Theory* 194. He clearly adds here (194–195) that this highest norm "must be *presupposed*, because it cannot be 'posited', that is to say: created, by an authority whose competence would have to rest on a still higher norm" [emphasis original].

168 Kelsen (n 161) *Pure Theory* 195. See also Kelsen (n 26) 111: "The reason for the validity of a norm is always a norm, not a fact. The quest for the reason of validity of a norm leads back, not to reality, but to another norm from which the first norm is derivable in a sense that will be investigated later."

169 Kelsen (n 161) *Pure Theory* 198.

our intuition."[170] And almost in the same breath we learn that "the true status of the basic norm" is "a neo-Kantian transcendental notion and answer to the ... juridico-transcendental question in the sense of Hermann Cohen's philosophy."[171]

These propositions are claimed to be made following Hermann Cohen, and hence are claimed to be in accordance or at least reconcilable with the so-called neo-Kantian school from Marburg.[172] One idea of neo-Kantianism was

[170] Gragl (n 16) 72 and 74: "In analogy to Kant's transcendental self, the *Grundnorm* is a *condition for* legal knowledge, and not an *object of* legal knowledge." On this see also Paulson (n 137) 313: "Kelsen would have his Pure Theory of Law understood as a theory of legal cognition, of legal knowledge. He writes again and again that the sole aim of the Pure Theory is cognition or knowledge of its object, precisely specified as the law itself." See also Bert van Roermund, "Norm-Claims, Validity, and Self-Reference" in Luís Duarte d'Almeida, John Gardner and Leslie Green (eds) *Kelsen Revisited: New Essays on the Pure Theory of Law* (Hart Publishing 2013) 11–42, who, however, makes the need explicit to differentiate between validity and bindingness. Beyond that, he argues that "Kelsen's own account of the basic norm commits him to the kind of 'recognition' theory of normativity which ... he professed to reject" (11).

[171] Gragl (n 16) 74. Besides the numerous contributions referring critically to or praising the work of Hans Kelsen, see also, particularly on the transcendental aspect, Gerhard Luf, "On the Transcendental Import of Kelsen's Basic Norm" in Stanley L Paulson and Bonnie Litschewski-Paulson (eds) *Normativity and Norms: Critical Perspectives on Kelsenian Themes* (Oxford Clarendon Press 1998) 221–234 (233), holding that "the familiar formulation of the basic norm ... point[s] to an altogether specific concept of law, a concept that is dependent on provisional methodological determinations and that does not possess a timeless quality at all"; and Stanley L Paulson, "The Great Puzzle: Kelsen's Basic Norm" in Luís Duarte d'Almeida, John Gardner and Leslie Green (eds) *Kelsen Revisited: New Essays on the Pure Theory of Law* (Hart Publishing 2013) 43–62 (49 ff), who, however, concludes that no Kantian transcendental argument undergirding the Kelsenian basic norm is sound.

[172] On this claim see Gragl (n 16) 64, n 62, quoting a letter from Kelsen to Treves, Hans Kelsen, "The Pure Theory of Law, 'Labandism', and Neo-Kantianism: A Letter to Renato Treves" in Stanley L Paulson and Bonnie Litschewski Paulson (eds) *Normativity and Norms: Critical Perspectives on Kelsenian Themes* (Clarendon Press 1998) 169–175 (171): "It is altogether correct that the philosophical foundation of the Pure Theory of Law is the Kantian philosophy, in particular the Kantian philosophy in the interpretation that it has undergone through Cohen." See also Hans Kelsen, *Hauptprobleme der Staatsrechtslehre* (Scientia 2nd ed 1923) vi and xvii. Cf Paulson (n 137). Cf Gragl (n 16) 65, n 74, claiming that Kelsen follows Cohen (n 141) *System der Philosophie, Zweiter Teil: Ethik des reinen Willens* 29; see also Hermann Cohen, *Logik der reinen Erkenntnis* (Cassirer 3rd ed 1922) 12, stating that for objective rules for the interpretation of meaning its logical structure must be an axiom. Otherwise, we would have to provide for the source of the necessary laws of logic based on either metaphysics or empirical facts. For this reference see Gragl (n 16) 59, nn 15 and 16 with further reference to Rintelen (n 142) 23–24, which, however, is more an overview of "German idealism" than a strict defense. For the critique that Kelsen would only seemingly connect to Marburgian neo-Kantianism (as the latter for instance clearly requires an existing object), see eg Voegelin (n 138) 109. For the qualification that only the earlier Kelsen was an adherent of (neo-) Kantianism and the later Kelsen was more Humean, see Andrei Marmor, "The Pure Theory of Law" in Edward N Zalta (ed) *Stanford Encyclopedia of Philosophy* (4 January 2016) available at https://plato.stanford.edu/entries/lawphil-theory/ [last accessed February 1, 2023], albeit with

to transport Kantian epistemology, which was mainly directed at the natural sciences, to other disciplines. The point was to discover the necessary preconditions of science (and thereby to confront empiricism[173] or, in positive terms, to emphasize the scientific nature of philosophy).[174] Nevertheless, friction is unavoidable when transplanting to the field of law and legal science ideas that were originally expressed with regard to natural sciences and knowledge in general and the external world in particular.[175] To Kelsen, it was obviously clear that law is a system of norms made by human beings for human beings.[176] In his words, "when we compare the objects that have been designated by the word 'law' by different peoples at different times, we see that all these objects turn out to be *orders of human behavior*." An "order," he goes on, "is a system of norms whose unity is constituted by the fact that they all have the same reason for their validity; and the reason for the validity of a normative order is a basic norm . . . from which the validity of all norms of the order are derived."[177] Within a Kantian tradition one thus has to argue why one thinks that scientific metaphysics, in other words a transcendental method, is considered necessary for cognizing the law. Kant himself

further reference to Paulson (n 171) and Michael S Green, "Marmor's Kelsen" in D A Jeremy Telman (ed) *Hans Kelsen in America* (Springer 2016) 31–55, who disagree.

[173] See Friedrich Lohmann, *Karl Barth und der Neukantianismus. Die Rezeption des Neukantianismus im "Römerbrief" und ihre Bedeutung für die weitere Ausarbeitung der Theologie Karl Barths* (De Gruyter 1995) ch 1 with many references.

[174] Cf Dreier (n 160) 70. Note that Kelsenian ideas must be differentiated from those of other neo-Kantian legal philosophers such as Rudolf Stammler and Emil Lask, as Kelsen postulated a very strict value neutrality from the perspective of legal science. See Jakab (n 35) 1045, n 4 with further reference to Rudolf Stammler, *Die Lehre vom richtigen Rechte* (De Gruyter 1902); Emil Lask, *Rechtsphilosophie* in id, *Gesammelte Schriften Vol 1* (Paul Siebeck 1923) 275 ff. See also Stanley L Paulson, "Zur neukantianischen Dimension der Reinen Rechtslehre. Vorwort zur Kelsen-Sander-Auseinandersetzung" in Stanley L Paulson (ed) *Die Rolle des Neukantianismus in der Reinen Rechtslehre. Eine Debatte zwischen Sander und Kelsen* (Scientia 1988) 7–26.

[175] See, however, Cohen (n 141) *System der Philosophie, Zweiter Teil: Ethik des reinen Willens* 66, qualifying legal science as the mathematics of the humanities in general and ethics in particular.Cf on Cohen, Lohmann (n 173) 65–129, and on this issue esp 84–87.For a critical perspective, see Jonathan Trejo-Mathys, "Neo-Kantianism in the Philosophy of Law: Its Value and Actuality" in Nicolas de Warren and Andrea Staiti (eds) *New Approaches to Neo-Kantianism* (Cambridge University Press 2015) 147–170 (164): "Intriguing as the idea is, few if any have found this analogy persuasive. It seems to go wrong from the beginning and to result from a forcing of the subject-matter of law and ethics into the structural requirements of Cohen's 'transcendental method,' which requires philosophical reflection to begin with the 'fact' of some 'science' or other."

[176] Kelsen (n 161) *Pure Theory* 3 ff, 30 ff.

[177] Kelsen (n 161) *Pure Theory* 31 [emphasis original].

apparently did not think it was.[178] Arguments are necessary for why the law, too, has a priori law-specific attributes.[179] Mere postulations that only then could law be cognized in a "pure way" are not sufficient as such claims result in a vicious metaphysical circle. Moreover, when following the Marburg neo-Kantian tradition, it is important to explain why this school of neo-Kantianism, more focused on the natural sciences, was chosen instead of the Badian approach focused on humanities. In addition, when following a neo-Kantian tradition, it is important to set out the social fact that has to be identified first. Only from this fact, in a second step, can objective validity be constituted according to neo-Kantianism, as briefly outlined above.[180] Moreover, this fact needs to be historically verifiable. Merely claiming that the term "law" has always turned out to be an order of human behavior determined "by different peoples at different times"[181] is rather weak in this regard.[182] In addition, neo-Kantians understood themselves as idealists. It does not seem that such a

[178] See the reference to Kelsenians admitting this below n 193.

[179] To be fair, Kelsen states in the first edition of his *Pure Theory of Law* (Hans Kelsen, *Introduction to the Problems of Legal Theory* (translated by Bonnie Litschewski Paulson and Stanley L Paulson Oxford Clarendon Press 1992 [*Reine Rechtslehre* 1934]) § 16, and sec § 50 (e)) that "the Pure Theory is well aware that one cannot prove the existence of the law as one proves the existence of natural material facts and the natural laws governing them, that one cannot adduce compelling arguments to refute a posture like theoretical anarchism, which refuses to see anything but naked power where jurists speak of the law." See, however, on the anarchist, 48.

[180] See Section 1.2.2.

[181] Kelsen (n 161) *Pure Theory* 31.

[182] See, however, Paulson (n 172) for an interesting interpretation of Kelsen starting from what he calls a "jurisprudential antinomy." Such antinomy follows from what Kelsen terms "natural law theory" and "empirico-positivist theory" as being "not only mutually exclusive, but also jointly exhaustive of the possibilities," and thus the refutation of both theories (Paulson n 172 314). In Paulson's words (n 172 314), "[f]or if one holds that the two traditional types of theory together exhaust the field, precluding any third type of theory, and if one holds, furthermore, that neither type of theory is defensible, then one faces an antinomy – the *jurisprudential antinomy*, as I shall call it" [emphasis original]. Based on this antinomy, Paulson interprets Kelsen as having offered a "regressive version of the Transcendental Argument" (n 172 329 ff), which basically holds that "the very possibility of cognition of legal norms presupposes the application of a category or normative imputation" as the only way "to anchor a legal philosophy that brings together the normativity thesis and the separability thesis." Paulson (n 172 332), however, reaches the conclusion that "the so-called regressive version of the transcendental argument, severed from the progressive version, collapses into a mere scheme of analysis." Beyond that, we could add that such an interpretation hinges on the persuasiveness of the refutation of "natural law theories" and "empirico-positivist theories." This is, first, quite a heavy load for the transcendental sphere, and second, faces the challenge that the modern version of the law vs morality debate is identified by some at least as false problems (*Scheinprobleme*), see eg Dietmar von der Pfordten, *Rechtsphilosophie. Eine Einführung* (C H Beck 2013) 66–78, esp 77.

classification would be accepted by Kelsenians. Rather, I suspect they would claim that their only idealization would be the purity of the law.

Beyond that, it is notable that Kelsen himself stated that no one can be forced to use the basic norm as a scheme to interpret the law.

> [A]n anarchist, for instance, who denied the validity of the hypothetical basic norm of positive law (theoretical anarchism always somehow shares the position of natural law, the theory of pure natural law that of anarchism), will view its positive regulation of human relationships (such as property, the hiring contract) as mere power relations and their description as "ought" norms a mere "fiction," as an attempt to supply a justifying ideology.[183]

This example shows that the Kelsenian basic norm is not a necessary condition for thinking about the law in a transcendental Kantian sense,[184] as the anarchist cognizes the very same act as, for instance, the police force. However, as Kelsen claims, to the anarchist this is not the law in action but brute illegitimate force. This understanding nourishes doubts that the Kelsenian position might collapse into a solipsistic understanding of the law where the subjective perception of the anarchist melts into the object – that is, the act he or she is cognizing. This even goes so far as Kelsen himself stating that international life might only be cognized via anarchy guided by power (instead of through a basic norm and thus monism with the primacy of international law, for instance).[185] If this is the case, however, how can we be sure that every lawyer will use this scheme? And, more importantly, if this is a personal decision depending on the Kantian assumption as referred to earlier, how can we ever be sure that this scheme is shared by different legal scholars, different legal cultures and so on? I submit that we cannot, especially if we remember the criticism advanced against the Kantian position by several philosophers, accusing it of falling short of solipsism.[186] Hence, if we take a skeptical stance towards the Kantian position and consider a development by Arthur Schopenhauer stating that "every man takes the limits of his own field of vision for the limits of the world,"[187] this critique becomes all the more

183 Kelsen (n 26) 413.

184 See on this Alexy (n 162) 200, who, however relativizes the relativization of the Kelsenian a priori.

185 See Jakab (n 35) 1047, n 14, with reference to Hans Kelsen, *Law and Peace in International Relations. The Oliver Wendell Holmes Lectures 1940–41* (Harvard University Press 1942) 48, 54.

186 See Section 1.2.1.

187 Arthur Schopenhauer, "Further Psychological Observations" in *Suffering, Suicide and Immortality. Eight Essays from The Parerga* (selected and translated by T Bailey Saunders Dover 2006 [*Parerga und Paralipomena. Kleine Philosophische Schriften* 1851]) 39–62 (46),

pressing. Hence, due to the Kantian assumptions, the critique these assumptions face, and these thoughts advanced by Kelsen himself, we have to classify the Kelsenian pure theory of law and its basic norm as "legal theoretical solipsism."[188] This critique might be responded to with a rather thick shared transcendental understanding of what legal validity and, hence, the law actually are. If we presumed such a thick legal a priori as given to any lawyer, we could establish a response to the legal solipsism reproach. This, however, becomes even more troublesome as it brings us into legal metaphysics – something that the pure theory of law claims to avoid. This critique is also illuminating. We can conclude that the more we aim for purity, the more we need to consult a priori legal knowledge. Only then can we ensure that lawyers will use the same scheme when interpreting the law.

Finally, with regard to neo-Kantianism, it has to be said that this philosophical movement was popular from around 1870 until the First World War.[189] The briefly outlined further developments, particularly concerning the linguistic turn in philosophy and epistemology alike, must be taken into account when a historical epistemological account such as Kantian or neo-Kantian epistemology is advocated in the twenty-first century.[190] And, in more general terms, there are philosophical voices stating that we cannot even be sure that we are not simply a computer simulation controlled by an advanced human society.[191] It is hard to establish certainty concerning a guarantee that what I see as what is there and what you see as what is there actually is there and that our perceptions are comparable. We need to account for that in our theoretical thinking if we want to fulfil scientific standards of philosophical thinking and argument. Yet the law is quite a special scientific discipline. Law's normativity is puzzling. It is hard to separate a description of facts and a prescription of how to act. Despite these difficulties, it is very likely a theoretical overload to mix these questions with epistemological puzzles.

Astonishingly, we can find arguments by convinced and well-established scholars who commit themselves to the pure theory of law, stating that even if Kant or neo-Kantians actually had a different project in mind or are simply

interpreting the noumenal and the phenomenal as one world with will and representation as different aspects of it.

188 See Jakab (n 35) 1047–1048, n 15, where he further doubts that the schemes of various legal scholars to interpret the law are the same. Much points in the direction that they are, indeed, not the same. This is even suggested by the Kelsenian standpoint that the interpretation of law includes a subjective element. See Kelsen (n 161) *Pure Theory* 348 ff.

189 Heis (n 140).

190 See Section 1.2.1.

191 Nick Bostrom, "Are You Living in a Computer Simulation?" (2003) 53 (211) Philosophical Quarterly 243–255.

misrepresented by the Kelsenian pure theory of law, this would not be a serious problem for the pure theory of law.[192] According to them, Kelsenian pure theory stands alone and even epistemological "realists" "today" (writing in 1991) would concede that knowledge (*Erkenntnis*) necessarily presupposes a combination of judgments a priori and a posteriori.[193] It is conceded that this understanding, which, certainly reflects an important insight, is nevertheless understood differently by the "realists" referred to above.[194] They consider the statement that the manner of cognizance constitutes the object not as a transcendental necessity, but as a consequence of scientific methodological procedure which entails – and this is by no means unimportant – that the methodology applied partly constructs the object. Therefore, science must use rigorous methodology. This, in turn, has the consequence that the methodology can and, depending on the progress of science, must be adapted. That the *act of choosing* a specific methodology has normative implications and must be appropriate is conceded by Kelsenian legal scholars[195] but without drawing the correct conclusions from doing so. On the contrary, this is taken as another confirmation of the pure theory of law[196] (and at the same time used to dismiss a contested view of analyzing the Austrian federal state as done by Peter Pernthaler, Theo Öhlinger, Karl Weber and others[197]).

[192] Rudolf Thienel, "Ein 'komplexer' oder ein normativer Bundesstaatsbegriff?" (1991) 42 Österreichische Zeitschrift für öffentliches Recht und Völkerrecht (ZÖR) 215–252 (240, n 88)

[193] Again Thienel (n 192) 240 in n 87, quoting besides Kant's *Critique of Pure Reason* (2nd ed 1787) 74 ff also Kant's Metaphysics of Morals (2nd ed 1789) 31 f. This readily departs from Kelsen himself and some Kelsenians. See n 137 above.

[194] See Thienel (n 192) 240, n 89, quoting Hans Albert, *Konstruktion und Kritik. Aufsätze zur Philosophie des kritischen Rationalismus* (Hoffmann und Campe 2nd ed 1975) 13 ff, esp 17 ff holding that "realists" would hold that the a priori only has a hypothetical character and, thus, can be criticized in the realm of specific scientific disciplines. However, this would change nothing with regard to the fundamental importance of the transcendental question of Kant.

[195] Thienel (n 192) 241, 90 and 91 with reference to Karl Popper, *Logik der Forschung* (Mohr Siebeck 8th ed 1984) 12 f; and Hans Albert, *Kritik der reinen Erkenntnislehre* (Mohr Siebeck 1987) 70 ff, esp 84 ff. See also Thienel (n 192) 218, holding that he is aware of the necessity, but also the free choice, of the specific direction of aiming at knowledge, the object of knowledge, and the method of cognizing knowledge providing further references in n 9 to Karl Popper (Thienel n 192 12–13); Albert (Thienel n 192 70 ff); Hans Albert, *Traktat über rationale Praxis* (Mohr Siebeck 1978) 33 ff; Victor Kraft, *Erkenntnislehre* (Springer 1960) 32. However, none of the quoted references supports the interpretation of the pure theory of law as the unique way of cognizing norms or as the unique legal method as advanced by Thienel.

[196] Thienel (n 192) 241.

[197] See eg Peter Pernthaler, "Der österreichische Bundesstaat im Spannungsfeld von Föderalismus und formalem Rechtspositivismus" (1969) 19 Zeitschrift für öffentliches Recht 361–379 (369); Theo Öhlinger, *Der Bundesstaat zwischen Reiner Rechtslehre und Verfassungsrealität* (Braumüller 1976); Peter Pernthaler, *Die Staatsgründungsakte der österreichischen Bundesländer: Eine staatsrechtliche Untersuchung über die Entstehung des Bundesstaates* (Braumüller 1979); Peter Pernthaler, *Allgemeine Staatslehre und*

The law is quite different from the question of what constitutes knowledge about the external world and how we acquire it. The law is simply a tool for organizing our social life. Thus, in the same way as it is not important for our daily life to reflect on whether a tiger we perceive as standing in front of us really is there (on the contrary, this is probably a bad moment to reflect on the existence of the external world), it is not of primary importance to reflect on what the law "actually" is and whether it "really" exists. Law is a practical tool. Whether law is good or bad depends to a considerable extent on whether it works or not – whether it is efficient. This was even acknowledged to some extent by Hans Kelsen.[198] Thus, it is very likely not the best choice to base our understanding of the law on a rather solipsistic understanding of epistemology holding that the method of cognizance fully constitutes the object of cognizance.

Law asks for a practical understanding of epistemology. To the same extent that I am satisfied if I ask you to bring me a red T-shirt and you – no matter what you perceive as red – manage to bring me a T-shirt that satisfies my "redness expectation," it is enough for our legal life that what we perceive as law is able to account for an intersubjective organization of social life.[199]

What it boils down to is that the Kelsenian pure theory of law and thus also Kelsenian monism is not a necessary condition for thinking about the law. It is a mere invitation to set up specific axioms to talk about law in a specific way. It has been and still is a radical way to claim that only this very specific way of thinking about the law can be called proper or pure legal scholarship, because

Verfassungslehre (Springer 1984) 404 ff; Karl Weber, *Kriterien des Bundesstaates: Eine systematische, historische und rechtsvergleichende Untersuchung der Bundesstaatlichkeit der Schweiz, der Bundesrepublik Deutschland und Österreichs* (Braumüller 1980) 79 ff; Peter Pernthaler and Karl Weber, "Bundesverfassung und Föderalismus" (1982) 21 (4) Der Staat 576–590; Peter Bußjäger, *Homogenität und Differenz: Zur Theorie der Aufgabenverteilung zwischen Bund und Ländern in Österreich* (Braumüller 2006).

198 Kelsen (n 161) 212: "A legal order is regarded as valid, if its norms are by and large effective (that is, actually applied and obeyed)." This statement, however, must not be interpreted as of effectiveness equaling validity for effectivity is a necessary but not a sufficient condition for validity. See Hans Kelsen, *Reine Rechtslehre* (Franz Deuticke 1934) 70. For the interpretation that the effectiveness of a normative order is an arbitrary criterion merely of heuristical value for the assumption of its validity, which is the basic norm, see Wolf-Dietrich Grussmann, "Grundnorm und Supranationalität – Rechtsstrukturelle Sichtweisen der europäischen Integration" in Thomas von Danwitz et al (ed) *Auf dem Wege zu einer europäischen Staatlichkeit* (1993) 47–64 (50) with further reference (n 10) to Adolf J Merkl, "Hans Kelsens System einer reinen Rechtslehre" (1921) 41 Archiv des öffentlichen Rechts 171–202 (179).

199 For an interesting and much more elaborated account of these questions relying on the late Wittgenstein, see Dennis Patterson, *Law and Truth* (Oxford University Press 1996). See also Poscher (n 134) for a discussion of the deflationary theory of truth without negating legal science as well as Miodrag A Jovanović, *The Nature of International Law* (Cambridge University Press 2019) for a prototype theory of concepts approach concerning international law.

this claim necessarily entails that if you do not agree on the axioms you are not doing legal science. You can do so as much as you are free to play tennis at the weekend in your leisure time, but when you want to talk about law at university, you must accept the axioms. This is quite a hostile way of doing science. However, due to its sharp contrast and its radicality it has attracted a lot of attention. The critique advanced here is, to repeat myself, not a blatant rejection of thinking and speaking like this about the law. However, the abovementioned criticism has made clear that, so far, no one has proven why the axioms chosen by the pure theory of law should be the only necessary conditions for thinking about the law. They were merely postulated. From this it follows that they are not hardwired in our brains as some sort of innate legal faculty; nor are they other commonly achieved preconditions for cognizing the law. It is simply an offer you can accept, which, on acceptance, provides you – admittedly – with a clear-cut language (with all its advantages and disadvantages). From this it follows, however, that you can also decline this offer, establish another methodology and still think and speak about the law.

In fact, the Kelsenian pure theory of law bears resemblance to *a* religion.[200] You can believe in it, or not. The high priests and true believers of Kelsenianism might tell you that this is the only truth and that there is no other true system of law. However, the mere existence of other religions with competing claims about the purpose of legal life and its claimed eternity simply show that this is one of many possible ways to think about the law. Moreover, the criticism advanced above forces us to draw the conclusion that it is not the most convincing way. In another metaphor, it is important to know the vocabulary of the Kelsenian language if you want to talk meaningfully to a Kelsenian. Yet it is by no means the only true legal language in the legal world. From this it follows that the claim that everything that is expressed in Kelsenian legal language represents legal science and, conversely, anything else is unscientific – or probably representing sociology, morality, but definitively not within the realm of legal science – is rather bold and should be rejected.[201]

200 See also Paulson (n 172) 322 as well as Paulson (n 171) 61, albeit admittedly in far less dramatic terms after having shown that while the pure theory of law cannot offer a convincing transcendental argument, it nevertheless "does not follow that Kelsen's Pure Theory of Law collapses with it. Rather the Pure Theory must simply take its place alongside other normativist legal theories, subjecting itself to the same evaluation they undergo. What will have changed, if the Pure Theory is evaluated in this way, is its claim to uniqueness, its claim to being the only possible normativist legal theory *sans* natural law. This claim – relying as it does on a transcendental argument that cannot be made to work – must be abandoned" [emphasis original]. See, however, n 34 for scholars who hold that the pure theory of law stands or falls with its epistemological premises.

201 For a critique of this particular feature of Kelsenian pure theory of law, see his pupil Voegelin (n 138) 117–118. See also Erich Voegelin, "Kelsen's Pure Theory of Law" (1927) 42 (2)

1.2.4 *Kelsenian Monism and the Solution of Norm Conflicts between Legal Orders*

Leaving the critique advanced against Kelsenian epistemology to one side, let us assume that we can accept the epistemological basis of legal monism. If we do so, we still need to provide arguments for why and how Kelsenian monism is superior when explaining the relationship between legal orders in general, and when looking for a convincing solution to norm conflicts in particular. Concerning the latter, Kelsen claims that the solution to norm conflicts between different legal orders follows "logically" from the theoretical stance of Kelsenian monism. This, however, faces a serious restriction due to its Kantian basis:

> Yet such a principle [of systematicity] does not prescribe any law to objects . . . but rather is merely a subjective law of economy for the provision of our understanding, so that through comparison of its concepts it may bring their universal use to the smallest number, without justifying us in demanding of objects themselves any such unanimity as might make things easier for our understanding or help it extend itself, and so give objective validity to its maxims as well.[202]

Against this background, it is notable that the norm conflict between "different systems of norms" is construed as a legal epistemological impossibility in Kelsenian legal monism.

> [T]he assumption of two truly different systems is revealed as false. If there should be two actually different systems of norms, mutually independent in their validity . . . both of which are related to the same object (in having the same sphere of validity), insoluble logical contradiction could not be excluded.

Political Science Quarterly 268–276, providing, however, more a positive overview than criticism. Günther Winkler is also critical of Kelsenian epistemology in *Rechtstheorie und Erkenntnislehre. Kritische Anmerkungen zum Dilemma von Sein und Sollen in der Reinen Rechtslehre aus geisteswissenschaftlicher und erkenntnistheoretischer Sicht* (Springer 1990), and was responsible for the republication of Voegelin's book. Beyond that we learn from Günther Winkler's preface (*Geleitwort*) in this republication that Voegelin's thesis supervisor (*Doktorvater*) was Othmar Spann and his second supervisor Hans Kelsen. For his habilitation thesis, too, the examiners were Spann and Kelsen. And while Kelsen offered some genuine praise, Voegelin was denied the *venia legendi* (the prerequisite for lecturing at Austrian and German Universities as a Professor) in the discipline of "state theory" (*Staatslehre*) in 1928, only receiving it in 1931. For this and more details on the relationship between Voegelin and Kelsen, see Günther Winkler, Geleitwort in Voegelin (n 138) v–vi.

202 Kant (n 36) A 306 / B 362. See Nicholas Rescher, *Epistemology. An Introduction to the Theory of Knowledge* (State University of New York Press 2003) 233, n 3, citing Kant as "the first philosopher clearly to perceive and emphasize this crucial point" and furthermore pointing to Peirce's "idea that the systematicity of nature is a regulative matter of scientific attitude rather than a constitutive matter of scientific fact." Charles Sanders Peirce, *Collected Papers Vol VII* (Harvard University Press 1958) sect 7.134.

> The norm of one system may prescribe conduct A for a certain person, under a certain condition, at a certain time and place. The norm of the other system may prescribe, under the same conditions and for the same person, conduct non-A. This situation is impossible for the cognition of norms.[203]

This is a rather astonishing thesis as it seems that, yet again, the a priori prerequisites are rather overloaded. It is thus important to take a closer look at this claim as well.[204] In cases of norm conflict, the monistic doctrine needs to deal with the question of which jurisdiction prevails – international or national law, and now international, EU or national law. However, a monistic doctrine with the so-called primacy of national law must be traced back to a highly nationalistic view of international law, which no longer can be considered suitable.[205] In other words, how could popular sovereignty in the form of national law (and thus one people only) rule over international or EU law without denying the validity of international or EU law? How should the validity of, say, EU law be based on the popular sovereignty of a single Member State's legal order and the popular sovereignty of one nation instead of all Member States' legal orders and their respective nations?[206] The failure

[203] Kelsen (n 26) 408.

[204] See Valentin Jeutner, *Irresolvable Norm Conflicts in International Law – The Concept of a Legal Dilemma* (Oxford University Press 2017) 121 ff with further references (esp 122 holding that "[i]ndeed, the law of non-contradiction and the explosion principle [which 'provides that a true contradictory statement causes the statement's normative reference system (a legal system, for example) to degenerate into triviality where any statement is true'] are by no means necessary principles of any logical system" [footnotes omitted]).

[205] Cf Lando Kirchmair, "The "Janus Face" of the Court of Justice of the European Union: A Theoretical Appraisal of the EU Legal Order's Relationship with International and Member State Law" (2012) 4 (3) Goettingen Journal of International Law 677–691 (688). Hans Kelsen, *Das Problem der Souveränität und die Theorie des Völkerrechts: Beitrag zu einer Reinen Rechtslehre* (JCB Mohr 2nd ed 1928) 317, himself equated the monistic doctrine with the primacy of national law as the "negation of all law". However, later on he left the decision up to politics, see Kelsen (n 17) 339 ff. Interestingly, Gragl (n 16) 33, 110–124, following some other members of the Vienna school of jurisprudence (Josef L Kunz, "On the Theoretical Basis of the Law of Nations" (1925) 10 Transactions of the Grotius Society 115–142 (139); Josef L Kunz, "La primauté de droit des gens" (1925) 6 Revue de droit international et de législation comparé 556–598 (572 ff); Josef L Kunz, *Völkerrechtswissenschaft und Reine Rechtslehre* (Deuticke 1923) 82; as well as Verdross (n 15) 33 ff; Alfred Verdross, "Grundlagen und Grundlegungen des Völkerrechts – ein Beitrag zu den Hypothesen des Völkerrechtspositivismus" (1921) 29 Niemeyers Zeitschrift für internationales Recht 65–91 (82–83)) – and deviating from Kelsen – claims that we have to rule out Kelsenian monism with primacy of national law for epistemological reasons as well.

[206] Compare also Walz (n 7) 40, who classified this perception of monism as "pseudomonistic"; see also Starke (n 11) 77, where he stated that "[r]educed to its lowest terms, the doctrine of State primacy is a denial of international law as law, and an affirmation of international anarchy."

of the monistic conception of the primacy of municipal law to answer these questions is left aside here.

Monism with the primacy of international law has attracted a lot more attention. In order to justify the primacy of international law, the monistic doctrine stipulated the premise of a hypothetical unity – being kept together by the "chain of validity."[207] The ultimate foundation of validity is Hans Kelsen's famous basic norm briefly touched on above.[208] It is a concept that accounts for the unifying foundation of law and its validity.[209] The basic norm is an attractive but problematic concept, which has found many diverging interpretations by admirers[210] and critics alike.[211] The concept of the "chain of validity" is even more troublesome.[212] Kelsen holds that

> [a] norm of general international law authorizes an individual or a group of individuals on the basis of an effective constitution, to create and apply as a legitimate government a normative coercive order. That norm [of general international law], thus, legitimates this coercive order [of a "state" in the meaning of international law] for the territory of its actual effectiveness as a valid legal order and the community constituted by this coercive order as a "state" in the sense of international law.[213]

Similarly, Verdross argues from the viewpoint of an international basic norm – which in Verdross' conception is *pacta sunt servanda*[214] – from which

[207] The term "chain of validity" stems from Joseph Raz, *The Concept of a Legal System: An Introduction to the Theory of Legal System* (Oxford University Press 2nd ed 1980) 105; Starke (n 11) 75; Catherine Richmond, "Preserving the Identity Crisis: Autonomy, System and Sovereignty in European Law" (1997) 16 (4) Law and Philosophy 377–420 (388).

[208] Kelsen (n 17) 196 ff.

[209] For a brief explanation, see Gragl (n 25) 671–673.

[210] Kelsen (n 213) 193 ff, 221; Robert Walter, "Entstehung und Entwicklung des Gedankens der Grundnorm" in Robert Walter (ed) *Schwerpunkte der Reinen Rechtslehre* (Manz 1992) 47–59 (47); Robert Walter, "Die Grundnorm im System der Reinen Rechtslehre" in Aulis Aarnio et al (eds) *Rechtsnorm und Rechtswirklichkeit: Festschrift für Werner Krawietz* (Duncker & Humblot 1993) 53–74 (85); Heinz Mayer, "Rechtstheorie und Rechtspraxis" in Clemens Jabloner and Friedrich Stadler (eds) *Logischer Empirismus und Reine Rechtslehre: Beziehungen zwischen dem Wiener Kreis und der Hans Kelsen Schule* (Springer 2002) 319–331; Ralf Dreier, "Bemerkungen zur Theorie der Grundnorm" in Hans Kelsen-Institut (ed), *Die Reine Rechtslehre in wissenschaftlicher Diskussion* (Manz 1982) 38–46 (39).

[211] Norbert Hoerster, *Was ist Recht? Grundfragen der Rechtsphilosophie* (C H Beck 2006) 134, 138 ff; Peter Koller, "Meilensteine des Rechtspositivismus im 20. Jahrhundert: Hans Kelsens Reine Rechtslehre und H. L. A. Harts 'Concept of Law'" in Ota Weinberger and Werner Krawietz (eds) *Reine Rechtslehre im Spiegel ihrer Fortsetzer und Kritiker* (Springer 1988) 129–178 (157 ff); Griller (n 11) Völkerrecht und Landesrecht, 87–89; Schroeder (n 2) 75 ff.

[212] For criticism, see András Jakab, "Problems of the Stufenbaulehre: Kelsen's Failure to Derive the Validity of a Norm from Another Norm" (2007) 20 (1) Canadian Journal of Law and Jurisprudence 35–67.

[213] Kelsen (n 161) *Pure Theory* 193–215, 215.

[214] Alfred Verdross, *Die Verfassung der Völkerrechtsgemeinschaft* (Springer 1926) preface, 21–23, and 30–31.

municipal law also derives: "The freedom of States is nothing else than a margin of discretion depending on international law."[215] According to him, the lawmakers of public international law are not States, but the international community, acting through an international organ with supranational power.[216]

Following this idea that norms can only derive from other norms, the conclusion drawn would have to be that any national law is derived from EU law, and EU and national law derive from international law. This, however, is an argument that does not reflect reality.[217] Indeed, the CJEU famously postulated the "autonomy of the Community legal order"[218] and introduced the "direct effect"[219] of EU law, which has been interpreted by some as a monistic approach.[220] Nevertheless, even for the most progressive EU constitutional lawyers it would be a step too far to argue that all Member State legal orders derive from EU law. Without the backup of the epistemological necessity of such claims, the postulation of such a chain of validity is exposed as the Emperor's new clothes: "But he has not got anything on!"[221]

The fatal blow for monism with regard to EU law is the relationship between EU law and international law, which appears to show even dualistic

[215] Verdross (n 214) 35 [translated by the author].

[216] Verdross (n 214) 48 ff. But see Krabbe (n 17) 305–309. For a more recent account taking sociological, ethical and political science perspectives into account, see Andreas L Paulus, *Die internationale Gemeinschaft im Völkerrecht. Eine Untersuchung zur Entwicklung des Völkerrechts im Zeitalter der Globalisierung* (CH Beck 2001). Also see Andreas L Paulus, "The Emergence of the International Community and the Divide between International and Domestic Law" in Janne E Nijman and André Nollkaemper (eds) *New Perspectives on the Divide between National and International Law* (Oxford University Press 2007) 216–250 (216), diagnosing that national courts consider international law not as a superior authority, but regard it "as formal authority only in the instance domestic law renders it binding for the court in question."

[217] For criticism of the other monistic concept with the primacy of national law (which would consequently make international and supranational law governed by almost 200 diverging national laws), see n 206. Cf Kirchmair (n 205) 681 n 12.

[218] Case C-6/64 *Costa v ENEL* ECLI:EU:C:1964:66; Case C-284/16 *Slovak Republic v Achmea BV* ECLI:EU:C:2018:158 para 33.

[219] Case-26/62 *Van Gend & Loos v Netherlands* ECLI:EU:C:1963:1.

[220] Kirchmair (n 205) 680 with further references in n 10.

[221] Hans Christian Andersen, "Des Kaisers neue Kleider" in Hans Christian Andersen (ed) *Gesammelte Märchen* I (Carl B Lorck 1847) 37–44 (43), "Aber er hat ja nichts an!" available at https://andersen.sdu.dk/vaerk/hersholt/TheEmperorsNewClothes_e.html [last accessed February 1, 2023].

elements.[222] This "Janus face" is a challenge for the unifying concept of Kelsenian monism – at least when trying to uphold its underlying assumptions to explain this reality. Hence, also concerning the relationship between international and EU law, Kelsenian monism faces a reality that challenges its theoretical assumptions. How can the relationship between international and EU law be explained as a unity by Kelsenian monism if the CJEU clearly conceives these two legal orders as being separate? Again, without the epistemological necessity of Kelsenian monism, this postulation becomes utterly fictitious and therefore is not a superior explanation of the relationship.[223]

1.3 WHY DUALISM AND KELSENIAN MONISM DO NOT RESOLVE THE QUESTION OF WHO HAS THE FINAL SAY

While it is important to consider the current dichotomy of legal sources of international, EU and national law, a common normative framework is equally important. Such a framework is necessary to acknowledge the entanglements of these three legal orders and to enable a solution to the norm conflicts arising from this entanglement. Hence, the changes in the legal landscape force us to leave behind the almost 100-year-old theories of monism and dualism. Major developments force us to seek an adequate theoretical framework that fits the reality of our time.

The main claims of dualism and monism are summarized in Table 1.1.

[222] Compare specifically Joined Cases C-402/05 P and C-415/05 P *Kadi and Al Barakaat International Foundation v Council and Commission* ECLI:EU:C:2008:461 para 125 defining UN law and EU law as "integrated but separate legal orders." Cf Kirchmair (n 205) 683–685 with further references.

[223] Compare in this regard also Friedrich Lohmann, "'Ethische Unruhe.' Die Funktion von Ethik bei der gesellschaftlichen Ordnungsbildung" in Helga Pelizäus and Ludwig Nieder (eds) *Das Risiko – Gedanken übers und ins Ungewisse. Interdisziplinäre Aushandlungen des Risikophänomens im Lichte der Reflexiven Moderne. Eine Festschrift für Wolgang Bonß* (Springer 2019) 95–125 (99–100), stating that the Kelsenian conception of normativity with the basic norm on top aims at achieving objectivity, order and clarity; however, the basic norm cannot fulfil this purpose. Rather, this seems to be like a rope out at sea which is grasped by somebody who has been shipwrecked in order to avoid drowning.

TABLE 1.1 *Overview of dualism as well as Kelsenian and Verdrossian monism*

	Dualism	Kelsenian monism	Verdrossian monism
Presuppositions	International and national law have: - different addressees; - different content (international law is purely inter-State law); - different sources.	- (neo-)Kantian epistemology ("manner of cognizance constitutes the object"). - Hypothetical unity – being kept together by the "chain of validity" and norms can only derive from other norms. - Norm conflict between "different systems of norms" is construed as a legal epistemological impossibility.	- Values based in natural law. - International basic norm: *pacta sunt servanda*.
Theoretical outcome	International and national legal orders are: - separated ("two circles, which possibly touch, but never cross each other," Triepel); - based on different grounds of validity.	- If international law is law, the logical consequence is that national, EU and international law must be seen as a unitary legal order. - Either international/EU law derives from national law or national law derives from international/EU law.	- "Unity of the legal world order"; - Municipal law derives from this international basic norm; - Lawmakers of public international law are not States, but the international community, acting through an international organ with supranational power.
Legal consequences	- Norms must be incorporated from one legal order into another. - The legal subjectivity of international organizations (be it the UN or the EU) would have one international and *x*-national ground of validity.	- Chain of validity (*Stufenbau nach der rechtlichen Bedingtheit*). - Ultimate ground of validity is the famous basic norm (*Grundnorm*). - If national law conflicts with international law, Kelsen earlier argued that national law is null and void whereas he later held that national law is voidable.	- Ultimate ground of validity is also the basic norm, which, however, is based on natural law. - If national law conflicts with international law, national law is voidable.
Failure	- Presuppositions outdated.	- Remains a theory focused on epistemology which does not hold its promise. - Norm conflict solution is highly hypothetical.	- Value-laden theory based on natural law. - Unity of the legal world order is highly fictitious.

2

Global Legal Pluralism and Constitutionalism

Another very prominent and more recent account of legal orders and their relationship is legal pluralism.[224] Hence, this chapter discusses some issues of global legal pluralism (Section 2.1) and also some issues related to its antagonist, global constitutionalism (Section 2.2). Both approaches will be analyzed to see whether they can provide a useful answer concerning our question as to how we can know who has the final say on the relationship between international, EU and national law in order to provide a solution for norm conflicts between these legal orders.

To grasp the idea of why global legal pluralism is no help in this regard, it is necessary to briefly outline the origins of the concept (Section 2.1.1). This will be followed by an analysis of the consequences of defining law for normative legal pluralism (Section 2.1.2), revealing the far-reaching importance of this definition. I aim to show that the specific notion of official and unofficial law within the frame of global legal pluralism is highly relevant for deciding how norm conflicts should be avoided and solved as well as why this is the case and why one solution might be better than another.

This analysis of the definition of law in global legal pluralism will lead us to the major argument of Section 2.1 on global legal pluralism, namely the importance of distinguishing between global legal pluralism as the description of recent factual developments, pointing, for example, to the massive increase in

[224] This chapter is partly based on Lando Kirchmair, "Descriptive vs. Prescriptive (Global) Legal Pluralism: A Gentle Reminder of David Hume's Is–Ought Divide" (2019) 51 (1) Journal of Global Legal Pluralism and Unofficial Law 48–71; for an overview of current pluralist scholars see Paul S Berman, *Global Legal Pluralism: A Jurisprudence of Law beyond Borders* (Oxford University Press 2012); Mireille Delmas-Marty, *Les forces imaginantes du droit (II): Le pluralisme ordonné* (Seuil 2006); English translation by Mireille Delmas-Marty, *Ordering Pluralism: A Conceptual Framework for Understanding the Transnational Legal World* (translated by Naomi Norberg Hart 2009) 44; Nico Krisch, *Beyond Constitutionalism: The Pluralist Structure of Postnational Law* (Oxford University Press 2010); for an overview see Ralf Michaels, "Global Legal Pluralism" (2009) 5 Annual Review of Law and Social Science 243–262.

international actors, norms and tribunals as well as adjudicators and, as a different issue, the question of how we ought to deal with or even solve those legal conflicts – based on a (common) framework – resulting from these plural, overlapping legal claims (Section 2.1.3). Fully acknowledging the difference between descriptive and prescriptive global legal pluralism is important to understand the consequences of this differentiation, clearly stating how normative conceptions of solving norm conflicts are justified. I contend that the literature on global legal pluralism falls short of doing this, which is a result of too broad a conception of law.

Moreover, the section on global legal pluralism holds that prescriptive proposals for solving legal norm conflicts are better not termed as "pluralistic." Instead, and this leads us directly to the following section on global constitutionalism (Section 2.2) and its potential to answer our question, I suggest that it is more accurate to refer to a necessarily common framework that addresses the question of how those conflicts should be resolved together or at least in a way acceptable to all parties (Section 2.3). As an outline of what I think is the most appropriate framework for handling norm conflicts in this pluralistic world, I argue with global legal pluralists that context is of the utmost importance when discussing the best common normative framework for dealing with legal norm conflicts from different legal orders. Universalist solutions, as presented by global constitutionalists, are likely to fall short of acknowledging the inevitable restrictions of context that are in place when dealing with legal norm conflicts on a global scale. In other words, global constitutionalism has to face the burden of universality, which is an unsurmountable challenge (except for some fundamental norms, namely *ius cogens* or a thin layer of global constitutionalism) (Section 2.2.2). With constitutional pluralism, however, I will submit that we will likely end up in a "constitutional stalemate" (Section 2.2.3).

I conclude this chapter by stating that neither global legal pluralism nor global constitutionalism can properly resolve our question as to how we can know who has the final say on the relationship between international, EU and national law (Section 2.4).

2.1 GLOBAL LEGAL PLURALISM: DESCRIPTIVE PERSUASIVENESS, BUT A LACK OF COMMON PRESCRIPTIVE SOLUTIONS

2.1.1 *The Origins of Global Legal Pluralism*

Eugen Ehrlich published his seminal *Grundlegung der Soziologie des Rechts* in 1913.[225] He studied, as he put it, the "living law" of the Bukovina. His main

[225] Eugen Ehrlich's book *Grundlegung der Soziologie des Rechts* (Duncker & Humblot 1913) was translated into English and published by Harvard University Press in 1936 *Fundamental Principles of Sociology of Law*.

observation was that alongside "positive law" there was also a sort of societal customary law, a distinct legal order, within the Austro-Hungarian Empire.[226] Ehrlich's ideas, though controversial at that time, found quite a broad audience. Because of his seminal studies, Ehrlich is nowadays considered a, if not the, founding father of legal sociology,[227] a field embedded in empirical science and interested in the social reality of the legal order. Resulting from the findings of Ehrlich, a common understanding of pluralism is nowadays "the presence in a social field of more than one legal order."[228]

Yet it took a while for his thoughts to become accepted and acknowledged by the global legal (sociological) mainstream. This is the case even though some scholars track traces of legal pluralist thinking back to Alberico Gentili, one of the founding fathers of international law in the sixteenth century.[229] Gentili's thoughts are interpreted to represent a "pragmatic pluralism" since he referred to the international society of "all organized political communities" in 1598.[230] However, instead of such a constructivist reading of Gentili, it is probably more appropriate to see in him an important intellectual figure rather than an early advocate of global legal pluralism.[231]

226 Ehrlich (n 225) 313.

227 Manfred Rehbinder, *Die Begründung der deutschen Rechtssoziologie durch Eugen Ehrlich* (Duncker & Humblot 2nd ed 1986).

228 John Griffiths, "What Is Legal Pluralism?" (1986) 24 Journal of Legal Pluralism 1–47; Sally Engle Merry, "Legal Pluralism" (1988) 22 Law & Society Review 869–896; Jacques Vanderlinden, "Le pluralisme juridique: essai de synthèse" in John Gilissen (ed) *Le Pluralisme juridique* (Université Libre de Bruxelles 1971) 19–56 (19). Cf Jacques Vanderlinden, "Return to Legal Pluralism: Twenty Years Later" (1989) 21 (28) Journal of Legal Pluralism 149–157 (156), who excluded from his understanding of legal pluralism "the existence, within a single legal order, of different mechanisms applied to similar situations [which] amounts to a plurality of legal mechanisms, not to legal pluralism." He continues by saying that "I realize today that in order to have pluralism, one must necessarily have many legal orders meeting in the same situation and making the individual not a 'sujet de droit' but a 'sujet de droits.'"

229 For more on Gentili see Merio Scattola, "Alberico Gentili (1552–1608)" in Bardo Fassbender and Anne Peters (eds) *The Oxford Handbook of the History of International Law* (Oxford University Press 2012) 1092–1097.

230 Benedict Kingsbury, "Confronting Difference: The Puzzling Durability of Gentili's Combination of Pragmatic Pluralism and Normative Judgment" (1998) 92 American Journal of International Law 713–723; William W Burke-White, "International Legal Pluralism" (2005) 25 (4) Michigan Journal of International Law 963–979 (978, n 69).

231 See eg Andreas Wagner, "Francisco de Vitoria and Alberico Gentili on the Legal Character of the Global Commonwealth" (2011) 31 (3) Oxford Journal of Legal Studies 565–582; Andreas Wagner, "Alberico Gentili: Sovereignty, Natural Law, and the System of Roman Civil Law" in Stefan Kadelbach, Thomas Kleinlein and David Roth-Isigkeit (eds) *System, Order, and International Law: The Early History of International Legal Thought from Machiavelli to Hegel* (Oxford University Press 2017) 92–114.

Another historical account of legal pluralism leads some scholars to regard legal pluralism as normality,[232] despite "legal centralism" taking over as a political and legal ideology as recently as the nineteenth century.[233] It was only in the 1960s that pluralism was rediscovered by sociological and anthropological legal scholarship and as recently as the 1990s that "pluralism" was (re)discovered and embraced by (international) legal scholarship. The development and debate of the "fragmentation" of international law opened the floor for discussion.[234]

From the vantage point of two different legal authorities present in the same social field, which can also be found to exist in colonial situations, "legal pluralism" also became a key concept in international law.[235] Berman describes the shift from anthropologically oriented studies towards what he terms "global *legal* pluralism" as follows: Formerly, studies were aimed at two distinct legal orders within the same territory, where one legal order was usually hierarchically superior to the other, even though this was not always the case in practice. Moving away from this hierarchical understanding, scholars, according to Berman, started to understand these different legal orders as "bidirectional, with each influencing (and helping to constitute) the other."[236] Boaventura de Sousa Santos describes three phases of pluralism:

[232] Sometimes this is used to make a normative argument against "legal centralism." However, I consider it rather a weak argument to say that legal pluralism was normal most of the time and it was only in the period of nation states that legal centralism gained the upper hand for a short period of time and now it is again time for global legal pluralism. I think that this greatly underestimates the advantages of modern State law, organized through a more or less democratic State, giving law legitimacy, people control, and so on.

[233] See specifically Brian Z Tamanaha, "Understanding Legal Pluralism: Past to Present, Local to Global" (2008) 30 (3) Sydney Law Review 375–411 (377 ff); cf Ralf Seinecke, "Recht und Rechtspluralismus: Forschungsperspektiven der 'Rechts'-Wissenschaften und 'Rechts'-Philosophie" in Carsten Bäcker and Sascha Ziemann (eds) *Junge Rechtsphilosophie* (Franz Steiner 2012) 143–158 (144 ff).

[234] Martti Koskenniemi, "Chairman of the Study Group of the ILC on Fragmentation of International Law: Difficulties Arising from the Diversification and Expansion of International Law" (2006) Report of the Study Group of the International Law Commission, UN Doc A/CN.4/L.682 paras 5 ff with reference to Wilfried C Jenks, "The Conflict of Law-Making Treaties" (1953) 30 British Yearbook of International Law 401–453 (403).

[235] Tamanaha (n 233) 390; Paul S Berman, "Global Legal Pluralism" (2007) 80 Southern California Law Review 1155–1238 (1170).

[236] Berman (n 235) 1171. See generally on the role of territory and boundaries in international law Daniel-Erasmus Khan, "Territory and Boundary" in Bardo Fassbender and Anne Peters (eds) *The Oxford Handbook of the History of International Law* (Oxford University Press) 225–249 (227–228 with further references), highlighting among other things the fact that "[t]here is strong evidence that long before the transition of mankind to a sedentary lifestyle, 'territoriality' as a type of intraspecific competition was already a distinctive feature of most (semi-)nomadic hunter-gatherer societies." See on the importance of territory for the law as

first the "colonial period," followed by the "post-colonial period in capitalist modern societies" and last the "post-modern legal plurality."[237] With the shift from the second to the latter phase, he relates a change in the definition of law, which leads to the identification of a differentiation in a "local," "national" and "transnational" analysis. Why this is problematic will be addressed first (Section 2.1.2).

Today the debate revolves around a pluralistic account of international law itself and its relation to national legal orders, which might be contrasted with those scholars arguing for a global constitutionalism (of international law) in a universalist sense.[238] In the following section I mostly focus on global legal pluralism as represented most commonly by Paul S. Berman,[239] Mireille Delmas-Marty,[240] Emmanuel Melissaris,[241] Nico Krisch,[242] Boaventura de Sousa Santos[243] and Gunther Teubner.[244] Yet this is by no means a review of pluralism scholars but rather a legal analysis, which addresses the question of

exemplified by Germany, Daniel-Erasmus Khan, *Die deutschen Staatsgrenzen. Rechtshistorische Grundlagen und offene Rechtsfragen* (Mohr Siebeck 2004), as well as Daniel-Erasmus Khan, "Das Staatsgebiet und die Grenzen der Bundesrepublik Deutschland" in Wolfgang Kahl, Christian Waldhoff and Christian Walter (eds) *Bonner Kommentar zum Grundgesetz* (C F Müller 2022); finally, see Daniel-Erasmus Khan, "Territory Taking Centre Stage in International Law. Some Preliminary Thoughts on the Rise of Territoriality to the Bedrock of Modern Statehood" in Société Française pour le droit international (ed) *Droit des Frontières internationals / The Law of International Borders* (Pedone 2016) 53–64 (53), for the "indeed somewhat disquieting news that, in all probability, the word territory must hence be considered as a close etymological relative of the word 'terrorist.'"

[237] Boaventura de Sousa Santos, *Toward a New Common Sense: Law, Science and Politics in the Paradigmatic Transition* (Routledge 1995) 117.

[238] Stefan Kadelbach, "Konstitutionalisierung und Rechtspluralismus – Über die Konkurrenz zweier Ordnungsentwürfe" in Jochen Bung and Armin Engländer (eds) *Souveränität, Transstaatlichkeit und Weltverfassung* ARSP-Beiheft 153 (Franz Steiner 2017) 97–108. For a differentiation between an internal international legal pluralism and another paradigm of legal pluralism external to the international legal order, see André Nollkaemper, "Inside or Out: Two Types of International Legal Pluralism" in Jan Klabbers and Touko Piiparinen (eds) *Normative Pluralism and International Law: Exploring Global Governance* (Cambridge University Press 2013) 94–139.

[239] Berman (n 224).

[240] Delmas-Marty (n 224).

[241] Emmanuel Melissaris, *Ubiquitous Law: Legal Theory and the Space for Legal Pluralism* (Ashgate 2009).

[242] Krisch (n 224).

[243] Boaventura de Sousa Santos (n 237).

[244] Gunther Teubner, "Globale Bukowina" (1996) 15 Rechtshistorisches Journal 255–290; Gunther Teubner, "Global Bukowina: Legal Pluralism in World Society" in Gunther Teubner (ed) *Global Law without a State* (Dartmouth 1997) 3–28.

how can we know who has the final say on the relationship between international, EU and national law. Thus, I will not even try to provide an overview of the different, and fascinating, accounts of those scholars, but simply pick out some core arguments to illustrate the points that I think are missing in the debate. This section therefore does not challenge the concept of legal pluralism as such, which has been fruitfully used to ask, for instance, why people in social interactions in some contexts opted for one legal order, and in other contexts for another.

2.1.2 *The Definition of Law*

Another important part of the shift from national to international legal pluralism as described by Berman was the readiness of legal scholars to embrace the idea of defining the "legal system" in a broader sense, "to include many types of nonofficial normative ordering, and therefore argu[ing] that such legal subgroups operate not just in colonial societies, but in advanced industrialized settings as well."[245] This shift in the acceptance of such a broad definition by legal scholars is a core point in the international legal pluralism debate as it illustrates on the one hand the claim of legal sociologists to overcome "the ideology of *legal centralism*"[246] to be able to analyze so-called non-State law as well.[247] This, however, is identified by its critics as the "core problem" of the debate.[248] It is also worth mentioning Gunther Teubner, who is very clear when he says:

[245] Berman (n 235) 1171 quoting Engle Merry (n 228) 870–871; cf Roger Cotterrell, *Law, Culture and Society: Legal Ideas in the Mirror of Social Theory* (Ashgate 2006) 37. See also Laura Nader, "The Anthropological Study of Law" (1965) 67 (6) The Ethnography of Law. American Anthropologist. New Series. Part 2 3–32 (4), who already discussed the implications of broad anthropological definitions of law explicitly referencing the empirically grounded reasons for such a definition (6); as well as Chris Fuller, "Legal Anthropology: Legal Pluralism and Legal Thought" (1994) 10 (3) Anthropology Today 9–12 (9), with reference, for instance, to Bronislaw Malinowski, *Crime and Custom in Savage Society* (Kegan Paul 1926), who equates law with social control in the widest sense.

[246] Griffiths (n 228) 3.

[247] Berman (n 235) 1171; Berman (n 224) 4: "This book seeks to grapple with the complexities of law in a world where a single act or actor is potentially regulated by multiple legal or quasi-legal regimes." Cf Berman (n 224, 17), who speaks of "a pluralist internationalisation that favours interactions between different legal systems, or ensembles (a more neutral term that takes into account currently forming ensembles that are too changing and unstable to constitute true legal systems)."

[248] Tamanaha (n 233) 391; Cotterrell (n 245) 37; see also Engle Merry (n 228) 878; and Sally Falk Moore, "Certainties Undone. Fifty Turbulent Years of Legal Anthropology, 1949–1999" (2001) 7 (1) Journal of the Royal Anthropological Institute 95–116 (106–107).

To avoid misunderstanding, I hasten to add that the binary code legal/illegal is not peculiar to the law of the nation state. This is in no way a view of "legal centralism" (Griffiths, 1986: 2ff.). It refutes categorically any claim that of the official law of the nation states, of the United Nations or of international institutions enjoy any hierarchically superior position. It creates instead the image of a heterarchy of diverse legal discourses.[249]

In the same vein, Nico Krisch leaves no doubt about the aim of his project entitled "beyond constitutionalism."[250] His clear goal is to envision "post-national law" and thus he is not "afraid of radical pluralism."[251] Similarly, Berman does not see an "intrinsic reason to privilege nation-state communities over others."[252] To the contrary, for Berman "the whole debate about law versus nonlaw is largely irrelevant in a pluralism context."[253] Klaus Günther portrays this with the "strikingly simple" definition of the law according to most global legal pluralists: "The debate on this question [the notorious problem of distinguishing legal orders from other kinds of normative orders] is for the most part irrelevant, for law is precisely what the agents

[249] Teubner (n 244) Global Bukowina. However, see the recent normative piece by Gunther Teubner, *Constitutional Fragments: Societal Constitutionalism and Globalization* (translated by Gareth Norbury Oxford University Press 2012), which soon faced criticism. See Teubner (n 244) 64.

[250] Krisch (n 224).

[251] Nico Krisch, "Who Is Afraid of Radical Pluralism? Legal Order and Political Stability in the Postnational Space" (2011) 24 (4) Ratio Juris 386–412; Melissaris (n 241) 4. Melissaris also explicitly advances his discourse-theory-based account of legal pluralism in order to "explore the possibility of understanding the law in dissociation from State." In his opinion (5), "legal pluralism seems like a promising alternative to a . . . monistic and necessarily hegemonic view of the law." Cf (46): "A basic assumption in this book is that there is nothing in the meaning of law that implies, presupposes or entails its necessary connection with the State." Yet Melissaris (47) is "asking whether it is possible to acquire some objective knowledge of what counts as law without, at the same time, abandoning the project of legal pluralism." See the earlier work by Emmanuel Melissaris, "The More the Merrier? A New Take on Legal Pluralism" (2004) 13 (1) Social & Legal Studies 57–79 (58): "[B]ecause of its inherent diversity, legal pluralism must be approached not as another legal theory but as *a radicalization of the way we think about the law, which must permeate and inform all theorizing of the law.* This means shifting the focus from strictly defined and hermetically closed *legal systems* to *legal discourses*" [emphasis original]. The problematic nature of such alternative approaches, as in this case Melissaris' approach, is highlighted by his suggestion (76) that "pluralistic knowledge of the legal cannot be acquired by or integrated in an institutionalized legal system.," but for Melissaris the "only available topos [where the meta-theoretical and meta-jurisprudential discourse should take place], at least at this stage, is legal scholarship."

[252] Berman (n 235) 1180; Berman (n 224) 62, with reference to Benedict Anderson, *Imagined Communities: Reflections on the Origins and Spread of Nationalism* (Verso 6th ed 2006).

[253] Berman (n 224) 54–55. For a critique of that account, see Michael Giudice, "Global Legal Pluralism: What's Law Got to Do with It?" (2014) 34 (3) Oxford Journal of Legal Studies 589–608 (600 ff).

involved each took to be law."[254] While the side arguing for a broad definition of *law* in terms of legal pluralism may confidently point to recent developments in international law, including a massive increase in international actors, norms and tribunals as well as adjudicators,[255] this picture contrasts with the problem of distinguishing "'law' from other forms of normative order."[256] The latter view has gained force through one of the most prominent advocates of legal pluralism, John Griffiths. He now holds the view that "the expression 'legal pluralism' can and should be reconceptualized as 'normative pluralism' or 'pluralism in social control,'" precisely because law "is not a theoretical concept in the sociology of law."[257]

The difficulty of defining law is acknowledged by Woodman when he states that "law covers a continuum which runs from the clearest form of state law through to the vaguest forms of informal social control."[258] Franz von Benda-Beckmann's concern in defining law is to "work with a concept that is broad enough to capture simple and complex legal configurations" and, hence, he prefers a "concept of law that is not linked to the state by definition and that is

[254] Günther (n 249) 2.

[255] Burke-White (n 230).

[256] Tamanaha (n 233) 392. Regarding criticism of Teubner see, for instance, Rupprecht Podszun, "Corporate Social Responsibility-Standards: Rechtstheoretische Aspekte und die Frage, was den 'Markenkern' der Rechtswissenschaft ausmacht" in Reto M Hilty and Frauke Henning-Bodewig (eds) *Corporate Social Responsibility: Verbindliche Standards des Wettbewerbsrechts?* (Springer 2014) 51–80 (66–67), who concedes that such an understanding makes law descriptively tangible, but a normative approach moves into the background. If the normative substance of law does not have to be defined, it is easier to integrate other regulating manifestations in a complex system. Yet Gunther Teubner, "Globale Zivilverfassungen: Alternativen zur staatszentrierten Verfassungstheorie" (2003) 63 Heidelberg Journal of International Law 1–28 (21), argues that secondary constitutional norms emerge, which transcend the validity paradox of self-made digital law and decide selectively about the quality of social norms as legal norms. This, however, seems rather vague, as Melissaris (n 241) 43, points out. Quite erroneously, this is also a criticism made against Melissaris' approach. See Derek McKee, "Review Essay – Emmanuel Melissaris's Ubiquitous Law: Legal Theory and the Space for Legal Pluralism" (2010) 11 (5) German Law Journal 573–584 (583). See also Andreas L Paulus, "Commentary to Andreas Fischer-Lescano & Gunther Teubner. The Legitimacy of International Law and the Role of the State" (2004) 25 (4) Michigan Journal of International Law 1047–1058, criticizing Andreas Fischer-Lescano and Gunther Teubner, "Regime-Collisions: The Vain Search for Legal Unity in the Fragmentation of Global Law" (2004) 25 (4) Michigan Journal of International Law 999–1046.

[257] John Griffiths, "The Idea of Sociology of Law and Its Relation to Law and to Sociology" in Michael Freeman (ed) *Law and Sociology: Current Legal Issues Vol 8* (Oxford University Press 2006) 49–68 (62–64); for a detailed analysis of this turn, see Tamanaha (n 232) 392–396; for an overview see Michaels (n 224) 250–252.

[258] Gordon R Woodman, "Ideological Combat and Social Observation: Recent Debate About Legal Pluralism" (1998) 30 (42) Journal of Legal Pluralism 21–59 (45).

broad enough to include 'legal pluralism' [as] a useful sensitising and analytical tool."[259] Consequently, when dealing with legal pluralism he offers a nuanced analytical conceptual understanding of law that allows him to differentiate legal orders on a number of dimensions.[260] Ralf Michaels suggests that "the three challenges from legal pluralism – non-state law, plurality and interaction – are related" and, thus, "[i]n order to assess any one of them, we must consider the other ones as well. We will not get an adequate concept of law beyond the state unless we address inter-relations between legal systems at the same time."[261]

I hold that the myriad definitions, understandings and concepts of law point strongly to the insight that there is no one single appropriate definition, understanding or concept of law. Instead, all definitions and concepts depend on the scientific background and goal, as well as the perspective of the analysis. It is thus important to be as clear and transparent as possible. This includes a distinct difference between modern State law, unofficial law and other normative forms within a normative approach. The point simply is that if law is defined very broadly, qualifying any commands or normative forces as law, then powerful developments such as the democratic legitimacy of the modern State law, guaranteed by constitutional review, and many more great legal achievements aimed at legitimizing legal normativity are lost if norm conflicts between official and unofficial law or other forms of normative authority collapse. In other words, we need to be careful to differentiate norm conflicts between official and unofficial law or other forms of normative authority in order to do justice to their diverse modes of legitimizing authority.

Highly differentiated concepts of law might be better equipped to do justice to such legitimacy issues when broadening the concept of law. Either way, it is important, as Franz von Benda-Beckmann suggests when he says that he is "perfectly aware that others dealing with law may need a different concept of law for different purposes."[262] This means that almost any definition or concept of law will have its advantages. For instance, with a broad

[259] Franz von Benda-Beckmann, "Who's Afraid of Legal Pluralism?" (2002) 34 (47) Journal of Legal Pluralism and Unofficial Law 37–83 (40).

[260] See eg von Benda-Beckmann (n 259) 44 with reference to Leopold Pospisil, *Anthropology of Law: A Comparative Perspective* (Harper and Row 1971) 39.

[261] Ralf Michaels, "Law and Recognition – Towards a Relational Concept of Law" in Nichole Roughan and Andrew Halpin (eds) *In Pursuit of Pluralist Jurisprudence* (Cambridge University Press 2017) 90–115 (95); cf Roger Cotterrell, "Does Global Legal Pluralism Need a Concept of Law?" in Upendra Baxi, Christopher McCrudden and Abdul Paliwala (eds) *Law's Ethical, Global and Theoretical Contexts – Essays in Honour of William Twining* (Cambridge University Press 2015) 303–319 (209–311).

[262] Von Benda-Beckmann (n 259) 40; Cotterrell (n 261) 316.

understanding of law, important normative forces are less likely to be missed when pursuing an empirical analysis of the role of the law in controlling social behavior. However, we should be aware of the prescriptive implications of such a broad concept of law when switching from a descriptive analysis to a prescriptive assessment. This does not mean that unofficial law or other forms of normative authority enjoy weaker legitimacy per se than modern State law. Unofficial law or other types of normative authority must not rest exclusively on pure force or mere habit, but might enjoy other modes of legitimacy. Separating official modern State law, unofficial law and other forms of normative authority, however, is necessary to highlight these differences. The argument simply holds that it is fruitful to acknowledge these differences when defining these various forms of normativity in order to ease the reference to the different modes of legitimacy.

2.1.3 *Description vs. Prescription and the "Normative Move" in the Global Legal Pluralism Debate*

If the goal is a descriptive analysis of the status quo, it is, of course, illustrative to work with a broad legal concept in order to obtain a "complete picture." This is important for social scientists as they look at legal obligations and conflicts. What the relevant law prescribes is an issue of great interest to social scientists. They go further than legal scholars in that they inquire how people actually use law in their interactions. So far, nobody would deny the explanatory force of pluralism. Social scientists usually do not say what the law should be like and how conflicts should be avoided and solved. In contrast to sociological or anthropological studies, legal scholars do not stop at this analytical point. They usually go further by analyzing the link between the collected data and the connected legal obligations and conflicts, aiming constantly at thinking how the law is but also what the law prescribes and how the law could or should be and how norm conflicts should be avoided or solved. However, at this point David Hume's warning still applies:

> In [almost all of the analyses of global legal pluralism], which I have hitherto met with, I have always remark'd, that the author proceeds for some time in the ordinary way of reasoning, and establishes [the existence of "global legal pluralism"], or makes observations concerning [the "global Bukowina" regarding international] human affairs; when of a sudden I am surpriz'd to find, that instead of the usual copulations of propositions, is, and is not, I meet with no proposition that is not connected with an ought, or an ought not. This change is imperceptible; but is, however, of the last consequence. For as this ought, or ought not, expresses some new relation or affirmation,

> 'tis necessary that it shou'd be observ'd and explain'd; and at the same time that a reason shou'd be given, for what seems altogether inconceivable, how this new relation can be a deduction from others, which are entirely different from it.[263]

Hume's powerful insight, of which this section endeavors to remind us, is the necessity of sharply distinguishing between the description of (recent) factual developments and, as a different issue, normative questions. While it is heavily disputed in philosophy whether David Hume actually proposed or discovered "Hume's Law" holding that it is logically impossible to directly conclude from an *is* towards an *ought*,[264] I wish to refer to Edgar Morscher, who articulated a modern version of three descriptive–normative dichotomies while leaving deliberately unanswered whether Hume actually proposed or discovered something like "Hume's Law."[265]

According to Morscher, we commit a naturalistic fallacy, first, if we do not "appropriately demarcate normative from descriptive discourse" (grammatical descriptive–normative dichotomy).[266] Second, we must not reduce normative to descriptive speech (in order to avoid the definitional descriptive–normative dichotomy).[267] Third, we would commit a naturalistic fallacy if we were to use

[263] Hume (n 59) 320.

[264] Cf Rachel Cohon, "Hume's Moral Philosophy" in Edward N Zalta (ed) *Stanford Encyclopedia of Philosophy* (August 20, 2018) available at https://plato.stanford.edu/entries/hume-moral/ [last accessed February 1, 2023]. Note, however, that relying on David Hume here does not necessarily imply that it is logically impossible to conclude an *ought* from an *is*. While such logical impossibility is the mainstream interpretation of David "Hume's law" attributed to the famous passage quoted in length above (68–69) Dirk Lüddecke, "Erstlingswerk: Der Konservatismus eines Radikalen. David Hume als Anatom politischer Loyalität" in Dirk Lüddecke and Felicia Englmann (eds) *Zur Geschichte des politischen Denkens. Denkweisen von der Antike bis zur Gegenwart* (J B Metzler 2014) 168–190 (176–179), provides a convincing argument for a less strong interpretation: Taking into account the explicit wording of the passage and where it is situated in the third book of the *Treatise of Human Nature*, Lüddecke concludes that Hume was about to clarify what will follow and the necessity – what has according to Hume not been done until then – to give a reason for concluding from an is towards an ought. For the interpretation that Hume had the move from true statements (irrespective of whether they are factual or moral) to motivational statements in mind, see John Finnis, *Natural Law and Natural Rights* (Oxford Clarendon Press 2nd ed 2011) 37–48; as well as Stephen Buckle, *Natural Law and the Theory of Property* (Oxford Clarendon Press 1991) 282–283. For controversial discussions see also William D Hudson (ed) *The Is–Ought Problem. A Collection of Papers on the Central Problem in Moral Philosophy* (Penguin 1969).

[265] Edgar Morscher, "The Descriptive-Normative Dichotomy and the So Called Naturalistic Fallacy" (2016) 38 (2) Analyse und Kritik 317–337.

[266] Morscher (n 265) 335–336.

[267] Morscher (n 265) 335–336.

arguments with exclusively descriptive premises and purely normative conclusions (the logical descriptive–normative dichotomy).[268]

What this means for us is that either we rest within a purely descriptive analysis of current facts and describe them as pluralistic, but of necessity end here,[269] or we take account of arguing now in the realm of *ought* by introducing, for instance, the thought that we *ought* to avoid conflicts, and that if they occur then we *ought* to cooperate somehow to deal with or solve them. This is what I think is the very first prescriptive step in the global legal pluralism debate.[270] By taking this step, one has to deliver reasons *why* one thinks we *should* or *should not* cooperate in a certain way in order to solve (or not solve) legal norm conflicts that occur in the plural legal realm. The same holds true for suggestions as to *how* and with which methods or mechanisms we *should* address these legal norm conflicts. I thus argue that we need to disclose the (normative) presuppositions underlying the claims that want to address possible legal solutions of these conflicts in the realm of *ought* (which also includes a clear differentiation between legal and normative pluralism). Claims that rest solely on the *description* of pluralistic orders do not suffice as a basis. Moreover, norm conflict identification and proper resolution must be based on a genuinely common normative framework that encompasses all affected legal orders. This means that a pluralistic picture without a common normative framework has no normative (legal) guidance for finding the final arbiter in legal norm conflicts.[271]

Once we see clearly the difference between descriptive and prescriptive global legal pluralism, it also becomes apparent that this differentiation is of utmost importance for the definition of law when speaking about global *legal* pluralism. So it makes sense in a descriptive account to define law openly, as many legal sociologists and anthropologists do when speaking about pluralism in order to capture all normative obligations and rights. While this works for descriptive pluralism, it is rather problematic if upheld in a prescriptive

[268] Morscher (n 265) 335–336.

[269] Yet it is important to concede that the description is informed by normative convictions, for example concerns about inequality and oppression, and that prescription, in turn, hinges on description. However, this does not exempt us from striving to sharply differentiate between both realms.

[270] For a powerful critique of the hidden "common point of reference" in pluralistic accounts, see Klaus Günther, "Normative Legal Pluralism – A Critique" in Jorge Luis Fabra Zamora (ed) *Jurisprudence in a Globalised World* (Edward Elgar 2020) 85–99. See also Klaus Günther, "Normativer Rechtspluralismus: Eine Kritik" in Thorsten Moos, Magnus Schlette and Hans Diefenbacher (eds) *Das Recht im Blick der Anderen: Zu Ehren von Eberhard Schmidt-Aßmann* (Mohr Siebeck 2016) 43–62.

[271] Gragl (n 25) 693–695.

account of global *legal* pluralism. This is because within a prescriptive account of legal pluralism, a broad definition of law (also including unofficial law or other forms of normative authority) involves (often implicitly) a very strong claim as to how things *ought* to be. If we do not differentiate within a prescriptive account between "official," mostly modern State law, and "unofficial law," or other forms of normative authority – that is, any authorities claiming normative force – we face the risk of blending their different modes of legitimacy.

An example would be to say that in norm conflicts, for instance between modern State law and another conflicting unofficial norm, there is no difference (in terms of their legitimacy and justification) and therefore we do not have any rules guiding this norm conflict. However, we could possibly try to settle this conflict by using various forms of conflict solutions. If advocated as such a prescriptive account, this blends those things that make official law "official" – namely, its specific forms of legitimacy, resulting from democratic structures and the rule of law (elections, division of powers, parliament, constitutional courts and their control mechanisms, fundamental rights, and so on) – with other modes of legitimacy of unofficial law or even in some instances brute force or mere habit. Thus, within a prescriptive account of global legal pluralism it is important to distinguish clearly between official and unofficial law and other forms of normative authority. Or again in the words of Klaus Günther:

> When the distinction between law and other social norms disappears, when every social actor who is creating social norms and who has the power to execute them is treated as a legislator, when the validity of positive law goes side by side with other types of legitimate validity (for example, factual acceptance by a majority), and, finally, when negotiating processes between various social actors make valid law – then it makes no more sense to speak of "the law," and one has to give up the principles of equal adjudication and of the democratic legitimacy of legislation.[272]

Yet this is not to say that official modern State law is in any sense better than unofficial law or other forms of normative authority. By highlighting this issue I simply want to emphasize that not differentiating between official and unofficial law or other forms of normative authority is a strong claim in the realm of *ought*, arguing that we *should* treat modern State law like other

[272] Klaus Günther, "Legal Pluralism or Uniform Concept of Law? Globalisation as a Problem of Legal Theory" (2008) 5 No Foundations – Journal of Extreme Legal Positivism 5–21 (15–16).

normative authorities, at least regarding norm conflict solutions.[273] I hold that it is important to differentiate between these forms of normativity because modern State law usually enjoys a considerable degree of legitimacy as its authority is founded on elections and constrained by checks and balances. Moreover, fundamental rights are guaranteed and constitutional review is in place. In other words, power exercised by the modern State is constrained by modern State law.[274] Other normative regulatory forces might not enjoy the same level of legitimacy in this regard. Unofficial law or other forms of normative authority might not enjoy the same safeguards and limitations to power as official law and official law might not enjoy the same legitimacy.

However, in some instances, unofficial law or other forms of normative authority might even enjoy a stronger form of legitimacy than official modern State law. It might well be the case, for instance, that some unofficial norms protect democratic values better than modern State law. Yet even in such a situation, it is preferable to distinguish between modern State law and unofficial law in order to clearly demonstrate that in this case unofficial law enjoys a stronger legitimacy than modern State law. If we treated both alike under one concept of law, we could not point to this difference. At least, it would be much more difficult to characterize this difference clearly. Either way, when proposing a broad definition of law blending official modern State law with other unofficial forms of normative power it is important to bear in mind the differences in legitimacy. It is not enough to bypass this legitimacy issue by holding that unofficial norms can also have an impact and, hence, can also be

[273] Compare, for instance, Melissaris (n 241) 45, who challenges that "law is necessarily associated with the state" and moreover claims that law is the vision of those theorists who associate law with the state "as coercively addressed by a small part of the population." I submit that this is a very strong accusation of the State as an institution being misused by "a small part of the population" coercing the majority to conform (at least implicitly against their will). Melissaris articulates an alternative approach based on discourse theory. However, it is difficult to see how such a thing as "shared normative experiences" might successfully substitute for the State. For this criticism see also McKee (n 256) 583.

[274] See eg Joseph Raz, "Why the State?" in Nichole Roughan and Andrew Halpin (eds) *In Pursuit of Pluralist Jurisprudence* (Cambridge University Press 2017) 136–162 (156–157). This can be questioned, of course. In the so-called rule-of-law crisis in the European Union, several Member States of the EU are suspected of violating fundamental EU values such as the rule of law or democracy. Generally, States may lack the fundamental modes of legitimacy I assume here for modern State law. My argument does not aim at protecting such wanting authorities. On the contrary, I think that for such forms of official law it is helpful to differentiate these forms of normativity from unofficial law that might clearly show a much stronger mode of legitimacy than the official law.

perceived as law.[275] That is because this is only an argument about the output – the impact – of the norm, not about its origin and legitimacy.[276]

Moreover, it is important to note that, depending on the context, for instance if we are dealing with horizontal relations (such as international law and international actors) and thus conflicts, the problem of blending official with unofficial law includes different prescriptive claims than if we are dealing with vertical relations (such as international and national law) and conflicts. It is the purpose of this book to emphasize that a clear line of argumentation should acknowledge this difference in any context. However, I do not wish to offer any substantial argument on a specific constellation. It should suffice to say that a sharp differentiation is always necessary in a prescriptive account of global legal pluralism. However, what this might look like specifically can vary depending on the context. I will return to this point later.

The difference between arguing within a prescriptive or a descriptive account of global legal pluralism is also important for proposing methods or mechanisms with which to solve norm conflicts of different legal orders. Global legal pluralists argue for different mechanisms to mediate conflicts between legal orders: "Sovereigntists" stand against "universalists"[277] and are then mediated by a "pluralist framework" that Berman, for instance, names "jurisgenerative constitutionalism."[278] "Utopian unity" is contrasted with an "illusion of autonomy" and is thus suggested to be solved or softened by "margins of appreciation."[279] In Krisch's account, a "foundational

[275] Paul S Berman, "From Legal Pluralism to Global Legal Pluralism" in Richard Nobles and David Schiff (eds) *Law, Society and Community Socio-Legal Essays in Honour of Roger Cotterrell* (Ashgate 2014) 255–271 (260–264).

[276] Paul S Berman, "The Evolution of Global Legal Pluralism" in Roger Cotterrell and Maksymilian Del Mar (eds) *Authority in Transnational Legal Theory: Theorising across Disciplines* (Edward Elgar 2016) 151–188 (154), even holds that "[g]lobal legal pluralism applies the insights of socio-legal scholarship and turns the gaze away from abstract questions of legitimacy and towards empirical questions of efficacy." Yet he adds that "[o]f course, questions of legitimacy and efficacy are inextricably linked … but the point is that once we come to recognize multiple sources of transnational and non-state authority, it is difficult to maintain any single abstract conception of legal authority."

[277] See the statement made by Berman (n 235) 1180, holding that sovereigntists "reject the legitimacy of all communities but the territorially-defined nation-state" and have "intrinsic reason to privilege nation-state communities over others," contrasting it with a radical universalist position stating (1189) that "[i]n contrast to a reassertion of territorial prerogative, a universalist vision tends to respond to normative conflict by seeking to erase normative difference altogether."

[278] Paul S Berman, "Jurisgenerative Constitutionalism: Procedural Principles for Managing Global Legal Pluralism" (2013) 20 (2) Indiana Journal of Global Legal Studies 665–695.

[279] Delmas-Marty (n 224) *Ordering Pluralism* 44.

constitutionalism" stands against "softer network forms of international cooperation" that are, again, mediated by pluralism.[280]

However, at the end of the day even Krisch, the most radical pluralist, bases the norm conflict resolution – at least in some cases – on what he calls "the *construction* of interface *norms*."[281] In his opinion, the "pluralist setting is concerned with orders that have established firm linkages and accepted forms of common decision-making."[282] Thus, also for him there *ought* to be certain *norms* ("interface norms"), which "regulate to what extent norms and decisions in one sub-order have effect in another."[283] Yet he immediately falls back on his radical pluralism (which is coherent in his "radical pluralistic" thinking) when saying that these "rules are set by each sub-order for itself, with a constant risk of conflict."[284] His main argument is that in the post-national sphere, "[u]nder conditions of strong fluidity and contestation, conflict rules face serious problems of adaptation to a changing environment" and "are unlikely to be able to truly settle conflicts – they might remain ineffectual or even enflame conflicts further."[285] Krisch is aware of the normative implications of his approach when saying that "postnational constitutionalism seeks to tap into the legitimating potential of its domestic counterpart" and therefore he is "only interested in normatively rich conceptions."[286] However, he holds that "[t]he pluralist setting distinguishes itself precisely by the fact that the conflict rules do *not* have an overarching legal character; they are normative, moral demands that find (potentially diverging) legal expressions only within the various sub-orders."[287]

Along these lines other pluralists also propose concepts that "instead of trying to erase conflict, seek ... to manage it," as Berman puts it.[288] However,

[280] Krisch (n 224) 300. Cf Krisch (n 224) 183: "pluralism helps steer a middle course between these positions – one that does not grant ultimate authority to any collective or process, but can help bring the competing visions into an informal balance." For criticism see Gregory Schaffer, "A Transnational Take on Krisch's Pluralist Postnational Law" (2012) 23 (2) European Journal of International Law 565–582.

[281] Krisch (n 224) 285 ff [emphasis added].

[282] Krisch (n 224) 288.

[283] Krisch (n 224) 285.

[284] Krisch (n 224) 286. Note also that Krisch states later (n 224 312) that these norms stem from the sub orders (286) and might clash.

[285] Krisch (n 251) 407.

[286] Krisch (n 224) 39.

[287] Krisch (n 224) 296 [emphasis original]. See also Krisch (n 224) 67: "Postnational constitutionalism is an attempt to establish continuity with central political concepts and domestic traditions; it tries to avoid the normative rupture often feared in discussions of globalization and global governance."

[288] Berman (n 235) 1192; Berman (n 224) 145.

thereby he is already engaging in the discussion of how we *ought* to deal with norm conflicts. To be fair, Berman admits to making prescriptive claims to a certain extent when he proposes what he calls "jurisgenerative constitutionalism" as a framework.[289] In fact, he explicitly suggests that "following the descriptive insights of legal pluralism, we might draw a normative lesson and *deliberately seek to create or preserve spaces for conflict among multiple, overlapping legal systems.*"[290] And to "manage" norm conflicts he reviews a series of "principles" that are, in his account, instead of being substantial, only of a procedural nature: namely "procedural mechanisms, institutions, and practices."[291] Miguel Poiares Maduro, too, speaks of the need to "manage" norm conflicts.[292] He offers the concept of interpretative and participative pluralism to handle norm conflicts. Yet, according to him, "[i]n a multi-level or federal system it is the vertical or federal conception of constitutionalism (as a form of limited government at the State and federal level) that requires the issue of 'who decides who decides' to be left unsolved."[293]

[289] Berman (n 276).

[290] Berman (n 235) 1164 [emphasis original]; see also Berman (n 275) 256; Berman (n 276) 154–155, 182. Yet Berman (n 235) 1166–1167 also holds that "Pluralism is thus principally a descriptive, not a normative, framework. It observes that various actors pursue norms and it studies the interplay, but it does not propose a hierarchy of substantive norms and values. Nevertheless, while it does not offer substantive norms, a pluralist approach may favor procedural mechanisms, institutions, and practices that provide opportunities for plural voices. . . . This commitment can, of course, have strong normative implications because it asks decision makers and institutional designers to at least consider the independent value of pluralism."

[291] Berman (n 235) 1192, and esp 1196 ff; Berman (n 224) 145, and esp 152 ff.

[292] See Miguel Poiares Maduro, "Contrapunctual Law: Europe's Constitutional Pluralism in Action" in Neil Walker (ed) *Sovereignty in Transition* (Hart 2003) 502–537 (523–524).

[293] Maduro (n 292) 522–523; he continues by stating that "[o]f course, all constitutional systems have historically developed forms of allocating the final authority as a way of preventing conflicts and guaranteeing that constitutional resolutions are accepted by all. But what if what makes the European legal order unique is that the open question should remain open?" Cf Miguel Poiares Maduro, "The Heteronyms of European Law" (1999) 5 (2) European Law Journal 160–168 (166): "I prefer Neil MacCormick's legal pluralism which leaves the open question open"; as well as Miguel Poiares Maduro, "European Constitution: What if This Is as Good as It Gets?" in Joseph H H Weiler and Marlene Wind (eds) *European Constitutionalism beyond the State* (Cambridge University Press 2003) 74–102 (97): "that requires the decision of 'who decides who decides' to be left open. The open question should be left open." Similarly, Mattias Kumm, "Who Is the Final Arbiter of Constitutionality in Europe? Three Conceptions of the Relationship between the German Federal Constitutional Court and the European Court of Justice" (1999) 36 (2) Common Market Law Review 351–386 (384), "refuses to answer the question." According to him, "within a pluralist framework, it does not make sense to speak of a final arbiter of constitutionality in Europe. In the approach outlined here the ECJ is conceived as the final arbiter of constitutionality at the level of the European

Likewise the French pluralist, Mireille Delmas-Marty, thinks that a national margin of appreciation is "key" to ordering pluralism and she goes on to mention, for instance, the principle of subsidiarity in the law of the European Union.[294] Samantha Besson suggests that democracy "ought rather to be the supercriterion: when its conditions are given, it subsumes all others as it were, as it constitutes the most legitimate way of deciding on the others."[295] Yet she is aware "of course, [that] identifying the democratic pedigree of each norm in conflict, whether of international or national law, remains extremely complex."[296] And, one might wish to add, democracy is not always the super-criterion of legal orders whose norms might be in conflict.

Thus, most of the global legal pluralists also think that there *should* be some rules to assist the resolution of norm conflict. Even though they are mostly rather restrictive and argue, for instance in the case of Berman, only in favor of some procedural rules (neglecting any hierarchical fundamental norms), this is a claim in the realm of *ought*. We can accordingly speak of a "normative move" in this quite recent global legal pluralism debate. This move is acknowledged sometimes explicitly and sometimes implicitly. Sometimes it is also neglected. In any case, it is important to justify such normative claims.[297] This section therefore gently reminds us of David Hume's insight referred to above. What is important when making this move is that global legal pluralists must justify why they think these rules should be valid in order to settle norm conflicts. Moving in the realm of *ought*, they are confronted with such problems as that even reductionist procedural mechanisms might be accused of having a strong liberal flavor – and are also somewhat overarching substantial value claims.[298]

Legal Order and the member state Constitutional Courts are conceived as the final arbiters of constitutionality at the national level."

[294] Delmas-Marty (n 224) *Ordering Pluralism* 44–46.

[295] Samantha Besson, "Whose Constitution(s)? International Law, Constitutionalism, and Democracy" in Jeffrey L Dunhoff and Joel P Trachtman (eds) *Ruling the World? Constitutionalism, International Law, and Global Governance* (Cambridge University Press 2009) 381–408 (405).

[296] Besson (n 295) 405. For a critique of democracy as the "objective, the end, of the European construct," see Joseph H H Weiler, "Europe: The Case against the Case of Statehood" (1998) 4 (1) European Law Journal 43–62 (60).

[297] For criticism in this regard, see also Mariano Croce and Marco Goldoni, "A Sense of Self-Suspicion: Global Legal Pluralism and the Claim to Legal Authority" (2015) 8 (1) Ethics & Global Politics 1–20 (11), saying that "How these [normative] demands are put forward and then channeled is a question which is left largely unexplored, except for the treatment of adjudicative processes."

[298] For this critique of Berman, see Alexis Galán and Dennis Patterson, "The Limits of Normative Legal Pluralism: Review of Paul Schiff Berman, Global Legal Pluralism: A Jurisprudence of

Almost everybody agrees that there are many diverse legal rules, stemming from different legal orders and authorities, which do conflict – at least sometimes, to a certain extent. In order to organize and minimize these uncertainties, even most pluralists agree that we need at least a minimum standard of *common* principles or rules to guide the resolution of these conflicts. Despite this implicit agreement, I think it is, nevertheless, important to emphasize explicitly that we are in need of a *common* normative concept (*ought*) that enjoys the highest possible approval among the parties concerned. I do not wish to present any specific solution here. However, I wish to highlight that, first, it is of utmost importance to state clearly that we want to avoid norm conflicts (and say why, or why not) and, second, that we want to deal with them preferably, because supposedly more easily, according to a *common* framework, which is – at best – already established. Equally, for the latter claim it must be crystal clear that this is a normative endeavor for which we need reasons and some form of agreement, or rather general legitimacy.

Although global legal pluralism may provide a coherent descriptive account of current legal developments, it lacks a satisfying common prescriptive account. Accordingly, claims (for how to solve or why not to solve norm conflicts) that rest solely on the *description* of pluralistic orders do not suffice as a basis for a normative account. If approaches of legal pluralism resort to some sort of "meta norms or principles" to solve norm conflicts,[299] they too will need to justify these principles and give reasons for such common accounts.

We need to distinguish merely descriptive accounts from prescriptive accounts in debates of global *legal* pluralism in order to enable a transparent discussion of the proposals made. By doing so, we have to acknowledge how difficult such common frameworks are, even if we envisage "only" procedural minimum requirements. This will lead us to the final claim of this chapter: Contextualization (Section 2.3). However, before dealing with

Law beyond Borders" (2013) 11 (3) International Journal of Constitutional Law 783–800 (esp 793 ff). For a response see Paul S Berman, "How Legal Pluralism Is and Is Not Distinct from Liberalism: A Response to Alexis Galán and Dennis Patterson" (2013) 11 (3) International Journal of Constitutional Law 801–808. See further critically also Ralf Michaels, "On Liberalism and Legal Pluralism" in Miguel Maduro, Kaarlo Tuori and Suvi Sankari (eds) *Transnational Law: Rethinking European Law and Legal Thinking* (Cambridge University Press 2014) 122–142 (141): "his [Berman's] managerialism also presupposes some superior position from which such management is possible." See, too, Groce and Goldoni (n 297) 8–9.

299 Compare Berman (n 278); Delmas-Marty (n 224) *Ordering Pluralism*. With regard to constitutional pluralism, see Mattias Kumm, "The Moral Point of Constitutional Pluralism" in Julie Dickson and Pavlos Eleftheriadis (eds) *Philosophical Foundations of European Union Law* (Oxford University Press 2012) 216–246 (220).

contextualization, we will see whether global constitutionalism can provide a helpful answer to our question.

2.2 GLOBAL CONSTITUTIONALISM: BETWEEN THE "BURDEN OF UNIVERSALITY" AND A "CONSTITUTIONAL STALEMATE"

2.2.1 *What Is (Understood by) Global Constitutionalism?*

Before moving on to my own proposal in Part II, another brief section devoted to global constitutionalism is in order. Constitutionalism on a global, supranational and national level is an important and wide-ranging concept. As a research topic, it has been around for some 100 years. Needless to say, it is hard to provide a general overview of constitutionalism.[300] Alfred Verdross was (one of) the first to speak of the constitution of the international legal community in 1926.[301] While this was quite progressive then, global constitutionalism has become a well-known concept recently, with its own journal, *Global Constitutionalism*, founded in 2012. Due to the successful emergence of "global constitutionalism" as an interdisciplinary movement in the twenty-first century, many diverging issues are being discussed under this influential label.[302] Global constitutionalism, as much as constitutionalism, shares the

[300] See eg Christine E J Schwöbel, *Global Constitutionalism in International Legal Perspective* (Martinus Nijhoff Publishers 2011) 4, identifying "five key themes of constitutionalization that shape the contemporary debate on global constitutionalism: the limitation of power, the institutionalization of power, social idealism (meaning an idea for the future that is based on societal values), the standard-setting capacity of constitutions in the sense of a systematization of law, and the recognition of individual rights." See also her categorization (49) as follows: "1) 'Social Constitutionalism' emphasizes the key theme of a limitation of the single locus of power through participation. 2) 'Institutional Constitutionalism' emphasizes the key themes of governance through institutionalization of power. 3) 'Normative Constitutionalism' emphasizes a common value system through the protection of individual rights and idealism. 4) And finally, 'Analogical Constitutionalism' includes the key themes that are seen as being incorporated in the respective domestic and regional constitutional orders. As was concluded, this dimension includes all key themes of constitutionalism, emphasizing the systematization of law (the fourth key theme)." For the distinction between "big-C" and "small-c" constitutionalism, see Mattias Kumm, "The Cosmopolitan Turn in Constitutionalism: On the Relationship between National Constitutional Law and Constitutionalism beyond the State" in Jeffrey L Dunoff and Joel P Trachtman (eds) *Ruling the World: Constitutionalism, International Law, and Global Governance* (Cambridge University Press 2009) 258–325 (260–265).

[301] Verdross (n 214).

[302] Anne Peters, "Constitutionalisation" in Jean d'Aspremont and Sahib Singh (eds) *Concepts for International Law – Contributions to Disciplinary Thought* (Edward Elgar 2019) 141–153. See also Schwöbel (n 300) ch 1, categorizing social, institutional, normative and analogical constitutionalism. For a broad understanding of constitutionalism, see Louis Henkin,

aspiration of establishment as well as the normative guidance and limitation of governmental power. In other words, constitutionalism "refers to governance according to constitutional principles."[303] We speak of a discourse which involves the "framing, constituting, regulating, and limiting [of] power"[304] – be it in a thin or thicker form.[305] The constitutionalization of international law is a project mainly interested in the substantial development of international law in the form of constitutional norms or principles (of the EU, for instance).[306] Constitutionalism is usually connected to certain key legal concepts such as the rule of law, human rights and democracy, and entails a materially substantiated form of what law should be like.[307] Very often a strong universal flavor is also attached to such concepts in a global perspective. This section does not challenge the finding that the EU legal order is a constitutional order. Instead, the aim is to discover whether the concept of global constitutionalism resolves the question of how we can know who has the final say on the relationship between the international, EU and national legal orders. This section will conclude that global constitutionalism is not very useful in guiding the relationship between legal orders because there must be some common agreement between those legal orders regarding how they interact, and in particular how norm conflicts between those legal orders can be solved. This is in contrast to the main aim of global constitutionalism,

"Elements of Constitutionalism" (1998) 60 (11) Special Issue of International Commission of Jurists. The Review 11–22 (11–12), stating that "Constitutionalism is nowhere authoritatively defined, but, as commonly used, a constitution designed to reflect constitutionalism will have common elements, with variations." For a narrower understanding see also Michael J Perry, *A Global Political Morality: Human Rights, Democracy, and Constitutionalism* (Cambridge University Press 2017) part III. For a functional approach see Jeffrey L Dunoff and Joel P Trachtman, "A Functional Approach to International Constitutionalization" in Jeffrey L Dunoff and Joel P Trachtman (eds) *Ruling the World: Constitutionalism, International Law, and Global Governance* (Cambridge University Press 2009) 3–35.

303 Jaako Husa, "Global Constitutionalism – Some Critical Remarks" (2017) 47 (1) Hong Kong Law Journal 73–88. See eg Mattias Kumm, "The Legitimacy of International Law: A Constitutionalist Framework of Analysis" (2004) 15 (5) European Journal of International Law 907–931.

304 Jean L Cohen, *Globalization and Sovereignty. Rethinking Legality, Legitimacy, and Constitutionalism* (Cambridge University Press 2012) 76.

305 Wil Waluchow, "Constitutionalism" in Edward N Zalta (ed) *Stanford Encyclopedia of Philosophy* (December 20, 2017) available at https://plato.stanford.edu/entries/constitutionalism/ [last accessed February 1, 2023].

306 For a critical overview of "world constitutionalism," see Oliver Diggelmann and Tilmann Altwicker, "Is There Something Like a Constitution of International Law? A Critical Analysis of the Debate on World Constitutionalism" (2008) 68 Heidelberg Journal of International Law 623–650.

307 For key legal concepts, see András Jakab, *European Constitutional Language* (Cambridge University Press 2016).

namely looking for sophisticated and substantial answers on how to constitute a specific (constitutional) order.

2.2.2 *Global Constitutionalism and the "Burden of Universality"*

Global constitutionalism is facing a challenge brought by descriptive legal pluralism: solutions to norm conflicts might differ depending on the context. Thus, according to the main argument of contextualization, another context asks for different solutions as different conditions are in place.[308] Once we reveal that the very first prescriptive question is what we *ought* to do with norm conflicts, there are likely to be very different solutions to different conflicts (and different legal orders involved) depending on the context.[309] This is acknowledged by understanding constitutionalism as a fragmented and contextualized concept,[310] as "a relatively consolidated form of global constitutionalism"[311] or, to a certain extent, as constitutional pluralism.[312]

[308] For a critique of Nico Krisch's pluralistic account of see also Schaffer (n 280) 579: "The positive, empirically-grounded study of transnational legal ordering, in contrast, is important for building a normative approach grounded in philosophical pragmatism which recognizes the need for institutional variation in response to different contexts."

[309] For a similar argument see also Melissaris (n 241) ch 3, relying on Robert M Cover, "The Supreme Court, 1982 Term-Foreword: Nomos and Narrative" (1983) 97 (4) Harvard Law Review 4–68; and Robert M Cover, "Violence and the Word" (1986) 95 (8) Yale Law Journal 1601–1629. However, it is important to highlight that my claim for contextualization is much simpler and thus less overladen than the claim Melissaris is making. While Melissaris' main target is a skeptical view of State law – or at least the link between State and law that is unnecessary in his eyes – my argument here is simply that when facing normative conflicts, there are likely to be various different solutions to dealing with the conflict depending on the context. Thus, I argue against a single – sometimes even not very clear prescriptive – claim of dealing with normative conflicts in the pluralistic world.

[310] Peters (n 302).

[311] Turkuler Isiksel, "Global Legal Pluralism as Fact and Norm" (2013) 2 Global Constitutionalism 160–195 (190).

[312] See Neil MacCormick, *Questioning Sovereignty. Law State and Nation in the European Commonwealth* (Oxford University Press 1999) 104; and Neil Walker, "The Idea of Constitutional Pluralism" (2002) 65 (3) Modern Law Review 317–359; as well as Neil Walker, "Constitutional Pluralism Revisited" (2016) 22 (3) European Law Journal 333–355. For an overarching analysis of all works that have appeared under the label of constitutional pluralism, see Klemen Jaklic, *Constitutional Pluralism in the EU* (Oxford University Press 2013). See also Mattias Kumm, "The Jurisprudence of Constitutional Conflict: Constitutional Supremacy in Europe before and after the Constitutional Treaty" (2005) 11 (3) European Law Journal 262–307 (266–267, 301); as well as Kumm (n 293) 375, 384. Kumm is a constitutional pluralist too. Furthermore, for a recent analysis focusing on the case law of the CJEU and constitutional courts of Member States, see Ana Bobić, *The Jurisprudence of Constitutional Conflict in the European Union* (Oxford University Press 2022) 59–71, distinguishing between constructive and destructive constitutional conflict.

In a similar fashion to dualism, the idea of constitutional pluralism constituted historical progress. It was Neil MacCormick who challenged the view, which he summarized as: "No sovereignty, no constitution; no constitution, no UK."[313] Against this dictum, he argued that "our passing beyond the sovereign state is to be considered a good thing."[314] Moreover, constitutional pluralism can be understood in the context of strong resistance to the rise of the federal states of Europe. If important actors do not agree with a wide-ranging transfer of sovereign rights bordering on the dissolution of sovereignty of Member States, then authority shall be safeguarded for a limited area. If the European final authority is not accepted, then at least both authorities, the European and the Member State, should be able to coexist. Letting both make their claims to constitutionalism defends the position that the EU is a constitutional order against those strong claims holding that only nation states, in our case EU Member States, can be constitutional orders.

We see this in the work of MacCormick when he states: "A pluralistic and interactive analysis of the relations between the legal systems of the Member States and their common system of EC law suggests instead that the highest court within each system retains interpretative competence-competence."[315] While according to MacCormick "sovereignty has not passed to the organs of the Union, the same analysis confirms that sovereignty has not remained with the individual Member States either."[316] Importantly, however, the European Community "constitutes in its own context and over the relevant range of topics a source of valid law superior to other sources recognised in each of the Member States."[317]

In a sense this is also the goal of Neil Walker when he warns that constitutionalism as such is under attack and proposes constitutional pluralism, predominantly as an epistemic tool to enable both EU Member States and the EU to lay their claims to constitutional authority.[318]

Both MacCormick's and Walker's versions of constitutional pluralism contribute to the theoretical discourse on how sovereignty or authority is distributed in Europe. Instead of giving all the power to the Member States or the EU as the final locus of political authority, they argue – in distinct ways – for a

313 Neil MacCormick, "Beyond the Sovereign State" (1993) 56 (1) Modern Law Review 1–18 (1).

314 MacCormick (n 313) 1.

315 Neil MacCormick, "The Maastricht-Urteil: Sovereignty Now" (1995) 1 (3) European Law Journal 259–266 (259).

316 MacCormick (n 315) 259.

317 MacCormick (n 315) 264.

318 Walker (n 312) The Idea of Constitutional Pluralism 317: "Constitutional discourse has perhaps never been more popular, nor more comprehensively challenged than it is today."

case in which both orders might enjoy, at least from their own perspective, their full autonomy, their claim to the last resort.[319]

And yet what is striking in both conceptions, though more in the latter than in the former,[320] is that from the outset these conceptualizations hold that both claims to foundational authority, those of the EU Member States and those of the EU, were incommensurable. What this fails to see – and therein lies another striking resemblance to long-ago dualist accounts – is that we are not talking about legal orders which are alien to each other. While this might well be true for the British common law and the French or German legal order, the legal order of the EU is significantly different in as much as it features an important commonality across the legal orders of its Member States, and that is the people. The EU legal order builds on the French, the German, the Polish people, and so on.[321] It is therefore incorrect to stipulate that the EU legal order be fundamentally different from these peoples.[322] It was also the French, the Germans, the Polish, and so on who engaged in establishing the EU legal order. To treat the EU legal order as incommensurably different in its claim to authority (for its given competences) is closer to denying that it might never be a constitutional order than these authors might wish.

What still remains problematic is the specific request for *constitutional* norms, rules and principles. The relationship between legal orders must not

[319] For an insightful analysis of both, see Jaklic (n 312) 13–68, situating both (at 50) in his categorization of constitutional pluralism accounts in the "theoretical discourse about the deepest foundations of the heterarchically as opposed to hierarchically related constitutional authorities and their sources."

[320] See, for instance, Walker (n 312) The Idea of Constitutional Pluralism 349, stating that "on a pluralist reading the assertion of rival plausible claims to have the last judicial word on an overlapping or disputed question of competence, provided these claims are also reasonably institutionally effective on their own terms, confirms rather than denies the interpretive autonomy of each of the polities or putative polities in question."

[321] Seeing this difference clearly, MacCormick (n 315) 262.

[322] For the critique that Walker does not provide arguments for his incommensurability-claim but "rather flatly state[s]" this axiom of his theory "as one aspect of the 'elementary circumstances of constitutional politics,'" see Jaklic (n 312) 54 (who offers candidates justifying this axiom at 54 ff). Or rather in Walker's (Neil Walker, "Late Sovereignty in the European Union" in Neil Walker (ed) *Sovereignty in Transition* (Hart 2003) 3–32 (28)) words, a sovereign ought to have its own constituting rules as well as rules of adjudication inter alia, as "[t]his is the irreducible core, the non-negotiable given of any sovereign order – . . . the 'vanishing point' of perspective from which its 'sovereign' vision of the world is constructed or assumed but which itself cannot be seen and cannot be questioned in the construction of that vision." For the critique that epistemic pluralism "undercuts itself" when trying to impose its axiom as the "least imposing" reciprocal claim as it thereby "implants the seeds of its own destruction.," see again Jaklic (n 312) 67.

always be of a constitutional dimension.[323] Moreover, despite the fact that a relationship between different legal orders does not have to be guided by one specific constitution, a legal relationship might still exist between certain legal orders. This holds true even if we can speak of an EU Member State legal order as a constitutional order and the EU legal order as a constitutional order.[324] It is challenging to determine the relationship between these legal orders as it requires establishing which constitutional system has the final say.

Additionally, global constitutionalism faces the challenge that the literature on constitutionalism comes from a specific legal culture, which casts doubt on its universality.[325] Finally, universalists face the critique of being too optimistic about intervening in others' affairs, which makes them more closely related to empires than they might wish.[326] Indeed,

> [the] constitutional project … seems to have lost some of its momentum in recent years. Constitutionalism's suggestion of a unitary international normative system struggles to deal with some of international law's main successes, namely with the increasing internationalization of national law, the development of highly integrated supranational legal orders such as the European Union, and an increasing specialization of international subsystems.[327]

In addition, more recent developments such as Russia's war of aggression against Ukraine and the shock emanating from this blatant violation of

[323] See Anne Peters, "Compensatory Constitutionalism: The Function and Potential of Fundamental International Norms and Structures" (2006) 19 (3) Leiden Journal of International Law 579–610 (597), asking whether discussions under the label of constitutionalism are not simply "thicker legalization and institutionalization, without any need to resort to the notion of constitution"; cf Dieter Grimm, "The Constitution in the Process of Denationalization" (2005) 12 (4) Constellations 447–463 (460).

[324] For the argument for a "double constitution" and "double state power" concerning the relationship between EU law and the Austrian legal order, see Peter Pernthaler, *Allgemeine Staatslehre und Verfassungslehre* (Springer 2nd ed 1996) 38.

[325] See Schwöbel (n 300) 5. For the more general question as to whether even international law is international, see Anthea Roberts, *Is International Law International?* (Oxford University Press 2017). See also with many references to the German tradition, Andreas L Paulus, "Zur Zukunft der Völkerrechtswissenschaft in Deutschland: Zwischen Konstitutionalisierung und Fragmentierung des Völkerrechts" (2007) 67 Heidelberg Journal of International Law 695–719. See on the different academic-dogmatic grasp of European law due to the languages, legal cultures and traditions, Armin Hatje and Peter Mankowski, "Nationale Unionsrechte. Sprachgrenzen, Traditionsgrenzen, Systemgrenzen, Denkgrenzen" (2014) 49 (2) Europarecht 155–169.

[326] Henning Ottmann, *Geschichte des politischen Denkens: Das 20. Jahrhundert – Von der kritischen Theorie bis zur Globalisierung* (J B Metzler 2012) 350.

[327] Andreas L Paulus and Johann Ruben Leiss, "Constitutionalism and the Mechanics of Global Law Transfers" (2018) 9 Goettingen Journal of International Law – 1 Special Issue: The Law behind Rule of Law Transfers 35–69 (39).

fundamental international norms make it even more difficult to argue for global constitutionalism as a sophisticated substantial answer on how to constitute the international order.

2.2.3 *Global Constitutionalism in a "Constitutional Stalemate"*

If global constitutionalism pays tribute to the "burden of universality" when asked for an answer on how we can know who has the final say on the relationship between international, EU and national law, and if global constitutionalism is understood as a fragmented and contextualized concept,[328] "a relatively consolidated form of global constitutionalism"[329] or, to a certain extent, also as constitutional pluralism,[330] we must fall back on a nonhierarchical relationship between the constitutional systems involved in order to avoid a subordination of one order by another. Trying to resolve these questions on a constitutional level might very likely lead to a "constitutional stalemate."

Therefore, I am skeptical about global constitutionalism being a helpful concept with regard to the challenge of resolving norm conflicts between overlapping international, EU and national legal orders. On a global scale, we are well advised to take the descriptive account of global legal pluralism seriously. The massive increase in international actors, norms and tribunals, as well as adjudicators, makes it very difficult to speak of global constitutionalism *de lege lata* (without definitely excluding the possible existence of a thin layer of global constitutionalism). A cautious assessment is that global

328 Peters (n 302).

329 Isiksel (n 311) 190.

330 For a critique, see, for instance, Martin Loughlin, "Constitutional Pluralism: An Oxymoron?" (2014) 3 (1) Global Constitutionalism 9–30, who looks at the origins of constitutional pluralism and finds that it is an "oxymoronic concept"; cf Alexander Somek, "Monism: A Tale of the Undead?" in Matej Avbelj and Jan Komárek (eds) *Constitutional Pluralism in the European Union and Beyond* (Hart 2012) 343–379, whose challenge to constitutional pluralism is neatly rephrased by Miguel Poiares Maduro, "Three Claims of Constitutional Pluralism" in Matej Avbelj and Jan Komárek (eds) *Constitutional Pluralism in the European Union and Beyond* (Hart 2012) 67–84 (72) as follows: "Somek argues that constitutional pluralists give up precisely where an answer is most needed: what happens when the constitutional conflict cannot be prevented or solved?" See also similarly, Andreas L Paulus, "Internationales, nationales und privates Recht. Hybridisierung der Rechtsordnungen" (2014) 46 Berichte der Deutschen Gesellschaft für Internationales Recht 7–46 (text at n 112).For a comparison of constitutional pluralism with what developmental psychologists call "parallel play," see R Daniel Kelemen, "On the Unsustainability of Constitutional Pluralism, European Supremacy and the Survival of the Eurozone" (2016) 23 (1) Maastricht Journal of European and Comparative Law 136–150 (136), stating that "constitutional pluralism is unsustainable, and just as children grow out of parallel play, so too must Europe's courts."

constitutionalism presumes too many substantial values for the envisaged common normative denominator so as to be a helpful general concept for norm conflict solution arising out of the relationship between international, EU and national law.[331]

If we agree that norm conflicts from different but overlapping legal orders should be avoided and if it appears as if they should be resolved, we need to look for appropriate concepts for the task. I argue that we are in need of a common normative (legal) framework for such a resolution. This would be common in the sense that this normative framework is brought about with agreement by all affected legal orders. In other words, if we agree that "stronger state[s should not be able to] lawfully force a constitutional position on another state or a stronger court on a weaker court, without any legal redress,"[332] we are in need of such a common normative concept. Still, this section contends that global constitutionalism is not directly helpful for our question of the relationship of legal orders either.[333] Constitutionalization is more interested in the substantial development of international law in the form of constitutional norms or principles (or of the constitutional norms or principles of the European Union for instance) than in explaining the relationship between international, EU and national law.[334] Our quest to resolve the question of who has the final say on the relationship between international, EU and national law, and along these lines the quest for a common framework to deal with norm conflicts from different legal orders, leads us to the need for contextualization.

331 See Perry (n 302), who envisages "agapic sensibility" as the foundation for human dignity. Perry's statement illustrates how difficult such universal legal standards are: "this book is about the *political morality* of human rights … not about the *international law* of human rights" (emphasis original), 2. For a critical account of the current state of EU "constitutionalization," see Dieter Grimm, "The Democratic Costs of Constitutionalization: The European Case" in Dieter Grimm, *Constitutionalism. Past, Present, and Future* (Oxford University Press 2015) 295–313.

332 Pavlos Eleftheriadis, "Cosmopolitan Legitimacy," paper presented at the 'Philosophical Foundations of Global Law' conference at the University of Cartagena, Colombia on August 25, 2016 (on file with the author).

333 See Alexander Somek, *The Cosmopolitan Constitution* (Oxford University Press 2014), who writes in the preface that "Greater 'constitutionalization' of supranational or even international law threatens to rob constitutionalism of its political core."

334 Jan Klabbers, *The Constitutionalization of International Law* (Oxford University Press 2009), simply presuming it; Thomas Kleinlein, *Konstitutionalisierung im Völkerrecht* (Springer 2012), refraining from strong normative claims. For a critical overview of "world constitutionalism," see Diggelmann and Altwicker (n 306).

2.3 THE NEED TO ACKNOWLEDGE CONTEXTUALIZATION

2.3.1 *Plurality of Contexts*

Instead of trying to come up with an overarching theory or model that aims at analyzing pluralism or constitutionalism worldwide, we should rather focus on the differences between all varying legal orders and thus norm conflicts at stake by taking context into account.

I am convinced that the search or struggle for common *prescriptive* guidelines for a norm conflict solution in our pluralistic world is much easier if we do not try to come up with one universal solution for all kinds of very different norm conflicts.[335] Hence, I argue with global legal pluralists that context is of utmost importance when discussing what is the best common normative framework to deal with legal norm conflicts.[336] Universalist solutions are likely to fall short of acknowledging the restrictions of context that exist when dealing with legal norm conflicts on a global scale. Therefore, I am convinced that we need to take the different contexts of all norm conflicts into account in order to find common solutions – before or after the conflict has emerged.

Acknowledging the fact that different contexts suggest different common frameworks for norm conflict solutions also applies to comparisons between historical examples of legal pluralism and current global legal pluralistic

[335] Compare Franz von Benda-Beckmann, "Anthropology and Comparative Law" in Keebet von Benda-Beckmann and Fons Strijbosch (eds) *Anthropology of Law in the Netherlands* (Foris 1966) 90–109 (92–93), asking "[w]hat is it we want to compare and why do we want to compare it?" See also Franz von Benda-Beckmann and Keebet von Benda-Beckmann, "The Dynamics of Change and Continuity in Plural Legal Orders" (2006) 53–54 Special double issue of the Journal of Legal Pluralism and Unofficial Law 1–44 (13–14), as well as F von Benda-Beckmann (n 258). See also William Twining, "A Post-Westphalian Conception of Law" (2003) 37 (1) Law and Society Review 199–258 (250). I am following F von Benda-Beckmann by suggesting that "the context and purposes of the inquiry supply criteria for distinguishing 'legal' from other normative orders." However, my suggestion here to focus on the context is not so much or only related to distinguishing law from nonlaw, but aims at grasping, depending on the context, different common concepts in order to address and hopefully deal with all varieties of legal normative conflicts.

[336] For an interesting conception in this regard, see Tom Flynn, *The Triangular Constitution. Constitutional Pluralism in Ireland, the EU and the ECHR* (Hart 2020) 53, holding that "interface norms under metaconstitutional pluralism are not universal, but rather context dependent." His version of interface norms, however, is different from Krisch's (n 224) 285 notion referred to above (see Flynn xxvii–iii). However, in Flynn's eyes (230–231), "a constitutionally pluralist conception of the relationship between the legal orders of Ireland, the EU and the ECHR as a deliberative polyarchy – a triangular constitution – is descriptively accurate *and* normatively desirable" [emphasis added]. Nevertheless, he sees that in this vein, "the universal and the particular seem to remain stubbornly separate."

settings. I previously referred to Berman's explanation of the shift from legal pluralism when describing the "living law" of the Bukovina or plural normative systems in some colonial settings – which were usually organized in a hierarchical way – towards "bidirectional" systems influencing each other without one constantly superior system. As already indicated, it is vital to look more closely at this shift. The living law of the Bukovina or some other colonial setting may be roughly summarized by noting that one people (colonial power) aimed at governing one specific territory (colony) where a different people (colonized people) lived by their own law, which was essentially "made" by them. The Bukovina and colonized peoples had their own, different law(s) ("living law") which was, at least in theoretical terms, not accepted by the dominant, colonizing people and was derogated by their legal order.[337] This means there was one territory with two exclusively different "authorities" (note especially that the law of the colonial power was largely not made by the people living in the colonies and thus also not legitimized by them in any way) with law making and enforcement power, whereby one was dominant over the other.

This constellation, however, is quite different from the way in which global legal pluralism is described nowadays – at least most "vertical" global legal pluralism. Yet the relation between the EU and international law as well as that between international law, EU law and (Member) State law are taken as examples by various pluralists.[338] We have again two different authorities with

[337] See, for instance, the discussion by Engle Merry (n 228) 869–870 of the repugnancy principle, which was used by colonial powers to "outlaw unacceptable African customs."

[338] Krisch (n 224) 109 ff; Berman (n 224) 154 ff; Delmas-Marty (n 224) *Ordering Pluralism* 83. Krisch (n 224) 109 ff, elaborates on European human rights law thereby focusing on the relationship between the European Convention on Human Rights and Member States as well as the example of UN sanctions (esp Kadi) and EU law (153 ff). Berman (n 224) 154 ff points to the relation between NAFTA panels and the US state courts. Similar to Krisch, Berman also picks the example of the relation between the European Court of Human Rights and constitutional courts of European Member States (155 ff). He also mentions "dialectical interactions . . . with regard to nonstate normative standards" (160). However, to be fair, Berman at least acknowledges (153) that "[d]escribing mechanisms for managing pluralism does not tell us how best actually to manage pluralism in particular cases." See also Delmas-Marty (n 224) *Ordering Pluralism* 83, who points to regional organizations (81 ff) such as NAFTA, the Andean Community, Caricom, Mercosur, the American Convention of Human Rights, the African Union, the European Convention of Human Rights as well as global organizations (97 ff), where she speaks about fragmentation and privatization as well as about (164) a "truly pluralist order" that is "hypercomplex" and "must combine horizontal and vertical interactions and correlate this variable-geometry integration with other movements." Delmas-Marty (n 224) *Ordering Pluralism* 17: her "hypothesis of ordered pluralism involves renouncing the binary opposition between hierarchical relationships (by subordination of one order to another) and non-hierarchical relationships (by coordination) and considering the

law making and (at least theoretical or rather weak) enforcement power which may possibly produce conflicting norms within the same territory. However, a decisive difference, which is not fully taken into account by the current debate, is that the people involved in the law-making procedure partly overlap. International law is – at least in theory – based on the participation in the law-making process of all those States that are bound by it afterwards. This means that when, for instance, international law conflicts with national law (two different legal orders) on the same territory (national State), there is a common element. This common element is the individuals of a modern State who are – at least indirectly – represented on both levels: at the level of the State as well as at the level of international law. In this sense, international law is a common law of all participating States. This is quite different from the situation where the Empire's center simply ignored the living law of the Bukovina or the law of colonies. Hence, the argument that international and national law are also to be seen as bidirectional does not hold. The context of these different examples varies too much. Vertical global legal pluralism dealing with norm conflicts between international, EU and national law is essentially different from the pluralism between the Empire and the living law of the Bukovina or the "relationship" between a colonial power and a colony. States make and thereby commit themselves to applying international law also at the national level – the Bukovina or colonies did not do so. Therefore, the law of the Empire enjoyed much less legitimacy concerning the Bukovina – at least in this regard. This difference is important when engaging with the discussion on how those norm conflicts should be addressed. In this regard, Müller states that "the EU has always been about *pluralism within common political parameters*. After all, the accession process itself did not aim at something like maximizing difference, but was explicitly and officially intended to ensure sameness in certain regards (democracy, rule of law, state capacity, etc.)."[339]

Yet this was just one example of how, in this case, possible solutions might look somewhat different as they involve certain specific conditions. Thus, a

process of interaction in a more nuanced fashion, a bit like the reflection of diverse pluralisms." For criticism against this stance see also Moritz Hartmann, "Review Essay: 'Lost in Disordered Clouds: Transnational Legal Pluralism and the Regulation of Global Asymmetries' – Mireille Delmas-Marty's Ordering Pluralism" (2009) 11 (9) German Law Journal 1025–1037 (1036).

339 Jan Werner Müller, "Protecting the Rule of Law (and Democracy!) in the EU. The Idea of a Copenhagen Commission" in Carlos Closa and Dimitry Kochenov (eds) *Reinforcing Rule of Law Oversight in the European Union* (Cambridge University Press 2016) 206–224 (221) [emphasis original].

different context, according to the main argument of contextualization, would require different solutions when different conditions exist.[340] Once we see that the very first prescriptive question is what to do with norm conflicts (*ought*), there are very likely to be very different solutions to different conflicts depending on the context.[341]

2.3.2 *An Individual or Institutional Setting for Norm Conflict Resolution?*

Another decisive issue regarding context is facing the question of which setting we consider more promising in the end to solve normative conflicts between competing legal orders: the "individual level" or the "institutional level"? If we were to choose the "individual level," we would leave individuals alone to resolve norm conflicts. In other words, context might inform our decision as to whether we share the skepticism of Kelsen when saying that we should try as hard as we can to avoid individuals finding themselves under different obligations at the same time: "A ought to be" and "A ought not to be."[342] Nowadays, however, the picture might be far more complex than when monism and dualism portrayed two rather simple, and thus clear pictures: either one unitary system (monism) or separated legal orders (dualism).[343] In numerous constellations it is difficult to speak of completely different legal orders. A commonality of both international and national law (as much as EU law – on both sides) is the people who are involved (at least to some degree) in each of the conflicting law-making procedures. It is the French, German, Italian, and other citizens who share the law-making process of national, European and even international law. Is this fact to be neglected when separating those legal orders because of different "sovereigns" ruling and controlling the different laws from different legal orders? It is important to

340 See again Schaffer (n 280) 579.

341 See similarly Melissaris (n 241) ch 3 relying on Cover (n 309).

342 Kelsen (n 26) 374–375; Kelsen (n 161) *Pure Theory* 205–206. See Martti Koskenniemi, *The Gentle Civilizer of Nations* (Cambridge University Press 2001) 240 with further reference to Kelsen (n 205). See also Neil MacCormick, "Risking Constitutional Collision in Europe?" (1998) 18 (3) Oxford Journal of Legal Studies 517–532 (530): This "problem is not logically embarrassing, because strictly speaking the answers are from the point of view of different systems. But it is practically embarrassing to the extent that the same human beings or corporations are said to have and not have a certain right. How shall they act? To which system are they to give their fidelity in action?" Regarding Neil MacCormick's shift from radical pluralism towards "pluralism under international law," see Krisch (n 251).

343 Kirchmair (n 205); Lando Kirchmair, "Is the EU Legal Order the Tombstone of the Dualistic and the Monistic Doctrine?" in Michael Thaler and Michel Verpeaux (eds) *La recherche en droit constitutionnel comparé* (L'Harmattan 2014) 71–86.

note that this argument is not another expression of a legal unity. It suffices to see that international (and also EU) law differs from the national law of Germany, Italy, France and so on quite obviously in relation to those individuals who actively (as indirect law makers) and passively (as subjects to the law) are related to the law. While Germans are subject to German national law as much as to EU and international law, Italians and French are not. They share EU and international law but not their own national laws. However, going back to the initial question, of which setting is the most promising to solve norm conflicts, between international and national legal orders for instance, we should take this insight into account. This might lead us to conclude that the individual level is not the appropriate level for norm conflict resolution in the context of these overlapping legal orders because this chapter holds that international, EU and national law generally should strive to avoid addressing individuals with conflicting norms holding, for instance, that "A ought to be" and at the same time "A ought not to be." In another context the answer could, however, look different. Moreover, facing the question whether we think we should or should not have a prescriptive common framework to deal with norm conflicts is the very first prescriptive claim dealt with above. I thus hold that we should deal with norm conflicts arising in the context of international, EU and national law generally speaking at an "institutional level," whereby I mean within the realm of international, EU or national law.

2.3.3 *Detecting the Common in Global Plural Legal Orders*

Independently of the question as to which setting, the individual or the institutional level, we consider more promising is the question whether norm conflicts between international, EU and national law "truly" arise. In order to answer this question in the affirmative, we need to operate from a common methodological point, namely a congruent (unifying both conflicting orders) definition and interpretation of law.[344] This common framework (understanding, definition) needs to be abstract enough to comprise all legal orders involved and it still needs to be concrete enough to deliver results. This is not an easy task. Independently of the concepts, methods, mechanisms or criteria that are to be used to decide on norm conflicts within "pluralistic" legal orders, these concepts must be encompassed by the *common* understanding of the law of all orders involved for the sake of legally solving norm conflicts arising between those different orders. These mechanisms or criteria

[344] See Somek (n 330) for the argument that the identification of a conflict necessarily implies an overarching system.

must be reflected in the common understanding of the conflicting legal norms. For such a common understanding, definition or concept of law, it is not enough that the identified legal concept, such as a principle of democracy, is given in only one of the conflicting legal orders. If the suggested principles are not reflected in the common understanding of law, they do not constitute a common framework. This must be taken into account if, for instance, some procedural mechanisms[345] or a super-criterion such as democracy[346] is suggested to guide or deal with conflicts of norms of plural orders.

However, while this does not mean that there must be one single, universal understanding of the law all over the world,[347] in relation to those legal orders involved in norm conflicts that should be solved, a *common* understanding and definition is essential to a *legal* solution. So when we discuss norm conflicts between EU and national law, we need to start from a common understanding of the law of both legal orders. When we discuss the relationship between international and national law we need a common definition of those two orders. And when norm conflicts between more legal orders, such as international, EU and national law, are at stake, our definition needs to be guided by a legal concept in accordance with all three legal orders. This implies that the criteria guiding the norm conflict resolution might look very different depending on the legal orders that are involved.

This is connected to a trivial but nonetheless crucial insight: it is not and never will be always possible to have legal means in order to solve (normative) conflicts. However, the question is whether in a world with rapidly growing interactions between different societies, and therefore different legal orders, we must leave the norm conflict solution between different legal orders purely to nonlegal mechanisms (or new legal mechanisms as suggested by systems theory, for instance), which might be too vague and possibly not sufficiently power resistant,[348] or market dominated and so on. There are legal means to deal with norm conflicts between different legal orders and the solution lies in finding the commonalities of those different legal orders.[349] Nobody would

[345] See the suggestion of Berman (n 235) 1192, and esp 1196 ff, Berman (n 224) 145, and esp 152 ff, for which he offers normative philosophical justifications.

[346] Besson (n 295) 405.

[347] See, however, Melissaris (n 241) 61, where he argues for a “thin but universal sense of law.”

[348] Günther (n 270) 5: “Historical experience teaches us that a pluralism of normative orders can rapidly become the victim of power asymmetries, or even bring forth such asymmetries.”

[349] For an interesting account focusing on authority, see Nicole Roughan, “The Relative Authority of Law: A Contribution to ‘Pluralist Jurisprudence’” in Maksymilian Del Mar (ed) *New Waves in Philosophy of Law* (Palgrave Macmillan 2011) 254–273; Nicole Roughan, *Authorities. Conflicts, Cooperation, and Transnational Legal Theory* (Oxford University Press 2013).

deny that the legal orders of the EU and a Member State overlap and the most important commonality of the EU and its Member States is the people. Nowadays, French, Germans, Greeks and so on are not only French, German and Greek citizens, they are also EU citizens. Being one and the same person, they belong to two somewhat distinct legal orders. Norm conflicts between these legal orders should be solved[350] because those "distinct" legal orders are unified to a certain extent by the very same subjects, namely the people.[351] Recent tendencies show that the international legal sphere also recognizes more actors than just States, as was the case in earlier days. The example of international criminal law shows that individuals are also subjects on the international plane.[352] More and more other areas of international law are developing in a similar direction. It is increasingly questioned whether only States are subjects of international law.[353] So even if we cannot (yet) speak of individuals as "world citizens," they are becoming more actively involved in international law and are increasingly being addressed directly. This shows that in those norm conflicts where individuals are also addressed directly by international law, norm conflicts between international law and national law have to be subject to legal resolution mechanisms in order to guarantee a legitimate regulation of those conflicts – at least if we want to avoid leaving the norm conflicts to nonlegal resolution techniques and forces such as (power) politics and market rules.

2.4 WHY GLOBAL LEGAL PLURALISM AND GLOBAL CONSTITUTIONALISM DO NOT RESOLVE THE QUESTION OF WHO HAS THE FINAL SAY

Pointing to *David Hume's* powerful insight, the section on global legal pluralism aimed to remind us of the necessity to distinguish clearly between global legal pluralism as the *description* of recent factual developments, pointing, on the one hand, towards the massive increase in international

[350] For a proposal, see von Bogdandy (n 29); Armin von Bogdandy, "Common Principles for a Plurality of Orders: A Study on Public Authority in the European Legal Area" (2014) 12 International Journal of Constitutional Law 980–1007.

[351] Jürgen Habermas, "Die Krise der Europäischen Union im Lichte einer Konstitutionalisierung des Völkerrechts – Ein Essay zur Verfassung Europas" (2012) 72 Heidelberg Journal of International Law 1–44 (5): "systemischen Zusammenwachsen einer multikulturellen Weltgesellschaft."

[352] See, generally, Elies Van Sliedregt, *Individual Criminal Responsibility in International Law* (Oxford University Press 2012).

[353] See, for instance, Anne Peters, *Beyond Human Rights. The Legal Status of the Individual in International Law* (Cambridge University Press 2016).

actors, norms and tribunals, as well as adjudicators, for example, and, on the other hand, the question of how we *ought to* deal with or even solve those legal conflicts – based on a (common) normative legal framework – resulting from these plural, overlapping legal claims. I argued that we need to disclose the presuppositions underlying the claims that address possible legal solutions for these conflicts in the realm of *ought* (which also includes a clear differentiation between legal and normative pluralism). Claims that rest solely on the *description* of pluralistic orders do not suffice as a basis. Thus, first, it is of utmost importance to be aware of the *is–ought* divide when defining what is law within studies of global *legal* pluralism. While a broad definition of the law might help to provide for a complete descriptive account of overlapping legal orders and legal obligations, a broad definition within a prescriptive account (often implicitly) includes a strong argument against any superiority of official modern State law over unofficial law. This, however, has to be clearly stated as well as underpinned with careful argumentation as to why, for instance, modern State law should not be enforced or is even invalid when some unofficial norms conflict.[354] The point is that the varying modes of legitimacy of official modern State law and unofficial law or other forms of normative authority must not be conflated. Pertinent issues and characteristics of modern State law such as democratic principles should be carefully differentiated from non-State law, which might not enjoy the same amount of legitimacy and thus might be diminished by a broad definition of a prescriptive account of global legal pluralism. This also pertains the other way round: a clear differentiation could be of help to show that unofficial law might enjoy an even stronger form of legitimacy than official law.

The section on global constitutionalism concludes that the *is–ought* divide is respected at best if prescriptive proposals to solve legal conflicts are differentiated depending on the context instead of resorting to universal solutions. In order to deal with conflicts of legal norms from different but overlapping legal orders, I suggested that we are more likely to come to a solution when we accept that different contexts make different solutions necessary. Global constitutionalism either faces the "burden of universality" or falls into the trap of a "constitutional stalemate." As a solution to such norm conflicts in legal

[354] Compare eg Piet Eeckhout, "The Integration of Public International Law in EU Law: Analytical and Normative Questions" in Piet Eeckhout and Manuel López-Escudero (eds) *The European Union's External Action in Times of Crisis* (Hart 2016) 189–204 (192), holding that "at its centre the idea [of legal pluralism] appears to be that the gap between legal systems is, in essence, unbridgeable. Each system has its own supreme authority – its own rules of recognition – and conflicts between systems cannot be resolved from within the law: ultimately, each system will give precedence to its own norms over those of the other system."

terms always deals with prescriptive claims, I finally argued that it is more precise to refer to a necessarily *common* framework that addresses the question of how those conflicts should be resolved *together* or at least in a way acceptable to all parties: this is neither reflected in the term plural nor provided by the concept of global constitutionalism.[355] Thus, global legal pluralism should rather focus on a descriptive account and global constitutionalism should pay tribute to contextualization (Table 2.1).

TABLE 2.1 *Overview of global legal pluralism and global constitutionalism*

	Global legal pluralism	Global constitutionalism
Presuppositions	- Norm conflicts are positive. - Focus on a descriptive account.	- Common values (and further necessities for constitutional unity). - Universality (at least for the claimed legal orders).
Theoretical outcome	- Description of pluralistic orders as the basis for a normative account for norm conflict solution.	- The Constitution guides all embraced legal orders/ norm conflicts.
Legal consequences	- Potential norm conflicts without a common solution (individuals might face contradictory claims).	- Always constitutional (depending on the content of the constitution).
Failure	- No satisfactory common account for norm conflict solution. - Descriptive accuracy, but normatively wanting. - Praise of norm conflicts without a common solution.	- Presuppositions are too demanding ("burden of universality"). - Not flexible enough for diverging contexts.

[355] Consider in this regard also the "deafening silence" asking whether there is anyone who is not a pluralist by Joseph H H Weiler, "Prologue: Global and Pluralist Constitutionalism – Some Doubts" in Graínne de Búrca and Joseph H H Weiler (eds) *The Worlds of European Constitutionalism* (Cambridge University Press 2012) 8–18 (14). See also the positive "reply" by Piet Eeckhout, "Human Rights and the Autonomy of EU Law: Pluralism or Integration?" (2013) 66 (1) Current Legal Problems 169–202 and further references at 171 in n 7 to like-minded scholars.

3

The "Autonomy" of the EU Legal Order as a Self-Standing Theory?

3.1 AUTONOMY UNIFIES THE EU LEGAL ORDER RELATING TO ITS MEMBER STATES

A long time ago, the CJEU postulated the creation of the Treaty's " own legal system," which later was explicitly framed as the "autonomy of the Community legal order".[356] This general statement was accompanied by the direct effect of EU law on the national laws of the Member States,[357] just like the primary application of EU law.[358] This was necessary to establish and guarantee the success of the EU by creating a strong and effective autonomous legal system.[359] Since then, autonomy has become a cornerstone of the EU

[356] See n 2. In Case 6/64 *Costa v ENEL* ECLI:EU:C:1964:66 p 594, the CJEU stated that the law stems from an "independent source" (in the French, German, Italian and Dutch language versions: une "source autonome" de droit, eine "autonom[e] Rechtsquelle," "una fonte autonoma" di diritto and "een autonome [rechts]bron"); the landmark ruling that sowed the seeds of "autonomy" as a legal concept, however, was Case 26/62 *Van Gend & Loos v Netherlands* ECLI:EU:C:1963:1. See eg Ingolf Pernice, "The Autonomy of the EU Legal Order – Fifty Years after Van Gend" in Antonio Tizzano, Juliane Kokott and Sacha Prechal (eds) *50th Anniversary of the Judgment in van Gend en Loos* (EU Publications Office 2013) 55–80 (56).

For a very early version of this section, see Lando Kirchmair, "The 'Janus Face' of the Court of Justice of the European Union: A Theoretical Appraisal of the EU Legal Order's Relationship with International and Member State Law" (2012) 4 (3) Goettingen Journal of International Law 677–691.

[357] See Case 26/62 *Van Gend & Loos v Netherlands* ECLI:EU:C:1963:1.

[358] Again Case C-6/64 *Costa v ENEL* ECLI:EU:C:1964:66; and Case 11/70 *Internationale Handelsgesellschaft* ECLI:EU:C:1970:114 para 3–4; Case 106/77 *Simmenthal II* ECLI:EU:C:1978:49.

[359] For an interesting argument defending the functional necessity of "autonomy" to ensure the independent legal personality of an international organization such as the EU but arguing "against a reading that gives normative content to autonomy in order to use it as a constitutional premise that elevates the pursuit of any and all objectives of the EU integration project above everything else," see Violeta Moreno-Lax and Katja S. Ziegler, "Autonomy of

legal order. Recently, for instance, the CJEU relied on the autonomous legal system of the EU to defend core values enshrined in Article 2 TEU vis-à-vis some Member States in the rule of law and democracy crisis.[360]

Considering the far-reaching effects on the national legal orders of EU Member States, it is important to base these decisions regarding the autonomy of the EU legal order on a theoretical foundation.[361] Bearing in mind the famous debate about the relationship between international and national law, scholarly debate began as soon as these CJEU rulings were established to analyze, in theoretical terms, the practical steps taken by the CJEU.[362] The unifying effect of autonomy in relation to Member State law has reminded many commentators of one of the grand old theories: monism. Consequently, some authors tried and still try to fit autonomy and the relationship between the EU and its Member States in general and the claim to autonomy in particular into a monistic scheme.[363]

the EU Legal Order – A General Principle? On the Risks of Normative Functionalism and Selective Constitutionalism" in Katja S. Ziegler, Päivi J. Neuvonen and Violeta Moreno-Lax (eds) *General Principles in EU Law. Constructing Legal Orders in Europe* (Edward Elgar 2022) 227–252 (227).

360 See Joined Cases C-357/19, C-379/19, C-547/19, C-811/19 and C-840/19 *Euro Box Promotion ea* ECLI:EU:C:2021:1034 para 254; and Case C-430/21 RS ECLI:EU:C:2022:99 para 73.

361 Speaking of a revolutionary new creation of the community legal order ("revolutionäre Neubildung der Gemeinschaftsrechtsordnung"), Theodor Schilling, "Das Verhältnis zwischen Völkerrecht, Gemeinschaftsrecht und staatlichem Recht" in Stefan Griller and Heinz Peter Rill (eds) *Rechtstheorie: Rechtsbegriff – Dynamik – Auslegung* (Springer 2011) 153–194 (170 ff) holding (172) that this revolution is from the perspective of a prerevolutionary legal order illegal, from the perspective of an external observer a relevant fact and from an interior perspective the foundation of a new legal order.

362 For a literature overview, see Koen Lenaerts, José A. Gutiérrez-Fons and Stanislas Adam, "Exploring the Autonomy of the European Union Legal Order" (2021) 81 Heidelberg Journal of International Law 47–87 (48, n 3).

363 See generally, for instance, the former president of the CJEU Gil C Rodríguez Iglesias, "Zu den Grenzen der verfahrensrechtlichen Autonomie der Mitgliedstaaten bei der Anwendung des Gemeinschaftsrechts" (1997) 24 (14–16) Europäische Grundrechtezeitschrift 289–295; Nicolas Michel, "L'imprégnation du droit étatique par l'ordre juridique international" in Daniel Thürer, Jean-François Aubert and Jörg Paul Müller (eds) *Verfassungsrecht der Schweiz* (Schulthess 2001) 63–69 (67); Stefan Griller, "Völkerrecht und Landesrecht – unter Berücksichtigung des Europarechts" in Robert Walter, Clemens Jabloner and Karl Zeleny (eds) *Hans Kelsen und das Völkerrecht: Ergebnisse eines internationalen Symposiums in Wien* (Manz 2004) 83–120 (109); Stefan Griller, "Der Stufenbau der österreichischen Rechtsordnung nach dem EU–Beitritt" (2000) 8 (4) Journal für Rechtspolitik 273–288 (284); Michael Potacs, "Zum Rang des Gemeinschaftsrechts gegenüber staatlichem Recht" in Clemens Jabloner, Otto Lucius and Alfred Schramm (eds) *Theorie und Praxis des Wirtschaftsrechts – Festschrift für H. René Laurer* (Springer 2009) 185–198 (196); Michael Potacs, "Das Verhältnis zwischen der EU und ihren Mitgliedstaaten im Lichte traditioneller Modelle" (2010) 65 (1) Zeitschrift für Öffentliches Recht 117–139 (120); Theo Öhlinger,

The main characteristic of monism – as we have seen, a theory developed most prominently by Georges Scelle, Hans Kelsen and Alfred Verdross at the beginning of the twentieth century[364] – is the assumption of a single unified legal system. This seems odd at first, since the first autonomy-related rulings of the CJEU were intended to establish and free the EU legal order from the legal orders of its Member States by claiming that the EU was built on an "independent" or "autonomous" source of law. However, the autonomy of the EU legal order could comprise such a unity of EU and Member State law at least in the sense the CJEU self-evidently meant: EU law is directly applicable in the Member State legal orders in respect of those competences that have been transferred to the EU. Promoted at the EU level, the autonomy would, similarly to a monistic doctrine, unify the EU legal order with the national legal orders of its Member States. Should norm conflicts arise between EU and national law, autonomy embedded in the monistic doctrine would need to deal with the question of which jurisdiction should prevail. While a monistic doctrine, with the so-called primacy of national law, must be traced back to a highly nationalistic view of international law that no longer can be considered suitable,[365] so would national autonomy. Autonomy with primacy of Member State law would not be autonomy; it would be self-contradictory. Each Member State's legal order could do what it sees fit.

Monism with the primacy of international law, and in our case EU law, could be more suitable. While the monistic doctrine stipulated the premise of

"Die Einheit des Rechts: Völkerrecht, Europarecht und staatliches Recht als einheitliches Rechtssystem?" in Stanley L Paulson and Michael Stolleis (eds) *Hans Kelsen: Staatsrechtslehrer und Rechtstheoretiker des 20. Jahrhunderts* (Mohr Siebeck 2005) 160–175 (169), concerning the highly abstract interpretation of Kelsen's monism that Öhlinger favors, this kind of interpretation is possible. However, one has to bear in mind that this abstract monism cannot provide a theoretical concept explaining, for instance, the primacy of EU law (Öhlinger 172); see also Schroeder (n 2) 113, 122; Pierre Pescatore, *L'ordre juridique des Communautés Européennes: Étude des sources du droit communautaire* (Liège 2nd ed 1975) 151. See also Kumm (n 293) speaking of a "European Monism," as well as more recently Gragl (n 16); Christina Eckes, "The Autonomy of the EU Legal Order" (2020) 4 (1) Europe and the World: A Law Review 1–19.

364 See above Section 1.2.

365 Walz (n 7) 40 classified this perception of monism as "pseudomonistic" (translation by the author). See also Starke (n 11) 77, where he stated: "[r]educed to its lowest terms, the doctrine of state primacy is a denial of international law as law, and an affirmation of international anarchy." For this reason the monistic conception with the primacy of municipal law is left aside here. Kelsen (n 205) 317, himself equated the monistic doctrine with the primacy of national law as the "*negation of all law.*" However, later on he left the decision up to political science, see Kelsen (n 161) *Pure Theory* 339 ff.

a hypothetical unity,[366] kept together by the "chain of validity,"[367] autonomy within the framework of monism would need to adopt such a stipulation. The ultimate ground for validity within Kelsenian monism is the famous basic norm of Hans Kelsen.[368] As a consequence, Member States and their law-making capacities were dependent on, or directly derived from, EU law.[369] This underlying premise does not fit the way EU Member States perceive the relationship of the EU legal order to their own legal orders.[370] Yet it still holds true that some other monistic arguments fit the interplay of EU and Member State law. The direct interaction between international or EU law and individuals, for example – an integral element of monism – has become increasingly relevant in light of current developments, which goes back to autonomy. Also, in a way, it was the postulated autonomy that paved the way to a deeper European integration. Autonomy as monism, however, does not seem to hold.

Nevertheless, autonomy is "part of the very DNA" of the EU legal order and has also been closely linked to the constitutionalization of the EU.[371] Others have emphasized the differences between EU law and the law of the Member States and have thus spoken of competing autonomous legal orders

[366] Compare Kelsen (n 161) *Pure Theory* 193 ff, 215: "A norm of general international law authorizes an individual or a group of individuals, on the basis of an effective constitution, to create and apply as a legitimate government a normative coercive order. That norm, thus, legitimizes this coercive order for the territory of its actual effectiveness as a valid legal order, and the community constituted by this coercive order as a 'state' in the sense of international law."

[367] See for the origin of the term "chain of validity" above n 207.

[368] Compare above n 210.

[369] See above n 365; compare also Verdross (n 214) 48 ff.

[370] For the critique that autonomy itself is not enough, see eg Dana Burchardt, *Die Rangfrage im europäischen Normenverbund. Theoretische Grundlagen und dogmatische Grundzüge des Verhältnisses von Unionsrecht und nationalem Recht* (Mohr Siebeck 2015) 81 ff. For a general critique, see Jörg Kammerhofer, *Uncertainty in International Law: A Kelsenian Perspective* (Routledge 2011) 192–193; Jörg Kammerhofer, "Kelsen – Which Kelsen? A Reapplication of the Pure Theory to International Law" (2009) 22 (2) Leiden Journal of International Law 225–249 (240 ff) with further references. See Trevor C Hartley, "National Law, International Law and EU Law – How Do They Relate?" in Patrick Capps, Malcolm Evans and Stratos Konstadinidis (eds) *Asserting Jurisdiction. International and European Legal Approaches* (Hart 2003) 65–81 (79), even holding that "As we have seen, Community provisions can have effect in Member States only by virtue of Member-State law, and the extent to which they prevail over domestic law also depends on a rule of Member-State law. However, all rules of Member-State law derive their validity from the national constitution: consequently, they cannot be valid if the constitution declares them invalid."

[371] Lenaerts, Gutiérrez-Fons and Adam (n 362) 49–52; for the understanding of autonomy as "embedded autonomy" within the framework of his "multilevel constitutionalism," see Pernice (n 356).

autonomies.[372] This, however, faces similar challenges to dualism. Aligning the concept of autonomy with other theories makes it vulnerable to the criticisms of those other theories too. However, if we are to think of autonomy as a theory in its own right, it is important to see that autonomy also needs a justification. Without proper justification, autonomy remains a mere postulate.

3.2 AUTONOMY SAFEGUARDS THE STABILITY OF THE EU LEGAL ORDER RELATING TO INTERNATIONAL LAW

Although the position of the CJEU regarding the internal relations of the EU to its Member States has been said to be driven by monistic arguments, the court does not seem to be convinced by such a theoretical conception. In relation to international law, the CJEU used the concept of autonomy rather as a shield. Opinion 1/91 demanded respect for the "autonomy of the Community legal order." This autonomy "must be assured exclusively by the Court of Justice."[373] The "constitutional charter of a Community based on the rule of law" contrasts with the European Economic Area based on an international agreement.[374] According to the CJEU, autonomy requires "that the essential character of the powers of the Community and its institutions as conceived in the Treaty remain unaltered" and that the procedures for ensuring uniform interpretation of the rules of international agreements and for the settlement of disputes do not bind the EU in the exercise of its internal powers.[375]

[372] See eg René Barents, *The Autonomy of Community Law* (Kluwer 2004) 268 ff, 299 ff, 176, speaking of that "the national territory is subject to two autonomous legal orders which, since they have the same scope, are thus competing."

[373] Opinion 1/91 *Draft agreement between the Community, on the one hand, and the countries of the European Free Trade Association, on the other, relating to the creation of the European Economic Area* ECLI:EU:C:1991:490 para 2; see also C-459/03 *Commission of the European Communities v Ireland* ECLI:EU:C:2006:345 para 2.

[374] Opinion 1/91 *Draft agreement between the Community, on the one hand, and the countries of the European Free Trade Association, on the other, relating to the creation of the European Economic Area* ECLI:EU:C:1991:490 para 21.

[375] Opinion 1/00 *Proposed agreement between the European Community and non-Member States on the establishment of a European Common Aviation Area* ECLI:EU:C:2002:231 paras 11–13 with reference to Opinion 1/91 *Draft agreement between the Community, on the one hand, and the countries of the European Free Trade Association, on the other, relating to the creation of the European Economic Area* ECLI:EU:C:1991:490 para 32, 41–46, 61–65 as well as Opinion 1/92 *Draft agreement between the Community, on the one hand, and the countries of the European Free Trade Association, on the other, relating to the creation of the European Economic Area* ECLI:EU:C:1992:189.

Faced with UN Security Council Resolutions on the violation of human rights, the Court emphasized in the famous *Kadi* cases that UN law and EU law "originate from distinct legal orders."[376] It was again autonomy that was key to justifying this stance.[377] More recently, the CJEU developed the concept of autonomy in more detail in its opinions on the accession of the EU to the ECHR (Opinion 2/13) and the conformity of the Comprehensive Economic and Trade Agreement (CETA) with EU law (Opinion 1/17).[378] The CJEU stated that autonomy requires that the interpretation of fundamental rights contained in the CFR, "the heart" of the EU legal structure, "be ensured within the framework of the structure and objectives of the EU."[379] An international agreement may be entered into by the EU only if "there is no adverse effect on the autonomy of the EU legal order."[380] More specifically, the CJEU stated again that an international agreement, in order to be compatible with the autonomy of the EU legal order, must not confer any power on international tribunals "to interpret or apply EU law" (except the power to interpret and apply the provisions of the agreement "having regard to the rules and principles of international law applicable between the Parties"). In addition, the awards issued by such tribunals must not "have the effect of

[376] Compare Joined Cases C-402/05 P and C-415/05 P *Kadi and Al Barakaat International Foundation v Council and Commission* EU:C:2008:461 paras 285 ff, 326–327; and Case C-548/09 P *Bank Melli Iran* ECLI:EU:C:2011:735 para 100: "It is important to note at the outset that Security Council resolutions and Council common positions and regulations originate from *distinct legal orders*" [emphasis added]. See also Fassbender (n 2) 336 ff. Cf Gráinne de Búrca, "The European Court of Justice and the International Legal Order after Kadi" (2010) 51 (1) Harvard International Law Journal 1–48 (2), "adopting a sharply dualist tone." For references to a more open, if not to say monistic, case law regarding international law in earlier terms see Kirsten Schmalenbach, "Normentheorie vs. Terrorismus: Der Vorrang des UN-Rechts vor EU-Recht" (2006) 61 (7) JuristenZeitung 349–353 (352).

[377] Joined Cases C-402/05 P and C-415/05 P *Kadi and Al Barakaat International Foundation v Council and Commission* ECLI:EU:C:2008:461 para 282.

[378] Opinion 2/13 *Draft international agreement – Accession of the European Union to the European Convention for the Protection of Human Rights and Fundamental Freedoms – Compatibility of the draft agreement with the EU and FEU Treaties* ECLI:EU:C:2014:2454; Opinion 1/17 *Comprehensive Economic and Trade Agreement between Canada, of the one part, and the European Union and its Member States, of the other part* (CETA) ECLI:EU:C:2019:341.

[379] Opinion 2/13 *Draft international agreement – Accession of the European Union to the European Convention for the Protection of Human Rights and Fundamental Freedoms – Compatibility of the draft agreement with the EU and FEU Treaties* ECLI:EU:C:2014:2454 para 169–170.

[380] Opinion 1/17 *Comprehensive Economic and Trade Agreement between Canada, of the one part, and the European Union and its Member States, of the other part* (CETA) ECLI:EU:C:2019:341 para 107–108.

preventing the EU institutions from operating in accordance with the EU constitutional framework."[381]

By stressing the concept of different legal orders, the CJEU evoked the opposite of a monistic doctrine. Some scholars have interpreted this case law as dualistic.[382] Indeed, this strongly reminds us of the famous phrase by Heinrich Triepel, stating that the international and national legal orders are "two circles, which possibly touch, but never cross each other."[383] Dualism divides international or EU law and national law into two different legal systems. Dualism, however, as we have seen previously, has considerable flaws. The division of legal systems in the dualistic doctrine was primarily based on the view that the law of international or EU and national legal systems emanates from different sources, leading to the supposition that international or EU law and national law have arisen from different legal orders relying on different grounds for validity.[384] If the autonomy of the EU legal order were linked with dualism, it would serve as a shield for EU law from international law. This might sound fitting at first. The main weakness of such an alignment between autonomy and dualism becomes clear when trying to establish a unitary legal subjectivity of international or supranational organizations (be it the UN or the EU) from a dualistic point of view. International norms are based on a national ground for validity within the dualistic doctrine. If autonomy were dualism in disguise then, as a consequence, international and supranational organizations would be based on international validity and, furthermore, on as many national grounds of validity as they have Member States.[385] This insecure starting point complicates the effect of the legal measures of these international organizations within EU or national law. In that light, the CJEU confronting the outside world with an explicit reference to different legal orders is open to criticism. This line of the autonomy case law is also vulnerable to this criticism and does not provide for a satisfying theoretical doctrine in this regard. It is similar to another element of dualism. Although it still holds true that international and

[381] Opinion 1/17 *Comprehensive Economic and Trade Agreement between Canada, of the one part, and the European Union and its Member States, of the other part* (CETA) ECLI:EU:C:2019:341 para 119.

[382] See eg Eckes (n 363) 7.

[383] Triepel (n 4) 111: "Völkerrecht und Landesrecht sind nicht nur verschiedene Rechtstheile, sondern auch verschiedene Rechtsordnungen. Sie sind zwei Kreise, die sich höchstens berühren, niemals schneiden" [emphasis omitted; translation in the text LK].

[384] Compare Anzilotti (n 5) 38–39.

[385] For this illustrative criticism, see Griller (n 363) Völkerrecht und Landesrecht 97; see also the general criticism by Starke (n 11).

national law emanate from different sources, dualism also assumes that the addressees and content of international and national law cannot be identical.[386] This argument no longer works. While the impossibility of identical addressees of international and EU law would lead to the exclusion of any kind of norm conflict between these two legal orders,[387] this obviously is not the case. Taking the *Kadi* cases[388] as an example, it becomes clear that international and EU law alike might well concern the same addressee as much as the same content. Kadi would not have been able to challenge the measures of the Security Council Resolution before the EU courts if he had not been the same person. Applying for protection under EU law against UN measures clearly shows that international and EU law alike deal with the same content. Furthermore, dualism turns a blind eye to the direct interaction between international law and individuals by stating that international law is purely inter-State law and can only stipulate obligations for States,[389] which does not share the same addressees with EU or national law.[390]

While some of these points could be justified on a pluralist reading of this autonomy case law, the criticisms of pluralism would still hold.[391] No matter which of the theories discussed is associated with the concept of autonomy, the criticism cannot be shaken off.

Does this also call into question the claimed autonomy and the protection of EU law from international law as an independent theory? The autonomy of the EU legal order not only encompasses the legal orders of the Member States, but apparently also shields EU law from international law.[392] Can this

386 See Triepel (n 4) 9, 11, 228–229; Anzilotti (n 5) 41–42.

387 See Triepel (n 4) 254 ff; Anzilotti (n 5) 42.

388 Compare above n 4.

389 See Triepel (n 4) 228–229, 119–120, 271; see also Anzilotti (n 5) 41 ff; cf Walz (n 7) 238–239, who was considered to be a moderate dualist, yet he did not postulate the impossibility of international law addressing individuals, but stated in 1933 that the character of international law at the time was mediatized through municipal law. Moreover, he proposed a differentiation between international law addressing States and international law created in order to address individuals (he called the former material and the latter formal international law), but this would still have to be mediatized through States (see Walz n 7 242–244).

390 This criticism was already expressed by Verdross (n 8) 432 ff; cf Mazzeschi (n 8) 42–43 with further references in n 12: "This means that international law now regulates *some* relationships between States and individuals *in a formal manner* (and not only in a substantive one)"; cf ICJ *LaGrand (Germany v USA)* Judgment ICJ Reports [2001] 466, 494 para 77.

391 See eg Pernice (n 356) linking autonomy with pluralism, if pluralism is considered a matter of realism (which may be close to conceding that pluralism is a descriptively helpful concept, as has been argued above). However, also for Pernice pluralism is flawed as it cannot offer a single legal solution in cases of norm conflict.

392 The Opinion 2/13 *Draft international agreement – Accession of the European Union to the European Convention for the Protection of Human Rights and Fundamental*

"Janus Face" of the CJEU be justified and what are the consequences for other theories of the relationship between international, EU and Member State law?

3.3 IS THIS "JANUS FACE" OF THE CJEU JUSTIFIABLE?

On the one hand, the CJEU borrowed monistic arguments in order to establish the "autonomy" of the EU legal order, unifying the legal order of its Member States with the legal system of the EU. On the other hand, the CJEU reprimanded the General Court[393] when that Court applied this monistic approach also to the relationship between EU law and international law.[394] Facing foreign law, which is possibly dangerous for the EU legal order, the CJEU prefers a dualistic argument separating its own autonomous legal systems from external legal systems.[395] This provokes the question of whether this "Janus Face" can be justified.

3.3.1 *Theoretical (In-)Appropriateness of the Position of the CJEU*

Is it possible to uphold a monistic argument concerning the inner relations of EU law while, at the same time, defending its autonomy by confronting the outside world with a dualistic view? In light of this situation, one and the same international organization – depending on its perspective and not on the different standpoint of the observer – would have to be categorized according to two completely diverging doctrines. Bearing in mind the controversy

Freedoms – Compatibility of the draft agreement with the EU and FEU Treaties ECLI:EU:C:2014:2454 is also paradigmatic in this sense.

393 Formerly known as the European Court of First Instance.

394 Compare Case T-315/01 *Yassin Abdullah Kadi and Al Barakaat International Foundation v Council and Commission* ECLI:EU:T:2005:332 para 214; as much as Case T-306/01 Ahmed Ali Yusuf and Al Barakaat International Foundation ECLI:EU:T:2005:332 para 265 applying the monistic doctrine also relating to international law. For a discussion see eg Daniel Halberstam, "Local, Global and Plural Constitutionalism: Europe Meets the World" in Gráinne de Búrca and Joseph H H Weiler (eds) *The Worlds of European Constitutionalism* (Cambridge University Press 2012) 150–202 (175 ff).

395 See Andreas Bergmann, *Zur Souveränitätskonzeption des Europäischen Gerichtshofs* (Mohr Siebeck 2018) 135–136, concerning the divergent handling of direct applicability of international agreements on the one hand, and EU law on the other. Cf Başak Çalı, *The Authority of International Law: Obedience, Respect, and Rebuttal* (Oxford University Press 2015) 137, for the argument that the concepts of monism and dualism developed a long time ago and are "conclusive statements of larger and more substantive theories one adopts on the nature of law, the nature of international law, the overlap between international law and domestic law, constitutional law, and more importantly, on the authority of international law."

between monists and dualists, it is far from easy to imagine that this question provoked by the CJEU would have met with positive support from either dualistic or monistic scholars. Monists are convinced by the unitarian legal (world[396]) order, which is structured as a hierarchical complex of norms.[397] Having this proclaimed unity in mind – inherently based on one fundamental basic norm from which all lower norms are delegated – an inevitable consequence arises: national law (also constitutional law) would have to be seen as delegated from EU law, and EU law in turn from international law. Dualists, in contrast, talk about the theoretical impossibility of the same addressees, content and sources of international or EU and national law. As a consequence, they were convinced that the separation of legal orders is not a choice to make but a theoretical necessity. These theoretical discrepancies between dualists and monists are far from being unified in one consistent position. Nevertheless, Maduro opined that the EU legal order is "a municipal legal order [postulating a dualistic separation in confrontation to international law] of trans-national dimensions, of which it forms the 'basic constitutional charter' [postulating a monistic unity of the EU and its Member States]."[398] If one is not willing to accept the view of the EU as a federal state, which would make a monistic view relating to its Member States no longer necessary,[399] the theoretical inconsistency of this position is faced with the abovementioned criticism. Yet at the beginning of this part of the book we also learned that both monism and dualism are 100-year-old theories. Hence, the theoretical demands of monism or dualism are very likely outdated, so neither the monistic nor the dualistic doctrine should be adopted concerning the internal as well as external relations of the EU. However, although this is clearly conceivable from a practical point of view, we need to be careful from a theoretical perspective not to throw out the baby with the bathwater. While it makes sense to discharge or at least considerably renew the 100-year-old theories of monism or dualism, we must be careful to keep a clear and consistent theoretical understanding of the relationship between international, EU and national law.

396 Compare Verdross (n 17); cf Kelsen (n 161) *Pure Theory* 328–329.

397 See above Section 1.2.

398 Joined Cases C-402/05 P and C-415/05 *P Kadi and Al Barakaat International Foundation v Council and Commission* ECLI:EU:C:2008:461 para 21.

399 For a reading of the relationship between the EU and Member State law along the lines of the Kelsenian three-circle theory he developed for a federal state, see Michael Thaler, "Rechtsphilosophie und das Verhältnis zwischen Gemeinschaftsrecht und nationalem Recht" (2000) 8 Journal für Rechtspolitik 75–84.

3.3.2 *The (In-)Appropriateness of the Grand Old Theories and Autonomy as an Independent Theory*

Given the theoretical flaws of the CJEU's position regarding the relationship of EU law with its Member States on the one hand and international law on the other, the question arises as to whether the underlying doctrines can still provide satisfactory explanations of current developments. By applying two diametrically opposed doctrines as one entity, the CJEU was criticized on theoretical grounds.[400] However, monism and dualism were developed before the rise of supranational organization(s). Furthermore, these doctrines have to be seen against the background of the historical conditions of the times in which they were formulated. In this respect, another crucial point of criticism is the political dimension of this question.[401] Already Hans Kelsen's indecisiveness over whether monism should be advocated with the primacy of international law or with the primacy of municipal law was triggered by the fact that from his point of view this question was a matter of politics.[402] However, in general it is possible to draw an analogy between the genesis of the aforementioned theories and the historical circumstances at that time. The origin of the monistic view governed by national law can be found in the eighteenth century and lasted until the late nineteenth century.[403] This period

[400] See above Section 3.3.1. See, however, Bruno de Witte, "European Union Law: How Autonomous Is Its Legal Order?" (2010) 65 Zeitschrift für Öffentliches Recht 141–155 (esp 149–155), arguing for a "relative autonomy" of the EU Legal Order also concerning international law.

[401] See also Janne E Nijman and André Nollkaemper, "Introduction" in Janne E Nijman and André Nollkaemper (eds) *New Perspectives on the Divide between National and International Law* (Oxford University Press 2007) 1–14 (9); see also Anne Peters, "Rechtsordnungen und Konstitutionalisierung: Zur Neubestimmung der Verhältnisse" (2010) 65 (1) Zeitschrift für Öffentliches Recht 3–63 (25–26). See the criticism of Gennady M Danilenko, "Application of Customary International Law to Municipal Law" in Grigory I Tunkin and Rüdiger Wolfrum (eds) *International and Municipal Law* (Duncker & Humblot 1988) 13 (23): "Experience indicates that positive results depend not only on the legal techniques used, but also on a number of political factors related to the attitude of a given State towards existing international law and relevant international obligations."

[402] See Hans Kelsen, *Reine Rechtslehre* (Franz Deuticke 1934) 142; and similarly Hans Kelsen, "Die Einheit von Völkerrecht und staatlichem Recht" (1958) 19 Heidelberg Journal of International Law 234–248 (246 ff); cf Jochen von Bernstorff, *The Public International Law Theory of Hans Kelsen: Believing in Universal Law* (Cambridge University Press 2010) 104 ff; and Nijman and Nollkaemper (n 401) 9, identifying the monists Scelle and Kelsen as value-driven defenders of democracy and the individual against State power. However, see Jakab (n 35).

[403] Compare major advocates of monism with the primacy of national law Hegel (n 14) §§ 330 ff; André Décencière-Ferrandière, "Considérations sur le Droit International dans ses Rapports avec le Droit de l'État" (1933) 40 (1) Revue Générale de Droit International Public 45–70

(and thus the theory) can be classified as extremely nationalistic, since a few authoritarian States ruled over the whole world and public international law was seen as "external State law."[404] Historical progress is represented by its successor: the dualistic doctrine. The following period of political moderation also influenced the theory governing the relationship between international and national law. The devolution of history in world politics and the parallel development of the two theories culminated in the monistic doctrine with the primacy of international law. So the monistic doctrine with primacy of international law, which was more or less developed after the First and Second World Wars, can be seen as the output of a pacifist worldview.[405] At least nowadays the identification of the theories with the political developments of the time leads to the conclusion that these theories, or at least fundamental elements of them, have to be qualified as inappropriate either way. On the one hand extremely nationalistic and on the other hand utopian worldviews left their traces in the diverging theories. This may disqualify them from providing an adequate theoretical explanation for the current relationship between international and EU law as much as EU and national law. In light of these connections, the diverging positions of the CJEU become far more understandable, at least in pragmatic terms. It is quite striking to see that the reason for adopting a dualistic point of view is driven by protectionism. The "smaller entity" prefers a reticent approach in order to safeguard itself against the "bigger entity." The high courts of Member States do not like too dominant a role of EU law,[406] while the CJEU does not want EU law to be

(64 ff); and also Georg Jellinek, *Die rechtliche Natur der Staatenverträge* (A Hölder 1880) 7, 40; however, on page 45 doubts were already expressed concerning this doctrine.

404 For this term (in German "äußeres Staatsrecht") see Hegel (n 14) § 330 ff.

405 See for a more detailed elaboration Antonio Cassese, *International Law* (Oxford University Press 2nd ed 2005) 213 ff.

406 Compare, for example, the Lisbon decision of the German Federal Constitutional Court, BVerfGE 123, 267 (*Lisbon*) para 339: "The primacy of application of European law remains, even with the entry into force of the Treaty of Lisbon, a concept conferred under an international treaty, i.e. *a derived concept* which will have legal effect in Germany only with the order to apply the law given by the Act Approving the Treaty of Lisbon. This derivative connection is not altered by the fact that the concept of primacy of application is not explicitly provided for in the treaties but was developed in the early phase of European integration in the case law of the Court of Justice by means of interpretation. It is a consequence of the continuing sovereignty of the Member States that in any case in the clear absence of a constitutive order to apply the law, the inapplicability of such a legal instrument to Germany is established by the Federal Constitutional Court" [emphasis added]. For further references, see Schroeder (n 2) 168 ff as well as for an overview, 248–249 with further references in n 270; cf Thaler (n 399) 77 with further references in n 5.

defenseless against international law.[407] While we have seen that the grand old theories cannot provide a solid framework for the postulated autonomy of the EU legal order, it may be the case that autonomy stands as an independent theory to explain the relationship between international, EU and Member State law.

In Opinion 1/17, the CJEU provided the most comprehensive explanation of how to understand the concept of autonomy. First, it is interesting to learn that the CJEU aims to establish autonomy as a holistic concept in as much as it states that it "exists with respect both to the law of the Member States and to international law."[408] Thus, the Court attempts to provide a concept that works both ways, thereby making itself vulnerable to the abovementioned criticisms. Autonomy cannot have two different versions depending on whether the EU is confronted with international law or Member State law. The CJEU goes on to say that autonomy "stems from the essential characteristics of the European Union and its law."[409] EU law in turn, according to the Court,

[407] Compare Joined Cases C-402/05 P and C-415/05 P *Kadi and Al Barakaat International Foundation v Council and Commission* EU:C:2008:461 paras 285 ff, 326–327; and Case C-548/09 P *Bank Melli Iran* ECLI:EU:C:2011:735 para 100: "It is important to note at the outset that Security Council resolutions and Council common positions and regulations originate from *distinct legal orders*" [emphasis added]. See also Fassbender (n 3) 336 ff. Cf the defensive attitude of the CJEU concerning WTO Dispute Settlement Body decisions within the EU legal order. Concerning the WTO Agreements in general see Case C-149/96 *Portugal v Council* ECLI:EU:C:1999:574; concerning DSB decisions and their direct effect on EU law see Case C-377/02 *Léon Van Parys* ECLI:EU:C:2005:121; cf Case C-351/04 Ikea ECLI:EU:C:2007:547 para 29 ff; Case C-120/06 P and Joined cases C-120/06 and C-121/06 P *Fabbrica italiana accumulatori motocarri Montecchio SpA (FIAMM) and Fabbrica italiana accumulatori motocarri Montecchio Technologies LLC (C-120/06 P), Giorgio Fedon & Figli SpA and Fedon America, Inc (C-121/06 P) v Council* ECLI:EU:C:2008:476 para 117 ff; cf Kirsten Schmalenbach, "Struggle for Exclusiveness: The ECJ and Competing International Tribunals" in Isabelle Buffard et al (eds) *International Law between Universalism and Fragmentation: Festschrift in Honour of Gerhard Hafner* (Martinus Nijhoff 2008) 1045–1068 (1056 ff). See also de Búrca (n 376) 5: "In fact, the broad language, carefully-chosen reasoning, and uncompromising approach of this eagerly-awaited judgment [*Kadi* case] by the plenary Court suggests that the ECJ seized this high-profile moment to send out a strong and clear message about the relationship of EC law to international law, and most fundamentally, about the autonomy of the European legal order."

[408] Opinion 1/17 *Comprehensive Economic and Trade Agreement between Canada, of the one part, and the European Union and its Member States, of the other part* (CETA) ECLI:EU:C:2019:341 para 109 [reference omitted].

[409] Opinion 1/17 *Comprehensive Economic and Trade Agreement between Canada, of the one part, and the European Union and its Member States, of the other part* (CETA) ECLI:EU:C:2019:341 para 109 [reference omitted].

> is characterised by the fact that it stems from an independent source of law, namely the Treaties, by its primacy over the laws of the Member States, and by the direct effect of a whole series of provisions that are applicable to their nationals and to the Member States themselves. Those characteristics have given rise to a structured network of principles, rules and mutually interdependent legal relations binding the European Union and its Member States reciprocally as well as binding its Member States to each other.[410]

This reasoning is somewhat circular if we want to distill from it a theoretical foundation for the concept of autonomy. Autonomy exists because of the independent source of law that was described in many different language versions as an "autonomous source of law" in one of the first judgments in which the CJEU established autonomy.[411] While the primacy of EU law and the direct effect are undoubtedly two concepts of EU law, they can hardly serve as a theoretical basis for autonomy (though as a functional justification, in order for primacy to be possible for example, EU law must be autonomous). A justification of autonomy based on these principles would be circular.

The CJEU furthermore stipulates:

> That autonomy accordingly resides in the fact that the Union possesses a constitutional framework that is unique to it. That framework encompasses the founding values set out in Article 2 TEU, which states that the Union "is founded on the values of respect for human dignity, freedom, democracy, equality, the rule of law, and respect for human rights," the general principles of EU law, the provisions of the Charter, and the provisions of the EU and FEU Treaties, which include, inter alia, rules on the conferral and division of powers, rules governing how the EU institutions and its judicial system are to operate, and fundamental rules in specific areas, structured in such a way as to contribute to the implementation of the process of integration described in the second paragraph of Article 1 TEU.[412]

This explanation sounds more like a functional explanation than a theoretical foundation. In short, the autonomy of EU law exists because the EU legal order is a constitutional legal order. This is fine in itself, but it is not a theoretical basis for autonomy. Rather, autonomy derives from the constitutionalization of the EU. This is consistent, but it does not provide an

[410] Opinion 1/17 *Comprehensive Economic and Trade Agreement between Canada, of the one part, and the European Union and its Member States, of the other part* (CETA) ECLI:EU:C:2019:341 para 109 [reference omitted].

[411] See above n 356.

[412] Opinion 1/17 *Comprehensive Economic and Trade Agreement between Canada, of the one part, and the European Union and its Member States, of the other part* (CETA) ECLI:EU:C:2019:341 para 110 [reference omitted].

independent theoretical basis for the relationship between international law, EU law and Member State law.

The autonomy is nevertheless pragmatically understandable. As a pragmatic functional doctrine, it might hold that the "concept of autonomy in no way implies that the EU and its law are euro-centric and that the Court of Justice seeks to insulate EU law from external influences by building legal walls that prevent the migration of ideas."[413] However, it is an inadequate theoretical approach to understanding the relationship between international, EU and Member State law.

3.4 WHY AUTONOMY IS NOT A SELF-STANDING THEORETICAL APPROACH

It can be concluded that the CJEU case law is best explained by two diametrically opposed doctrines regarding the relationship of legal orders to one another. From a theoretical perspective, this is inconceivable. The same organization cannot follow two different approaches, one based on a dualistic view and one on a monistic view. From a pragmatic perspective, however, this Janus Face of the CJEU is quite understandable. Considering the historical background of the origins of the two doctrines and the dimension of political influences, they both have their merits. Monism, on the one hand, is an expression of legal unity, which is absolutely necessary for the EU to safeguard its integration process. On the other hand, dualism helps to secure the stability of this integration process by separating the EU legal order from far-reaching international influences. As Janus is known as the god representing the beginning and the end, the monistic face regarding the relationship of the EU to its Member States may represent the end of an integration process while the dualistic face might indicate the beginning of broader integration into international law. However, whereas this cannot be a conclusion in absolute terms, it is necessary to emphasize that none of these integration processes is absolute. Nor is autonomy. The EU has not turned into a federal state representing a "municipal legal order"; nor is it possible to separate the EU legal order – itself representing a supranational organization – so strictly from international law. It would be wise not to build up absolute structures regarding other legal systems while in a phase of transformation. However, at the same time, this is the reason why almost 100-year-old theories might not offer the theoretical framework capable of accompanying a reasonable

[413] Lenaerts, Gutiérrez-Fons and Adam (n 362) 87.

balance between the legal spheres involved. Likewise, autonomy as an independent theory cannot provide for an adequate replacement either. As a theory, it is a mere postulate without a sophisticated basis. As a pragmatic functional tool for the EU constitutional order, however, it serves its purpose well. It is only as an overarching theory of the relationship between international law, EU law and Member State law that it is not helpful.

4

An Intermediate Conclusion

A critical approach to the theories of dualism and monism is now quite common.[414] However, this does not mean that some elements of these theories cannot be applied in a meaningful way and thereby might still be useful tools to understand specific processes of the relationship between international, EU and national law.[415] And, despite all the criticism these theories have faced, their persistence is remarkable. Dualism and monism alike are still referred to in many textbooks;[416] they are present in case law[417] and in scholarly work.[418] Also in practice, many (national) legal orders are still often referred to as being "dualistic" or "monistic." Thus, there is a need to make the critical points as clearly as possible in order to explain why they are of no help in answering the question posed by this book.

Moreover, the preceding chapter holds that (global) legal pluralism cannot offer a satisfying normative account for norm conflict resolution between international, EU and national law either. Hence, prescriptive proposals to solve legal conflicts arising from different legal orders on the global plane are better not termed "pluralistic." Rather, this chapter suggests that it is more precise to refer to a necessarily *common* framework which addresses how those conflicts should be resolved *together* or at least in a way acceptable to all parties.

[414] Von Bogdandy (n 29) 400 denoted those theories "intellectual zombies"; Kirchmair (n 205); Kirchmair (n 343) with further references.

[415] Jakab (n 212).

[416] See eg Ramses A Wessel, "The EU and International Law" in Ramses A Wessel and Joris Larik (eds) *EU External Relations Law. Text, Cases and Materials* (Hart 2nd ed 2020) 139–174 (148 ff).

[417] The German Federal Constitutional Court, BVerfGE 111, 307 (*Görgülü*).

[418] Gragl (n 16); Gragl (n 25); as well as Paul Gragl, "In Defence of Kelsenian Monism: Countering Hart and Raz" (2017) 8 (2) Jurisprudence 287–318.

Finally, this chapter holds that such a common framework depends hugely on the context. Thus, solutions are more likely to be found if we focus on specific contexts instead of trying to provide universal solutions for different situations. That is why global constitutionalism or global law cannot provide universal solutions for norm conflict resolution between international, EU and national law. They do not take the "burden of universality" seriously enough or would end in a "constitutional stalemate." Broadly speaking, this is because it is usually far too difficult in our highly complex and dynamic world to come up with global or truly universal solutions. A brief analysis of autonomy has also shown that it is not an independent theory that can explain and guide norm conflicts in the relationship between the international, EU and Member State legal orders.

If my analysis so far is correct, then all major theories on the relationship between legal orders suffer from serious flaws when trying to answer the question of where to find the decisive source in legal norm conflicts. At the same time, a sound theoretical concept is essential for the relationship between legal orders. Hence, I propose my own theoretical concept: consent-based monism. Arguably, this concept provides a sound theoretical foundation without becoming ensnared in the flaws attributed to the existing theories, and it should provide a credible answer to the question posed.

PART II

Consent-Based Monism

A Structural Answer

My aim with what I call consent-based monism (Chapter 6) is to conceptualize in a highly abstract way how we could understand the structural relationship between legal orders in general. The goal is to identify a common denominator that is abstract enough to capture principal issues of relationships between legal orders but still provides enough normative guidance to bring about concrete results. How particular situations are analyzed might then differ significantly depending on which context we are looking at. Only then can we resolve the question of who has the final say.

In order to identify the common denominator of international, EU and national law, the theory of consent-based monism adopts an old approach dressed in new clothes. The generic legal principle *pacta sunt servanda* will be identified as the common denominator. *Pacta sunt servanda* has already been taken as the basic norm, most famously by Alfred Verdross but also by others (including even Hans Kelsen). Verdross based this norm on substantial values and can therefore be classified as being within the natural law tradition. The underlying understanding of law for our purposes (Chapter 5), however, will require an in-depth look at current research in such fields as neurobiology, evolutionary and developmental psychology, as well as philosophy to learn what is currently *perceived* as the most plausible biological setup that enables normativity in general and morality in particular. After critically analyzing the approach termed "Universal Moral Grammar" (Section 5.3), advanced, among others, by John Mikhail, and outlining the problems this concept is facing, we will turn to what I call (innate) intersubjectivity (Section 5.5). I submit that (innate) intersubjectivity is a more plausible biological setup enabling normativity and morality. On this basis, the prelegal normative principle *pacta sunt servanda* will be established as the foundation of consent-based monism (Section 5.6).

5

The Underlying Understanding of Law

5.1 PROLEGOMENA

In order to analyze the relationship between international, EU and national law properly, I will establish a working hypothesis: a common denominator of international, EU and national law must be stipulated to enable a transparent and methodologically coherent analysis of the relationship. The legal concept underlying consent-based monism concentrates on those legal aspects especially relevant for the relationship between international, EU and national law. Because international law, EU law and national law are somewhat different legal fields, an abstract understanding of law is necessary to include all three fields under one common denominator. The common denominator is vital because it enables a comparison of those different fields.

The definition of law as well as its origins start in the "legal desert."[1] The legal desert can be understood as a legal vacuum, a neutral, prelegal status without any further specification. Of course, such a starting point provokes immediate associations with social contract theories, which have a specific way of thinking about the organization of a state in common. However, there

[1] Compare the theories of the social contract summarized by Peter Koller, *Neue Theorien des Sozialkontrakts* (Duncker & Humblot 1987); Patrick Riley, *Will and Political Legitimacy* (Harvard University Press 1982); and Michael Lessnoff (ed) *Social Contract Theory* (New York University Press 1990); for an overview, see also Ann Cudd and Seena Eftekhari, "Contractarianism" in Edward N Zalta (ed) *Stanford Encyclopedia of Philosophy* (March 15, 2017) available at https://plato.stanford.edu/entries/contractarianism/ [last accessed February 1, 2023]; as well as Elizabeth Ashford and Tim Mulgan, "Contractualism" in Edward N Zalta (ed) *Stanford Encyclopedia of Philosophy* (April 20, 2018) available at https://plato.stanford.edu/entries/contractualism/ [last accessed February 1, 2023]. See for an overview of different understandings of law in relation to public international law, Ulrich Fastenrath, *Lücken im Völkerrecht – Zu Rechtscharakter, Quellen, Systemzusammenhang, Methodenlehre und Funktionen des Völkerrechts* (Duncker & Humblot 1991) 32 ff.

are also notable differences between various conceptions of social contract theories. The legal desert was, for instance, considered empirically as an anarchic state in which everyone is at war with everyone else, famously expressed as the "state of nature" by Thomas Hobbes.[2] In contrast, natural rights were conceived by John Locke to already exist and to be protected by a social contract.[3] Jean-Jacques Rousseau, in turn, thought expropriation necessary to enable the formation of the "*volonté générale*,"[4] which is considered to be a prerequisite for the formation of common interests.

As I am not focusing on how a just society can be conceived, the following outline will suffice: in the legal desert, a consensus between two or more individuals is widely considered to be *the* possibility that allows the establishment of a binding legal rule to organize social life.[5] Consensus is thereby understood to serve as a tool for unifying individual interests[6] and does not aim to establish any values or tools that might indicate how a just society would be organized. While the point of departure is very similar to most social contract theories – the "legal desert" – the aim of this analysis contrasts sharply with the aim of political philosophy as the goal of this book is much more moderate.

Choosing this basis aims at modeling the structural relationship between international, EU and national law without saying how society or the State or a supranational organization should be organized (or without arguing, for

2 Thomas Hobbes, *Leviathan* (Three-Text Edition of *Thomas Hobbes's Political Theory. The Elements of Law, De Cive and Leviathan*, edited by Deborah Baumgold Cambridge University Press 2017 [1651]) ch 13.

3 John Locke, *Two Treatises of Government* (*Two Treatises of Government and A Letter Concerning Toleration*, edited by Ian Shapiro Yale University Press 2003 [1690]) book 2, ch 2.

4 Jean-Jacques Rousseau, *The Social Contract* (*The Social Contract and The First and The Second Discourses*, English translation and edited by Susan Dunn Yale University Press 2002 [1762] *Du Contract Social; Ou Principes du Droit Politique*) book 1, ch 6; Koller (n 1) 25.

5 Compare also Weinberger's argument aiming at disclosing natural law-based theories and arguing that legal positivism originates from non-cognitivism, holding that it is impossible to cognize the right law and justify norms cognitively: Ota Weinberger, *Norm und Institution. Eine Einführung in die Theorie des Rechts* (Manz 1988) 72–73.

6 Compare also Robert Alexy, "Diskurstheorie und Menschenrechte" in Robert Alexy (ed) *Recht, Vernunft, Diskurs – Studien zur Rechtsphilosophie* (Suhrkamp 1995) 127–164 (129), who circumscribes discourse theory as a procedural theory of practical validity. Jürgen Habermas, *Die Einbeziehung des Anderen* (Suhrkamp 2nd ed 1997) 299–300; Jürgen Habermas, *Die postnationale Konstellation* (Suhrkamp 1998) 175; and Jürgen Habermas, *Faktizität und Geltung – Beiträge zur Diskurstheorie des Rechts und des demokratischen Rechtsstaats* (Suhrkamp 1992) 138, stating that those regulations are legitimate that all possibly affected persons might approve of as participants in rational discourse. Seyla Benhabib, "Another Universalism: On the Unity and Diversity of Human Rights" (2007) 81 Proceedings and Addresses of the American Philosophical Association 7–32 (21). This, however, is not meant to suggest that international, EU or national law is the result of a power-free rational discourse. It merely indicates the need to unify individual interests.

instance, whether the EU has a constitution or not). Yet it is not merely a descriptive theory. Consent-based monism is a proposal for normative guidance of norm conflict resolution between different legal orders. Whether the legal desert is best understood by imagining a natural disaster or other events is left to the reader's imagination. This starting point guarantees a consistent definition of law for our purposes. That is, the definition of international *law*, EU *law* and national *law* must be uniform. For if it is not, the norm conflict resolution between the different legal orders cannot work with *common* normative standards and is therefore left to brute force – at least from the perspective of one legal order.[7]

Analogous to the historical idea of social contract theory, the consensus element is based on the abstract principles of *pacta sunt servanda* and *pacta tertiis*.[8] Natural law theories also originally conceived of *pacta sunt servanda* as the basic norm of international and national law as, for instance, in the case of Alfred Verdross.[9] However, in this tradition it is also the case that more prelegal values than the principle of *pacta sunt servanda* are found to exist which can derogate positive law. In Verdross' parlance, natural law exists "in the objective realm of values,"[10] of which *pacta sunt servanda* is the basic

7 Yet it is important to clarify that this definition of law is not supposed to be superior to any other definition of law. Consent as a source of law, in particular, has been criticized recently. See eg, rather recently, Andrew T Guzman, "Against Consent" (2012) 52 (4) Virginia Journal of International Law 747–790. My response regarding this so-called consent problem points to the purpose for which the definition of law made in this book is decisive. The purpose is not to find a superior way of legitimizing law or understanding the specific nature of, say, international law but to find a definition of law abstract enough to serve as a common denominator of international, EU and national law. See for a deconstruction of force as a necessary element of public international law, Fastenrath (n 1) 45–52.

8 Koller (n 1) 12–13.

9 See Alfred Verdross, *Die Verfassung der Völkerrechtsgemeinschaft* (Springer 1926) preface, 21–23, and 30–31; see also Alfred Verdross, *Die Einheit des rechtlichen Weltbildes auf Grundlage der Völkerrechtsverfassung* (Mohr 1923) 6–8; Dionisio Anzilotti, *Corso di diritto internazionale* (Athenaeum 2nd ed 1912) 49–50. See also Hans-Martin Pawlowski, *Methodenlehre für Juristen. Theorie der Norm und des Gesetzes* (C F Müller 3rd ed 1999) para 661, arguing that the justification of politics enables the voter to form and maintain consens of community. This consens, in turn, is of vital importance for the existence of a state (or our system) because it justifies the possibility of law as law as a prerequisite for community. See also Pawlowski para 840 ff with further references. See Heribert-Franz Köck, "Der erste Staatszweck in einer pluralistischen Gesellschaft" in Herbert Miehsler et al (eds) *Ius Humanitas. Festschrift zum 90. Geburtstag von Alfred Verdross* (Duncker & Humblot 1980) 87 (95); Gerhard Luf, "Zur Problematik des Wertbegriffes in der Rechtsphilosophie" in Herbert Miehsler et al (eds) *Ius Humanitas. Festschrift zum 90. Geburtstag von Alfred Verdross* (Duncker & Humblot 1980) 127–146; Josef Isensee, "Ethische Grundwerte im freiheitlichen Staat" in Ansgar Paus (ed) *Werte – Rechte – Normen* (Kevelaer et al 1979) 132 (134).

10 Verdross (n 9) *Die Verfassung der Völkerrechtsgemeinschaft* 23.

norm.[11] The approach advanced here holds that these values must not simply be postulated but rather be made plausible by looking at interdisciplinary research. This has not been the case for the values presupposed by Alfred Verdross. Moreover, despite his natural law approach, Alfred Verdross also advocates his monist conception along with the Kelsenian chain of validity. According to this approach, any EU and national law is derived from international law and the basic norm, and thus, for Verdross, "[t]he freedom of States is nothing else than a margin of discretion depending on international law."[12] This faces the criticism advanced above, however, and hence has to be rejected. Beyond that, and in contrast to Kelsenian legal monism as outlined and criticized, consent-based monism is not based on epistemological assumptions that either collapse into solipsism or demand thick hypothetical a priori concepts.

Modern social contract theories most prominently represented by John Rawls presuppose reasonable people.[13] This also pertains to older

[11] Alfred Verdross, "Grundlagen und Grundlegungen des Völkerrechts – ein Beitrag zu den Hypothesen des Völkerrechtspositivismus" (1921) 29 Niemeyers Zeitschrift für internationales Recht 65–91; Alfred Verdross, "Le fondement du droit international" (1927) 16 Recueil des cours I 247–323 (286–287). Cf Verdross (n 9) *Die Verfassung der Völkerrechtsgemeinschaft* 37, where Verdross unfolds his version of monism holding the primacy of international law over national law based on his natural law conception, but with a moderate twist which does not declare national law conflicting with international law as invalid per se but only provides for its voidability. On this see also Alfred Verdross, "Droit international public et droit interne" (1954) 32 Revue de Droit International, de Sciences Diplomatiques et Politiques 219 (221–223).

[12] Verdross (ch 1 n 214) 35 [translation by LK]. See Section 1.2. See, however, Otto Pfersmann, "La production des normes : production normative et hiérarchie des normes" in Michel Troper and Dominique Chagnollaud (eds) *Traité international de droit constitutionnel. Distribution des pouvoirs, Vol 2* (Dalloz) 483–528 (519) for a modern interpretation.

[13] For the purpose of his political conception of justice, John Rawls associates with the reasonable "first, with the willingness to propose and honor fair terms of cooperation, and second, with the willingness to recognize the burdens of judgment and to accept their consequences." With rational human beings, according to John Rawls, *Political Liberalism* (Columbia University Press expanded ed 2005) 48, n 1, "knowing that people are rational we do not know the ends they will pursue, only that they will pursue them intelligently." Rawls makes this differentiation by following Kant's *Metaphysik der Sitten* (on this see William M Sibley, "The Rational versus the Reasonable" (1953) 62 (4) Philosophical Review 554–560 (554 ff); and Thomas M Scanlon, "Contractualism and Utilitarianism" in Amartya Sen and Bernard Williams (eds) *Utilitarianism and Beyond* (Cambridge University Press 1982) 103–128, reprinted in Thomas M Scanlon, *The Difficulty of Tolerance: Essays in Political Philosophy* (Cambridge University Press 2003) 124–150 (137 ff). This differentiation seems to become all the more negligible to the extent that human beings are perceived as social beings which are cooperative by nature. For evidence that intuitions seem to prefer non-egoistic action, see for instance David G Rand, Joshua D Greene and Martin A Nowak, "Spontaneous Giving and Calculated Greed" (2012) 489 Nature 427–430 (427 ff). That this seemed to be the case for Rawls (*Political Liberalism*

conceptions.[14] Jürgen Habermas, too, can be mentioned in this line of thinking – for instance, his orientation towards reason that is obvious in the presuppositions of communicative competence as a basis for a typology of rationality.[15] The pragmatic presupposition, which we do have to assume for participants of a rational discourse, is an aspiration (from an observer perspective we learn that rational discourse is only rarely perceived in pure form); the real situation, however, must not be too distant from this assumption. Hence, conscious manipulations and lies, for instance, cannot be brought in line with the presuppositions of communicative competence as a basis for a typology of rationality.[16] This is of relevance because, according to Habermas, "[o]nly

1998, 123–124) too becomes possible, as he ascribes to rational human beings a particular form of moral sensibility that underlies the desire to participate in cooperation on terms that others can reasonably be expected to agree to as well and rational beings with strongly egoistic behavior as being close to psychopaths. For a critique of the notion of reasonableness in Rawls, which is said to imply a certain tendency towards political cooperation, see for instance A John Simmons, "Justification and Legitimacy" (1999) 109 (4) Ethics 739–771, reprinted in A John Simmons, *Justification and Legitimacy – Essays on Rights and Obligations* (Cambridge University Press 2001) 122–157 (150–151).

[14] Immanuel Kant, *Metaphysische Anfangsgründe der Rechtslehre* (1797) part II, ch 2, § 19 especially 100–101 stating that holding a promise is a postulate of pure reason.

[15] Jürgen Habermas, "Was heißt Universalpragmatik?" in Karl-Otto Apel (ed) *Sprachpragmatik und Philosophie* (Suhrkamp 1976) 174–272. However, see for instance Matthias Mahlmann, "Mind and Rights: Neuroscience, Philosophy, and the Foundations of Legal Justice" in Mortimer N Sellers (ed) *Law, Reason, and Emotion* (Cambridge University Press 2017) 80–137 (104), who holds that "[a] discourse in the technical sense is a normatively loaded enterprise." Concerning contractualism Mahlmann asks: "Contractualism leaves the questions of the normative foundations of the contract open, more precisely: Why is it legitimate that human beings are only bound by obligations that can be imagined as accepted by free and equal persons? Where do the noncontractarian preconditions of contractualism stem from?" [footnotes omitted].

[16] Habermas (n 15). Compare to the current situation the speech of Jürgen Habermas at the "New Perspectives for Europe" conference at Goethe University Frankfurt, which appeared as online article. The speech starts as follows: "I am invited to talk about New Perspectives on Europe, but new ones fail me, and the Trumpian decay afflicting even the core of Europe makes me seriously question my old perspectives." Importantly, however, Habermas speaks about European integration (and not about preconditions of communicative competence), yet it is instructive to learn that "[i]f the suspected link between the economic drifting apart of the eurozone member economies on the one hand and the strengthening of right-wing populism on the other hand in fact holds, then we're sitting in a trap in which the necessary social and cultural preconditions for a vital and safe democracy face further damage." Compare also "Interview with Jürgen Habermas" in Andre Bächtiger et al (eds) *The Oxford Handbook of Deliberative Democracy* (Oxford University Press 2018) 871–882 (871 ff). See also Karl-Otto Apel, "Das Apriori der Kommunikationsgemeinschaft und die Grundlagen der Ethik: Zum Problem einer rationalen Begründung der Ethik im Zeitalter der Wissenschaft" in Karl-Otto Apel (ed) *Transformation der Philosophie Vol 2* (Suhrkamp 1973) 358–435 (400) who states that lying and even the refusing to critically understand or explain and justify arguments would make dialogue impossible.

those norms can claim to be valid that meet (or could meet) with the approval of all affected in their capacity as participants in a practical discourse."[17] For Thomas Scanlon, in turn, it is not reasonable consensus, but the condition that nobody could reasonably disagree with a specific action, which provides for its legitimacy.[18]

The approach advanced in this book holds that those prelegal principles must not be chosen arbitrarily. Their origin needs to be disclosed because the starting point should not deviate from, or rather should be able to be brought in line with, scientifically plausibilized conditions of us as human beings. The prelegal application of the *pacta sunt servanda* rule according to consent-based monism derives from the finding that all individuals generally strive for cooperation.[19] Another motivation not to violate the achieved consensus is that any violation could endanger the successful adoption of a future consensus, which again is important for cooperation not as a static one-off act but as a continuous process. Cooperation, in turn, relies on participating in a consensus from which one must not deviate in order not to compromise cooperation. When searching for the biological setup that undergirds cooperation, this book will point to innate intersubjectivity, which will be outlined later in this section. This includes the moral obligation born out of the innate intersubjectivity of individuals that leads to a reciprocal duty to form legal rules to coordinate social order and to act cooperatively, which provides for positive effects for all participating individuals. Yet again, contrary to social contract theories, this starting point does not aim to establish principles of justice[20] or to legitimize specific forms of societal organization.[21] Without proposing a material content of *just* law, structural arguments regarding the connection of individuals through consensus – in other words, law – will dominate the articulated understanding of law.

[17] Jürgen Habermas, "Discourse Ethics: Notes on Philosophical Justification" in Jürgen Habermas, *Moral Consciousness and Communicative Action* (MIT Press 1990) 43–115 (66). See critique by Seyla Benhabib, "In the Shadow of Aristotle and Hegel: Communicative Ethics and Current Controversies in Practical Philosophy" (1989) 21 (1) Philosophical Forum 1–31.

[18] Thomas M Scanlon, *What We Owe to Each Other* (Harvard University Press 1999).

[19] See on this below Section 5.6.

[20] John Rawls, *A Theory of Justice* (Harvard University Press 1971); John Rawls, *The Law of Peoples* (Harvard University Press 1999).

[21] Koller (n 1) 17, who indicates that social contract theories have – on the one hand – to determine an acceptable starting point allowing for a fair agreement. On the other hand, these social contract theories aim to show which principles find reasonable acceptance by all participants.

In order to analyze the relationship between international, EU and national law, it is necessary to outline the underlying concept of law. Following the aforementioned conditions, law is simply defined as a binding consensus (*Willensübereinkunft*) between all participating individuals. The consensus element may be fulfilled by different actions, such as explicit, implied or tacit acceptance.[22] However, only consensus between two or more individuals may produce a common legal rule in the legal desert.[23] The consensus unifies the individual interests of the participants. The resulting overlapping interest – for example, a common rule to organize cohabitation – becomes valid through the binding consensus. Consensus is furthermore understood in an abstract way, with collective interest being the central idea. The conviction of the individuals concerned as to whether they can establish a consensus is assumed to be a sufficiently stabilizing element for this legal concept and its binding character.[24] The prelegal, reasonable *pacta sunt servanda* principle reflects this. While we will now look at the biological setup that enables this chosen definition, the move from innate intersubjectivity to moral duty to the *pacta sunt servanda* principle clearly outlines the normative element of this understanding. However, as the connection between innate intersubjectivity and the *pacta sunt servanda* principle is made explicit, and due to its thin normative account, consent-based monism is submitted as a concept well-suited to answer our question of how we can know who has the final say.

The idea expressed here is that *pacta sunt servanda* is fundamental for the law. In other words, the argument that the (moral) obligation to obey the law is constituted by consensus is by no means new. This became clear after the brief overview of various accounts of social contract theories. Indeed, concerning arguments on the moral obligation to obey the law, it is "[p]erhaps most famous [to] focus on the idea that people consent in some fashion to the operations of their legal-governmental systems."[25] However, this position has

[22] For such an understanding of consensus compare also Rüdiger Wolfrum and Jakob Pichon, "Consensus" in Rüdiger Wolfrum (ed) *Max Planck Encyclopedia of Public International Law* (2010) para 3.

[23] Weinberger (n 5) 73.

[24] The binding character is considered to be an implied element of the consensus. Eugenio Bulygin, "Das Problem der Geltung bei Kelsen" in Stanley L Paulson and Michael Stolleis (eds) *Hans Kelsen – Staatsrechtslehrer und Rechtstheoretiker des 20. Jahrhunderts* (Mohr Siebeck 2004) 80–95 (88–89) with further references at 95; Matthias Knauff, *Der Regelungsverbund: Recht und Soft Law im Mehrebenensystem* (Mohr Siebeck 2010) 25, who speaks of a specific characteristic of law that legal validity rests on useful conventions.

[25] Matthew H Kramer, "Legal and Moral Obligation" in Martin P Golding and William A Edmundson (eds) *The Blackwell Guide to the Philosophy of Law and Legal Theory* (Blackwell 2005) 179–190 (180); for another overview see Leslie Green, "Law and

also attracted a lot of criticism. Concerning the purpose of finding an answer to the legitimacy of law in general and governmental power in particular, skeptical voices doubt the force of consent as a moral obligation to obey the law. Today, "although theories of political obligation focused on consent have not altogether vanished, they have largely lost favor among political and legal philosophers."[26] What therefore seems necessary is to revisit, albeit briefly, the major criticism of consent as a (moral) obligation to obey the law.

The major lines of criticism against consent include the argument that (1) it is implausible that all people affected by governmental power have actually consented to the exercise of such power – whether explicitly or implicitly. Beyond that, (2) such consent can hardly include a mandate for all legal norms usually enforced on us in today's societies. Moreover, consent has its limits: for instance, one cannot enslave oneself. In addition, and unfortunately quite pressing in our times, (3) critics ask: What is the force of consent that was once given to a regime that subsequently "declines into corrupt odium"? "[A]ny binding force previously conferred on its directives by undertakings of obedience would dissipate."[27] Hence, to what do we actually consent and what might dissolve our consent?

The first point of criticism (1) has largely been answered in the form of a concession. The consent envisaged by social contract theories is not explicit consent in the form of a public referendum, but a hypothetical construction as, for instance, framed in the question whether reasonable people would agree to a specific form of government. Immanuel Kant already openly admitted to the fictitious nature of such a contract.[28] From the work of John

Obligations" in Jules Coleman and Scott Shapiro (eds) *The Oxford Handbook of Jurisprudence & Philosophy of Law* (Oxford University Press 2002 reprinted in 2011) 514–547 (525–531); Brian Bix, *Jurisprudence: Theory and Context* (Sweet & Maxwell 5th ed 2009) 178–180.

26 Kramer (n 25) 180.

27 Kramer (n 25) 180 with reference to J W Harris, *Legal Philosophies* (Butterworths 1997) ch 16; John Horton, *Political Obligation* (Macmillan 1992); and Jonathan Wolff, *An Introduction to Political Philosophy* (Oxford University Press 1996) ch 2, who, for instance, provide other reasons for obligations to obey the law; see also Green (n 25) 525–526; Bix (n 25) 179. See also the argument by Herbert L A Hart, "Are There Any Natural Rights?" (1955) 64 (2) Philosophical Review 175–191 (185), holding that "[w]hen any number of persons conduct any joint enterprise according to rules, and thus restrict their liberty, those who have submitted to these restrictions when required have a right to similar submission from those who have benefited by their submission." See also Norbert Hoerster, *Was ist Recht? Grundfragen der Rechtsphilosophie* (CH Beck 2006) 133, holding that justification of legal evaluation is reliant on ethical premises, which, in turn, are related to a compromise between individual interests.

28 See Koller (n 1) 14, who makes reference to Immanuel Kant, *Über den Gemeinspruch: "Das mag in der Theorie richtig sein, taugt aber nicht für die Praxis"* (Berlinische Monatsschrift 1793) 153.

Rawls, it also clearly follows that the original position is not a state that is actually feasible. Beyond that, with regard to the EU, and to a large extent to international law, we can rely on written treaties with explicit procedures where authorized representatives gave their explicit consent. For the purpose of this book, that is rather a strong argument, as we focus on the relationship between international, EU and national law.

An answer to the second line of criticism (2) proceeds along similar lines when holding that this founding consensus of EU Treaties and international legal agreements provides fruitful ground for spelling out more detailed rules on the basis of the founding consensus.

The third line of skepticism (3) is much more difficult to accommodate. In this case it is, roughly speaking, necessary to admit that consensus has its limits and cannot cover brute force exerted by the government. This is a complicated issue which obliges us to spell out concretely what might be part of consensus and what falls short of it. For our purposes here, we can neglect this objection as we are dealing with the relationship of established legal orders. This is possible because we are not concerned with the typical question of political contractualism, namely asking what makes a government legitimate. Rather, we are concerned with the relationship between legal orders. The approach advanced in this book claims to be able to exclude legitimacy issues against the background of the question asked. The question of how we can know who has the final say in norm conflicts between international, EU and national law arguably only discusses legal orders involving a sophisticated conception of legitimacy – though with differences. Therefore, in terms of legitimacy, we must rely on the conception of the legal orders involved in the relationship.[29] Hence, if the prelegal principles are also reflected in positive law, they become a declaratory regulation that renews but does not establish their validity. However, a congruence between the prelegally valid *pacta sunt servanda* principle and its mirror image in positive law – for instance, the fact that consensus has been positivized as an important

[29] This might be justified as we learn from Bix (n 25) 177 that "most writers who discuss a moral obligation to obey the law are considering quite modest claims: (1) *not* that one must obey laws however unjust the legal system – the discussion usually assumes a generally just legal system; and (2) *not* that one must obey the law whatever the circumstances – the obligation is at most a presumptive or "prima facie" obligation, which can be overridden if a stronger moral obligation requires a contrary action" [emphasis original]. In n 1 to (2) Bix clarifies that "[j]ust as one is justified in violating the moral obligation to keep a promise to meet a friend for lunch in order to keep a stronger moral obligation to tend to a sick parent, so one would be morally justified in violating a law if some more important matter is involved (e.g. violating the speed limit to get a seriously ill friend to the hospital)."

source of law in international law[30] – confirms or rather reinforces the importance of these principles.[31] Moreover, EU law is actually the prime example of a legal order that is based on a real (founding) consensus: the Treaties.

These rather brief answers to what are surely major challenges that have long been subject to intense academic discussions are not meant to finally settle the dispute. Rather, this only provides a loose frame for advancing a new line of undergirding consensus as a prelegal obligation to obey the law. Yet, and this is a very important caveat, what follows is not meant to reestablish consensus as the single force to legitimize the force of any type of law. Contrary to most literature on consensus as the way to establish a moral duty to obey the law, the approach of consent-based monism advanced by this book only takes the relationship between legal orders into account. Hence, it is openly admitted that in order to legitimize, for instance, the duty to obey national law, other approaches, such as constitutionalism broadly speaking, are highly likely to be much better equipped for such a purpose.

In order to elaborate on the moral duty to adhere to the *pacta sunt servanda* principle, we will first look at what is the most sophisticated account of engaging with the biological setup of morality.[32] This is arguably the thesis of an innate Universal Moral Grammar (UMG) that relies on an analogy to the thesis in linguistics of a universal grammar of the human faculty of

[30] Art 26 and 35 VCLT.

[31] Compare also John L Brierly, *The Law of Nations* (Oxford University Press 1963) 56: "The ultimate explanation of the binding force of all law is that man, whether he is a single individual or whether he is associated with other men in a state, is constrained, in so far as he is a reasonable being, to believe that order and not chaos is the governing principle of the world in which he has to live." Cf [even though relating to *pacta sunt servanda* and international treaties] Georg Dahm, *Völkerrecht Vol I* (De Gruyter 1958) 12, especially n 17 holding that the minimum set of international legal order must include *pacta sunt servanda*, which holds true for practical reasons. See also Jost Delbrück, "Begriff, Geltung u. Erscheinungsformen des Völkerrechts" in Georg Dahm et al (eds) *Völkerrecht Vol I/1* (De Gruyter 2nd ed 1989) 27 (37), by saying who counts consensus as a source of law implies *pacta sunt servanda*. See Jost Delbrück, "Verbindlichkeit und Geltungsbereich der Verträge" in Georg Dahm et al (eds) *Völkerrecht Vol I/3* (De Gruyter 2nd ed 2002) 600 (600 f), stating that *pacta sunt servanda* and *pacta tertiis* are self-evident "ius necessarium." See also Jules Basdevant, "Règles generals du droit de la paix" (1936) 58 Recueil des Cours Vol IV 471–715 (642). See Hans Wehberg, "Pacta Sunt Servanda" (1959) 53 (4) American Journal of International Law 775–786 (782) and, providing an overview, Kirsten Schmalenbach, "Article 26" in Oliver Dörr and Kirsten Schmalenbach (eds) *Vienna Convention on the Law of Treaties – A Commentary* (Springer 2nd ed 2018) paras 13–22 with further references.

[32] This chapter significantly builds on Lando Kirchmair, "Morality between Nativism and Behaviorism. (Innate) Intersubjectivity as a Response to John Mikhail's 'Universal Moral Grammar'" (2017) 37 (4) Journal of Theoretical and Philosophical Psychology 230–260.

language. Drawing on this faculty, John Mikhail, among others, argues that we humans have an inborn moral grammar. However, we will not simply borrow the concept of a UMG for our purposes. On the contrary, in this chapter that fascinating thesis is first critically juxtaposed with counter-perspectives from the various fields on which it is based. By confronting this approach with substantial criticism from fields such as neurobiology, evolutionary and developmental psychology and philosophy, we will discover that there is ample space for doubting UMG and especially its claimed innateness. In methodological terms, Mikhail suggested using collective evidence from the various disciplines to prove the hypothesis of an innate UMG as there is not sufficient support for UMG within each discipline alone. This multi- and interdisciplinary approach is also contested in this chapter as it does not provide a stable basis for what we envisage as a moral duty to support the *pacta sunt servanda* principle.

However, in lieu of UMG, this chapter submits that intersubjectivity is more suitable for conceptualizing the origins and development of the biological setup of human morality. We will refer to Colwyn Trevarthen's concept of primary, secondary and tertiary intersubjectivity, which is gaining in popularity. This enables us, it is argued, to align morality and its development with core concepts of (developmental) psychology. Such an understanding of morality finally lays bare the origins of moral normativity, which is essential for us as a basis for the *pacta sunt servanda* principle.

5.2 ASCERTAINING THE MORAL DUTY TO ADHERE TO THE *PACTA SUNT SERVANDA* PRINCIPLE VIA THE CONCEPT OF AN INNATE "UNIVERSAL MORAL GRAMMAR"

The concept of the "Moral Gene" provoked many headlines in the early 2000s in some of the most prestigious scientific journals, such as *Nature*[33] and *Science*,[34] but this "breakthrough" also attracted the attention of the general public.[35] Philosophers had been speculating about this idea for

33 Paul Bloom and Izzat Jarudi, "The Chomsky of Morality? A View of Morality as the Product of an Innate Mental Faculty – Rather Like Language" (2006) 443 Nature 909–910.

34 Greg Miller, "The Roots of Morality: Neurobiologists, Philosophers, Psychologists, and Legal Scholars Are Probing the Nature of Human Morality Using a Variety of Experimental Techniques and Moral Challenges" (2008) 320 (5877) Science 734–737.

35 Richard Rorty, "Born to Be Good" (August 27, 2006) New York Times, available at www.nytimes.com/2006/08/27/books/review/Rorty.t.html?pagewanted=all&_r=0 [last accessed February 1, 2023]; Jörg Blecha and Rafaela von Bredow, "Die Grammatik des Guten" (July 30, 2007) Spiegel, available at www.spiegel.de/spiegel/print/d-52417856.html [last accessed

centuries;[36] it took until the 1970s, however, for political philosopher John Rawls to cautiously suggest a fascinating analogy. He speculated whether the theory of a "universal grammar," suggesting that humans possess an innate "human language faculty," which had been successfully and influentially articulated by Noam Chomsky and other linguists since the late 1950s, could be a valuable starting point for biological origins of human morality.[37] The idea of thinking about an analogous moral grammar, as articulated by John Rawls, was first taken seriously, in their PhD theses, by the two legal philosophers John Mikhail[38] and Matthias Mahlmann,[39] who both studied with Chomsky. Admittedly, it is an exciting idea that, if proven correct, would definitely be of great interest, not just for science and our purposes, but for humanity in general (including, for instance, lawyers). Yet it seems there is still quite a long way to go.

To set up the argument, I shall first briefly sum up the core thesis of an innate UMG (Section 5.3.2). In order to illustrate that we are at the very beginning of the long journey to discover whether human beings are actually equipped "genetically" with UMG, I will give a short overview of counterarguments from such varied scientific branches as neurobiology, evolutionary psychology and anthropology as well as philosophy, thus establishing a firm criticism of the concept of UMG (Section 5.3.3). Mikhail's problematic understanding of multi- and interdisciplinarity, which allows him to sum up results collectively that are not convincing proof for UMG within each discipline alone, is the fatal blow for UMG (Section 5.3.3.4). The result of such an inquiry will be that UMG is not likely to be the best hypothesis or framework within which to analyze the biological setup that enables moral decisions, with research on the astonishing behavior of nonhuman great apes

February 1, 2023]; Jörg Blecha, "Mit Anstand auf die Welt" (December 18, 2006) Spiegel, available at www.spiegel.de/spiegel/print/d-49929836.html [last accessed February 1, 2023]; Hubertus Breuer, "Das Moral-Gen: Ist das Gute im Menschen angeboren? Wissenschafter meinen: ja" (March 31, 2007) Profil, available at www.profil.at/home/das-moral-gen-ist-gute-menschen-wissenschafter-169043 [last accessed February 1, 2023].

36 John Mikhail and Matthias Mahlmann, "Cognitive Science, Ethics and Law" in Zenon Bankowski (ed) *Epistemology & Ontology: IVR-Symposium Lund 2003* (Franz Steiner 2005) 95–102 (95 esp nn 1–4).

37 Rawls (n 20) section 9, 46 ff with reference to Noam Chomsky, *Aspects of the Theory of Syntax* (MIT Press 1965) 3–9.

38 Mikhail's Cornell Philosophy PhD dissertation dates back to 2000 and his Stanford JD thesis to 2002. His work has also been published in an extended version as John Mikhail, *Elements of Moral Cognition: Rawls' Linguistic Analogy and the Cognitive Science of Moral and Legal Judgment* (Cambridge University Press 2011).

39 Matthias Mahlmann, *Rationalismus in der praktischen Theorie: Normentheorie und praktische Kompetenz* (Nomos 2nd ed 2008).

and "their morality" significantly informing this conclusion. Finally, I suggest that something like an (innate) intersubjectivity might be more appropriate for our purposes (Sections 5.4 and 5.5). By relying on Colwyn Trevarthen's work on intersubjectivity and thus the division into primary, secondary and tertiary intersubjectivity, I aim to propose a psychologically robust concept embedded in developmental psychology research in order to clarify the origins and development of morality, which enables us to establish the moral duty undergirding the *pacta sunt servanda* principle (Section 5.6).

5.3 WHAT IS "UNIVERSAL MORAL GRAMMAR"?

5.3.1 *Introduction*

For his account of A *Theory of Justice*, John Rawls presupposed that human beings are rational and reasonable agents.[40] While such assumptions can be found in many accounts of legal and political philosophers as well as legal theorists and,[41] albeit unconsciously, also in many accounts of legal practitioners, Rawls suggested that these presuppositions might be understood analogously to "universal generative linguistics" famously advocated by Noam Chomsky.[42] This fascinating suggestion would – if successfully demonstrated to be scientifically defensible – satisfy many philosophers and lawyers who for centuries have been speculating about such a "nativist" basis for human morality (and rule obedience).[43]

Yet it is important to note that the suggestion of this analogy made by Rawls is far more modest and cautious than the approach put forward by John Mikhail. Mikhail himself acknowledges that Rawls' argument "is not the same thing as defending the empirical claim ... that all humankind shares a common moral nature, in the form of a Universal Moral Grammar. That claim, understood as a hypothesis of natural science, goes far beyond anything Rawls actually defends in A *Theory of Justice*."[44] The claim made by Mikhail will be of central interest for this chapter and the criticisms echoed here.

40 Rawls (n 20) 11 ff and 142 ff, which give an elucidating overview suggesting that these presuppositions are strongly connected to the account of Immanuel Kant. See also Stefan Bird-Pollan, "Rawls: Construction and Justification" (2009) 1 (2) Public Reason 12–30; Sibley (n 13).

41 See above 127.

42 Noam Chomsky, *Syntactic Structures* (Mouton 1957). For a detailed account of the Rawlsian argument, see Mikhail (n 38).

43 See, for instance, the overview provided by Mikhail and Mahlmann (n 36) 95.

44 Mikhail (n 38) 73.

His claim is driven by the question whether the "mind's properties are genetically determined." The argument is based on a simple claim reminding us of the earlier discussion of Kant,[45] which states that "[e]ven if one accepts the traditional Empiricist assumption that the mind is a general-purpose learning device, this still implies a very specific inborn mental capacity – namely, the capacity to acquire any type of knowledge, and to do so more or less uniformly."[46] In his work, Mikhail sets out to use the astonishing results of some trolley problems to strengthen the suggestion of the linguistic analogy.[47] His main claim is that the "descriptive problem" highlighted by these trolley problems is best explained by "the moral grammar hypothesis." As Mikhail suggests, the trolley problems might serve as proof of the fact that moral judgments depend on how "action is mentally represented."[48]

Generative linguistics is organized around five questions, which are also taken as a frame for the idea of UMG.[49] A major consequence of this analogy is that moral grammar is universal and innate. In order to back up the suggested innateness, reference is made to various research fields such as cognitive sciences, especially (neuro)biology, anthropology, (evolutionary and developmental) psychology and linguistics.[50] However, as will be shown in Section 5.3.3, most scientists in each field are quite cautious about the innate thesis, which is – to be fair – also mentioned by Mikhail. Yet he suggests that if the results from those different fields are thought of "collectively," the innateness of Universal Moral Grammar becomes at least a plausible understanding.[51]

45 See above Section 1.2.1.

46 Mikhail and Mahlmann (n 36) 97.

47 Philippa Foot, *The Problem of Abortion and the Doctrine of the Double Effect in Virtues and Vices* (Basil Blackwell 1978), originally appearing as Philippa Foot, "The Problem of Abortion and the Doctrine of Double Effect" (1967) 5 Oxford Review 5–15; Judith Jarvis Thomson, "Killing, Letting Die, and the Trolley Problem" (1976) 59 (2) The Monist 204–217; Judith Jarvis Thomson, "The Trolley Problem" (1985) 94 (6) Yale Law Journal 1395–1415.

48 Mikhail (n 38) 38–39.

49 For an overview see John Mikhail, "Universal Moral Grammar: Theory, Evidence and the Future" (2007) 11 (4) Trends in Cognitive Sciences 143–152.

50 Mikhail (n 49) 143.

51 Mikhail (n 49) 143: "initial evidence for UMG comes from multiple sources, including psychology, linguistics, anthropology and cognitive neuroscience. Although none of this evidence is univocal or conclusive, collectively it provides at least modest support for the hypothesis that humans possess an innate moral faculty that is analogous, in some respects, to the language faculty that has been postulated by Chomsky and other linguists."

5.3.2 *Key Elements of UMG*

5.3.2.1 The Linguistic Analogy

In analogy to "generative linguistics" and its universal grammar, the basis of the thesis of an innate UMG is the "moral grammar" argument.[52] Like universal grammar in linguistics, UMG is modeled around five main questions. According to Mikhail, they are to be answered one after another.[53] The first, and thus most basic, question is: (Q1) "What constitutes moral knowledge?" Mikhail answers: "[B]y a particular generative moral grammar (or theory of moral competence): a theory of the steady or acquired state of the mind/brain of a person who possesses a system of moral knowledge, or what one might refer to informally as a 'sense of justice', 'moral sense', 'moral faculty', or 'conscience.'"[54]

The next question is (Q2): "How is moral knowledge acquired?" Here the answer is: "*Universal Moral Grammar* (UMG): a theory of the initial state of the moral faculty, assumed to be a distinct subsystem of the mind/brain, along with an account of how the properties UMG postulates interact with experience to yield a mature system of moral knowledge."[55]

The third question (Q3), "How is moral knowledge put to use?," is no longer a primary focus of Mikhail's research. He differentiates this question from the first one by making a "competence–performance distinction." While *moral competence* means "an individual's moral knowledge … the term *moral performance* … refer[s] to how that knowledge is put to use."[56] Regarding the answer to the third question, Mikhail is already very cautious and states that,

[52] Mikhail (n 38); Mahlmann (n 39) 101–102 expects from a rationalist starting point, that UMG, according to him a predisposition of certain essential elements of moral knowledge, shares characteristics with the universal grammar of language.

[53] Mikhail (n 38) 71: "[W]e cannot even formulate [Q1] until a presumptively adequate answer to [Q2] is in hand. … As Rawls [John Rawls, "The Independence of Moral Theory" (1975) 48 Proceedings and Addresses of the American Philosophical Association 5–22 (10)] correctly observes, we must resist the temptation to answer questions before we are adequately prepared to do so."

[54] Mikhail (n 38) 15.

[55] Mikhail (n 38) 15.

[56] Mikhail (n 38) 18; Mikhail explains further (n 38 19) that by distinguishing [Q1] and [Q3] he is attempting to "shift (or begin to shift) the focus of moral theorists away from behaviourism and toward mentalism. In my judgment, the theory of moral cognition has not yet fully recovered from the damage that was done to it by behaviourism. Part of what [he] hope[s] to accomplish in [t]his book is to begin to repair this damage, by showing how a mentalistic approach to moral cognition might work." This particular point remains uncontested by the criticism advanced in this chapter.

"if available, [the answer] would be given by a theory of *moral performance*: a theory of how moral knowledge enters into the actual representation and evaluation of human acts and institutions and other forms of actual behavior."[57]

Neither (Q4) "How is moral knowledge physically realized in the brain?" nor (Q5) "How did moral knowledge evolve in the species?" is part of the main focus of Mikhail. Here thinks it would be "premature" to attempt to answer them before having an "adequate grasp of plausible answers" to (Q1)–(Q3).[58] Thus, they are not of central interest here either.

5.3.2.2 The Hypothesis of a Moral Grammar

UMG rests, according to Mikhail's approach, on the hypothesis of a moral grammar:

> The argument for moral grammar holds that the properties of moral judgment imply that the mind contains a moral grammar: a complex and possibly domain-specific set of rules, concepts, and principles that generates and relates mental representations of various types. Among other things, this system enables individuals to determine the deontic status of an infinite variety of acts and omissions.[59]

Mikhail seems to support this thesis, at least partly, with "functional imaging and patient studies [which] have led some researchers to conclude that a fairly consistent network of brain regions is involved in moral cognition."[60] He further bases his moral grammar hypothesis on the fact that people make intuitive moral judgments when faced with trolley problems.[61] Trolley problems are designed to ask people to judge whether they think that a certain –

57 Mikhail (n 38) 15.

58 Mikhail (n 38) 24: "Put differently, we cannot seriously ask how moral knowledge is realized in the brain or how it evolved in the species until what constitutes moral knowledge and how it is acquired and put to use by each individual are better understood." However, it is questionable how we can know what constitutes moral knowledge and how we acquire it, and speculate about its innateness, if we do not know, and we cannot know in advance, how moral knowledge is physically realized in the brain. It is furthermore likely that the last question (Q5), as to how moral knowledge evolved in the species, is heavily interwoven with Mikhail's previous questions and I am pretty sure that, as we have learned from other discoveries in the natural sciences, an appropriate answer to this question, or at least an educated guess on how to answer it, certainly will reveal important insights into how things work out in our "mind/brain" nowadays.

59 Mikhail (n 38) 88; Mikhail (n 49) 144.

60 Mikhail (n 49) 143.

61 Mikhail (n 38) 78 ff.

hypothetical – action is morally permissible or not.[62] The most famous trolley problem covers the following scenario: a trolley's brakes have stopped working and it is heading towards five innocent workers who are working on the tracks with their backs turned to the trolley. The test subject is now asked whether it would be morally permissible to flip a switch to change the direction of the trolley, which would result in the death of one innocent person working on the other track. While most people would trigger the switch to change the trolley's direction in order to save five innocent people while killing one innocent person instead, they would not throw a fat man in front of the trolley (another trolley problem constellation) in order to stop the trolley and achieve the very same utilitarian result of saving five people instead of one person. This is astonishing because it reveals that the same utilitarian logic – save five instead of one – does not apply in both cases. When asked, most people fail to come up with an explanation for their decision,[63] which indicates that intuitive guidelines are at work.[64] This suggests that people judge according to some rules or principles (for instance, the doctrine of double effect) that they themselves cannot explain or sometimes would not even recognize.[65] Within the realm of moral competence, people have moral knowledge that is inaccessible to their consciousness but implicitly guides their decisions. People make moral judgments of moral permissibility and impermissibility "that far outstrip their own capacities to reflectively identify, explain, or justify."[66]

[62] Foot (n 47); Thomson (n 47).

[63] See Mikhail (n 38) 83: "When experimental subjects are asked to justify or explain their judgments, they appear unable to express the principles on which their judgments are based. We are thus led to a further surprising hypothesis: some of the operative principles of moral grammar appear to function below actual or even potential consciousness, at least in this context. The content of these principles, in other words, appears to be nonintrospectible" [footnotes omitted].

[64] Mikhail (n 38) 82–83: Those moral judgments "are not made by a conscious application of moral rules or principles, so far as this may be determined by observation or introspection. Nonetheless, the judgments appear to be principled, as evidenced by the fact that, despite being relatively immediate and spontaneous, they are stable, stringent, and highly structured, amenable to constituent manipulation, and intuitively consistent with judgments rendered in structurally similar scenarios. In addition, the judgments are typically made with a high degree of certitude and, indeed, are often experienced as being 'objective' rather than a matter of subjective taste or preference from a phenomenological perspective. We thus appear led to the hypothesis that, as is the case with grammaticality judgments, which also possess similar properties, the moral judgments elicited by [the trolley problems] involve the use of unconscious principles or algorithms" [footnotes omitted].

[65] Mark Alfano and Don Loeb, "Experimental Philosophy" in Edward N Zalta (ed) *Stanford Encyclopaedia of Philosophy* (August 9, 2018), available at http://plato.stanford.edu/entries/experimental-moral/ [last accessed February 1, 2023].

[66] Alfano and Loeb (n 65).

5.3.2.3 The Poverty of the Moral Stimulus

The main support for this hypothesis relies on the argument of the poverty of the moral stimulus. This argument

> holds that the manner in which this grammar is acquired implies that at least some of its core attributes are innate, where "innate" is used in a dispositional sense to refer to cognitive systems whose essential properties are largely predetermined by the inherent structure of the mind, but whose ontogenetic development must be triggered and shaped by appropriate experience and can be impeded by unusually hostile learning environments.[67]

An example of the poverty of the moral stimulus, as indicated by Mikhail, would be that children at a very young age do make surprising and quite complicated moral decisions, which are unlikely to derive solely from learning experience. This argument is backed up by Mikhail with findings from developmental psychology when he gives a variety of examples highlighting the capabilities of young children between the ages of three and six.[68] He points out, for example, that "human children also appear biologically predisposed to comfort others who are experiencing emotional distress and, more broadly, to help others achieve their goals, to share valuable resources with them, and to provide them with helpful information."[69] He also quotes findings suggesting, for example, that "3–4-year-old children use intent or purpose to distinguish two acts that have the same result."[70] Yet Mikhail acknowledges that "[b]oth arguments are nondemonstrative and presuppose a familiar set of idealizations and simplifying assumptions."[71]

In brief, the research program of UMG is about explaining trolley problems, which "suggest[s] that individuals are intuitive lawyers who are capable of drawing intelligent distinctions between superficially similar cases, although their basis for doing so is often obscure."[72]

[67] Mikhail (n 38) 88; Mikhail (n 49) 144.

[68] Mikhail (n 38) 104–105; Mikhail (n 49) 143.

[69] John Mikhail, "Moral Grammar and Human Rights – Some Reflections on Cognitive Science and Enlightenment Rationalism" in Ryan Goodman, Derek Jinks and Andrew K Woods (eds) *Understanding Social Action, Promoting Human Rights* (Oxford University Press 2012) 160–202 (174).

[70] Mikhail (n 49) 143.

[71] Mikhail (n 49) 144.

[72] Mikhail (n 49) 150.

5.3.3 *Criticism of (the Thesis of an Innate) UMG*

The hypothesis of UMG is astonishing and impressive, attracting a lot of attention from admirers or followers and also – quintessentially for scientific debates – critics. What follows will classify as the latter.

5.3.3.1 A Working Analogy? Differences between the Linguistic and Moral Grammar and a Skeptical Neurobiological View

Marc Hauser also investigated Rawls' linguistic analogy, touching on Mikhail and Mahlmann. His book *Moral Minds* will not be dealt with here though.[73] However, in their review of Hauser's *Moral Minds*, Paul Bloom and Izzat Jarudi discussed and questioned some elements of the linguistic analogy. They are not fundamentally against the "idea of an innate moral faculty" and consider it "well worth investigating."[74] Yet they stress that, "[f]or instance, some arguments for linguistic innateness are based on assumptions about the generative nature of language; these might not export well to the moral domain."[75] Emmanuel Dupoux and Pierre Jacob are similarly critical when they "argue that the formal grammatical concepts proposed by Chomsky are unlikely to throw much light onto the psychological mechanisms that underlie moral judgments, moral development and moral diversity."[76] They basically hold that those unquestioned similarities between "generative linguistics" and UMG are not enough to show "that the mechanisms underlying moral

[73] Marc D Hauser, *Moral Minds: How Nature Designed Our Universal Sense of Right and Wrong* (Ecco 2006). For the sake of clarification: not dealing with this book here is not because of the reported scientific misconduct that led to his resignation. Furthermore, this book was not one of his many works reportedly affected. For a discussion as to whether, or better to what extent, Hauser's *Moral Minds* constitutes plagiarism of Mikhail's work, see Gilbert Harman, "Does Marc Hauser's Moral Minds Plagiarize John Mikhail's Earlier Work?," as well as Hauser's response: Marc D Hauser, "Response to Gil Harman's 'Did Marc Hauser's Moral Minds Plagiarize John Mikhail's Earlier Work?,'" formerly available at www.princeton.edu. Steven Pinker's work is not dealt with in this chapter either, as Mikhail's work is considered the most sophisticated argument for the innate morality of human beings. However, compare Steven Pinker, *The Blank Slate: The Modern Denial of Human Nature* (Viking 2002) and the review of John Dupré, "Making Hay with Straw Men. Book Review of Pinker, Steven. The Blank Slate" (2003) American Scientist, available at www.americanscientist.org/article/making-hay-with-straw-men [last accessed February 1, 2023] for a general account of nativism and its critique.

[74] Bloom and Jarudi (n 33) 910; Emmanuel Dupoux and Pierre Jacob, "Universal Moral Grammar: A Critical Appraisal" (2007) 11 (9) Trends in Cognitive Sciences 373–378 (373).

[75] Bloom and Jarudi (n 33) 909–910.

[76] Dupoux and Jacob (n 74) 373.

judgments make use of moral information encoded in a dedicated moral grammar."[77] Furthermore, there is no parallel to "native languages" in morals, which is related to the fact that individuals' moral opinions might change over time, whereas a mother tongue does not change as easily.[78] Thus, the linguistic analogy is maybe not the best way to explore the relation between moral competence and human biology.[79] This does not, however, mean that morality and its origins are not to be traced back to nature in any way.[80]

Mikhail anticipates and thus reacts to such criticism, holding that "[t]he point … is not to deny that there are significant differences between moral theory and linguistics. On the contrary, [he] not only accept[s], but insist[s], that these two disciplines, and the theoretical problems they seek to solve, are dissimilar in many fundamental respects."[81] Yet he also admits that if he "were to begin again today from scratch, [he] would probably write a very different book, one geared less toward fitting [his] own ideas about moral theory into the format of Rawls' brief remarks on the linguistic analogy in *A Theory of Justice* and more toward the independent development of a naturalistic moral psychology within broad scientific parameters."[82] Mikhail then devotes a large part of his book to "answering" criticisms that were raised by prominent philosophers against the linguistic analogy suggested by Rawls in Section 9 of his preeminent *A Theory of Justice*. This, however, is not relevant for the astonishing claim Mikhail raises with his UMG. Mikhail himself admits that Rawls never intended to suggest any specific innate moral grammar when drawing his analogy.[83] Mikhail's claim goes much further than Rawls'. The criticism raised here does not aim at the general link between morality and human biology, but is addressed to the specific design of UMG. In this regard, it is striking that, as Patricia Churchland stresses, "[j]ust as the brain did not evolve to read [in our Middle Stone Age human ancestors 300,000–50,000 years ago], but to do complex pattern recognition to help guide action, so it is entirely possible it did not evolve to favor universal human rights, or trial by

77 Dupoux and Jacob (n 74) 374.

78 Alfano and Loeb (n 65). However, people can lose their mother tongue quite significantly if they move to another country and, for whatever reason, stop speaking their first language. I am grateful to Helen Heaney for this point.

79 Jesse Prinz, "Resisting the Linguistic Analogy: A Commentary on Hauser, Young, and Cushman" in Walter Sinnott-Armstrong (ed) *Moral Psychology. The Cognitive Science of Morality: Intuition and Diversity Vol II* (MIT Press 2008) 157–170.

80 Dupoux and Jacob (n 74) 377–378.

81 Mikhail (n 38) 33.

82 Mikhail (n 38) Preface xvii. His book is based on his PhD thesis, which he defended in 2000 (n 38 Preface xvi).

83 Mikhail (n 38) 73.

jury."[84] This is to say, "we need to be cautious about ascribing such values as a yearning for moral progress to early *Homo sapiens*, and hence to our basic nature here and now."[85] She goes on to clarify that "[t]he capacity for problem-solving, whatever that really involves in terms of brain circuitry, allows for the emergence of novel behaviors, without the aid of new genes."[86]

She further points out:

> Evidence for some genetic changes within the last 10,000 years does exist, but so far these changes pertain not to brain circuitry, cognition, or social temperament, but to properties that are arguably more amenable to evolutionary change without triggering a deleterious cascade of changes. An important example is the genetic change that allowed adult humans to digest animal milks.[87]

For her, too, "[t]here is no doubt that our genes are massively important in what we are and for the variability among us, but from that observation, nothing very specific can be concluded, such as that there is a 'gene for' fairness or religion or wanderlust."[88]

Briefly, none of the arguments presented here definitely rules out UMG and its claimed innateness.[89] Similar to many other scientific questions, this debate will very likely not find any black or white arguments either. Hence, probability and relative argumentative strengths play an important role. After

84 Patricia S Churchland, *Braintrust: What Neuroscience Tells Us about Morality* (Princeton University Press 2011) 18–19.
85 Churchland (n 84) 19.
86 Churchland (n 84) 20.
87 Churchland (n 84) 21.
88 Churchland (n 84) 22.
89 What might be of interest here as well is the case of epigenetics. For a potentially interesting analogy compare Brian G Dias and Kerry J Ressler, "Parental Olfactory Experience Influences Behavior and Neural Structure in Subsequent Generations" (2014) 17 (1) Nature Neuroscience 89–98, who have shown, for instance, that "[p]arental olfactory experience influences behavior and neural structure in subsequent generations." In other words, mice can pass on behavioral sensitivity towards a particular odor to subsequent generations via an epigenetic modification of their gene pool (and not via learned behavior). However, see Jacek Debiec and Regina Marie Sullivan, "Intergenerational Transmission of Emotional Trauma through Amygdala-Dependent Mother-to-Infant Transfer of Specific Fear" (2014) 111 (33) Proceedings of the National Academy of Sciences of the United States of America 12222–12227, for a social fear-learning paradigm as a condition-stimulus-specific fear response for transmission to offspring in rats. Debiec and Sullivan (12226) also show that "maternal physical presence is not necessary for fear learning to occur." However, the odor of the fear-conditioned mother in combination with the neutral odor (condition stimulus) is. Hence, the picture, at least in this case, still seems to be rather complex, leaving various possibilities instead of one simple way to transmit fear in rodents. I am grateful to Jacek Debiec for pointing out to me that the studies do not contradict each other, but are actually complementary.

having concentrated on the "linguistic analogy" and a neurobiological perspective, I would rather doubt that innate UMG is the most convincing explanation for the origins of morality. However, for more clarity, I will further investigate perspectives from philosophy as well as psychology.[90]

5.3.3.2 Fundamental Misconceptions of UMG? The Perspective of Skeptical (Legal) Philosophy and the Empiricist Challenge

One main concern that has been raised against the very foundations of UMG is the counterargument voiced by Dennis Patterson, who questions in a Wittgensteinian manner the idea of "locat[ing] moral knowledge in a 'place', that place being the mind."[91] By doubting this basis, Patterson addresses what he thinks is a "conceptual deficiency" of UMG, which of necessity has to be clarified before exploring the truth.[92] This is because "any empirical inquiry that proceeds from conceptual confusion cannot yield satisfactory results."[93] The fundamental problem according to Patterson is that the mind (which in Mikhail's approach contains a moral grammar that is part of "the inherent structure of the mind") cannot be located in any place within the human body,[94] but needs to be understood as following from social action, as argued by Ludwig Wittgenstein.

Mikhail contends, however, that "[b]ehaviorism in ethics fails for the same reason that behaviorism in linguistics fails: it is simply unable to account for the fact that the operation of a specific mental capacity, in an identifiable cognitive domain, is characterized by potential novelty and

90 A nicely put metaphor by David Eagleman, *Incognito: The Secret Lives of the Brain* (Pantheon 2011) 221, which he named the "'radio theory' of brains," explains the fundamental point very well: "Imagine that you are a Kalahari Bushman and that you stumble upon a transistor radio in the sand. You might pick it up, twiddle the knobs, and suddenly, to your surprise, hear voices streaming out of this strange little box. If you're curious and scientifically minded, you might try to understand what is going on. You might pry off the back cover to discover a little nest of wires. Now let's say you begin a careful, scientific study of what causes the voices. You notice that each time you pull out the green wire, the voices stop. When you put the wire back on its contact, the voices begin again. The same goes for the red wire. Yanking out the black wire causes the voices to get garbled, and removing the yellow wire reduces the volume to a whisper. You step carefully through all the combinations, and you come to a clear conclusion: the voices depend entirely on the integrity of the circuitry. Change the circuitry and you damage the voices. … Your conclusions are limited by the fact that you know absolutely nothing about radio waves and, more generally, electromagnetic radiation."

91 Dennis Patterson, "On the Conceptual and the Empirical – A Critique of John Mikhail's Cognitivism" (2008) 73 (2) Brooklyn Law Review 611–623 (611 and 614).

92 Patterson (n 91) 611–612.

93 Patterson (n 91) 612.

94 Patterson (n 91) 620–621.

unboundedness."[95] That is why, for him, "the guiding assumption of this hypothesis [moral grammar] is the classical rationalist idea, suitably reinterpreted, that certain basic moral and legal notions and precepts are engraved in the mind, presumably as a kind of innate instinct."[96]

Patterson disagrees:

> Like all forms of rationalism, Mikhail's premise is that the object of explanation (in this case, moral knowledge) is located in a place. In Mikhail's view, moral knowledge is in the mind. This claim is confused because "knowledge" is an ability and not a thing. "Know" is a success verb, not a referent. To "know" something is neither to be in a certain state nor is it to be in possession of a particular structure of mind or brain. Like all abilities, the ability to know moral rules is exhibited in behavior.[97]

However, Mahlmann comes to Mikhail's aid by stressing that we can also detect at least some (internal) subjective consciousness of rule-following in Wittgenstein,[98] which is at least ignored if not deemed to be wrong by him when accounting for the basis of rules in (external) social practice. Therefore, in the end, even Wittgenstein has to presuppose some sort of faculty or capacity to understand rules initially on a subjective level. Mahlmann bases his claim on unusual cases and the astonishing capacity of humans to deal with rules shortly after having learned them and without any prior experience.[99] However, this argument does not exclude with reasonable certainty the possibility that we have *learned* to generalize and thereby use knowledge and adapt it to new situations that are similar to those situations in which we learned knowledge beforehand. The argument of the astonishing capability of humans to learn is simply not enough to claim that the only plausible or most convincing explanation is an innate UMG. What we need to remember for the latter reasoning, and the main point of this chapter, is that we are dealing with hypotheses and possible interpretations here. The innateness of UMG is therefore anything but uncontested and secure. Other possible explanations – such as an innate learning capacity, which is very abstract (and thus less likely to be demonstrated as false) – cannot be excluded.[100]

95 Mikhail (n 38) 95.

96 Mikhail (n 38) 101.

97 Patterson (n 91) 620.

98 Mahlmann (n 39) 151–152 summarizing that one can only follow an internal rule, but not an external rule and, thus, external rules require internal rules.

99 Mahlmann (n 39) 139–140.

100 Compare, for instance, Churchland (n 84) 11, who puts it this way: "The hypothesis on offer is that what we humans call *ethics* or *morality* is a four-dimensional scheme for social behaviour that is shaped by interlocking brain processes: (1) *caring* (rooted in attachment to kin and kith

Yet, in the end, Mahlmann seems to be correct insofar as he states that the "nature/nurture" debate regarding human morality is not a question of whether the human mind is innate or not, but about which behaviors or faculties are innate, which ones are learned and the extent of both.[101] I assert that this question, namely the extent of the innateness of human morality, is still unclear and it is difficult to tell whose approach is finally correct: Mikhail's and Mahlmann's nativism or Patterson's empiricism. This chapter does not aim to change that. Yet probabilities and relative argumentative strengths can be evaluated. Even though the nature/nurture debate about morality is still unresolved, which this chapter surely will not change, I shall illustrate that quite radical approaches such as innate UMG are appealing, albeit questionable. By highlighting further criticisms against UMG I aim to underpin this claim.

5.3.3.3 Humans as "Intuitive Lawyers"? Methodological Problems of UMG as Exposed by Psychologists: A Criticism of Unconscious Principles as the Basis of UMG

5.3.3.3.1 Unconscious Moral Decisions as the Basis of UMG Mikhail holds that "[t]he existence of ... unconscious [operative] principles [of moral competence] is a core insight of Universal Grammar."[102] Indeed, "humans as 'intuitive lawyers'" is a key argument of UMG. This insight is not unfamiliar to a number of philosophers, who for centuries have speculated about such an intuitive basis for moral judgments.[103] Mikhail seeks to capture these unconscious moral judgments by following Chomsky's differentiation between moral competence and moral performance. The former aims only at elucidating "the relatively simple problem of explaining the properties of people's rapid and spontaneous intuitive moral judgments (ie, the problem of moral perception), not the more complex problem of explaining how people choose to act."[104] Mikhail also stresses that "UMG draws a fundamental distinction between an individual's *operative* moral principles – the principles she

and care for their well-being), (2) *recognition of others' psychological states* (rooted in the benefits of predicting the behaviour of others), (3) *problem-solving in a social context* (e.g., how we should distribute scarce goods, settle land disputes; how we should punish the miscreants), and (4) *learning social practices* (by positive and negative reinforcement, by imitation, by trial and error, by various kinds of conditioning, and by analogy)" [footnotes omitted].

[101] Mahlmann (n 39) 103.

[102] Mikhail (n 38) 99.

[103] Mikhail (n 38) 99.

[104] Mikhail (n 69) 170.

actually uses in making her considered moral judgments – and her *express* principles – those statements she makes when she attempts to explain or justify those judgments."[105]

These methodological clarifications are the basis for the claim that unconscious moral judgments are most likely to be held as demonstrating innate moral grammar. I already highlighted that the linguistic analogy has been severely criticized and that research results in cognitive neuroscience are far from conclusive with regard to innate UMG.[106] Now I would like to address what I think is Mikhail's most fundamental, manifest error when appraising evidence, namely his interpretation of research results from psychology.

Mikhail quotes Felix Warneken and Michael Tomasello when saying that "[h]uman children also appear biologically predisposed to comfort others who are experiencing emotional distress and, more broadly, to help others achieve their goals, to share valuable resources with them, and to provide them with helpful information."[107] Mikhail continues by citing their summary, which concludes that "from an early age human infants are naturally empathetic, helpful, generous, and informative."[108] He refers to other psychologists who also found that children, at a very young age ranging from three to four years, show some astonishing behavior, such as the "*mala in se/mala prohibita* distinction when making moral judgments," or that they "use information about an actor's intent or purpose to distinguish two acts with the same result."[109] Mikhail's conclusion of these research results is astonishing for several reasons. He suggests that "[i]n all of these cases and others like them, to explain the observable data scientists must be willing to attribute unconscious knowledge and complex mental operations to the child that go well beyond anything she has been taught."[110] Yet this seems odd because the children in the studies Mikhail refers to are already rather old to conclude that

[105] Mikhail (n 69) 170: "just as individuals are often unaware of or mistaken about the principles that guide their linguistic intuitions, so too they are often unaware of or mistaken about the principles that guide their moral intuitions." He continues (n 69 173) by highlighting that "moral cognition may be compared not only to language perception but also to numerous other cognitive capacities such as vision, depth perception, musical cognition, and face recognition, all of which also depend on unconscious mental operations. The central challenge facing cognitive scientists in all of these domains is to extract and understand the operation of the mind's hidden rules of intuitive judgment."

[106] See Section 5.4.3.1.

[107] Mikhail (n 69) 174; Felix Warneken and Michael Tomasello, "Varieties of Altruism in Children and Chimpanzees" (2009) 13 Trends in Cognitive Sciences 397–402.

[108] Mikhail (n 69) 174 quoting Warneken and Tomasello (n 107) 401.

[109] Mikhail (n 38) 174–175 with further references.

[110] Mikhail (n 69) 176; Mikhail (n 38) 176.

these are innate features. The very same psychologists that Mikhail quotes are much more cautious than he is and strive to design studies in sophisticated ways in order to test much younger children, at the age of twelve to eighteen months, for example, and are still very reluctant to conclude any inborn features from their results. Furthermore, their aim is not directed at proving an innate UMG or something similar, but at quite different, more specific, goals such as clarifying whether the toddlers they tested understand the beliefs of others,[111] and do understand and share intentions.[112] This contradicts Mikhail's interpretation, which holds that "[i]t seems implausible to think that they [the concepts and principles of children at the age of three to six] are acquired by means of explicit instruction; examples in the surrounding environment; or any known processes of imitation, internalization, socialization, and the like."[113]

Another fundamental, methodological problem of UMG is that trolley problems, even if specified and slightly modified, cannot support the innateness thesis of UMG. This is because they require too challenging a skill, such as reading, or at least verbal skills, which children only develop at quite a late age, so it does not allow any conclusions to be drawn about innate behavior. This is why evolutionary and developmental psychologists have developed studies over the last few years that try to reduce construct-irrelevant skills (reading skills, verbal skills, and so on), to a minimum. Quite recently psychologists discovered that toddlers aged twelve to eighteen months are able to understand the beliefs of others by looking at their eye movements and, more actively, whether tested toddlers engaged in helping behavior.[114] It is

[111] Kristine H Onishi and Renée Baillargeon, "Do 15-Month-Old Infants Understand False Beliefs?" (2005) 308 (5719) Science 255–258; David Buttelmann, Malinda Carpenter and Michael Tomasello, "Eighteen-Month-Old Infants Show False Belief Understanding in an Active Helping Paradigm" (2009) 112 (2) Cognition 337–342; David Buttelmann et al, "Eighteen-Month-Olds Understand False Beliefs in an Unexpected-Contents Task" (2014) 119 Journal of Experimental Child Psychology 120–126.

[112] Michael Tomasello et al, "Understanding and Sharing Intentions: The Origins of Cultural Cognition" (2005) 28 (5) Behavioral & Brain Sciences 1–61.

[113] Mikhail (n 69) 176.

[114] See eg Buttelmann et al (n 111). The ontogeny of moral behavior in general and toddlers' willingness to help others is the subject of a large and very dynamic body of research which cannot be represented here in any comprehensive manner. However, see Moritz Köster et al, "Cultural Influences on Toddlers' Prosocial Behavior: How Maternal Task Assignment Relates to Helping Others" (2016) 87 (6) Child Development 1727–1738, highlighting "the role of caregivers' socialization practices for the early ontogeny of helping behavior" suggesting inter alia "culture-specific developmental pathways"; as well as Marta Giner Torréns, Kristin Dreizler and Joscha Kärtner, "Insight into Toddlers' Motivation to Help: From Social Participants to Prosocial Contributors" (2021) 64 Infant Behavior and Development 101603, proposing that "initially, toddlers start helping in ongoing chores driven by their interest in

unlikely that trolley problems could be modified sufficiently to test children younger than five or six (with limited reading skills). It is thus highly problematic to infer any appropriate conclusions about innate features.[115]

Mikhail himself addresses a less fundamental problem with this. He attempts to answer the criticism directed against the usefulness of trolley problems for advancing knowledge about UMG, such as the fact that they deal with highly uncertain outcomes.[116] In trolley problems, people are only asked if an act is morally permissible or not (as a sort of idealization). This is problematic, however. While they might believe with a high degree of certainty that triggering the switch should change the direction of the trolley, in other cases (for example, pushing the fat man off the bridge) the certainty of the outcome (and thus the decision about the moral permissibility of the outcome) is more doubtable. Thus it might obscure the real process in people's minds when deciding about the moral permissibility of a certain action.[117] That is why I am quite convinced there would be several nuances,

social interactions." For an overview article, see Markus Paulus, "The Emergence of Prosocial Behavior: Why Do Infants and Toddlers Help, Comfort, and Share" (2014) 8 (2) Child Development Perspectives 77–81, discussing four models aiming to explain the emergence of prosocial behavior (emotional contagion and empathic concern, goal alignment, social interactionist accounts and social learning) concluding (at 80) that "different instances of prosocial behavior are likely brought about by different mechanisms."

[115] To say nothing of the ethical issues which could be involved in confronting children with such dilemmas.

[116] Mikhail (n 38) 94 ff.

[117] Consider, for instance, the different percentages for the permissibility of various trolley problem constellations: Mikhail (n 38) 127 figure 6.1(a). When Walter triggering the switch makes "a footbridge overlooking the tracks collapse" and as a side effect kills a man standing on the footbridge (Mikhail n 38 109, scenario 12 "collapse bridge") this is judged to be permissible by almost 70 percent. Contrast this with Victor, who can trigger a switch dropping a heavy object, a man, "into the path of the train ... thereby preventing it from killing the men" (Mikhail n 38 109, scenario 11 "drop man"), judged to be permissible for almost 40 percent. Similarly, for roughly 60 percent of participants it is judged permissible for Oscar to trigger a switch which directs the train to the side track where a heavy object stops the train, with "a man standing on the side track in front of the heavy object with his back turned" (Mikhail n 38 108, scenario 7 "man-in-front"). Mikhail"s explanation rests on whether "the agent's goal presumably is to save the men by causing the train to hit the object but not the man" (Mikhail n 38 126). However, at least to me, it seems that the implausibility of a heavy object, ie a fat man, stopping a train might influence judgment of the permissibility of a certain act to a considerable extent as well. If I am certain that by triggering a switch redirecting a train and thus saving five persons instead of sacrificing one, I could be inclined to judge this rather as morally permissible in comparison with a situation where I have to sacrifice one person for sure by triggering a switch, thus dropping this fat man into the path of the train in order to achieve something which is in reality rather implausible. To be fair, Mikhail is aware of such objections when discussing the "marginal calculus of risk" and, thus, holds that "not all of the variance in these six cases can be explained" with "different utilities of the risk"

such as between how permissible or forbidden it is for Alice (a doctor in another scenario) to save the most seriously injured patient instead of saving five less severely injured persons (who would also die without treatment) in contrast to Frank pushing the fat man onto the track in order to stop the trolley, not to mention the transplantation scenario which asks whether it is permissible to "harvest" Bob and thus kill a perfectly healthy and innocent person who went to see a doctor for a health check, in order to distribute his organs to five different people in need of an organ transplant. While this should not be the main issue in this chapter, I am not entirely convinced by Mikhail's answer regarding the uncertainty criticism.[118] What would happen, for instance, if people were allowed to decide on a scale of one to five when judging the morality of the abovementioned acts? It could be that the results would reflect this uncertainty. To change the focus, another promising interpretation of why people judge differently (and do not use purely utilitarian logic related to how many people they would save) might be trust. I am quite sure that if people were asked to judge whether a certain trolley problem action is permissible or not on a scale of one to five, as suggested, the organ transplant case would be considered far more impermissible than, for instance, a doctor being kept busy saving one seriously injured person instead of five slightly less seriously injured people who would also die without help. To continue further, I think that this modification would quite likely reveal differences, showing that there is no such thing as a moral grammar but that a variety of issues (relevant for moral decisions) are involved that influence the participants' ability to make a decision. Moreover, a different study showed that if people are asked in a foreign language whether they would push the fat man onto the tracks in order to stop the trolley, they answer in the affirmative more than 50 percent more frequently than when asked in their native tongue.[119] And recently the so-called Moral Machine experiment, an online platform where anyone worldwide can make life-or-death decisions about several different characters (women, men, children, the elderly, doctors, homeless persons, and so on), came to the conclusion that there might be some "global moral preferences."[120] However, a critical "comment" on this

(Mikhail n 38 141–144). However, just mentioning other factors that also influence the judgment is not enough. The implausibility of certain highly artificial scenarios is still a worrisome objection, at least to some extent.

[118] Mikhail (n 38) 98 ff.

[119] Albert Costa et al, "Your Morals Depend on Language" (2014) 9 (4) Public Library of Science ONE 1–7.

[120] Edmond Awad et al, "The Moral Machine Experiment" (2018) 563 (7729) Nature 59–64 (60), despite also finding variances along what they coined "cultural clusters" (61).

experiment has shown that the results change considerably if participants are not forced to choose between saving two different subjects, a man or a woman for example, but are also given the possibility of treating both subjects equally.[121] Yet, for the sake of addressing the idea of UMG – in addition to the methodology of trolley problems – I shall continue.

Mikhail is right when he notes it seems clear that in trolley problems, for instance, people know whether a certain act is morally right or wrong but often cannot explain why they think so. This might suggest that their judgment is based unconsciously on certain moral issues. Whether this is because of guiding, innate principles or a moral grammar, however, seems more than questionable.

This somewhat simplified argument regarding the relation between intuitive decisions, as shown by some trolley problems, and the argument for inborn principles/inborn UMG as the only or most plausible explanation for these unconscious decisions is dubious. Whereas unconscious decisions undoubtedly exist, it does not follow automatically that any unconscious behavior has to be innate by default.[122] Joshua Greene, for instance, refers to "genetic transmission, cultural transmission, and learning from personal experience" as the "only mechanisms known to endow human automatic cognitive processes."[123] Rather, humans exhibit many impressive unconscious skills, such as driving cars, riding bicycles and so on, which are incontestably learned rather than innate.[124] And just to foreshadow a categorical argument from the nativist camp: yes, there need to be some innate capabilities that allow us to learn such complex actions. However, instead of taking car driving or bicycle riding to be inborn faculties based on an inborn grammar, these examples make it clear that the inborn preconditions for learning such skills

Cf Edmond Awad et al, "Universals and Variations in Moral Decisions Made in 42 Countries by 70,000 Participants" (2020) 117 (5) Proceedings of the National Academy of Sciences (2332–2337).

[121] See Yochanan E Bigman and Kurt Gray, "Life and Death Decisions of Autonomous Vehicles" (2020) 549 (7797) Nature E1–E2. For a discussion of both studies, see Norbert Paulo, Leonie Möck and Lando Kirchmair, "The Use and Abuse of Moral Preferences in the Ethics of Self-Driving Cars" in Fernando Aguiar, Antonio Gaitán and Hugo Viciana (eds) *Experiments in Moral and Political Philosophy* (Routledge 2024) 290–309.

[122] Joshua D Greene, "Beyond Point-and-Shoot Morality: Why Cognitive (Neuro)Science Matters for Ethics" (2014) 124 (4) Ethics 695–726 (698): "automatic settings need not be 'innate' or 'hardwired.'"

[123] Greene (n 122) 714.

[124] Churchland (n 84) 10: "Moral values need not involve rules, though they sometimes do; they need not be explicitly stated, but may be implicitly picked up by children learning to get along in their social world, just as they implicitly pick up how to keep a fire going or how to tend goats."

are highly abstract and difficult to grasp, let alone to categorize.[125] Most reasonably innate properties are better understood as a specific abstract human learning capability.[126] And only in a second step can we try to trace back specific human actions to certain innate capabilities, which must not always directly correlate with the unconscious behavior.

In this regard, it is striking to see that Mikhail himself admits that UMG must be "triggered," which at least indicates a sort of undetermined – and possibly undeterminable – difference between the abstract inborn capability and its expression (still within the realm of the (moral) competence).[127] Interestingly, Kahneman's metaphor explaining the functioning of the human brain with the symbolic picture of two systems might well illustrate the point made here.[128] Fast, intuitive thinking can do many astonishing things, albeit not without making some errors, which might be corrected by the other type of slow, rational and conscious thinking. This is just to indicate that quite a few things in life are done unconsciously, which does not mean that all this behavior is innate behavior by default. Take, for example, trained sportsmen, who improve their ability by training for such a long time until they just act without "thinking."

5.3.3.3.2 Criticism of the Argument of the Poverty of the (Moral) Stimulus Mikhail admits that his "argument is not conclusive ... and more research is needed to clarify the relevant conceptual and evidentiary issues."[129] I take this opportunity to address what I think is another methodological deficiency of Mikhail's research, which he deems to be promising for further investigations of a UMG. Even though he admits some uncertainties regarding his hypothesis, he still claims that "'it suffices' to note the novelty and unboundedness of moral judgment." This "attempt at *scientific* explanation," which does not rule out alternative explanations, as Mikhail states, "claim[s] only to be [a] more reasonable or adequate explanation ... of a given body of evidence than [its] rivals."[130] In my eyes, this approach includes a forbidden shift of the burden of proof, which Mikhail indirectly introduces

[125] This difficulty strengthens the criticism voiced above in Section 5.3.3.

[126] Joshua D Greene and Jonathan Haidt, "How (and Where) Does Moral Judgment Work?" (2002) 6 (12) Trends in Cognitive Sciences 517–523 (519), who argue for a human capacity as a "sophisticated abstract reasoning that can be applied to any subject matter." See also Churchland (n 84) 22, who points out that "[w]hat is stunning about humans is how easily we learn such a vast range of things, things that, given the culture, we would not have had an opportunity to learn 200,000 years ago."

[127] Mikhail (n 38) 88.

[128] Daniel Kahneman, *Thinking, Fast and Slow* (Penguin 2012).

[129] Mikhail (n 69) 176.

[130] Mikhail (n 38) 68–69 citing Rawls (n 20) 46.

with this argument. If we cannot explain every single instance of moral decision making, he suggests, this is because the unexplainable instances for us, such as unintentional moral decisions in the trolley problems, must simply be innate. Interestingly, Chomsky puts this argument on the poverty of the stimulus of linguistics a bit differently. He says that we *know*; it must thus be evidently clear that we cannot explain how, for instance, children know why some phrases are grammatically correct and some are wrong.[131] Put differently, according to Chomsky the very little information children have cannot account for their astonishing capability to sense what sentences are grammatically correct or wrong. If we can definitively rule out that there is no possible alternative explanation, then, and only then, does this suggest a universal grammar. Yet I am quite convinced that no such certainty beyond any reasonable doubt exists for moral judgments. There is no way to reasonably exclude with certainty that people – or young children – cannot have acquired such a deep knowledge of moral rules in the short time since they were born.[132] Scientifically speaking, we cannot (yet) rule out definitively that in the first three years of their lives, these children could not have acquired this differentiation by learning from others.[133]

For this reason, I cannot help but think of the argument of the "poverty of the moral stimulus" as an equivalent to or replacement of an early nativist

[131] Chomsky (n 37) 58: "It seems plain that language acquisition is based on the child's discovery of what from a formal point of view is a deep and abstract theory – a generative grammar of his language – many of the concepts and principles of which are only remotely related to experience by long and intricate chains of quasi-inferential steps. A consideration of the character of the grammar that is acquired, the degenerate quality and narrowly limited extent of the available data, the striking uniformity of the resulting grammars, and their independence of intelligence, motivation, and emotional state, over wide ranges of variation, leave little hope that much of the structure of the language can be learned by an organism initially uninformed as to its general character." Cf Fiona Cowie, "Innateness and Language" in Edward N Zalta (ed) *Stanford Encyclopedia of Philosophy* (January 16, 2008), available at http://plato.stanford.edu/entries/innateness-language/ [last accessed February 1, 2023] with further illustrating examples and explanations. Just for the sake of clarification, I want to stress that I am not dealing with the question of whether this argumentation works for language acquisition here. See Stephen Laurence and Eric Margolis, "The Poverty of the Stimulus Argument" (2001) 52 (2) British Journal for the Philosophy of Science 217–276 (221): "the general idea behind the Poverty of the Stimulus Argument is clear. It is that the knowledge acquired in language acquisition far outstrips the information that is available in the environment … or as philosophers sometimes put it, the output of the language acquisition process is radically underdetermined by the input."

[132] See again Greene and Haidt (n 126) 519 and Churchland (n 84) 22, who rather emphasize the capacity to learn new tasks quickly (instead of an inborn capacity).

[133] See Jesse J Prinz, "Is Morality Innate?" in Walter Sinnot-Armstrong (ed) *Moral Psychology. Evolution of Morality: Adaptations and Innateness Vol I* (MIT Press 2007) 367–406 (391–395), giving further alternative examples for prima facie universal moral behavior.

argument. Some things that are as astonishing as young children showing impressive skills regarding moral judgments thus seem unexplainable (in our case with such behavioral, empirical arguments as acquiring fundamental moral knowledge by learning) such that the unique plausible explanation which remains is their innateness. To put it slightly more provocatively, UMG seems to be compensation for the "God made" argument of earlier times.

5.3.3.4 "Is the Whole Greater than the Sum of Its Parts?" Methodological Issues with Interdisciplinary Arguments

Now, finally, I would like to address how Mikhail draws conclusions from various research fields. He puts it this way:

> None of this evidence [coming from developmental and social psychology, experimental philosophy, ethology, cognitive neuroscience, comparative linguistics, deontic logic, legal anthropology and comparative law] is conclusive, and all of it is open to competing interpretations. Collectively, however, this evidence provides considerable support for the innate and universal moral capacities presupposed by many leading human rights instruments.[134]

This argument reminds me of the well-known phrase that "the whole is greater than the sum of its parts," the sense of which has already been questioned within the discipline of "Gestalt psychology."[135] If each individual discipline cannot come to a robust conclusion regarding UMG, why should we be able to outweigh the doubts and criticisms raised within the borders of each discipline by adding up the evidence? What is the reason that only supportive indications are to be added up, but not doubts and criticisms? I am convinced that in fact the opposite is true. Using results from one discipline in another, leading to multidisciplinary and interdisciplinary findings, is very promising and is maybe the easiest way in science to enhance knowledge. This is because if, for instance, a problem we have been confronted with for only a short time in one discipline has been investigated in

[134] Mikhail (n 69) 174. For a slightly more cautious wording, see Mikhail (n 38) 104: "Initial evidence for this basic approach comes from multiple sources, including developmental psychology, comparative linguistics, legal anthropology, and cognitive neuroscience. While none of this evidence is univocal or conclusive, collectively it provides at least modest support for the hypothesis that humans possess an innate moral faculty that is analogous, at least in some respects, to the language faculty postulated by Chomsky and other linguists."

[135] See Kurt Koffka's early criticism in *Principles of Gestalt Psychology* (Harcourt-Brace 1935) 176: "It has been said: The whole is more than the sum of its parts. It is more correct to say that the whole is something else than the sum of its parts, because summing up is a meaningless procedure, whereas the whole-part relationship is meaningful."

another discipline for quite some time already, we can draw on those findings without doing all the work again. However, this does not come without cost. Different disciplines are different in relation to the presuppositions they are constructed on and they also differ regarding the methodology used to achieve meaningful results. In order to transplant research findings from one discipline into another we have to ensure that we fulfil the standards of both disciplines in order, for instance, not to conflate presuppositions, methodology or definitions from one discipline in an inconsistent manner with those of another discipline. If we do not do that, to stay within the transplant metaphor, the body's immune system will reject the new organ. To transfer knowledge safely from one discipline to another, quality – that is, methodological tests – from both disciplines must be fulfilled. In our case here, for instance, the methodology used in the field of neurobiology must be applied correctly and the tests in this field must be fulfilled almost uncontestably (and not summed up collectively). In other words, the decision as to whether something seems to be valid knowledge within one field must be clear before its findings are transferred to other fields. The same applies to evolutionary psychology or anthropology in relation to the question of whether "facts" – that is, results established in those fields – are valid knowledge to be used (trustworthily) within another research discipline. Moreover, even if the benchmarks of those original fields are fulfilled, they need to stand the test of the discipline they are intended to be transplanted to.

Thus, in brief, adding up results (so that the whole is more than the sum of its parts) does not work if the results themselves do not represent secure knowledge and therefore do not suffice to make a convincing argument in their original field.

5.4 BRIDGING NATIVISM AND BEHAVIORISM: (INNATE) INTERSUBJECTIVITY

So far, I have suggested some objections to innate UMG, including Mikhail's problematic interdisciplinary account favorably interpreting research results for UMG from various scientific disciplines. Tomasello and Vaish, for instance, "speculate" about the origins of human cooperation and morality, and their most educated guess is that, rather than an innate moral grammar, the special human "norm-based morality," as they call it, is acquired by learning while living in complex cultural environments.[136] They understand

[136] Michael Tomasello and Amrisha Vaish, "Origins of Human Cooperation and Morality" (2013) 64 Annual Review of Psychology 231–255.

human cooperation and morality as a two-step process. The first step, which humans share with nonhuman great apes, is "mutualistic collaboration and prosocially motivated interactions with specific other individuals."[137] Only the second step, which constitutes a "more abstract, agent-neutral, norm-based morality,"[138] is uniquely human.

This second step – and this is important for the reasoning behind this chapter – is explained within the frame of human ontogenesis. "[L]arge-scale cultural worlds full of impersonal and mutually known conventions, norms, and institutions" are, according to Tomasello and Vaish, the reason for the development of norm-based morality.[139] The second step starts roughly at the age of three and their best guess is that "human teaching" and quite likely "cooperative breeding," also in contrast to nonhuman great apes, are mainly responsible for the development of this "norm-based morality."[140] Tomasello and Vaish call this the "interdependence hypothesis": quite likely a change in their environment forced humans to respond, which they did with a special "group-mindedness."[141] This is "underlain by skills of collective intentionality, [which] engendered truly im-personal, agent-neutral, objective social norms."[142] To put it differently, according to Tomasello and Vaish, the important point is what the significant reasons are for the "ontogenetic origins of human morality." For them, the development of a "second-person morality" (which humans share with nonhuman great apes) towards the "norm-based morality" (uniquely human, and decisive in our case) happens mainly because "young children are born into a cultural world already full of all kinds of moral norms and institutions."[143] Just to be clear, the point is not to give weight to a purely behavioral explanation of the origins of human morality. However, that abstract thing we call "morality" is quite likely not "hardwired" as such into the human mind/brain but is best understood as a complex interplay between inborn and learned features. How to measure or determine the exact weighting between the two is still unknown in relation to

[137] Tomasello and Vaish (n 136) 232.
[138] Tomasello and Vaish (n 136) 232.
[139] Tomasello and Vaish (n 136) 232 and 250.
[140] Tomasello and Vaish (n 136) 238, with reference to Sarah Blaffer Hrdy, *Mothers and Others* (Harvard University Press 2009); Gergely Csibra and György Gergely, "Natural Pedagogy" (2009) 13 (4) Trends in Cognitive Sciences 148–153; see also Colwyn Trevarthen and Jonathan Delafield-Butt, "Biology of Shared Meaning and Language Development: Regulating the Life of Narratives" in Maria Legerstee, David W Haley and Marc H Bornstein (eds) *The Infant Mind: Origins of the Social Brain* (Guilford Press 2013) 167–199 (181).
[141] Tomasello and Vaish (n 136) 239.
[142] Tomasello and Vaish (n 136) 239.
[143] Tomasello and Vaish (n 136) 240 ff and 250.

morality.[144] However, a lot points towards the conclusion that as there is no such thing as a "car driving grammar," there is quite likely also no such thing as a UMG.[145] Yet Tomasello and Vaish, using the "logic of overjustification," suggest that "young children's motivation to help is intrinsic and not dependent on concrete extrinsic rewards, and indeed it is undermined by such rewards."[146]

Hence, Tomasello and Vaish are also interested in the nature/nurture debate:

> One question that arises is what contributes to the ontogenetic shift from a second-personal to a norm-based morality. A part of the answer certainly lies in social-cognitive development: In order to engage in a norm-based morality, children must move from seeing individuals and social interactions purely in interpersonal terms to additionally seeing all individuals from an agent-neutral or bird's-eye perspective. They must also develop the capacity to see themselves as individuals just like all other individuals, to evaluate their own behavior, and to understand that others evaluate them in the same way that they evaluate others.[147]

5.4.1 *Intuitions and the Supposed Impossibility of Unconscious Rule-Following*

UMG bases a major claim of its innateness thesis on the observation that humans are "intuitive lawyers" and make moral judgments partly unconsciously. Not only UMG but also various other approaches to morality point to intuitions and emotions as major driving forces.[148] A challenging objection to such claims is the "impossibility" of unconscious norm obedience.

[144] Churchland (n 84) 22; Patricia S Churchland, "The Neurobiological Platform for Moral Values" (2014) 151 Behaviour 283–296 (293).

[145] For an instructive illustration of the process of learning to drive "automatically," see Charles Duhigg, *The Power of Habit: Why We Do What We Do in Life and Business* (Random House 2012) 19–20.

[146] Tomasello and Vaish (n 136) 240–241, with reference to Mark R Lepper, David Greene and Richard E Nisbett, "Undermining Children's Intrinsic Interest with Extrinsic Rewards: A Test of the 'Overjustification' Hypothesis" (1973) 28 (1) Journal of Personality & Social Psychology 129–137.

[147] Tomasello and Vaish (n 136) 250, with reference to Thomas Nagel, *The View from Nowhere* (Oxford University Press 1989).

[148] See eg Jesse J Prinz, *The Emotional Construction of Morals* (Oxford University Press 2008).

Patterson holds that "[i]t is difficult to see how these normative activities are possible when we are unconscious of the existence of the rule."[149] He identifies two problems connected with the idea of

> explain[ing] moral cognition with the claim that the mind follows rules by unconsciously interpreting their requirements in particular cases. The first involves the claim that to understand what a rule requires we need to interpret it. The second involves the claim that "following a rule" is something a person does "unconsciously." Neither of these claims makes sense; and, lacking sense, neither is amenable to empirical testing (that is, experiment).[150]

As a consequence, for him

> [t]he distinction between correct and incorrect rule-following is a matter of community agreement in judgments over time. If Wittgenstein is correct, then the idea of unconscious rule-following is nonsensical. Following a rule, making judgments about what a rule requires, and the very idea of normativity itself require a role for others in the intersubjective constitution of norms of correctness.[151]

This criticism connects to the research results and the accompanying interpretation of psychologists such as Michael Tomasello, who argue that the specific human "norm-based morality" springs from human cohabitation (instead of an inborn faculty or grammar). An account arguing that our rule-following capacity rests in social practice could thus rely on the contention that unconscious rule-following (the case when people know something is definitely morally wrong, but cannot explain why or differ significantly in their reasoning) is simply a very well-trained social practice.

[149] Patterson (n 91) 619. Patterson further says: "Of course, we may act in a manner *consistent* with a rule. But that is not to say that we are following the rule, for to do that would require that we do all the things I just mentioned. Thus Mikhail's claim that a person follows a rule unconsciously is untenable" [emphasis original] cf Michael S Pardo and Dennis Patterson, *Minds, Brains, and Law: The Conceptual Foundations of Law and Neuroscience* (Oxford University Press 2013) 14.

[150] Patterson (n 91) 615–616. Patterson continues by pointing at the "infinite regress" argument, relying on Wittgenstein. By doubting "understanding" a rule means "interpreting" it, "rule-following" as a "mental phenomenon" is questioned as such (Patterson n 91 617–618, with reference to Ludwig Wittgenstein, *Philosophical Investigations* (translated by G E M Anscombe 2nd ed Blackwell 1958) §§ 139–242). Succinctly, Patterson (n 91) 618: "the agreement of rule-followers over time is the ground of understanding. … This harmony in reaction and application is constitutive of all practices, including legal practice. It is the basis of our legal judgments."

[151] Patterson (n 91) 618.

However, was rule-following as a social practice not confronted with Mahlmann's insight such that even Wittgenstein has to presuppose a sort of internal, subjective consciousness of rule-following?[152] Unconscious rule-following must not necessarily be "accidental" rule-following in the sense that a certain behavior was by coincidence identical to what a certain rule required. Rule-following is nonsensical when we are not aware of the rule at all. Nevertheless, it is conceivable that we possess or have developed an unconscious drive or need to act in a certain way, for instance because we were conditioned in this way or it is hardwired in our mind/brain. For either alternative, such a process might well be unconscious. Is there thus space for an unconscious innate UMG? I still answer this question in the negative. Tomasello and Vaish's interpretation seems more cautious and reasonable and is in line with Churchland's description.[153] Yet Mahlmann's criticism of Wittgenstein seems to be thorough. A prudent attempt to describe this process might be an understanding of an innate abstract human capacity to understand the beliefs of others, sharing intentions and the like.[154] Thus, we are well advised to seek a more abstract, more fundamental biological setup instead of looking for a "moral gene." A more promising approach seems to start at the bottom when thinking of which features are innate or not. That is to say, we had better not take such an advanced concept as morality, which is a highly controversial construct, to frame the search for our inborn features in the natural sciences.[155] If we want to understand these innate

[152] See text above at n 98.

[153] Tomasello and Vaish (n 136).

[154] This is already shown by toddlers at the age of twelve to eighteen months (see Tomasello et al (n 112); Onishi and Baillargeon (n 111) 255–258; Buttelmann, Carpenter and Tomasello (n 111); Buttelmann et al (n 111). But this understanding is, of course, open to further research, refinement and even reevaluation. Cf Churchland's (n 84) 11 understanding of morality. At this stage it is important to highlight that it is still disputed whether those young children can understand beliefs, or whether it is something much less sophisticated, such as learning behavior rules without any representation of mental states. See, for instance, Sophie J Milward, Sotaro Kita and Ian A Apperly, "The Development of Co-Representation Effects in a Joint Task: Do Children Represent a Co-Actor?" (2014) 132 (3) Cognition 269–279; Sophie J Milward, Sotaro Kita and Ian A Apperly, "Individual Differences in Children's Corepresentation of Self and Other in Joint Action" (2017) 88 (3) Child Development 964–978. For an overview of the mental state research and different explanations, see Jason Low and Josef Perner, "Implicit and Explicit Theory of Mind: State of the Art" (2012) 30 (1) British Journal of Developmental Psychology 1–13. See also the two-systems theory by Ian Apperly and Stephen Butterfill, "Do Humans Have Two Systems to Track Beliefs and Belief-Like States?" (2009) 116 Psychological Review 953–970, which argues that the evidence for early understanding of beliefs is not the same as for what older children understand. I am grateful to Sophie Milward for drawing my attention to this.

[155] If we do so, we also have to confront findings suggesting that nonhuman great apes are also able to understand other beings (even humans!) beliefs. See David Buttelmann et al, "Great

preconditions for developing morality and rule-following, we should investigate in depth what could be cautiously conceived of as a sort of innate intersubjectivity of human beings.

5.4.2 *Intersubjectivity*

Colwyn Trevarthen, for instance, has spoken for many years about an "innate intersubjective sympathy that an alert infant can show shortly after birth."[156] His standpoint on intersubjectivity relies on intentions and emotions as causal preconditions for shared experience of referential signs;[157] he argues that

Apes Distinguish True from False Beliefs in an Interactive Helping Task" (2017) 12 (4) PLoS ONE.

[156] Colwyn Trevarthen, "What Is It Like to Be a Person Who Knows Nothing? Defining the Active Intersubjective Mind of a Newborn Human Being" (2011) 20 (1) Infant and Child Development 119–135 (119); see Colwyn Trevarthen and Penelope Hubley, "Secondary Intersubjectivity: Confidence, Confiding and Acts of Meaning in the First Year" in Andrew Lock (ed) *Action, Gesture and Symbol* (Academic Press 1978) 183–229; Colwyn Trevarthen, "Communication and Cooperation in Early Infancy. A Description of Primary Intersubjectivity" in Margaret Bullowa (ed) *Before Speech: The Beginning of Human Communication* (Cambridge University Press 1979) 321–347; Colwyn Trevarthen, "Development of Intersubjective Motor Control in Infants" in Michael G Wade and H T A Whiting (eds) *Motor Development in Children: Aspects of Coordination and Control* (Martinus Nijhof 1986) 209–261; Colwyn Trevarthen, "The Concept and Foundations of Infant Intersubjectivity" in Stein Bråten (ed) *Intersubjective Communication and Emotion in Early Ontogeny* (Cambridge University Press 1998) 15–46; Colwyn Trevarthen, "The Neurobiology of Early Communication: Intersubjective Regulations in Human Brain Development" in Alex Fedde Kalverboer and Albert Gramsbergen (eds) *Handbook on Brain and Behavior in Human Development* (Kluwer 2001) 841–882; Colwyn Trevarthen and Ken Aitken, "Infant Intersubjectivity: Research, Theory, and Clinical Applications" (2001) 42 (1) Journal of Child Psychology and Psychiatry 3–48; Colwyn Trevarthen, "First Things First: Infants Make Good Use of the Sympathetic Rhythm of Imitation, Without Reason or Language" (2005) 31 (1) Journal of Child Psychotherapy 91–113; Colwyn Trevarthen, "The Intersubjective Psychobiology of Human Meaning: Learning of Culture Depends on Interest for Co-Operative Practical Work and Affection for the Joyful Art of Good Company" (2009) 19 Psychoanalytic Dialogues 507–518; Colwyn Trevarthen, "Embodied Human Intersubjectivity: Imaginative Agency, to Share Meaning" (2012) 4 (1) Cognitive Semiotics 6–56; Trevarthen and Delafield-Butt (n 140); Colwyn Trevarthen, Maya Gratier and Nigel Osborne, "The Human Nature of Culture and Education" (2014) 5 (2) Cognitive Science 173–192; Colwyn Trevarthen and Jonathan Delafield-Butt, "Intersubjectivity in the Imagination and Feelings of the Infant: Implications for Education in the Early Years" in E Jayne White and Carmen Dalli (eds) *Under-Three Year Olds in Policy and Practice* (Springer 2017) 17–39; for a schematic overview see Colwyn Trevarthen and Jon-Roar Bjørkvold, "Life for Learning. How a Young Child Seeks Joy with Companions in a Meaningful World" in Darcia Narvaez et al (eds) *Contexts for Young Child Flourishing: Evolution, Family, and Society* (Oxford University Press 2016) 28–60 (46).

[157] And, hence, the work of Walter J Freeman, "Nonlinear Brain Dynamics and Intention According to Aquinas" (2008) 6 (2) Mind and Matter 207–234; Jaap Panksepp, "At the

infants are capable of "intentional and emotional factors of meaning making."[158] Along with Reddy,[159] Trevarthen holds that "[b]asic complex emotions are evident in accurate descriptions of how infants know our minds."[160] Narvaez, too, is convinced that "emotions, cognitions, and behaviors are linked" and emotion and cognition co-occur and even co-develop.[161] Trevarthen and his colleagues base their arguments on various sources, such as the prenatal development of the embryo,[162] as well as on observations of newborn infants and their emotional expressions. According to them, attempts to imitate "reveal that the infant is being intentional."[163] According to

Interface between the Affective, Behavioral and Cognitive Neurosciences: Decoding the Emotional Feelings of the Brain" (2003) 52 (1) Brain and Cognition 4–14; Jaap Panksepp and Colwyn Trevarthen, "The Neuroscience of Emotion in Music" in Stephen Malloch and Colwyn Trevarthen (eds) *Communicative Musicality: Exploring the Basis of Human Companionship* (Oxford University Press 2009) 105–146.

158 Trevarthen and Delafield-Butt (n 140) 169, 181; cf Colwyn Trevarthen, "The Generation of Human Meaning: How Shared Experience Grows in Infancy" in Alex Seemann (ed) *Joint Attention: New Developments in Philosophy, Psychology, and Neuroscience* (MIT Press 2011) 73–135; Trevarthen (n 156) What Is It Like to Be a Person Who Knows Nothing? 123; Colwyn Trevarthen, "How Control of Movements Develops" in H T A Whiting (ed) *Human Motor Actions: Bernstein Reassessed* (Elsevier 1984) 223–261.

159 Vasu Reddy, *How Infants Know Minds* (Harvard University Press 2008).

160 Trevarthen (n 156) What Is It Like to Be a Person Who Knows Nothing?

161 Darcia Narvaez, *Neurobiology and the Development of Human Morality. Evolution, Culture, and Wisdom* (W W Norton & Company 2014) 39–41, with reference to Stanley Greenspan and Stuart Shanker, *The First Idea* (Da Capo Press 2004).

162 Trevarthen and Delafield-Butt (n 140) 214; Colwyn Trevarthen, Jonathan Delafield-Butt and Benjamin Schögler, "Psychobiology of Musical Gesture: Innate Rhythm, Harmony and Melody in Movements of Narration" in Anthony Gritten and Elaine King (eds) *Music and Gesture II* (Ashgate 2011) 11–43; Trevarthen (n 156) What Is It Like to Be a Person Who Knows Nothing? 126–129; Trevarthen (n 156) The Intersubjective Psychobiology of Human Meaning; Trevarthen and Aitken (n 156) 6–8.

163 Trevarthen and Delafield-Butt (n 140) 173, with further reference to Heidelise Als, "Social Interaction: Dynamic Matrix for Developing Behavioral Organization" in Ina Č Užgiris (ed) *Social Interaction During Infancy: New Directions for Child Development Vol 4* (Jossey-Bass 1979) 21–39; T Berry Brazelton, "Evidence of Communication During Neonatal Behavioural Assessment" in Margaret Bullowa (ed) *Before Speech: The Beginning of Human Communication* (Cambridge University Press 1979) 79–88; T Berry Brazelton and J Kevin Nuget, *The Neonatal Behavioral Assessment Scale* (Mac Keith Press 1995); Emese Nagy and Peter Molnár, "Homo Imitans or Homo Provocans? Human Imprinting Model of Neonatal Imitation" (2004) 27 (1) Infant Behavior and Development 54–63; Emese Nagy, "Innate Intersubjectivity: Newborns' Sensitivity to Communication Disturbance" (2008) 44 (6) Developmental Psychology 1779–1784; Emese Nagy, "The Newborn Infant: A Missing Stage in Developmental Psychology" (2011) 20 (1) Infant and Child Development 3–19. Trevarthen and Delafield-Butt (n 140) 180 hold furthermore that "[b]abies are born with many 'anticipatory adaptations for cultural learning,' of which a capacity for joint attention to share consciousness of objects is just one and not the earliest or most beguiling" [references omitted] As well as Trevarthen and Delafield-Butt (n 140) 182: "The cortical tissue for cultural

Trevarthen and Delafield-Butt, "[t]he infant wants an exchange, is seeking imitative dialogue, and is responding with emotions that evaluate a 'good' exchange, one that is courteously timed and intimately shared. This proves that a human child does not need to learn how to communicate 'thoughtfully' in a human way."[164] The authors are aware of remaining uncertainties and ascribe them to still lacking technology for studying pre- and postnatal child development in detail.[165] With reference to earlier work,[166] they nevertheless hold that

> [r]esearch on the coordination and regulation of infants' body movements and on engagements between infants and parents proves that human beings are born with *subjectivity*, or coherent self-awareness in movement, and a drive for *intersubjectivity*, or cooperation in intimate coordination with other persons. The movements of the two partners become affectively attuned to one another as they respond in a reciprocal exchange.[167]

Similarly, Rochat holds that "immediately after birth, infants are capable of demonstrating already a sense of their own body as a differentiated entity: an entity among other entities in the environment."[168] Hence, newborns do not have zero self-awareness, but are able to differentiate themselves from the

learning can be changed and functions can be increased, relocated, or weakened by experience, but how the human brain grows before birth, and what infants can do shortly after they are born, shows that basic rules – for object perception, for purposeful movement, and for motive states that construct time and space for action and that might become conscious of other bodies and their behaviours – all begin their differentiation without benefit of experience, and they have a program of development that expects human company. This program is laid down in the core of the brain in association with systems of autonomic self-regulation."

[164] Trevarthen and Delafield-Butt (n 140) 173.

[165] Trevarthen and Delafield-Butt (n 140) 185.

[166] Trevarthen (n 156) Communication and Cooperation in Early Infancy; Trevarthen (n 158) How Control of Movements Develops; Trevarthen (n 156) Development of Intersubjective Motor Control in Infants; Colwyn Trevarthen, "Form, Significance and Psychological Potential of Hand Gestures of Infants" in Jean-Luc Nespoulous, Paul Perron and André Roch Lecours (eds) *The Biological Foundation of Gestures: Motor and Semiotic Aspects* (Erlbaum 1986) 149–202.

[167] Trevarthen and Delafield-Butt (n 140) 189 [emphasis original] with reference to Daniel N Stern, *The Interpersonal World of the Infant. A View from Psychoanalysis and Development Psychology* (Basic Books 1985); cf Philippe Rochat, Cláudia Passos-Ferreira and Pedro Salem, "Three Levels of Intersubjectivity in Early Development" in Antonella Carassa, Francesca Morganti and Giuseppe Riva (eds) *Enacting Intersubjectivity. Paving the Way for a Dialogue between Cognitive Science, Social Cognition and Neuroscience* (Da Larioprint 2009) 173–190.

[168] Philippe Rochat, "Five Levels of Self-Awareness as They Unfold Early in Life" (2003) 12 Consciousness and Cognition 717–731 (722).

world around them.[169] They show the "creative experience of being alone with the feelings of the body." The newborn is thus a self-explorer who reflectively engages with his or her own body.[170] In Trevarthen and Delafield-Butt's parlance, this is labeled "subjectivity,"[171] which is a necessary precondition for intersubjectivity. If I do not have any sense of my subjectivity, I cannot relate to other subjects in a meaningful way. Following Trevarthen, Reddy,[172] Rochat,[173] and Legrain and colleagues[174] it seems reasonable to take for granted a sense of subjectivity necessary for engaging in first intersubjective relations. Further development of children and thus the development of intersubjectivity is, however, a process in flux. "The baby becomes increasingly demonstrative, seductive and self-conscious as 'self–other' awareness grows."[175] Capturing this process with clear categories is therefore a difficult task. Nevertheless, we have to work with categories and labels. Hence, the goal is to be as precise as possible when aiming at correctly attributing scientific facts of major shifts in children's development to meaningful categories and labels.

Trevarthen classifies intersubjectivity into three major steps, beginning with "primary intersubjectivity," which he used to denote affective, dyadic interactions with others that are very likely to be considered innate features of newborns.[176] Neonates, who "adjust their behavior according to the social responsiveness of their interaction partner," underpin that assumption.[177] The fact that infants differentiate between animate and inanimate objects as well as between biological and nonbiological movement further points to early intersubjectivity.[178] "Turn-taking contingency,"[179] which has been shown by six- to eight-week-old infants, who prefer live video exchanges with their mothers to

[169] Rochat (n 168) 722–723.

[170] Trevarthen (n 156) What Is It Like to Be a Person Who Knows Nothing? 130.

[171] Trevarthen and Delafield-Butt (n 140) 189.

[172] Reddy (n 159).

[173] Rochat (n 168).

[174] Leon Legrain, Axel Cleeremans and Arnaud Destrebecqz, "Distinguishing Three Levels in Explicit Self-Awareness" (2011) 20 (3) Consciousness and Cognition 578–585.

[175] Jonathan Delafield-Butt and Colwyn Trevarthen, "Theories of the Development of Human Communication" in Paul Cobley and Peter J Schultz (eds) *Theories and Models of Communication* (Mouton De Gruyter 2013) 199–222 (211).

[176] Trevarthen (n 156) Communication and Cooperation in Early Infancy.

[177] Nagy (n 163) Innate Intersubjectivity 1779.

[178] Vincent M Reid and Tricia Striano, "The Directed Attention Model of Infant Social Cognition" (2007) 4 (1) European Journal of Developmental Psychology 100–110.

[179] Lynne Murray and Colwyn Trevarthen, "Emotional Regulation of Interactions between Two-Month-Olds and their Mothers" in Tiffany M Field and Nathan A Fox (eds) *Social Perception in Infants* (Ablex 1985) 177–197.

videotaped exchanges, strongly underpins this assumption. Hence, contingent exchange with their mothers is preferred to videotaped images of the mother, and thus preferred over nonresponsive exchange, which does not take the infants' (re)action into account. Rochat and Striano also speak of intersubjectivity due to an "innate sensitivity to social stimuli" as well as a "sense of shared experience and reciprocity with others."[180] Further support comes from neonates' preference "to look at a face with open eyes as opposed to a face with closed eyes."[181] Finally, primary intersubjectivity strongly relates to the concept of "protoconversations," which begin at around two months.[182] Even though Michael Tomasello opted for a more demanding understanding of intersubjectivity,[183] Trevarthen's approach finds increasing attention and approval.[184] After all, also for Tomasello, "these early interactions are deeply social in that they have emotional content and turn-taking structure."[185]

180 Phillipe Rochat and Tricia Striano, "Social-Cognitive Development in the First Year" in Philippe Rochat (ed) *Early Social Cognition: Understanding Others in the First Months of Life* (Lawrence Erlbaum 1999) 3–34 (4).

181 Gergely Csibra, "Recognizing Communicative Intentions" (2010) 25 (2) Infancy, Mind and Language 141–168 (144).

182 Mary C Bateson, "The Epigenesis of Conversational Interaction: A Personal Account of Research Development" in Margaret Bullowa (ed) *Before Speech: The Beginning of Human Communication* (Cambridge University Press 1979) 63–77 (65); cf Delafield-Butt and Trevarthen (n 175) 211; Trevarthen and Delafield-Butt (n 140) 174; Trevarthen (n 156) What Is It Like to Be a Person Who Knows Nothing? 129; cf Csibra (n 181) 148, speaking of "motherese" as the "prosody of infant-directed speech."

183 Michael Tomasello, *The Cultural Origins of Human Cognition* (Harvard University Press 1999) 59–62.

184 See, for instance, Narvaez (n 161) 87: "Expressive body signs develop before speech, from proto-conversations of 'primary intersubjectivity' and 'cooperative awareness' with protolanguage by the end of the first year" (with reference to Trevarthen and Hubley (n 156) 183–229; Penelope Hubley and Colwyn Trevarthen, "Sharing a Task in Infancy" (1979) 4 Social Interaction during Infancy: New Directions for Child Development 57–80. See also Narvaez (n 161 44): "Indeed, at birth infants are ready for intersubjectivity, which develops into the capacity for joint attention by about ten months." Compare also Daniel N Stern, *The Interpersonal World of the Infant. A View from Psychoanalysis and Developmental Psychology* (Basic Books 1st paperback ed 2000) nxxii, who states that: "[i]n light of new evidence of other-centered participation shown by infants in their many forms of imitation, as well as the new findings on mirror neurons and adaptive oscillators, I am now convinced that early forms of intersubjectivity exist almost from the beginning of life." Recent pieces of evidence "suggest that, probably from the beginning of life, infants have the capacity for what Bråten (1998) terms altero-centric participation or what Trevarthen has long called primary intersubjectivity" (xx). See also Rochat, Passos-Ferreira and Salem (n 167) 173–190, as well as Dan Zahavi, *Self and Other: Exploring Subjectivity, Empathy, and Shame* (Oxford University Press 2014) 232–233, n 17.

185 Tomasello (n 183) 59.

Starting at around nine months, infants make a remarkable developmental leap. They start including objects in their intersubjective relations. "Secondary intersubjectivity" captures this shift in "cooperative awareness."[186] This significant increase in awareness of what others are doing boils down to rising intention and pleasure at knowing, deriving from how other persons deal with objects.[187] Hence, "a cooperative 'person–person–object' awareness comes into being," which is also reflected by parents and others in the manner of engaging and talking to the child.[188] Similarly, Selby and Bradley speak of a "general relational capacity," which comprises the interaction of trios of six- to nine-month-olds as well as the dyadic engagement of infants.[189] When tasks become shared at around nine months, this constitutes a true "turning point."[190] In other words, triadic joint attention, the capacity to include an object or subject in the dyadic relation between two subjects, enters the stage. Joint attention "turns a mutually experienced event into an *interaction*, into something joint."[191] This "awareness of attending together"[192] is constituted either by "interpersonally coordinated affective states"[193] building on the capacity "to adopt the bodily anchored psychological stance of another person"[194] or "via communication."[195]

[186] Trevarthen and Hubley (n 156); Trevarthen (n 156) The Intersubjective Psychobiology of Human Meaning 512.

[187] Trevarthen and Hubley (n 156).

[188] Trevarthen (n 186) The Intersubjective Psychobiology of Human Meaning 512.

[189] Jane M Selby and Ben S Bradley, "Infants in Groups: A Paradigm for the Study of Early Social Experience" (2003) 46 (4) Human Development 197–221.

[190] Delafield-Butt and Trevarthen (n 175) 211–212; Trevarthen (n 186) The Intersubjective Psychobiology of Human Meaning 512; see also Tomasello (n 183) 61: "The Nine-Month Revolution"; see also Zahavi (n 184) 231. However, for a brief discussion on the controversy of when joint attention "kicks in," see Zahavi (n 184 232–233), with reference to Reddy (n 159) 92, 98. See also Vasu Reddy, "Joining Intentions in Infancy" (2015) 22 (1–2) Journal of Consciousness Studies 24–44 (24), for the claim that "joint intentional actions are best understood as the processes through which intention awareness develops rather than just as the products of such awareness."

[191] Malinda Carpenter and Kristin Liebal, "Joint Attention, Communication, and Knowing Together in Infancy." In Axel Seemann (ed) *Joint Attention: New Developments in Psychology, Philosophy of Mind, and Social Neuroscience* (MIT Press 2011) 159–181 (168) [emphasis original].

[192] Zahavi (n 184) 232.

[193] R Peter Hobson and Jessica Hobson, "Joint Attention or Joint Engagement? Insights from Autism" in Alex Seemann (ed) *Joint Attention: New Developments in Psychology, Philosophy of Mind, and Social Neuroscience* (MIT Press 2011) 115–136 (116).

[194] Jessica A Hobson and R Peter Hobson, "Identification: The Missing Link between Joint Attention and Imitation?" (2007) 19 (2) Development and Psychopathology 411–431 (411).

[195] Carpenter and Liebal (n 191) 167.

"Tertiary intersubjective understanding"[196] develops from around two or three to six years (or maybe even a bit earlier, in the middle of the second year).[197] Bråten and Trevarthen include a broad range of capacities, such as "second-order understanding of others' minds and emotion," under this tertiary stage.[198] Rochat and colleagues join Trevarthen and propose additionally that "a third level of intersubjectivity" comprises jointly represented and negotiated values leading to an "ethical stance accompanying emerging theories of mind."[199] In their view, this third stage represents "the foundation and main constitutive element of human sociality."[200] A major extension is that "objects and situations in the environment are not just jointly attended to (secondary intersubjectivity), they become also *jointly evaluated* via negotiation, until eventually some kind of a mutual agreement is reached."[201] Hence, while secondary intersubjectivity and joint attention as well as joint tasks ask for more than a simple parallel execution of certain actions, tertiary intersubjectivity, in addition to reflecting other people's actions, refers to actively shaping the representation of another person's understanding. Secondary emotions such as embarrassment or guilt illustrate that children begin to be aware of and care about how others perceive and evaluate them. This richer understanding of themselves as social beings finds parallels in a continuous development in their self-awareness.[202]

5.4.3 *Is Intersubjectivity Innate?*

Considering the increased age at which children enter this stage of tertiary intersubjectivity and the immense learning process children have made until then, it is already almost impossible to differentiate neatly between innate features and socially learned behavior. At least it is hard to deny that unfavorable environmental conditions can impede the "normal" social and moral

[196] With overviews in Stein Bråten and Colwyn Trevarthen, "Prologue. From Infant Intersubjectivity and Participant Movements to Simulation and Conversation in Cultural Common Sense" in Stein Bråten (ed) *On Being Moved: From Mirror Neurons to Empathy* (John Benjamins North America 2007) 21–34; Trevarthen and Aitken (n 156) 4–8; cf Philippe Rochat and Cláudia Passos-Ferreira, "From Imitation to Reciprocation and Mutual Recognition" in Jaime A Pineda (ed) *Mirror Neuron Systems: The Role of Mirroring Processes in Social Cognition* (Humana Press Springer 2008) 191–212.

[197] Rochat and Passos-Ferreira (n 196) 185.

[198] Bråten and Trevarthen (n 196) 23, 26.

[199] Rochat, Passos-Ferreira and Salem (n 167) 177.

[200] Rochat, Passos-Ferreira and Salem (n 167) 174.

[201] Rochat, Passos-Ferreira and Salem (n 167) 185 [emphasis original].

[202] See below Section 5.6.3.

development of a child.[203] However, with the expression "innate intersubjective drive/natural sympathy,"[204] Trevarthen suggests that what unfolds only later explicitly in protoconversations, joint attention and joint actions at least are dependent on and develop due to innate features.[205] "Protocultural intelligence" might thus be imagined to be on some sort of rail tracks insofar as the "intersubjective intentions and perceptions that it depends on can be already found in the active agency and sociable awareness of an alert and contented newborn."[206] Similarly, Trevarthen and Aitken speak of "prenatally drafted motives that are adapted for intelligent life in the company of other subjects, not the first appearance of the adaptive behaviours."[207]

Hence, while some elements of intersubjectivity, such as subjectivity itself, are arguably already found in newborn infants, tertiary intersubjectivity consists of a highly complex combination of innate features that have to be triggered and shaped by a caring environment. To depict clearly and exclusively what is innate and what is shaped by the environment is immensely difficult and possibly not the most important task.[208] Claims for innate features have to provide evidence for an insensitivity to environmental influences. This troubles any strong innateness claim for complex cognitive and behavioral traits, such as morality.[209] Clear attributions to nativism or behaviorism in a black or white fashion are likely to fall short of representing reality correctly. Focusing on developmental steps, such as the attempt to subsume the origins and development of morality under the concept of intersubjectivity, might be more promising. However, also by taking such a stance, we have to bear in mind that those specific capacities or features might be present in

203 See Narvaez (n 161) ch 6 and 7.

204 Trevarthen (n 156) First Things First 93, n 1: "This is what I mischievously called 'innate intersubjectivity' in the early 1970s. Now, though it has served its purpose well, that rather ponderous, indeed intellectually pedantic, term is something like an albatross round my neck, but maybe useful to baffle experts in machine intelligence. I prefer, in fact, innate interpersonality, but that is little better, so I am settling for natural 'sympathy', which turns out to have excellent historical and philological credentials."

205 See Trevarthen (n 156) First Things First 93.

206 Trevarthen (n 156) What Is It Like to Be a Person Who Knows Nothing? 130, with reference to Colwyn Trevarthen, "An Infant's Motives for Speaking and Thinking in the Culture" in Astrid H Wold (ed) *The Dialogical Alternative: Towards a Theory of Language and Mind. Festschrift für Ragnar Rommetveit* (Scandinavian University Press/Oxford University Press 1992) 99–137.

207 Trevarthen and Aitken (n 156) 10.

208 See also Narvaez (n 161) 20, who finds "'nature versus nurture' to be a false dichotomy because of the constant interaction of the two elements."

209 L Christopher Suhler and Patricia S Churchland, "Can Innate, Modular 'Foundations' Explain Morality? Challenges for Haidt's Moral Foundations Theory" (2011) 23 (9) Journal of Cognitive Neuroscience 2103–2116 (2105).

infants but we simply were/are not able to "measure" or "identify" them. Major scientific progress throughout history through the invention of new technologies or methodologies and the overturn of former scientific truisms teaches us decency for what we consider as our current "scientific truths."[210] An example for a complex combination of innate features and socially learned behavior, which we find in studies on the fear conditioning of rodents,[211] might further complicate the picture. This example shows that we might even face parallel processes of innate and learned features for similar or even identical tasks, actions or conduct. In the case of rodents, fear conditioning was shown to be transmitted epigenetically[212] as well as through social transmission.[213]

5.5 INTERSUBJECTIVITY AND MORALITY

Behaviorism was very strong throughout the last century. However, in recent years nativism – also due to the increase in new technological insights – has again gained considerable strength. From both camps, sophisticated approaches exist that aim at explaining core concepts of human sociality. A radical denial of either behaviorism or nativism is thus not convincing. This general stance also holds true concerning human morality. Radical approaches arguing for either a hardwired morality in our minds/brains or pictures of moral blank slates are not wholly credible. An essential and sophisticated concept of human life such as morality very likely benefits greatly from some innate features or capacities of our mind/brain. However, at the same time a caring environment, which triggers and shapes this neurobiological foundation, is essential. I think it is safe to say that most people can agree with this general stance. The details are a matter of controversy, but a lack of technological means further complicates the discussion. Hence, the current arguments are about weighing up probabilities, which remain open until scientific facts based on uncontroversial technological

[210] Think only how the age of children accomplishing false-belief studies has dropped since the first false-belief study (Heinz Wimmer and Josef Perner, "Beliefs About Beliefs: Representation and Constraining Function of Wrong Beliefs in Young Children's Understanding of Deception" (1983) 13 (1) Cognition 103–128; Josef Perner, *Understanding the Representational Mind* (MIT Press 1991)), with a reported age for accomplishing the false-belief task of four to six years of age (for 57 percent of tested children and six to nine years for 86 percent of tested children) towards most recent false-belief studies (eg Buttelmann et al (n 111)) finding that even eighteen-month-old toddlers can accomplish false-belief tasks.

[211] See above n 89.

[212] Dias and Ressler (n 89).

[213] Debiec and Sullivan (n 89).

methodological tools bring clarity.[214] Arguably, intersubjectivity is the essential basis for both.

A caveat is necessary before testing intersubjectivity as the core concept for looking at the origins and further development of morality. Any definition of what morality actually is influences the search for its innate features.[215] If we conceive of morality as the product of reason, we will almost automatically put emphasis on the emergence of consciousness and reason-related capacities as a landmark in its origins. However, if emotions and intuitions are thought to be the only basis of moral decisions, very likely we would tend to underrate the difficult search for consciousness and look at the neurobiological emergence of emotions instead. Similar to radical behavioral or nativist accounts, the answer with regard to reason or emotion being exclusive foundations for morality is not a radical but an inclusive approach: Moral phenomena can only be explained "in terms of diverse cognitive components that are not specific to morality."[216] Similarly Sahakian and Gottwald hold when reviewing fMRI studies looking for the "morality network" that there is not "a single brain area of morality that is not also active during other processes" and thus "moral decision-making appears to rely on many parallel, co-operating systems and brain areas."[217] Undoubtedly, emotions play a vital role for morality. However, reason certainly affects our moral life as well. Thus Narvaez states that "[t]he agile moral person uses a range of capacities from extremely controlled (deliberate, conscious, intentional) to extremely automatic (nondeliberate, unconscious or preconscious, nonintentional, habit-based), selecting what is appropriate for the situation."[218] Acknowledging this, the approach proposed here seeks to find a middle way. Such an approach seems to be more easily defensible than more radical and detailed approaches to, for instance, innate moral features such as UMG. Of course, proposing a more abstract concept brings the risk of remaining utterly trivial. In order to avoid such superficiality concerns, I aim to identify and then ascribe cornerstones of human morality to the three major shifts in intersubjectivity referred to above. Thus, the goal is to embed the origins and development of morality in the rich literature on intersubjectivity in child development. This is

[214] See eg an analysis of "how fMRI reveals what really goes on in our minds [and what fMRI does not reveal]" in Barbara J Sahakian and Julia Gottwald, *Sex, Lies, and Brain Scans. How fMRI Reveals What Really Goes On in Our Minds* (Oxford University Press 2017).

[215] For an overview see Jean Decety and Jason M Cowell, "Friends or Foes: Is Empathy Necessary for Moral Behavior?" (2014) 9 (4) Perspectives on Psychological Science 525–537.

[216] Joshua D Greene, "The Rise of Moral Cognition" (2015) 135 Cognition 39–42 (39).

[217] Sahakian and Gottwald (n 214) 60–61.

[218] Narvaez (n 161) 125.

arguably helpful to explain how, finally, at around thirty-six months, infants generally have a grasp of good and bad, which is (then still) primarily based on their relationship with caregivers.[219]

5.5.1 *Primary Intersubjectivity as the Precursor of Morality*

Primary intersubjectivity is manifested in protoconversations and reciprocal sympathetic imitation displayed in the first weeks of life. These "primary intersubjective dialogues of protoconversation and reciprocal sympathetic imitation exhibited in the first weeks of life … lead to more lively jokes and games rich in emotions of 'other awareness.'"[220] In other words, "[w]hen the mammalian offspring are born, they depend for survival on the mother. So the mammalian brain has to be organized to do something completely new [in contrast to self-care]: take care of others in much the way she take care of herself."[221] The hormones oxytocin and vasopressin play a crucial role for "social bonding" and "mammalian other-care" at a neurobiological level,[222] whereby oxytocin "facilitates attachment of mother to baby. And of baby to mother"[223] and vasopressin "triggers a different cascade of events so that the mother protects offspring, defending them against predators, for example."[224] However, Churchland still cautiously frames that "[a]lthough it is known that oxytocin and vasopressin are critical in social behavior, much about their roles as well as the circuitry with which they interact remains unknown."[225] Hence, we might record at the stage of primary intersubjectivity that social bonding primarily guided by the hormones oxytocin and vasopressin plays a crucial role

[219] Narvaez (n 161) 66, with reference to Robert N Emde et al, "The Moral Self of Infancy: Affective Core and Procedural Knowledge" (1991) 11 (3) Developmental Review 251–270.

[220] Bråten and Trevarthen (n 196) 22, with reference to Reddy (n 159).

[221] Churchland (n 144) 284.

[222] Churchland (n 144) 286–291.

[223] Churchland (n 144) 287 with reference to Eric B Keverne and James P Curley, "Vasopressin, Oxytocin and Social Behaviour" (2004) 14 (6) Current Opinion in Neurobiology 777–783; Kevin D Broad, James P Curley and Eric B Keverne, "Mother-Infant Bonding and the Evolution of Mammalian Social Relationships" (2006) 361 (1476) Philosophical Transactions of the Royal Society B 2199–2214.

[224] Churchland (n 144) 286, with reference to Eric B Keverne, "Genomic Imprinting and the Evolution of Sex Differences in Mammalian Reproductive Strategies" (2007) 59 Advances in Genetics 217–243; Stephen W Porges and Carol Sue Carter, "Neurobiology and Evolution: Mechanisms, Mediators, and Adaptive Consequences of Caregiving" in Stephanie L Brown, R Michael Brown and Louis A Penner (eds) *Self-Interest and Beyond: Toward a New Understanding of Human Caregiving* (Oxford University Press 2007) 53–71; Yawei Cheng et al, "Love Hurts: an fMRI Study" (2010) 51 (2) Neuro Image 923–929.

[225] Churchland (n 144) 295.

in strengthening the relationship between the newborn infant and his/her mother. A sense of intersubjectivity is also given while a more sophisticated relation with other subjects awaits development. So even if we hold that "[m]orality begins with the development of implicit procedural knowledge, based on pattern recognition," which "underlies all of cognitive functioning and undergoes continual refinement throughout life,"[226] we have to admit that at the level of primary intersubjectivity such knowledge is very limited. So when Narvaez suggests that "'[t]he early self is a moral one,' built on the trust (or mistrust) and social commitment (or lack thereof) learned procedurally in early life," this is an optimistic assessment.[227] Morality is yet to start developing. Alternatively, at most it only becomes apparent at a later point. However, important core elements of what essentially becomes human morality are already present at birth. Innate primary intersubjectivity is a very important precursor for morality:

> The infant's brain develops from an "interpersonal neurobiology," that is, collaborative, reciprocal communication that allows the child to connect to others, regulate emotions, establish a self-story, engage the world with vitality, and reflect on mental states (D. J. Siegel, 1999). Interactions with caregivers form traces, creating embodied "representations" of the social world to be carried forward and used in future relations. In terms of adult morality, Mikulincer and Shaver (2005) find consistent patterns between secure attachment and compassionate behavior.[228]

What it takes for morality to arise is a shift from receiving care towards caring about the other, which will primarily be the caregiver. Therefore, primary intersubjectivity is needed; that is, a distinction of oneself from the other as well as an identification of the other (versus an object). This is the first instance of extending care about oneself towards someone else's well-being.[229]

[226] Narvaez (n 161) 64.

[227] Narvaez (n 161) 64.

[228] Narvaez (n 161) 72, with reference to Daniel J Siegel, *The Developing Mind: How Relationships and the Brain Interact to Shape Who We Are* (Guilford 1999); as well as Mario Mikulincer and Phillip R Shaver, "Attachment Theory and Research: Resurrection of the Psychodynamic Approach to Personality" (2005) 39 (1) Journal of Research in Personality 22–45.

[229] I think that this shift is necessarily included in the definition of morality and thus excludes what Narvaez calls safety ethics. While ethics (which she equates with morality) might have quite diverging definitions, I have trouble subsuming anything like "modes of self-protection" ("It's about me and my survival") (Narvaez n 161 189) under morality. I think that morality necessarily involves an interpersonal element, albeit not only in the sense of, for instance, self-protection in social relations due to fear, but more in a way of having in mind the well-being of the other person I am in a social relation with.

Such care for other familiar others' well-being must not be fully conscious. Hence, some sort of innate features resulting from primary intersubjectivity might be relevant for early caring behaviors such as helping or consoling others.[230] However, I think that some sort of sophisticated understanding of the other subject is necessary for further development of such caring behavior. Why should we care much about someone else if we do not understand that other person's being/mind?

5.5.2 *Secondary Intersubjectivity and Important Steps towards Morality*

"Secondary intersubjective attunement" refers to the landmark development at around nine months of adding an object to the primary between-two-subjects relation. Joint attention to objects and emotional referencing become center stage, strengthening "mutual attention within trusting relations of companionship."[231] Nevertheless, while this might very well be the case it is not clear how this general statement leads to morality in humans. In other words, we can ask, as Patricia Churchland does: "But how do we get from a general disposition to care about others, to specific moral actions, such as telling the truth, respecting the goods of others, and keeping promises?"[232] For Churchland, learning and problem solving is decisive.[233] For Narvaez, perspective taking is key.[234] While infants at the stage of secondary intersubjectivity are quick learners and make rapid progress, it is still hard to clearly align key components of this stage with morality. Hence, while the capacity to include objects in an interpersonal relation is necessary for morality, as it does extend the primary intersubjective relation, it is not sufficient. More advanced perspective taking is essential for consideration of the morality or the well-being of others.

[230] See eg J Kiley Hamlin, Karen Wynn and Paul Bloom, "3-Month-Olds Show a Negativity Bias in Their Social Evaluations" (2010) 13 (6) Developmental Science 923–929; J Kiley Hamlin, "The Case for Social Evaluation in Preverbal Infants: Gazing toward One's Goal Drives Infants' Preferences for Helpers over Hinderers in the Hill Paradigm" (2015) 5 (1563) Frontiers in Psychology 1–9; for criticism see Eliala Salvadori et al, "Probing the Strength of Infants' Preference for Helpers over Hinderers: Two Replication Attempts of Hamlin and Wynn (2011)" (2015) 10 (11) PLOS ONE 1–10.

[231] Bråten and Trevarthen (n 196) 22.

[232] Churchland (n 144) 291.

[233] Churchland (n 144) 291.

[234] Narvaez (n 161) 100.

5.5.3 *Tertiary Intersubjectivity and the Origin of Morality*

Besides conversational and narrative speech, "a sense of verbal or narrative self and other in first-order modes of symbolic communication, and (from 3 to 6 years) second-order understanding of others' minds and emotion (theory or simulation of mind) opens for perspective-taking and emotional absorption."[235] What is necessary for morality is the capacity to extend the caring relationship between a caregiver and the infant to others.[236] If this other is not another caregiver (the father, grandparents or similar), but a stranger, then a disentanglement from the caring relationship towards a more general sense of well-being for this stranger is necessary. For such a disentanglement, the ability for a third-order perspective is necessary. Additionally, an understanding of others' minds, at least in an abstract way, is important for grasping norm-guided morality. It is quite difficult to pinpoint at what specific age children develop such an understanding of others' minds. This is because the theory of mind itself is a highly complex concept that is not present spontaneously at a certain age but develops steadily over time.[237] However, I think it is less controversial to assume that the development of an understanding of others' minds is connected closely with the stage of tertiary intersubjectivity and the development of norm-guided morality. Hence, a probable starting point could be identified at around eighteen to twenty-two months.[238] The concept of self-awareness also plays a major role in relating oneself and one's own actions to others. Similarly to the capacity of understanding others' minds, "self-awareness is not a monolithic, all-or-none ability but rather consists in at least three different levels."[239] A mask task conducted by Legrain and colleagues indicates that the "most sophisticated level of self-awareness, the external self" is present at around twenty-two months.[240] In the course of tertiary intersubjectivity, first prosocial behavior such as helping and consoling takes place. This brings "the child to the threshold of moral development and the progressive construction of an explicit sense of justice."[241]

235 Bråten and Trevarthen (n 196) 23.

236 See also Churchland (n 144) 289. Cf Meredith Allen, Conrad Perry, and Jordy Kaufman, "Toddlers Prefer to Help Familiar People" (2018) 174 Psychology 90–102, reporting experiments demonstrating that toddlers are significantly more likely to help a person they had previously become familiar with.

237 See n 154.

238 See eg Buttelmann et al (n 111).

239 Legrain, Cleeremans and Destrebecqz (n 174) 584, based on Rochat (n 168).

240 Legrain, Cleeremans and Destrebecqz (n 174) 584.

241 Rochat et al (n 167) 186, with reference to William Damon, "Fair Distribution and Sharing: The Development of Positive Justice" in Bill Puka (ed) *Fundamental Research in Moral Development* (Garland Publishing 1994) 189–254.

A second shift, which might more adequately be described as a process rather than a spontaneous shift, is the extension of care for well-being towards an unfamiliar other. This is most likely facilitated by an extended caring environment.[242] A precondition for this extension is disentanglement from one specific caregiver towards many diverse caregivers. Such an extension might even lead to an abstract potentiality of future caregivers. Hence, even though this might not be the driving force, we can rationalize both shifts by a motivation to secure care by caring for familiar and then unfamiliar others.

While secondary intersubjectivity is important to broaden the scope of attention to objects in interpersonal relations, it is particularly the development of tertiary intersubjectivity that underpins and deepens this extension. In order to be able to imagine (in the crudest version) potential future caregivers and cooperation partners (one might add), an understanding of others' minds is immensely important. While the innate drives of a social being might suffice for such care even for unfamiliar others' well-being, due to our development in highly complex and interacting societies with cooperative breeding, it is the development of understanding others that truly enforces or at least strengthens the motivation to care also for unfamiliar others' well-being. And the capacity for a third-person perspective is immensely helpful in improving such understanding. This is the place for empathy in morality.[243] The capacity to put oneself in others' shoes can support caring for unfamiliar others' well-being. However, it is not the core of morality as such.

5.5.4 *Consequences and Objections I: A Dark Picture of Our Amoral Species?*

Understanding the origins and development of morality as described makes us see more clearly the constant extension of what is and what becomes important in a growing child. This includes the downside that we will quite likely never reach a full extension in terms of the quality and quantity of caring for unfamiliar others' well-being in comparison to the way we care for familiar others' well-being.[244] Whether we agree on this insight or not is a very different question to whether we like it, and if we do not like it, what we

[242] See, for instance, Tomasello and Vaish (n 136) 238, pointing to cooperative breeding.

[243] See Section 5.6.4.

[244] See eg the "spotlight effect" caused by empathetic focusing on a particular fate in Paul Bloom, *Against Empathy: The Case for Rational Compassion* (Ecco 2016); compare also, for instance, Jean-François Bonnefon, Iyad Rahwan and Azim Shariff, "The Social Dilemma of Autonomous Vehicles" (2016) 352 (6293) Science 1573–1576, on defining algorithms for helping autonomous vehicles make moral decisions and the reported change of attitudes of tested individuals when family members are involved.

should change and how. We can claim, for instance, that our caring for unfamiliar others is underdeveloped, should be strengthened, extended to specific groups, and so on. I am convinced that such endeavors – from some desperately needed ones to some more controversial – benefit greatly from the insight just described. While it might be, to some extent, disturbing to understand morality in this way, I think a more nuanced understanding, with different layers of morality, can actually be very helpful. From this perspective it is truly fascinating to see that human life, lived in highly complex and cooperative societies, has brought about some quite amazingly universal moral norms that we display even towards unfamiliar others. However, while moral standards supposedly show an amazing form of universality, a closer look reveals quite astonishing differences.[245] Instead of lamenting the innate amorality of our species, we can say that the glass is already more than half full by taking our current moral stance as a great achievement of civilization, thereby embracing the normativity of morality. Instead of understanding morality as undermining such normativity, we can improve our morality by active sociality – rather than putting our hopes in moral genes. We can identify dangers and address them more easily if we admit (and do not overlook) various diverging views of what someone has learned as a good decision/act (morality). In Narvaez's terms, we can safely say that "[e]veryone has morality." However, she adds that this means "everyone aims for what she perceives to be good in the moment."[246]

> In comparison to a well-formed self, a malformed self just sees the "good" differently. The personal beliefs a person has about the social world plays a large role in perception of the "good". Those with limited social experience in the evolutionary sense (evolved developmental niche) develop misconstruals of the good life. Instead of openhearted relational attunement, they "know" distance and distrust. What feels rewarding (good and right) is quite different from our human heritage.[247]

Nevertheless, Narvaez, too, has a positive outlook for us: "Contrary to Hobbesian views that nature is red in tooth and claw (Dawkins, 2006), there is overwhelming evidence that the natural world itself is much more infused with cooperation than competition, on all levels and through time – 4 billion years of it (Weiss & Buchanan, 2009)."[248]

[245] For a critical assessment of "universal moral rules" see Prinz (n 133) 372–387.
[246] Narvaez (n 161) 206.
[247] Narvaez (n 161) 206.
[248] Narvaez (n 161) 220 [references omitted].

5.5.5 *Consequences and Objections II: Intersubjectivity vs. Empathy*

However, intersubjectivity faces an immediate objection if understood to be the core of morality: intersubjectivity per se is neutral towards good or bad decisions or the well-being of others. Thus, intersubjectivity does not comprise the quintessence of morality. In order to deal with this objection, I suggest looking at empathy first, which is often taken as the core of morality.[249]

For de Waal, "an interest in others is fundamental." He rhetorically asks where human morality would be without it.[250] Rifkin even holds that the "maturation of empathy and the development of a moral sense are one and the same thing."[251] However, while there is "a relationship between morality and empathy," it is problematic to use the concepts interchangeably.[252] Whether empathy must necessarily be tied to morality and well-being is not as clear as might be thought at first glance. Intuitively we might tend to approve of such an approach; however, a closer look makes a refutation of this common assumption more likely. We can, for instance, feel empathy for a person without any involvement of moral sentiment or concern for the well-being of that person but in a more abstract way of simply understanding the (emotional) situation of the other.[253] Another critique of empathy as the core foundation of morality is that empathy might involve bias towards specific persons or groups with whom identification is easier.[254] Furthermore, empathy is quite a vague concept. Therefore, Decety and Cowell ask for more precision, "perhaps abandoning the muddy concept of empathy."[255] For instance, the study by Batson and colleagues has clearly shown important limitations to empathy being the foundation of morality.[256] Finally, Prinz doubts that empathy is necessary for morality,[257] and Bloom even made a case *Against Empathy*.[258]

[249] See for instance Jeremy Rifkin, *The Empathic Civilization. The Race to Global Consciousness in a World in Crisis* (Penguin 2009); Frans De Waal, *The Age of Empathy: Nature's Lessons for a Kinder Society* (Crown/Archetype 2010); Peter Bazalgette, *The Empathy Instinct: How to Create a More Civil Society* (John Murray 2017).

[250] De Waal (n 249) 9.

[251] Rifkin (n 249) 119.

[252] See Decety and Cowell (n 215).

[253] Jesse J Prinz, "Is Empathy Necessary for Morality?" in Amy Coplan and Peter Goldie (eds) *Empathy: Philosophical and Psychological Perspectives* (Oxford University Press 2011) 211–229.

[254] Decety and Cowell (n 215) with further references.

[255] Decety and Cowell (n 215).

[256] C Daniel et al, "Immorality from Empathy-Induced Altruism: When Compassion and Justice Conflict" (1995) 68 Journal of Personality and Social Psychology 1042–1054.

[257] Prinz (n 253).

[258] Bloom (n 244).

While this criticism is certainly justified, I argue that embedding the origins and development of morality in the rich concept of intersubjectivity in child development with its differentiation in at least three major stages helps us to better grasp the various stages in moral development, thereby providing space for accommodating the criticism advanced against empathy. In contrast to putting myself in someone else's shoes (empathy), intersubjectivity is the more abstract ability to relate to someone else. However, the most important step – the extension of caring for the well-being of an unfamiliar other, which has been said to take place in the stage of tertiary intersubjectivity – clearly deserves more attention and might even lead to further differentiation within the concept of tertiary intersubjectivity. Relating moral origins and further development to intersubjectivity is not to say that morality necessarily involves an intersubjective relation between two persons. This would even contradict a specific feature of morality's normativity, which is more general and abstract. However, as a starting point, primary and secondary intersubjectivity is necessary. The more abstract norm-based morality is succinctly captured by developing tertiary intersubjectivity, which is mostly constituted by a bird's-eye view. Thus, the important shift described by tertiary intersubjectivity is necessary for the normativity of morality to unfold, which is by definition more general and abstract than a simple relation between two subjects. The ability to switch to a third-person perspective and to negotiate values with others enables us to see ourselves from a bird's-eye view and thus reflect on/judge our acts in a more abstract way than when only concerning one person (empathy). Whether the approach is based on emotions or reason, (socially learned) conditioning towards other unfamiliar people's needs is necessary.[259]

Finally, the phenomenon of intersubjectivity, and in particular what has been identified as tertiary intersubjectivity, could also be connected to philosophical accounts, such as the approach advanced by Peter Gärdenfors, who captured intersubjectivity as "sharing and representing of other's mentality."[260] For him, "[a] prerequisite of an animal (or a human) entertaining any form of intersubjectivity is that it has an *inner world*, ie, an ability to

[259] See, for instance, the illustration of caring and its neurobiological roots in Churchland (n 144) 286–291; see also Narvaez (n 161) 194–195.

[260] Peter Gärdenfors, "The Role of Intersubjectivity in Animal and Human Cooperation" (2008) 3 (1) Biological Theory 1–12 (2); cf Peter Gärdenfors, "Slicing the Theory of Mind" (2001) 36 Danish Yearbook of Philosophy 7–34; Peter Gärdenfors, *How Homo Became Sapiens: On the Evolution of Thinking* (Oxford University Press 2003); Peter Gärdenfors, "Evolutionary and Developmental Aspects of Intersubjectivity" in Hans Liljenström and Peter Århem (eds) *Consciousness Transitions: Phylogenetic, Ontogenetic and Physiological Aspects* (Elsevier 2007) 281–305.

imagine objects and situations also in their absence. The crucial issue as regards cooperation is whether an individual has any representation of other individuals' inner worlds."[261] However, for Gärdenfors, intersubjectivity is not a simple yes or no capacity but is subdivided into five capacities: representing the emotions of others (empathy); representing the attention of others; representing the intentions of others; representing the beliefs and knowledge of others; and representing the desires of others.[262] Besides, intersubjectivity is a well-known philosophical concept that might be used fruitfully to continue building on and hence might work as a connecting concept for neurobiological, psychological and philosophical approaches to morality.[263]

5.5.6 *Consequences and Objections III: Hardwired Intersubjectivity?*

A nuanced understanding of intersubjectivity, divided into primary, secondary and tertiary elements according to major developments in infants, enables us to answer similar objections as entertained by Patterson.[264] This is the objection that "intersubjectivity is not something that is located inside people's heads and that intersubjectivity is not 'mind reading.'"[265] Whereas we do not have an intersubjectivity gene and nor is intersubjectivity hardwired in our mind/brain as such, the differentiated perspective on intersubjectivity nevertheless allows us to identify its innate features. Thus, the detailed descriptions of what is embraced by primary intersubjectivity are, to a high degree, features already present at birth, which enable newborn infants to develop a relationship with caregivers.

[261] Gärdenfors (n 260) The Role of Intersubjectivity in Animal and Human Cooperation 3; compare Tomasello's more demanding understanding of intersubjectivity referred to above, 156.

[262] Gärdenfors (n 260) The Role of Intersubjectivity in Animal and Human Cooperation 3.

[263] Yet clearly this is a superficial and early interpretation that requires further elaboration. Still, I am convinced that this is a promising way to bridge the nature/nurture debate in relation to morality and obeying rules. For the concept of intersubjectivity in phenomenology, see Edmund Husserl, *Cartesian Meditations: An Introduction to Phenomenology* (Martinus Nijhoff 1960) [originally published under the title Méditations cartésiennes: Introduction à la phénoménologie 1931], especially the 5th meditation: "Transcendental Being as Monadological Intersubjectivity." See also the work of Zahavi (n 184). For intersubjectivity in psychoanalysis, see George E Atwood and Robert D Stolorow, *Structures of Subjectivity: Explorations in Psychoanalytic Phenomenology and Contextualism* (Routledge 2nd ed 2014).

[264] See above Section 5.4.3.2.

[265] Maricela Correa-Chávez and Amy L D Roberts, "A Cultural Analysis Is Necessary in Understanding Intersubjectivity" (2012) 18 (1) Culture & Psychology 99–108 (99).

5.6 THE MORAL DUTY TO ADHERE TO THE *PACTA SUNT SERVANDA* PRINCIPLE AND THE UNDERLYING UNDERSTANDING OF THE LAW

The thesis of an innate Universal Moral Grammar by analogy with the famous thesis of a "universal grammar" in linguistics has attracted a lot of attention. Admittedly, it is an exciting idea that, if proven correct, would definitely be of great interest, not just for science, but also for humanity (including lawyers, of course).[266] Yet the detailed criticism outlined suggests that there is still a long way to go. That is because this fascinating thesis, which I have addressed here mainly in the version advocated by John Mikhail, does not stand up to the criticism. The aim of this chapter was to highlight new counterarguments as well as to compile and evaluate some of the most substantial criticisms from fields such as neurobiology, evolutionary and developmental psychology and philosophy. Instead of UMG, this thesis suggests an "innate intersubjectivity" as a more detailed and refined, but also more abstract and thus less demanding, approach to dealing with the biological setup that enables humans to make moral judgments.

The threefold approach to intersubjectivity is, arguably, the basis on which we humans develop "norm-based" morality. The rich research and literature on intersubjectivity provide a good account to embed nativist elements of moral origins and development in behavior learned by experience and social practice. This is not completely different to how Mikhail sees UMG. However, what is important to retain here is that there is no such thing as a direct relation between the final norm-based morality and the innate preconditions. We know far too little about it to make any sense of it.

[266] See Mikhail's suggestion (n 38) 101 that this "mentalist theory of ethics may be able to vindicate a core insight of the natural law tradition: the existence of natural normative yardsticks, accessible to all, against which to measure the legitimacy of positive law" and similarly Mikhail (n 69). For criticism of that approach, see Lando Kirchmair, "How (Not) to Argue for the Relation between Natural Sciences and Law: Why the Thesis of an Innate 'Universal Moral Grammar' and Its Relevance for Law as Argued by John Mikhail Fails" (2019) 105 (4) Archiv für Rechts- und Sozialphilosophie 523–535. For another careful analysis of the relevance of the constitution of our mind for our rights, see Mahlmann (n 15) 134–135, holding that "it is perhaps a plausible idea that there is a great distance between the human moral faculty and the Universal Declaration of Human Rights, or other concrete, historically shaped catalogues of rights in constitutions and international bills of rights. But the moral faculty could turn out … to be the cognitive precondition for the possibility ultimately to frame something like the Universal Declaration of Human Rights and the aspirations it implies." Mahlmann (n 15 135) is extremely careful, and rightly so, when answering the question as to the "*normative* importance" of a potential "mentalist account of morality and law" [emphasis original]. His clear answer is that "[i]t has no normative consequences as such because one needs normative arguments to justify any normative point."

What seems quite clear by now is that a full-blown human morality is not hardwired in our minds/brains. Without clear evidence, it is difficult to argue that innate capacities lead straightforwardly to a full-blown human morality. Yet this finding might be subject to change in the light of new insights in the field of moral psychology and, in particular, moral cognition. However, for now it is more appropriate to refer to well-known concepts in child development instead of entertaining exciting but fictitious concepts such as UMG. What is important to remember in any case is that interdisciplinary arguments might support such a quest and the quest to understand the origins and development of human morality needs to be informed by various disciplines. However, if this interdisciplinary quest to unravel the remaining mysteries of morality is carried out in the manner criticized above, this is more a contribution to confusion than a proof.

Despite being less daring than UMG, the proposal of intersubjectivity still has a controversial starting point. The innateness of intersubjectivity is far from being established science. Proponents of this concept are aware of that and offer – convincing – reasons why they think intersubjectivity in its various forms and stages has innate features, laying the tracks for further developments. Support for intersubjectivity is rising.[267] However, further work is needed in particular on the relationship between intersubjectivity research and morality to be able to present more detailed insights. Despite potential intuitive disappointment on account of human nature lacking clear innate moral features, such a concept, which ascribes most parts of human morality to a complex mix of innate features and learned behavior, should not be a disappointing picture of our species. First, our current moral stance as a species, no matter how dark or bright the picture might be, is what we have achieved – through evolution, thus (epi)genes *and* civilization. Briefly, we can say that

> [t]he capacity for moral behaviour is rooted in the neurobiology of sociality, and in mammals depends on nonapeptides oxytocin and vasopressin, as well as on elaborated cortical structures that interface with the more ancient structures mediating motivation, reward, and emotion. The neural mechanisms supporting social behavior are tuned up epigenetically by social interactions and by learning the social practices of the group, and by figuring out how to best deal with new social problems.[268]

[267] See Daniel N Stern, *Forms of Vitality. Exploring Dynamic Experience in Psychology and the Arts* (Oxford University Press 2010); Stern (n 184) xi–xxxvii; Philippe Rochat, *Others in Mind. Social Origins of Self-Consciousness* (Cambridge University Press 2009); as well Narvaez (n 161).

[268] Churchland (n 144) 295.

This is not questioned by a concept arguing for innate or learned features either. However, how we tackle our current stance on morality is intertwined with its origins and development. The picture proposed here is rather optimistic if we consider changing or improving morality. What we perceive as moral downsides are not set in (genetic) stone, but open for (societal) change.[269] Thus, what we might wish to change can be learned. This, arguably, is a challenge that can be addressed more easily with an emphasis on learned behavior. It can be subject to change, for instance, through education and by the further shaping of human beings.

At the same time, the detailed analysis arguably provides plausible and fruitful ground for our aim to establish a prelegal *pacta sunt servanda* principle. Intersubjectivity is suitable for conceptualizing the origins and development of the biological setup of human morality and, in an abstract way, also undergirding what constitutes human cooperation. By referring to Colwyn Trevarthen's concept of primary, secondary and tertiary intersubjectivity we find a convincing concept allowing us to ground human cooperation and, inextricably related to cooperation, the duty to find and keep a consensus. This enables us – so runs the argument – to align morality and its development with core concepts of (developmental) psychology. Such an understanding of morality finally lays bare the origins of moral normativity, which is essential for us as the moral duty to stand by the *pacta sunt servanda* principle. In other words, these scientifically plausible findings offer the image that we humans are no Robinson Crusoes and therefore need to cooperate reliably. Yet what is important is to clearly admit the normative move implemented at this stage. While we did our best to take a close look at neurobiology and (developmental) psychology in order to find stable ground for our claims in the natural sciences, we find astonishing research that is continuing apace. Hence, it is highly likely that our knowledge about this process will improve and maybe change. Moreover, we have to admit the move from findings in natural sciences to normative principles. This is an intricate issue and, according to the understanding of the *is–ought* divide expressed in this book, we need to offer reasons for such a move. Finally, we must acknowledge that this normative move has consequences for our understanding of the law. It is once again important to remind ourselves of the research question of this thesis, which is how we can know who has the final say on norm conflict resolution of international, EU and national law. The

[269] See, in this regard, also with many examples and an emphasis on the role of emotions, Philipp Hübl, *Die aufgeregte Gesellschaft. Wie Emotionen unsere Moral prägen und die Polarisierung verstärken* (C Bertelsmann 2019).

understanding of the law developed here does not suggest a general theory of law or a universal definition of law. While the approach advanced here might prove fruitful for further analysis, this book expressly limits itself to the structural analysis of the relationship between international, EU and national law. Bearing this in mind, we will now go on to elaborate what is here termed consent-based monism in order to solve norm conflicts between international, EU and national law.

6

The Theory of Consent-Based Monism

6.1 DEFINITION

Consent-based monism relies on the idea of a circle of two or more individuals, which originates in the creation of one single binding consensus.[270] In other words, this circle – on which the idea of consent-based monism is built – originates through the creation of law at an abstract level, which rests on the consensus of individuals. If the very same individuals create another consensus, this is to be considered a supplement to the same circle. As a consequence, individuals may only create a binding consensus for themselves. Accordingly, law creators in this abstract conception are only the individuals, who are simultaneously the creators and the addressees of the consensus.

Because this book aims to find a common denominator for resolving norm conflicts between international law, EU law and national law, an abstract understanding of law is necessary to include all three fields under one common denominator. The common denominator is vital because it enables a comparison of those different fields (thus monism). In terms of their

[270] For a very early account of this theory, which I called originally *Die Theorie des Rechtserzeugerkreises* (TREK) in German and "the theory of the law creators' circle" in English, as applied to the relationship between public international law and the Austrian legal order, see Lando Kirchmair, *Die Theorie des Rechtserzeugerkreises – eine rechtstheoretische Untersuchung des Verhältnisses von Völkerrecht zu Staatsrecht am Beispiel der österreichischen Rechtsordnung* (Duncker & Humblot 2013). For an introduction to the theory (and further references) and its application to international treaties and their relationship to the Austrian as well as the Hungarian legal order as well as the former abbreviation TREK, from the German term "Die Theorie des Rechtserzeugerkreises," see Lando Kirchmair, "The Theory of the Law Creators' Circle: Re-Conceptualizing the Monism–Dualism–Pluralism Debate" (2016) 17 (2) German Law Journal 179–214, and finally a preliminary application of this theory to the relationship between international, EU and national law can be found in Lando Kirchmair, "Who Has the Final Say? The Relationship between International, EU and National Law" (2018) 10 European Journal of Legal Studies 47–100.

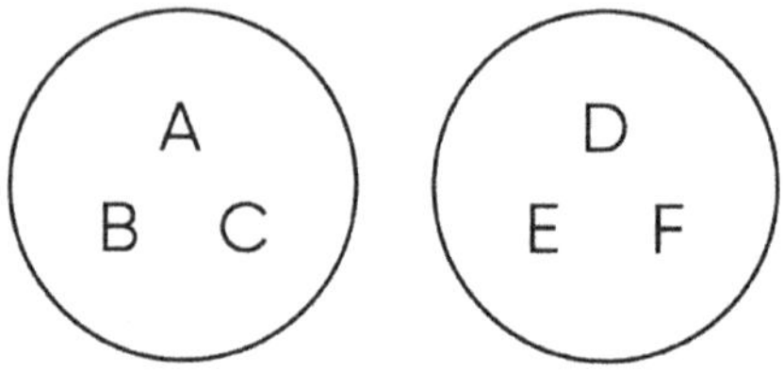

FIGURE 6.1 Two law circles constituted by different individuals

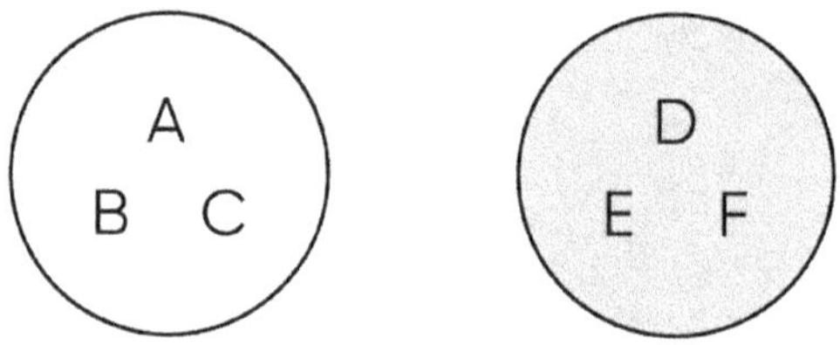

FIGURE 6.2 Two law circles with nonidentical content constituted by different individuals

relationship to each other, the individuals who do not share a single circle remain in the legal desert. Figure 6.1 illustrates two law circles that are constituted by wholly different individuals – for example, individuals A, B and C on the one hand and D, E and F on the other.

However, this does not imply any judgment of the legal desert, which is a neutral, prelegal status. Furthermore, there is a need to stress once again that one single consensus on a specific matter suffices to constitute law between the participating individuals as represented by a circle.

6.2 CONFLICTS BETWEEN DIFFERENT CIRCLES

Individuals who do not share the same circle are, in relation to each other, in the legal desert (see Figure 6.2; the different colors – white and grey – illustrate that these two circles established law with nonidentical content). However, this is only theoretically relevant because nowadays *ius cogens* rules – even though in a very basic and limited sense – provide practically for universal fundamental rules by the largest possible circle.[271] Naturally, the status of a legal desert regarding a specific subject matter lasts only until individuals join a circle and consent on this specific subject matter.

Different circles are less of a concern. Yet if they overlap, problems may arise. Circles overlap if an individual is, at the same time, a member of two

[271] See, albeit briefly, below Section 7.2.3.1. See Kirchmair (n 270) 141 ff.

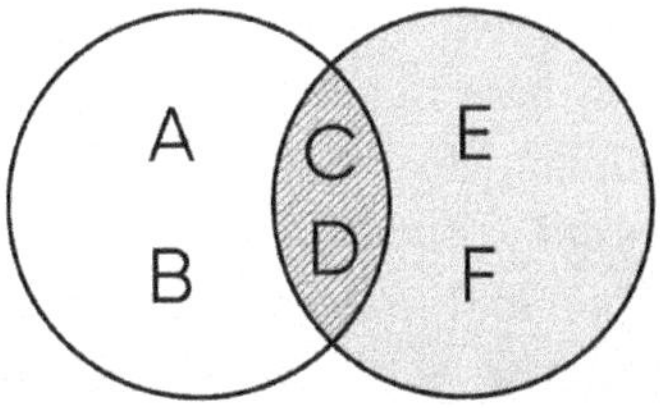

FIGURE 6.3 Two law circles with nonidentical content constituted by partly identical individuals

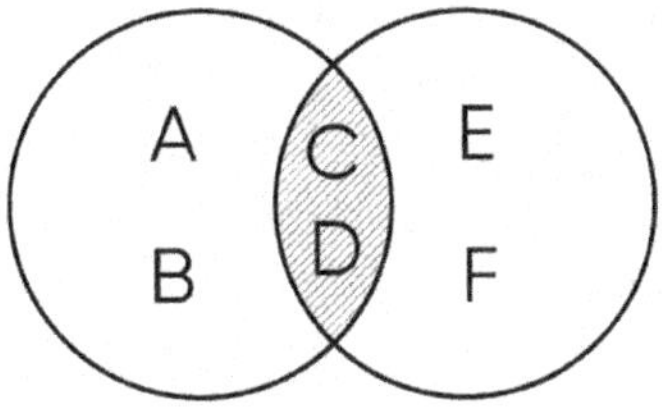

FIGURE 6.4 Two law circles with identical content constituted by partly identical individuals

different circles whose total members are not fully identical (see Figure 6.3). This would be the case, for instance, if the white circle includes individuals A and B as well as *C* and *D* and the grey circle includes individuals *C* and *D* as well as E and F. Recall that individuals participating in one circle are by definition creators and addressees of the consensus.

Overlapping circles are unproblematic if they include completely diverging subject matters (see the different tones of the circles in Figure 6.3, which indicate that the white and grey circles relate to different subject matters). However, if one or more individuals are at the same time members of different but partly overlapping circles regulating the same subject matter, they are possibly conflicting (see Figure 6.4).

A norm conflict between circles arises "between norms, one of which may be permissive, if in obeying or applying one norm [from one circle], the other norm [from another circle of which the same individual is also a member] is necessarily or potentially violated" (see Figure 6.4).[272] Once a consensus has

[272] See also Erich Vranes, "The Definition of 'Norm Conflict' in International Law and Legal Theory" (2006) (2) 17 European Journal of International Law 395–418 (418), who also argues in favor of a broad definition of norm conflicts. See Hans Kelsen, *Allgemeine Theorie der Normen* (Manz 1979) 99; Hans Kelsen, *Reine Rechtslehre* (Franz Deuticke 2nd ed 1960) 209; as well as Ewald Wiederin, "Was ist und welche Konsequenzen hat ein Normkonflikt" (1990) 22 Rechtstheorie 311–333 (318), who specified the definition of Kelsen by stating that also conflicts between commanding and permitting norms are norm conflicts (324). This also applies in cases of de facto inability (316). See also Kirsten Schmalenbach, "Article 53" in Oliver Dörr and Kirsten Schmalenbach (eds) *Vienna Convention on the Law of*

been established by several individuals, it must not be infringed on by a single individual, either by simply breaching the consensus without the acceptance of the other members of this circle, or by creating a conflicting consensus with other individuals (*pacta sunt servanda* as well as *pacta tertii*).[273] Otherwise, the prelegally found *pacta sunt servanda* principle previously established would be violated.[274] In other words, if A, B, C and D agree that x is a forbidden action, C, D, E and F must not allow x either. However, regarding the solution of this conflict of norms, we remain in the legal desert. As far as different circles are concerned, the well-known norm conflict solution rules such as the maxim *lex posterior* and *lex specialis* do not provide a solution. It is important to emphasize that these norm conflict solution rules may only provide for a solution within one and the same circle. This, however, does not prevent a norm conflict solution circle from being created which embraces both conflicting circles (see Figure 6.5).

Treaties – A Commentary (Springer 2nd ed 2018) para 54; and Valentin Jeutner, *Irresolvable Norm Conflicts in International Law – The Concept of a Legal Dilemma* (Oxford University Press 2017) 29–30, adapting this definition; cf Karl Engisch, *Die Einheit der Rechtsordnung* (Winter 1935) 46; and Karl Engisch, *Einführung in das juristische Denken* (Kohlhammer 7th ed 1977) 162; Thomas Zoglauer, *Normenkonflikte – zur Logik und Rationalität ethischen Argumentierens* (Frommann-Holzboog 1998) 125 ff; as well as Lars Lindahl and David Reidhav, "Conflict of Legal Norms: Definition and Varieties" in Michał Araszkiewicz and Krzysztof Płeszka (eds) *Logic in the Theory and Practice of Lawmaking* (Springer 2015) 49–96 (53), who state that "there are conflicts between prohibitions and permissions," which includes not only potential breaches, but "If it is prohibited to do X, this means the same as that it is not permitted to do X. Thus, in the case under consideration, a consequence of the set of norms is that it is both permitted to do X and not permitted to do X. As this conjunction is contradictory, there is a conflict in the set of norms. With respect to the simple cases discussed here, no distinction is made between potential and actual conflicts: in these cases, if there is conflict, it is conflict *tout court*. In case of prohibition, N1, and permission, N2, the existence of conflict is independent of whether someone makes use of the permission or not." For a narrower definition, which is often used at the international level, see Wilfred Jenks, "The Conflict of Law-Making Treaties" (1953) 30 British Yearbook of International Law 401–453 (426): "A conflict in the strict sense of direct incompatibility arises only where a party to the two treaties cannot simultaneously comply with its obligations under both treaties"; Wolfram Karl, "Conflicts between Treaties" in Rudolf Bernhardt (ed) *Encyclopedia of Public International Law Vol VII* (North-Holland 1984) 467–473 (468): "there is a conflict between treaties when two or more treaty instruments contain obligations which cannot be complied with simultaneously"; and also Gabrielle Marceau, "Conflicts of Norms and Conflicts of Jurisdictions: The Relationship between the WTO Agreement and MEAs and Other Treaties" (2001) 35 (6) Journal of World Trade 1081–1131 (1084).

[273] Erich Vranes, "Lex superior, lex specialis, lex posterior – Rechtsnatur der 'Konfliktlösungsregeln'" (2005) 65 Heidelberg Journal of International Law 391– 405 (402, n 48).

[274] See above Section 5.6.

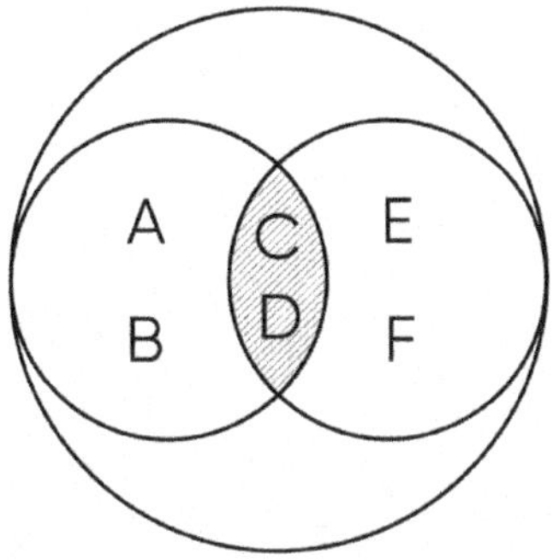

FIGURE 6.5 Two law circles with identical content constituted by partly identical individuals embraced by a norm conflict solution circle

If there is no embracing conflict-solving circle, those individuals remain in the norm conflict-solving legal desert. Of course, this does not mean that conflicts might not be solved peacefully and satisfactorily. But there is no legal norm conflict solution rule. Consent-based monism does not provide any solution for the constellation of partly overlapping and conflicting circles either.

6.3 CONSENT-BASED MONISM AND THE THEORY OF THE LARGER CIRCLE

The theory of the larger circle is based on the aforementioned prelegal assumptions, which are the principles *pacta sunt servanda* and *pacta tertiis*. These prelegal principles are fundamental for all agreed consensuses. If a legal rule has been created by a consensus, unilateral abrogation is no longer possible. The rule of the larger circle always prevails over the rule of the smaller circle, *if* – and this is important – *all* members of the smaller circle are also members of the larger circle – which means that the smaller circle is absorbed by the larger circle. (See Figure 6.6, which illustrates that A, B, and C constitute the smaller circle that is completely absorbed by the larger circle of A, B, C, D, and further individuals and so on.)

To illustrate this, I will discuss an example: if A, B and C (the larger circle) ban smoking in their shared flat, then A and B alone (the smaller circle) may not reinstate smoking or smoke in their flat without C's acceptance. Consequently, the content of the agreed rule is decisive. The consensus of the larger circle must not be violated or hindered by a conflicting rule set up by the smaller circle. If the consensus were to be violated by one or more individuals, this would be a clear breach of the consensus of the larger circle and would thereby violate the prelegal principle *pacta sunt servanda*.

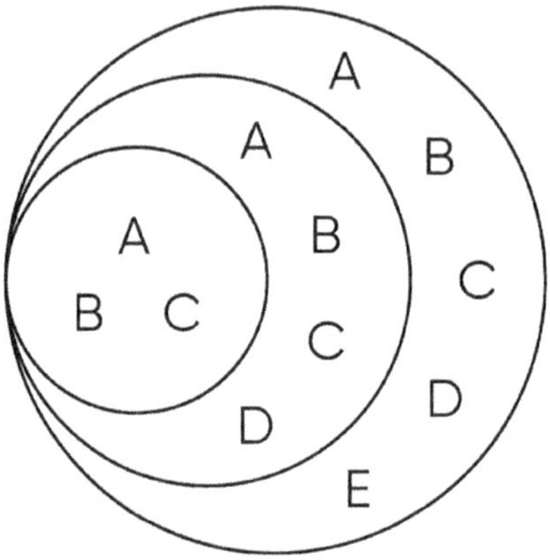

FIGURE 6.6 Three law circles where all members of the smaller circle are also members of the larger circle

If the smaller circle does not break a rule of the larger circle, then the smaller circle is free to agree on whatever rules its members would like. For instance, it may agree on further, more specific rules as long as they do not conflict with a rule of the larger circle. To illustrate this, I revisit the "smokers" example: in this scenario, A, B and C ban smoking again, not only in their flat but also in the pub they frequent. At first glance, it seems less likely that A and B should not be allowed to smoke a cigarette in the pub if they wish to do so when going out one evening without C. To understand this, it is important to take a close look at the consensus agreed between A, B and C. It is essential to know whether they agreed to stop smoking in general or just when in each other's company. If the agreed consensus aims at preventing them from smoking in general – regardless of the place and whose company they are in – it is only possible for all three of them together to change or end their agreed consensus.

The change of location from their flat to a public bar is intended to show that the content of the agreed consensus is crucial. It is much more likely that they would agree to a ban on smoking in their flat, even if for different reasons, than they would do in general (also in the pub). Therefore, one might think that A and B are free to smoke in the bar if the consensus agreed on by A, B, and C does not contain any specifications or any explicit command forbidding them to do this. But if it does include a specification or an explicit command and it is clear that the consensus is a general ban on smoking, they may only override or change it by all three acting together. The command not to deviate from the agreed consensus might, furthermore, be implicitly found in the smoking ban in relation to the shared flat. Without any further specification of

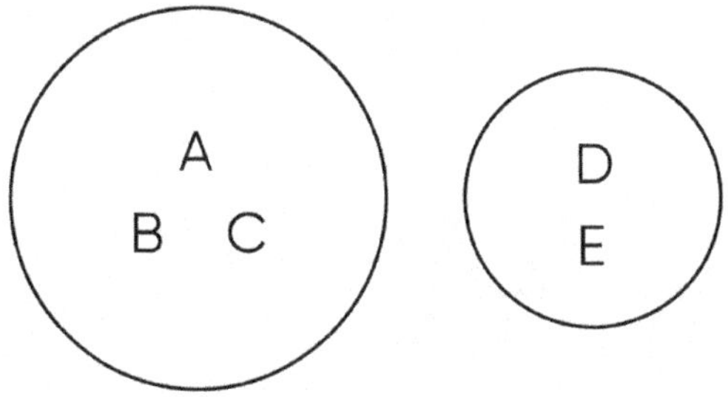

FIGURE 6.7 Two law circles of different size constituted by different individuals

the consensus, we can only assume that the command not to deviate originated from the consensus itself. In the pub example, an explicit command stating that a deviation from the agreed ban is or is not allowed might be seen as necessary to clarify that A and B, alone or together, might deviate from the ban. Without this explicit command, one could assume that A and/or B are allowed to smoke when C is not present. However, if an explicit command not to smoke in the pub, whether alone or with others, has been agreed by all three, it is clear that, according to the theory of the larger circle, any agreement by A and/or B (the smaller circle) to allow smoking in the pub would violate the consensus of A, B and C (the larger circle). Consequently, it is paramount to know whether the smaller circle has simply established a more specific rule that does not conflict with the consensus of the larger circle, or whether the smaller circle rule directly violates the consensus of the larger circle.

While a mere specification of a rule is not problematic, a norm conflict is. A norm conflict caused by the rule of the smaller circle conflicting with a rule of the larger circle contravenes the theory of the larger circle and the pre-legally established principle of *pacta sunt servanda* on which it is based. If the larger circle gives a material command, the smaller circle must obey this command. If the larger circle agrees on a certain consensus, this same consensus may only be changed or deviated from on the same level as it was agreed (the larger circle). This also applies to the legal consequences and effects of the consensus on the members of the smaller circle.

According to the theory of the larger circle, if the members of the different circles are not identical or fully included in a larger circle, it is not possible for the smaller circle to be overruled by the larger circle. This larger circle is not related to the smaller circle because the members of the different circles are not identical (see Figure 6.7). Therefore, it does not matter if those circles include conflicting rules regarding their subject matters because both apply the *pacta tertii* principle. The circles are, in relation to each other, in the legal desert.

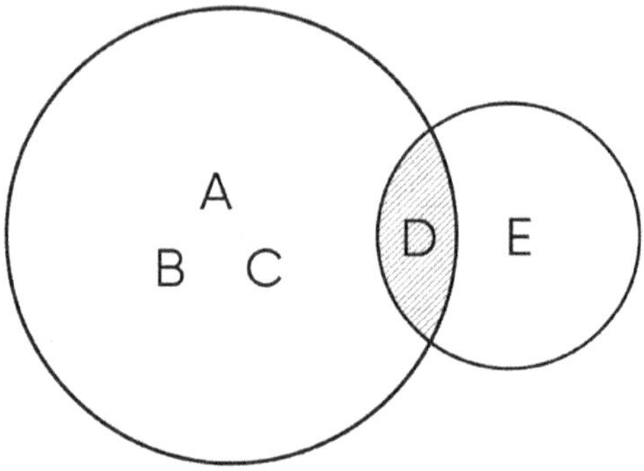

FIGURE 6.8 Two law circles with identical content of different size constituted by partly identical individuals

If some, but not all, of the members of both circles with conflicting subject matters are identical, the case is different (see Figure 6.8). The constellation of Figure 6.8 is very close to the constellation of Figure 6.4. The question is whether the size difference between constellation 4 and constellation 8 is relevant. It is important to note that the constellation in Figure 6.8 is impossible with regard to the relationship between international, EU and national law because the state (the smaller circle) participates in the making of law in the EU and the international sphere (the larger circle) as a unity, acting on behalf of its individuals. Yet, theoretically speaking, it is important to note that the case of Figure 6.8 is not the primary application of the theory of the larger circle. The difference from the constellation illustrated in Figure 6.4 is too insignificant. Therefore, either a larger circle embracing both circles governs the conflict (see Figure 6.5) or the individuals concerned remain in the legal desert as regards the solution of the norm conflict.

6.4 LEGAL CONSEQUENCES RESULTING FROM A VIOLATION OF THE CONSENSUS OF THE LARGER CIRCLE

In terms of the relationship between international, EU and national law, consent-based monism and the theory of the larger circle forces us to analyze the content of the rulings of the larger, international (or EU with regard to national) circle. Contrary to prevailing theories on this relationship,[275] there is no general, blanket legal consequence leading to an absolute or otherwise standardized legal consequence or effect of international law within the legal order of the EU or of EU law within the national legal order. Consent-based

[275] For criticism see Chapters 1 and 2.

monism does not stipulate a single absolute legal consequence. Generally speaking, the smaller circle lacks the ability to create a rule that conflicts with any rule of the larger circle (*rechtliches Können*). The larger circle is free to change this general situation.

Concerning the relationship between EU and Member State law, the primacy of EU law stipulates that Member States can make law conflicting with EU law (*rechtliches Können*). They are not allowed to make such law, but if they do anyhow, the conflicting Member State law is not applicable (*rechtliches Dürfen*). In order to identify the effect of EU law within the Member State legal orders, the doctrine of direct effect is very well known.[276]

Before coming to the peculiarities of the supranational EU legal order, a brief discussion of the relationship between international and EU or national law will further illustrate what I have in mind. Using the relationship between international and EU or national law as an example, EU law or national law (the smaller circle) lacks the ability to create rules conflicting with *ius cogens* norms. EU or national rules conflicting with *ius cogens* are null and void *ex tunc*. The existence of *ius cogens*, however, suggests that the smaller circle (EU law or national law, both concerning international law) has the ability to create EU or national rules that conflict with general international law without a *ius cogens* character (*rechtliches Können*), but lacks the authorization to do so (*rechtliches Dürfen*). This implies that the focus should be on the emergence of international law. More recent EU or national law lacks the authorization to subsequently change – or even deviate from – international law by incorporating it into the EU or national legal order via reception theories. Therefore, it becomes crucial to analyze the content of the international rulings of the larger circle. The consensus of the larger, international circle is decisive when the legal consequences or effects of international law are analyzed in relation to EU and national law.

Having said this, it is important to note that most of the international rules do not stipulate a far-reaching effect on national law: Solely applicable international rules (Section 6.4.1) must, therefore, be differentiated from directly applicable (Section 6.4.2) and individualizing rules (Section 6.4.3).

6.4.1 *Solely Applicable Rules*

Solely applicable rules, also called interstate laws, leave it up to the discretion of the national legal order to decide how to implement these rules

[276] For a more detailed discussion see Chapter 7.

domestically. Typical wording for such provisions is quite abstract, formulating only general obligations, which are then subject to further specification by national laws. Even today, most of the international rules are still solely applicable, which means that they do not have a direct effect within the national legal order. Therefore, further specification of the international rule, for instance by national acts, is necessary. The EU or national Act concretizes and thereby "implements" the general – that is, solely applicable – international rule. Consent-based monism does not challenge this. The approach advanced by this thesis is not an ideological project aimed at advancing international law to have more effect within EU or national law. With regard to the relationship between EU and Member State law, this category, very roughly speaking, fits directives in EU law (Article 288 TFEU).[277]

6.4.2 *Directly Applicable Rules*

In contrast, directly applicable rules – in other words, self-executing rules – give no discretion to the national legal order in deciding how to implement these rules domestically. Directly applicable norms take effect within the EU or national legal order without any EU or national Act except for ratification, and consequently simply do not leave discretion to the national legal order.[278]

[277] However, as is well known: badly implemented or directives implemented too late can, nevertheless, have direct effect. See Case C-6/90 and C-9/90 *Francovich v Italy* ECLI:EU:C:1991:428. Yet a detailed analysis of the legal acts of EU law on Member States' legal orders when thinking about consent-based monism will follow in Part III.

[278] Alfred Verdross and Bruno Simma, *Universelles Völkerrecht – Theorie und Praxis* (Duncker & Humblot 3rd ed 1984) 550; Stefan Griller, *Die Übertragung von Hoheitsrechten auf zwischenstaatliche Einrichtungen* (Springer 1989) 355, who defines direct applicability (even related to the EU) as national validity of individual international law norms with direct legal effect without any interference of an additional national act. Compare August Reinisch, "Zur unmittelbaren Anwendbarkeit von EWR-Recht" (1993) Zeitschrift für Europarecht, Internationales Privatrecht und Rechtsvergleichung 11–30 (15), with further references in n 40; and Yuji Iwasawa, "The Doctrine of Self-Executing Treaties in the United States: A Critical Analysis" (1986) 26 Virginia Journal of International Law 627–692 (632, n 27); compare also Thomas Buergenthal, "Self-Executing and Non-Self-Executing Treaties in National and International Law" (1992) 235 Recueil des Cours Vol IV 303–400 (317). See also André Nollkaemper, "The Duality of Direct Effect of International Law" (2014) 25 (1) European Journal of International Law 105–125 (107 with further references), pointing to the fact, that "[i]nstances of direct effect, where international law was used as a direct basis for a decision, have been reported in about 30 states outside the EU." He, states, however (108–109), that international law would defer the choice between two identified functions of direct effect, namely "pierc[ing] the boundary of the national legal order and protect individual rights" in contrast to "shield[ing] the national legal order from the effects of international law," to national courts, thereby exposing the "political function of domestic

In this case, no further national Act is needed and EU or national law-applying organs – such as the courts – have to apply it directly.[279] If an international treaty or a provision of it is directly applicable, the smaller (EU or national) circle has already accepted this effect by agreeing to the consensus at the international level. A subsequent unilateral EU or national derogation of the deliberately consented direct applicability of the international treaty is opposed according to consent-based monism. Again, very cautiously, this category relates best to EU regulations (Article 288 TFEU).

6.4.3 *Individualizing Rules*

A third category of international rules, which can be distinguished from solely and directly applicable rules, is individualizing rules. Individualizing rules are those international rules that directly address individuals without the need for an EU or national organ to enforce or apply them. They bind or grant rights to individuals directly without the EU or a State intervening (again, except for the making of this international norm).[280] Individualizing international rules are rules that are not directed towards the EU or the State, but directly towards the individual without using the EU or the State as a mediator. Several international criminal law norms or – with regard to national law only – also Article 34 of the European Convention on Human Rights (institution of proceedings) as well as similar provisions constitute examples of individualizing rules. In this case again, there is no need for any incorporation, adoption or transformation of the international rule into the EU or national legal order. The Charter of Fundamental Rights of the EU as well as the possibility of individuals to launch actions for annulment (Article 263 (4) TFEU) come to mind when speaking about individualizing rules of EU law.

courts at the intersection of legal orders." Cf André Nollkamper, *National Courts and the International Rule of Law* (Oxford University Press 2011) 117 ff.

[279] Karen Kaiser, "Treaties, Direct Applicability" in Rüdiger Wolfrum (ed) *Max Planck Encyclopedia of Public International Law* (2011) para 1; Karel Vasak, "Was bedeutet die Aussage, ein Staatsvertrag sei 'self-executing'? Zum Erkenntnis des Verfassungsgerichtshofs vom 27.6. 1960, B 469/59" (1961) 24 Juristische Blätter 352 (352).

[280] Compare the enumeration made by Jost Delbrück, "Das Individuum im Völkerrecht" in Georg Dahm et al (eds) *Völkerrecht Vol. I/2* (De Gruyter 2nd ed 2002) 259 (263 f) with further references. Stefan Griller, "Völkerrecht und Landesrecht" in Robert Walter et al (eds) *Hans Kelsen und das Völkerrecht – Ergebnisse eines Internationalen Symposiums in Wien* (Manz 2005) 83–120 (96, 98 ff); Anne Peters, *Beyond Human Rights. The Legal Status of the Individual in International Law* (Cambridge University Press 2016).

6.5 THE CONNECTION BETWEEN CIRCLES

Based on the analysis in the previous sections, the larger the circle, the thinner the regulation density becomes.[281] The consensus also tends to become more abstract and fundamental the larger a circle is. However, this is not a theoretical restriction on the regulatory possibility of the larger or even largest possible circle. Rather, it is a practical phenomenon. The more individuals that are involved, the more difficult it is to reach a consensus. But, theoretically, if all legal rules stemmed from the same largest conceivable circle embracing all individuals, no smaller circles would exist. Practically, this is not (yet) the case. Therefore, many subject matters are not embraced by an international, or even a very large EU, circle. Hence, only the most fundamental rules are embraced by the largest possible circle. All but these rules are left to smaller circles at the next smaller level. This continues until the smallest possible level of two individuals. The only condition coming with consent-based monism is that the rules of the smaller circle must not conflict with a rule of the larger circle.

In reading this, one might be tempted to compare the thoughts articulated here with the *Kelsenian* "chain of validity"[282] (in German, *Delegationszusammenhang*, on which the hierarchy of norms, *Stufenbau nach der rechtlichen Bedingtheit*, is based).[283] The main characteristic of this chain of validity is that a norm can derive its validity only from another norm.[284] As a consequence of this conviction, monism with primacy of international law stipulates that all national law derives validity from the higher international law.[285] Similarly, the "competence-theory" of Verdross holds that state sovereignty is a competence derived from international

[281] Of those circles of which the larger circle includes all members of the smaller circle. See Figure 6.6.

[282] Joseph Raz, *The Concept of a Legal System: An Introduction to the Theory of Legal System* (Oxford University Press 2nd ed 1980) 105; Joseph G Starke, "Monism and Dualism in the Theory of International Law" (1936) 17 British Yearbook of International Law 66–81 (75).

[283] Kelsen (n 272) *Reine Rechtslehre* 196 ff, 221–222.

[284] Kelsen (n 272) *Reine Rechtslehre* 196 ff, 221–222. For a critical account of the *Stufenbaulehre* see, for example, András Jakab, "Problems of the Stufenbaulehre: Kelsen's Failure to Derive the Validity of a Norm from Another Norm" (2007) 20 (1) Canadian Journal of Law and Jurisprudence 35–67.

[285] Kelsen (n 272) *Reine Rechtslehre* 221; Verdross (n 9) *Die Verfassung der Völkerrechtsgemeinschaft* 35. Compare for criticism thereof (using the legal order of the EU as an example) Lando Kirchmair, "Die autonome Rechtsordnung der EU und die Grenzen von Monismus und Dualismus" in Matthias C Kettemann (ed) *Grenzen im Völkerrecht – Grenzen des Völkerrechts* (Jan Sramek 2013) 275–291.

law and thus the existence of an international constitution is assumed.[286] Besides other crucial differences between the "chain of validity" and consent-based monism, it is especially important to emphasize that the connection between the larger and the smaller circle according to the approach advanced here requires only that the smaller circle must not infringe any rule of the larger circle. If a specific subject matter is not regulated by a consensus at the level of the larger circle, the smaller circle is free to agree on any consensus as its members wish. Consequently, the smaller circle is not derived from the larger circle and the validity of the rule of the smaller circle does not stem – at least not theoretically – from the larger circle. Only to the extent that a consensus has been established at the level of the larger circle, the smaller circle must not violate this consent. Besides that, consent-based monism does not hinge on dubious transcendental a priori methodology, as does Kelsenian legal monism (Table 6.1).[287]

[286] Verdross (n 9) *Die Einheit des rechtlichen Weltbildes auf Grundlage der Völkerrechtsverfassung* 31–35. This assumption of the "*Kompetenz-Kompetenz*," located at the international sphere becomes even more clear by the statement of Verdross (n 11) Le fondement du droit international 319. Compare generally concerning the "competence–theory" of Verdross Anke Brodherr, *Alfred Verdross' Theorie des gemäßigten Monismus* (Herbert Utz 2004) 75 ff.

[287] For detailed criticism see Section 1.2.

TABLE 6.1 *Consent-based monism in contrast to other approaches*

	Kelsenian monism	Verdrossian monism	Dualism	Global legal pluralism	Global constitutionalism	Consent-based monism
Presuppositions	- (Neo-)Kantian epistemology ("manner of cognizance constitutes the object"). - Hypothetical unity – being kept together by the "chain of validity" and norms can only derive from other norms. - Norm conflict between "different systems of norms" is construed as a legal epistemological impossibility.	- Values based on natural law. - International basic norm: *pacta sunt servanda.*	- International and national law have: - different addressees; - different content (international law is purely inter-State law); - different sources.	- Norm conflicts are positive. - Focus on a descriptive account.	- Common values (and further necessities for constitutional unity). - Universality (at least for the claimed legal orders).	- Prelegal *pacta sunt servanda* (based on innate intersubjectivity) [consent-element]. - Common understanding of the law (however, only in case we want norm conflict solution) [monistic-element].
Theoretical outcome	If international law is law, the logical consequence is that national, EU and international law must be seen as a unitary legal order. - Either international/EU law derives from national law or national law derives from international/EU law.	- "Unity of the legal world order." - Municipal law derives from this international basic norm. - Lawmakers of public international law are not States but the international community, acting through an international organ with supranational power.	- International and national legal orders are: - separated ("two circles which possibly touch, but never cross each other", Triepel) and - based on different grounds of validity.	- Description of pluralistic orders as the basis for a normative account for norm conflict solution.	- The Constitution guides all embraced legal orders/norm conflicts.	- Common denominator for norm conflict solution. - Authorization for norm creation of the smaller circle in the larger circle (if the smaller circle is part of the larger circle).

Legal consequences	- Chain of validity (*Stufenbau nach der rechtlichen Bedingtheit*). - Ultimate ground of validity is the famous basic norm (*Grundnorm*). - If national law conflicts with international law, the earlier Kelsen argued, national law is null and void, the later Kelsen held that national law is voidable.	- Ultimate ground of validity is also the basic norm, which, however, is based on natural law. - if national law conflicts with international law, national law is voidable.	- Norms must be incorporated from one legal order into another. - Legal subjectivity of international organizations (be it the UN or the EU) would have one international and cross-national ground of validity.	- Potential norm conflicts without a common solution (individuals might face contradictory claims).	- Always constitutional (depending on the content of the Constitution).	- Larger circle's consensus trumps (identical) smaller circle's consensus and, hence, the smaller circle must not unilaterally derogate from the consensus of the larger circle. - Content is decisive (in terms of analyzing whether the smaller circle is bound by a consensus of the larger circle).
Failure	- Remains a theory focused on epistemology which does not hold its promise. - Norm conflict solution is highly hypothetical.	- Value-laden theory based in natural law. - Unity of the legal world order is highly fictitious.	- Presuppositions outdated.	- No satisfactory common account for norm conflict solution. - Descriptive accuracy, but normatively wanting. - Praise of norm conflicts without a common solution.	- Presuppositions are too demanding ("burden of universality"). - Not flexible enough for diverging contexts.	

PART III

A Practical Application of Consent-Based Monism

Now that the theory has been spelled out, this final part aims to test its applicability using the example of the European Union and its relationship with its Member States (Chapter 7) as well as with other (international) legal orders (Chapter 8). I am convinced that a theory-based argument analyzing the relationship between international, EU and Member State law will contribute fruitfully to key issues in EU law such as the doctrine of direct applicability, the primacy question between EU law and the fundamental constitutional law of its Member States as well as the relationship between EU and international law.[1] It could provide convincing theoretical argumentation, solving potential tensions between the constitutional courts of some Member States and the CJEU as well as other international courts and tribunals. For example, arguments embedded in a sound theoretical explanation may help to clarify such questions as the tension between European integration and (German) "constitutional identity," which, according to the German Constitutional Court, is resistant to integration.[2] Moreover, the famous "Kadi saga"[3] could be seen in a slightly different light as well.

[1] See, however, for an interesting "radically empirical way how national courts 'react' to disputes involving international organizations" focusing on "'real world' problems," August Reinisch, *International Organizations before National Courts* (Cambridge University Press 2000) xi. See for an overview of important cases of domestic courts applying international law, André Nollkaemper and August Reinisch, *International Law in Domestic Courts. A Casebook* (Oxford University Press 2018). For a general overview on the relationship between EU law and national law, see Paul Craig and Gráinne de Búrca, *EU Law. Text, Cases, and Materials* (Oxford University Press 7th ed 2020) 314 ff.

[2] On this, see eg Mattias Kumm, "Rebel without a Good Cause: Karlsruhe's Misguided Attempt to Draw the CJEU into a Game of "Chicken" and What the CJEU Might Do About It" (2014) 15 (2) German Law Journal 203–215.

[3] Joined Cases C-402/05 P and C-415/05 P *Kadi and Al Barakaat International Foundation v Council and Commission* ECLI:EU:C:2008:461; C-584, C-593, & C-595/10P *Commission v Kadi* ECLI:EU:C:2013:518. Cf Matej Avbelj, Filippo Fontanelli and Giuseppe Martinico (eds) *Kadi on Trial: A Multifaceted Analysis of the Kadi Trial* (Routledge 2014).

7

EU Law and Member State Law

7.1 HOW IT ALL BEGAN

The European Court of Justice famously declared in *Van Gend & Loos* as early as 1963 that the "Community constitutes a new legal order of international law for the benefit of which the states have limited their sovereign rights, albeit within limited fields, and the subjects of which comprise not only the Member States but also their nationals."[4] In addition, the CJEU stipulated that this law enjoys direct effect and creates individual rights which Member States and their courts must respect.[5] A year later, the CJEU added something important. In *Costa v ENEL* the Court stated that the law of the European Community is itself a legal order by postulating the "autonomy of the Community legal order" when holding that "[b]y contrast with ordinary international treaties, the EEC Treaty has created its own legal system which, on the entry into force of the Treaty, became an integral part of the legal systems of the Member States and which their courts are bound to apply."[6] The autonomous EU legal order was born.[7]

[4] Case 26/62 *Van Gend & Loos v Netherlands* ECLI:EU:C:1963:1 p 12.

[5] Case 26/62 *Van Gend & Loos v Netherlands* ECLI:EU:C:1963:1 pp 13, 16.

[6] Case 6/64 *Costa v ENEL* ECLI:EU:C:1964:66 p 593; the German version states "*Rechtsordnung*"; the French version uses "*ordre juridique*"; cf Opinion 1/91 *Draft agreement between the Community, on the one hand, and the countries of the European Free Trade Association, on the other, relating to the creation of the European Economic Area* ECLI:EU:C:1991:490 para 2 postulated the "autonomy of the Community legal order," compare the German version "*Autonomie des Rechtssystems der Gemeinschaft*"; see furthermore on this Werner Schroeder, *Das Gemeinschaftsrechtssystem: Eine Untersuchung zu den rechtsdogmatischen, rechtstheoretischen und verfassungsrechtlichen Grundlagen des Systemdenkens im Europäischen Gemeinschaftsrecht* (Mohr Siebeck 2002) 104–105 (with further references in nn 6 and 7). See also Case C-284/16 *Slovak Republic v Achmea BV* ECLI:EU:C:2018:158 para 33.

[7] See above Chapter 3.

Moreover, the CJEU continued by saying:

> The integration into the laws of each Member State of provisions which derive from the Community, and more generally the terms and the spirit of the Treaty, make it impossible for the States, as a corollary, to accord precedence to a unilateral and subsequent measure over a legal system accepted by them on a basis of reciprocity. Such a measure cannot therefore be inconsistent with that legal system. The executive force of Community law cannot vary from one State to another in defence to subsequent domestic laws, without jeopardizing the attainment of the objectives of the Treaty set out in Article 5 (2) and giving rise to the discrimination prohibited by Article 7.[8]

Thus, the primacy of EU law over Member State law was established.

Based on this foundation, some years later, in *Internationale Handelsgesellschaft* of 1970, the Court explicitly claimed the primacy of EU law even over the constitutional law of its Member States, no matter whether fundamental rights or structural principles are involved:

> Recourse to the legal rules or concepts of national law in order to judge the validity of measures adopted by the institutions of the Community would have an adverse effect on the uniformity and efficacy of Community law. The validity of such measures can only be judged in the light of Community law. In fact, the law stemming from the Treaty, an independent source of law, cannot because of its very nature be overridden by rules of national law, however framed, without being deprived of its character as Community law and without the legal basis of the Community itself being called in question. Therefore the validity of a Community measure or its effect within a Member State cannot be affected by allegations that it runs counter to either fundamental rights as formulated by the constitution of that State or the principles of a national constitutional structure.[9]

In 1978, in *Simmental II*, this primacy of EU law over conflicting Member State law was finally explicitly spelled out in positive terms:

> Furthermore, in accordance with the principle of the precedence of Community law, the relationship between provisions of the Treaty and directly applicable measures of the institutions on the one hand and the

8 Case 6/64*Costa v ENEL* ECLI:EU:C:1964:66 pp 593–594.

9 Case 11/70 *Internationale Handelsgesellschaft* ECLI:EU:C:1970:114 para 3; see in this regard also Case C-409/06 *Winner Wetten GmbH v Bürgermeisterin der Stadt Bergheim* ECLI:EU:C:2010:503 para 61: "Rules of national law, even of a constitutional order, cannot be allowed to undermine the unity and effectiveness of Union law." See also Case C-399/11 *Stefano Melloni v Ministerio Fiscal* ECLI:EU:C:2013:107 para 59.

> national law of the Member States on the other is such that those provisions and measures not only by their entry into force render automatically inapplicable any conflicting provision of current national law but – in so far as they are an integral part of, and take precedence in, the legal order applicable in the territory of each of the Member States – also preclude the valid adoption of new national legislative measures to the extent to which they would be incompatible with Community provisions.[10]

In 1998, in judgment *IN.CO.GE.'90 and others*, the CJEU finally clarified the legal consequences of a conflict between EU law and Member State law. According to the CJEU, EU law enjoys primacy (*Anwendungsvorrang*) but does not invalidate conflicting Member State law (*Geltungsvorrang*):

> It cannot therefore, contrary to the Commission's contention, be inferred from the judgment in Simmenthal that the incompatibility with Community law of a subsequently adopted rule of national law has the effect of rendering that rule of national law non-existent. Faced with such a situation, the national court is, however, obliged to disapply that rule, provided always that this obligation does not restrict the power of the competent national courts to apply, from among the various procedures available under national law, those which are appropriate for protecting the individual rights conferred by Community law.[11]

This primacy creates the effect of forcing national courts to disapply national law contradicting EU law only where the latter has direct effect.[12]

In 2018, in another landmark decision, the CJEU decided that a national high court, the French Conseil d'État, had breached its obligation to submit a preliminary reference according to Article 267 (3) TFEU.[13] Soon after, the CJEU clarified the CILFIT doctrine by adding the requirement that a

[10] Case 106/77 *Amministrazione delle Finanze dello Stato v Simmenthal SpA* ECLI:EU:C:1978:49 para 17.

[11] Case C-10/97 *IN.CO.GE.'90 and others* ECLI:EU:C:1998:498 para 21.

[12] To this end see Case C-573/17, *Popławski* ECLI:EU:C:2019:530 esp para 60–62. See too Dawid Miasik and Monika Szwarc, "Primacy and Direct Effect – Still Together: Poplawski II" (2021) 58 (2) Common Market Law Review 571–590.

[13] Case C-416/17 *Commission v France* ECLI:EU:C:2018:811 para 112, stating that "the existence of reasonable doubt concerning that interpretation [concerning Article 49 and 63 TFEU] could not be ruled out when the Conseil d'État (Council of State) delivered its ruling." For an analysis, see Vincent Delhomme and Lucie Larripa, "C-416/17 Commission v France: Failure of a Member State to Fulfil its Obligations under Article 267(3) TFEU" (November 22, 2018) European Law Blog, available at https://europeanlawblog.eu/2018/11/22/c-416-17-commission-v-france-failure-of-a-member-state-to-fulfil-its-obligations-under-article-2673-tfeu/ [last accessed February 1, 2023].

national high court must give reasons for not referring a case to the CJEU.[14] Yet there is no need to submit a second preliminary reference to check whether the national court of last resort has applied EU law correctly.[15]

In the *Rimšēvičs* case handed down in 2019, however, the CJEU potentially took another major step in the process of European integration. For the first time in the history of the EU, the CJEU declared void an act of a Member State, namely the decision of the Republic of Latvia to relieve the Governor of the Latvian Central Bank, Mr. Ilmārs Rimšēvičs, of his post.[16] While Article 14 (2) of the Statute of the European Central Bank provides for the possibility to refer such a decision to the CJEU "on grounds of infringement," and a cautious reading of this case might point to the specificity of this type of action in the realm of EU banking law, commentators have already described this judgment as a "constitutional moment,"[17] which "should send shockwaves through the circles participating in the discourse on European constitutional law."[18] The "Mephistophelian power of a court to nullify an act of public authority has always been regarded as the ultimate expression of its superior position."[19] This is certainly true in symbolic terms; however, considering the primacy of EU law and the so-called *Rechtsbereinigungspflicht* of Member

[14] Originally, see Case 283/81 *Srl CILFIT and Lanificio di Gavardo SpA v Ministry of Health* ECLI:EU:C:1982:335; for the clarification, see Case C-561/19 *Consorzio Italian Management e Catania Multiservizi and Catania Multiservizi* ECLI:EU:C:2021:799. For a brief analysis, see Imelda Maher, "The CILFIT Criteria Clarified and Extended for National Courts of Last Resort under Art. 267 TFEU" (2021) 7 (1) European Papers 265–274.

[15] Case C-261/21 *F. Hoffmann-La Roche Ltd ea v Autorità Garante della Concorrenza e del Mercato* ECLI:EU:C:2022:534 para 60, stating that "where the supreme court of the administrative system of that Member State gives a decision settling a dispute in which it had made a request to the Court of Justice for a preliminary ruling under Article 267 TFEU, the parties to that dispute may not seek a revision of that decision of the national court based on the contention that the latter disregarded the interpretation of EU law provided by the Court of Justice in response to that request."

[16] Case C-202/18 and C-238/18 *Ilmārs Rimšēvičs and European Central Bank v Republic of Latvia* ECLI:EU:C:2019:139 para 66. Cf Michael Dougan, "The Primacy of Union Law over Incompatible National Measures: Beyond Disapplication and towards a Remedy of Nullity" (2022) 59 (5) Common Market Law Review 1301–1332 (1309 ff), pointing also to Case C-219/17 *Silvio Berlusconi and Finanziaria d'investimento Fininvest SpA (Fininvest) v Banca d'Italia and Istituto per la Vigilanza Sulle Assicurazioni (IVASS)* ECLI:EU:C:2018:1023 as well as (1317 ff) Case C-487/19 W Ż ECLI:EU:C:2021:798 and asking whether "a new Union law remedy of nullity" were on the rise (1321 ff).

[17] Daniel Sarmiento, "Crossing the Baltic Rubicon" (March 4, 2019) Verfassungsblog, available at https://verfassungsblog.de/crossing-the-baltic-rubicon/ [last accessed February 1, 2023].

[18] Jürgen Bast, "Autonomy in Decline? A Commentary on Rimšēvičs and ECB v Latvia" (May 13, 2019) Verfassungsblog, available at https://verfassungsblog.de/autonomy-in-decline-a-commentary-on-rimsevics-and-ecb-v-latvia/ [last accessed February 1, 2023].

[19] Bast (n 18).

States, it is not that different to the CJEU simply declaring the Member State had not acted in conformity with EU law. It was already settled case law that national legislators must not enact new national law conflicting with EU law, which includes the duty to adjust national law to EU law.[20]

Primacy in its typical form as developed by the CJEU is now settled case law.[21] However, "for all its uniqueness and despite the fact that most legal actors have accepted it to a large extent, primacy remains sensitive and contested. This is witnessed by the fact that the attempt to codify it in the Constitutional Treaty failed."[22] Only Declaration No. 17 annexed

[20] See eg Case C-290/94 *Commission v Greece* ECLI:EU:C:1996:265 para 2, on "the principle of the free movement of workers and the abolition of all discrimination based on nationality between workers of the Member States"; Case 104/86 *Commission v Italy* ECLI:EU:C:1988:171 para 12: "As the Court has held on a number of occasions, the primacy and direct effect of the provisions of Community law do not release member states from their obligation to remove from their domestic legal order any provisions incompatible with community law, since the maintenance of such provisions gives rise to an ambiguous state of affairs in so far as it leaves persons concerned in a state of uncertainty as to the possibilities available to them of relying on Community law." Case C-162/99 *Commission v Italy* ECLI:EU:C:2001:35 para 36 maintaining in force of national provisions Italy "has failed to fulfil its obligations under Articles 48 and 52 of the Treaty." Case C-314/08 *Krzysztof Filipiak v Dyrektor Izby Skarbowej w Poznaniu* ECLI:EU:C:2009:719 para 81 with further references: "In accordance with settled case-law, a national court which is called upon, within the exercise of its jurisdiction, to apply provisions of Community law is under a duty to give full effect to those provisions, if necessary refusing of its own motion to apply any conflicting provision of national legislation, even if adopted subsequently, and it is not necessary for the court to request or await the prior setting aside of such provision by legislative or other constitutional means." This is generally acknowledged by national courts, for instance, by the Austrian Constitutional Court: VfSlg 19.632/2012 para 5.8 (*Grundrechtecharta Erkenntnis*). For the literature and the duties of national administrative authorities, see Maartje Verhoeven, *The Costanzo Obligation. The Obligations of National Administrative Authorities in the Case of Incompatibility between National Law and European Law* (Intersentia 2011); and for the duties of national courts, see Monica Claes, *The National Courts' Mandate in the European Constitution* (Hart 2006).

[21] See eg Case C-409/06 *Winner Wetten GmbH* ECLI:EU:C:2010:503 para 55 with further references.

[22] Monica Claes, "The Primacy of EU Law in European and National Law" in Damian Chalmers and Anthony Arnull (eds) *The Oxford Handbook of European Union Law* (Oxford University Press 2015) 178–211 (178). However, see more recently Joined Cases C-357/19, C-379/19, C-547/19, C-811/19 and C-840/19 *Euro Box Promotion ea* ECLI:EU:C:2021:1034 para 248, where the court points to Declaration No 17 of the Treaty of Lisbon concerning primacy and the fact that "essential characteristics of the EU legal order and the importance of compliance with that legal order were ... confirmed by the ratification, without reservation, of the Treaties amending the EEC Treaty and, in particular, the Treaty of Lisbon," and para 249: "Article 4(2) TEU provides that the Union is to respect the equality of Member States," which can only be achieved "if the Member States are unable, under the principle of the primacy of EU law, to rely on, as against the

to the Treaty of Lisbon provides an anchor for this concept in EU primary law.

What is more, on the sixtieth anniversary of *Van Gend & Loos* and soon *Costa ENEL*, and with the help of hindsight, another driving force behind the success of European integration has been detected in the preliminary reference procedure and the ready acceptance of important players in Member State legal orders which apply EU law to give that law its designed effect within Member State legal orders.[23] Hence, the strong position of the CJEU claiming the unconditional primacy of EU law over Member State law depends in a way on organs applying national law.[24] Especially with regard to self-confident national constitutional courts, and unfortunately, one has to

EU legal order, a unilateral measure, whatever its nature." In addition, see Case C-430/21 *RS* ECLI:EU:C:2022:99 para 47, where the court held that the principle of primacy also "constitutes an expression of the principle of sincere cooperation set out in Article 4(3) TEU." For a discussion, see Christoph Krenn, "Warum Unionsrecht Vorrang hat: Zur aktualisierten Begründung des Vorrangprinzips in den Urteilen Euro Box Promotion und RS" (2024) Europarecht (in press).

[23] See in this regard Morten Rasmussen, "Revolutionizing European Law: A History of the *Van Gend en Loos* Judgment" (2014) 12 (1) International Journal of Constitutional Law 136–163 (136), holding that "[t]he new enforcement system remained highly fragile, however, due to the dependency on the cooperation of national courts through the preliminary reference system. As a result, the full effects of the Van Gen den Loos judgment [and EU primacy introduced in *Costa v ENEL*] were only felt after the Single European Act (1986) pushed reluctant national governments and courts to finally come to terms with the legal order the ECJ had developed." For instance, the Austrian Constitutional Court is quite active in this regard and sent its first preliminary reference request only four years after Austria's accession to the EU, VfSlg 15.450/1999.

[24] See in particular the Portuguese Constitutional Tribunal, Tribunal Constitucional, Decision of July 15, 2020, No 422/2020 (Rapporteur: Justice José António Teles Pereira), English translation available at www.tribunalconstitucional.pt/tc/en/acordaos/20200422.html [last accessed February 1, 2023], para 2.3.2.3, stating after reconstructing the European case law on primacy that "in federal systems the unity of the legal order is ensured by the judicial power of the federation – therein lies the *supremacy* of federal law – whereas the primacy of EUL depends entirely on the priority given to its application by national courts. In the event that they refuse to recognise primacy, the only safeguards available to the European Union are the mechanisms of liability for non-compliance. The primacy of EUL therefore lies midway between the supremacy of federal law and the guarantee of international law, reflecting the particular nature of the European integration process." While basically Member States accept the primacy of EU law concerning nonconstitutional Member State law, a lack of knowledge of EU law and more trivial reasons might actually undermine the basic acceptance of the primacy of EU law at least to some extent. See, in this regard Claes (n 22) 187–193 with examples and further references.

add, with captured constitutional courts in illiberal Member States,[25] this adds another perspective that is still of uncertain outcome.[26]

7.2 IT TAKES TWENTY-SEVEN TO TANGO

First, it must be clearly emphasized that this strong position of EU law is bound at the level of EU law by other principles. These principles, which also

[25] In relation to Poland see eg Wojciech Sadurski, *Poland's Constitutional Breakdown* (Oxford University Press 2019) chs 3 and 4; Piotr Bogdanowicz and Maciej Taborowski, "How to Save a Supreme Court in a Rule of Law Crisis: The Polish Experience" (2020) 16 (2) European Constitutional Law Review 306–327; for more details on the situation in Hungary, see eg Gábor Halmai, "A Coup against Constitutional Democracy. The Case of Hungary" in Mark A Graber, Sanford Levinson and Mark Tushnet (eds) *Constitutional Democracy in Crisis?* (Oxford University Press 2018) 243–256; as well as András Jakab, "Informal Institutional Elements as Both Preconditions and Consequences of Effective Formal Legal Rules: The Failure of Constitutional Institution Building in Hungary" (2020) 68 (4) American Journal of Comparative Law 760–800; and Pál Sonnevend, András Jakab and Lóránt Csink, "The Constitution as an Instrument of Everyday Party Politics: The Basic Law of Hungary" in Armin von Bogdandy and Pál Sonnevend (eds) *Constitutional Crisis in the European Constitutional Area* (CH Beck et al 2015) 33–109. Unfortunately, Hungary and Poland are not the only countries affected by this development. See in this regard Seán Hanley and Milada Anna Vachudová, "Understanding the Illiberal Turn: Democratic Backsliding in the Czech Republic" (2018) 34 East European Politics 276–296; as well as David Kosař, Jiří Baroš and Pavel Dufek, "The Twin Challenges to Separation of Powers in Central Europe: Technocratic Governance and Populism" (2019) 15 (3) European Constitutional Law Review 427–461; as well as in the same issue on "Populism and Constitutionalism", Silvia Suteu, "The Populist Turn in Central and Eastern Europe: Is Deliberative Democracy Part of the Solution?" (2019) 15 (3) European Constitutional Law Review 488–518; Paul Blokker, "Populist Counter-Constitutionalism, Conservatism, and Legal Fundamentalism" (2019) 15 (3) European Constitutional Law Review 519–543; and Martin Krygier, "Institutionalisation and Its Trials. (Anti-) Constitutional Populism in Post-Communist Europe" (2019) 15 (3) European Constitutional Law Review 544–573.

[26] Besides a voluminous case law within the realm of the rule of law and democracy crisis in Europe, two pending cases in particular might provide for future groundbreaking steps: Case C-629/21 P(R) *Puigdemont i Casamajó ea v Parliament and Spain* ECLI:EU:C:2022:413, in relation to democracy and the infringement action brought by the Commission against Hungary (Case C-769/22) on December 19, 2022 concerning a potential direct applicability of Article 2 TEU. For a recent analysis of case law, see eg Koen Lenaerts, "The Rule of Law and the Constitutional Identity of the European Union" (March 5, 2023) part of the speech delivered by the president of the CJUE Koen Lenaerts on February 17, 2023 at the conference organized by the Bulgarian Association for European Law in Sofia, available at https://evropeiskipravenpregled.eu/the-rule-of-law-and-the-constitutional-identity-of-the-european-union/#_ftnref49 [last accessed February 1, 2023]; Luke Dimitrios Spieker, *EU Values before the Court of Justice. Foundations, Potential, Risks* (Oxford University Press 2023). Cf Bruno De Witte, "Direct Effect, Primacy and the Nature of the Legal Order" in Gráinne de Búrca and Paul Craig (eds) *The Evolution of EU Law* (Oxford University Press 2011) 323–362 (352–356), pointing to the rulings of various national constitutional courts to establish "counterlimits" of EU primacy indicating a "two-dimensional reality" (356). Cf Claes (n 22) 179, following De Witte by speaking of a "principle of EU law, and . . . national conceptions of the primacy of EU law."

have to be taken into account at EU level, are the principle of loyalty,[27] respect for national identities, respect for the constitutional and procedural autonomy of Member States,[28] as well as the principle of conferral.[29] Second, Article 2 TEU clearly states that "[t]he Union is founded on the values of respect for human dignity, freedom, democracy, equality, the rule of law and respect for human rights, including the rights of persons belonging to minorities." These values are not alien to the Member States, but "are common to the Member States in a society in which pluralism, non-discrimination, tolerance, justice, solidarity and equality between women and men prevail." Finally, the EU Fundamental Rights Charter guarantees that EU law is in conformity with human rights. Before the Treaty of Lisbon, fundamental rights were distilled from the legal orders of the Member States as general principles of EU law as the CJEU was reluctant to consider EU fundamental rights first. As early as 1969, in *Stauder*, fundamental human rights were already represented in the realm of general principles of Community law.[30] Hence, EU law is, in manifold ways, constrained by fundamental legal principles well-known to its Member States. Therefore, a serious violation of national fundamental rights by EU law has become quite unlikely. Finally, Article 4 (2) TEU provides respect for the equality of Member States and their "national identities, inherent in their fundamental structures, political and constitutional, inclusive of regional and local self-government." Moreover, the EU is not an abstract alien entity enforcing strange and evil things on the innocent Member States, a fact that is often forgotten by some national politicians and other actors. Rather, the decisions taken by the EU are well-connected to the Member States acting in the Council and the European Council. The European Parliament is also strongly connected to European citizens.

Despite these guarantees, the absolute primacy of any EU provision over Member State law including constitutional law has, nevertheless, provoked several reactions from national constitutional courts, with the German Federal Constitutional Court spearheading the resistance.

27 See on this generally Marcus Klamert, *The Principle of Loyalty in EU Law* (Oxford University Press 2014).

28 Concerning the former, see Monika Polzin, *Verfassungsidentität: Ein normatives Konzept des Grundgesetzes?* (Mohr Siebeck 2018). Concerning procedural autonomy, see Christoph Krönke, *Die Verfahrensautonomie der Mitgliedstaaten der Europäischen Union* (Mohr Siebeck 2013).

29 See Claes (n 22) 186, who emphasizes these principles.

30 Case 29/69 *Erich Stauder v Stadt Ulm – Sozialamt* ECLI:EU:C:1969:57.

In a decision on June 9, 1971, the German Federal Constitutional Court clearly expressed understanding and accepted the sole responsibility of the CJEU for interpreting the EU Treaties.[31] In that decision, the German Federal Constitutional Court pointed to Article 24 of the German Basic Law, which includes the constitutional authorization to transfer sovereign rights to international institutions. By ratifying the Treaty of Rome, the European Communities, and consequently an originary legal order, was created, which permeates national legal orders.[32]

Yet the transfer of sovereign rights via Article 24 of the German Basic Law is not without limits. This relates particularly to the protection of national fundamental rights that are an inalienable part of the German Basic Law and the constitutional identity of Germany. This was the message delivered to the CJEU in a famous decision by the German Federal Constitutional Court from May 29, 1974 (*Solange I*). According to this decision, EU primacy is only given as long as (*solange*) national fundamental rights pertaining to the national constitutional identity are not violated.[33] In this case, the German Federal Constitutional Court decided that EU secondary law has to be assessed for its conformity with German fundamental rights. Moreover, Article 24 (1) of the German Basic Law does not allow for a transformation of sovereign rights if

[31] BVerfGE 31, 145 (168) (*Lütticke*); see also BVerfGE 22, 293 (295–296) (*EWG Verordnungen*), holding that no constitutional complaint would be admissible against EU secondary law as EU acts originate not from a German authority but from a supranational public authority.

[32] BVerfGE 31, 145 (172–173) (*Lütticke*).

[33] BVerfGE 37, 271 (278–279) (*Solange I*); English translation available at (1974) 11 (2) Common Market Law Review 540 (549): "Article 24 of the Constitution deals with the transfer of sovereign rights to inter-state institutions. This ... does not open the way to amending the basic structure of the Constitution, which forms the basis of its identity, without a formal amendment to the Constitution, that is, it does not open any such way through the legislation of the inter-state institution. ... But Article 24 of the Constitution limits this possibility in that it nullifies any amendment of the Treaty which would destroy the identity of the valid constitutional structure of the Federal Republic of Germany by encroaching on the structures which go to make it up. ... The Community still lacks a democratically legitimated Parliament directly elected by general suffrage which possesses legislative powers and to which the Community organs empowered to legislate are fully responsible on a political level. It still lacks in particular a codified catalogue of fundamental rights, the substance of which is reliably and unambiguously fixed for the future in the same way as the substance of the Constitution. ... Provisionally, therefore, in the hypothetical case of a conflict between Community law and ... the guarantees of fundamental rights in the Constitution ... the guarantee of fundamental rights in the Constitution prevails as long as the competent organs of the Community have not removed the conflict of norms in accordance with the Treaty mechanism."

such a transformation amends the fundamental structure of the German Constitution on which its identity is based.[34]

Nevertheless, this was not the end of history. In the *Solange II* decision of October 22, 1986, the German Federal Constitutional Court confirmed that the transformation of sovereign rights according to Article 24 (1) of the German Basic Law has limits enshrined in the German Constitution.[35] Concretely, Article 24 (1) of the German Basic Law does not allow interference with German constitutional identity, the very fabric of its constitutional structure.[36] However, in *Solange II* the German Federal Constitutional Court accepted that the protection of fundamental rights at EU level is adequate.[37]

The Italian Constitutional Court also stood up against the bold dictum in *Internationale Handelsgesellschaft* in a decision of December 18, 1973, stating that if EU law were to conflict with fundamental principles of the Italian constitutional order or with the inalienable rights of the human person enshrined in the Italian Constitution,[38] the primacy of EU law would end.

34 BVerfGE 37, 271 (279–280) (*Solange I*).

35 BVerfGE 73, 339 (*Solange II*).

36 BVerfGE 73, 339 (375–376) (*Solange II*). Interestingly, this statement was made without reference to Article 79 (3) German Basic Law, the so-called eternity clause, providing that specific fundamental principles cannot be changed by amendment. This is important as Article 24 (1) German Basic Law allows the transfer of sovereign rights via law; hence, a constitutional amendment is not necessary. See Rupert Stettner, "Europäisches Gemeinschaftsrecht als Quelle der Rechtsfindung deutscher Gerichte 1974–1984" (1986) 111 (3 and 4) Archiv des öffentlichen Rechts 359–413 and 537–594 (559). For a detailed discussion, see Polzin (n 28) 45–48 with further references.

37 BVerfGE 73, 339 (387) (*Solange II*); English translation (1987) 24 (3) Common Market Law Review 225: "In view of these developments, it must be held that, so long as the European Communities, and in particular the case law of the European Court, generally ensure an effective protection of fundamental rights as against the sovereign powers of the Communities which is to be regarded as substantially similar to the protection of fundamental rights required unconditionally by the Constitution, and in so far as they generally safeguard the essential content of fundamental rights, the Federal Constitutional Court will no longer exercise its jurisdiction to decide on the applicability of secondary Community legislation cited as the legal basis for any acts of German civil courts or authorities within the sovereign jurisdiction of the Federal Republic of Germany, and it will no longer review such legislation by the standard of the fundamental rights contained in the Constitution." See also BVerfGE 102, 147 (162 ff) (*Bananenmarktordnung*) (esp 164), specifying that the protection of fundamental rights by the EU must be effective and in principle comparable to the German Basic Law.

38 Italian Constitutional Court, Corte costituzionale, decision 183/73 of December 27, 1973 *Frontini* ECLI:IT:COST:1973:183 para 9; English translation available (1974) 2 Common Market Law Review 372. Cf Italian Constitutional Court, Corte costituzionale, decision 170/84 of June 8, 1984 *Granital* ECLI:IT:COST:1984:170; English translation available (1984) 21 Common Market Law Review 756. Cf Marta Cartabia, "The Italian Constitutional Court and the Relationship between the Italian Legal System and the European Community" (1990) 12 Michigan International Law Journal 173–203 (203), suggesting more focus on the general

Interestingly, and similarly to the German Federal Constitutional Court, in Italy, too, the argument was made that these principles were already limited by Italian legislation, which is – according to Article 11 of the Italian Constitution (*controlimiti*, that is, counter-limits in the Italian Constitutional Court doctrine) – not allowed to violate these principles and rights. Thus, these principles and rights must not be exposed to potential violation by the transferal of sovereign rights to an international institution either.

In both cases, the emancipation of the European integration project was presumably not foreseen by the constitutional architecture or, at the very least, was advancing at a faster pace than expected. Hence, to keep up with these developments in Germany, a new *Europa-Artikel*, Article 23 of the German Basic Law, was enacted in 1992 to allow for the signing of the Maastricht Treaty in the same year.[39] This article explicates the limits of the transfer as laid down in the German Basic Law by referring to Article 79 (3), the eternity clause (Ewigkeitsklausel). Article 23 states that in order to realize a unified Europe, the Federal Republic of Germany is willing to contribute to the development of the EU, which is obliged to ensure democratic, social and federal principles as well as the principle of subsidiarity and the rule of law. Moreover, this provision stipulates that the EU should provide for the protection of fundamental rights comparable to the German Basic Law.[40] Germany is not the only Member State to have established a proper "Europe clause" in its constitution, with Sweden, Portugal and Lithuania following suit.[41] In Austria,

relationship between the institutions rather than on particular norms and pleading for a strong autonomy of the European system in order to avoid "'nationalization' of Community law."

39 See eg Rudolf Streinz, "Artikel 23" in Michael Sachs (ed) *Grundgesetz* (CH Beck 7th ed 2014); cf Kirsten Schmalenbach, *Der neue Europaartikel 23 des Grundgesetzes im Lichte der Arbeit der Gemeinsamen Verfassungskommission* (Duncker & Humblot 1996).

40 Article 23 (1) German Basic Law: "With a view to establishing a united Europe, the Federal Republic of Germany shall participate in the development of the European Union that is committed to democratic, social and federal principles, to the rule of law and to the principle of subsidiarity and that guarantees a level of protection of basic rights essentially comparable to that afforded by this Basic Law. To this end the Federation may transfer sovereign powers by a law with the consent of the Bundesrat. The establishment of the European Union, as well as changes in its treaty foundations and comparable regulations that amend or supplement this Basic Law or make such amendments or supplements possible, shall be subject to paragraphs (2) and (3) of Article 79" (Law from December 21, 1992, BGBl I, p 2086 amended by BGBl. I 2008 p 1926) [official translation by Professor Christian Tomuschat, Professor David P Currie, Professor Donald P Kommers and Raymond Kerr, in cooperation with the Language Service of the German Bundestag, including the amendment(s) to the Act by the Act of June 28, 2022 (Federal Law Gazette I p 968)].

41 See Claes (n 22) 197 with further references.

Article 23a–k of the Austrian Constitution was enacted before Austria's accession to the EU in 1995.[42]

Thus, Article 23 (1) of the German Basic Law served as a legal basis for the ratification of the Treaty of Maastricht. In the *Maastricht* decision of October 12, 1993, the German Federal Constitutional Court clearly emphasized the limits of the transformation of sovereign rights to the EU:

> An interpretation of Article F(3) which would give the Union a power to extend its powers would also contradict the consistently expressed intention of the Contracting Parties to define by Treaty provisions the principle of restricted specific empowerment and to set clear limits to individual rules conferring powers. If Article F(3) were the basis for a power to take powers, it would cut across the whole system of competences under the Union Treaty, as well as the Treaties establishing the European Communities, the subsequent Treaties, and the Acts amending or supplementing them, and make them largely meaningless. Such an interpretation is also contradicted by Article M, which excludes any implied amendment of the existing Treaties by the Union Treaty.[43]

Moreover, the German Federal Constitutional Court determined the limits of the transformation of sovereign rights according to Article 79 (3) of the German Basic Law and the enshrined democracy principle as well as statehood.[44] This includes that "[p]articipation in the democratic process must not be voided of content through too all-embracing a transfer of the functions and powers of the German parliament."[45] The starting point is the constitutive people of the Member States accounting for statehood, which in turn democratically legitimates the EU as well.[46] Article 79 (3) of the German Basic Law provides the guarantee for that as it is only to be amended in the

[42] The accession was made possible via a proper Constitutional Law which was, according to Article 44 (3) of the Austrian Constitution, approved by an obligatory public referendum. The Austrian Constitution was amended by introducing a new section B "Europäische Union" including six new Articles, since increased to eleven Articles. For an overview of the process in 1995, see Christoph Grabenwarter, "Änderungen der österreichischen Bundesverfassung aus Anlaß des Beitritts zur Europäischen Union" (1995) 55 Heidelberg Journal of International Law 166–190.

[43] BVerfGE 89, 155 (173) (*Maastricht*) English translation (1994) 31 (1) Common Market Law Review 57 para 68.

[44] BVerfGE 89, 155 (188 ff) (*Maastricht*).

[45] BVerfGE 89, 155 (172, 186) (*Maastricht*) English translation (1994) 31 (1) Common Market Law Review 57.

[46] BVerfGE 89, 155 (186) (*Maastricht*) English translation (1994) 31 (1) Common Market Law Review 57.

case of a (legal) revolution. Moreover, the German Federal Constitutional Court declared:

> Inasmuch as the Treaties establishing the European Communities, on the one hand, confer sovereign rights applicable to limited factual circumstances and, on the other hand, provide for Treaty amendments (through a normal procedure and a simplified one) this distinction is also important for the future treatment of the individual powers. Whereas a dynamic extension of the existing Treaties has so far been supported on the basis of an open-handed treatment of Article 235 of the EEC Treaty as a "competence to round-off the Treaty" as a whole, and on the basis of considerations relating to the "implied powers" of the Communities, and of Treaty interpretation as allowing maximum exploitation of Community powers ("effet utile"), in future it will have to be noted as regards interpretation of enabling provisions by Community institutions and agencies that the Union Treaty as a matter of principle distinguishes between the exercise of a sovereign power conferred for limited purposes and the amending of the Treaty, so that its interpretation may not have effects that are equivalent to an extension of the Treaty. Such an interpretation of enabling rules would not produce any binding effects for Germany.[47]

Later on the German Federal Constitutional Court specified that this only holds true for "obvious" and "substantive" violations of the competences.[48]

What is interesting to us is that the discussion revolves – roughly speaking – around the question of what is included in the transfer of sovereignty from a Member State to the EU. This question did not concern only the German and Italian Constitutional Courts. They were further joined by other constitutional or supreme courts of EU Member States.[49]

47 BVerfGE 89, 155 (210) (*Maastricht*) English translation (1994) 31 (1) Common Market Law Review 57 [footnotes omitted].

48 BVerfGE 126, 286 (304) (*Honeywell*) "offensichtlich" and "hinreichend qualifiziert"; *Honeywell* with reference to BVerfGE 123, 267 (353) (*Lisbon*), holding that, first, the CJEU must be consulted with a preliminary reference. For a comparative analysis see also Maja Walter, "Integrationsgrenze Verfassungsidentität – Konzept und Kontrolle aus europäischer, deutscher und französischer Perspektive" (2012) 72 Heidelberg Journal of International Law 177–200 (200), concluding that in 2012 the discourse on national constitutional identity by national constitutional courts in France and Germany are mere "smoke signals" instead of practical decision-making strategies.

49 See, for instance, the Danish Supreme Court, Højesteret, Decision of April 6, 1998 – I 361/1997 (*Maastricht*) and thereto Frederik Thomas, "Das Maastricht-Judgment des dänischen Obersten Gerichtshofs vom 6. April 1998" (1998) 58 Heidelberg Journal of International Law 879–906 with further references and a partial German translation of the judgment. See also the Belgian Cour d'Arbitrage, Decision of October 16, 1991– 26/91, printed in (1992) Journal des Tribunaux 6670, and thereto Franz C Mayer, *Kompetenzüberschreitung und*

In its Lisbon judgment of June 30, 2009, the German Federal Constitutional Court confirmed that "it must be possible within the German jurisdiction to assert the responsibility for integration if obvious transgressions of the boundaries occur when the European Union claims competences."[50] This assertion can also serve "to preserve the inviolable core content of the Basic Law's constitutional identity by means of an identity review."[51]

Moreover,

> [t]he [German] Federal Constitutional Court has already opened up the way of the ultra vires review for this, which applies where Community and Union institutions transgress the boundaries of their competences. If legal protection cannot be obtained at the Union level, the [German] Federal Constitutional Court examines whether legal instruments of the European institutions and bodies keep within the boundaries of the sovereign powers accorded to them by way of conferral whilst adhering to the principle of subsidiarity under Community and Union law (Article 5.2 ECT; Article 5.1 second sentence and 5.3 Lisbon TEU).[52]

The German Federal Constitutional Court continues by noting: "Furthermore, the [German] Federal Constitutional Court reviews whether

Letztentscheidung. Das Maastricht-Urteil des Bundesverfassungsgerichts und die Letztentscheidung über Ultra vires-Akte in Mehrebenensystemen. Eine rechtsvergleichende Betrachtung von Konflikten zwischen Gerichten am Beispiel der EU und der USA (CH Beck 2000) 179 ff with a comparative overview of the then fifteen EU Member States and the impact of the *Maastricht* decision of the German Federal Constitutional Court. See Mayer (228 ff) with reference also to the Spanish Constitutional Tribunal, Tribunal Constitutional, Decision of July 1, 1992, 108/1992, reprinted in (1993) Europäische Grundrechte-Zeitschrift 285, in which the Spanish Constitutional Tribunal also held that it has the competence to review whether Community law is in compliance with the Spanish Constitution. For another overview see Mattias Wendel, *Permeabilität im europäischen Verfassungsrecht: verfassungsrechtliche Integrationsnormen auf Staats- und Unionsebene im Vergleich* (Mohr Siebeck 2011). See also Julio Baquero Cruz, "The Legacy of the Maastricht-Urteil and the Pluralist Movement" (2008) 14 (4) European Law Journal 389–422 (389), stating that the *Maastricht* decision of the German Federal Constitutional Court "has left a deep mark on EU law."

50 BVerfGE 123, 267 (353–354) (*Lisbon*) para 240 (English translation available on the homepage of the German Constitutional Court: www.bundesverfassungsgericht.de/SharedDocs/Entscheidungen/EN/2009/06/es20090630_2bve000208en.html [last accessed February 1, 2023]). On the judgment see Daniel Thym, "In the Name of Sovereign Statehood: A Critical Introduction to the Lisbon Judgment of the German Constitutional Court" (2009) 46 (6) Common Market Law Review 1795–1822.

51 BVerfGE 123, 267 (353–354) (*Lisbon*) para 240 with further reference to BVerfGE 75, 223 (235) (*Kloppenburg*); 89, 155 (188) (*Maastricht*); 113, 273 (296) (*European Arrest Warrant*).

52 BVerfGE 123, 267 (353–354) (*Lisbon*) para 240 with further reference to BVerfGE 58, 1 (30–31) (*Eurocontrol I*); 75, 223 (235, 242) (*Kloppenburg*); 89, 155 (188) (*Maastricht*).

the inviolable core content of the constitutional identity of the Basic Law pursuant to Article 23.1 third sentence in conjunction with Article 79.3 of the Basic Law is respected."[53] The origin of this is laid down:

> The exercise of this review power, which is rooted in constitutional law, follows the principle of the Basic Law's openness towards European Law (*Europarechtsfreundlichkeit*), and it therefore also does not contradict the principle of sincere cooperation (Article 4.3 Lisbon TEU); otherwise, with progressing integration, the fundamental political and constitutional structures of sovereign Member States, which are recognised by Article 4.2 first sentence Lisbon TEU, cannot be safeguarded in any other way. In this respect, the guarantee of national constitutional identity under constitutional and under Union law go hand in hand in the European legal area. The identity review makes it possible to examine whether due to the action of European institutions, the principles under Article 1 and Article 20 of the Basic Law, declared inviolable in Article 79.3 of the Basic Law, have been violated. This ensures that the primacy of application of Union law only applies by virtue and in the context of the constitutional empowerment that continues in effect.[54]

The Lisbon judgment of the German Federal Constitutional Court finally unfolds the concept of constitutional identity as a "uniform abstract absolute concept," which, at the same time, sets limits to the transformation of sovereign rights to the EU and the primacy of EU law.[55] Article 79 (3) of the German Basic Law is "the limit of the inviolable constitutional identity."[56] Moreover, "the constituent power has not granted the representatives and bodies of the people a mandate to dispose of the identity of the constitution."[57] Beyond that, the German Federal Constitutional Court once again emphasized the international law character of the EU.[58]

[53] BVerfGE 123, 267 (*Lisbon*) para 240 with further reference to BVerfGE 113, 273 (296) (*European Arrest Warrant*).

[54] BVerfGE 123, 267 (353–354) (*Lisbon*) para 240.

[55] Polzin (n 28) 48–49.

[56] BVerfGE 123, 267 (344) (*Lisbon*) para 219.

[57] BVerfGE 123, 267 (343–344) (*Lisbon*) para 218. Confirming BVerfGE 132, 195 (238) (*ESM einstweiliger Rechtsschutz*); BVerfGE 135, 317 (413) (*ESM*).

[58] BVerfGE 123, 267 (eg 328) (*Lisbon*). See also affirmatively in this regard Ewald Wiederin, "Deutschland über alles: Das Lissabon-Urteil des Bundesverfassungsgerichts" (2010) 48 (9) Österreichische Juristenzeitung 398–406 (402). See also Armin von Bogdandy and Stephan Schill, "Overcoming Absolute Primacy: Respect for National Identity under the Lisbon Treaty" (2011) 48 (5) Common Market Law Review 1417–1454, according to whom the "revised identity clause [in the Treaty of Lisbon compared to the Maastricht Treaty] can help to reconceptualize the relationship between EU law and domestic constitutional law and guide the way to a more nuanced understanding beyond the categorical positions of the ECJ

In its *Lisbon* judgment in 2013, the Danish Supreme Court held that the CJEU has authority on the interpretation of EU law. This, however, "must not result in a widening of the scope of Union powers."[59] Moreover, the "Danish authorities are obliged to ensure that this [that no new powers are transferred to the EU] is observed." This national control of the *Kompetenz-Kompetenz* was further confirmed by the Danish Supreme Court in the *Ajos* case on December 6, 2016.[60] "In essence, *Ajos* is illustrative of a turn towards a greater national patrolling of the limited mandate given to the EU, including its judicial organ."[61] The Polish Constitutional Court also held that EU primacy has its limits.[62]

on the one side, which supports the doctrine of absolute primacy of EU law even over the constitutional law of Member States, and that of most domestic constitutional courts on the other, which largely follow a doctrine of relative primacy in accepting the primacy of EU law subject to certain constitutional limits" [footnotes omitted]. They do so by also emphasizing a nonhierarchical, but pluralist understanding of the relationship between the EU and Member State legal orders. Thus, they see their suggested understanding to be in line with "multilevel approaches, the network concept and – especially in Germany – the concept of Verbund (i.e., a composite structure)" (1419–1420 with further references in nn 8–10). On national identities, see Ingolf Pernice, "Der Schutz nationaler Identität in der Europäischen Union" (2011) 136 (2) Archiv des öffentlichen Rechts 185–221; Alejandro Saiz Arnaiz and Carina Alcoberro Llivina (eds) *National Constitutional Identity and European Integration* (Intersentia 2013); and Christian Calliess and Gerhard van der Schyff, *Constitutional Identity in a Europe of Multilevel Constitutionalism* (Cambridge University Press 2019) in general; Constance Grewe, "Methods of Identification of National Constitutional Identity" in Alejandro Saiz Arnaiz and Carina Alcoberro Llivina (eds) *National Constitutional Identity and European Integration* (Intersentia 2013) 37–48; and Monica Claes, "National Identity: Trump Card or Up for Negotiation?" in Alejandro Saiz Arnaiz and Carina Alcoberro Llivina (eds) *National Constitutional Identity and European Integration* (Intersentia 2013) 109–139 in particular.

59 Danish Supreme Court, Højesteret, Decision of February 20, 2013 – 199/2012 (*Lisbon*) part III confirming Danish Supreme Court, Højesteret, Decision of April 6, 1998 – I 361/1997 (*Maastricht*). See on the Lisbon judgment Helle Krunke, "The Danish Lisbon Judgment: Danish Supreme Court, Case 199/2012, Judgment of 20 February 2013" (2014) 10 (3) European Constitutional Law Review 542–570; as well as Henrik Palmer Olsen, "The Danish Supreme Court's Decision on the Constitutionality of Denmark's Ratification of the Lisbon Treaty" (2013) 50 (5) Common Market Law Review 1489–1503. Cf Helle Krunke, "Impact of the EU/EEA on the Nordic Constitutional Systems" in Helle Krunke and Björg Thorarensen (eds) *The Nordic Constitutions. A Comparative and Contextual Study* (Hart 2018) 167–202.

60 Danish Supreme Court, Højesteret, Decision of December 6, 2016 – 15/2014 (*Dansk Industri (DI) on behalf of Ajos A/S vs Estate of Karsten Eigil Rasmussen*). See thereto Helle Krunke and Sune Klinge, "The Danish *Ajos* Case: The Missing Case from *Maastricht* and *Lisbon*" (2018) 3 (1) European Papers 157–182.

61 Mikael Rask Madsen, Henrik Palmer Olsen and Urška Šadl, "Legal Disintegration? The Ruling of the Danish Supreme Court in AJOS" (January 30, 2017) Verfassungsblog, available at https://verfassungsblog.de/legal-disintegration-the-ruling-of-the-danish-supreme-court-in-ajos/ [last accessed February 1, 2023].

62 Polish Constitutional Tribunal, Trybunal Konstytucyjny, Decision of November 24, 2010, K 32/09 (*Lisbon Treaty*), English translation available at www.trybunal.gov.pl/eng/index.htm

The Italian Constitutional Court finally engaged in a direct dialogue with the CJEU after the Tribunale di Cuneo (District Court of Cuneo, Italy) sent a preliminary reference request to the CJEU in 2014. The CJEU decided in the *Taricco I* case[63] that Article 325 TFEU, namely the obligation of the EU and its Member States to "counter fraud and any other illegal activities affecting the financial interests of the Union," is directly applicable and that the primacy of EU law entails that certain provisions of Italian criminal law contradict this aim.[64] The sensitive matter of a substantive tax criminal law provision and previous case law of the Italian Constitutional Court led to a rare preliminary reference request by the Italian Constitutional Court in which it essentially questioned the *Taricco I* judgment when asking the CJEU, could you "say it again, please?"[65] According to the Italian Constitutional Court, the issue concerned, namely "the principle of non-retroactivity of criminal law affirmed by Article 25 of the Italian

[last accessed February 1, 2023], holding that (2.6) "[f]rom the point of sovereignty and the protection of other constitutional values, what is significant is the limitation of conferral of competences 'in relation to certain matters' (and thus without infringing the 'core' competences, which allow for sovereign and democratic determination of the fate of the Republic of Poland, pursuant to the Preamble of the Constitution)." In this judgment, the Polish Constitutional Tribunal noted the differences between the German and Polish Constitutions. Nevertheless, it made explicit reference to the concept of "constitutional identity" in the Lisbon judgment of the German Federal Constitutional Court (*Lisbon Treaty* 3.3); cf the decision of the Polish Constitutional Tribunal, of November 16, 2011 SK 45/09 (Re Brussels Regulation – Council Regulation (EC) No 44/2001) 2: "The secondary legislation of the European Union as the subject of constitutional review". See also Paul Craig, "Constitutional Identity in the United Kingdom: An Evolving Concept" in Christian Calliess and Gerhard van der Schyff (eds) *Constitutional Identity in a Europe of Multilevel Constitutionalism* (Cambridge University Press 2019) 284–302 (301), noting that "[t]here are clear indications that the [UK] Supreme Court has been influenced by German law when framing UK jurisprudence on relations between the UK and the EU, more especially concerning constitutional limits to the grant of power to the EU."

63 Case C-105/14 *Criminal proceedings against Ivo Taricco and Others* ECLI:EU:C:2015:555.

64 For an analysis of the "Taricco saga," see Giovanni Piccirilli, "The 'Taricco Saga': the Italian Constitutional Court Continues Its European Journey" (2018) 14 (4) European Constitutional Law Review 814–833; as well as Matteo Bonelli, "The Taricco Saga and the Consolidation of Judicial Dialogue in the European Union: CJEU, C-105/14 Ivo Taricco and others, ECLI: EU:C:2015:555; and C-42/17 M.A.S., M.B., ECLI:EU:C:2017:936 Italian Constitutional Court, Order no. 24/2017" (2018) 25 (3) Maastricht Journal of European and Comparative Law 357–373.

65 For this wording, see Pietro Faraguna, "The Italian Constitutional Court in re Taricco: 'Gauweiler in the Roman Campagna'" (January 31, 2017) Verfassungsblog, available at https://verfassungsblog.de/the-italian-constitutional-court-in-re-taricco-gauweiler-in-the-roman-campagna/ [last accessed February 1, 2023]. Italian Constitutional Court Order No 24 of 2017, available at www.giurcost.org/decisioni/2017/00240-17.html; English translation www.cortecostituzionale.it/documenti/download/doc/recent_judgments/O_24_2017.pdf [last accessed February 1, 2023].

Constitution[,] applies also to provisions regulating limitation periods."[66] However, precisely those provisions were found to be against Article 325 of the TFEU by the CJEU in the first place. On December 5, 2017, the CJEU solved the issue diplomatically rather than dogmatically. It expressed understanding essentially by stating that Article 325 of the TFEU would not apply to already committed tax crimes, but only to future misconduct.[67] On a positive note, we can hold that the Italian Constitutional Court did not engage in a *controlimiti* or constitutional identity language, nor did the CJEU ignore substantial provisions of the law of a Member State. However, the quite pragmatic solution also provokes criticism in as much as it "might have opened a Pandora's box for an even broader trend towards constitutional exceptionalism among EU Member States."[68]

Interestingly, and in contrast to this line, for instance,[69] the Austrian Constitutional Court principally acknowledges the primacy of EU law over national constitutional law.[70] However, the core principles of the Austrian

[66] Bonelli (n 64) 361.

[67] Case C-42/17 *Criminal proceedings against MAS und MB* ECLI:EU:C:2017:936.

[68] Dana Burchardt, "Belittling the Primacy of EU Law in Taricco II" (December 7, 2017) Verfassungsblog, available at https://verfassungsblog.de/belittling-the-primacy-of-eu-law-in-taricco-ii/ [last accessed February 1, 2023].

[69] Also "Dutch courts, unlike some of their foreign counterparts, have never expressed *Solange*-type limits to the supremacy of EU law." See thereto André Nollkaemper and Rosanne van Alebeek, "Netherlands" in Fulvio Maria Palombino (ed) *Duelling for Supremacy: International Law vs. National Fundamental Principles* (Cambridge University Press 2019) 255–276 (256). See for the finding that the "principle of consistent interpretation proves to be effective and of great practical importance for public international as well as then European Community law, especially in Dutch courts, Gerrit Betlem and André Nollkaemper, "Giving Effect to Public International Law and European Community Law before Domestic Courts. A Comparative Analysis of the Practice of Consistent Interpretation" (2003) 14 (3) European Journal of International Law 569–589 (569).

[70] See already VfSlg 14.886/1997. See Christoph Grabenwarter, "National Constitutional Law Relating to the European Union" in Armin von Bogdandy and Jürgen Bast (eds) *Principles of European Constitutional Law* (Hart et al 2nd ed 2011) 95–144 (97 n 6) with reference to the Austrian Constitutional Court, VfSlg 15.427/1999, "on the replacement of the organisational provision of Art 133 No 4 of the Federal Constitution by a Directive." On this see also Theo Öhlinger, "Übernahme des Vertrages von Lissabon in die österreichische Rechtsordnung" in Waldemar Hummer and Walter Obwexer (eds) *Der Vertrag von Lissabon* (Nomos 2009) 411–425 (417), who adds that the Austrian Constitutional Court did accept the primacy of EU law without even questioning it; as well as Konrad Lachmayer, "The Constitution of Austria in International Constitutional Networks: Pluralism, Dialogues and Diversity" in Anneli Albi and Samo Bardutzky (eds) *National Constitutions in European and Global Governance: Democracy, Rights, the Rule of Law. National Reports* (Springer 2019) 1271–1322, pointing to the case law in which the Austrian Constitutional Court set aside constitutional law due to the primacy of EU law already four years after Austria's accession to the EU, VfSlg 15.427/1999; see also VfSlg 17.065/2003, 19.632/2012.

Constitution, the so-called *Baugesetze* or *Grundprinzipien*, which can only be amended by public referendum according to Article 44 (3) of the Austrian Constitution (*Bundes-Verfassungsgesetz, B-VG*), are not considered to be subordinate to EU law by Austrian constitutional experts.[71] Nevertheless, an ultra vires act would only be declared if the act in question were obviously without any justification.[72] Concerning the Charter of Fundamental Rights of the European Union (CFR) the Austrian Constitutional Court declared in 2012 that the CFR will be used as a standard of constitutional review by the Austrian Constitutional Court.[73] In 2018 the Belgian[74], French[75] and in

[71] See, for instance, Peter Pernthaler, *Der Verfassungskern. Gesamtänderung und Durchbrechung der Verfassung im Lichte der Theorie, Rechtsprechung und europäischen Verfassungskultur* (Manz 1998) 14, who speaks of a double constitution (Peter Pernthaler, "Die neue Doppelverfassung Österreichs" in Herbert Haller et al (eds) *Staat und Recht. Festschrift für Günther Winkler* (Springer 1997) 773–796), whereas, however, the core of the constitution – which he equates with the fundamental principles (Pernthaler, *Der Verfassungskern* 27) – constitutes the outermost limit of supranational development of the law (with explicit reference to BVerfGE 89, 155 (Maastricht) in n 61. See also Theo Öhlinger, "Die Transformation der Verfassung. Die staatliche Verfassung und die europäische Integration" (2002) 124 (1) Juristische Blätter 2–11 (2) as well as Theo Öhlinger, "Die österreichische Verfassung und die europäische Integration" in Waldemar Hummer (ed) *Paradigmenwechsel im Europarecht zur Jahrtausendwende* (Springer 2004) 67–85, who also emphasizes that these core principles have obviously been changed by Austria's accession to the EU (this accession necessitated a public referendum according to Article 44 (3) of the Austrian Constitution and thereby fundamentally changed the core principles of the Austrian constitution).

[72] See Theo Öhlinger and Michael Potacs, *EU-Recht und staatliches Recht. Die Anwendung des Europarechts im innerstaatlichen Recht* (Linde 6th ed 2017) 19–20, which notes that the prevailing view accepts the Court's monopoly on interpretation as well as its sweeping powers, since Austria somehow knew what it was getting into when it joined the EU. Furthermore, it provides the example that only such a judgment of the Court would be qualified as an absolutely null and void act if it certified that a secondary law act is covered by EU competences which it is not in a quite obviously unjustifiable manner ("ganz offenkundig unvertretbarer Weise").

[73] VfSlg 19.632/2012. See for an overview Gisela Kristoferitsch, "The Charter of Fundamental Rights of the European Union to Be Treated like Constitutional Law. Austrian Constitutional Court Judgment of 14 March 2012, U 466/11 et al" (2013) 7 (1) Vienna Journal on International Constitutional Law 88–92; for a critical analysis, see eg Magdalena Pöschl, "Verfassungsgerichtsbarkeit nach Lissabon Anmerkungen zum Charta-Erkenntnis des VfGH" (2012) 67 (3) Zeitschrift für Öffentliches Recht 587–609; Reinhard Klaushofer and Rainer Palmstorfer, "Austrian Constitutional Court Uses Charter of Fundamental Rights of the European Union as Standard of Review: Effects on Union Law" (2013) 19 (1) European Public Law 1–11; as well as Stefan Kieber and Reinhard Klaushofer, "The Austrian Constitutional Court Post Case-Law after the Landmark Decision on Charter of Fundamental Rights of the European Union" (2017) 23 (2) European Public Law 221–236.

[74] Belgium Constitutional Court, Cour Constitutionnelle, 15 March 2018 No 29/2018 B.9, B.10.5, B.15 ff.

[75] French Constitutional Court, Conseil Constitutionnel, 26 July 2018 No 2018-768 DC para 10, 12, 38. For an analysis, see Laurence Burgorgue-Larsen, "La mobilisation de la Charte des

2019 also the Italian[76] and German[77] Constitutional Courts followed suit. While this case law on the CFR is complex and profound, for our purposes two striking commonalities deserve to be highlighted. First, this case law shows the struggle of Member State constitutional courts that actively seek and advocate for their position in the application of European constitutional law in general and European fundamental rights law in particular, even if this includes quite progressive judgments not explicitly supported by provisions in the respective Member State constitutions.[78] Yet it clearly stated that the CJEU has the final say on the interpretation of the CFR.[79] In essence, the relationship between EU human rights law and Member State constitutional courts can be described as rather trusting.[80]

However, in the *Honeywell* judgment of July 6, 2010 the German Federal Constitutional Court granted the CJEU development of the law, albeit methodologically limited:[81] "Ultra vires review may only be exercised in a manner

droits fondamentaux de l'Union européenne par les juridictions constitutionnelles" (2019) Titre VII (2) De l'intégration des ordres juridiques: droit constitutionnel et droit de l'Union européenne 31–40.

76 Italian Constitutional Court, Corte costituzionale, January 23, 2019 No 20/2019 para 2.1, 2.3. For an analysis, see Oreste Pollicino and Giorgio Repetto, Not to Be Pushed Aside: The Italian Constitutional Court and the European Court of Justice (February 27, 2019) Verfassungsblog, available at https://verfassungsblog.de/not-to-be-pushed-aside-the-italian-constitutional-court-and-the-european-court-of-justice/ [last accessed February 1, 2023], highlighting, among other things in the judgment, the statement that "the Charter 'is a part of Union law that is endowed with particular characteristics due to the typically constitutional stamp of its contents,'" and therefore "it cannot be left to the ordinary judges to enforce its contents in domestic law."

77 BVerfGE, 152, 216 (*Recht auf Vergessen II*). For an analysis, see eg Thomas Kleinlein, "Neue starke Stimme in der europäischen Grundrechts-Polyphonie" (December 1, 2019) Verfassungsblog, available at https://verfassungsblog.de/neue-starke-stimme-in-der-europaeischen-grundrechts-polyphonie/ [last accessed February 1, 2023]; as well as Marten Breuer, "Wider das Recht auf Vergessen … des Bundesverfassungsgerichts!" (December 2, 2019) Verfassungsblog, available at https://verfassungsblog.de/wider-das-recht-auf-vergessen-des-bundesverfassungsgerichts/ [last accessed February 1, 2023].

78 See eg the German Federal Constitutional Court, BVerfGE 152, 216 (*Recht auf Vergessen II*) para 53–61, quite frankly admitting that this is in order to avoid its loss of significance. Admittedly, legally the decision is motivated by a diagnosed gap in the legal protection of EU fundamental rights as there is no European constitutional complaint mechanism. This gap must be closed according to the duty of integration in Art 23 (1) of the German Basic Law.

79 See, again, the German Federal Constitutional Court BVerfGE, 152, 216 (*Recht auf Vergessen II*) para 69, also with explicit reference to the preliminary reference procedure according to Art 267 (3) TFEU and the respective case law Case 283/81 *Srl CILFIT and Lanificio di Gavardo SpA v Ministry of Health* ECLI:EU:C:1982:335 para 21.

80 See eg Andreas Paulus, "Horizontale und vertikale Aufgabenteilung beim Grundrechtsschutz in Europa" in Thomas Groh et al (eds) *Verfassungsrecht, Völkerrecht, Menschenrchte – Vom Recht im Zentrum der Internationalen Beziehungen. Festschrift für Ulrich Fastenrath* (C F Müller 2019) 79–88 (85) speaking of mutual trust (*gegenseitigem Vertrauen*).

81 BVerfGE 126, 286 (303–306) (*Honeywell*).

which is friendly towards European law."[82] Quite generously, the German Federal Constitutional Court acknowledged:

> The Union understands itself as a legal community; it is in particular bound by the principle of conferral and by fundamental rights, and it respects the constitutional identity of Member States (see in detail Art. 4 sec. 2 sentence 1, Art. 5 sec. 1 sentence 1 and Art. 5 sec. 2 sentence 1, as well as Art. 6 sec. 1 sentence 1 and Article 6 sec. 3 TEU). According to the legal system of the Federal Republic of Germany, the primacy of application of Union law is to be recognised and it is to be guaranteed that the powers of control which are constitutionally reserved for the [German] Federal Constitutional Court are only exercised in a manner that is cautious and friendly towards European law. This means for the ultra vires review at hand that the [German] Federal Constitutional Court must in principle comply with the rulings of the Court of Justice as a binding interpretation of Union law.

In addition, the CJEU must be vested with the opportunity to provide its opinion on the matter: "Prior to the acceptance of an ultra vires act by European bodies and institutions, the Court of Justice is therefore to be afforded the opportunity to interpret the Treaties, as well as to rule on the validity and interpretation of the legal acts in question, in the context of preliminary ruling proceedings according to Art. 267 TFEU." Moreover:

> Ultra vires review by the [German] Federal Constitutional Court can ... only be considered if it is manifest that acts of European institutions and agencies have taken place outside the transferred powers (see BVerfGE 123, 267 <353, 400>). A breach of the principle of conferral is only manifest if the European bodies and institutions have transgressed the boundaries of their powers in a manner specifically violating the principle of conferral (Article 23.1 of the Basic Law), the breach of powers is, in other words, sufficiently qualified.

Hence, "the act of authority of the European Union must be manifestly in violation of powers and that the impugned act is highly significant for the allocation of powers between the Member States and the Union with regard to the principle of conferral and to the binding nature of the statute under the rule of law."[83] This passage was quoted at length in the *OMT* decision of January 14, 2014.[84] Moreover, in that decision the German Federal

[82] BVerfGE 126, 286 (303) (*Honeywell*) with further reference to BVerfGE 123, 267 (354) (*Lisbon*).

[83] BVerfGE 126, 286 (303 and 304) (*Honeywell*).

[84] BVerfGE 134, 366 (*OMT*) para 24, English translation available at www.bundesverfassungsgericht.de/SharedDocs/Entscheidungen/EN/2014/01/rs20140114_

Constitutional Court clarified that German constitutional identity is not identical to the national identities respected by the TEU as the German constitutional identity provided for by Article 79 (3) of the German Basic Law is absolute and the national identity according to Article 4 (2) TEU is subject to balancing.[85] Beyond that, the German Federal Constitutional Court further concretized how constitutional identity sets limits to the primacy of EU law (albeit without declaring in the specific cases that the constitutional identity would have been violated by an act of the EU).[86] In the decision of December 15, 2015, the German Federal Constitutional Court admitted a constitutional complaint with the purpose of an identity control. The message is clear and withdraws the trust expressed in the *Solange II*. Article 23 (1) in connection with Article 79 (3) of the German Basic Law establishes a protection that allows for control on a case-by-case basis.[87] Identity control includes human dignity as enshrined in Article 1 of the German Basic Law in addition to the principles of democracy, the rule of law, the welfare state principle and the federal principle as guaranteed by Article 20 of the German Basic Law.[88]

2_runhead; [last accessed February 1, 2023]. See thereto the special issue (2014) 15 (2) German Law Journal.

85 BVerfGE 134, 366 (386) (*OMT Vorlage*) confirming BVerfGE 123, 267 (343) (*Lisbon*); see also BVerfGE 142, 123 (202) (*OMT Decision*). See on the difference Polzin (n 28) 62–67 with further references. On national identity, see Elke Cloots, *National Identity in EU Law* (Oxford University Press 2015).

86 BVerfGE 140, 317 (354–366) (*Identitätskontrolle*); BVerfGE 142, 123 (*OMT Decision*); BVerfGE 146, 216 (para 57) (*PSPP Vorlage*).

87 BVerfGE 140, 317 (341) (*Identitätskontrolle*); confirmed by BVerfGE 142, 123 (194–195) (*OMT Decision*). In this judgment (BVerfGE 142, 123 (207–208)), the German Federal Constitutional Court established also a duty of constitutional organs to face potential violations of EU organs of the constitutional identity. In this regard see also more recently BVerfGE 151, 202 paras 1–320 (94) (*Europäische Bankenunion*). See also Christian Walter and Markus Vordermayer, "Verfassungsidentität als Instrument richterlicher Selbstbeschränkung in transnaitonalen Integrationsprozessen. Vergleichende Überlegungen anhand der Rechtsprechung von EuGH und EGMR" (2015) 63 Jahrbuch des öffentlichen Rechts der Gegenwart 129–166 (131–132) with further references and diagnosing a tendency of establishing constitutional identity control mechanisms in European constitutional courts which they consider critically if they are applied unilaterally: Member States as keepers of the grail cannot exist in an integrated community. Critically also Christoph Schöneberger, "Identitäterä – Verfassungsidentität zwischen Widerstandsformel und Musealisierung des Grundgesetzes" (2015) 63 Jahrbuch des öffentlichen Rechts der Gegenwart 41–62; Dana Burchardt, "Die Ausübung der Identitätskontrolle durch das Bundesverfassungsgericht – Zugleich Besprechung des Beschlusses 2 BvR 2735/14 des BVerfG vom 15.12.2015 ('Solange III'/'Europäischer Haftbefehl II')" (2016) 76 Heidelberg Journal of International Law 527–551; as well as Polzin (n 28) 59–61.

88 BVerfGE 142, 123 (195) (*OMT Decision*); BVerfGE 143, 65 (para 59) (*CETA einstweiliger Rechtsschutz I*); see also recently BVerfGE 151, 202 paras 1–320 (204) (*Europäische

Finally, the German Federal Constitutional Court also states that such identity control has to be exercised in friendliness to EU law.[89] From this follows that the CJEU has to be asked first in a preliminary reference according to Article 267 (3) TFEU.[90] Importantly, the German Federal Constitutional Court also outlines the difference between an identity control and an ultra vires control although both are connected to Article 79 (3) of the German Basic Law.[91] This also constitutes a deviation from the Maastricht judgment as formerly the control of an ultra vires act was solely related to the competences transferred to the EU in the statute with which the Treaty had been ratified.[92] This also includes, via the reference to Article 79 (3) of the German Basic Law, the democracy principle enshrined in Article 20 (2) of the German Basic Law.[93]

Even though the Czech Constitutional Court declared a judgment by the CJEU to be ultra vires in 2012,[94] it was the judgment by the German Federal

Bankenunion) confirming that the ultra vires control and the identity control are self-standing measures of control (albeit both are related to Article 79 (3) German Basic Law). While the former controls for the action of EU organs and institutions for potentially overstepping the authorization according to Article 23 (1) German Basic Law (and the doctrine of the "*ausbrechender Rechtsakt*"), the latter does not control the conformity of this authorization, but the absolute limit ("*absolute Grenze*") provided by Article 79 (3) German Basic Law. The ultra vires control is a particular case of the identity control focused on the principle of democracy (BVerfGE 151 para 205 with further reference to BVerfGE 142, 123 (203 para 153) (*OMT Decision*)).

89 BVerfGE 140, 317 (338) (*Identitätskontrolle*); BVerfGE 142, 123 (203–204) (*OMT Decision*).

90 BVerfGE 142, 123 (204) (*OMT Decision*); also in this regard BVerfGE 146, 216 (para 58) (*PSPP Vorlage*).

91 BVerfGE 142, 123 (202) (*OMT Decision*).

92 BVerfGE 89, 155 (188) (*Maastricht*).

93 BVerfGE 142, 123 (188, 190–195, 202) (*OMT Decision*); BVerfGE 143, 65 (paras 50–51, 59) (*CETA einstweiliger Rechtsschutz I*); BVerfGE 146, 216 (para 44 ff, 63, 124) (*PSPP Vorlage*).

94 Czech Constitutional Court, Ústavní soud České republiky, Decision of February 14, 2012 – Pl Ús 5/12 declaring ultra vires Case C-399/09 *Marie Landtová v Česká správa socialního zabezpečení* ECLI:EU:C:2011:415. See thereto Jan Komárek, "Playing with Matches: The Czech Constitutional Court Declares a Judgment of the Court of Justice of the EU Ultra Vires; Judgment of 31 January 2012, Pl. ÚS 5/12, Slovak Pensions XVII" (2012) 8 (1) European Constitutional Law Review 323–337; as well as Attila Vincze, "Das tschechische Verfassungsgericht stoppt den EuGH. Zum Urteil des tschechischen Verfassungsgerichts Pl. ÚS 5/12 vom 14.2.2012" (2013) 48 (2) Europarecht 194–204. Interestingly the Polish Constitutional Tribunal also assessed the conformity of secondary EU law with the Polish Constitution, coming to the conclusion, however, that secondary EU law under scrutiny did not violate the Polish Constitution. See Decision of November 16, 2011 – SK 45/09 (*Re Brussels Regulation – Council Regulation (EC) No 44/2001*). Cf Katarzyna Granat, "Kontrolle des EU-Sekundärrechts durch den polnischen Verfassungsgerichtshof. Anmerkung zum Beschluss des polnischen Verfassungsgerichtshofs vom 16. November 2011, SK 45/09" (2013) 48 (2) Europarecht 205–214 (214), who concludes that the cautious decision by the Polish

Constitutional Court on May 5, 2020 that created a great deal of fuss. Until May 5, 2020, the relationship between the CJEU and the German Federal Constitutional Court could indeed be described – despite all the ups and downs and small ruptures – as a "fruitful dialogue."[95] Yet, despite all its intricacies, this harmonious relationship has been shaken to the core by the so-called PSPP judgment of the German Federal Constitutional Court.[96] For the first time in the history of the EU, the German Federal Constitutional Court declared a judgment of the CJEU ultra vires, stating that it had acted "objectively arbitrarily" when "interpreting the treaties in a way which was no longer comprehensible."[97] Calling the CJEU judgment "arbitrary," so ran the justification by the then president of the Court, Andreas Voßkuhle, in an interview,[98] might sound harsh to a layperson but it was legally necessary, as this was the hurdle self-imposed by the German Federal Constitutional Court in the *Honeywell* judgment.[99] The corresponding judge in this case, Peter M. Huber, also explained in two newspaper interviews that this finding had been "legally mandatory."[100] Despite the lengthy judgment, it is more than questionable whether the CJEU judgment on the PSPP program of the European Central Bank[101] must actually be mandatorily qualified as ultra vires in terms of structurally expanding the competences of the EU, in this case by exceeding the ECB's mandate. In an unparalleled critique of the judgment, several lawyers and EU civil servants as well as German and Austrian law professors formulated a critical comment, which was then signed in an open letter – by further law professors, national civil servants and lawyers. This critique challenged the finding that it was "mandatory."[102] Without

Constitutional Tribunal can be interpreted as a signal for a harmonious relationship between EU and Member State law. See also Koen Lenaerts, "Kooperation und Spannung im Verhältnis von EuGH und Verfassungsgerichten" (2015) (1) Europarecht 3–27 (16 ff), identifying a conflict between the German Federal Constitutional Court and the CJEU concerning the ultra vires control and the division of competences between the EU and its Member States – although Lenaerts (3) emphasizes that despite some martial language being used in public debate, he prefers a sober and responsible analysis of the shared responsibility in the multilevel system of the EU.

95 In this vein, Paulus (n 80) 86.

96 BVerfGE 154, 17 (*PSPP*).

97 BVerfGE 154, 17 (*PSPP*) para 112, 116.

98 Interview with Andreas Voßkuhle, Erfolg ist eher kalt, *Die Zeit* May 14, 2020.

99 BVerfGE 126, 286 (*Honeywell*), and above 205 and 212–213.

100 Interview with Peter M Huber, "Das EZB-Urteil war zwingend," *Frankfurter Allgemeine Zeitung* May 12, 2020; as well as Corinna Budras, EZB hätte kooperativer sein müssen, *Frankfurter Allgemeine Zeitung* June 29, 2020.

101 Case C-493/17 Weiss et al ECLI:EU:C:2018:1000.

102 Jan Dietze et al, "Europa – Quo Vadis? Ein kritischer Kommentar zum EZB-Urteil des BVerfG" (2020) 31 (12) Europäische Zeitschrift für Wirtschaftsrecht 525–530. This comment

delving into the intricacies of this complex topic, it is noteworthy for the purposes of this book that the judgment was unprecedented in the sense that the constitutional court of a Member State declared a judgment by the CJEU in a matter of substance to be ultra vires and thereby strongly questioned the autonomy of the CJEU in authoritatively interpreting the Treaties. On this point, the critique of the PSPP judgment of the German Federal Constitutional Court is largely justified.[103]

This judgment arguably has inspired several other Member State constitutional courts, which have subsequently delivered similar judgments. The French Conseil d'État declared in April 2021 that – despite the primacy of EU law – the French Constitution was at the top of the French legal order. Article 88-1 of the French Constitution integrated the EU legal order. The consequence thereof is that if the application of a European directive or regulation, as interpreted by the CJEU, would have the effect of removing the effective guarantees of the French Constitution (without equivalent protection at EU level), the administrative judge must set aside EU law.[104] In a decision of the Polish Constitutional Tribunal delivered on October 7, 2021, the Polish Constitutional Tribunal has stated that Union law does not take precedence over (Polish) national constitutional law.[105] On the contrary, the attempt of

was published in connection with and signed by "Professor Dr. Dr. h.c. mult. Jürgen Basedow, Hamburg – Professor Dr. Peter Behrens, Hamburg – Rechtsanwalt Dr. Georg Berrisch, Brüssel – Jan Ceyssens, Brüssel – Professor Dr. Stefan Griller, Salzburg – Professor Dr. Herwig Hofmann, Luxemburg – Professor Dr. Susanne Kalss, Wien – Professor Dr. Katja Langenbucher, Frankfurt a. M. – Professor Dr. Leander D. Loacker, Zürich – Professor Dr. Theo Öhlinger, Wien – Professor Dr. Dr. h.c. Ingolf Pernice, Berlin – Professor Dr. Jessica Schmidt, Bayreuth – Professor Dr. Francesco Schurr, Innsbruck – Rechtsanwalt Dr. Gerd Schwendinger, Hamburg – Professor Dr. Daniel Thym, Konstanz – Rechtsanwalt Dr. Andreas von Bonin, Brüssel – Rechtsanwalt Professor Dr. Robin van der Hout, Brüssel."

[103] See the almost immediate post by Franz C Mayer, "Auf dem Weg zum Richterfaustrecht? Zum PSPP-Urteil des BVerfG" (May 7, 2020) Verfassungsblog, available at https://verfassungsblog.de/auf-dem-weg-zum-richterfaustrecht/ [last accessed February 1, 2023], asking whether we are on the way to the "law of the jungle of judges"; or András Jakab and Pal Sonnevend, "The Bundesbank Is under a Legal Obligation to Ignore the PSPP Judgment of the Bundesverfassungsgericht" (May 25, 2020) Verfassungsblog, available at https://verfassungsblog.de/the-bundesbank-is-under-a-legal-obligation-to-ignore-the-pspp-judgment-of-the-bundesverfassungsgericht/ [last accessed February 1, 2023], concluding that it is "more than likely that this new sort of judicial politics [introduced by the PSPP judgment when 'flagrantly giving up on a paradigm that ensured peace between two of the most important courts in Europe'] will equally hurt European integration and the rule of law." See furthermore the critical analysis offered in the special issue "The German Federal Constitutional Court's PSPP Judgment" (2020) 21 (5) German Law Journal.

[104] French State Council, Conseil d'État, Decision of April 21, 2021, No 393099, paras 4 and 5.

[105] Polish Constitutional Tribunal, Decision of October 7, 2021, K 3/21. For an impressive rebuke by twenty-seven retired judges of the Polish Constitutional Tribunal, see Stanisław

the CJEU to "interfere" in the Polish judiciary would violate the rule of supremacy of the Polish Constitution and the rule that sovereignty must be preserved in the process of European integration. The Hungarian and Romanian Constitutional Courts have reasoned in a similar way too.[106] In the case of Hungary, for instance, the Hungarian government is constitutionally empowered to disapply EU law if it considers that it would violate Hungarian constitutional identity. Due to these events and the preceding developments, "the functioning of the EU legal order itself is in jeopardy."[107]

It seems that by declaring the CJEU judgment ultra vires, these constitutional courts have finally proven that the ultra vires control by Member States should not be in the hands of quite a small number of judges speaking in the name of democracy and sovereignty but rather in the sphere of politics. Hence, when a Member State holds that an EU act is ultra vires, this should rather be expressed by a democratic decision of the Member State because the CJEU has, judicially speaking, the last word on matters of EU competence.[108]

7.3 THE PREVAILING DOCTRINE, ALTERNATIVE APPROACHES AND CRITIQUE

In the literature, these cases have been hotly debated, with countless arguments and various approaches being advanced. A very interesting and

Biernat et al, "Statement of Retired Judges of the Polish Constitutional Tribunal" (October 11, 2021) Verfassungsblog, available at https://verfassungsblog.de/statement-of-retired-judges-of-the-polish-constitutional-tribunal/ [last accessed February 1, 2023].

[106] Hungarian Constitutional Court, Alkotmánybíróság, Decision of December 20, 32/2021 (XII. 20.) AB; for an analysis, see Attila Vincze, "Unsere Gedanken sind Sprengstoff – Zum Vorrang des Euro-parechts in der Rechtsprechung des ungarischen Verfassungsgerichts" (2022) 49 Europäische Grundrechte Zeitschrift 13–21. Rumanian Constitutional Court, Curtea Constituțională a României, Decision of June 8, 2021, No 390 (published in the official Gazette no. 612 of June 22, 2021 and in English translation, available at www.ccr.ro/wp-content/uploads/2021/07/Decizie_390_2021_EN.pdf [last accessed February 1, 2023]) para 74 ff.

[107] Thomas Ackermann et al, "Editorial Comments: Clear and Present Danger: Poland, the Rule of Law & Primacy" (2021) 58 (6) Common Market Law Review 1635–1648 (1648).

[108] See Thomas von Danwitz, "Einheitliche Auslegung und Vorrang des Unionsrechts im Dialog der Gerichte" Verfassunbslog (October 27, 2022), available at https://verfassungsblog.de/einheitliche-auslegung-und-vorrang-des-unionsrechts-im-dialog-der-gerichte/ [last accessed February 1, 2023], noting from the point of view of EU law that the discussion concerning the uniform interpretation and the primacy of EU law "is now beginning with renewed vehemence [and] seems strangely out of step with the times" [translation by LK].

influential concept is that of multilevel constitutionalism by Ingolf Pernice.[109] In his words:

> Multilevel constitutionalism is based on the assumptions that the *contrat social*, the concept developed by Rousseau, does not necessarily lead to one unitary State, and that the notion of constitution is not necessarily bound to a rigid concept of the State. This new conception creates room for a pluri- or multilevel organization of public authority and responsibilities. Federal States are a classic example that a society can be organized in a two-level State structure, in which limited public authority is entrusted to bodies called "states", both on the national and subnational level; powers are divided between two levels of government according to their respective constitutions. They are an example not only of the possibility of such division but also of the variety of ways in which the relationship between the two levels of original and basically autonomous public authority can be organized. However, multilevel constitutionalism does not necessarily imply statehood at each level. The essential feature of a two or multilevel constitutional (federal) system is that the legitimacy of the various levels of government is not derived from one another. Rather, each level of government has "original" legitimacy, insofar as it is democratically founded on the general will of the people affected by its policies, on the one hand, and has direct jurisdiction over the people (citizenry) from which its legitimacy is derived, on the other. Multilevel constitutionalism bridges the apparent conflict between European constitutionalism and the constitutionalism of the Member States.[110]

The idea of this concept can be read as an answer to the Maastricht judgment of the German Constitutional Court.[111] In this spirit, European and Member

[109] For the German designation *Verfassungsverbund* (as an alternative concept to the *Staatenverbund* as used by the German Federal Constitutional Court) and a particular emphasis on the European citizens, see Ingolf Pernice, "Die Dritte Gewalt im europäischen Verfassungsverbund" (1996) 31 (1) Europarecht 27–43; Ingolf Pernice, "Multilevel Constitutionalism and the Treaty of Amsterdam: European Constitution-Making Revisited?" (1999) 36 (4) Common Market Law Review 703–750; Ingolf Pernice, "Europäisches und nationales Verfassungsrecht" (2001) 60 Veröffentlichungen der Vereinigung der Deutschen Staatsrechtslehrer 148–193; Ingolf Pernice, "The Treaty of Lisbon: Multilevel Constitutionalism in Action" (2009) 15 (3) Columbia Journal of European Law 349–407; as well as a tool for criticizing current state of affairs in times of crisis, see Ingolf Pernice, "Multilevel Constitutionalism and the Crisis of Democracy in Europe" (2015) 11 (3) European Constitutional Law Review 541–562.

[110] Pernice (n 109) Multilevel Constitutionalism and the Treaty of Amsterdam 709 [footnotes omitted].

[111] See Matthias Jestaedt, "Der Europäische Verfassungsverbund – Verfassungstheoretischer Charme und rechtstheoretische Insuffizienz einer Unschärferelation" in Rüdiger Krause,

State law are two levels, which, however, form a unitary system due to material, functional and institutional interdependence: the European Constitution.[112] Hence, in every single case there is a legal answer to a norm conflict.[113] Interestingly, it is precisely this unity of the system that asks for the acceptance of a collision norm for norm conflicts, which is the primacy principle defended by the CJEU.[114] Nevertheless, this does not result in a subordination of either the European or a national constitutional law because "[t]he development of the European Union is an open and dynamic constitutional process of (re)allocation and (re)definition of powers in a multilevel system of political governance. The goal is not a 'super State.'"[115]

Parallels from this approach to consent-based monism are quite evident, especially when we consider that Ingolf Pernice speaks of a "European social contract"[116] and points to two separately legitimized legal orders.[117] Differences lie in the materially requested substance of the legal orders – both conceptualized

Winfried Veelken and Klaus Vieweg (eds) *Recht der Wirtschaft und der Arbeit in Europa: Gedächtnisschrift für Wolfgang Blomeyer* (Duncker & Humblot 2004) 637–674 (641) [wiederabgedruckt in Christian Calliess (eds) *Verfassungswandel im europäischen Staaten- und Verfassungsverbund. Beiträge der Ersten Göttinger Gespräche zum deutschen und europäischen Verfassungsrecht vom 15. bis 17. Juni 2006* (Mohr Siebeck 2007) 93–128]. See also Stefan Griller, "Fragmentierungen im Öffentlichen Recht: Diskursvergleich im internationalen und nationalen Recht" (2018) 77 Veröffentlichungen der Vereinigung der Deutschen Staatsrechtslehrer 237–283 (254).

112 Pernice (n 109) Europäisches und nationales Verfassungsrecht 153, 173–174; Pernice (n 109) Multilevel Constitutionalism and the Treaty of Amsterdam 728. See, however, Joseph Weiler, "Epilogue. The European Courts of Justice: Beyond 'Beyond Doctrine' or the Legitimacy Crisis of European Constitutionalism" in Anne-Marie Slaughter, Alex Stone Sweet and Joseph H H Weiler (eds) *The European Court and National Courts – Doctrine and Jurisprudence: Legal Change in Its Social Context* (Hart 1998) 365–391 (366): "After all, as has been evident for some time now . . . national Sleeping Beauty has woken up and discovered that she did not like the European Union Prince at all."

113 Pernice (n 109) Dritte Gewalt 31–32; Pernice (n 109) Europäisches und nationales Verfassungsrecht 172; see also Pernice (n 109) Multilevel Constitutionalism and the Treaty of Amsterdam 712. See also Joseph H H Weiler and Ulrich Haltern, "The Autonomy of the Community Legal Order – Through the Looking Glass" (1996) 37 (2) Harvard International Law Journal 411–448 (447): "The constitutional discourse in Europe must be conceived as a conversation of many actors in a constitutional interpretive community, rather than a hierarchical structure with the ECJ at the top. . . . A feature of neo-constitutionalism in this case would be that the jurisdictional line (or lines) should be a matter of constitutional conversation, not a constitutional *diktat*" [emphasis original].

114 Pernice (n 109) Europäisches und nationales Verfassungsrecht 182; Pernice (n 109) Multilevel Constitutionalism and the Treaty of Amsterdam 713–714.

115 Pernice (n 109) Multilevel Constitutionalism and the Treaty of Amsterdam 729; see also Pernice (n 109) Europäisches und nationales Verfassungsrecht 185.

116 Pernice (n 109) Multilevel Constitutionalism and the Treaty of Amsterdam 749–750.

117 On the autonomous validity of EU law ("autonome Geltung"), see Theo Öhlinger, "Verfassungsrechtliche Aspekte der Übernahme von Gemeinschaftsrecht und Unionsrecht in

as constitutional (which somehow limits the concept concerning the relationship of international and EU law unless one is ready also to conceptualize international law as constitutional) – as well as in the conceptualization of the norm conflict solution. Multilevel constitutionalism in Pernice's conception presupposes "a constitution made up of the constitutions of the Member States bound together by a complementary constitutional body existing of the European Treaties."[118] This conception has attracted many followers in Germany[119] and

die österreichische Rechtsordnung" in Waldemar Hummer and Michael Schweitzer (eds) *Österreich und das Recht der Europäischen Union* (Manz 1996) 169–197 (171–172); as well as Theo Öhlinger, "Unmittelbare Geltung und Vorrang des Gemeinschaftsrechts und die Auswirkungen auf das verfassungsrechtliche Rechtsschutzsysttem" in Stefan Griller, Karl Korinek and Michael Potacs (eds) *Grundfragen und aktuelle Probleme des öffentlichen Rechts. Festschrift für Heinz Peter Rill zum 60. Geburtstag* (LexisNexis 1995) 359–379 (361), making a comparison holding that EU law is valid in its Member States, as is Austrian federal law in its federal states, in order to demonstrate that EU law certainly must not be transformed (*übernommen*) in the legal orders of its Member States. This is not to say that the EU is a federal state, but is well described by Anna Katharina Mangoldt, *Gemeinschaftsrecht und deutsches Recht. Die Europäisierung der deutschen Rechtsordnung in historisch-empirischer Sicht* (Mohr Siebeck 2011) 494, as the reconstruction – in her case – of the German legal order as a Member State legal order (as we do not speak of the legal order of federal states, for instance the legal order of Baden Württemberg and the German legal order, we should not speak of the EU and the German legal orders but of a Member State legal order). See also Theo Öhlinger, "Die Auswirkungen der Europäischen Integration auf die Rechtssysteme der Mitgliedstaaten" in Fritz Breuss, Gerhard Fink and Stefan Griller (eds) *Vom Schumann-Plan zum Vertrag von Amsterdam* Vol 2 (Springer 2000) 51–68 (58 ff); Öhlinger and Potacs (n 72) 57–58, with a comparison to a federal state and the validity of the law of the federation in a state. Cf Michael Potacs, "Zum Rang des Gemeinschaftsrechts gegenüber staatlichem Recht" in Clemens Jabloner, Otto Lucius and Alfred Schramm (eds) *Theorie und Praxis des Wirtschaftsrechts. Festschrift für H. René Laurer* (Springer 2009) 185–198 (188 ff), holding that for this reason EU law cannot be integrated in the chain of validity of the Austrian legal order (*Stufenbau der österreichischen Rechtsordnung*). In this regard also Theo Öhlinger, "EU-Beitritts-BVG in Karl Korinek et al (eds) *Österreichisches Bundesverfassungsrecht* (Verlag Österreich 2016) para 75. However, see Stefan Griller, "Der Stufenbau der österreichischen Rechtsordnung nach dem EU-Beitritt" (2000) 8 Journal für Rechtspolitik 273–288 (284), who states that the relationship between EU law and the Austrian legal order can be conceptualized with monism or dualism. For an early critical view stating that Austrian law could derogate EU law according to the principle *lex posterior derogat legi priori*, see Hans René Laurer, "Europarecht und österreichische Rechtsordnung – Rechsnormen in einem einheitlichen Stufenbau? – Ein 'Vorwort'" (1997) 52 (21) Österreichische Juristenzeitung 801–810.

118 Pernice (n 109) Multilevel Constitutionalism and the Treaty of Amsterdam 707.

119 See for instance Franz C Mayer, "Verfassung im Nationalstaat: Von der Gesamtordnung zur europäischen Teilordnung?" (2016) 75 Veröffentlichungen der Vereinigung der Deutschen Staatsrechtslehrer 7–63 (28 ff), who speaks, however, of a "cooperative constitutional pluralism" (38 ff), and also holds that we should differentiate between supremacy (and a normative hierarchy) and primacy (a nonhierarchical priority (*Vorrang*)) of EU law which does not entail primacy of validity (*Anwendungsvorrang* is not a *Geltungsvorrang*) but merely a right of way as in traffic (*Vorfahrtsregel* or *Vorzugsregel*, as termed by Anne Peters, *Elemente einer Theorie der Verfassung Europas* (Duncker & Humblot 2001) 219). This metaphoric

beyond.[120] By way of a sort of reconciliation, even the former president of the German Federal Constitutional Court, Andreas Voßkuhle, advanced a nonhierarchical understanding of a *Verfassungsgerichtsverbund* – in his words, a "multilevel cooperation of the European constitutional courts."[121]

It is, however, the claim of this unity that provokes criticism. One of the critiques by Matthias Jestaedt accuses the concept of being an "oxymoron" from the perspective of legal theory.[122] The point of departure of this criticism

language, however, is quite telling. For we are left figuring out what is the legal meaning of this traffic rule. For a critique of the limited potential of the notion of multilevel constitutionalism (*Staatenverbund, Verfassungsverbund*), which cannot enhance our knowledge, see eg Armin von Bogdandy, "Konstitutionalisierung des europäischen öffentlichen Rechts in der europäischen Republik" (2005) 60 (11) JuristenZeitung 529–540 (533, n 43): "Das Manko dieser Begriffsbildungen ist, dass sie keine Ebene des Vergleichs eröffnen und damit nur begrenzt erkenntnisstiftend sind." Dana Burchardt, *Die Rangfrage im europäischen Normenverbund. Theoretische Grundlagen und dogmatische Grundzüge des Verhältnisses von Unionsrecht und nationalem Recht* (Mohr Siebeck 2015); Dana Burchardt, "The Relationship between the Law of the European Union and the Law of Its Member States – A Norm-Based Conceptual Framework" (2019) 15 (1) European Constitutional Law Review 73–103, put forward another interesting conception which aligns in a way with the multilevel conceptualizations when claiming that a mere analysis of the legal orders should be extended to an additional analysis of involved norms – a so-called *Normenverbund*.

120 For Austria, see for instance, Pernthaler (n 71) Die neue Doppelverfassung; Öhlinger (n 117) EU-Beitritts-BVG para 74–75; Öhlinger and Potacs (n 72) 9; cf Gunnar Folke Schuppert, "Europa im Verfassungsfieber – Bemerkungen zu Sinn und Unsinn der europäischen Verfassungsdebatte" in Ines Katenhusen and Wolfram Lamping (eds) *Demokratien in Europa: Der Einfluss der europäischen Integration auf Institutionenwandel und neue Konturen des demokratischen Verfassungsstaates* (Springer 2003) 91–116 (106), who differs by asking "Doppelverfassung, Verfassungsverbund oder multilevel constitutionalism?"

121 Andreas Voßkuhle, "Multilevel Cooperation of the European Constitutional Courts: Der Europäische Verfassungsgerichtsverbund" (2010) 6 (2) European Constitutional Law Review 175–198; see also Andreas Voßkuhle, "'European Integration through Law': The Contribution of the Federal Constitutional Court" (2017) 58 (1) European Journal of Sociology 145–168, going further down this line by speaking of the "Basic Law's openness to integration," "as well as the co-operation between the [German] Federal Constitutional Court and the European Court of Justice in the execution of European Union law and the protection of fundamental rights." For a conceptualization as a network and a judicial dialogue respectively, see eg another (former) justice of the German Federal Constitutional Court, Andreas L Paulus, "Human Rights Protection in a European Network of Courts" (2013) 107 Proceedings of the American Society of International Law 174–182; as well as Andreas L Paulus, "Engaging in Judicial Dialogue" in Amrei Müller (ed) *Judicial Dialogue and Human Rights* (Cambridge University Press 2017) 258–266. Finally, speaking also of cooperation, see again two (former) justices, Peter M Huber and Andreas L Paulus, "Cooperation of Constitutional Courts in Europe: The Openness of the German Constitution to International, European, and Comparative Constitutional Law" in Mads Andenas and Duncan Fairgrieve (eds) *Courts and Comparative Law* (Oxford University Press 2015) 281–299.

122 Jestaedt (n 111) 657–673, holding that the concept of multilevel constitutionalism does not withstand the "stresstest" from the perspective of legal theory (658). See also critically Griller (n 111) 264, n 105, who, however, expresses his criticism less "sharply" and not in full

is the Kelsenian assumption that the specific normative existence of law is its validity, which is the attributability of a norm to a legal order.[123] From such a perspective, a norm from another autonomous legal order, in our case EU law, is perceived as nonlaw from the perspective of a Member State legal order. This holds true as long as the EU norm is not received, or in other words created, by the Member State legal order.[124] This also excludes the possibility of an "interactive exchange" or "one dialogue" but two separate normative processes.[125]

Another major objection refers to two contradictory claims: The principle of primacy constituting the unity of the EU and Member State legal orders on the one hand and the claim of a heterarchical, nonhierarchical relation of these legal orders on the other.[126] Indeed, the Kelsenian perspective, which is taken by Jestaedt, has been criticized in this book.[127] The critique of multilevel constitutionalism being dealt with here, however, has a point. The most problematic issue is the claimed unity constituted by the primacy of EU law. This arguably cannot provide for a common denominator of EU and Member State law. Beyond that, this seriously questions the claim of heterarchical legal orders as well. According to consent-based monism, the primacy of EU law is not the common denominator but simply ensures that those competences that have been transferred to the EU level can be exercised and are enforced in case of conflicts with Member State law. In that sense, this is a clearly hierarchical relationship. However, for those competences that still remain at the national level of the Member States, such a hierarchy does not exist. Delineating the fine line between the division of competences, which is due

agreement with Kelsen in the sense that monism would be a precondition for the application of norm conflict solution rules.

[123] Jestaedt (n 111) 658, with reference to Hans Kelsen, *Allgemeine Theorie der Normen* (Manz 1979) 2, 3, 22–23, 39, 136–137, 139, 167–168, 171.

[124] Jestaedt (n 111) 659–660.

[125] Jestaedt (n 111) 660–662, interestingly (albeit consistent as both theories – the pure theory of Hans Kelsen and the systems theory of Niklas Luhmann – treat human beings as mere objects in order to preserve their purity and system) with references to Luhmanian systems theory (Niklas Luhmann, *Rechtssoziologie* (Westdeutscher Verlag 3rd ed 1987) 356–357, 359; Niklas Luhmann, *Das Recht der Gesellschaft* (Suhrkamp 1993) 76 ff) and its conceptualization of "autopoietic systems."

[126] Jestaedt (n 111) 662–666, holding that norm conflicts can only occur within one legal order as a norm conflict presupposes two conflicting claims of validity. Moreover, for Jestaedt, who advocates a monistic understanding of the relationship between EU and Member State law, from the perspective of legal theory, primacy of EU law and Member State law is justifiable. This conflict, which constitutes the difference between a federal state (*Staatenbund*) and multilevel constitutionalism (*Verfassungsverbund*) cannot – consistent with Kelsen – be solved on legal grounds (667–670).

[127] See above Section 1.2.

to the progressive development of EU law by EU organs and replies by national organs not being static but on the move, is thus key to conceptualizing the relationship.[128] Multilevel constitutionalism does not provide for a convincing argument in this regard. Hence, an ultra vires claim by Member States, for instance through their constitutional courts, is comprehensible. Any claim, be it in the name of identity or human rights, would have to show that this actually is an ultra vires act, transgressing the competences once transferred to the EU.[129] For if this is not the case, constitutional identity provides a dangerous blueprint allowing for many questionable derogations from established EU law.[130]

In Austria, the reference point for the question of potential limits to the transformation of competences, and thus also of "integration barriers," is the constitutional law with which the accession of Austria to the EU was legally made possible: the so-called *Beitritts-BVG*.[131] The decisive question in this

[128] For the vast literature, see eg Gerard Conway, "Conflicts of Competence Norms in EU Law and the Legal Reasoning of the ECJ" (2010) 11 (9) German Law Journal 966–1005, applying a framework of norm conflicts and the concept of competence norms; see eg Sacha Garben and Inge Govaere (eds) *The Division of Competences between the EU and the Member States. Reflections on the Past, the Present and the Future* (Hart 2017).

[129] For the argument that a unification of fundamental rights, ultra vires, and identity control is conceivable, see Hans-Georg Dederer, "Die Grenzen des Vorrangs des Unionsrechts – zur Vereinheitlichung von Grundrechts-, Ultra-vires- und Identitätskontrolle" (2014) 69 (7) Juristenzeitung 313–322.

[130] For an example of how the concept of constitutional identity is also used by the Hungarian Constitutional Court, see Alkotmánybíróság, Decision 22/2016 (XII. 5.) AB on November 30, 2016, as well as the analysis by Renata Uitz, "National Constitutional Identity in the European Constitutional Project: A Recipe for Exposing Cover Ups and Masquerades" (November 11, 2016) Verfassungsblog, available at https://verfassungsblog.de/national-constitutional-identity-in-the-european-constitutional-project-a-recipe-for-exposing-cover-ups-and-masquerades/ [last accessed February 1, 2023]; Tímea Drinóczi, "Hungarian Constitutional Court: The Limits of EU Law in the Hungarian Legal System: Judgment of 5 December 2016, No 22/2016" (2017) 11 (1) Vienna Journal on International Constitutional Law 139; and Gábor Halmai, "The Hungarian Constitutional Court and Constitutional Identity" (October 1, 2017) Verfassungsblog, available at https://verfassungsblog.de/the-hungarian-constitutional-court-and-constitutional-identity/ [last accessed February 1, 2023]. For a general analysis, see R Daniel Kelemen and Laurent Pech, "Why Autocrats Love Constitutional Identity and Constitutional Pluralism. Lessons from Hungary and Poland" (2018) 2 RECONNECT working paper; R Daniel Kelemen and Laurent Pech, "The Uses and Abuses of Constitutional Pluralism: Undermining the Rule of Law in the Name of Constitutional Identity in Hungary and Poland" (2019) 21 Cambridge Yearbook of European Legal Studies 59–74. For a critique that constitutional identity is actually national sovereignty, see eg Lando Kirchmair, "Nationale Souveränität als Verfassungsidentität. Warum der EuGH Letztentscheider über den Gehalt nationaler Identität sein sollte" (2021) 73 (8) Die Öffentliche Verwaltung 321–326 with further references.

[131] Bundesverfassungsgesetz über den Beitritt Österreichs zur Europäischen Union (BGBl 1994/744). Cf Stefan Griller, "Verfassungsfragen der österreichischen EU-Mitgliedschaft" (1995)

regard is – and this constitutes an interesting difference from those Member States that have been involved in the EU integration process from the beginning – whether the constitutional law allowing for the accession of Austria to the EU includes "integration barriers." The law plainly states in Article I that on the approval of the Austrian people of the *Beitritts-BVG* the competent organs are authorized to conclude the international treaty on the accession of Austria to the EU.[132] From the explanatory remarks to the government bill, we learn that this constitutional law should open up the Austrian legal order in a way that accommodates the special claim for the validity – including primacy (also over constitutional law) and direct effect – of EU law.[133] Interestingly, the explanatory remarks to the government bill also refer to substantive "integration barriers." The question was whether – in analogy to Article 23 of the German Basic Law – it would be necessary to include reservations relating to certain fundamental values of the Austrian Constitution in the constitutional law authorizing the accession to the EU.[134] However, such "constitutional 'integration barriers'" or a provision securing the basic structure of the Austrian Constitution could be "politically desirable, but are legally not necessary."[135]

The reasons for this standpoint were as follows: (1) Fundamental principles (the democratic principle, the separation of powers, the rule of law and the federal principle) of the Austrian Constitution would be amended, but not derogated, by the accession. Hence, these principles would remain standard for the control of future developments (including amendments of the EU Treaties). If future acts were qualified again as a total revision of these principles (*Gesamtänderung*), another public referendum according to

9 Zeitschrift für Europarecht, internationales Privatrecht & Rechtsvergleichung 98–115; Griller (n 117) 276 ff; Öhlinger (n 117) EU-Beitritts-BVG.

[132] See Article I holding that with the approval of the *Beitritts-BVG*, the organs responsible under federal constitutional law are authorized to conclude the Accession Treaty to the EU in accordance with the outcome of the negotiations determined by the accession referendum on April 12, 1994.

[133] ErläutRV 1546 BlgNR 18. GP 4 and specifying at 7 that the primacy of EU law has the consequence that all national organs of legislation and execution in Austria have to disregard national legal provisions if they are in conflict with directly applicable legal acts of EU law. This explicitly includes also constitutional law and, thus, the otherwise existing monopoly of the Austrian Constitutional Court to review and possibly repeal legal provisions is broken.

[134] ErläutRV 1546 BlgNR 18. GP 6.

[135] ErläutRV 1546 BlgNR 18. GP 6: "Eine solche Festschreibung in Form von verfassungsrechtlichen 'Integrationsschranken' oder eines besonders abzusichernden 'integrationsfesten Verfassungskernes' bzw. einer 'Struktursicherungsklausel' könnte politisch wünschenswert erscheinen, ist jedoch aus rechtlicher Sicht nicht erforderlich."

Article 44 (3) of the Austrian Constitution would become necessary.[136] (2) Substantive modifications of EU primary law via EU secondary law are already violations of EU primary law and thus illegal. The CJEU is in charge of monitoring for such violations. (3) Ultra vires acts of EU organs are – with or without constitutional integration barriers – to be considered null and void. This understanding is covered by the international law principle *clausula rebus sic stantibus* and further confirmed by the understanding in other EU Member States.[137] (4) Acts of EU organs, which would overstep the competences transferred to the EU and which obviously conflict with the fundamental principles of the Austrian Constitution as modified by the accession to the EU, would be absolutely void and thus insignificant.[138] (5) To avoid misunderstandings, it is finally emphasized that the EU – also without writing this explicitly in the *Beitritts B-VG*, the Austrian constitutional law to accede the EU – is self-evidently an institution that is obliged to keep democratic principles and the rule of law and guarantees a comparable protection of fundamental rights. Moreover, the EU does not challenge the Republic of Austria as a democratic federal state that adheres to the rule of law.[139]

From this clearly follows that the amendment of the Treaty of Lisbon or a new treaty that qualified as a total revision of the fundamental principles of the Austrian Constitution (*Baugesetze*), as was the case in the Austrian accession to the EU, would necessitate a public referendum according to Article 44 (3) of the Austrian Constitution.[140] This is confirmed in Article 50 (4) of the Austrian Constitution, which since the constitutional amendment of 2008 has included the phrase "irrespective of Article 44 (3) of the Austrian

[136] ErläutRV 1546 BlgNR 18. GP 6.

[137] ErläutRV 1546 BlgNR 18. GP 7.

[138] ErläutRV 1546 BlgNR 18. GP 7. There is a pleonasm "contradictory contradiction," (*kontradiktorischem Widerspruch*) in the original which somehow indicates the high threshold of such a conflict. The special section Article I of the explanatory remarks to the government bill (8) furthermore explicitly states that the authorization of acceding to the EU entails all duties and obligations that come with the supranational character of EU law and the related limitations of sovereignty.

[139] ErläutRV 1546 BlgNR 18. GP 7.

[140] This is the dominant opinion in Austrian scholarship: Pernthaler (n 71) Doppelverfassung 795; Peter Pernthaler and Gerhard Baumgartner, "Der Rang des Gemeinschaftsrechts im Stufenbau der Rechtsordnung" (2000) 8 Journal für Rechtspolitik 84–99 (86, n 22); Peter Bußjäger and Gregor Heißl, "Nationaler Souveränitätsanspruch versus autonome Rechtsordnung? Integrationsschranken im Spannungsverhältnis zur Vorrangjudikatur" (2008) 34 (8) Österreichische Juristenzeitung 307–315 (312–213); Öhlinger and Potacs (n 72) 58–59; Öhlinger (n 117) EU-Beitritts-BVG para 77 with further references (also to some voices who have a different view); Rainer Palmstorfer, "Bundesverfassungsrechtliche Integrationsschranken und Unionsrecht" in Clemens Jabloner et al (eds) *Scharfsinn im Recht. Liber Amicorum für Michael Thaler* (Jan Sramek 2019) 417–428 (419).

Constitution." Therefore, according to Article 44 (3) of the Austrian Constitution, any amendment to EU Treaties that would qualify as a total revision of the Constitution (*Gesamtänderung*) would again be in need of a public referendum.[141]

According to some scholars, this also holds true for an amendment via secondary EU law.[142] Other scholars disagree, arguing that would not be the case.[143] This is quite a theoretical debate, however. In light of the development of the EU, it is unlikely that secondary EU law would violate the fundamental principles of the Austrian Constitution but not EU primary law.[144] Thus, the question as to whether a public referendum should be held on EU secondary law or on a constitutional law amending the Austrian Constitution in order to provide the basis for such a secondary EU law is highly theoretical.[145] In the event that this type of secondary EU law existed, it would first be the task of the EU legal order and its organs to deal with such a questionable secondary law. Only in the case that the CJEU confirmed secondary EU law that fundamentally violated the basic principles of the Austrian Constitution would there be an act of an EU organ that could

[141] See Theo Öhlinger and Andreas Müller, "Artikel 50 B-VG" in Karl Korinek et al (eds) *Österreichisches Bundesverfassungsrecht* (Verlag Österreich 2018) para 69 with further references to the fact that if EU treaties would be amended to such an extent that this constitutes a total revision of the Austrian Constitution, the necessary public referendum needs to be about the new European treaty or a special constitutional law amending the Austrian Constitution by authorizing competent organs to ratify the treaty.

[142] Öhlinger and Potacs (n 72) 60; Öhlinger (n 117) EU-Beitritts-BVG para 81 with further references; Bußjäger and Heißl (n 140) 314, stating that EU secondary law which would violate the fundamental principles of Austrian constitutional law would simply not be applicable in Austria (albeit the Austrian Constitutional Court could not derogate such EU secondary law or declare it unapplicable); Theo Öhlinger and Harald Eberhard, *Verfassungsrecht* (facultas 11th ed 2016) para 191: "Unionsrecht unterliegt daher nicht der Normenkontrolle des VfGH"; Andreas Janko, *Gesamtänderung der Bundesverfassung* (Verlag Österreich 2004) 433, explicitly extending this to secondary EU law which is in conformity with primary EU law.

[143] Palmstorfer (n 140) 419–420 with further references in n 8 and 9 among others to Hubert Isak, "Kompetenzüberschreitende Akte von Organen der Europäischen Union – Die Sicht des österreichischen Verfassungsrechts" in Bruno Simma and Constanze Schulte (eds) *Völker- und Europarecht in der aktuellen Diskussion* (Linde 1999) 33–58 (34), voicing the presumption of lawfulness of EU secondary law. However, Isak (39–41) holds also that a judgment by the CJEU, confirming ultra vires secondary EU law, would be null and void – yet this would be a rather theoretical academic train of thought; Stefan Griller, "Blockademöglichkeiten gegen die Einführung des Euro" (1997) 4 Journal für Rechtspolitik 221–233 (230), with the exception of a serious ultra vires act which is not covered by EU primary law.

[144] See also in this regard Öhlinger and Potacs (n 72) 60.

[145] See Öhlinger (n 117) EU-Beitritts-BVG para 81–82 with further references discussing the technical difficulties of how to administer such a public referendum on EU secondary law.

constitute an act ultra vires also according to the explanatory remarks to the government bill of the Act granting the accession of Austria to the EU. In such a highly unlikely event, it would be up to Austrian Courts, be it the Constitutional Court, the Administrative Court or the Supreme Court, to decide on such an ultra vires act.[146] Interestingly in this regard, while Theo Öhlinger and Michael Potacs hold that a differentiation between ultra vires acts of the CJEU and constitutional integration barriers would not be possible because of the autonomous validity of EU law,[147] Peter Bußjäger suggests exactly such a differentiation.[148] Yet, as has been noted, this is quite a theoretical question.

At the same time, this means that in Austria there are no unsurmountable barriers for further integration, as, for instance, argued by the German Federal Constitutional Court with reference to Article 23 (1) and 79 (3) of the German Basic Law.[149] The high threshold of a *Gesamtänderung* – that is, a

146 Öhlinger (n 117) EU-Beitritts-BVG para 83, emphasizing, however, that before such a move, every judicial organ in Austria would have to consult the CJEU via the preliminary reference procedure. Only in the unlikely event that the CJEU were to declare an EU secondary law compatible with EU law, but at the same time this EU secondary law would violate fundamental Austrian constitutional law, this EU secondary law would not be applicable in Austria; nor would the decision by the CJEU. Cf Öhlinger (n 117) EU-Beitritts-BVG 85 ff; Potacs (n 117) 193–194; Griller (n 131) 100.

147 Öhlinger and Potacs (n 72) 60.

148 Peter Bußjäger, "Folgerungen aus dem Lissabonurteil des Bundesverfassungsgerichts" (2010) 132 (5) Juristische Blätter 273–283 (280), stating that ultra vires acts which violate fundamental principles of the Austrian Constitution would be resistant against "integration," hence *integrationsfeste Schranken*, whereas ultra vires acts which do not violate this core principles would be a sole matter of EU law.

149 Griller (n 131) 96–97; Roland Winkler, *Integrationsverfassungsrecht: Das österreichische Verfassungsrecht und das Recht der Europäischen Union – Koordination, Kooperation, Konflikt* (Springer 2003) 54–55, emphasizing that according to Article 44 (3) of the Austrian Constitution no unsurmountable barriers for further integration exist if – given that further integration has to be qualified as a *Gesamtänderung* (that is, a total revision of the fundamental principles) of the Austrian Constitution according to Article 44 (3) – a public referendum takes place. Heinz Schäffer, "Österreich und die Europäische Union – Erfahrungen und Leistungen des österreichischen VfGH" (2005) 60 Zeitschrift für Öffentliches Recht 345–388 (355–356, 359); Christoph Grabenwarter, "Offene Staatlichkeit: Österreich" in Armin von Bogdandy, Cruz Villalón and Peter M Huber (eds) *Handbuch Ius Publicum Europaeum. Vol 2 Offene Staatlichkeit – Wissenschaft vom Verfassungsrecht* (2008) 211–241 (231); Stefan Griller, "Executive Summary" in European Parliament and Directorate-General for International Policies (ed) *National Constitutional Law and European Integration* (European Parliament 2011) 11–31 (18), summarizing the Austrian constellation as follows: "On the grounds of these constitutional amendments, primacy of EU law is generally accepted by the courts, even primacy over constitutional provisions. The resulting *barriers for further European integration* are as follows: amendments of primary EU law must be approved by qualified majority in the Austrian parliament. An explicit amendment of formal constitutional law is not necessary even if the new treaty provisions are of a constitutional nature in a material sense.

total revision of the fundamental principles of the Austrian Constitution – is further exemplified by the fact that so far, rather uncontroversially, the Treaty of Amsterdam, the Treaty of Nice, the accession of new Member States and the Treaty of Lisbon were not considered to constitute a total revision of the Austrian Constitution. Thus, no public referendum was necessary.[150]

It is nevertheless important to emphasize that claims which hold that the validity and primacy of EU law ultimately depend on Member State law are actually problematic. In a way, this resembles Brexit. You simply cannot "have your cake and eat it." Unilaterally withdrawing from reciprocally established EU law means leaving the EU.[151] It is unimaginable to withdraw the "national basis of validity of EU law" and remain in the EU at the same time. How would this work practically? Hence, to claim that the final validity of EU law depends on national laws enabling a country's accession to the EU (and implicitly stating that therefore a unilateral withdrawal would be possible) are simply threats to leave the EU. For you cannot have the benefits of (valid) EU law in the one case but not in another (except for claims holding that a specific act is ultra vires).[152] In other words, the supervision of EU law and the

As mentioned, this is how the Lisbon Treaty was handled. The procedure applies as long as future amendments do not essentially affect the fundamental principles of the Austrian constitution – mainly the principles of democracy, rule of law, liberal state (fundamental rights protection), separation of powers, federal state, and Republican state. Several of them (democracy, rule of law, separation of powers) were already changed on the occasion of Austria's accession to the EU. In this amended version they continue to form part of the fundamental principles of the Austrian Constitution. Should a new EU Treaty (again) essentially affect those principles, it could only be ratified after the previous total amendment of the Austrian Constitution, meaning an amendment by formal Constitutional Act which must be accepted by a (mandatory) referendum. It is, however, not easy to define the borderline between such a total amendment and the previously mentioned 'simple' amendment of the Austrian Constitution. The mentioned constitutional barriers consist in more or less burdensome procedural requirements for the approval and ratification of future EU primary law amendments. However, contrary to several other EU Member States, the Austrian Constitution does not include any 'eternity clause.' Consequently, at least from a legal point of view, any future steps in European integration through treaty amendments are admissible."

150 See only Öhlinger (n 70) 417 ff; Öhlinger and Potacs (n 72) 58–59, with reference to Walter Berka, *Verfassungsrecht* (Verlag Österreich 6th ed 2016) para 302, holding furthermore that participation in the European integration is not a fundamental principle of the Austrian Constitution.

151 See Federico Fabbrini, "After the OMT Case: The Supremacy of EU Law as the Guarantee of the Equality of the Member States" (2015) 16 (4) German Law Journal 1003–1023, defending the principle of supremacy of EU law arguing that it is in the interest of all Member States as it preserves their equality and prevents "each country of the EU from cherry-picking which provisions of EU it likes or not."

152 See also R Daniel Keleman, "On the Unsustainability of Constitutional Pluralism: European Supremacy and the Survival of the Eurozone" (2016) 23 (1) Maastricht Journal of European

CJEU by national constitutional courts, unless they overstep their competences, is hardly justifiable.[153] What is preferable is to address and adjust potential shortcomings at the actual level of their origin rather than invoking a national legal order.[154]

Less straightforwardly, some aim to differentiate primacy from supremacy. While the former only constitutes the *Anwendungsvorrang* of EU law – that is, the primacy of applicability – the latter would imply hierarchy in the sense of validity primacy (*Geltungsvorrang*), which invalidates conflicting Member State law.[155] The latter would, it is argued, only be the case in "truly federal systems" such as Germany, with its principle of "Bundesrecht bricht Landesrecht," or the United States.[156] This, however, is hard to understand.

and Comparative Law 136–150 (149): "[T]he only appropriate and feasible remedy that national constitutional courts can apply, should they conclude that acts of EU institutions are ultra vires and/or threaten their inviolable constitutional identity, is to declare that their state's continued membership in the European Union is unconstitutional (*Verfassungswidrig*)" [emphasis original]. Even some pluralists hold that the freedom of the constitutional courts of the Member States is not endless and they ought to show respect for EU law. See Miguel Poiares Maduro, "Contrapunctual Law: Europe's Constitutional Pluralism in Action" in Neil Walker (ed) *Sovereignty in Transition* (Hart 2003) 502–537 (533–534), stating that "[i]n fact, I would argue that their claim of ultimate authority should only be exercised in the event of a systemic conflict arising between the European legal order and the integrity of the national constitution. In that case, national constitutional courts could still affirm their ultimate authority either at a moment of constitutional ratification or by creating a situation of constitutional exit. In the latter case, the constitutional conflict could be established by a national constitutional court in a specific case but would have to be of such importance as to affect the entire constitutional relationship between the European Union and the Member State and, therefore, to raise the issue of exit. Only such an understanding of national constitutional authority by national constitutional courts is capable of respecting the principles of contrapuntal law highlighted. In the exchange of this adjustment of the national constitutional claims of authority to the claim of authority of EU law, the European Court of Justice ought to recognise an enhanced role for national courts and national constitutionalism in the interpretation and application of EU law." To others like Ana Bobić, *The Jurisprudence of Constitutional Conflict in the European Union* (Oxford University Press 2022) 39, such a line of argument "resembles Cold War logic."

153 For the critique that the approach the German Federal Constitutional Court has taken with regard to the Lisbon Treaty is "dualism cloaked as pluralism," see Andreas L Paulus, "From Dualism to Pluralism: The Relationship between International Law, European Law, and Domestic Law" in Pieter H F Bekker, Rudolf Dolzer and Michael Waibel (ed) *Making Transnational Law Work in the Global Economy. Essays in Honour of Detlev Vagts* (Cambridge University Press 2010) 132–153.

154 See also in this regard Andreas L Paulus, "Internationales, nationales und privates Recht. Hybridisierung der Rechtsordnungen" (2014) 46 Berichte der Deutschen Gesellschaft für Internationales Recht 7–46 (text at n 108).

155 See above (n 119); see also eg Matej Avbelj, "Supremacy or Primacy of EU Law: (Why) Does it Matter?" (2011) 17 (6) European Law Journal 744–763; Claes (n 22) 182.

156 Claes (n 22) 182.

While there is an obvious difference between primacy of application and primacy of validity, this difference is nevertheless rather negligible.[157] In case of a conflict, either way Member State law is inferior and has to give way to EU law. Only if the conflicting EU law ceases to exist because the relevant provision is cancelled would the formerly suppressed national provision come to life again. Beyond this rare situation the duty of all Member State organs exists to refrain from conducting conflicting measures with EU law.[158] Hence, depending on the function of the organ, this also includes the duty of national legislators not to enact new national law which conflicts with EU law. Moreover, this also extends to adjusting national law to comply with EU law, which comes close to a primacy of validity – except for the fact that the Member State has to do it by itself (*Rechtsbereinigungspflicht*).[159] Beyond that, this comparison is flawed as, for instance, the highly developed Austrian federal state does not know supremacy of the federation, the *Bund*, over the federal states, the *Länder*.[160]

Monica Claes holds "that there is not one principle of primacy but many, European and national principles. There is therefore no shared rule of conflict and no encompassing, external perspective or 'law of laws' on the basis of which it can be decided what provision or standard should give way in a concrete case."[161] This conclusion is somewhat hasty, however. Simply because several constitutional courts in Member States challenged

157 See Dougan (n 16) 1301, arguing that the obligation of Member State courts to "regard certain incompatible national measures as null and void" is "evolutionary rather than revolutionary."

158 The national organ, however, remains free to choose the appropriate national procedure, see above n 11.

159 See above n 20.

160 See generally Ewald Wiederin, *Bundesrecht und Landesrecht. Zugleich ein Beitrag zu Strukturproblemen der bundesstaatlichen Kompetenzverteilung in Österreich und in Deutschland* (Springer 1995); cf the three circles theory by Hans Kelsen, "Die Bundesexekution – Ein Beitrag zur Theorie und Praxis des Bundesstaates, unter besonderer Berücksichtigung der deutschen Reichs- und der österreichischen Bundes-Verfassung" in Zaccaria Giacometti and Dietrich Schindler (eds) *Festgabe für Fritz Fleiner zum 60. Geburtstag* (J C B Mohr 1927) 127–187; Hans Kelsen, *General Theory of Law and State State* (translated by Anders Wedberg Harvard University Press 1945) 316, to accommodate a unitary legal order nonetheless (basically referring to the division of competences included in a third overarching circle); see in this regard Michael Thaler, "Rechtsphilosophie und das Verhältnis zwischen Gemeinschaftsrecht und nationalem Recht" (2000) 8 Journal für Rechtspolitik 75–84.

161 Claes (n 22) 202. For a differentiation of four functions of the principle of primacy, see Clara Rauchegger, "Four Functions of the Principle of Primacy in the Post-Lisbon Case Law of the European Court of Justice" in Katja S Ziegler, Päivi J Neuvonen and Violeta Moreno-Lax (eds) *General Principles in EU Law. Constructing Legal Orders in Europe* (Edward Elgar 2022) 157–172.

unconditional EU primacy does not mean that there is no shared rule of conflict. Beyond that, many similarly pluralistic attempts to conceptualize the relationship between EU and Member State law suffer from the shortcomings outlined.[162] This provides the basis for a new understanding of this relationship that is theoretically sound and able to explain the undergirding structural relationship between EU law and Member State law.

7.4 INTERPRETATION ACCORDING TO CONSENT-BASED MONISM

According to consent-based monism, the EU is the larger circle with regard to its Member States. All EU Member States in turn are independent smaller circles that are also part of the EU circle. This is illustrated by Figure 6.6 in Part II. The consensus established at the level of the larger EU circle must not be violated unilaterally by a smaller Member State circle. However, this only concerns the content that has been consented to. For any further consensus, the smaller circles remain free to consent on what they wish. This stands in contrast to a monist understanding of the relationship between EU and Member State law of a Kelsenian or Verdrossian nature. Consent-based monism does not hold that Member State law is delegated from EU law. Nor does consent-based monism assume that in order to conceive of both EU law and Member State law as law, it is logically necessary to understand them as a unitary legal order.[163] Consent-based monism only states that once a consensus has been reached at the level of a larger circle (which in our case here is EU law), then it must not be derogated unilaterally by a smaller circle. If the aim is to solve norm conflicts as defined above, then and only then is a common denominator – a common definition of law – necessary. This, however, is no question of logic or epistemology but of consensus. In contrast to dualism or

[162] See Section 2.1. See, however, Kelemen and Pech (n 130) Why Autocrats Love Constitutional Identity and Constitutional Pluralism, who state that "[t]hough the theory of constitutional pluralism was developed with the best of intentions in mind, it is having destructive consequences that threaten the EU legal order. The theory of constitutional pluralism had inherent flaws, but could function as a serviceable fudge to avert inter-court conflict so long as all the courts involved engaged in sincere cooperation, dialogue and mutual accommodation." Thus, to them, "with the emergence and ongoing consolidation of competitive authoritarian regimes in Hungary and Poland, the days when one could assume all national judiciaries would engage in sincere cooperation have ended and the dangers that were always inherent in the concept of constitutional pluralism and the connected concept of constitutional identity have become manifest."

[163] Paul Gragl, "The Pure Theory of Law and Legal Monism – Epistemological Truth and Empirical Plausibility" (2015) 70 (4) Zeitschrift für Öffentliches Recht 665–736 (674, 685); Paul Gragl, *Legal Monism: Law, Philosophy, and Politics* (Oxford University Press 2018). See also Jestaedt (n 111) 667–670.

pluralism, consent-based monism holds that such a common normative basis for solving norm conflicts is essential to solve any such conflict by legal means. Moreover, consent-based monism provides an argument on where to look for such common ground, namely consensus at the level of the larger circle. This common denominator, however, does not have to be of constitutional quality.

Reaching a consensus at the level of the larger circle might be eased by formal procedures such as majority ruling or the authorization of certain specific organs to create law. This has often happened in the EU to date as it has developed into a supranational organization with constitution-like traits.[164] Lawmaking in the EU shows roughly all the basic rule-of-law criteria. However, it is important to emphasize that consent-based monism is not about triggering yet another argument as to whether the EU is truly a constitutional or even state-like community or what is missing in order for it to become one. Consent-based monism is simply a structural argument that indicates where to seek answers to questions such as how we can know who has the final say on certain matters. Hence, it is of utmost importance to understand clearly what EU Treaties and the accepted development of EU law actually involve.

The EU competence regime is decisive in this regard.[165] It is vital to pinpoint exactly which competences have been shifted to the European level. To answer this question, it is important to define where the competence regime is regulated and who decides in the case of a dispute about specific competences. The competences in Articles 2–6 TFEU are the starting point and, in the case of conflict, the CJEU has the final say on matters of competences (Article 19 TEU). Member States are required to file an action for annulment before the CJEU if they think the EU lacks competence in a particular field because they themselves are not authorized to void EU acts.[166] Roughly speaking, if the EU has competence for a specific matter, the EU circle may adopt legal acts. EU legal acts within the framework of EU competences are legally binding and, in the case of conflict with Member State law, they enjoy primacy.[167] This is largely uncontested. Moreover, it is

[164] Case 294/83 *Parti ecologiste "Les Verts" v European Parliament* ECLI:EU:C:1986:166 para 23: "the basic constitutional charter, the Treaty." See also, more recently, eg Case C-284/16 *Slovak Republic v Achmea BV* ECLI:EU:C:2018:158 para 33: "the constitutional structure of the EU."

[165] See similarly also Paul Craig, "The ECJ and Ultra Vires Action: A Conceptual Analysis" (2011) 48 (2) Common Market Law Review 395–437.

[166] Case 314/85 *Foto-Frost v Hauptzollamt Lübeck-Ost* ECLI:EU:C:1987:452.

[167] See Case 6/64 *Costa v ENEL* ECLI:EU:C:1964:66; as well as Case C-10/97 *IN.CO.GE.'90 and others* ECLI:EU:C:1998:498; Case C-409/06 *Winner Wetten GmbH* ECLI:EU:C:2010:503 para 55.

also uncontested that the EU has no *Kompetenz-Kompetenz*.[168] Hence, the EU must not enlarge its catalogue of given competences on its own terms.

The intriguing question is whether this primacy has limits – that is, whether there is a core of a national "constitutional identity" which is resistant to this primacy. In other words, as we have briefly seen already, it is not the case that all Member States, or rather their national constitutional courts, recognize the CJEU's institutional supremacy.[169] A case in point is the German Federal Constitutional Court and its famous position on the core of German Basic Law that is said to be resistant concerning full integration.[170] Similarly, just as consent-based monism does not say anything about the question of which political system or which specific norm might be just, nor does it say whether there should or should not be something like a core that is resistant to integration. Consent-based monism is neutral towards the content. It does, however, say that once a consensus has been taken at the level of a larger circle, this consensus must not be violated unilaterally by a smaller circle. Therefore, it is crucial to analyze the norms of the smaller circle that have authorized and still authorize consensus formation in the larger circle. At the very beginning of the EU, these were national norms on the *authorization* to conclude and ratify international treaties.[171] This authorization does not, however, constitute the foundation of the consensus of the larger circle. It merely enables representatives from the smaller circle to consent to a rule

[168] However, see András Jakab, *European Constitutional Language* (Cambridge University Press 2016) ch 6 on sovereignty and European integration with further references. Yet see Thaler (n 160) 79 ff, who differentiates the legislative *Kompetenz-Kompetenz* from a judicial *Kompetenz-Kompetenz* of the CJEU.

[169] Thomas Horsley, *The Court of Justice of the European Union as an Institutional Actor: Judicial Lawmaking and Its Limits* (Cambridge University Press 2018) 223 with further references in n 21. See generally his ch 6.

[170] German Federal Constitutional Court, BVerfGE 123, 267 (*Lisbon*). For an overview, see Polzin (n 28); as well as Kassandra Wetz, *Funktionen von Verfassungsidentität als gerichtliches Konzept in der Europäischen Union* (Mohr Siebeck 2021), mapping the evolution of constitutional identity in Germany, France, Spain, Poland, the Czech Republic as well as Hungary, concluding that the term constitutional identity is ambiguous and misleading. She therefore suggests that the term should be replaced by constitutional core (*Verfassungskern*); and Bobić (n 152) 138 ff (looking into Poland, France, Spain, Italy and Portugal); as well as Gerhard van der Schyff, "EU Member State Constitutional Identity: A Comparison of Germany and the Netherlands as Polar Opposites" (2016) 76 Heidelberg Journal of International Law 167–191.

[171] For the designation authorization (instead of incorporation, implementation or the like), compare Lando Kirchmair, "The Theory of the Law Creators' Circle: Re-Conceptualizing the Monism–Dualism–Pluralism Debate" (2016) 17 (2) German Law Journal 179–214.

at the level of the larger circle. By now, the EU regulates how its own legal edifice changes autonomously (Article 48 TEU on ordinary and simplified revision procedures). Major changes such as the introduction of completely new treaties, for instance, are subject to ratification by all Member States.[172] In effect, this means that they have to be ratified unanimously by the larger EU circle (in the sense of abolishing or extending the old consensus at this level). A unilateral derogation by only a few Member States would clearly violate the consensus of the larger circle (which, of course, is not to say that such a violation is not possible). An "integration-resistant core," on the one hand, must not violate any consensus that has been obtained at the level of the larger EU circle. On the other hand, the larger circle must not autonomously add competences without authorization by all of the smaller circles. This also holds true for the interpretation of the scope of application of EU law, which, essentially, must be reflected in the consensus of the larger circle. This refers to questions on the scope of applicability of the Charter of Fundamental Rights, such as[173] the rule of law crisis in the EU and judicial independence,[174] as

[172] Dieter Grimm, "The Role of National Constitutions in a United Europe" in Dieter Grimm, *Constitutionalism. Past, Present, and Future* (Oxford University Press 2015) 271–294 (274), who holds "that within the purview of European law the latter [national law] can no longer act in a self-determined manner." Nevertheless, "the EU has not yet acquired the right to determine its own legal basis."

[173] Case C-617/10 *Åkerberg Fransson* ECLI:EU:C:2013:105; see also Case C-206/13 *Siragusa* ECLI:EU:C:2014:126; C-198/13 *Hérnandez ea v Reino de España* ECLI:EU:C:2014:2055 C-42/17 *Criminal proceedings against MAS und MB* ECLI:EU:C:2017:936; C-612/15 *Kolev ea* ECLI:EU:C:2018:392, regarding the scope of applicability of the Charter of Fundamental Rights, which, again, triggered a debate about judicial activism. See, for instance, Allan Rosas, "When Is the Charter of Fundamental Rights Applicable at National Level?" (2012) 19 (4) Jurisprudence 1269–1288 (1270), holding that the "introduction of a fundamental rights regime into EU law is essentially a story of judge-made law." See Benedikt Pirker, *Grundrechtsschutz im Unionsrecht zwischen Subsidiarität und Integration. Zur Anwendung der Unionsgrundrechte auf die Mitgliedstaaten* (Nomos 2018).

[174] Case C-64/16 *Associação Sindical dos Juízes Portugueses v Tribunal de Contas* ECLI:EU: C:2018:117, holding basically that the CJEU is competent – relying on the principle of effective judicial protection enshrined in second subparagraph of Article 19 (1) TEU – to evaluate the guarantee of independence of national courts and tribunals if this "may concern the application or interpretation of EU law" (para 39). This too is a prime example of how to understand the competence regime of the EU, as the appointment and removal of judges actually is an exclusive Member State competence. Establishing a doctrine of nonregression in relation to Article 2 TEU values, see eg Case C-896/19 *Repubblika v Il-Prim Ministru* ECLI: EU:C:2021:311, paras 60 ff (and cited case law). Without going into details, what exactly is comprised and prescribed by EU law in relation to respect for the rule of law in Member States is an essential question in the realm of many "rule of law decisions" of the CJEU.

much as to the scope of autonomy of the EU legal order.[175] Hence, consent-based monism does not offer a blanket solution that would enable us to finally answer the grand question in this book by giving the final say in any question, for example, to the EU or to its Member States. Rather, it aims at providing some guidance by indicating how we can know who has the final say. Hence, answering the question might, in some cases, be a painstaking task. However, this is unavoidable given the ongoing process of European integration with its many constitution-like dynamics. Yet what becomes clear is that subsequently created integration barriers that were not apparent from the outset are a unilateral derogation of the rule of the larger circle. Whether some specific concepts, such as national constitutional identity, have always been present and have never changed in a Member State constitution, and thus have also limited the authorization on the extent to which accession to the EU was legally mandated, is thus identified as the important question to be answered. However, as consent-based monism is neutral towards the content, unfortunately this concept cannot do more than point in the right direction.

Consent-based monism, nevertheless, puts emphasis on the question of how to interpret the content of a consensus. The Vienna Convention on the Law of Treaties (VCLT) offers rules for the interpretation of international treaties. Again, by now, the CJEU, based on Article 19 TEU, has developed its own array of interpretation techniques[176] (as there is no provision clearly stipulating which interpretation technique shall be used or be supreme in the case of conflict[177]). The interpretation techniques employed by the CJEU largely correspond to "classical techniques" well-known in national law or those mentioned in the VCLT.[178]

[175] See Case C-284/16 *Slovak Republic v Achmea BV* ECLI:EU:C:2018:158 and the confirmation that investment arbitration in an intra-EU context is part of EU law (and thus within the competence of the EU and the jurisdiction of the CJEU). Therefore, investment tribunals in such a context lack jurisdiction as Art. 267 and 344 TFEU preclude provisions establishing arbitral tribunals (para 62) as they could "interpret or indeed apply EU law" (para 42) and thereby endanger the unity, primacy and effectiveness of EU law. While this decision has caused an upheaval in academia and the "arbitration world," consent-based monism actually suggests simply looking at the competence of the larger law creators' circle, the EU legal order and whether we find there sufficient support for the approach taken – in the case at hand – by the CJEU. If one does, it seems indeed that EU law covers the approach taken.

[176] Koen Lenaerts and José A Gutiérrez-Fons, "To Say What the Law of the EU Is: Methods of Interpretation and the European Court of Justice" EUI Working Paper AEL 2013/9, available at http://cadmus.eui.eu/bitstream/handle/1814/28339/AEL_2013_09_DL.pdf?sequence=1&isAllowed=y [last accessed February 1, 2023].

[177] Giulio Itzcovich, "The Interpretation of Community Law by the European Court of Justice" (2009) 10 (5) German Law Journal 537–560.

[178] Lenaerts and Gutiérrez-Fons (n 176).

8

International Law and EU Law

Consent-based monism concerns natural persons reaching a consensus. If A, B and C agree on a consensus, this must not subsequently be violated by B and C without A. What has just been said about the relationship between EU and Member State law also applies to the relationship between international and EU law. Once the circle of the EU has agreed on a consensus with a larger, international circle, it must not violate this consensus unilaterally. It is thus decisive to, first, clearly identify how the EU circle can establish a consensus at the larger international level. This implies on the one hand that the EU is a subject of international law[179] and, on the other hand, that the EU is competent to act concerning the subject matter (Articles 3–6 TFEU).[180] Both conditions are clearly satisfied by now.[181] International organizations count as subjects of international law since the ICJ reparations advisory opinion[182] and the EU, according to Article 47 TEU in connection with Article 335 TFEU, has established legal subjectivity – in other words, it has legal personality as enshrined in Article 47 TEU.[183] Moreover, which

179 See eg Matthias Ruffert, "Artikel 47 EUV" in Christian Calliess and Matthias Ruffert (eds) *EUV/AEUV* (CH Beck 6th ed 2022) para 7, emphasizing that the legal subjectivity of the EU concerning international law is – as with any international organization – functionally limited. See also Werner Schroeder, "Die Europäische Union als Völkserrechtssubjekt" in Walter Obwexer (ed) *Die Europäische Union im Völkerrecht* 2 (2012) Europarecht-Beiheft 9–23; and Jan Klabbers, *The European Union in International Law* (Editions A Pedone 2012) 22–28.

180 Concerning the external relations of the EU, see Piet Eeckhout, *EU External Relations Law* (Oxford University Press 2nd ed 2012) part I.

181 For an overview of how the EU is understood from the perspective of international law in scholarship, see Jed Odermatt, *International Law and the European Union* (Cambridge University Press 2021) ch 1.

182 ICJ, *Reparation for Injuries Suffered in the Service of the United Nations* Advisory Opinion ICJ Reports [1949] 174.

183 Schroeder (n 179); for more details see Carolin Damm, *Die Europäische Union im universellen Völkergewohnheitsrecht* (Mohr Siebeck) 10–19. From a theoretical micro-

organ is authorized to conclude an international norm (Article 216–219 TFEU) is decisive. Second, it is important to determine the content of the consensus. This interpretation process is primarily the task of the level at which the consensus has been agreed, namely the international level. For instance, in *Achmea BV*, the CJEU confirmed that, in principle, EU law allows for an international agreement establishing a court that would interpret the provisions of such an agreement with a binding nature for the CJEU.[184] This is also accurate when thinking along the lines of consent-based monism. Yet the CJEU added the conditionality that this holds true "provided that the autonomy of the EU and its legal order is respected."[185] I would add – again thinking along the lines of consent-based monism – that this condition must be respected by those organs authorized by the EU legal order when concluding international agreements (and international law more generally). However, this conditionality may not serve as an excuse for breaches of the concluded international agreements, in the form of unilateral subsequent derogations for instance, because international law as such does not allow provisions of internal law to be invoked as a justification for a failure to perform a treaty (Article 27 VCLT). Third, subject to the consensus, the effect of this consensus on the level of the smaller circle depends on whether the norm of the international circle is solely applicable, directly applicable or individualizing.[186]

The international circle knows four different types of legal sources. These are, according to Article 38 of the Statute of the International Court of Justice, (a) international conventions, (b) international custom and (c) general principles of law. In addition, (d) legal acts of international organizations can now be a source of international law as well.[187] Depending on each source, different rules are applicable about their making, interpretation and legal effect. In order to determine their effect within the level of the smaller, in our case, the EU circle, it is necessary to look closely at the process of making and interpreting them. In what follows, I will demonstrate how the effect of an

constitutionalist perspective discussing differentiated integration, ie international agreements between EU Member States, and their implication for the legal personality of the EU, see Jonathan Bauerschmidt, *Die Rechtsperson der Europäischen Union im Wandel. Auswirkungen differenzierter Integration durch Völkerrecht auf die Europäische Union* (Mohr Siebeck 2019).

184 Case C-284/16 *Slovak Republic v Achmea BV* ECLI:EU:C:2018:158 para 57.

185 Case C-284/16 *Slovak Republic v Achmea BV* ECLI:EU:C:2018:158 para 57.

186 Part II.

187 Jörg Polakiewicz, "International Law and Domestic (Municipal) Law, Law and Decisions of International Organizations and Courts" in Rüdiger Wolfrum (ed) *Max Planck Encyclopedia of Public International Law* (2012) para 1.

international treaty (Section 8.1) and customary international law (Section 8.2) unfold within the EU legal order.

What I would like to emphasize again as a general remark is that consent-based monism is not about the content but about the structural relationship between circles. If there is a consensus at the level of the larger circle, the smaller circle must not unilaterally violate this consensus. For instance, in the famous *Kadi* saga, the CJEU annulled an EU regulation because this regulation implemented United Nations Security Council resolutions sanctioning suspected terrorists without respecting EU fundamental rights.[188] The individual concerned, Yassin Abdullah Kadi, was associated with Osama bin Laden or the Al-Qaeda network and was therefore listed by the UN Sanctions Committee that was installed in the aftermath of terrorist attacks on the US embassies in Kenya and Tanzania in 1998. A consequence of this listing was the freezing of Kadi's and other individuals' or entities' European assets, which was implemented by an EU Regulation in 2002.[189] Kadi challenged this listing at several EU courts due to alleged violations to him using his property freely as well as the breach of his rights to effective judicial review and a fair trial according to Article 6 ECHR. The Court of First Instance decided in 2005, however, that the Court has no authority to call into question the lawfulness of UN SC Resolutions (except for *ius cogens*, which was not found applicable in this case).[190] While this judgment was associated with a monist understanding of the relationship between EU and international law, the CJEU did not follow this direction. On September 3, 2008, the Court annulled the regulation concerning Kadi, finding that the CJEU has jurisdiction to review the lawfulness of the contested regulation as it has to ensure a full review of the lawfulness of all EU acts "in the light of the fundamental rights forming an integral part of the general principles of Community law."[191] By doing so the CJEU found a breach of "the rights of defence, especially the right to be heard, and of the principle of effective judicial

[188] Joined Cases C-402/05 P and C-415/05 P *Kadi and Al Barakaat International Foundation v Council and Commission* ECLI:EU:C:2008:461; and C-595/10 P *Commission and others v Kadi* ECLI:EU:C:2013:518. For an overview, see Clemens Feinäugle, "Kadi Case" in Rüdiger Wolfrum (ed) *Max Planck Encyclopedia of Public International Law* (2014); Peter Hilpold, "EU Law and UN Law in Conflict: The Kadi Case" (2009) 13 Max Planck Yearbook of United Nations Law 141–182.

[189] Council Regulation 881/2002 of May 27, 2002.

[190] Case T-315/01 *Yassin Abdullah Kadi and Al Barakaat International Foundation v Council and Commission* ECLI:EU:T:2005:332 ECLI:EU:T:2005:332 para 225.

[191] Joined Cases C-402/05 P and C-415/05 P *Kadi and Al Barakaat International Foundation v Council and Commission* ECLI:EU:C:2008:461 para 326.

protection."[192] Moreover, the Court found that Kadi's fundamental right to respect for property had been violated.[193] Following this decision, the UN Sanctions Committee provided Kadi with reasons for his listing and gave him the possibility to comment. Thereafter the Sanctions Committee decided to list Kadi again, which was again implemented by Committee Regulation.[194] Kadi brought a case against this regulation before the General Court.[195] Now the General Court followed the reasoning of the CJEU, conducted a full review of the challenged regulation and annulled it on September 30, 2010. The explanation given was that the information and evidence regarding the reasons for Kadi's listing had not been disclosed to him and so his right to defense and effective judicial review and to property were still violated. Even though the Sanctions Committee delisted Kadi on October 5, 2010, the European Committee, the Council of the European Union and the United Kingdom appealed. Finally, in *Kadi I*, on July 18, 2013, the CJEU held that the improvement of the UN Sanctions Committee procedure was not enough to change this holding.[196]

Very briefly, as a kind of introduction to what follows, according to consent-based monism, the smaller circle should have invoked an ultra vires competence of the larger circle, stating that the UN Security Council (to put it delicately) had overstated its competence. Alternatively, it should have considered the resolution faulty because *UN* human rights had been violated (which would have necessarily implied – admittedly difficult – arguments for the application of human rights, in this case effective judicial protection, at UN level).[197] This is a first indication of what consent-based monism implies

[192] Joined Cases C-402/05 P and C-415/05 P *Kadi and Al Barakaat International Foundation v Council and Commission* EU:C:2008:461 para 353.

[193] Joined Cases C-402/05 P and C-415/05 P *Kadi and Al Barakaat International Foundation v Council and Commission* EU:C:2008:461 para 371.

[194] Commission Regulation (EC) 1190/2008 November 28, 2008 amending Council Regulation (EC) No 881/2002.

[195] Case T-85/09 *Kadi v Commission* ECLI:EU:T:2010:418.

[196] Case C-595/10 P *Commission and others v Kadi* ECLI:EU:C:2013:518 para 66.

[197] For such an argument (albeit without consent-based monism as a basis), see Martin Scheinin, "Is the ECJ Ruling in Kadi Incompatible with International Law?" (2009) 28 (1) Yearbook of European Law 637–653. See also Gráinne de Búrca, "The Road not Taken. The European Union as a Global Human Rights Actor" (2011) 105 (4) American Journal of International Law 649–693 (680), generally holding that "[t]he ECJ has been notoriously reluctant, however, to cite or rely on other international and regional human rights treaties apart from the ECHR"; see also Gráinne de Búrca, "The ECJ and the International Legal Order: A Re-Evaluation" in Gráinne de Búrca and Joseph H H Weiler (eds) *The Worlds of European Constitutionalism* (Cambridge University Press 2012) 105–149 (140); Andrea Bianchi, "Assessing the Effectiveness of the UN Security Council's Anti-Terrorism Measures: The Quest for Legitimacy and Cohesion" (2017) 17 (5) European Journal of International Law

in contrast to grand old theories. I hope that the direction in which an application of consent-based monism goes has been made visible and understandable. I will now make this more explicit by showing how international treaties (Section 8.1) and customary international law (CIL) (Section 8.2) relate to the EU legal order according to consent-based monism.

8.1 THE INTERNATIONAL AGREEMENT

The international agreement, or international treaty, is a written agreement that is carried by a consensus between two or more subjects of international law. Subjects of international law are foremost states and international organizations.[198] The expression of will is left to State representatives expressing the will of individuals represented by the State. EU or national law provides for the *norms of authorization* to conclude an international agreement as a legal basis for the expression of the representatives.

These norms of authorization are reflected at an international level in Article 46 of the Vienna Convention on the Law of Treaties (VCLT).[199] Article 46 of the VCLT allows a State to "invoke the fact that its consent to be bound by a treaty has been expressed in violation of a provision of its internal law regarding the competence to conclude treaties as invalidating its consent" only if, cumulatively, "that violation was manifest and concerned a rule of its internal law of fundamental importance." In other words, Article 46 is restricted to violations of national law on the national *process* of expressing its will to be bound by an international treaty. A possible violation of the *content* of national law by an international treaty was excluded on purpose.[200]

881–919; Juliane Kokott and Christoph Sobotta, "The Kadi Case – Constitutional Core Values and International Law – Finding the Balance?" (2012) 23 (4) European Journal of International Law 1015–1024, arguing that the Court indicated a possible opening towards the precedence of Security Council measures if human rights enjoy sufficient safeguards.

198 The Holy Sea, the Red Cross and the Order of Malta are not treated here. For a historical overview of the Red Cross, see eg Daniel-Erasmus Khan, *Das Rote Kreuz: Geschichte einer humanitären Weltbewegung* (CH Beck 2013).

199 Article 46 "Provisions of internal law regarding competence to conclude treaties:

> 1. A State may not invoke the fact that its consent to be bound by a treaty has been expressed in violation of a provision of its internal law regarding competence to conclude treaties as invalidating its consent unless that violation was manifest and concerned a rule of its internal law of fundamental importance.
> 2. A violation is manifest if it would be objectively evident to any State conducting itself in the matter in accordance with normal practice and in good faith."

200 See Thilo Rensmann, "Article 46" in Oliver Dörr and Kirsten Schmalenbach (eds) *Vienna Convention on the Law of Treaties – A Commentary* (Springer 2nd ed 2018) para 33, n 87. See also Mark E Villiger, "Article 46" in Mark E Villiger (ed) *Commentary on the 1969 Vienna*

If Article 46 is not applicable, Article 27 of the VCLT is fully pertinent.[201] Article 27 stipulates that "[a] party may not invoke the provisions of its internal law as justification for its failure to perform a treaty." As a consequence, no material violations of national law may be invoked based on Article 46 or Article 27 at the international level.[202]

When international agreements deal with fundamental matters, consent to be bound by a treaty is expressed by ratification. The international agreement is negotiated and then opened to signature. Then, the adequate organ in the EU or national legal order has to consent before a State representative can sign and ratify the agreement (Article 14 (1) VCLT).[203] The relevant rules on how international agreements are concluded according to international law

Convention on the Law of Treaties (Brill 2009) para 8; Georg Ress, "Wechselwirkungen zwischen Völkerrecht und Verfassung bei der Auslegung völkerrechtlicher Verträge" in Georg Ress and Christoph Schreuer (eds) *Wechselwirkungen zwischen Völkerrecht und Verfassung bei der Auslegung völkerrechtlicher Verträge* (CF Müller 1982) para 23–24, n 7, 102–103. Also compare the commentary in the discussion of the presentation by Ress, by Karl Zemanek at 101, as well as Bruno Simma disputing at 110–111. There is a reference to the "einstigen Vater . . . des ILC-Entwurfs." See Special Rapporteur of the ILC to the VCLT, *Waldock*, YILC Vol. II, 4th report of the special rapporteur Sir Humphrey Waldock from March 19, March 25, June 17, 1965, at 71, para 6. See Luzius Wildhaber, *Treaty-Making Power and Constitution – An International and Comparative Study* (Helbing and Lichtenhahn 1971) 347–348. It is rightly feared that making the validity of agreements depend on their accord with each and every norm of constitutional law, written or customary, notorious or obscure, would gravely endanger the security of international transactions. States would feel encouraged to invoke their constitutional law to eliminate undesirable agreements or to "internationalize" conflicts between municipal state organs or interest groups. See also Andreas L Paulus, "Kompetenzüberschreitende Akte von Organen der Europäischen Union – Die Sicht des Völkerrechts" in Bruno Simma and Constanze Schulte (eds) *Völker- und Europarecht in der aktuellen Diskussion* (Linde 1999) 49–58, applying insights from international law on the relationship between EU and Member State law. Cf Ulrich Fastenrath, *Kompetenzverteilung im Bereich der auswärtigen Gewalt* (CH Beck 1986) esp 220.

201 Article 27 Internal law and observance of treaties. A party may not invoke the provisions of its internal law as justification for its failure to perform a treaty. This rule is without prejudice to Article 46. See Kirsten Schmalenbach, "Article 27" in Oliver Dörr and Kirsten Schmalenbach (eds) *Vienna Convention on the Law of Treaties – A Commentary* (Springer 2nd ed 2018); Rensmann (n 200) para 22.

202 See supra n 200.

203 Article 14 Consent to be bound by a treaty expressed by ratification, acceptance, or approval.

> 1. The consent of a State to be bound by a treaty is expressed by ratification when: (a) the treaty provides for such consent to be expressed by means of ratification; (b) it is otherwise established that the negotiating States were agreed that ratification should be required; (c) the representative of the State has signed the treaty subject to ratification; or (d) the intention of the State to sign the treaty subject to ratification appears from the full powers of its representative or was expressed during the negotiation.
> 2. The consent of a State to be bound by a treaty is expressed by acceptance or approval under conditions similar to those which apply to ratification.

between states and international organizations are generally said to be customary international law.[204] The Vienna Convention on the Law of Treaties between States and International Organizations (VCLT II)[205] – even though this treaty has not yet entered into force – essentially reflects these customary rules.[206] In the following sections, I will focus on this process.[207]

8.1.1 *The International Agreement and the EU Legal Order*

In order to find out how the EU concludes international agreements and how an international agreement concluded by the EU affects the EU legal order, we have to look at "by whom" and "in which subject matters" the EU is willing to conclude international agreements with other subjects of international law.[208] The EU's competence regime is quite complex and will not

See eg Frank Hoffmeister, "Article 14" in Oliver Dörr and Kirsten Schmalenbach (eds) *Vienna Convention on the Law of Treaties – A Commentary* (Springer 2nd ed 2018).

[204] See, generally, Olivier Corten and Pierre Klein, "Are Agreements between States and Non-State Entities Rooted in the International Legal Order?" in Enzo Cannizzaro (ed) *The Law of Treaties beyond the Vienna Convention* (Oxford University Press 2011) 3–24.

[205] Vienna Convention on the Law of Treaties between States and International Organizations (VCLT II), 21. 3. 1986 (1986) ILM 25 543. See eg Cases C-386/08 *Firma Brita GmbH v Hauptzollamt Hamburg-Hafen* ECLI:EU:C:2010:91 paras 40–45 referring to Article 31 and 34 of the VCLT as binding on the EU as rules of CIL; as well as T-512/12 *Front populaire pour la libération de la saguia-el-hamra et du rio de oro (Front Polisario) v Council of the European Union* ECLI:EU:T:2015:953 paras 92–93.

[206] See also Kirsten Schmalenbach, "Art. 218 AEUV" in Christian Calliess and Matthias Ruffert (eds) *EUV/AEUV* (CH Beck 6th ed 2022) para 3 with further references. For the customary international law nature of Art 31 (3) VCLT, see, for instance, ICJ, *Kasikili/Sedudu Island (Botswana/Namibia)* Judgment) ICJ Reports [1999] 1075 para 18; ICJ, *Certain Questions of Mutual Assistance in Criminal Matters (Djibouti v France)* Judgment ICJ Reports [2008] 177 para 112. Cf Pieter Jan Kuijper, "The European Courts and the Law of Treaties: The Continuing Story" in Enzo Cannizzaro (ed) *The Law of Treaties beyond the Vienna Convention* (Oxford University Press 2011) 256–278.

[207] For the purpose of this book, which is to provide a fresh look at the general relationship between international and EU law, it is sufficient to show the applicability of consent-based monism concerning two of the most important sources of international law, namely treaty law and customary international law. Yet the idea behind this book is not to provide a handbook-style comprehensive look at every single aspect of this relationship. This is the reason why, for instance, mixed agreements are not specifically analyzed here. On the CJEU's exclusive jurisdiction concerning mixed agreements, see eg Tobias Lock, *The European Court of Justice and International Courts* (Oxford University Press 2015) esp 92–134. On mixed agreements in general, see eg Nicolas Levrat et al (eds), *The EU and Its Member States Joint Participation in International Agreements* (Hart 2022).

[208] This section does not deal with international agreements between EU Member States. For such an analysis, see Bruno de Witte and Thibault Martinelli, "Treaties between EU Member States as Quasi-Instruments of EU Law" in Marise Cremona and Claire Kilpatrick (eds) *EU Legal Acts. Challenges and Transformations* (Oxford University Press 2018) 157–188.

be dealt with in detail here.[209] This book will simply assume that if the EU acts on the international plane it has competence in the subject matter concerned.

8.1.1.1 The Competence to Confirm the Will of the EU to Be Bound by an International Agreement

First, it is decisive to look at the circumstances under which the EU might conclude international agreements. Article 216 (1) TFEU provides in this regard that:

> The Union may conclude an agreement with one or more third countries or international organisations where [a] the Treaties so provide or where [b] the conclusion of an agreement is [ba] necessary in order to achieve, within the framework of the Union's policies, one of the objectives referred to in the Treaties, or is [bb] provided for in a legally binding Union act or is [bc] likely to affect common rules or [bd] alter their scope.

Moreover, Article 3 (2) TFEU states that "[t]he Union shall also have exclusive competence for the conclusion of an international agreement when its conclusion is provided for in a legislative act of the Union or is necessary to enable the Union to exercise its internal competence, or in so far as its conclusion may affect common rules or alter their scope."[210]

[209] For a detailed analysis of the EU's competences in the field of international relations, see Panos Koutrakos, *EU International Relations Law* (Hart 2nd ed 2015) part I; see also Graham Butler, *Constitutional Law of the EU's Common Foreign and Security Policy: Competence and Institutions in External Relations* (Hart 2019); as well as the contributions in Eleftheria Neframi and Mauro Gatti (eds) *Constitutional Issues of EU External Relations Law* (Nomos 2018); and in Marise Cremona (eds) *Structural Principles in EU External Relations Law* (Hart 2018). For a general analysis of the foreign policy objectives of the EU, see Joris Larik, *Foreign Policy Objectives in European Constitution* (Oxford University Press 2016); see also Geert de Baere, *Constitutional Principles of EU External Relations* (Oxford University Press 2008); for an analysis of the division of powers between the EU and its Member States with regard to regulating and protecting investments, see eg August Reinisch, "The Division of Powers between the EU and Its Member States 'After Lisbon'" in Marc Bungenberg, Joern Griebel and Steffen Hindelang (eds) *International Investment Law and EU Law* (2011) 43–54.

[210] Pointing to differences between Article 3 (2) TFEU and Article 216 (1) TFEU, Koutrakos (n 209) 128–129 criticizes that "Articles 216(1) and 3(2) TFEU fail to capture the subtlety and the dynamic nature of the Court's interpretation of competence and risk introducing generalisations in an area that least requires them." Yet it is a general truism that norms necessarily are more general than concrete cases. This particularly holds true for norms enshrining competences. Hence, it seems rather understandable when Paul Craig, *The Lisbon Treaty. Law, Politics and Treaty Reform* (Oxford University Press 2010) 400, states that these differences are marginal: "The specific categories listed in Article 216 TFEU as to when the EU is empowered to make an international agreement do not 'map' perfectly on to the

The CJEU clarified, concerning Article 228 (1) TEC, that the term "agreement" is used "in a general sense to indicate any undertaking entered into by entities subject to international law which has binding force, whatever its formal designation."[211] This understanding also applies to the Treaty of Lisbon[212] and clearly also includes international organizations as subjects of international law.[213] It is in this sense that I have spoken so far and will continue to speak of international agreements. Moreover, this broad understanding of agreements, which does not hinge on formal qualification as an agreement, is consistent with the understanding of Article 2 (1) (a) VCLT holding that "'Treaty' means an international agreement concluded between States in written form and governed by international law, whether embodied in a single instrument or in two or more related instruments and whatever its particular designation."[214]

The first competence constellation (see [a] above) in Article 216 (1) TFEU is quite clear. Where treaties so provide, the EU is competent to conclude an agreement with other subjects of international law. The treaties that are most relevant in this context are the common commercial policy (Article 207 (3) TFEU), the central banking system (Article 219 (3) TFEU), scientific collaboration (Article 186 TFEU), environmental policy (Article 191 (4) TFEU), development cooperation (Article 212 (3) TFEU), association

wording used in Article 3(2). There is nonetheless a significant overlap between the two. It is unlikely that the differences in wording will lead to differences in result."

211 Opinion 1/75 ECLI:EU:C:1975:145 p 1360. See also C-327/91 *France v Commission* ECLI:EU:C:1994:305 para 27.

212 Opinion of advocate general Sharpston of May 15, 2014 in Joined Cases C-103/12 and C-165/12, *Parliament and Commission v Council (Venezuelan Fishing Opportunities)* ECLI:EU:C:2014:334 para 96, also clarifying that the notion agreement "does not cover the circumstance where the EU expresses its intention to be bound by the terms of its declaration without the need for acceptance by the third State in whose favour that declaration is made. Nor does it apply to instruments whereby no binding commitment is entered into." Regarding the latter, see also C-233/02 *France v Commission* ECLI:EU:C:2004:173 paras 43–45. For the literature, see eg Alan Dashwood, "EU Acts and Member State Acts in the Negotiation, Conclusion, and Implementation of International Agreements" in Marise Cremona and Claire Kilpatrick (eds) *EU Legal Acts. Challenges and Transformations* (Oxford University Press 2018) 189–249 (194–198). Cf Allan Rosas, "Recent Case Law of the European Court of Justice Relating to Article 218 TFEU" in Jenő Czuczai and Frederik Naert (eds) *The EU as a Global Actor – Bridging Legal Theory and Practice: Liber Amicorum in Honour of Ricardo Gosalbo Bono* (Brill Nijhoff 2017) 365–379 (366–369).

213 Case C-327/91 *France v Commission* ECLI:EU:C:1994:305 paras 25 and 27.

214 On this similarity, see also Rudolf Mögele, "Art 216" in Rudolf Streinz (ed) EUV/AEUV (CH Beck 3rd ed 2018) para 5; cf Kirsten Schmalenbach, "Art 2" in Oliver Dörr and Kirsten Schmalenbach (eds), *Vienna Convention on the Law of Treaties – A Commentary* (Springer 2nd ed 2018) paras 5–7.

agreements (Article 217 TFEU) and common foreign and security policy (Article 37 TEU).[215]

The first subgroup of the second competence constellation (see [ba] above) is actually a natural correlate giving the EU competence to conclude treaties if this is "necessary in order to achieve, within the framework of the Union's policies, one of the objectives referred to in the Treaties." If the competence to conclude an international agreement is not spelled out, as, for instance, in Article 79 (3) TFEU, but the competence is necessary to achieve a treaty objective, an implied competence is given. This is, of course, subject to interpretation in the sense that the CJEU must, first, identify a treaty objective and, second, hold that the competence to conclude an international agreement is necessary to achieve this objective. This competence is essentially a codification of CJEU case law.[216] In the Joined Cases 3, 4 and 6/76 *Cornelis Kramer and Others*, the CJEU spelled out this competence constellation when holding that "[i]n the absence of specific provisions of the Treaty authorizing the Community to enter into international commitments in the sphere of conservation of the biological resources of the sea, one must turn to the general system of Community law in the sphere of the external relations of the Community."[217] This competence relates to the internal implied competences of the EU.[218]

Similarly, the second, third and fourth subgroup of the second competence constellation have their origin in the case law of the CJEU. In the second

[215] For this list see Philipp Terhechte, "Article 216 TFEU" in Jürgen Schwarze (eds) *EU-Kommentar* (Nomos 4th ed 2018) para 5; see also Rudolf Geiger, "Article 216 TFEU" in Rudolf Geiger, Daniel-Erasmus Khan and Markus Kotzur (eds) *European Union Treaties. A Commentary. Treaty on European Union. Treaty on the Functioning of the European Union* (CH Beck and Hart 2015) para 9 with further reference to Art 6 (2) TEU; Art 165 (3) TFEU; Art 167 (3) TFEU; Art 168 (3) TFEU; Art 211 TFEU; Art 212 (3) TFEU; Art 219 TFEU.

[216] See Eeckhout (n 180) 112–113, pointing, however, to the fact that the codification of case law was "copied from the Constitution for Europe." Therefore, he holds that "one may assume that the Court will keep a certain freedom as regards developing its implied-powers case law." However, see also Koutrakos (n 209) 126, holding that the interpretation of this competence constellation must not be interpreted too broadly. For criticism holding that the codification of the principles developed in the case law of the CJEU has hardly improved the situation as case law is rather complex and context specific, see Geert De Baere and Panos Koutrakos, "The Interactions between the Legislature and the Judiciary in EU External Relations" in Phil Syrpis (ed) *The Judiciary, the Legislature and the EU Internal Market* (Cambridge University Press 2012) 243–273.

[217] ECLI:EU:C:1976:114 para 16 as well as paras 19/20 and 21/25. See also Opinion 1/76 *Draft Agreement Establishing a European Laying-up Fund for Inland Waterway Vessels* ECLI:EU:C:1977:63 paras 3 and 4; Case C-476/98 *Commission v Germany* ECLI:EU:C:2002:631 para 82.

[218] See Geiger (n 215) para 10 with further references.

subgroup [bb] the competence rests on a legally binding Union act.[219] The third subgroup [bc] focuses on the likelihood of common rules being affected[220] and the fourth subgroup [bd] states the possibility that these rules might be altered regarding their scope.[221] Alternatives [bc] and [bd] aim at ensuring that individual or collective actions by Member States do not impair EU legal acts. Therefore, an implied EU competence is given should this impairment occur.[222]

The decision as to which of these constellations the competence to conclude an international agreement shall be based on has to fulfil the general standards of all legal decisions and thus has to have legal foundation.[223] Hence, "the choice of legal basis for an EU measure must rest on objective factors that are amenable to judicial review," which includes the aim and content of that measure and thus, in our case, the agreement.[224] This is important because a decision on the approval of an international agreement by the Council based on the wrong competence renders the decision invalid. This is, in turn, a severe impairment of the authorization of the relevant organ to conclude an international agreement on behalf of the EU. Yet this refers

[219] Opinion 1/94 *Competence of the Community to conclude international agreements concerning services and the protection of intellectual property* ECLI:EU:C:1994:384 para 95 (WTO): "Whenever the Community has included in its internal legislative acts provisions relating to the treatment of nationals of non-member countries or expressly conferred on its institutions powers to negotiate with non-member countries, it acquires exclusive external competence in the spheres covered by those acts." See also Opinion 2/92 *Competence of the Community or one of its institutions to participate in the Third Revised Decision of the OECD on national treatment* ECLI:EU:C:1995:83 para 33.

[220] Case 22/70 *Commission v Council* ECLI:EU:C:1971:32 paras 16–18 and 22 (ERTA). On the "ERTA doctrine," pre- and post-Lisbon case law as well as the critical position of some Member States, see Mirka Kuisma and Joris Larik, "The Continuing Contestation of ERTA. Conferral, Effectiveness and the Member States' Participation in Mixed Agreements" in Nicolas Levrat et al (eds) *The EU and Its Member States' Joint Participation in International Agreements* (Hart 2022) 43–58.

[221] Opinion 1/03 ECLI:EU:C:2006:81 para 133: "It follows from all the foregoing that a comprehensive and detailed analysis must be carried out to determine whether the Community has the competence to conclude an international agreement and whether that competence is exclusive. In doing so, account must be taken not only of the area covered by the Community rules and by the provisions of the agreement envisaged, insofar as the latter are known, but also of the nature and content of those rules and those provisions, to ensure that the agreement is not capable of undermining the uniform and consistent application of the Community rules and the proper functioning of the system which they establish."

[222] See Kirsten Schmalenbach, "Art. 216 AEUV" in Christian Calliess and Matthias Ruffert (eds) *EUV/AEUV* (CH Beck 6th ed 2022) para 16 with further reference to case law in n 66.

[223] Schmalenbach (n 222) para 24. Also with reference to case law for constellations when different and equivalent aims shall be achieved by one agreement which might then be based on different competence constellations.

[224] Case C-137/12 *Commission v Council* ECLI:EU:C:2013:675 para 52.

only to internal EU procedures to authorize the correct organ. In terms of the international validity of this agreement, the general rules of the VCLT, *in concreto* Article 46 and 27 VCLT, are applicable. These rules only allow for the invocation of the invalidation of a consent to be bound by an agreement if that violation of the internal process of authorization was a manifest violation of a law of fundamental importance.[225] This is a high threshold, which, given the complexity of the EU competence regime, will very likely not be met when a decision to approve an international agreement has been based on a wrong competence.[226]

For historical reasons, the executive is in charge of a state's external relations.[227] Even though much younger than most states, the EU is no exception to this (historical) rule. Article 218 TFEU lays out the procedure for the conclusion of an international agreement by the EU and is of "constitutional scope."[228] Article 218 (2) TFEU authorizes the Council to open negotiations (3), adopt negotiating directives (4), authorize the signing (5) as well as the

[225] See above Section 8.1.

[226] See implicitly Case C-211/01 *Commission v Council* ECLI:EU:C:2003:452 para 55, holding that "[i]t is common ground that the content of international agreements cannot be amended unilaterally, without new negotiations being undertaken by the contracting parties." Cf Opinion 2/20 *Cartagena Protocol* ECLI:EU:C:2001:664 para 5. With concrete reference to the VCLT see Schmalenbach (n 222) para 24; Frank Hoffmeister, "The Contribution of EU Practice to International Law" in Marise Cremona (ed) *Developments in EU External Relations Law* (Oxford University Press 2008) 37–127 (62–63) giving further examples. See also generally (albeit with the traditional distinction between international and EU law), Anne Peters, "The Position of International Law within the European Community Legal Order" (1997) 40 German Yearbook of International Law 9–77 (76): "The question of the *hierarchical status* of international law within the Community legal order is answered differently by international law and by Community law. In the external (international law) perspective, international law prevails over primary and secondary Community law. In contrast, the Community perspective is that the EC Treaty takes priority over international law (with the exception of *ius cogens*). Nevertheless, the ECJ has no jurisdiction to declare Community agreements that are incompatible with the EC Treaty invalid with binding force as against the Contracting Parties. The Court merely invalidates the internal act of conclusion of an agreement with the consequence that the agreement is inapplicable within the Community, but remains valid on the international plane" [emphasis original].

[227] See generally Theo Öhlinger, *Der Völkerrechtliche Vertrag im Staatlichen Recht – Eine Theoretische, Dogmatische und Vergleichende Untersuchung am Beispiel Österreichs* (Springer 1973) esp 12–13.

[228] Case C-425/13 *Commission v Council* ECLI:EU:C:2015:483 para 62, holds that "[i]t is apparent from the Court's case-law that Article 218 TFEU constitutes, as regards the conclusion of international treaties, an autonomous and general provision of constitutional scope, in that it confers specific powers on the EU institutions." On the "specific provisions" of Art 207 (3, 4) TFEU as referred to in Art 218 (1) TFEU within the common commercial policy, see Dashwood (n 212) 191–192. See also Art 219 TFEU on the conclusion of exchange rates and monetary agreements.

conclusion (6) of agreements. Article 218 (10) TFEU ensures that the European Parliament is "immediately and fully informed at all stages of the procedure."

Again, this internal process is also reflected at international level. International law provides for the rules guiding the process of concluding an international agreement. On the international plane these rules are laid down in the VCLT II, which reflects mostly customary international law.[229] Article 11 (2) VCLT II establishes the process of a formal confirmation, which is the pendant to the ratification of a treaty by states.[230] With this formal confirmation, the EU expresses its will to be bound by the international agreement and hands in the decision of approval made by the Council together with the certificate of the agreement with the depositary.

This internal process has to be complied with so that we can safely speak of a proper authorization to express the will of the EU to be bound by an international agreement. Yet, from the perspective of international law, the correctness of this internal process is only reflected in the abovementioned Article 46 VCLT. Only manifest violations of rules with fundamental importance are relevant. This is also acknowledged by the CJEU.[231] Otherwise Article 27 VCLT, which holds that "[a] party may not invoke the provisions of its internal law as justification for its failure to perform a treaty," is fully applicable. Hence, the Treaties – as much as the constitutional provisions of States – are not a good reason for not fulfilling the obligations concluded in international agreements either.[232]

[229] Holding that the VCLT II is binding for the EU as customary international law, see eg Philipp Terhechte, "Article 218 TFEU" in Jürgen Schwarze (ed) *EU-Kommentar* (Nomos 4th ed 2018) para 1.

[230] See Schmalenbach (n 206) para 8.

[231] See, for instance, Case C-327/91 *France v Commission* ECLI:EU:C:1994:305 paras 41–3 declaring void the act of the Commission on the basis of which the Commission concluded the agreement instead of the application to declare void the agreement itself. On this see also Anthony Aust, *Modern Treaty Law and Practice* (Cambridge University Press 3rd ed 2013) 314; Koutrakos (n 209) 158–160; and Hoffmeister (n 226) 62–64.

[232] This is also practically acknowledged by the court to some extent. See Joined Cases C-317 and 318/04 *Parliament v Council and Commission* ECLI:EU:C:2006:346 para 73. On this see also Pieter Jan Kuijper, "The Case Law of the Court of Justice and the Allocation of External Relations Powers: Whither the Traditional Role of the Executive in EU Foreign Relations?" in Marise Cremona and Anne Thies (eds) *The European Court of Justice and External Relations Law – Constitutional Challenges* (Hart 2016) 95–114 (112–113).

8.1.1.2 The Initiation, Negotiation and Conclusion of International Agreements

According to Article 218 (3) TFEU, the Commission may initiate the negotiation of international agreements as it also initiates legislative acts according to Article 17 (2) TEU.[233] If the agreement relates to common foreign and security policy, however, the initiative is the responsibility of the High Representative of the Union for Foreign Affairs and Security Policy (again Article 218 (3) TFEU). Both can initiate the process with a recommendation on the basis of which they invite the Council to authorize taking up negotiations.[234] These recommendations might also include draft negotiating directives according to Article 218 (4) TFEU, which are not – despite the English terminology – directives according to Article 288 TFEU.[235] Despite this fact, they are legally binding.[236] Authorization by the Council is a decision without specific addressees according to Article 288 (4) TFEU, which is subject to review under Article 263 TFEU.[237] Depending on the subject matter, either the Commission or the High Representative might be appointed as negotiators of the agreement (Article 218 (3) TFEU).[238]

[233] For an exemplary case study on CETA, see Jelena Bäumler, "Vom Vertragstext zum Inkrafttreten: Das Vertragsschlussverfahren im Mehrebenensystem am Beispiel CETA" (2016) 51 (6) Europarecht 607–631. On the particularities of CETA as a mixed agreement, see Manon Damestoy and Nicolas Levrat, "The Mixed Nature of the EU–Canada FTA. Between Competences Distribution and Democratic Legitimacy" in Nicolas Levrat et al (eds) *The EU and Its Member States' Joint Participation in International Agreements* (Hart 2022) 77–95.

[234] See Dashwood (n 212) 199, who highlights that this recommendation has to be distinguished from a proposal, which, according to Article 293 (1) TFEU, might be amended by the Council by unanimous action.

[235] See Eeckhout (n 180)197, with reference to the fact that in other language versions of Article 218 (3) TFEU the terminology differs.

[236] C-425/13 *Commission v Council* ECLI:EU:C:2015:483 paras 28–30. Cf Dashwood (n 212) 199, who highlights that these draft negotiating directives might be amended by the Council and should, for practical reasons, be formulated broadly in order to enable the negotiator to pursue their task effectively without breaching the directives (206). In this regard see also the Opinion of advocate general Wathelet C-425/13 *Commission v Council* ECLI:EU:C:2015:174 para 105. Yet these directives should not provide for "detailed negotiating positions" that "bind the negotiator" in a sense contrary to their role according to Article 218 (4) TFEU. For this finding and their binding effect, see C-425/13 *Commission v Council* ECLI:EU:C:2015:483 paras 86–90.

[237] C-114/12 *Commission v Council* ECLI:EU:C:2014:2151 paras 39–41.

[238] Dashwood (n 212) 201–203, argues that the language of Article 218 (3) TFEU and it being different from its predecessor provisions might entail a discretion for the Council also to adopt, for instance, the current holder of the Presidency as Union negotiator or head of the Union's negotiating team. See also Eeckhout (n 180) 117, pointing to the importance that according to

Once the agreement is negotiated, the Council may adopt, on proposal by the negotiator, another decision authorizing the signing and, potentially also, the provisional application of the agreement (Article 218 (5) TFEU).[239] At this stage of the process, the European Parliament must not consent; however, it must be fully informed according to Article 218 (10) TFEU. Usually the signature does not render an international agreement binding.[240] However, if it does so, exceptionally, the decision by the Council must be based on Article 218 (6) TFEU instead of Article 218 (5) TFEU.

Finally, the negotiated and signed agreement has to be concluded by another decision of the Council according to Article 218 (6) TFEU.[241] The voting rule that generally applies is a qualified majority rule, except for agreements covering fields for which unanimity is required and those which are listed in Article 218 (8) TFEU.[242]

For Council decisions on the conclusion of an international agreement, the participation of the European Parliament plays a vital role in safeguarding the democratic control of important external actions of the executive power.[243] As in most national legal orders, this involvement of the European Parliament begins with the process of authorizing the Council to formally confirm the agreement when it has already been negotiated and signed. Article 218 (6) (a)

Article 218 TFEU "the Commission is no longer the sole negotiator" (n 148), which is important because of "the antagonism between the Commission and the Council, which in the domain of international negotiations and the conclusion of international agreements, epitomizes the struggle between supranationalism and intergovernmentalism" (117). He sees this to be mediated in practice, however, by choosing mixed agreements if there is doubt as to the scope of EU competences (ch 7). Yet for matters of institutional balance he holds that "the choice for the negotiator is between the Commission and the High Representative" and that his choice ought to be guided so that the Commission is the negotiator except for common foreign and security policy agreements (196). See also Koutrakos (n 209) 141, suggesting that if the agreement is related to the common foreign and security policy, the common security and defence policy as well as to other EU policies, then, "in principle, it is to be negotiated by both the Commission and the High Representative." See also Mauro Gatti and Pietro Manzini, "External Representation of the European Union in the Conclusion of International Agreements" (2012) 49 (5) Common Market Law Review 1703–1734 (1708–1709).

239 On its provisional application, see eg Koutrakos (n 252) 13–16 with further references.

240 See text above at n 230 concerning the process established in Article 11 ff. VCLT II.

241 Holding that the conclusion is equivalent to ratification or accession, see Koutrakos (n 209) 147.

242 See Koutrakos (n 209) 147–149.

243 Case 138/79 SA *Roquette Frères v Council* EU:C:1980:249 para 33: the involvement of the parliament reflects "the fundamental democratic principle that the peoples should take part in the exercise of power through the intermediary of a representative assembly"; Case C-130/10 *Parliament v Council* ECLI:EU:C:2012:472 para 81. On improvements in terms of democratic control after the Lisbon Treaty of the EU diagnosed external relations as similar developments "of the foreign policy sector as its Member States," see Kuijper (n 232) 113.

TFEU lists the agreements that need the approval of the European Parliament. These are (i) association agreements, (ii) the agreement on Union accession to the European Convention for the Protection of Human Rights and Fundamental Freedoms (ECHR), (iii) agreements establishing a specific institutional framework by organizing cooperation procedures, (iv) agreements with important budgetary implications for the Union, and (v) agreements covering fields to which either the ordinary legislative procedure applies or the special legislative procedure where consent by the European Parliament is required.[244] This enumeration is quite extensive and, hence, the requirement of consent by the European Parliament can be considered the rule and its weaker institutional standing, where it must only be consulted or informed, the exception.[245] Yet the European Parliament is not formally involved in initiating an international agreement or negotiating its text, which is a serious limitation of the democratic control of international agreements.[246] This limitation is weakened by an inter-institutional agreement between the European Parliament and the Commission (based on Article 295 TFEU) ensuring that the Commission informs the European Parliament about its intentions to propose the beginning of negotiations, give the European Parliament insights into the draft negotiating directives and take due account of the European Parliament's comments in the negotiation phase about which the European Parliament is duly informed by the Commission.[247] Article 218 (6) (b) TFEU states that concerning agreements other than those listed in (a), the European Parliament has at least to be consulted and given the possibility to deliver an opinion on the agreement. However, when the agreement relates exclusively to the common foreign and security policy of the EU, the European Parliament is precluded from participating in the conclusion of such an agreement.[248] This is rather problematic,

[244] Koutrakos (n 209) 150–154.

[245] For such a classification and with further explanations on earlier versions of this requirement in former treaties, see Dashwood (n 212) 224–226.

[246] See Eeckhout (n 180) 199, who points to a case where the European Parliament managed to considerably shape the text of an international agreement with the United States on the exchange of financial information for anti-terrorist purposes by threatening not to give its consent to the final version of the agreement. See Koutrakos (n 209) 153–154 with further references in this regard.

[247] Framework Agreement on Relations between the European Parliament and the European Commission OJ L 304, 20.11.2010, 47–62. See Eeckhout (n 180) 199–200 with further reference to criticism of the Council on this agreement by stating that it would undermine the institutional balance in the treaties. See also Terhechte (n 229) para 16, with further references to former interinstitutional agreements such as the Luns-Westerterp-Procedure from 1973.

[248] C-130/10 *Parliament v Council* ECLI:EU:C:2012:472 para 82.

particularly concerning potential future developments in the EU's defense capacity and military cooperation.[249] Generally, the "distinction is designed to reflect externally the division of powers between institutions that applies internally."[250] "Exclusively" in this regard does not mean that no elements other than that of the common foreign and security policy must be dealt with in the agreement. Rather, the CJEU decided that "the main ... [aim] for the purposes of determining the legal basis of the contested decision" is decisive.[251] Finding the substantive legal basis of the decision on the conclusion of the agreement is key for choosing which procedure under Article 218 (6) TFEU is applicable to ensure the institutional balance provided for by the Treaties.[252]

Even if the European Parliament must not consent to the agreement or be consulted and give an opinion on the agreement, it nevertheless shall be "immediately and fully informed at all stages of the procedure" (Article 218 (10) TFEU).[253] Defiance of this provision is a ground for annulment of a Council decision on the conclusion of the agreement.[254] This is important because "[t]hat rule is an expression of the democratic principles on which the European Union is founded."[255] Yet it is a thin line between balancing the

[249] See Eeckhout (n 180) 211, who holds that the exclusion of the European Parliament on international agreements in common foreign and security policy matters "is clearly untenable" because "[t]he EU is developing its defence capacity, it is setting up military operations, it is concluding international agreements regarding such operations, and no parliamentary organ is formally involved in the process."

[250] C-658/11 *Parliament v Council* ECLI:EU:C:2014:2025 para 55. On this see also Eeckhout (n 180) 118, holding that a uniform internal and external competence regime of the EU is important, also in terms of safeguarding the "uniform interpretation of EU law."

[251] C-658/11 *Parliament v Council* ECLI:EU:C:2014:2025 para 45.

[252] C-263/14 *European Parliament v Council* ECLI:EU:C:2016:435 para 42–44 speaking of a "constitutional significance"; see also C-658/11 *Parliament v Council* ECLI:EU:C:2014:2025 paras 56–62. More recently on issues of the institutional balance concerning the process of concluding international agreements, see Panos Koutrakos, "Institutional Balance and the Duty of Cooperation in Treaty-Making under EU Law" (2018) 68 (1) International and Comparative Law Quarterly 1–33; see on this Geert De Baere and Tina Van den Sanden, "Interinstitutional Gravity and Pirates of the Parliament on Stranger Tides: The Continued Constitutional Significance of the Choice of Legal Basis in Post-Lisbon External Action" (2016) 12 (1) European Constitutional Law Review 85–113; as well as Pieter Jan Kuijper, "The Court and the New EU Foreign Relations Law: Institutional Balance?" in Jenő Czuczai and Frederik Naert (eds) *The EU as a Global Actor – Bridging Legal Theory and Practice: Liber Amicorum in Honour of Ricardo Gosalbo Bono* (Brill Nijhoff 2017) 48–64.

[253] C-658/11 *Parliament v Council* ECLI:EU:C:2014:2025 para 85 holding that this "applies to any procedure for concluding an international agreement, including agreements relating exclusively to the CFSP."

[254] C-658/11 *Parliament v Council* ECLI:EU:C:2014:2025 paras 75–78, 80.

[255] C-658/11 *Parliament v Council* ECLI:EU:C:2014:2025 para 81.

need for confidentiality in negotiating international agreements and the need for democratic control.[256] An inter-institutional agreement between the European Parliament and the Council concerning the forwarding to and handling by the European Parliament of classified information held by the Council on matters other than those in the area of the common foreign and security policy further serves to mediate the issue.[257]

The Council's decision to conclude an international agreement must rest on a substantive legal basis, which applies to any legal Act in the EU legal order. More precisely, this decision "must rest on objective factors amenable to judicial review, which include the aim and content of that measure."[258] Preferably, a single legal basis shall be identified if this is possible according to a "predominant purpose or component" in case of a "twofold purpose" or "component" of the agreement.[259] If this is not possible, the "measure must be founded on the various corresponding legal bases" if the "procedures required by each legal basis" are not incompatible with each other.[260]

8.1.1.3 The Binding (Direct) Effect of the International Agreement within the EU Legal Order: Simple Applicability and Direct Applicability

The success of international agreements depends on how their effect unfolds in the legal order of the participating state or international organization. Article 216 (2) TFEU holds in this regard that "[a]greements concluded by the Union are binding upon the institutions of the Union and on its Member States." This is rather brief but actually quite clear. If the EU has formally

[256] See on this Deirdre Curtin, "Official Secrets and the Negotiation of International Agreements: Is the EU Executive Unbound?" (2013) 50 (2) Common Market Law Review 423–457.

[257] Inter-institutional Agreement of March 12, 2014 between the European Parliament and the Council concerning the forwarding to and handling by the European Parliament of classified information held by the Council on matters other than those in the area of the common foreign and security policy, OJ C 95, 1.4.2014, 1–7.

[258] C-377/12 *Commission v Council* ECLI:EU:C:2014:1903 para 34.

[259] C-377/12 *Commission v Council* ECLI:EU:C:2014:1903 para 34. See Dashwood (n 212) 211–217, for further explanations and examples with reference to case law and the "centre of gravity" test. On this see also Peter Van Elsuwege, "The Potential for Inter-Institutional Conflicts before the Court of Justice: Impact of the Lisbon Treaty" in Marise Cremona and Anne Thies (eds) *The European Court of Justice and External Relations Law-Constitutional Challenges* (Hart 2016) 115–136 (117–119). For criticism of the "use of the so-called 'centre of gravity test' as a means to delineate areas of competence," see De Baere and Van den Sanden (n 252).

[260] C-377/12 *Commission v Council* ECLI:EU:C:2014:1903 para 34 with further reference to Case C-130/10 *Parliament v Council* ECLI:EU:C:2012:472 paras 42–45 and the case law cited. For a review of the case law, see Dashwood (n 212) 218–221.

confirmed and thereby officially declared its will to be bound by an international treaty, this treaty is binding on the EU. Nothing else is expected by international law: Article 26 VCLT, also known as one, if not the, fundamental norm of international law, requests that *pacta sunt servanda*.[261] The CJEU concretized this general command when holding that provisions of such agreements "form an integral part of community law."[262] Since 1974 this is settled case law and the CJEU clarified that Member States also have "to ensure compliance with the obligations arising from such agreements."[263] Since 1986 the CJEU has specified that international agreements form part of the EU legal order when they enter into force according to international law.[264]

Despite being rather straightforward, this provokes the question as to *how* international agreements form part of the EU legal order. An important question in this regard is whether such agreements are directly applicable.[265] In order to avoid confusion I will consistently speak about direct applicability and simple applicability as distinguished in Part II. I will refer to the very same concept and will thus be using "direct effect" as a synonym for "direct applicability" concerning the relationship between international and EU law.[266] What is more, direct applicability should be distinguished from the

[261] See also Eeckhout (n 180) 325.

[262] Case 181/73 *R & V Haegeman v Belgium* ECLI:EU:C:1974:41 para 5.

[263] See only Case 104/81 *Hauptzollamt Mainz v CA Kupferberg & Cie KG a.A.* ECLI:EU:C:1982:362 para 11. See also para 13 with explicit reference to *Haegeman*; see further case law in n 264.

[264] Case 12/86 *Meryem Demirel v Stadt Schwäbisch Gmünd* ECLI:EU:C:1987:400 para 7, again with explicit reference to *Haegeman* and mentioning explicitly that this is the case from when the agreement entered into force; Case 30/88 *Hellenic Republic v Commission* ECLI:EU:C:1989:422 para 12 with explicit reference to *Demirel*; as well as recently Joined Cases C-464/13 and C-465/13 *Oberto* ECLI:EU:C:2015:163 para 29, again with explicit reference to *Demirel*.

[265] Eeckhout (n 180) 329–330 argues for a distinction between the direct effect of international agreements and the direct effect of "internal" EU law. His argument for distinctiveness relies on the primacy of application of EU law concerning conflicting Member State law, however, whereas the direct effect of international law would have to be distinguished from the direct effect of "internal" EU law because in this case the question would be whether international agreements have primacy over "internal" EU law. This conflation of two separate doctrines is, however, quite unfortunate. The question of whether a legal order enjoys primacy over another legal order is simply different from the question of whether an agreement, a specific provision in this agreement or a specific norm have a direct effect.

[266] See Section 6.4 above. This is proposed also in the light of the seemingly synonymous use of direct effect and direct applicability in 26/62 *Van Gend & Loos v Netherlands* ECLI:EU:C:1963:1, also embracing the statements by various governments. Cf Peters (n 226), holding that "[p]rovisions of international agreements concluded by the Community have *direct effect* when Community and Member State courts can derive concrete legal rights or obligations

question of whether an agreement or a specific provision of it confers subjective rights on individuals, which is a sub-question of direct applicability.[267] This has been acknowledged for quite some time now in the case law of the CJEU.[268] Hence, not all provisions that are directly applicable confer

from them. The precondition for this is the Contracting Parties' respective intent, normally manifested in the provisions' language. The Communitarian notion of direct effect of Community agreements (external Community law) builds on the traditional notion of direct effect of international agreements in the domestic order of States, and on the Communitarian notion of direct effect of internal Community law" [emphasis original]. However, see also Francesca Martines, "Direct Effect of International Agreements of the European Union" (2014) 25 (1) European Journal of International Law 129–147 (137), pointing to the exceptional fact "that it is the legal order itself that stands out for its inherent feature of being addressed to private subjects as a default rule." This sets apart *Van Gend en Loos* from classical international law agreements.

[267] See Joined Cases 21/72 to 24/72 *International Fruit Company NV and Others* ECLI:EU:C:1972:115 para 8, for misleadingly asking for an agreement to confer rights on citizens which could be invoked before courts as a precondition for invalidating an EU provision. See Koutrakos (n 209) 259–278, with further reference to case law in which the CJEU has not always applied the same test in order to determine whether an international agreement or a provision in such an agreement has a direct effect. See also Peters (n 226) 76: "Some cases and much writing implicitly or explicitly associate direct effect with procedural standing or substantive rights of individuals. In contrast, this paper argues that direct effect is best understood as an objective prerequisite for application of international rules by courts."

[268] See, for instance, the case law on the interpretation of EU law in the light of international agreements which are not directly applicable in Joined Cases C-300/98 and C-392/98 *Parfums Christian Dior SA v TUK Consultancy BV and Assco Gerüste GmbH and Rob van Dijk v Wilhelm Layher GmbH & Co KG and Layher BV* ECLI:EU:C:2000:688 para 45; C-431/05 *Merck Genéricos – Produtos Farmacêuticos Ld[a] v Merck & Co Inc and Merck Sharp & Dohme Ld[a]* ECLI:EU:C:2007:496 para 35; C-428/08 *Monsanto Technology LLC v Cefetra BV* ECLI:EU:C:2010:402 para 72. See also Joined Cases C-288/09 and C-289/09 *British Sky Broadcasting Group plc (C-288/09) and Pace plc (C-289/09) v The Commissioners for Her Majesty's Revenue & Customs* ECLI:EU:C:2011:248 para 83, expressly stating that "it should be borne in mind that, according to settled case-law, even though the provisions of a treaty such as the ITA are not such as to create rights upon which individuals may rely directly before the courts under European Union law, where the European Union has legislated in the field in question, the primacy of international agreements concluded by the European Union over provisions of secondary Community legislation means that such provisions must, so far as is possible, be interpreted in a manner that is consistent with those agreements"; cf Joined Cases C-320/11, C-330/11, C-382/22 and C-383/11 *Digitalnet OOD and Others v Nachalnik na Mitnicheski punkt – Varna Zapad pri Mitnitsa Varna* ECLI:EU:C:2012:745 para 39. Cf also Öhlinger and Potacs (n 72) 62–66, who point out that with regard to EU law and its applicability in Member State law the CJEU does not speak of "subjective rights" (which is rather a German notion) but of "individual rights": Case 26/62 *Van Gend & Loos v Netherlands* ECLI:EU:C:1963:1 13; Case 6/64 *Costa v ENEL* ECLI:EU:C:1964:66, "rights of individuals" or "citizens' rights" (Case 33/76 *Rewe-Zentralfinanz eG and Rewe-Zentral AG v Landwirtschaftskammer für das Saarland* ECLI:EU:C:1976:188) or simply of "rights" (C-329/97 *Sezgin Ergat v Stadt Ulm* ECLI:EU:C:2000:133 para 40) C-112/00 *Eugen Schmidberger, Internationale Transporte und Planzüge v Republik Österreich* ECLI:EU:C:2003:333 paras 74, 80; C-426/05 *Tele2 Telecommunication GmbH v Telekom-Control-Kommission* ECLI:EU:

subjective rights on individuals, but all provisions that confer subjective rights on individuals are directly applicable. In order to determine whether an international agreement enjoys direct applicability, the CJEU adjudicated the following: "[R]egard must be simultaneously paid to the spirit, the general scheme and the wording of the Convention and of the provision concerned."[269] For if a specific provision in an agreement provides for direct applicability, it must "contain ... a clear and precise obligation which is not subject, in its implementation or effects, to the adoption of any subsequent measure" by a (legislative) EU organ.[270]

First, it is up to the international agreement, and hence to the parties of the agreement, to determine whether the agreement shall be directly applicable. The CJEU generally holds that "[i]t is true that the effects within the Community of provisions of an agreement concluded by the Community with a non-member country may not be determined without taking account of the international origin of the provisions in question."[271] Therefore, the international agreement is decisive when determining whether its provisions are directly applicable. "In conformity with the principles of public international law Community institutions which have power to negotiate and conclude an agreement with a non-member country are free to agree with that country what effect the provisions of the agreement are to have in the

C:2008:103. This is not intended to limit direct applicability, which is not only pertinent when the Treaty confers rights on individuals but also when it entails obligations for Member States and their organs (Case 28/67 *Firma Molkerei-Zentrale Westfalen/Lippe GmbH v Hauptzollamt Paderborn* ECLI:EU:C:1968:17 "the EEC Treaty produces direct effects *and* creates individual rights" [emphasis added]).

269 Case 87/75 *Conceria Daniele Bresciani v Amministrazione Italiana delle Finanze* ECLI:EU:C:1976:18 para 16. For discussion of the evolution of the CJEU's case law on the direct effect of international agreements, see Mario Mendez, *The Legal Effects of EU Agreements. Maximalist Treaty Enforcement and Judicial Avoidance Techniques* (Oxford University Press 2013) 94–106.

270 See Case 17/81 *Pabst & Richarz KG v Hauptzollamt Oldenburg* ECLI:EU:C:1982:129 para 27. Note that this does not primarily rest on the absence of specific implementation measures but rather refers to the nature of the provision and the question of whether it can be applied without further legal acts. In this regard see also Eeckhout (n 180) 336, with reference to "classic direct-effect reasoning" on the relationship between EU law and Member State law. For a discussion, see Mendez (n 269) 100, who highlights the ease with which the CJEU declared for the second time in history that an international agreement has direct effect. Also in this regard see 12/86 *Meryem Demirel v Stadt Schwäbisch Gmünd* ECLI:EU:C:1987:400 para 14. For further references to earlier case law, see Eeckhout (n 180) 340, n 58; and on more recent case law see 342, n 66.

271 Case 104/81 *Hauptzollamt Mainz v CA Kupferberg & Cie KG a A* ECLI:EU:C:1982:362 para 17.

internal legal order of the contracting parties."[272] Yet this is not a blank cheque because "only if that question has not been settled by the agreement does it fall for decision by the courts having jurisdiction in the matter, and in particular by the Court of Justice within the framework of its jurisdiction under the Treaty, in the same manner as any question of interpretation relating to the application of the agreement in the Community" to determine whether an international agreement is directly applicable.[273] The CJEU furthermore acknowledges the (bona fide) duty of all parties to an agreement to take responsibility for executing the agreement fully while nevertheless emphasizing that the appropriate legal means to do so are left to the parties.[274] However, again, the CJEU added the exception that this holds true unless the agreement specifies those legal means.[275]

Second, if the agreement does not provide for an explicit reference as to whether its provisions are directly applicable, it is a matter of interpretation to determine the effect of such an agreement. International principles on the interpretation of international treaties are the primary reference point. Yet the CJEU also aimed at ensuring uniformity in the sense that those international agreements which reflect EU law are also to a certain extent interpreted in a way that leads to the same or similar results.[276]

[272] Case 104/81 *Hauptzollamt Mainz v CA Kupferberg & Cie KG a A* ECLI:EU:C:1982:362 para 17. See also C-149/96 *Portugal v Council* ECLI:EU:C:1999:574 para 34 with explicit reference to *Hauptzollamt*.

[273] Case 104/81 *Hauptzollamt Mainz v CA Kupferberg & Cie KG a A* ECLI:EU:C:1982:362 para 17. See also C-149/96 *Portugal v Council* ECLI:EU:C:1999:574 para 34 with explicit reference to *Hauptzollamt*.

[274] Case 104/81 *Hauptzollamt Mainz v CA Kupferberg & Cie KG a A* ECLI:EU:C:1982:362 para 18. See also C-149/96 *Portugal v Council* ECLI:EU:C:1999:574 para 35 with explicit reference to *Hauptzollamt*.

[275] Case 104/81 *Hauptzollamt Mainz v CA Kupferberg & Cie KG a A* ECLI:EU:C:1982:362 para 18. See also C-149/96 *Portugal v Council* ECLI:EU:C:1999:574 para 35 with explicit reference to *Hauptzollamt* adding that the agreement shall be interpreted "in the light of its subject-matter and purpose" in order to find out whether the agreement itself specifies the appropriate legal means to execute the agreement fully.

[276] See with further references, Eeckhout (n 180) 335. See also Koutrakos (n 207) 274–275, pointing to the fact that the CJEU denied "any automatic extension of the interpretation of EC Treaty prohibitions in the area of free movement of goods to similarly or identically worded provisions of FTAs" in Case 270/80 *Polydor Limited and RSO Records Inc v Harlequin Records Shops Limited and Simons Records Limited* ECLI:EU:C:1982:43, 104/81 *Hauptzollamt Mainz v CA Kupferberg & Cie KG a A* ECLI:EU:C:1982:362 and C-312/91 *Procedural issue relating to a seizure of goods belonging to Metalsa Srl* ECLI:EU:C:1993:279 on the one hand. However, on the other hand, the CJEU in C-207/91 *Eurim-Pharm GmbH v Bundesgesundheitsamt* ECLI:EU:C:1993:278 and C-163/90 *Administration des Douanes et Droits Indirects v Léopold Legros and others* ECLI:EU:C:1992:326, "suggests that the effectiveness of prohibitions set out in the latter would be undermined if the liberal

Moreover, the CJEU clarified that the courts of the contracting parties interpreting the agreement differently, in the sense that one court would hold a certain provision to be directly applicable while another court would disagree, does not "constitute a lack of reciprocity."[277] While the CJEU concluded in *Kupferberg* that the provision of the international agreement concerned is directly applicable,[278] its later GATT and WTO case law is known to be less "friendly" to international law.[279] In 1994, the CJEU concluded that GATT is not directly applicable[280] and in 1999 it relied on a "considerable importance to negotiation between the parties" in WTO agreements. This included the fact that compensation might be granted for the time when the "immediate withdrawal of the measures is impracticable" or, if the member "fails to fulfil its obligation to implement," a recommendation of the dispute settlement body follows.[281] Hence, "to require the judicial organs to refrain from applying the rules of domestic law which are inconsistent with the WTO agreements would have the consequence of depriving the legislative or executive organs of the contracting parties of the possibility . . . of entering into negotiated agreements."[282] From this follows that WTO agreements do not, "interpreted in the light of their subject-matter and purpose," "determine the appropriate legal means of ensuring that they are applied in good faith in the legal order of the contracting parties."[283] This general

interpretation of the analogous EU prohibitions were not transposed." Koutrakos (n 207), however, comes to the conclusion that if these judgments are viewed in their "specific factual and legal context," this differentiation might be justified.

277 Case 104/81 *Hauptzollamt Mainz v CA Kupferberg & Cie KG a A* ECLI:EU:C:1982:362 para 18.

278 Case 104/81 *Hauptzollamt Mainz v CA Kupferberg & Cie KG a A* ECLI:EU:C:1982:362 para 27.

279 See thereto in detail Koutrakos (n 207) 280–307.

280 Joined Cases 21/72 to 24/72 *International Fruit Company NV and Others* ECLI:EU:C:1972:115 para 19; 9/73 *Carl Schlüter v Hauptzollamt Lörrach* ECLI:EU:C:1973:110 para 18; C-280/93 *Germany v Council* ECLI:EU:C:1994:367 paras 109–110.

281 Case C-149/96 *Portugal v Council* ECLI:EU:C:1999:574 paras 36–39.

282 Case C-149/96 *Portugal v Council* ECLI:EU:C:1999:574 para 40.

283 Case C-149/96 *Portugal v Council* ECLI:EU:C:1999:574 para 41. On provisions of TRIPS see Joined Cases C-300/98 and C-392/98 *Parfums Christian Dior SA v TUK Consultancy BV and Assco Gerüste GmbH and Rob van Dijk v Wilhelm Layher GmbH & Co KG and Layher BV* ECLI:EU:C:2000:688 paras 42–44, holding that settled case law (with reference to *Hauptzollamt* and *Demirel*) states that agreements "must be regarded as being directly applicable when, regard being had to the wording, purpose and nature of the agreement, it may be concluded that the provision contains a clear, precise and unconditional obligation which is not subject, in its implementation or effects, to the adoption of any subsequent measure," which is (with reference to *Portugal v Council*) not the case for WTO agreements and also holds *mutatis mutandis* for TRIPS. See also C-307/99 *OGT Fruchthandelsgesellschaft mbH v Hauptzollamt Hamburg-St. Annen* ECLI:EU:C:2001:228 para 26, concluding that the

finding, however, might be reversed if "the Community intended to implement a particular obligation assumed in the context of the WTO, or where the Community measure refers expressly to precise provisions of the agreements and understandings contained in the annexes to the WTO Agreement."[284] Finally, the CJEU also concluded "that the nature and the broad logic of UNCLOS [United Nations Convention on the Law of the Sea] prevent the Court from being able to assess the validity of a Community measure in the light of that Convention" and hence also that UNCLOS does not enjoy direct applicability.[285] The latter was based on the reasoning that UNCLOS would not confer rights on individuals but only to ships, and the legal status of ships is dependent on the flag State.[286]

This CJEU case law on GATT and the WTO attracted a lot of attention and criticism because it was said to be a departure from EU friendliness towards international law.[287] If an international agreement does not state

same "must apply, for the same reasons, to the provisions of GATT 1994." Confirming WTO jurisprudence, see also Joined Cases C-27/00 and C-122/00 *The Queen v Secretary of State for the Environment, Transport and the Regions, ex parte Omega Air Ltd (C-27/00) and Omega Air Ltd, Aero Engines Ireland Ltd and Omega Aviation Services Ltd v Irish Aviation Authority (C-122/00)* ECLI:EU:C:2002:161 para 93; C-93/02 P *Biret International SA v Council of the European Union* ECLI:EU:C:2003:517 para 52. Again concerning TRIPS, see C-245/02 *Anheuser-Busch Inc v Budějovický Budvar, národní podnik* ECLI:EU:C:2004:717 para 54; again generally Joined Cases C-120/06 and C-121/06 P *Fabbrica italiana accumulatori motocarri Montecchio SpA (FIAMM) and Fabbrica italiana accumulatori motocarri Montecchio Technologies LLC (C-120/06 P), Giorgio Fedon & Figli SpA and Fedon America, Inc (C-121/06 P) v Council* ECLI:EU:C:2008:476 para 111.

284 Case C-76/00 P *Petrotub SA and Republica SA v Council of the European Union* ECLI:EU:C:2003:4 paras 53–54; C-93/02 P *Biret International SA v Council of the European Union* ECLI:EU:C:2003:517 para 53, with reference to Case 70/87 *Fediol v Commission* ECLI:EU:C:1989:254 paras 19–22; and C-69/89 *Nakajima v Council* ECLI:EU:C:1991:186 para 31 concerning GATT; and regarding WTO agreements, C-149/96 *Portugal v Council* ECLI:EU:C:1999:574 para 49. See Eeckhout (n 180) 357–365, calling this "the principle of implementation."

285 Case C-308/06 *The Queen, on the application of International Association of Independent Tanker Owners (Intertanko) and Others v Secretary of State for Transport* ECLI:EU:C:2008:312 para 65.

286 Case C-308/06 *The Queen, on the application of International Association of Independent Tanker Owners (Intertanko) and Others v Secretary of State for Transport* ECLI:EU:C:2008:312 para 61. The same holds true for the Kyoto Protocol. See C-366/10 *Air Transport Association of America and Others v Secretary of State for Energy and Climate Change* ECLI:EU:C:2011:864. Cf Koutrakos (n 209) 263–264.

287 See Schmalenbach (n 222) para 31 with further references in nn 126 and 128 and an interesting argument in para 41 holding that an exemption from general direct applicability in previous CJEU case law concerning the WTO could have been justified from an international law perspective considering that the Council of Ministers of the EC stated in the Uruguay Round that individuals will not be able to rely directly on GATT 1994 due to the nature of the

clearly what effect its provisions are supposed to have in the legal orders of its parties, it is up to the Court to determine whether the agreement confers subjective rights.[288] To this end, the Court assesses the direct applicability of the provisions of an international agreement according to the criteria it uses to determine the direct applicability of a directive.[289] Hence, the nature and the broad logic of the international agreement must not preclude its direct applicability and its provisions must be unconditional and sufficiently precise.[290] The interpretation of whether a provision is unconditional and sufficiently precise is determined by "the specific context" of the provision of an international agreement.[291] This fits in particularly well with the analysis in Part I and the relevance of contextualization.

However, if an international agreement that has been concluded is published in the *Official Journal of the EU* and is found to be directly applicable, then the organs applying EU and national law have to apply it in the same way as a regulation.[292]

regulation. For further references on literature on this topic, see Eeckhout (n 180) 343, n 68, as well as 375 for a nuanced defense of this case law.

[288] See concerning GATT 1947, Joined Cases 21/72 to 24/72 *International Fruit Company NV and Others* ECLI:EU:C:1972:115 para 19; and Joined Cases C-120/06 and C-121/06 P *Fabbrica italiana accumulatori motocarri Montecchio SpA (FIAMM) and Fabbrica italiana accumulatori motocarri Montecchio Technologies LLC (C-120/06 P), Giorgio Fedon & Figli SpA and Fedon America, Inc (C-121/06 P) v Council* ECLI:EU:C:2008:476 para 109.

[289] 12/86 *Meryem Demirel v Stadt Schwäbisch Gmünd* ECLI:EU:C:1987:400 para 14. Case C-167/17 *Klohn v An Bord Pleanála* ECLI:EU:C:2018:833 para 33 with explicit reference to *Demirel*.

[290] See especially Case C-344/04 *The Queen, on the application of International Air Transport Association and Others v Secretary of State for Transport* ECLI:EU:C:2006:10 para 39; Case C-308/06 *The Queen, on the application of International Air Transport Association and Others v Secretary of State for Transport* ECLI:EU:C:2008:312 para 45; and Joined Cases C-120/06 and C-121/06 P *Fabbrica italiana accumulatori motocarri Montecchio SpA (FIAMM) and Fabbrica italiana accumulatori motocarri Montecchio Technologies LLC (C-120/06 P), Giorgio Fedon & Figli SpA and Fedon America, Inc (C-121/06 P) v Council* ECLI:EU:C:2008:476 para 110; C-135/10 *Società Consortile Fonografici (SCF) v Marco Del Corso* ECLI:EU:C:2012:140 para 43; C-363/12 *Z v A Government department and The Board of management of a community school* ECLI:EU:C:2014:159 paras 87–88, holding that the obligations in the United Nations Convention on the Rights of Persons with Disabilities only address contracting parties due to their "programmatic" nature. See recently C-207/17 *Rotho Blaas Srl v Agenzia delle Dogane e dei Monopoli* ECLI:EU:C:2018:840 para 43. See also Koutrakos (n 207) 259–267 on the "precondition for direct effect: the nature and logic of the agreement" as well as 267–278 on "the application of the principle of direct effect." See also Martines (n 266) 138.

[291] For this argument see Koutrakos (n 209) 275.

[292] See eg Case C-192/89 *S. Z. Sevince v Staatssecretaris van Justitie* ECLI:EU:C:1990:322 para 26. In this judgment the CJEU holds furthermore that individuals can claim subjective rights from an international agreement even without publication in the Official Journal (para 24).

8.1.1.4 Which Rank for International Agreements in the EU Legal Order?

It is settled case law of the CJEU that international agreements concluded by the EU take precedence over EU secondary law.[293] According to Article 216 (2)

However, unpublished international agreements cannot cause negative effects for individuals. Cf Schmalenbach (n 222) para 37 with further references in n 160 and with the qualification that the case law of the CJEU on the direct applicability of international agreements is generally not questioned by scholarship (para 40).

[293] Joined Cases 21/72 to 24/72 *International Fruit Company NV and Others* ECLI:EU:C:1972:115 para 14: "It follows from the Community nature of such provisions that their effect in the Community may not be allowed to vary according to whether their application is in practice the responsibility of the Community institutions or the Member States and, in the latter case, according to the effects in the internal legal order of each Member State which the law of that State assigns to international agreements concluded by it." The CJEU further continued to hold that "Therefore it is for the Court, within the framework of its jurisdiction in interpreting the provisions of agreements, to ensure their uniform application throughout the Community." For the first explicit mention of the primacy of international agreements, albeit still in the context of interpretation, see C-61/94 *Commission v Germany* ECLI:EU:C:1996:313 para 52, holding that "the primacy of international agreements concluded by the Community over provisions of secondary Community legislation means that such provisions must, so far as is possible, be interpreted in a manner that is consistent with those agreements"; C-286/02 *Bellio F.lli Srl v Prefettura di Treviso* ECLI:EU:C:2004:212 para 33; C-228/06 *Mehmet Soysal und Ibrahim Savatli v Germany* ECLI:EU:C:2009:101 para 59; C-344/04 *The Queen, on the application of International Air Transport Association and European Low Fares Airline Association v Department for Transport* ECLI:EU:C:2006:10 para 35; C-311/04 *Algemene Scheeps Agentuur Dordrecht BV v Inspecteur der Belastingdienst – Douanedistrict Rotterdam* ECLI:EU:C:2006:23 para 25; C-308/06 *The Queen, on the application of International Association of Independent Tanker Owners (Intertanko) and Others v Secretary of State for Transport* ECLI:EU:C:2008:312 para 42; C-366/10 *Air Transport Association of America and Others v Secretary of State for Energy and Climate Change* ECLI:EU:C:2011:864 para 50; Joined Cases C-288/09 and C-289/09 *British Sky Broadcasting Group plc (C-288/09) and Pace plc (C-289/09) v The Commissioners for Her Majesty's Revenue & Customs* ECLI:EU:C:2011:248 para 83; Joined Cases C-320/11, C-330/11, C-382/22 and C-383/11 *Digitalnet OOD and Others v Nachalnik na Mitnicheski punkt – Varna Zapad pri Mitnitsa Varna* ECLI:EU:C:2012:745 para 39; Joined Cases C-335/11 and C-337/11 *HK Danmark, acting on behalf of Jette Ring v Dansk almennyttigt Boligselskab (C-335/11) and HK Danmark, acting on behalf of Lone Skouboe Werge v Dansk Arbejdsgiverforening, acting on behalf of Pro Display A/S (C-337/11)* ECLI:EU:C:2013:222 para 28; Joined Cases C-335/11 and C-337/11 *HK Danmark* ECLI:EU:C:2013:222 para 28; C-414/11 *Daiichi Sankyo Co Ltd and Sanofi-Aventis Deutschland GmbH v DEMO Anonymos Viomichaniki kai Emporiki Etairia Farmakon* ECLI:EU:C:2013:520 para 22; C-363/12 *Z v A Government department and The Board of management of a community school* ECLI:EU:C:2014:159 para 71; C-356/12 *Wolfgang Glatzel v Freistaat Bayern* ECLI:EU:C:2014:350 para 70; Joined Cases C-401/12 P to C-403/12 P *Council v Vereniging Milieudefensie and Stichting Stop Luchtverontreiniging Utrecht* ECLI:EU:C:2015:4 para 52; C-543/14 *Ordre des barreaux francophones et germanophone and Others* ECLI:EU:C:2016:605 para 49; C-207/17 *Rotho Blaas Srl v Agenzia delle Dogane e dei Monopoli* ECLI:EU:C:2018:840 para 43.

TFEU, the CJEU holds that such international agreements "are binding on its institutions."[294] Hence, EU legislation also has to take international agreements into account and must not ignore, let alone derogate, them.[295] This could be seen as quite a friendly position towards international law, as in several EU Member States international treaties share the same rank as national laws and thus might also be derogated by national laws.[296] Yet international agreements clearly stand behind EU primary law because the EU has no competence to alter the Treaties.[297] This hierarchy is only said to be reversed in case EU primary law contradicted *ius cogens* (Article 53 VCLT).[298]

[294] Case C-363/12 *Z v A Government department and The Board of management of a community school* ECLI:EU:C:2014:159 para 71.

[295] On the duty to interpret (secondary but probably not primary) EU law in the light of international law, see C-61/94 *Commission v Germany* ECLI:EU:C:1996:313 para 52, holding that "the primacy of international agreements concluded by the Community over provisions of secondary Community legislation means that such provisions must, so far as is possible, be interpreted in a manner that is consistent with those agreements." See Teresa Weber, "Die völkerrechtskonforme Auslegung von Unionsrecht – primär nur bei Sekundärrecht, nur sekundär bei Primärrecht?" (2013) 68 Zeitschrift für öffentliches Recht 389–416.

[296] See for Germany BVerfGE 141, 1 (*Völkerrechtsdurchbrechung*). For a critical analysis, see Ulrich Fastenrath, "Anmerkung" (2016) 71 (12) JuristenZeitung 636–640, who holds that this judgment is "an unprecedented disregard of public international law of Faustian quality" [translation by LK]; cf Lando Kirchmair, "Ist Art. 59 Abs. 2 GG tatsächlich dualistisch? Ein Beitrag zur Stärkung der innerstaatlichen Wirkung völkerrechtlicher Verträge und gleichzeitig einer stärkeren Einbindung der Legislative auf völkerrechtlicher Ebene" (2017) 72 (3) Zeitschrift für öffentliches Recht 515–547 with further references. On Art 59 (2) of the German Basic Law, see eg Ulrich Fastenrath and Thomas Groh, "Art 59 GG" in Karl Heinrich Friauf and Wolfram Höfling (eds) *Berliner Kommentar zum Grundgesetz* (Erich Schmidt 22 2007).

[297] Opinion 2/94 *Accession by the Community to the European Convention for the Protection of Human Rights and Fundamental Freedoms* ECLI:EU:C:1996:140 para 4, holding that an agreement "incompatible with the provisions of the Treaty could not fail to provoke, not only in a Community context but also in that of international relations, serious difficulties and might give rise to adverse consequences for all interested parties, including third countries." Opinion 3/94 *GATT – WTO – Framework agreement on bananas* ECLI:EU:C:1995:436 para 17. However, for criticism concerning this rank below EU primary law of international agreements that have not been concluded by the EU, such as the UN Charta in the Kadi cases, see Koutrakos (n 209) 222.

[298] See in this regard the Court of First Instance Case T-315/01 *Yassin Abdullah Kadi and Al Barakaat International Foundation v Council and Commission* ECLI:EU:T:2005:332 para 226–242. On this question see the discussion by Kirsten Schmalenbach, "Normentheorie vs. Terrorismus: Der Vorrang des UN-Rechts vor EU-Recht" (2006) 61 (7) JuristenZeitung 349–353.

8.1.1.5 Interpretation of International Agreements by the CJEU

In view of the preceding argument, it seems logical that the CJEU considers itself competent to interpret international agreements. They are acts performed by EU organs and form an integral part of the EU legal order. Thus the CJEU is competent to interpret international agreements in the light of Article 267 (1) (b) TFEU.[299] It is, however, at the same time compatible with EU law if an international agreement provides for "the creation of a court responsible for the interpretation of its provisions" whose decisions are binding on the European Union (if the autonomy of the EU legal order remains intact).[300] Hence, if the CJEU interprets international agreements it must be aware of their international origin.[301] If not explicitly indicated so, it is simply not possible to request from other contracting parties that they implicitly agree to the CJEU as the competent interpreter of the international agreement.[302] Therefore, the VCLT I & II and the rules on interpretation contained therein, especially Articles 31 and 32, which are also considered to reflect customary international law, are applied by the CJEU.[303] These rules put at their center

[299] Case 181/73 *R & V Haegeman v Belgium* ECLI:EU:C:1974:41 para 5: "The provisions of the Agreement, from the coming into force thereof, form an integral part of Community law." Thus, (para 6) "[w]ithin the framework of this law, the Court accordingly has jurisdiction to give preliminary rulings concerning the interpretation of this Agreement." Concerning treaties between Member States and non-Member States the jurisdiction of the CJEU, in principle, is not given, see C-533/08 *TNT Express Nederland BV v AXA Versicherung AG* ECLI:EU:C:2010:243 para 61 with further references to previous case law.

[300] Opinion 1/17 *Comprehensive Economic and Trade Agreement between Canada, of the one part, and the European Union and its Member States, of the other part (CETA)* ECLI:EU:C:2019:341 para 106 ff with many references to previous case law, and especially to Opinion 2/13 *Draft international agreement – Accession of the European Union to the European Convention for the Protection of Human Rights and Fundamental Freedoms – Compatibility of the draft agreement with the EU and FEU Treaties* ECLI:EU:C:2014:2454. See thereto Kieran Bradley, "Investor–State Dispute Tribunals Established under EU International Agreements: Opinion 1/17 (EU-Canada CETA)" in Graham Butler and Ramses A Wessel (eds) *EU External Relations Law. The Cases in Context* (Hart 2022) 959–969.

[301] See also Eeckhout (n 180) 304 stating that "it would be wrong to conclude from the fact that agreements form part of the EU legal order that they are automatically and fully assimilated to 'internal' EU law, in particular as regards methods of interpretation. The agreement, despite being integrated in the EU legal order, remains an act of international law."

[302] Eeckhout (n 180) 304. See also Marise Cremona, "External Relations and External Competence of the European Union" in Paul Craig and Gráinne de Búrca (eds) *The Evolution of EU Law* (Oxford University Press 2nd ed 2011) 217–268 (234–235), holding that "as long as both parties perform their obligations, it does not affect the reciprocity of the agreement if one does so by attributing direct effect to its provisions while the other does not."

[303] Case C-61/94 *Commission v Germany* ECLI:EU:C:1996:313 para 30, referring to "the general rule of international law requiring the parties to any agreement to show good faith in its performance"; C-312/91 *Metalsa Srl* ECLI:EU:C:1993:279 para 12 with explicit reference to

the ordinary meaning of the provisions in the context of the Treaty and in the light of its object and purpose.[304] This is generally sound; however, particularly those provisions of international agreements that are also reflected in EU law occasionally provide grounds for criticism in terms of the interpretation of the CJEU not paying sufficient respect to the international origin of the international agreement.[305]

8.1.1.6 Consistent Interpretation of EU Law with International Agreements

The CJEU has adjudicated that similarly to the consistent interpretation of secondary EU law with the Treaties, "the primacy of international agreements concluded by the Community over provisions of secondary Community legislation means that such provisions must, so far as is possible, be interpreted in a manner that is consistent with those agreements."[306] The phrase so far as is possible has been described as "when the wording of secondary Community legislation is open to more than one interpretation."[307] In such a narrow sense, this is simply a rule giving preference to one of several possible interpretations if the usual methods of interpretation do not suggest a specific interpretation.[308] In particular when international agreements are not found

Art 31 VCLT; Opinion 1/91 *Draft agreement between the Community, on the one hand, and the countries of the European Free Trade Association, on the other, relating to the creation of the European Economic Area* ECLI:EU:C:1991:490 para 14 with explicit reference to Art 31 VCLT; 104/81 *Hauptzollamt Mainz v CA Kupferberg & Cie KG a A* ECLI:EU:C:1982:362 para 17: "It is true that the effects within the Community of provisions of an agreement concluded by the Community with a non-member country may not be determined without taking account of the international origin of the provisions in question." The CJEU added with this origin in mind (para 18) that, "[a]ccording to the general rules of international law there must be *bona fide* performance of every agreement" [emphasis original]. Moreover, the CJEU holds in this respect that the agreement is to be interpreted "in the light of its subject-matter and purpose." See thereto also Schmalenbach (n 222) para 55, with further reference to literature in n 219. See also Philippe Manin, "The European Communities and the Vienna Convention on the Law of Treaties between States and International Organizations or between International Organizations" (1987) 24 (3) Common Market Law Review 457–481.

304 See in detail Oliver Dörr, "Art 31 and 32" in Oliver Dörr and Kirsten Schmalenbach (eds) *Vienna Convention on the Law of Treaties – A Commentary* (Springer 2nd ed 2018) esp with reference in para 6 to the customary international law nature of both provisions.

305 See Eeckhout (n 180) 306–319 for an overview of case law and a nuanced critique.

306 Case C-61/94 *Commission v Germany* ECLI:EU:C:1996:313 para 52.

307 Case C-61/94 *Commission v Germany* ECLI:EU:C:1996:313 para 52.

308 In such a sense Eeckhout (n 180) 355 qualified this principle as being "logical and obvious," because "[t]he coherence of a legal system requires that its various provisions are as much as possible interpreted in the light of each other, so as to avoid conflict between them, and consistent interpretation is a preferred judicial technique for such conflict prevention."

to be directly applicable, this technique can be used by the CJEU to avoid violations of international agreements.[309]

8.1.1.7 The Suspension and Termination of International Agreements

Article 218 (9) TFEU states that the provisions on concluding international agreements essentially also apply to the suspension of international agreements.[310] The explicit possibility in the Treaties of suspending international agreements has to be seen against the background of human rights clauses in international economic agreements.[311] While the suspension of an international agreement due to serious violations of human rights might principally be appreciated by the European Parliament as well, paragraph 9 of Article 218 TFEU is applicable to any suspension. In this regard, it is noteworthy that there is one major exception to the analogous application of the provisions on the conclusion of international agreements. The European Parliament has no say concerning the suspension of an international agreement.[312] Again, this exclusion of the European Parliament is also the case in quite a few national legal orders. Yet this is a severe lacuna in terms of democratic safeguards. Moreover, the EU Treaties remain silent on the termination of an international agreement and thus the question of whether the European Parliament has a say in the termination of an international agreement is unanswered, at least by the EU Treaties. This lacuna, it is submitted, shall be filled by the *actus contrarius* doctrine.[313] Hence, the same

[309] See Eeckhout (n 180) 355, n 124 with further references on the use of this technique as regards GATT, the WTO and UNCLOS.

[310] In Case C-687/15 *Commission v Council* ECLI:EU:C:2017:803 para 47, the court holds that Article 218 (9) TFEU has to be understood literally by emphasizing that a suspension must be based on a decision of the Council and not in conclusions taken in meetings as has been the practice concerning the International Telecommunication Union. On the scope of Article 218 (9) TFEU, see Wolfgang Weiß, "Verfassungsanforderungen und Integrationsverantwortung bei beschließenden Vertragsorganen in Freihandelsabkommen" (2016) Europäische Zeitschrift für Wirtschaftsrecht 286–291 (288). See also C-399/12 *Germany v Council* ECLI:EU:C:2014:2258 para 52, where the court holds that Article 218 (9) TFEU applies also when the EU "did not take part in the international agreement." See also the comment by Florian Jung, "Reben, Wein und der EuGH: Zur Auslegung von Art. 218 Abs. 9 AEUV – Anmerkungen zum Urteil des EuGH vom 07.10.2014, Rs. C-399/12 – Deutschland/Rat" (2015) 50 (6) Europarecht 735–745.

[311] See on this Koutrakos (n 209) 155 with further references.

[312] See Eeckhout (n 180) 209.

[313] For this argument see also Waldemar Hummer, "Art 218" in Christoph Vedder and Wolff Heintschel von Heinegg (eds) *Europäisches Unionsrecht. Handkommentar* (Nomos et al 2nd ed 2018) para 34 (albeit without explicitly extending this understanding to a necessary approval by the European Parliament. See Dirk Wouters, "The External Relations of the European Union Since Lisbon: A Practitioner's Perspective" in Jenő Czuczai and Frederik Naert (eds) *The EU as a Global Actor – Bridging Legal Theory and Practice: Liber Amicorum in Honour of*

provisions shall apply to the termination of international agreements as to the conclusion of international agreements[314] because in the case of termination of an international agreement there is no good reason for excluding the European Parliament. Excluding the European Parliament from the termination of international agreements would go against the democratic principle of including the European Parliament in the process in the first place. In terms of internal legislative competences, the administration is not allowed to cancel legislation of the parliament either. There is no good reason why this should be any different with international agreements.

8.1.1.8 Pre-Conclusion Review of International Agreements on Their Conformity with Primary EU Law by the CJEU According to Article 218 (11) TFEU

Article 218 (11) TFEU holds that "[a] Member State, the European Parliament, the Council or the Commission may obtain the opinion of the Court of Justice as to whether an agreement envisaged is compatible with the Treaties. Where the opinion of the Court is adverse, the agreement envisaged may not enter into force unless it is amended or the Treaties are revised."

This possibility of requesting an opinion from the CJEU is not a toothless tiger but an important instrument that might prevent the conclusion of an international agreement by the EU. Hence, contrasting with the terminology of a seemingly non-binding opinion, the second sentence of Article 218 (11) TFEU indicates that such an opinion enjoys binding force.[315] A famous case at hand is Opinion 2/13 on the accession of the EU to the ECHR.[316]

Ricardo Gosalbo Bono (Brill Nijhoff 2017) 65–86 (85), suggesting also a recourse to "constitutional principles common to Member States, EU practice and institutional balance considerations."

[314] See on this also Kuijper (n 232) 110–111. For further references to the disparate practice of the Member States, see also Jan A Wouters et al (eds), *The Law of EU External Relations: Cases, Materials, and Commentary on the EU as an International Legal Actor* (Oxford University Press 3rd ed 2021) 83 ff; see also Eeckhout (n 180) 209. See generally – albeit on the determination of the voting rule in Article 218 (8) and (9) TFEU – Case C-244/17 *Commission v Council* ECLI:EU:C:2018:662 para 21: "In order to satisfy requirements of clarity, consistency and rationalisation, Article 218 TFEU lays down a single procedure of general application concerning, in particular, the negotiation and conclusion of international agreements which the European Union is competent to conclude in the fields of its activity, including the CFSP, except where the Treaties lay down special procedures."

[315] See also in this regard Eeckhout (n 180) 268–269 with further references in n 4.

[316] Opinion 2/13 *Draft international agreement – Accession of the European Union to the European Convention for the Protection of Human Rights and Fundamental Freedoms –*

Those organs that are eligible to request an opinion from the CJEU might even do so before negotiations commence if the purpose of the envisaged agreement is known.[317] This is necessary to guarantee effective control and an effective negotiation process.[318]

If the controversial issue is not the competence to negotiate and conclude the agreement, which can also be subject to a request for an opinion,[319] but whether the agreement itself is in conformity with the EU Treaties, the request for an opinion has to identify those provisions in question.[320]

Requesting an opinion is only possible for "envisaged agreements," which includes agreements until they are finally concluded by the Council.[321] Hence, a post-ratification control, as is the case in some national legal orders, is not established by Article 218 (11) TFEU. Yet, after an agreement has

Compatibility of the draft agreement with the EU and FEU Treaties ECLI:EU:C:2014:2454 para 145, holding that "[t]hat provision has the aim of forestalling complications which would result from legal disputes concerning the compatibility with the Treaties of international agreements binding upon the EU." On the accession generally, see Paul Gragl, *The Accession of the European Union to the European Convention on Human Rights* (Hart 2013). Further examples are Opinions 2/94 ECLI:EU:C:1996:140 para 3; 1/08 *General Agreement on Trade in Services (GATS)* ECLI:EU:C:2009:739 para 107; and 1/09 *Draft agreement – Creation of a unified patent litigation system* ECLI:EU:C:2011:123 para 47.

317 Opinion 1/78 *International Agreement on Natural Rubber* ECLI:EU:C:1979:224 para 35, explicitly also taking the interests of non-Member States into account for having competences to negotiate and conclude agreements clarified; Opinion 2/94 *Accession by the Community to the European Convention for the Protection of Human Rights and Fundamental Freedoms* ECLI:EU:C:1996:140 paras 10–18; Opinion 1/03 *Competence of the Community to conclude the new Lugano Convention on jurisdiction and the recognition and enforcement of judgments in civil and commercial matters* ECLI:EU:C:2006:81 para 111.

318 See Opinion 1/03 *Competence of the Community to conclude the new Lugano Convention on jurisdiction and the recognition and enforcement of judgments in civil and commercial matters* ECLI:EU:C:2006:81 para 111.

319 See Article 196(2) of the Rules of Procedure of the Court of Justice of September 25, 2012 (OJ L 265, 29.9.2012), as amended on June 18, 2013 (OJ L 173, 26.6.2013, p 65) and on July 19, 2016 (OJ L 217,12.8.2016, p 69): "A request for an Opinion may relate both to whether the envisaged agreement is compatible with the provisions of the Treaties and to whether the European Union or any institution of the European Union has the power to enter into that agreement."

320 Opinion 2/94 *Accession by the Community to the European Convention for the Protection of Human Rights and Fundamental Freedoms* ECLI:EU:C:1996:140 paras 19–20; Opinion 2/13 *Draft international agreement – Accession of the European Union to the European Convention for the Protection of Human Rights and Fundamental Freedoms – Compatibility of the draft agreement with the EU and FEU Treaties* ECLI:EU:C:2014:2454 paras 145–146.

321 Opinion 1/94 *Competence of the Community to conclude international agreements concerning services and the protection of intellectual property* ECLI:EU:C:1994:384 para 12: "The Court may be called upon to state its opinion pursuant to Article 228(6) of the Treaty at any time before the Community's consent to be bound by the agreement is finally expressed. Unless and until that consent is given, the agreement remains an envisaged agreement."

entered into force, the Council decision to conclude the agreement can be challenged with an action for annulment reviewing the legality of an Act adopted by an EU institution according to Article 263 TFEU,[322] or the interpretation of the agreement might be clarified by the preliminary rulings procedure according to Article 267 TFEU.[323] However, the fact that no post-ratification control of the international agreement is possible further strengthens the stance that the international agreement is binding on the EU until its obligations have been changed or removed on the international plane. A post-ratification contradiction with EU law that might be found after the Council decision has been challenged successfully does not change the international obligation stemming from the international agreement.

The review of international agreements by courts is a controversial topic.[324] On the one hand, pragmatic reasons might speak for early monitoring by a court in order to avoid unconstitutional international agreements.[325] Article 46 VCLT II only allows invoking the invalidation of the consent to be bound by an agreement if that violation of the internal process of authorization was a manifest violation of a law of fundamental importance.[326] On the other hand, such preemptive controls might represent interference by the judiciary in the competences of the legislative and the executive.[327]

8.1.2 *Critique of the Prevailing Doctrine: Monistic "Adoption" or Dualistic "Transformation" of International Agreements in the EU Legal Order?*

Scholarship often laments that the most important information is missing in Article 216 (2) TFEU.[328] Article 216 (2) TFEU does not state which rank

[322] See in this regard, for instance, Joined Cases C-317/04 and C-318/04 *European Parliament v Council and Commission* ECLI:EU:C:2006:346 para 50. Cf Eeckhout (n 180) 287–292.

[323] See on the latter with further references Eeckhout (n 180) 274–287, as well as Koutrakos (n 209) 235–250.

[324] For a comparative overview see Eleonora Mesquita Ceia, *Die verfassungsgerichtliche Kontrolle völkerrechtlicher Verträge. Eine rechtsvergleichende Untersuchung zwischen Brasilien und Europa* (Nomos 2011). For references to similar special procedures of other international organizations, see Koutrakos (n 209) 230.

[325] See in this regard Opinion 1/75 *Understanding on a Local Cost Standard* ECLI:EU:C:1975:145 p 1360–1361. Cf Koutrakos (n 209) 233–334, highlighting the significance of this provision and giving further references.

[326] See above Section 8.1. See on this also Eeckhout (n 180) 270; as well as Terhechte (n 229) para 32.

[327] See Schmalenbach (n 206) para 41 with further references to critical voices in n 104.

[328] See eg Koutrakos (n 209) 212: "Whilst Article 216(2) TFEU affirms the binding effect of international agreements concluded by the Union, it does not do so exhaustively." Cf Koutrakos (n 209) 219. See, however, Jan Wouters, Jed Odermatt and Thomas

international agreements shall have within the EU legal order if they form an integral part of it.[329] Yet complaints about the open texture of Article 216 (2) TFEU can be quickly countered and the lacuna is readily answered by scholarship,[330] usually by referring – sometimes explicitly, rather more often implicitly – to the old theories on the relationship between international and national law dealt with in Part I. The general statement that agreements are binding on the EU is interpreted to point at a monistic relationship between international agreements and the EU legal order.[331] This qualification hinges

Ramopoulos, "Worlds Apart? Comparing the Approaches of the European Court of Justice and the EU Legislature to International Law" in Marise Cremona and Anne Thies (eds) *The European Court of Justice and External Relations Law – Constitutional Challenges* (Hart 2016) 249–279 (254), stating that it is not the silence of the Treaties, but the Court's failure "to make use of existing provisions putting emphasis on the EU's respect for international law" or its restrictive interpretation of such provisions.

[329] See eg Eeckhout (n 180) 327: "The provision [Art 216 (2) TFEU] is limited to expressing the binding character of agreements concluded by the EU, and it does not describe the legal consequences or effects of this characteristic."

[330] See eg Eeckhout (n 180) 189, who even optimistically holds that "[t]he core question of when international agreements have direct effect in EU law has long since been fully explored, and appears, at least at a level of principle, to be more or less answered."

[331] See, in this regard, for instance, Ramses A Wessel, "Reconsidering the Relationship between International and EU Law" in Enzo Cannizzaro, Paolo Palchetti and Ramses A Wessel (eds) *International Law as Law of the European Union* (Martinus Nijhoff 2012) 7–33 (12). However, he also notes that the monism–dualism dichotomy might be less helpful in determining the complexities of EU law, such as the effect of international law within the EU legal order (12–13) and concludes, after discussing the modern versions of pluralism and constitutionalism, with the diagnosis of a shift from "a systemic to a more substantive approach" (33); see also the conclusion by Vlad Constantinesco and Denys Simon, "Quelques problèmes de relations extérieures des Communautés Européennes" (1975) 11 Revue trimestrielle de droit européen 432–469 (442), stating that in the absence of express provisions, the agreements validly concluded by the EU would be automatically introduced into the EU legal order; Schmalenbach (n 222) para 32; Kirsten Schmalenbach, "Struggle for Exclusiveness: The ECJ and Competing International Tribunals" in Isabelle Buffard et al (eds) *International Law between Universalism and Fragmentation: Festschrift in Honour of Gerhard Hafner* (Brill 2008) 1045–1068 (1058): "The Court's settled case law regarding the incorporation of international customary law and international agreements follows a monistic concept in order to enable the EC and its organs to comply with international obligations." See also Enzo Cannizzaro, "The Neo-Monism of the European Legal Order" in Enzo Cannizzaro, Paolo Palchetti and Ramses A Wessel (eds) *International Law as Law of the European Union* (Martinus Nijhoff 2012) 35–58 (35), who holds that "the idea of developing a coherent and all-embracing theoretical model, capable of explaining all the complexities and the infinite theoretical and practical issues arising from [the troubled relationship between international law and EU law] seems more and more questionable." Despite this caution, he considers "neo-monism," employing notions and techniques instead of a fully fledged account in order to (36) "enhance the autonomy of the internal legal experience [of the EU] vis-à-vis international law." Cf Andrés Delgado Casteleiro, *The International Responsibility of the European Union. From Competence to Normative Control* (Cambridge University Press 2018)

on the fact that agreements are "adopted" automatically by the EU legal order once they are concluded internationally. In other words, there is no additional EU legal Act to "transform" the agreement into EU law except for the authorization of the competent EU organ to conclude the agreement.

This stands in stark contrast to a dualistic interpretation of the relationship, which would insist on an additional act of transformation. In the opinion of those who interpret this relationship as dualistic, it is the decision on approval of the competent organ to conclude the international agreement that transforms the international agreement into the EU legal order.[332]

More moderate voices talk about a "general transformation" or a "general adoption," relying basically on a dualistic separation of the EU and the international legal order, but actually allowing for an abstract connection.[333]

32–33; as well as Andreas Bergmann, *Zur Souveränitätskonzeption des Europäischen Gerichtshofs* (Mohr Siebeck 2018) 119 with further references to German language scholarship in n 5. Critically, however, see Eeckhout (n 180) 326–327, and at 374, casting doubt about the helpfulness of monism and dualism "as they supply only black and white answers to what is in fact a set of nuanced and diverse issues"; as well as Armin von Bogdandy, "Pluralism, Direct Effect, and the Ultimate Say: On the Relationship between International and Domestic Constitutional Law" (2008) 6 (3-4) International Journal of Constitutional Law 397–413. Generally for a monistic qualification of the relationship between EU and Member State law see part I, n 363.

332 See, for instance, Robert Uerpmann-Wittzack, "The Constitutional Role of International Law" in Armin von Bogdandy and Jürgen Bast (eds) *Principles of European Constitutional Law* (Hart et al 2nd ed 2011) 131–167 (135 in general terms and 147 with regard to WTO law, as well as 177 with regard to Article 6(2) TEU, which he understands too as stipulating an "incorporation"). See also Daniel-Erasmus Khan, "Art 216" in Rudolf Geiger, Daniel-Erasmus Khan and Markus Kotzur (eds) *EUV/AEUV* (CH Beck 6th ed 2017) para 18, speaking of a "genereller Vollzugsbefehl"; see, however, Daniel-Erasmus Khan and Lando Kirchmair, "Art 216" in Rudolf Geiger et al (eds) *EUV/AEUV* (CH Beck 7th ed 2023) para 18; see also Matthias Müller, *Das Rechtsprechungsmonopol des EuGH im Kontext völkerrechtlicher Verträge. Untersucht anhand der Rechtsprechung des Gerichtshofs der Europäischen Union* (Nomos 2012) 102, holding that the decision of the Council would be constitutive for the effect of the international agreement within the EU legal order. However, he explicitly states that the international agreement is not "unionized" and remains thus an international agreement in the sense, for instance, that international rules on treaty interpretation would apply instead of EU rules.

333 See, for instance, Albert Bleckmann, "Die Position des Völkerrechts im inneren Rechtsraum der EG. Monismus oder Dualismus der Rechtsordnungen?" (1975) 18 German Yearbook of International Law 300–319 (315); Khan (n 332) para 18; Olivier Jacot-Guillarmod, *Droit communautaire et droit international public. Etude des sources internationales de l'ordre juridique des Communautés européennes* (Librairie de l'Université Genève 1979) 104–109, with further references and a typical underestimation of the relevance of the theoretical standpoint: "Le Conseil renvoie dos à dos les monistes, qui ne sont pas privés de la satisfaction intellectuelle d'appliquer la règle internationale elle-même, et les dualistes, qui s'imaginent – avec une satisfaction intellectuelle sans doute comparable – appliquer un authentique règlement. Quelle que soit sa propre conviction, on ne peut s'empêcher de penser que ces

The reason for referring to either monism or dualism is rarely theoretical in nature. The motivation is usually result driven. Either an automatic adoption or a more controlled transformation guides the choice for labeling the relationship between international agreements and the EU legal order. Finally, in this interpretation the difference is not that important. In the end, most scholars from either camp argue that international agreements rank within the EU legal order between primary EU legislation – that is, the Treaties – and secondary EU law.[334] Finally, most scholars nevertheless hold that, principally, EU law is friendly towards international law.[335] Usually, the CJEU case law on GATT, the WTO, UNCLOS and the Kadi saga is mentioned as an exception to this friendliness.[336]

Piet Eeckhout cautiously asks whether legal pluralism might provide a fitting theoretical framework for the relationship between international and EU law. However, he does not seem to want to commit himself to such a

querelles d'écoles importent peu. En effet, l'essentiel est que l'efficacité des accords conclus par la Communauté soit garantie de manière optimale dans l'ordre juridique communautaire, sous le contrôle d'interprétation uniforme de La Cour de justice."

334 See only Schmalenbach (n 331) 1048; or Allan Rosas, "International Responsibility of the EU and the European Court of Justice" in Malcolm Evans and Panos Koutrakos (eds) *The International Responsibility of the European Union. European and International Perspectives* (Hart 2013) 139–159 (158).

335 Eeckhout (n 180) 435: "After nearly forty years of case law one can certainly not conclude that the EU legal order is hostile towards international law."

336 See eg de Búrca (n 197) The ECJ and the International Legal Order; see, however, also Gráinne de Búrca, "International Law before the Courts. The EU and the US Compared" (2015) 55 (3) Virginia Journal of International Law 685–728 (685), noting "a great many more commonalities between the approaches" of the CJEU and the US Supreme Court than are generally assumed; see also Jan Klabbers, "Straddling the Fence: The EU and International Law" in Anthony Arnull and Damian Chalmers (eds) *The Oxford Handbook of European Union Law* (Oxford University Press 2017) 52–71 (71), holding "that the EU has always employed an ambivalent attitude towards international law." See Klabbers (n 179) 71: "the ECJ has held, since the early days, that with respect to the effect of EU law within the domestic legal orders of the member states, monism is the only way to go; dualism is unacceptable, as it would probably undermine the unity of EU law." He further adds that "[t]his position has no doubt contributed to the image of the EU as an actor that is friendly disposed towards international law, but the image is deceptive: the EU is friendly disposed towards EU law, and while it may have been fashionable to regard EU law as an emanation of international law, this is no longer habitually done. The fact that EU law prescribes monism with respect to its own domestic effect is understandable and has in all likelihood contributed greatly to the longevity and success of the EU, but is not based on a particularly friendly attitude towards international law." For the critique that the CJEU's approach to international law assembles a court focused on national sovereignty of Triepel's coinage, see Lando Kirchmair, "Europäische Souveränität? Zur Autonomie des Unionsrechts im Verhältnis zum Völkerrecht sowie den Mitgliedstaaten am Beispiel der Corona Krise" (2021) 56 (1) Europarecht 28–39.

position.[337] Rather he holds that "the integration of international law into EU law is a more appropriate paradigm, characterizing the relationship as it currently stands, and as it ought to evolve."[338] Panos Koutrakos could be interpreted as being similarly amenable to legal pluralism when subtitling part II of his treaties "The Management of EU International Relations Law." As we saw in Part II, this is quite close to the language of Paul Berman, who suggests within the realm of his global legal pluralism that norm conflicts shall be "managed."[339] Yet Koutrakos already clarifies in his introduction that "[t]he term 'management' is used in its broadest sense and refers to the various ways in which the Union and the Member States, on the one hand, and the Court of Justice, on the other, translate the constitutional principles of external competence into practice."[340] This is no reference to the legal pluralist literature. Nevertheless, Panos Koutrakos holds that in concluding an international agreement, the Council would carry out two functions, namely an external function in binding the EU to the international obligation and an internal function acting "under the constitutional powers given in the Treaties and under the procedure laid down therein."[341] This unfortunately reminds us of a dualistic thinking that artificially separates the international from the EU legal order.[342] This is not necessary and also not predetermined by any provision, in international or EU law. While it is true that the Council is authorized by the Treaties to bind the EU externally by concluding international agreements, the act of conclusion melts this authorization into an expression of the will of the EU to conclude the international agreement concerned. However, even if this is seen to reflect the role of international agreements being "an instrument for influence in the world, but also a tool for the consolidation of EU law and the coherence between EU and international action," that is hardly to be understood as a dualistic argument.[343]

Eileen Denza holds that, despite the unique feature of the autonomous EU legal order and its constitutional character, the foundations of the EU – from

[337] Eeckhout (n 180) 374–375

[338] Eeckhout (n 180) 191.

[339] Koutrakos (n 209) part II.

[340] Koutrakos (n 209) 3.

[341] Koutrakos (n 209) 147.

[342] Even though Koutrakos (n 209) 257 explicitly refers to literature which contests the "analytical usefulness" of the dichotomy between monism and dualism, he goes without making it "a point of reference" for his chapter on the Enforcement of International Law in the EU Legal Order.

[343] For such an understanding see also Panos Koutrakos, "The European Union" in Michael J Bowman and Dino Kritsiotis (eds) *Conceptual and Contextual Perspectives on the Modern Law of Treaties* (Cambridge University Press 2018) 933–965 (965).

the perspective of national courts and governments – still have the character of international law.[344] The approach of the CJEU towards international law might, thus, be characterized in a similar way to that of national courts.[345] Christina Eckes, too, argues with a particular focus on the autonomy of the EU legal order that the primacy of EU law over international law "has an external dimension" in as much as it is "relevant for protecting the EU legal order and the cooperation of the CJEU and national courts from direct, unfiltered external pressure."[346]

Concerning the direct applicability of international agreements, Francesca Martines holds that the "double test [to determine the direct applicability of an international agreement] does not seem to fit the control of validity of secondary legislation or Member State law where private parties are those who might benefit from the international (less strict) provisions but who cannot claim a subjective right in a proper sense."[347] She rather argues that

> in these cases the ECJ should analyze only the content and the scope of the international rule to verify whether it can be applied in the case (*Pêcheurs de l'Etang de Berre*) by the national court (setting aside national incompatible measures), or whether it may be applied as a benchmark by which to assess the compatibility of national (or the validity of European) legislation (Biotech, Intertanko, IATA, and ATAA).[348]

This argument receives strong theoretical support from consent-based monism, as I will show in the next section.[349] As she argues, it is "the clear and precise character of the obligation, which does not require for its implementation the adoption of any subsequent measure," which should be decisive for determining the direct applicability of an international agreement.[350]

[344] Eileen Denza, "Placing the European Union in International Context: Legitimacy of the Case Law" in Maurice Adams et al (eds) *Judging Europe's Judges: The Legitimacy of the Case Law of the European Court of Justice* (Hart 2013) 175–196 (176).

[345] See Rosas (n 334) 158.

[346] Christina Eckes, *EU Powers under External Pressure. How the EU's External Actions Alter Its Internal Structures* (Oxford University Press 2019) 97. See also 31, claiming that the "CJEU's narrative of the normative autonomy of EU law is best understood as absolute and hence as a binary choice rather than a matter of degree." Eckes (31) claims – with Kaarlo Tuori in *European Constitutionalism* (Cambridge University Press 2015) – that it is "[t]he autonomy narrative [which] allows the CJEU to depart in *all its case law* from the standpoint that EU law is domestic law" [emphasis original].

[347] Martines (n 266) 141 with further references to case law.

[348] Martines (n 266) 141.

[349] See Section 8.1.3.

[350] Martines (n 266) 141. The CJEU occasionally follows such an approach, for instance in C-280/93 *Germany v Council* ECLI:EU:C:1994:367 paras 61 and 66. See further also the case

The Court's reasoning why UNCLOS does not enjoy direct applicability because it would not confer rights on individuals but only on ships is to be criticized as well.[351] Direct applicability is not to be conflated with the subjective rights of individuals. The only test, rather, should be whether the provision is sufficiently precise and unconditional.[352]

What is also important is to see that the CJEU might have more leeway when interpreting differently various international agreements depending on their parties and purposes. The Court could easily be more willing to take up a dominant interpretative approach on association agreements since the international party to such agreements will very likely accept the Court's dominant stance on interpretation, as the next step will be the accession and hence total submittance of this party to the jurisdiction of the Court. In this light, it is also understandable that the CJEU might likewise be more willing to accept that association agreements are directly applicable.[353] This might be different in the case of other international agreements that are "proper" international agreements, however, in the sense that it is clear that the parties – the EU and other states or international organizations for example – will not initiate a strong association likely to end in the accession of the third state or organization to the EU but will remain Treaty partners. In such a case, the other party will, understandably, be much less willing to accept a dominant stance of the CJEU on the interpretation of such an agreement, in the same way as the German Federal Constitutional Court would be much less willing to accept a

law affirming direct applicability without the conferral of subjective rights for individuals above n 268.

351 C-308/06 *The Queen, on the application of International Association of Independent Tanker Owners (Intertanko) and Others v Secretary of State for Transport* ECLI:EU:C:2008:312 para 61. For criticism see also Piet Eeckhout, "Case C-308/06 The Queen, on the Application of International Association of Independent Tanker Owners (Intertanko) and Others v Secretary of State for Transport, Judgment of the Court of Justice, (Grand Chamber) of 3 June 2008" (2009) 46 (6) Common Market Law Review 2041–2057 (2053). Cannizzaro is also critical (n 331) 49. The same holds true for the Kyoto Protocol. See C-366/10 *Air Transport Association of America and Others v Secretary of State for Energy and Climate Change* ECLI:EU: C:2011:864 para 77: "Article 2(2) of the Kyoto Protocol . . . provides that the parties thereto are to pursue limitation or reduction of emissions of certain greenhouse gases from aviation bunker fuels, working through the ICAO. Thus, that provision, as regards its content, cannot in any event be considered to be unconditional and sufficiently precise so as to confer on individuals the right to rely on it in legal proceedings in order to contest the validity of Directive 2008/101."

352 This is all the more relevant as Wouters, Odermatt and Ramopoulos (n 328) 262 diagnose that it is recent case law of the court which looks at the fact whether provisions confer rights on individuals.

353 See also Klabbers (n 336) 81.

dominant interpretation of the US Supreme Court on an international treaty between Germany and the United States.

Moreover, advocate general Kokott clearly pointed out:

> Whether or not the provisions in question are directly applicable and – correlatively – whether they confer rights on individuals is not conclusive for the purpose of responding to the request for a preliminary ruling. Even the legal bases of the Treaties are in principle not directly applicable in the sense that individuals can derive from them rights or legal consequences to their benefit. Nevertheless, individuals may question the legality of rules of secondary law by contesting the legal basis thereof.[354]

Mario Mendez has pointed out that there seems to be a difference in the likelihood of leading the CJEU to declare the direct applicability of an international agreement.[355] While the CJEU remains reluctant to declare a provision of an international agreement to be directly applicable when evaluating the actions of EU organs (where the criterion is whether a subjective right is provided by the international agreement), this reluctance changes when the CJEU is to assess the actions of Member States in terms of international agreements concluded by the EU. In the latter case, the CJEU seems to be more willing to acknowledge direct applicability.[356]

8.1.3 *Interpretation According to Consent-Based Monism*

According to consent-based monism, the international agreement remains what it is at EU or national level, namely international law and thereby a consensus of a larger circle. The prevailing doctrine regarding the relationship between international and EU law interprets relevant EU norms as so-called reception norms or incorporation norms of international law that aim to integrate international law into the EU legal order. However, consent-based monism questions this integration and the legal consequences that stem from the confrontation of international norms with the hierarchy of the EU or national legal orders.

Most importantly, I wish to remind readers of the criticism advanced against the prevailing theories on the relationship between international law and the EU or national legal order.[357] This criticism showed for each theory that old

[354] Opinion of advocate general Kokott C-308/06 *The Queen, on the application of International Association of Independent Tanker Owners (Intertanko) and Others v Secretary of State for Transport* ECLI:EU:C:2007:689 para 66.

[355] Mendez (n 269).

[356] Mendez (n 269).

[357] Part I.

and (still) current theories on the relationship have serious flaws. Arguably, this precludes them from being used as guiding instruments or tools of interpretation when dogmatically analyzing the relationship between international and EU law. These theories simply should no longer be used because they do not serve as correct reference points. This is not only of theoretical importance. It is, for instance, a consequence of dualistic and monistic thinking to associate a certain rank of the international agreement with the EU or national legal order. This is unfortunate, however. From consent-based monism I submit that it is still more accurate to refer to the international agreement as international law, even though it is an "integral part" of EU law. A consequence is that this international agreement must not be "ranked" within the EU or national legal order. What is important, however, is how a potential violation of an international agreement of EU primary law is, nevertheless, conceptualized. In this regard I submit that, if the norms of the EU legal order – which regulate the conclusion of international agreements – are interpreted under consent-based monism as EU norms of authorization, it is important to define the limits of this authorization: A limit on the authorization to ratify international agreements is provided by the external competences of the EU. Yet, concerning this limitation, it must always be borne in mind that Article 46 VCLT is rather restrictive and, otherwise, Article 27 VCLT is fully pertinent. This, however, is already basically accepted by the prevailing doctrine.

Another major consequence of the application of consent-based monism is that pertinent EU norms (in the case of international agreements particularly, Articles 216 and 218 TFEU) are interpreted as norms of *authorization* and thus allow competent EU organs to create international law. Following consent-based monism, the legal consequences of public international law within the EU legal sphere then have to be qualified according to (the content of) international law – that is, the sphere of the larger circle. Correspondingly, international law distinguishes between three kinds of norms: solely applicable, directly applicable and individualizing norms.[358] Solely applicable norms – or, simply, interstate law – allow subjects of international law to choose how they wish to implement international agreements. However, directly applicable – self-executing – norms, which have "direct effect" within the EU or national legal order without any EU or national Act except the ratification, simply do not.[359] As a direct consequence of this interpretation, a

[358] See Section 6.4 above.

[359] See eg Alfred Verdross and Bruno Simma, *Universelles Völkerrecht* (Duncker & Humblot 3rd ed 1984) 550; Stefan Griller, *Die Übertragung von Hoheitsrechten auf zwischenstaatliche*

directly applicable international agreement has a "direct effect" in the EU and the national legal order without any further EU or national Act except the ratification.[360] If an international agreement or a provision of it is directly applicable, the smaller circle has already accepted this effect by agreeing to the consensus at the international level. Consent-based monism opposes any subsequent unilateral national derogation of the deliberately consented direct applicability of the international treaty. Hence, the quest for an analogous application of the doctrine of "direct effect" of EU norms and their effect in national legal orders concerning international agreements must be rejected too. While most commentators hold that it would not be logical to use different tests or methods of adjudication, such an argument entails the bold assertion that international agreements concluded by the EU would also constitute EU law. This, however, cannot be the result of such agreements being an "integral part" of EU law. International agreements concluded by the EU remain what they are, international agreements. And thus they ought to be interpreted as international agreements. If they explicitly say so, they are directly applicable. If they do not, then international methods of interpretation, which are enshrined in Article 31 ff VCLT and generally enjoy the

Einrichtungen (Springer 1989) 355, defining direct applicability [related to the EU] as "die innerstaatliche Geltung der einzelnen Völkerrechtsnormen . . . ohne Dazwischentreten eines weiteren staatlichen Aktes" mit "Durchgriffswirkung"; August Reinisch, "Zur Unmittelbaren Anwendbarkeit von EWR-Recht" (1993) Zeitschrift für Europarecht, Internationales Privatrecht und Rechtsvergleichung 11–30 (15 n 40); Yuji Iwasawa, "The Doctrine of Self-Executing Treaties in the United States: A Critical Analysis" (1986) 26 Virginia Journal of International law 627–692 (632, n 27); Thomas Buergenthal, "Self-Executing and Non-Self-Executing Treaties in National and International Law" (1992) 235 Recueil des Cours IV 303–400 (317–321). See also André Nollkaemper, "The Duality of Direct Effect of International Law" (2014) 25 (1) European Journal of International Law 105–125 (107 with further references), pointing to the fact that "[i]nstances of direct effect, where international law was used as a direct basis for a decision, have been reported in about 30 states outside the EU." He states, however (108–109) that international law would defer the choice between two identified functions of direct effect, namely "pierc[ing] the boundary of the national legal order and protect[ing] individual rights" in contrast to "shield[ing] the national legal order from the effects of international law," to national courts, thereby exposing the "political function of domestic courts at the intersection of legal orders." See André Nollkamper, *National Courts and the International Rule of Law* (Oxford University Press 2011) 117 ff.

360 Karen Kaiser, "Treaties, Direct Applicability" in Rüdiger Wolfrum (ed) *Max Planck Encyclopedia of Public International Law* (2011) para 1: "A treaty is 'self-executing' or 'directly applicable' in domestic law, when its provisions will be applied by courts or executive agencies as provisions of domestic law without the need of further legislative or administrative measures" [internal citations omitted]. Even if Vasak subsumes two different things to "self-executing," he seems to share this notion. Karel Vasak, "Was bedeutet die Aussage, ein Staatsvertrag sei 'self-executing'? – Zur Erkenntnis des Verfassungsgerichtshofs vom 27.6.1960, B 469/59" (1961) 24 Juristische Blätter 352 (352).

status of customary international law, ought to be applied in order to find out whether the international sphere is aimed at a directly applicable agreement or provision despite not explicitly saying so.[361] If the result of this inquiry is negative, there is still the possibility of reading such an effect into the agreement by a court of a party to the agreement. This, however, must then follow the corresponding international law rules. In such a case, the CJEU is only a "national" court providing for one possible interpretation of a party to the international agreement. Individualizing international norms bind or grant rights to individuals directly without an intervening state.[362] In *Intertanko*, for instance, the issue was not direct applicability but whether the convention confers rights on individuals.[363] This is different from direct applicability as the former – even in the case law of the court – and also in the realm of consent-based monism requires only that the convention might be followed by an organ applying EU law without any further act but the authorization for the conclusion of the agreement. This must not always lead to individual – that is, subjective – rights.[364]

8.2 CUSTOMARY INTERNATIONAL LAW

This section first discusses the nature of customary international law, thereby drawing on the paradox of the two-element approach to the emergence of CIL, as many have done before.[365] Due to the disputed nature of CIL, which has been described as being a "theoretical minefield,"[366] it is necessary to

[361] Similarly, the international law rules on the termination of an international agreement are decisive (and not EU or national rules). See on the "limits of *pacta sunt servanda*" at the international level, Christina Binder, *Die Grenzen der Vertragstreue im Völkerrecht* (Springer 2012).

[362] See Jost Delbrück, "Das Individuum im Völkerrecht" in Georg Dahm, Jost Delbrück and Rüdiger Wolfrum (eds) *Völkerrecht* 1 (De Gruyter 2002) 259 (263–264); see also Stefan Griller, "Völkerrecht und Landesrecht" in Robert Walter et al (eds) *Hans Kelsen und das Völkerrecht – Ergebnisse eines Internationalen Symposiums in Wien* (Manz 2005) 83–120 (96, 98 ff).

[363] C-308/06 *The Queen, on the application of International Association of Independent Tanker Owners (Intertanko) and Others v Secretary of State for Transport* ECLI:EU:C:2008:312.

[364] For criticism of *Intertanko* for being too formalistic, see Eeckhout (n 180) 382–383. However, for a general appraisal of focusing on the "question of whether a provision confers rights, or intended to confer rights, on private parties," see also Eeckhout (n 180) 436.

[365] The first part of this section draws on Lando Kirchmair, "What Came First: The Obligation or the Belief? A Renaissance of Consensus Theory to Make the Normative Foundations of Customary International Law More Tangible" (2017) 59 German Yearbook of International Law 289–319.

[366] Martti Koskenniemi, "The Pull of the Mainstream" (1990) 88 (6) Michigan Law Review 1946–1962 (1947).

briefly elaborate on my understanding of CIL. How can a State or, in more general terms, a subject of international law, acting in a certain way, be convinced of its legal obligation to behave in that manner if this particular act has not yet been established as CIL but is merely in the process of emerging? By stepping out of CIL theory and looking at similar conundrums, I conclude in this section, first, that consensus theory – in close alignment with consent-based monism – is the most prominent candidate for providing a solution to this question. Against the common view, the argument offered here suggests that the most obvious flaws of this explanation are, in fact, its greatest strengths.

In brief, this understanding enables us to see Article 38 ICJ Statute, the basic reference point for all sources of international law, as a means to identify the final CIL norm, which is to be distinguished from its formal source. An unwritten meta-norm, as the argument goes, guides the process of CIL emergence. This meta-norm is the correct place to discuss what practice and *opinio iuris* must look like to count as making an offer and accepting that offer so as to finally give rise to a CIL norm. Consensus theory thus teaches us that we need to state more clearly how to evince state practice[367] with its accompanying legal conviction. Based on that understanding, this section also aims to propose a formula grounded in theory to guide the genesis of CIL. Clearly, asking for more specific rules guiding the emergence and succinct identification of state practice and *opinio iuris* undermines the fluidity and dynamics of CIL. However, it is consensus theory that teaches us that legal certainty has its price.

Second, after having outlined this basic understanding of CIL, I will discuss the relationship between customary international law and the EU legal order, first by highlighting the approach that is to be found in case law and the prevailing doctrine, and second by offering a somewhat different reading from consent-based monism.

8.2.1 *Introduction to the Nature of Customary International Law*

Even though so-called modern customary international law has revolted against its traditional methodological underpinning, general (state) practice and *opinio iuris* are still the two elements necessary to identify CIL.[368] But

[367] As this is established terminology I will keep using state practice, which is meant to also include the practice of other established subjects of international law such as international organizations like the EU.

[368] See ICJ, *North Sea Continental Shelf Cases (Federal Republic of Germany v Denmark; Federal Republic of Germany v Netherlands)* Judgment ICJ Reports [1969] 3 para 77; as well as ICJ, *Jurisdictional Immunities of the State (Germany v Italy: Greece Intervening)* Judgment ICJ

how do we deal with the paradox that "the acts concerned amount to a settled practice," and only become CIL if and when this practice is accompanied by "evidence of a belief that this practice is rendered obligatory by the existence of a rule of law requiring it"[369] (Section 8.2.2)? Hence, what came first: the obligation or the belief? This constitutes a conundrum that was already posed by Aristotle (at least implicitly), albeit with regard to the question of whether the chicken or the egg came first. However, we can still learn from this for our debate and understand CIL as an evolutionary process (Section 8.2.3). First, we learn that lines are always hard to draw and legal definitions in particular are based on legally introduced conceptions to a great extent. Yet we need to draw the line somewhere. As the argument goes, this is best illustrated by consensus theory, the most obvious flaws of which are defended here, namely the fiction of "tacit agreement" and the question why new subjects of international law are bound by CIL (Section 8.2.4). However, consensus theory is not advocated as a superior truth but as an approach that best explains core questions relating to the normative foundations of CIL. Moreover, consensus theory also reflects what is here understood as the core feature of consent-based monism. As a consequence of this understanding, it follows that Article 38 Statute of the International Court of Justice (ICJ Statute)[370] should not be understood as the definition of the "formal source" of CIL and its genesis but as a means to identify the already established rule of CIL. A formal, unwritten meta-norm of creating CIL is assumed to exist as the normative foundation, which is related to but not identical with Article 38 ICJ Statute. This meta-norm is the correct place to discuss the genesis of CIL and possibly inbuilt mechanisms such as "tacit agreement," "persistent objectors" and why new subjects of international law are bound by CIL (Section 8.2.5). The frame of this meta-norm is consensus theory understood as an ongoing, evolutionary process, which is simply required so as to be able to call a norm customary. In the end, the suggested understanding of the genesis of CIL as an offer and acceptance within the framework of consensus theory helps make CIL more tangible when identifying it. Having defined the context, questions about the content of a CIL norm or the burden of proof might be seen more clearly

Reports [2012] 99, para 55 with further references. In this regard see also the Draft Conclusions on Identification of Customary International Law, with commentaries, adopted by the ILC at its seventieth session in 2018, submitted to the General Assembly as a part of the Commission's report covering the work of that session (A/73/10), Yearbook of the International Law Commission (2018) Vol II, Part Two, General Commentary (3).

369 ICJ, *North Sea Continental Shelf Cases (Federal Republic of Germany v Denmark; Federal Republic of Germany v Netherlands)* Judgment ICJ Reports [1969] 3 para 77.

370 Statute of the International Court of Justice, June 26, 1945, UNCIO 15, 355 (ICJ Statute).

(Section 8.2.6). We might even face such claims as proposed here that we need evidence of state practice following a specific formula as a guideline, asking, for instance, for a specific frequency of practice by a quarter of all potentially participating subjects of international law, accompanied by statements reflecting *opinio iuris* – as a minimum. Clearly, this undermines the fluidity and dynamics of CIL. Yet we learn from consensus theory that legal certainty has its price.

8.2.2 *The Classical Two-Element Approach and the Prominent Paradox*

General (state) practice and *opinio iuris* are the two elements necessary to identify CIL. They are to be found in Article 38 ICJ Statute, and have been succinctly confirmed by the jurisprudence of the ICJ, which clearly stated in the *North Sea Continental Shelf* cases that "two conditions must be fulfilled [for] the acts concerned to amount to a settled practice," namely practice must be accompanied by "evidence of a belief that this practice is rendered obligatory by the existence of a rule of law requiring it."[371] Finally, the International Law Commission (ILC) and its special rapporteur Sir Michael Wood also favor the two-element approach, asking for general (State) practice (*consuetudo*) and *opinio iuris*.[372] Thus, the starting point for this section is the two-element approach.

The element of general (State) practice can be succinctly summarized as a longer lasting[373] (*ratione temporis*) "constant and uniform" practice[374]

[371] See above n 368.

[372] See Draft Conclusions on Identification of Customary International Law (n 368) General Commentary (3).

[373] See ICJ, *North Sea Continental Shelf Cases (Federal Republic of Germany v Denmark; Federal Republic of Germany v Netherlands)* Judgment ICJ Reports [1969] 3 para 74: "the passage of only a short period of time is not necessarily, or of itself, a bar to the formation of a new rule of customary international law on the basis of what was originally a purely conventional rule." Cf James Crawford, *Brownlie's Principles of Public International Law* (Oxford University Press 8th ed 2012) 24; Anthony D'Amato, *The Concept of Custom in International Law* (Cornell University Press 1971) 56 ff; and Michael Akehurst, "Custom as a Source of International Law" (1974–75) 47 British Yearbook of International Law 1–53 (14).

[374] Cf ICJ, *Asylum Case (Columbia v Peru)* Judgment ICJ Reports [1950] 266, 276: "that the rule invoked ... is in accordance with a constant and uniform usage practiced by the States in question." See also ICJ, *North Sea Continental Shelf Cases (Federal Republic of Germany v Denmark; Federal Republic of Germany v Netherlands)* Judgment ICJ Reports [1969] 3 para 74: "State practice, including that of States whose interests are specially affected, should have been both extensive and virtually uniform in the sense of the provision invoked"; and ICJ, *Military and Paramilitary Activities in and against Nicaragua (Nicaragua v United States)* Judgment ICJ Reports [1986] 14 para 186: "The Court does not consider that, for a rule to be established as customary, the corresponding practice must be in absolutely rigorous conformity

(*ratione materiae*) (possibly) related to a geographical space (*ratione loci*).[375] These components are relative with respect to each other, which is to say that they might be present in differently weighted proportions without diminishing the prerequisite of practice.[376] Second, this practice must be sustained by the conviction that it reflects a legal obligation (*opinio iuris*) in order to be considered as *law* rather than a practice that is legally irrelevant.[377] In addition, it is possible that a CIL norm is limited regionally in terms of the presence of its elements.[378]

Thus, a CIL norm according to Article 38 (1) ICJ Statute is a general practice (*consuetudo*) sustained by the conviction that it reflects a legal obligation (*opinio iuris*). The subjective element of *opinio iuris* is the conviction of States and other subjects of international law that they must follow a particular practice because they are legally obliged to do so. Yet if we do not concentrate on the identification of CIL alone but also consider its genesis, this understanding proves to be contradictory. How is it possible for a new norm to arise in CIL if any practice must already be supported by the belief of subjects of international law that they are obliged to act in this way by an already existing rule of CIL?

A well-known way to pass by this contradiction was simply to suppose[379] that this first belief of subjects of international law to be legally obliged to act in a

with the rule. In order to deduce the existence of customary rules, the Court deems it sufficient that the conduct of States should, in general, be consistent with such rules, and that instances of State conduct inconsistent with a given rule should generally have been treated as breaches of that rule, not as indications of the recognition of a new rule." Cf Crawford (n 373) 24 ff.

375 See Robert Kolb, "Selected Problems in the Theory of Customary International Law" (2003) 50 (2) Netherlands International Law Review 119–150 (133); Malcolm N Shaw, *International Law* (Cambridge University Press 7th ed 2014) 58 ff. For omission counting as State practice see Akehurst (n 373) 10 ff; and Jörg Kammerhofer, *Uncertainty in International Law: A Kelsenian Perspective* (Routledge 2011) 67 with further references in n 40.

376 See ICJ, *North Sea Continental Shelf Cases (Federal Republic of Germany v Denmark; Federal Republic of Germany v Netherlands)* Judgment ICJ Reports [1969] 3 para 74; ICJ, *Military and Paramilitary Activities in and against Nicaragua (Nicaragua v United States)* Judgment ICJ Reports [1986] 14 para 186; as well as Kolb (n 375) 133 ff.

377 See ICJ, *North Sea Continental Shelf Cases (Federal Republic of Germany v Denmark; Federal Republic of Germany v Netherlands)* Judgment ICJ Reports [1969] 3 para 77: *opinio iuris* is "evidence of a belief that this practice is rendered obligatory by the existence of a rule of law requiring it. The need for such a belief, ie, the existence of a subjective element, is implicit in the very notion of the *opinio juris sive necessitates*."

378 See Shaw (n 375) 65 ff.

379 Or, as John Tasioulas, "*Opinio Juris* and the Genesis of Custom: A Solution to the 'Paradox'" (2007) 26 Australian Yearbook of International Law 199–205 (199) added, "states *mistakenly* believing, or successfully pretending mistakenly to believe" [emphasis original].

certain way is an erroneous belief.[380] This, however, was understandably criticized by Hans Kelsen as an unconvincing basis for the emergence of CIL norms.[381] Another understanding offered by Kelsen himself comes close to an evolutionary process – which I will discuss below[382] – but nonetheless falls short of offering a solution to the core problem: He simply stated that the individuals "must believe that they apply a norm, but they need not believe that it is a legal norm which they apply."[383] The problem is only displaced. How this norm – whatever source it might have – evolves to a legal norm remains unclear. Hiroshi Taki still defended Kelsen's approach.[384] To overcome the "problem of error" and to explain how customary norms become international customary *law*, he simply refers to a material distinction of practice: "[G]eneral and consistent usage becomes customary international law when its content is related to 'a matter of international law', but it remains as international comity and so forth when this is not the case."[385] Hence, the subjective element of *opinio iuris* is simply discharged and even though Taki himself offers the objection of Alfred Verdross[386] pointing towards the high

380 See David Lefkowitz, "(Dis)solving the Chronological Paradox in Customary International Law: A Hartian Approach" (2008) 21 (1) Canadian Journal of Law and Jurisprudence 128–148 (129), identifying François Gény, *Methode d'interpretation et sources en droit prive positif* (Librairie Générale de Droit et de Jurisprudence 2nd ed 1919) 367–371; with reference to Peter Benson, "François Gény's Doctrine of Customary Law" (1982) 20 Canadian Yearbook of International Law 267–281, as the first person to have proposed such an understanding. See Hans Kelsen, "Théorie du Droit International coutumier" (1939) 1 (NS) Revue International de la Théorie du Droit 253–274 (263). See also Bin Cheng, "United Nations Resolutions on Outer Space: 'Instant' Customary International Law?" (1965) 5 Indian Journal of International Law 23–48 (45, especially in n 107); as well as D'Amato (n 373) 66 ff.

381 See Kelsen (n 160) *General Theory of Law and State* 114: "The usual interpretation of this requirement [*opinio iuris*] is that individuals constituting by their conduct the law-creating custom must regard their acts as determined by a legal rule; they must believe that they perform a legal duty or exercise a legal right. This doctrine is not correct. It implies that the individuals concerned must act in error: since the legal rule which is created by their conduct cannot yet determine this conduct, at least not as a legal rule." This famous critique of the traditional understanding was labeled "the problem of error" by Hiroshi Taki, "*Opinio Juris* and the Formation of Customary International Law: A Theoretical Analysis" (2008) 51 German Yearbook of International Law 447–466 (452).

382 See Section 8.2.3.

383 See Hans Kelsen, *Principles of International Law* (Rinehart 1952) 307. However, not very far from what he criticized (and Taki labeled) as the problem of error, for Kelsen (308), "custom is unconscious and unintentional lawmaking."

384 Taki (n 381) 447.

385 See Taki (n 381)461. Finally, Taki (466) joins Kelsen again by writing that "in order to determine that customary international law has been established, one does not need to prove the presence of *opinio juris*, but only the presence of consciousness of 'any norm whatever.'"

386 See Taki (n 381)463, referring to Alfred Verdross, "Das völkerrechtliche Gewohnheitsrecht" (1963) 7 Japanese Annual of International Law 1–7 (4).

relativity of the judgment with regard to what is important for making something international law instead of a simple usage, he nevertheless seems to be satisfied with referring to the "entire positive international law"[387] as sufficient guidance for such judgment. John Tasioulas' solution to the paradox suffers from a similar problem despite being quite different in nature.[388] His proposal to answer the challenge[389] seems to overvalue the other element. *Opinio iuris*, for him, can be characterized as "the creation of an international legal rule according to which the specified pattern of behaviour would be lawful is *ethically justified*. Such a legal rule should be created by means of a process that involves general state practice consistent with it and an ethical endorsement by states of its establishment as a legal rule."[390] He thereby simply shifts the problem to the presupposition of "a broader, systemic ethical commitment on the part of a state."[391] Where the "moral attractiveness of a customary norm" as "a matter of objective truth"[392] comes from and how it can be identified remains unclear. This might be an interesting approach for CIL norms in the realm of global justice,[393] but very likely must fail as a universal explanation for the emergence of CIL.

Hence, we are still left with the problem of explaining how a binding norm becomes law.[394] David Lefkowitz seeks to grapple with this by reference to

[387] See Taki (n 381) 461.

[388] See Tasioulas (n 379); John Tasioulas, "Custom, Jus Cogens, and Human Rights" in Curtis A Bradley (ed) *Custom's Future: International Law in a Changing World* (Cambridge University Press 2016) 95–116.

[389] Tasioulas (n 379) does not call it a paradox, but a "serious flaw" because if States mistakenly believe that a specific behavior is already legally valid this is not "self-contradictory" strictly speaking.

[390] Tasioulas (n 379) [emphasis added].

[391] To be fair to him, his goal seems to be to "harness customary international law to a global justice agenda": Tasioulas (n 379).

[392] See Tasioulas (n 388) 105, n 20.

[393] Which is – to be fair – apparently a key goal of Tasioulas (n 379). However, his critique of a rational choice theory of CIL solely focusing on preferences of States Tasioulas (n 388) 98 ff: "But a preference, thus broadly understood, does not necessarily purport to identify a consideration that is even in principle capable of justifying the claim to legitimacy (moral bindingness) inherent in law" can be returned to him. How to identify morally irrelevant customary norms as law? He seems to be aware of this when considering "an objection to the foregoing analysis, one that takes issue with the liberal use of the adjective 'ethical' in characterising the beliefs and commitments" of States (Tasioulas n 379).

[394] See Emily Kadens and Ernest A Young, "How Customary Is Customary International Law?" (2013) 54 (3) William & Mary Law Review 885–920 (907): "The central problem of custom concerns the 'extra ingredient' necessary to transform a repetitive practice into a binding norm. And a central lesson of our historical discussion is that this has always been the central problem."

Hart's rule of recognition.[395] Arguably, his approach is the most sophisticated one in terms of aiming at an explanation for how mere usage becomes customary *law*. Lefkowitz explains that the paradox arises from the confusion that the agents who first have to believe in the existence of a customary rule (the first step) are the same agents whose adherence to the rule of recognition turns (in a second step) the customary rule into a legal rule of customary international *law*. Hence, he displaces the "law or not law" question not towards some external, objective morality (Tasioulas) or the entire body of international law (Taki), but "(dis)solves" it within one and the same agent. Whether we deem this to be a satisfactory solution or not is actually not particularly important for my argument here.[396] My point here is that all these "solutions" proposed refer – some more, some less implicitly – to an evolutionary process.

In other words, the two-element approach always was and still is faced with the paradoxical question of what came first: the obligation or the belief to be bound?[397] This is also the subject of the following conundrum, which is said to have been first expressed by Aristotle in this way: "If there has been a first man ... he must have been born without father or mother – which is repugnant to nature. ... [For] there could not have been a first egg to give a beginning to birds, or there should have been a first bird which gave a beginning to eggs; for a bird comes from an egg."[398]

8.2.3 *The Way Out: An Evolutionary Perspective*

This question has perplexed humanity for quite some time. One of the first said to have discussed this paradox, Aristotle proposed that the "actual"

[395] See Lefkowitz (n 380).

[396] To the contrary, I think for the purpose of my argument here it is safe to say that more precise criteria for identifying what the law, in our case customary international law, is, would be also welcome within the *Hartian* approach to which Lefkowitz (n 380) adheres.

[397] Cf Shaw (n 375) 62 ff; and D'Amato (n 373) 66 ff.

[398] It is very likely that this famous quote stems from François Fénelon, *Lives of the Ancient Philosophers* (Knight and Lacey 1825) 202 (translated from *Abrégé des vies des anciens philosophes*, Paris 1726, 314), while aiming to explain Aristotle's thoughts as expressed in his Metaphysics, book Theta (9. 1049b: "since we have distinguished the several senses of priority, it is obvious that actuality is prior to potentiality"). Thus, Plutarch was very likely the first person to expressly use the example of the chicken and the egg in Quaestiones Convivales (2.3.2); see Plutarch, *Morals* (corrected and revised by William W. Goodwin, 1874), available at www.perseus.tufts.edu/hopper/text?doc=Perseus%3Atext%3A2008.01.0312%3Abook%3D2%3Achapter%3D3%3Asection%3D2 [last accessed February 1, 2023]. I am grateful to Miklós Könczöl for pointing me to Plutarch.

chicken came before the "potential" egg.[399] The bible also suggests an easy way out as on day five God created "every winged bird according to its kind."[400] Finally, in 2010, the bible's view was supposedly supported by its – assumed – opponent: hard science. An article on the protein ovocleidin-17 by researchers at the universities of Warwick and Sheffield, who used a supercomputer based in Edinburgh, were credited in the popular media for finally having settled the question.[401] However, for us as lawyers, the final say in this discussion is in fact not important. This holds especially true as the actual paradox is very much related to a core issue of us as lawyers, namely labelling and defining concepts and notions, something that is quintessential for us to be able to use and work with the concepts and definitions we constructed previously. Thus, the chicken might be first, as we call this particular bird a chicken if it has specific chicken-like attributes, and the egg might be second, as we ascribe the "chicken egg" attributes (including a specific characteristic of the eggshell which can only be produced by the protein ovocleidin-17). As a consequence, the chicken precedes the "chicken egg."[402] However, if we open up our definition of the "chicken egg" slightly, being less strict about the concept of what we conceive as a "chicken egg" and simply asking for a

399 See eg Edward Halper, *Aristotle's Metaphysics: A Reader's Guide* (Continuum 2012) 87. Cf Theosophy, "Ancient Landmarks: Plato and Aristotle" (1939) 27 (11) Theosophy 483–491. Cf Aristotle, *Metaphysics, Book Theta* and the discussion of actuality and potentiality at 1049b.

400 See Genesis 1:21.

401 University of Warwick researchers Mark Rodger and David Quigley, in collaboration with colleagues at the University of Sheffield, were able to apply a powerful computing tool called metadynamics and the UK national supercomputer in Edinburgh to crack this egg problem. The conclusion was that the chicken had won the race as it claimed that it produced this special protein which is indispensable for creating eggshells. However, this can also be seen as a textbook example of how the popular media sometimes overstate research results in order to make them understandable and possibly also a bit sexier. The crucial point of this chemistry article was quite different and the interesting point for us here is that this special protein was indispensable for creating *chicken* eggshells. Thus, this research project did not solve the question of the chicken/bird and the egg, but the chicken and the chicken egg (and to be fair to the researchers, they did not claim to have done so). See University of Warwick, Researchers Apply Computing Power to Crack Egg Shell Problem, July 9, 2010, available at: www2.warwick.ac.uk/newsandevents/pressreleases/researchers_apply_computing/ [last accessed February 1, 2023]. See Colin L Freeman et al, "Structural Control of Crystal Nuclei by an Eggshell Protein" (2010) 49 (30) Angewandte Chemie International Edition 5135–5137.

402 See also for a concise explanation, Christopher M Langan, *The Art of Knowing: Expositions on Free Will and Selected Essays* (Mega Press 2002) 97 ff. First, in order to prevent ambiguities, he rephrases the question into four, more precise questions: "1. Which came first, the chicken or (just any old) egg? 2a. Which came first, the chicken or an egg laid by a chicken? 2b. Which came first, the chicken or an egg containing a chicken? 2c. Which came first: the chicken, or an egg laid by and containing a chicken?" The answers to these questions are "(1) The egg. (2a) The chicken. (2b) The egg. (2c) The chicken."

certain – albeit very thin – (egg)shell in which chickens can develop, we have to start from scratch.[403] Thus, we rather strive for a different understanding, acknowledging an answer that is already to be found in the contradiction expressed in the statement attributed to Aristotle.

To cut a long story short: We have known since Darwin that Adam and Eve were not the first humans but that we developed slowly but steadily from *homininae* to *homini*. The scientific perspective enables us to overcome the creationist position of Adam and Eve as the first humans by thinking of the genesis of humans as an evolutionary process. In the same vein, it is obvious that the chicken neither fell from heaven nor hatched from a mysterious first egg but has its ancestors in other creatures. Thus, we as lawyers do not have to take up the solution offered by Aristotle;[404] nor do we have to deal with what natural scientists found.[405] We can stop the natural science debate here,[406] learning for our case that neither a preexisting obligation nor a mistaken belief is the key to our puzzle. Instead, the evolutionary process is as follows: A certain practice of a State might be adequate practice without supporting the belief that the subject of international law is legally obliged to act in this way. The subjective element *opinio iuris* might be added as time goes by and other subjects of international law act similarly and thus adjust their acts.[407] Slowly but steadily, as time passes, a subjective conviction of a legal obligation can arise. Nothing else is expressed by the term "custom," which implies a sort of repetitive, spatial component. This evolving process is the prerequisite for the emergence of a CIL norm.

However, the paradox is not fully solved by this differentiated perspective. The fast pace of current times also provides challenges for the law as a regulatory phenomenon. Even if custom implies a certain duration, the rapidly changing world supports the call for a more rapidly emerging CIL.[408] However, the faster the process is, the more questionable the

[403] See Langan (n 402) 97 ff.

[404] See supra nn 398 and 399.

[405] See supra n 400.

[406] For those interested in an overview, see Renée Schroeder, *Die Henne und das Ei: Auf der Suche nach dem Ursprung des Lebens* (Residenz 2011) 81 ff.

[407] See Brian D Lepard, *Customary International Law: A New Theory with Practical Implications* (Cambridge University Press 2010) 112, who suggested that "*opinio juris* be interpreted as a requirement that states generally believe that it is desirable now or in the near future to have an authoritative legal principle or rule prescribing, permitting, or prohibiting certain state conduct." See also Brian D Lepard, "Customary International Law as a Dynamic Process" in Curtis A Bradley (ed) *Custom's Future: International Law in a Changing World* (Cambridge University Press 2016) 62–94.

[408] See Cheng (n 380) 23.

explanation just given becomes. The more spontaneous or quicker the evolution of a CIL norm is, the more important the requirements for a *conscious* legal process will be. Guidance for the identification of quick and consciously emerging CIL norms (as well as for more slowly emerging ones) is – as the central argument of this section goes – provided by consensus theory.

8.2.4 A *Renaissance of Consensus Theory*

What we can learn from this evolutionary perspective is the importance of distinguishing between the emergence of CIL norms and the identification of that final product. The latter is only possible once the process of genesis has been finalized. While the line between emerging and existing customary international *law* is hard to draw,[409] precisely such a line is at the core of any lawmaking process: We need to call norms law at some point in order to ascribe them their special consequences (like their binding nature, often combined with sanctions or the threat of them in the event of noncompliance).[410] The argument in this section is that consensus theory does the best job of, first, highlighting that this point is crucial, and second, even proposing guidance as to how such line-drawing with regard to customary law is best addressed.

Consensus theory here is simply understood as the need for acceptance of the formation (or modification) of a CIL norm in order to create customary international *law*, whereas for the identification (and preservation) of a CIL norm a belief that some customary norm is law is sufficient.[411] Understood in

[409] See also Kammerhofer (n 375) 80 ff.

[410] See Niklas Luhmann, *Soziale Systeme. Grundriß einer allgemeinen Theorie* (Suhrkamp 1984), which reduces law to a binary code of law and nonlaw.

[411] See ILC, Second Report on Identification of Customary International Law by the Special Rapporteur Sir Michael Wood, UN Doc A/CN.4/672 (2014) para 66: "In particular, some have debated whether the subjective element does indeed stand for the belief (or opinion) of States, or rather, for their consent (or will)." With further reference in footnote 206 to the ILA London Statement of Principles, 30: "It is possible to achieve an elision or apparent reconciliation of these two approaches by using such terms as 'accepted' or 'recognized' as law." For a critique of explicit consent as unanimity requirement with regard to CIL, see Andrew T Guzman and Jerome Hsiang, "Reinvigorating Customary International Law" in Curtis A Bradley (ed) *Custom's Future: International Law in a Changing World* (Cambridge University Press 2016) 275–304 (281 ff). See also Oliver P Hauser et al, "Cooperating with the Future" (2014) 511 Nature 220–223. However, see also Andreas L Paulus and Matthias Lippold, "Customary Law in the Postmodern World (Dis)Order" (2018) 112 American Journal of International Law Unbound 308–312 (308), holding that "If one accepts that any legal order requires a degree of effectiveness in the sense of general adherence to its rules, states' consent, in particular the consent of powerful states, will be of central importance for the effectiveness of international law, given the way the world is likely to remain structured for the foreseeable future" [footnotes omitted].

this way, consensus theory is not as demanding as explicit consent theory with regard to CIL. Whereas the latter asks for straightforward consent to a rule, the former is more open towards tacit agreement of some subjects of international law complementing explicit consent expressed by other subjects of international law.[412] The consent of those subjects of international law that do not explicitly consent to a certain CIL norm is according to consensus theory included already in the meta-norm of regulating CIL emergence.[413] The subjective element of *opinio iuris* is understood as explicitly or implicitly expressing the acceptance of the offer of a specific practice by its repetition (or nonobjection).[414] Instead of asking for explicit consent of a subject of international law, the offer of a raised claim can also be accepted through tacit agreement. To be more specific, the formula proposed below implies that a specific fraction of subjects of international law has to accept via practice and *opinio iuris*, and other potential actors give their tacit agreement if they do not persistently object.[415] Such broad understanding including the concept of acquiescence is consistent with the notion of "acceptance as law" as opposed to "belief that something is the law" and, hence, is consistent with the approach of the ILC.[416] However, note that the ILC draft conclusions speak of "accepted as law," which, of course, is only accurate in terms of identifying CIL, but traps into the CIL paradox with regard to CIL emergence.

[412] See Lefkowitz (n 380) 142: "It is consensus, not consent, that provides the basis for social norms." However, see critically Tasioulas (n 388) 103, in particular n 17: "The failure to distinguish consent from consensus is ubiquitous, even among critics of voluntarism."

[413] See infra, 296–298.

[414] See infra Section 8.2.5.3, on the persistent objector rule. See James A Green, *The Persistent Objector Rule in International Law* (Oxford University Press 2016) 273, quoting Max Sørensen, "Theory and Reality in International Law" (1981) 75 Proceedings of the American Society of International Law 140–149 (147): "the persistent objector rule can 'reasonably claim a permanent place [in the system] even when the positive emphasis in the law-creating process is shifted from consent to the less rigid notion of consensus.'"

[415] See Alain Pellet and Daniel Müller, "Article 38" in Andreas Zimmermann et al (eds) *The Statute of the International Court of Justice: A Commentary* (Oxford University Press 3rd ed 2018) para 226, with further reference to the *travaux préparatoires* of the Statute of the Permanent Court of International Justice in footnote 641 quoting Baron Descamps and Root. See also Karol Wolfke, *Custom in Present International Law* (Tow Nauk 1964) 56, who holds that CIL is "a continuous process of raising mutual claims and the adoption of an attitude to such claims."

[416] See Draft Conclusions on Identification of Customary International Law (n 368) General Commentary (3). The wording in Article 38 (1) (b) ICJ Statute speaks of "accepted as law," which is solely expressing the applicable law for the ICJ and guides the identification of a CIL norm (see infra n 449 and accompanying text). For the emergence of a CIL norm we have to reconstruct the actual meta-norm for CIL emergence according to the identification of CIL regulated in Art 38 ICJ Statute. Therefore, the notion of "acceptance as law" for CIL emergence is the most suitable one.

Consensus theory, the argument goes, is the only convincing theory to handle the aforementioned paradox, while still remaining within the two-element approach.[417] Yet consensus theory is not advocated as a superior truth but as an approach that best explains core questions of the normative foundations of CIL.[418] The suggested understanding of the genesis of CIL as offer and acceptance within the framework of consensus theory should help, in the end, to make CIL more tangible.[419] Hence, I do not aim at a theoretical "solution" of the paradox. I am satisfied with highlighting the troublesome point of CIL norm emergence in theoretical terms and as a consequence ask for practical guidance to diminish uncertainty with regard to CIL norm emergence and, subsequently, identification.[420] Consensus theory forces us to provide more concrete criteria for clarifying when exactly a certain CIL norm came to existence. Without such clarification the identification of CIL norms is nebulous and remains troublesome. This does not exclude the possibility that a subject of international law might act in the erroneous belief that it is legally obliged to behave in a certain manner (as was proposed to explain the emergence of CIL).[421] However, the evolutionary view minimizes such erroneous acts to a negligible degree.

With regard to this book, a formal source of law is simply understood as the settlement of procedural criteria aimed at making law.[422] Such a formal source thus eases the identification of law as it regulates which procedures or elements might deliver legal rules (and which might not). In the process some relevant features of lawmaking, such as majority voting, might be established.[423] Again, it is important to differentiate sharply between the

[417] See above Section 8.2.3.

[418] See Alfred Verdross, "Entstehungsweisen und Geltungsgrund des universellen völkerrechtlichen Gewohnheitsrechts" (1969) 29 Heidelberg Journal of International Law 635–653 (636).

[419] See below Section 8.2.5.

[420] Hence, the aim is not "to try to fit the round peg of voluntarism in the square hole of social reality," as Green (n 414) 249, has eloquently put it.

[421] See above n 380.

[422] See also Lando Kirchmair, *Die Theorie des Rechtserzeugerkreises. Eine rechtstheoretische Untersuchung des Verhältnisses von Völkerrecht zu Staatsrecht am Beispiel der österreichischen Rechtsordnung* (Duncker & Humblot 2013) 68 ff.

[423] See also Maurice H Mendelson, "The Subjective Element in Customary International Law" (1996) 66 British Yearbook of International Law 177–208 (190): "But given that States have in fact consented to the existence of a system of international law as a whole … it does not necessarily follow that the creation and binding force of each individual rule in the system is dependent on the consent of each and every subject at each and every moment. … It is States, as the principal subjects of the systems, who decide what processes will be recognized as generating rules of law. If they chose, they could recognize papal pronouncements or the randomly generated choices of a computer, say, as sources of legal obligation."

process of emergence and the identification of the new CIL rule. In this vein – as a by-product – it is interesting to see that it is important to distinguish between the content of a rule, or better, what someone wants the content to be (that is, the final result), and the process describing how we can achieve this result. As a consequence of this insight, we need to strive to somehow disconnect the result of the process from what we want the result to look like.[424]

Sharply distinguishing between the emergence and identification of a CIL norm is crucial but rather problematic as CIL is largely unwritten and even the weighting of both necessary elements is controversial.[425] This gives rise to many uncertainties regarding, for instance, which acts qualify as state practice,[426] which in turn makes it harder to identify the element as such.[427] With regard to CIL, the difficulties are connected with those formal criteria as they are not clearly regulated. Thus, as a consequence, identification is a virulent problem, too.[428] The identification of a CIL norm is, at its core, a cognitive problem, which can be eased by describing the procedure by which certain acts qualify as CIL. This description of certain criteria is usually accomplished by a formal source of law. Consensus theory presses us to acknowledge this.

The goal of this section is to propose that consensus theory can help to overcome or at least deal with these well-known difficulties more easily if its theoretical pursuit is taken serious in the practical realm. Thus, simply put (and idealized), by acting in a certain way, a subject of international law is suggesting that this specific *consuetudo* could become law if it is accepted by further subjects of international law.[429] Those subjects of international law that adjust their behavior to the offer agree and as a consequence CIL

[424] See Jeremy Waldron, *Law and Disagreement* (Oxford University Press 1999) 88–118.

[425] See also Jörg Kammerhofer, "Uncertainty in the Formal Sources of International Law: Customary International Law and Some of Its Problems" (2004) 15 (3) European Journal of International Law 523–553.

[426] For an overview on the discussion see Kammerhofer (n 375) 62 ff.

[427] See Kammerhofer (n 375) 68 ff.

[428] See Martti Koskenniemi, *From Apology to Utopia: The Structure of International Legal Argument* (Cambridge University Press 2005) 431, who asks hypothetically whether uncertainty with regard to CIL would diminish if it were clear which acts count as State practice and how they can be evinced.

[429] See Raphael M Walden, "The Subjective Element in the Formation of Customary International Law" (1977) 12 (3) Israel Law Review 344–364 (355): "The tacit consent theory, in all its forms, has the great merit of recognising the constitutive nature of custom."

emerges.[430] In theory, the paradox is explained, even in the event of spontaneously emerging CIL.[431] In this manner, CIL is established by confirming state practice borne by the will to accept the offer. This understanding is reflected by consensus theory.[432] The importance of this insight is not only theoretical. On the contrary, the theoretical challenges reflect practical problems.[433] Hence, this section seeks to demonstrate what such practical consequences of taking consensus theory seriously might look like.

8.2.5 *Practical Implications of Consensus Theory*

8.2.5.1 The Challenge of Tacit Agreement and the Necessity to Distinguish the Identification of CIL Regulated in Article 38 ICJ Statute from the Emergence of CIL Guided by a Meta-Norm

Probably the most common and obvious criticism directed against consensus theory to explain CIL is that a large number of subjects of international law which do not actively engage in practice are nonetheless bound by the

430 Similarly Shaw (n 375) 62: "If a state proclaims a twelve-mile limit to its territorial sea in the belief that although the three-mile limit has been accepted law, the circumstances are so altering that a twelve-mile limit might now be treated as becoming law, it is vindicated if other states follow suit and a new rule of customary law is established. If other states reject the proposition, then the projected rule withers away and the original rule stands, reinforced by state practice and common acceptance." See Sir Humphrey Waldock, "The Legal Basis of the Continental Shelf" (1950) 36 Transactions of the Grotius Society 115–148 (138 ff), who describes the process as "an invitation to other States to join in a deliberate and legislative development of customary law."

431 For the thesis that erroneous belief is necessary for the emergence of customary law see above n 380.

432 For a recent overview with further references see Green (n 414) 239–273. See also Verdross (n 418) 636 ff. See Grigory I Tunkin, "Remarks on the Juridical Nature of Customary Norms of International Law" (1961) 49 (3) California Law Review 419–430; Gennady M Danilenko, "The Theory of Customary International Law" (1988) 31 German Yearbook of International Law 9–47; Olufemi Elias, "The Nature of the Subjective Element in Customary International Law" (1995) 44 (3) International and Comparative Law Quarterly 501–520; Karol Wolfke, *Custom in Present International Law* (Springer 2nd ed 1993) 57. For a critical view see Kolb (n 375) 144: "some form of organic law-making through practice … involving some mixture of will-elements (*opinio iuris*) and non-will elements (general practice binding all states)."

433 However, see ILC, Second Report on Identification of Customary International Law (n 411) para 66: "The subjective element of customary international law has, however, 'created more difficulties in theory than in practice', and the theoretical torment which may accompany it in the books has rarely impeded its application in practice." For a critique of such "knee-jerk pragmatism," see Tasioulas (n 388) 95. The Draft Conclusions on Identification of Customary International Law (n 368) follow a similar strategy by excluding the emergence of CIL. This, however, is not only a theoretical, but a very practical issue and problem.

established norm.[434] First, we have to distinguish this desire for active practice from active practice in the form of an omission (still counting as practice).[435] However, considering the rather limited frame of omissions, the objection still holds. Thus, second, another response to this challenge is that a subject of international law might express its objection against the emerging norm. If it does so persistently, it is not bound by the new CIL norm. Overstating the point, one could argue that a subject of international law might even opt to remain silent and thereby agree to be bound. Whether this is a good illustration of a tacit agreement remains to be seen. However, the relevance of consensus decreases (and the objection against tacit agreement increases) as subjects of international law participate less actively in practice.[436] This becomes especially obvious if the topics concerned are deemed to be of utmost relevance although they have not yet been regulated in positive law. Hence, the temptation is strong to deem such fundamental norms as "given" CIL,[437] thereby bypassing the evidence of such norms.[438] As an answer, some scholars proposed that only those subjects of international law might *acquiesce* silently which knew or could have known of the emerging CIL norm[439] ("potentially affected subjects of international law"[440]). Still, critical voices question silent acquiescence.[441]

[434] See for example Kelsen (n 383) 311. Cf Ian C MacGibbon, "Customary International Law and Acquiescence" (1958) 33 British Yearbook of International Law 115–145 (130): "[I]n the early stages of the development of a customary right other States are faced with the choice of objecting or remaining passive. From their inaction the inference of consent in and acceptance of the validity of the claim may be drawn."

[435] See above n 375.

[436] See Kammerhofer (n 375) 77.

[437] Kammerhofer (n 375) 78 ff.

[438] See similarly D'Amato (n 373) 218 ff: "The root of the problem may involve an age-old device of political philosophers who, to add to their own persuasiveness, claim that the behavioral norms they set forth are in fact obeyed by mankind in general. Marx, Hobbes, Hegel, and Austin, among many others, have attempted to show 'scientifically' that what ought to be the case is in fact the case, and that nothing the reader may do will derail what the writer perceives as historically inevitable. So too McDougal argues that the Lasswellian values not only should be accepted by all reasonable and decent men, but in fact they are so accepted throughout the world. What, then, if someone rejects them? McDougal would consign such men to the extra-legal world, much as Rousseau, for example, solved the problem of dissent in his Social Contract by banishing the dissenters from the body politic." I leave it to the reader's imagination at this point as to which norms of modern CIL could be particularly affected.

[439] See Mendelson (n 423) 186 with reference to ICJ, *Fisheries Case (United Kingdom v Norway)* Judgment ICJ Reports [1951] 116 paras 138 ff; see also Shaw (n 375) 63 ff.

[440] See below n 493 and accompanying text.

[441] Kammerhofer (n 375) 78 regards acquiescence as a "legal fiction." See also Michael Byers, *Custom, Power and the Power of Rules: International Relations and Customary International Law* (Cambridge University Press 1999) 143 ff; as well as Mendelson (n 423) 186 ff; and

To satisfy these critical voices, an additional response is to point to the freedom of subjects of international law to establish a formal source with regard to CIL allowing for such a tacit agreement.[442] Thus, once such a formal source has been established, it is possible that tacit agreement features CIL in a similar way as it is possible to establish a formal source for "majority decisions." If we include the idea of acquiescence in the frame of the formal source, we can deal with this sort of criticism. In positive words, the formal source includes an authorization for "active subjects of international law" and their practice, giving them the power to bind inactive subjects of international law as well (if they do not disagree persistently).[443]

To address remaining skepticism, an analogy to the "first constitution" of a subject of international law might be persuasive. Social contract theory is confronted with similar objections. Criticism holds that such a fundamental consensus (empowering active subjects of international law in our case) is utopian and thus fictive. However, this was already answered by Immanuel Kant when he openly admitted the fictive element of such a contract.[444] In fact the very first consensus, as the argument goes, is (fictively) assumed and deals with accepting a majority decision even with regard to the very first constitution.[445] This preceding consensus is based on the assumption that all subjects involved are in agreement that having any constitution is in the interests of all. In other words, the very first consensus (whether fictive or tacit is blurry and not of utmost importance) is that we need some agreement, which is better than unregulated chaos. Thus, even if the "first constitution" is not the desired result of all subjects involved, people are united in the belief that they are in need of a constitution.[446] As a consequence,

Torsten Gihl, "The Legal Character of Sources of International Law" (1957) 1 Scandinavian Studies in Law 51–92 (79).

[442] See above n 423.

[443] For a pragmatic description, see Gerald G Fitzmaurice, "The Law and Procedure of the International Court of Justice 1951–54: General Principles and Sources of Law" (1953) 30 British Yearbook of International Law 1–70 (68): "Where a general rule of customary international law is built up by the common practice of States, although it may be a little unnecessary to have recourse to the notion of agreement (and a little difficult to detect it in what is often the uncoordinated, independent, if similar, action of States), it is probably true to say that consent is latent in the mutual tolerations that allow the practice to be built up at all; and actually patent in the eventual acceptance (even if tacit) of the practice, as constituting a binding rule of law."

[444] See Peter Koller, *Neue Theorien des Sozialkontrakts* (Duncker & Humblot 1987) 14, who makes reference to Immanuel Kant, *Über den Gemeinspruch: "Das mag in der Theorie richtig sein, taugt aber nicht für die Praxis"* (Berlinische Monatsschrift 1793) 153.

[445] Whether explicit, tacit or fictive might be left open here.

[446] For an interesting line of a similar argument regarding majority decisions and the authority of legislation see Waldron (n 424) 159–160.

we should not ask those individuals who did not vote for the concrete result ("the actual first constitution") whether they agree on the specific content of this very first constitution. Rather, the question should be whether the very first (tacit) consensus (acceptance of the majority decision in order to have any constitution) leading to the first constitution is to be opposed with the alternative of unregulated chaos. Being confronted with the choice of chaos or constitution, most of the disagreeing minority will probably agree. Yet if the result of the majority "consensus" goes too far, forcing a minority to prefer chaos, for instance, we are faced with a (smaller but still existent) problem regarding the "first constitution." Luckily we can step out of our metaphor now, because with regard to CIL we have the concept of persistent objection to deal with this problem.[447]

Returning to our topic, we have learnt three things from the theoretical discussion on the foundations of CIL. First, the necessity of CIL for a working international legal order can be perceived as a common foundation unifying all subjects of international law so important that the concept of silent *acquiescence* is accepted. Second, the danger of being bound by inactive behavior is relativized by the possibility of expressing persistent objection.[448] If a subject of international law persistently objects, it simply rejects the offer. Third, uncertainty with regard to silent acquiescence can also be differentiated from the metaphoric example of the "first constitution" as the formal source of CIL has its basis in positive international law. Hence, with regard to CIL, such a formal source in positive law does exist, but it is not Article 38 (1) (b) ICJ Statute, which regulates how CIL emerges. Thus, it does not deal

[447] See ICJ, *Fisheries Case (United Kingdom v Norway)* Judgment ICJ Reports [1951] 116 (131); ICJ, *Asylum Case (Columbia v Peru)* Judgment ICJ Reports [1950] 266 (277 ff). See Akehurst (n 373) 25 with further references in nn 5 and 6; as well as Ted L Stein, "The Approach of the Different Drummer: The Principle of the Persistent Objector in International Law" (1985) 26 (2) Harvard International Law Journal 457–482. For a critical perspective see Jonathan Ian Charney, "The Persistent Objector Rule and the Development of Customary International Law" (1985) 56 British Yearbook of International Law 1–24. For a recent, comprehensive account see Green (n 414).

[448] See Charney (n 447) 16: "It is difficult to see how the acceptance of the [persistent objector] rule does not reflect an acceptance of the consent theory of international law. If a mere objection to an evolving rule of law can prevent application of that rule to the State, then each State has the unilateral power to decide whether or not to be bound by the rule." However, see Kolb (n 375) 144, who asserts that "[i]f customary law were really voluntary, the whole doctrine of the persistent objector would be useless." Yet it is possible to understand the doctrine of *persistent objectors* – analogously to the burden of proof – as a sheet anchor. As Nils Petersen, "The Role of Consent and Uncertainty in the Formation of Customary International Law" in Brian D Lepard (ed) *Reexamining Customary International Law* (Cambridge University Press 2018) 111–130, points out, treaty law can be perceived as an "opt in," and customary law as an "opt out" system.

directly with the process of how CIL emerges.[449] Still, Article 38 determines how to identify the result of the formal CIL source and can and must, therefore, be used to reconstruct the formal source leading to this result.[450] In other words, Article 38 is a cornerstone for the identification of CIL and at least a touchstone regarding the emergence of CIL. And it allows for a reconstruction of this formal source as it establishes how to identify CIL, outlining the prerequisites of emerging CIL norms. The foundational consensus regarding CIL as a source of international law includes the concept of acquiescence with regard to emerging CIL norms.[451]

This is also very much related to the paradox discussed above. That paradox was the reason why many commentators have described the formulation of Article 38 (1) ICJ Statute as unfortunate.[452] However, considering the arguments just presented, this is not convincing. The definition in Article 38 presupposes what some commentators want to get out of it: As the ICJ might only identify already existing norms of CIL, the purpose of the ICJ Statute is "only" to define how to identify the result of the formal sources of international law.[453] In other words, the nature of the ICJ Statute is to define applicable legal sources and not to establish or regulate the genesis process of the same sources. Thus, a court only needs to find "whether the fruit is ripe, not when it ripened."[454] This is also an important difference with regard to national

[449] See also with regard to Article 38 ICJ Statute in general Pellet and Müller (n 415) para 80, with further reference in n 187, among others to Robert Y Jennings and Arthur Watts, *Oppenheim's International Law* (Oxford University Press 9th ed 1992) 24; Gerald Fitzmaurice, "Some Problems Regarding the Formal Sources of International Law" in Frederik Mari van Asbeck et al (eds) *Symbolae Verzijl* (Martinus Nijhoff 1958) 153–176 (176); Jean d'Aspremont, *Formalism and the Sources of International Law: A Theory of the Ascertainment of Legal Rules* (Oxford University Press 2011) 149.

[450] However, see ICJ, *Jurisdictional Immunities of the State (Germany v Italy: Greece Intervening)* Judgment ICJ Reports [2012] 99 para 55: "It follows that the Court must *determine*, in accordance with Article 38 (1) (b) of its Statute, the *existence* of 'international custom, as evidence of a general practice accepted as law' conferring immunity on States and, if so, what is the scope and extent of that immunity. To do so, it must apply the criteria which it has repeatedly laid down for identifying a rule of customary international law" [emphasis added].

[451] See above n 414.

[452] See for instance Verdross (n 418) 649, especially in n 67.

[453] For a similar argument (albeit with Art 53 Vienna Convention on the Law of Treaties, May 23, 1969, UNTS 1155, 331 (VCLT) in mind) see Ulf Linderfalk, "The Creation of Jus Cogens: Making Sense of Article 53 of the Vienna Convention" (2011) 71 Heidelberg Journal of International Law 359–378.

[454] For such a metaphor see Mendelson (n 423) 179 in n 9: "[A] court need only decide whether the rule had come into being for the parties at the 'critical date' (or equivalent) – in other words, whether the fruit is ripe, not when it ripened." See also Fitzmaurice (n 449) 173, for whom Article 38 "does not really profess to contain an abstract statement of the sources of international law." He goes on by saying that "Article 38 is simply a sort of standing directive to

constitutional orders, where usually the lawmaking process of national laws is clearly regulated, or with regard to international treaties as a source of law, which are governed by the Vienna Convention on the Law of Treaties. The unwritten formal source of CIL stands in contrast to this.[455] From Article 38 (1) ICJ Statute we can only reconstruct the formal source of CIL and thus the emergence procedure.[456] This reconstruction, however, can lead us to the formal source, which is an unwritten meta-norm. This meta-norm is the correct place to discuss the normative foundation and practical implications of CIL. Also the work of the ILC on this subject is of utmost importance and would be well-advised to deal with the process of the emergence of CIL instead of focusing only on the identification of CIL.

Consensus is thus a characteristic element in the process of CIL emergence, though CIL is characteristically modified – if we do not speak simply of a supplementary norm – by a breach of existing practice.[457] In the frame of consensus theory this is to be understood as a conscious breach of existing laws with the (legally allowed) aim of modifying existing laws. If a critical number of subjects of international law follow the suggested modification of the former, the breach is healed. If the suggested modification is not successful, the illegality of the proposed change remains and is confirmed by the majority

the Court as to what it is to apply in deciding cases brought before it." From a critical perspective, Gennady M Danilenko, *Law-Making in the International Community* (Brill 1993) 36, states that "[e]xamples of state practice indicating a wide acceptance of Art. 38 as an authoritative enumeration of sources of international law are numerous."

455 See Louis Henkin, *International Law, Politics and Values* (Brill 1995) 31 ff: "The international system implies a number of assumptions and conceptions of axiomatic 'constitutional' character."

456 However, see also erroneously ICJ, *Military and Paramilitary Activities in and against Nicaragua (Nicaragua v United States)* Judgment ICJ Reports [1986] 14 para 207, quoting ICJ, *North Sea Continental Shelf Cases (Federal Republic of Germany v Denmark; Federal Republic of Germany v Netherlands)* Judgment ICJ Reports [1969] 3 para 77: "[F]or a new customary rule to be formed, not only must the acts concerned 'amount to a settled practice', but they must be accompanied by the *opinio juris sive necessitatis*. Either the States taking such action or other States in a position to react to it, must have behaved so that their conduct is 'evidence of a belief that this practice is rendered obligatory by the existence of a rule of law requiring it. The need for such a belief, i.e., the existence of a subjective element, is implicit in the very notion of the *opinio juris sive necessitates*.'" Critically also Mendelson (n 423) 183. See recently ICJ, *Jurisdictional Immunities* (n 368) para 55: "It follows that the Court must determine, in accordance with Article38 (1) (b) of its Statute, the *existence* of 'international custom, as evidence of a general practice accepted as law'" [emphasis added].

457 This is the other extreme of a simple extension. Of course a sort of middle way between both extremes is conceivable. Thus, "bending" an existing rule instead of breaching it might also be a way of amending an existing norm. This would fit in very well with the offered understanding of an evolutionary process. However, for the sake of clarity, I refer to a breach of the existing norm in the text. I am grateful to Gábor Sulyok for the idea of "bending" norms.

of subjects of international law.[458] A conscious expression of *opinio iuris* might be helpful to clearly identify the current status and thus contributes to legal certainty.[459]

8.2.5.2 Inductive vs. Deductive Approach and Consensus Theory

What has been discussed so far is closely related to the question of whether CIL is generated and subsequently identified by an inductive[460] or a deductive[461] approach. Induction can be characterized as inferring a general rule from individual instances.[462] A consistent, long-lasting process is more likely to be accounted for by an inductive approach, empirically collecting acts of practice. Quicker, or even instant CIL, however, may be more easily explained as an answer to the spontaneously emerging necessities of a global world with reference to the deduction of legal convictions derived from "universal pre-existing" norms or opinions.[463] Deduction can be qualified as inferring a specific rule from an overarching rule or principle.[464]

Both methods of identifying CIL very likely lead, in a radical way, to the omission of one of the two elements of CIL.[465] The deductive approach – in a radical version – first interprets state practice as a simple proof for the existence of the CIL norm in question, which is said to rest on the foundation of a universal legal conviction.[466] Thus, from this perspective only the element of

[458] See ICJ, *Military and Paramilitary Activities in and against Nicaragua (Nicaragua v United States)* Judgment ICJ Reports [1986] 14 para 207: "Reliance by a State on a novel right or an unprecedented exception to the principle might, if shared in principle by other States, tend towards a modification of customary international law." See Kammerhofer (n 375) 74 ff, who introduces a meta-level to substantiate the possibilities of modification.

[459] See also Akehurst (n 373) 8.

[460] See Anthea E Roberts, "Traditional and Modern Approaches to Customary International Law: A Reconciliation" (2001) 95 (4) American Journal of International Law 757–791 (758), who calls the inductive process traditional.

[461] The deductive process is referred to as modern by Roberts (n 460) 758 ff. Critically, Bruno Simma and Philip G Alston, "The Sources of Human Rights Law: Custom, Jus Cogens, and General Principles" (1988–89) 12 Australian Yearbook of International Law 82–108 (88).

[462] See Stefan Talmon, "Determining Customary International Law: The ICJ's Methodology between Induction, Deduction and Assertion" (2015) 26 (2) European Journal of International Law 417–443 (420).

[463] See Alberto Alvarez-Jiménez, "Methods for the Identification of Customary International Law in the International Court of Justice's New Millennium Jurisprudence: 2000–2009" (2011) 60 (3) International & Comparative Law Quarterly 681–712 (686).

[464] See Talmon (n 462) 420.

[465] With regard to the one-element approach, see critically Kammerhofer (n 375) 61 ff.

[466] See Cheng (n 380); as well as Karl Strupp, "Les règles générales du droit international de la paix" (1934) 47 Recueil des Cours I 259–595. Also Tasioulas (n 388). For the same

opinio iuris is deemed to be constitutive for the emergence of CIL.[467] The affirming practice of other subjects of international law or their tacit agreement is swept away in favor of a strong focus on a universal legal conviction (*opinio iuris*), which, for instance, is derived – in a modern version – from multilateral treaties or UN resolutions.[468] To exaggerate a bit, we could hold that a deductive approach does not need or care about the agreement of other subjects of international law because even the first practice is only deduced from a preexisting norm that was already transcendentally present in the legal consciousness of all subjects of international law. It is thus only made visible. The proximity to natural law, completely detached from consensus, is obvious. Hence, early approaches to CIL saw first practice as simple "recognition" of a transcendentally present norm.[469] The "modern," deductive approach to identifying CIL does at least substitute the transcendental, natural norm with the legal conviction of subjects of international law proving practice and its binding nature. Still, the spatial element, which is at least related to the semantic interpretation of the word "custom," remains neglected.[470] As a consequence, the designation of "customary" becomes questionable.[471] Accordingly, the proposal to subordinate such law emanating from a universal *opinio iuris* to another legal source, namely general principles,[472] is entirely understandable. Having spoken of Article 38 (1) (b) ICJ

qualification of Tasioulas' approach, see Lepard (n 407) Customary International Law as a Dynamic Process 75, n 45.

[467] Note again that it is still important to distinguish the case of omissions, which can be clear practice if demonstrated convincingly. See above n 375.

[468] See Roberts (n 460) 758 ff (referring to ICJ, *Military and Paramilitary Activities in and against Nicaragua (Nicaragua v United States)* Judgment ICJ Reports [1986] 14 para 186): "The court did not make a serious inquiry into state practice, holding that it was sufficient for conduct to be generally consistent with statements of rules, provided that instances of inconsistent practice had been treated as breaches of the rule concerned rather than as generating a new rule." See Jonathan Ian Charney, "Universal International Law" (1993) 87 (4) American Journal of International Law 529–551 (545 ff). However, it is doubtful whether the ICJ actually had such a modern deductive approach in mind (despite the wording). See Shaw (n 375) 55; as well as Alvarez-Jiménez (n 463) 688.

[469] See Kammerhofer (n 375) 78 ff.

[470] See also Simma and Alston (n 461) 89 ff. Critically Akehurst (n 373) 14.

[471] See Robert Y Jennings, "What Is International Law and How Do We Tell It When We See It?" (1981) 37 Annuaire Suisse de Droit International 59–88 (67): "Perhaps it is time to face squarely the fact that the orthodox tests of custom – practice and *opinio juris* – are often not only inadequate but even irrelevant for the identification of much new law today. And the reason is not far to seek: much of this new law is not custom at all, and does not even resemble custom."

[472] With regard to fundamental human rights, see Simma and Alston (n 461). See Nils Petersen, "Customary Law without Custom? Rules, Principles, and the Role of State Practice in

Statute before – not as the legal source of CIL but as the definition of how to identify CIL – this is enough to clearly refute a radical deductive approach.

In contrast, the inductive approach – again in a radical version – may also amount to a one-element approach, this time neglecting the subjective element of *opinio iuris* however.[473] This leads us to the problematic situation that behavior under the flag of courtesy or other (than legal) means cannot be distinguished from mandatory legal actions.[474] However, a more moderate version of inductive identification allows space for the legal conviction of subjects of international law. Thus, CIL emerges inductively by looking at the new practice of a subject of international law supported by legal conviction of proposing a new law (*opinio iuris*) as well as a quantifiable number of further subjects of international law who – by following this proposal – accept the offer and thereby establish law. This is supplemented by silence from inactive subjects of international law.[475] Thus, empirical facts lead to the induction of a legal rule.

A modest version of the inductive and deductive approach combined (that is, an acknowledgment of both elements) might thus lead to the emergence and succinct identification of CIL.[476] The relationship between the element of state practice and *opinio iuris* might be described as somewhat relative, as the concentrated presence of one of the two could compensate for a slightly

International Norm Creation" (2007–2008) 23 (2) American University International Law Review 275–310.

473 See Kelsen (n 383) 264–266, who, however, revised it to solely refer to State practice later, in Hans Kelsen, *Principles of International Law* (Rinehart 2nd ed 1966) 450 ff; see Paul Guggenheim, *Traité de droit international public* (Librairie de l'Université 1953) 46 ff; Paul Guggenheim, "Les deux éléments de la coutume en droit international" in Librairie générale de droit et de jurisprudence (ed) *La technique et les principes du droit public: Études en l'honneur de Georges Scelle* I (Librairie générale de droit et de jurisprudence 1950) 275–284; this was later revised in Paul Guggenheim, *Traité de droit international public* I (Librairie de l'Université 2nd ed 1967) 103 ff; see also Lazare Kopelmans, "Custom as a Means of the Creation of International Law" (1937) 18 British Yearbook of International Law 127–151 with some exceptions (135); see also Gihl (n 441) 53 and 84.

474 See D'Amato (n 373) 57: "Finally, a failure to protest might manifest not acquiescence but a belief that the usage was simply outside the legal realm, belonging to the realm of social courtesy or comity."

475 See also Shaw (n 375) 63: "Customary law is thus established by virtue of a pattern of claim, absence of protest by states particularly interested in the matter at hand and acquiescence by other states," with further references to ICJ, *Land, Island and Maritime Frontier Dispute (El Salvador/Honduras: Nicaragua intervening)* Judgment ICJ Reports [1992] 3 para 405.

476 See also William T Worster, "The Inductive and Deductive Methods in Customary International Law Analysis: Traditional and Modern Approaches" (2014) 45 (2) Georgetown Journal of International Law 445–521; Alvarez-Jiménez (n 463) 689 ff. See also Talmon (n 462) 417, who concludes "that the main method employed by the Court [ICJ] is neither induction nor deduction but, rather, assertion."

less clear presence of the other element.[477] However, this relativity is not absolute. The strong presence of one element might not compensate for the complete absence of the other element.[478] As a consequence, relying on consensus theory and interpreting the identification of CIL according to Article 38 (1) (b) ICJ Statute asks for the presence of both elements for CIL to emerge. The emergence of CIL on the basis of just one element might only work if Article 38 (1) ICJ Statute were to be changed. This is an effect of the reconstruction of the formal source of CIL emergence from the definition of how CIL norms are identified.

Recent tendencies in the case law of international criminal tribunals have led scholars to focus on and propagate a "modern" CIL, very often leading to the neglect of one element, whether this be *consuetudo* or *opinio iuris*.[479] Still I am convinced that – even though it is a fascinating field for analysis – this must be seen as an exception to the rule rather than the opposite – that is, indicating a ground-breaking shift in the normative foundations of CIL. Reasons for these exceptions might be, for instance, the vague, if not to say nonexistent (international criminal) law regarding some problems that have been and still are subject to adjudication by international criminal tribunals (from which, nonetheless, results were/are expected). This has almost unavoidably provoked a highly problematic use of traditional methods for CIL identification or – if we take up the perspective of those who want to ring in a new age of CIL – simply shows the shift in CIL identification.[480] Hence, even though we are facing striking examples and challenges from this area of international law for CIL, this is to be perceived much more as a warning (and yet an understandable example) for the need to have a clearer framework for CIL emergence and identification rather than a revolution in terms of international sources. The reason is simply that adjudication is not the right place for lawmaking (even though the lines are often blurred).[481]

[477] See Frederick L Kirgis, "Custom on a Sliding Scale" (1987) 81 (1) American Journal of International Law 146–151 (149), who, however, extends his "sliding scale" to the replacement of one element. See also Oskar Schachter, "Entangling Treaty and Custom" in Yoram Dinstein and Mala Tabory (eds) *International Law at a Time of Perplexity: Essays in Honour of Shabtai Rosenne* (Martinus Nijhoff 1989) 717–738 (731).

[478] See above n 373.

[479] For an extensive overview of the case law, see Thomas Rauter, *Judicial Practice, Customary International Criminal Law and Nullum Crimen Sine Lege* (Springer 2017).

[480] For a detailed analysis see Rauter (n 479).

[481] See also Tamás Hoffmann, "The Gentle Humanizer of Humanitarian Law: Antonio Cassese and the Creation of the Customary Law of Non-International Armed Conflicts" in Carsten Stahn and Larissa van den Herik (eds) *Future Perspectives on International Criminal Justice* (Asser Press 2010) 58–80. For the argument that judges, beyond identifying custom, also have

Needless to say, it is utopian to hold that the judge is only "*la bouche de la loi*," as Montesquieu once famously stated.[482] Sometimes this is more evident; sometimes it is less so. And the matter is one of degree. However, far too often an analysis stops at this point, already satisfied with having – albeit sometimes very convincingly – blurred the lines (in this case of lawmaking and adjudication). Having done so, it is far too easy to forget that the point simply is that we need lines. Our whole thinking works in categories and labels. This holds true even though the lines are very often hard to draw. Thus, to cut it short: Adjudication sometimes might be a bit too active, blurring the line between interpreting and making the law. However, blurring the lines is not a sufficient argument for abolishing the lines. In our case, the arguments are not even good enough to shift the lines by openly awarding international adjudicators the role and competence of lawmaking (even if they sometimes overstepped their competence and their activism was welcomed by commentators and even subjects of international law). Especially so-called hard cases (mostly blurring the lines) are difficult to handle because they cannot be solved to a satisfactory degree (or with one "right" answer) in contrast to more clear-cut cases. However, using the benchmark of the clear-cut cases for the hard cases might blur the lines, which is problematic. This does not mean that we should refrain from thinking critically about the lines or even from shifting them when, after due consideration and well-grounded reasoning, they have to be moved (at best to minimize hard cases and – often overlooked – not to create new ones). But even if we abolish some lines, in general we need these boundaries, at least at some point.

8.2.5.3 The Challenge of "New Subjects of International Law," Consensus Theory and What We Can Learn to Make CIL More Tangible

Yet another challenge consensus theory faces is new subjects of international law joining the international community and the question of how they could

the power to define what custom is as a source of law, see Vassilis Tzevelekos, "Juris Dicere: Custom as a Matrix, Custom as a Norm, and the Role of Judges and (Their) Ideology in Custom Making" in Nikolas M Rajkovic et al (eds) *Power of Legality: Practices of International Law and Their Politics* (Cambridge University Press 2016) 188–208. According to this view, what judges want is decisive for whether custom is the result of a tacit agreement or not.

482 In this regard it is striking to see that even one of the most prominent positivistic scholars, Hans Kelsen, understood judicial decisions (within their narrow frame as guided by the law) as making the law, and he himself was a very active and progressive constitutional judge. See Ewald Wiederin, "Der österreichische Verfassungsgerichtshof als Schöpfung Hans Kelsens und sein Modellcharakter als eigenständiges Verfassungsgericht" in Thomas Simon and Johannes Kalowada (eds) *Schutz der Verfassung: Normen, Institutionen, Höchst- und Verfassungsgerichte* (Duncker & Humblot 2013) 283–315.

possibly be bound by existing CIL without having explicitly expressed their consent. This challenge is different from the argument presented before as the "new subjects of international law" did not have the chance to object to a rule while it was emerging. Thus, they are faced with being bound by existing CIL norms when they join the community. However, first, we can hold that this is no longer a pressing practical question[483] as the international legal order is more or less stable with regard to territory. Second, this point of criticism can be counteracted with a slightly different but generally similar answer as previously posed in favor of tacit agreement. One can argue that new subjects of international law might be said to agree tacitly to existing norms in order to be able to profit from the stability of the existing legal order.[484] The price, as the argument goes, is to accept the existing laws.[485]

Hence, instead of understanding this as a flaw of consensus theory we can turn the issue upside down: Consensus theory is helpful as it clearly highlights where the real problems lie. It shows us what is problematic and important for the normative foundations of CIL. Thus, we learn from consensus theory that it is crucial to know when the offer has been accepted. Made clear with regard to new subjects of international law, this insight also holds true for "normal" cases of CIL emergence. Consensus theory draws our attention clearly to the need for specifying quantitative criteria in order to determine an offer and its acceptance. To simply ask for a specific number, saying that the offer is accepted if five subjects of international law agree to the invitation, is very likely not to do justice to the complicated and demanding events in this rapidly changing international legal order. However, a more complex formula might do. To grapple better with the question of which behavior should count when looking at state practice, it was suggested to look at those subjects of international law that were actively involved or at least aware of a specific practice and capable of intervening.[486] A corresponding but slightly different

483 The literature quoted regarding this problem mostly dates back to the 1960s. See, for instance, Tunkin (n 432) 429; Georges Abi-Saab, "The Newly Independent States and International Law: An Outline" (1962) 8 (2) Howard Law Journal 97–121; Richard A Falk, "The New States and International Legal Order" (1966) 118 Recueil des Cours 1–103; Michael Schweitzer, *Das Völkergewohnheitsrecht und seine Geltung für neuentstehende Staaten* (Gehlen 1969).

484 Note that this is different from the argument above as these new States could not have consented (even hypothetically) to the underlying formal source of the CIL and the analogous consensus of the "first constitution" mentioned, at least not in the form of the very same State as is subject to being bound now. Thus, the concept of a fictitious consent regarding the first consensus is not a very convincing tool in this case.

485 See eg Grigory I Tunkin, *Theory of International Law* (translated by W E Butler George Allen & Unwin 1974) 129.

486 See supra n 440.

point is to focus on those subjects of international law that actually have an interest in the practice concerned. Well-known examples are the law of the sea (where subjects of international law without access to the sea are an example of at least very limited interest) or space law (where some subjects of international law are not able to participate in space missions due to financial and/or technical constraints), both demonstrating that some subjects of international law are prevented from consenting.[487]

It is interesting to see how such arguments are similar to the problem of how to bind new subjects of international law. One could ask how subjects of international law can be bound by a certain CIL norm if they did not even have the chance (due to limited access to and/or interest in the law of the sea) to object to a CIL norm, let alone consent consciously and freely to such a norm. And, more specifically, how can we explain or say that this problem is guided by consensus theory with regard to CIL emergence? However, this is a rather one-sided perspective. If we take up the perspective of those subjects of international law engaging in a certain field, for instance the law of the sea, we can ask why they should worry about possible future actors in the present. Or, to put it a bit more specifically, why should we not be able to find a customary legal solution to a certain problem at present just because, in the future, some new actors might possibly appear? And, slightly more provocatively, should a space mission not be regulated by any CIL norm just because there is still one small subject of international law that is not able or does not want to engage financially in space missions?[488] Regarding space, we can understand that any nonparticipating State may, all of a sudden, finally find the financial means or otherwise simply decide to participate in a space mission as a new subject of international law. And thus we can argue in a similar way as we did regarding new States in the 1960s. We could hold that those new subjects of international law do consent to the existing CIL norms by participating in the legal order. Thus, they could also consent to the existing CIL regime regarding space when they start their own space missions. Furthermore, those new subjects of international law are not completely subjected to the existing regime. They can even propose new CIL norms, thereby extending or bending and so modifying the current regime, which might be successful if they find enough other subjects of international law willing to accept their offer.

The point is that at present we also strive for the legal regulation of a specific act or field, such as in the abovementioned example of outer space. It is not a

[487] See Petersen (n 448).

[488] However, note the difference here between whether we are speaking of those States that have an interest in a certain practice or those that are simply unable to act in a certain way.

very strong argument to prevent a regulation in the present by saying that in the future the case might be different (especially if we are speaking about vague future actors). This is the perspective of currently active subjects of international law (be it with regard to space, the sea or some other possibly narrower field). Admittedly, this does not solve the potentially problematic issue that new subjects of international law or subjects of international law starting to become active in a certain field are faced with existing CIL norms concerning a given CIL regime. However, even though the question of "fairness" might pop up here, it is not the task of CIL (or not exclusively at least) to provide for a fair solution in this regard. How could that be? CIL emerges via actors and thereby guides their relationship to each other. CIL is based on action. That is why it is rather limited in scope and content and – importantly here – regarding new actors. How could you behave with regard to something nonexistent? So, CIL as such is not able to respond to this demand for a "fair solution" independently of time. (Concerning a time-dependent status quo – depending on the notion and understanding of fairness – CIL does provide for a more or less fair solution to the extent that consensus might deliver such a solution.) Hence, we should rather praise consensus theory for clearly pointing towards a sensitive topic, namely how to bind new subjects of international law (with regard to their existence or potential to act in a certain field). Yet it is not the purpose of a theory to solve this issue. That is left to practice. The theory did its job if we were clearly directed towards the problem.

Thus, this is no weakness of consensus theory aiming to explain or give a framework to the emergence of CIL. Rather the opposite is true: It is the strength of consensus theory to point out these difficulties and some of its impossibilities. It is the great merit of consensus theory to clearly highlight that on the one hand we cannot demand too much from CIL (quite a likely fallacy for many lawyers and scholars), unless we completely abolish the concept as such and argue for what is often called a "modern" CIL emergence process with only one element driven by a higher reasoning and based on *opinio iuris* having its source in a (sometimes vague, sometimes undefined) transcendental authority[489] (likely to be as fallible as wishful thinking or to represent the interests of strong individual actors).[490] On the other hand, it is exactly this

489 See supra Section 8.2.5.2.

490 See Lepard (n 407) Customary International Law as a Dynamic Process 80: "Perhaps the biggest problem with *opinio juris*-focused theories is that they risk treating *lex ferenda* as *lex lata*. They are particularly prone to 'wishful thinking'. Without the confirmation of consistent state practice, there is at least the possibility that states do not actually endorse the norm as a legal norm that should or does bind them; it may be merely aspirational."

insight that puts us in a position to come up with criteria to make CIL more tangible in practice. Against this background Conclusion 3, concretizing the "assessment of evidence for the two constituent elements," of the draft conclusions of the ILC is very welcome (even though – as argued here – such criteria belong to the normative framework on how CIL emerges rather than how it is identified).[491] In accordance with this attempt to concretize CIL, even more precise criteria could help to make CIL emergence more tangible and, hence, its identification less uncertain.

In a nutshell, the formula I wish to propose to make CIL norm emergence more tangible must focus on potentially active subjects of international law.[492] Thus, the point of departure is the number of subjects of international law that are potentially able to act in a certain field (be it the sea, space or a narrower field). The decisive point when CIL emerged and can be identified as such (that is, the point when the offer is accepted) is thus a specific fraction of this number. This should – ideally – be subject to empirical research on case law in order to obtain an educated estimate, which has proven to be a rather effective number. However, for the sake of the argument, I wish to offer here a guess, namely that 25 percent as a minimum number of potentially active subjects of international law shall suffice. Whether this guess is educated remains to be seen. Thus a CIL norm emerges if and when, out of twenty potentially active subjects of international law, we have the consistent practice of five subjects of international law supported by *opinio iuris*.

[491] Draft Conclusions on Identification of Customary International Law (n 368) Conclusion 3.

[492] Note that this is different from the concept of "States whose interests are specially affected" (see supra n 439 and accompanying text) to which the ICJ referred in *North Sea Continental Shelf Cases (Federal Republic of Germany v Denmark; Federal Republic of Germany v Netherlands)* Judgment ICJ Reports [1969] 3 para 74. Specially affected States are thought to have a particular weight in terms of considering a certain practice within a "short period of time," nonetheless "both extensive and virtually uniform." Yet, of course, both concepts might overlap as a specially affected State is within the category of potentially active states. However, vice versa this is not always the case. See for specially affected States also Mark E Villiger, *Customary International Law and Treaties: A Study of Their Interactions and Interrelations with Special Consideration of the 1969 Vienna Convention on the Law of Treaties* (Martinus Nijhoff 1985) 13 ff, with reference in nn 112 and 113 to Max Sørensen, "Principes de droit international public" (1960) 101 Recueil des Cours III 1–254 (40); and Verdross (n 418) 650, suggesting to focus on those States which had "the opportunity to engage in such practice." However, such a limitation might also prove to be too narrow unless the opportunity to engage is defined quite broadly, for instance including also articulating an interest in a certain practice (compare the example of Villiger, 14, that "'unaffected' States, such as landlocked countries, have taken a keen interest in the rules on the exploitation of the EEZ or the continental shelf"). Thus, I wish to propose as an even slightly broader framework for potentially active states.

Whether they are new as such or are engaging in a new field, new subjects of international law are thus confronted with an existing CIL regime guiding the world or a specific field of it. This is just being realistic. In the past, exploring new territories was also rewarded with the possibility of acquiring the unexplored area. First come, first served. Or in slightly different words, offering rewards to explorers is a principle we still refer to rather often in many different legal and nonlegal ways. Why not with regard to CIL?

Yet this has to be seen as a guiding standard rather than an absolute number or formula.[493] Thus, exceptions might be possible. Furthermore, the figure of 25 percent of potentially active subjects of international law clearly depends on what we perceive as an active subject of international law and, more specifically, what the attribute "potentially" refers to. This is also subject to a clear definition to make CIL more tangible. Similarly, this understanding could help in terms of who shall be charged with the question of proof. The framework of this meta-norm is consensus theory. But we have also learned that we as lawyers have a special need to work with concepts and definitions and so we have to draw lines. The meta-norm is the place where we should start drawing them. The ILC and its reports might wish to take up this issue and suggest even more specific guidelines than the vague formula proposed here in order to give CIL more (legal) certainty, thereby highlighting and emphasizing an important element in the genesis of CIL that is often overlooked but is of utmost importance, namely trust. Nevertheless, this section aims to highlight a framework within which we could make CIL more tangible and remains quite abstract in its proposals as the main focus of this book lies somewhere else.

8.2.6 *Conclusion on the Understanding of CIL*

Whether the chicken preceded the egg or the egg the chicken is a tricky question. Even though there have been prolific and fascinating attempts by philosophers and other scientists to give an answer, its charm of masterly illustrating circularity remains. I took up this conundrum in order to provide arguments for resurrecting or, even better, reanimating consensus theory as the theoretical framework for CIL and its normative foundations, which is essential to subsequently discuss the relationship between CIL and the EU legal order. The point, in a nutshell, is that the commonly perceived flaws of consensus theory are actually not its flaws, but rather its great strengths: Consensus theory,

[493] See eg Petersen (n 448), highlighting different variations requiring different solutions.

as the argument goes, shows the basic logic and problems or potential conflicts of CIL and its normative foundations more clearly than other theories. Dealing with a formal source of international law creates problems without a clearly regulated written framework defining which processes and to what extent actions and convictions are decisive. Thus, acknowledging the evolutionary process of CIL emergence makes clear, first, that Article 38 ICJ Statute is an important reference point. It is the cornerstone for identifying CIL. Yet it is only a touchstone for how CIL emerges, which still remains vague, relying as it does on a positive, but unwritten, formal source of international law that can only be reconstructed by using the illustration of Article 38 ICJ Statute. Second, seeing the situation more clearly, it is a different question from how we should deal with the virulent problems of such a vague lawmaking process. What are the consequences of such a seemingly self-perpetuating evolutionary process of CIL emergence? Just as the question of the chicken and the egg becomes easier to solve if we know whether we are talking about any old egg, a chicken egg or an egg containing a chicken without having been laid by a chicken, consensus theory tells us that we need to focus on some (somewhat arbitrary) lines in order to be able to have a common understanding of when a CIL rule is emerging and when it becomes a valid and binding norm.

Thus, instead of waiting too long, as the Montagues and Capulets did in Shakespeare's *Romeo and Juliet* (to use another example of self-perpetuating circles), continuing their feud by blaming each other for having started it, until tragically suffering the loss of their beloved, we should rather aim to understand that we need to step out of this self-perpetuating circle. Consensus theory forces us to define more precisely what an offer is in the realm of CIL and when it is accepted. This section has proposed a formula stating how much state practice and *opinio iuris* is needed for the emergence of a CIL norm and what framework might be suitable as a guideline. Clearly, this is debatable. The need to make CIL more tangible in the correct place, namely with reference to its meta-norm, which is to be reconstructed according to the definition of the result (the definition of how to identify CIL according to Article 38 ICJ Statute), is less debatable. Only the future will tell whether we "shall be pardon'd, and some punished" or whether the following will still apply to us:

> [F]or never was a story of more woe
> Than this of Juliet and her Romeo?[494]

[494] See William Shakespeare, *Romeo and Juliet* (John Danter 1597) lines 331–332.

8.2.7 *Customary International Law and the EU Legal Order*

In order to find out how the EU contributes to the creation of CIL and how the effect of CIL unfolds for and within the EU legal order, we have to look at "by whom" and "in which subject matters" the EU contributes to the formation of CIL.[495] In addition, because of the special nature of CIL, we have to look at how CIL – with or without the contribution of the EU – becomes binding for the EU. Again, as has been stated for international agreements, this book will not deal with the EU competence regime but will simply assume that if the EU acts on the international plane, it has competence in the subject matter concerned.

8.2.7.1 The Competence to Contribute to the Emergence of a CIL Norm

Due to the nature of CIL as described above, we do not find regulations for the formation of CIL norms analogous to those for the competence to confirm the will of the EU to be bound by an international agreement. CIL norms are, in their origin, typically informal. Establishing a formal competence would therefore also be of limited effect. Yet we do have to find some sort of legal guidance for the contribution of the formation of CIL norms by organs of the EU.[496] For the EU, such guidance can be found in Article 3 (5) TEU and Article 21 (1) and (2) (b) TEU. While the former generally prescribes the fashion of the relations of the EU to the "wider world," which arguably also imply its capacity to contribute to the formation of CIL,[497] the latter specifies that the principles "which have inspired" the creation of the EU shall also guide the Union's actions "on the international scene" by seeking "to develop relations and build partnerships with third countries, and international, regional or global organisations which share the principles referred to in the first subparagraph."[498] In contrast to the expression of the will to be bound by

[495] For the general possibility that international organizations can – within the limits of their competences – contribute to the formation of CIL, see Michael Wood, Special Rapporteur of the ILC, *Third Report on Identification of Customary International Law*, 67th Session, General Assembly, UN Doc A/CN.4/682 para 77, who explicitly refers to the example of the EU.

[496] See also Damm (n 183) 134, who adds that this is also of importance for applying the content of the CIL norm within the EU legal order.

[497] See in this regard Matthias Ruffert, "Artikel 3 EUV" in Christian Calliess and Matthias Ruffert (eds) *EUV/AEUV* (CH Beck 6th ed 2022) para 18, pointing to the EU's capacity as an actor to participate in the formation and implementation of international law.

[498] See Wolfram Cremer, "Artikel 21 EUV" in Christian Calliess and Matthias Ruffert (eds) *EUV/AEUV* (CH Beck 6th ed 2022) para 5, emphasizing the commitment of the EU and the Member States to making these standards more effective "worldwide."

an international agreement, we do not have clearly established competences for concrete organs. It is, therefore, of importance to see which acts count as state practice and which count as *opinio iuris* on the international plane in order to determine which acts of EU organs might contribute to the formation of CIL norms. Potentially, certain acts might be attributable to the EU even though there is no clear competence for every single case of state practice or *opinio iuris*.[499] This, however, is not a specific defect in the EU's competences on the formation of CIL. The nature of CIL implies a vague competence ascription, which is also the case for States.[500] While this is problematic in terms of democratic legitimacy, the typical content of CIL norms, which is far more relevant for the relation between the typical subjects of international law, cushions this negative effect to some extent.[501]

Generally speaking, the contribution of the EU to the formation of CIL is imaginable for once by extending the addressees of CIL norms from States to international organizations, or by the formation of CIL norms directly by international organizations.[502] While the former category is more general in nature and concerns – for instance, CIL norms about the conclusion of

499 See Damm (n 183) 148, stating that a visible act, which counts as state practice and carries *opinio iuris*, is enough in this regard.

500 See Kirchmair (n 422) 197–199 concerning Austria.

501 See Kuijper (n 232) 105, holding that "the problem of democratic legitimacy ... is stronger than in the case of international agreements, since parliaments normally have had nothing to do with the gestation to these rules of international law." He goes on to emphasize that "[t]his democratic deficit of customary international law is all the more acute, as customary international law is nowadays often derived by international courts and tribunals from declarations, UN resolutions and multilateral conventions that are insufficiently ratified (also by the EU) to have entered into force." See Pieter Jan Kuijper, "Customary International Law, Decisions of International Organisations and other Techniques for Ensuring Respect for International Legal Rules in European Community Law" in Jan Wouters, André Nollkaemper and Erika de Wet (eds) *The Europeanisation of International Law* (TMC Asser Press 2008) 87–106 (87–88), criticizing that the lack of provisions in EU primary law on the "adoption and reception of general international law" and the consequence of "judge-made" law in this regard "raises delicate issues of democratic legitimization."

502 See Kirsten Schmalenbach, "Die Europäische Union und das universelle Völkerrecht" in Werner Schroeder (ed) *Europarecht als Mehrebenensystem* (Nomos/facultas 2008) 67–88 (69). For the argument that international organizations in general and the EU in particular are capable of contributing to CIL, see Jed Odermatt, "The European Union's Role in the Making and Confirmation of Customary International Law" in Fernando Lusa Bordin, Andreas Th Müller and Francisco Pascual-Vives (eds) *The European Union and Customary International Law* (Cambridge University Press 2022) 66–94 (68 ff concerning IOs in general and 80 ff concerning the EU).

international agreements – the latter relates more to the common (institutional) law of international organizations.[503]

8.2.7.2 The Binding (Direct) Effect of CIL within the EU Legal Order: Simple Applicability and Direct Applicability

With regard to international agreements we do not have a clear and precise statement on their binding (direct) effect within EU law. However, Article 216 (2) TFEU provides some guidance. Concerning CIL we do not have any such guidance at all.[504] Despite this "silence of the treaties,"[505] we can safely assume that CIL, as much as general international law, including general principles of international law and unilateral declarations, is binding for the EU. Moreover, Article 3 (5) TEU obliges the EU to contribute to the "strict observance and the development of international law."[506] This is hard to imagine if the EU would not consider itself to be bound by international law.[507] Finally, the CJEU confirmed in *Racke* that the EU "must respect international law in the exercise of its powers." Therefore, the EU is "required to comply with the rules of customary international law" and thus EU legal acts also have to be in compliance with CIL.[508] This finding was confirmed in subsequent case law[509] and later on also with reference to Article 3 (5)

[503] For an example of the latter category, Henry G Schermers and Niels M Blokker, *International Institutional Law* (Brill 6th ed 2018) § 1339, mention, for instance, the abstention of permanent members of the security council which now constitutes approval.

[504] Astrid Epiney, "Die Bindung der EU an das allgemeine Völkerrecht" in Walter Obwexer (ed) *Die Europäische Union im Völkerrecht* (2012) Europarecht-Beiheft 25–48 (26).

[505] Paul Gragl, "The Silence of the Treaties: General International Law and the European Union" (2014) 47 German Yearbook of International Law 375–410.

[506] For an analysis in this regard, see Eleftheria Neframi, "Customary International Law and the European Union from the Perspective of Article 3(5) TEU" in Piet Eeckhout and Manuel López-Escudero (eds) *The European Union's External Action in Times of Crisis* (Hart 2016) 205–222.

[507] See eg Eeckhout (n 180) 383, holding that "[i]t is plain that the EU cannot take part in international treaty-making without respecting and applying general international law."

[508] Case C-162/96 *Racke v Hauptzollamt Mainz* ECLI:EU:C:1998:293 paras 27, 29, and 45. See Cases C-286/90 *Anklagemindigheden v Poulsen and Diva Navigation* ECLI:EU:C:1992:453 para 9, where the CJEU already stipulated that the EU "must respect international law in the exercise of its powers"; as well as C-405/92 *Etablissements Armand Mondiet SA v Armement Islais SARL* ECLI:EU:C:1993:906 para 13 on "customary international maritime law." See also T-115/94 *Opel Austria v Council* ECLI:EU:T:1997:3 para 90, referring to the "principle of good faith" as recognized by the ICJ as CIL, which, therefore, is also binding on the EU. For more details on case law, see Eeckhout (n 180) 384–393.

[509] Case C-308/06 *The Queen, on the application of International Association of Independent Tanker Owners (Intertanko) and Others v Secretary of State for Transport* ECLI:EU:C:2008:312 para 51–52, albeit with a negative finding in this concrete case. On the CIL

TEU.[510] The CJEU stipulated that "it should be examined first whether the principles ... are recognised as forming part of customary international law." If this question is answered in the affirmative, "it should, secondly, then be determined whether and to what extent they may be relied upon by individuals to call into question the validity of an act of the European Union."[511] This is very important because here the CJEU is confirming, correctly, that CIL norms might be individualizing in the sense defined here[512] and thereby provide rights for individuals. Moreover, advocate general Jacobs confirmed that individualizing CIL norms do exist.[513]

Importantly, advocate general Jacobs also expressed that it would not be advisable to analogously apply the case law concerning the direct effect of international agreements.[514] Yet he established that "the particular rules in issue must contain clear and precise obligations."[515] In contrast, advocate general Kokott held that the case law on the direct effect of international agreements would be transferable to CIL.[516] In her eyes, there is no "good reason why individuals should be permitted to rely on principles of customary international law under less stringent conditions than when relying on

nature of some provisions of the VCLT, see Case C-386/08 *Firma Brita GmbH v Hauptzollamt Hamburg-Hafen* ECLI:EU:C:2010:91 para 42; C-364/10 *Hungary v Slovak Republic* ECLI:EU:C:2012:630 para 44; see also T-231/04 *Greece v Commission* ECLI:EU:T:2007:9 paras 85–87 on the CIL nature of the "principle of good faith"; as well as C-203/07 P *Greece v Commission* ECLI:EU:C:2008:606 para 64.

510 Case C-366/10 *Air Transport Association of America and others v Secretary of State for Energy and Climate Change* ECLI:EU:C:2011:864 para 101. Cf Wouters, Odermatt and Ramopoulos (n 328) 252.

511 Case C-366/10 *Air Transport Association of America and others v Secretary of State for Energy and Climate Change* ECLI:EU:C:2011:864 para 102.

512 See Section 6.4.3.

513 Opinion of advocate general Jacobs, C-162/96 *Racke v Hauptzollamt Mainz* ECLI:EU:C:1997:582 para 84: "It may be noted in passing that there may be other types of rules of customary international law which do intend to confer rights on individuals, for example rules of international humanitarian law." See, however, Martines (n 266) 143–144, who holds that "[a]lthough international customary law could be self-executing (clear and precise), for its intrinsic characteristics this source of law does not create subjective rights that can be invoked before a national court." Yet the only reason she provides to support this bold claim is that human rights norms with the nature of CIL would only be addressed to states, leaving private parties "as beneficiaries" (Martines n 266 144 n 42).

514 Opinion of advocate general Jacobs, C-162/96 *Racke v Hauptzollamt Mainz* ECLI:EU:C:1997:582 para 83.

515 Opinion of advocate general Jacobs, C-162/96 *Racke v Hauptzollamt Mainz* ECLI:EU:C:1997:582 para 85.

516 Opinion of advocate general Kokott, C-366/10 *Air Transport Association of America and others v Secretary of State for Energy and Climate Change* ECLI:EU:C:2011:637 para 110 ff.

international agreements";[517] "many principles of customary international law have now been codified in international agreements" and therefore "[i]t would make no sense if, when individuals are relying on one and the same principle of international law, different conditions were to apply according to whether it was being relied on as a principle of customary international law or as a principle under an international agreement."[518] On these grounds, advocate general Kokott submitted that, in order to be deemed directly effective, CIL norms, too, must be binding on the EU and the "nature and broad logic of that particular principle of customary international law must not preclude such a review of validity; the principle in question must also appear, as regards its content, to be unconditional and sufficiently precise."[519] This, however, meets with strong criticism pointing to the unique nature of CIL norms, which are obviously different from international agreements.[520] Otherwise we would not speak of different types of sources of international law. This influences the way in which CIL norms can be determined and hence the request that those norms have to pass the same test of "unconditionality" and being "sufficiently precise." Finally, the argument that many CIL norms are to be found in multilateral agreements blurs the difference between international agreements and CIL. Only if a specific norm is binding for the EU because it is regulated in an international agreement and simultaneously in CIL and their content is identical might it be the case that a double standard would arise. Still, if the CIL norm in this case is found to be more demanding in the sense that it is directly effective (but the norm in the international agreement is not), then there is no good reason to limit the CIL norm because of the norm contained in the international agreement. As a result, we are left with a self-standing test of directly effective and individualizing CIL norms that have to follow the standards of international law.[521] Any limitation by a test introduced on the EU level would potentially

[517] Opinion of advocate general Kokott, C-366/10 *Air Transport Association of America and others v Secretary of State for Energy and Climate Change* ECLI:EU:C:2011:637 para 111.

[518] Opinion of advocate general Kokott, C-366/10 *Air Transport Association of America and others v Secretary of State for Energy and Climate Change* ECLI:EU:C:2011:637 para 112.

[519] Opinion of advocate general Kokott, C-366/10 *Air Transport Association of America and others v Secretary of State for Energy and Climate Change* ECLI:EU:C:2011:637 para 113.

[520] Damm (n 183) 217.

[521] See also Geert De Baere and Cedric Ryngaert, The ECJ's Judgment in Air Transport Association of America and the International Legal Context (2013) 18 (3) European Foreign Affairs Review 389–409 (397): "if principles of customary international law appear, as regards their content, to be unconditional and sufficiently precise, individuals should be able to rely on them in the same way as with respect to international agreements and a full review should take place."

limit the international norm. In turn, the argument was made by the Court that due to the fact that "a principle of customary international law does not have the same degree of precision as a provision of an international agreement,"[522] the review of secondary EU law and its compliance with CIL would be limited to "whether, in adopting the act in question, the institutions of the European Union made manifest errors of assessment concerning the conditions for applying those principles."[523] The introduction of the necessity of a manifest violation was established by advocate general Jacobs analogous to the restrictions of the direct effectivity of international agreements.[524] However, if, as a consequence of such an approach, the standard of review of secondary EU law is even more restrictive than with international agreements, this is also to be criticized.[525] While it is understandable for pragmatic reasons that the identification of CIL norms is difficult and their concrete content is sometimes hard to establish, this is not a sufficient reason to restrict the compliance of EU law with CIL for manifest errors only.[526] In fact, any violation of a CIL norm constitutes a violation of international law and, as such, is to be avoided or corrected. Hence, the manifest error test must be reinterpreted.[527] If this is to describe a vague realm of CIL formation and identification, where it is simply not clear whether a CIL norm provides for a specific regulation or not, then of course this needs to be taken into account by the Court as well.[528] The same holds true when the "purpose and nature" test of international agreements is analogously applied to CIL norms.[529]

[522] C-366/10 *Air Transport Association of America and others v Secretary of State for Energy and Climate Change* ECLI:EU:C:2011:864 para 110.

[523] C-366/10 *Air Transport Association of America and others v Secretary of State for Energy and Climate Change* ECLI:EU:C:2011:864 para 110. For this manifest error test, see C-162/96 *Racke v Hauptzollamt Mainz* ECLI:EU:C:1998:293 para 52.

[524] Opinion of advocate general Jacobs, C-162/96 *Racke v Hauptzollamt Mainz* ECLI:EU:C:1997:582 para 71.

[525] Wouters, Odermatt and Ramopoulos (n 328) 265.

[526] See also De Baere and Ryngaert (n 521) 398, who make the point – concerning the *Air Transport Association of America* judgment of the CJEU – that "from the affected individual's point of view" they "should arguably be allowed to invoke *all* rules of jurisdiction under customary law in domestic/EU proceedings" independently of a potential distinction between "*validity* and *scope*" [emphasis original].

[527] See also Nicolas A J Croquet, "The Import of International Customary Law into the EU Legal Order: The Adequacy of a Direct Effect Analysis" (2013) 15 Cambridge Yearbook of European Legal Studies 47–81.

[528] As somehow implied by Eeckhout (n 180) 394, when holding that "[t]he Court is also right to limit review to manifest violations."

[529] See again Eeckhout (n 180) 395, arguing that rules of international humanitarian law, which were mentioned as an example by advocate general Jacobs, "should have direct effect, and it

In addition, if the following passage in the judgment of the CJEU is interpreted as a restriction on the application of CIL within the EU legal order, then this is also a problematic restriction. The CJEU stipulated that

> [t]he principles of customary international law mentioned in paragraph 103 of the present judgment may be relied upon by an individual for the purpose of the Court's examination of the validity of an act of the European Union in so far as, first, those principles are capable of calling into question the competence of the European Union to adopt that act . . . and, second, the act in question is liable to affect rights which the individual derives from European Union law or to create obligations under European Union law in his regard.[530]

Hence, for the CJEU, CIL norms must not provide for subjective rights in the strict sense in order to tentatively identify a potential violation by an EU law norm.[531]

8.2.7.3 Which Rank for CIL in the EU Legal Order?

Also concerning CIL, the CJEU holds that CIL norms take precedence over EU secondary law.[532] Whether they take also precedence over EU primary law has not yet been explicitly settled by the CJEU. Some indication can be drawn

should be possible for private parties to challenge EU acts which violate such rules, if that were ever the case."

[530] Case C-366/10 *Air Transport Association of America and others v Secretary of State for Energy and Climate Change* ECLI:EU:C:2011:864 para 107. Labeling this test "rigorous . . . but also realistic," see Eileen Denza, "International Aviation and the EU Carbon Trading Scheme: Comment on the Air Transport Association of America Case" (2012) 37 (3) European Law Review 314–326 (323).

[531] See also Theodore Konstadinides, "When in Europe: Customary International Law and EU Competences in the Sphere of External Action" (2012) 13 (11) German Law Journal 1177–1201 (1195). For further discussion, see also Damm (n 183) 218–224.

[532] See eg C-162/96 *Racke v Hauptzollamt Mainz* ECLI:EU:C:1998:293 para 27, 29, and 45; C-308/06 *The Queen, on the application of International Association of Independent Tanker Owners (Intertanko) and Others v Secretary of State for Transport* ECLI:EU:C:2008:312; C-366/10 *Air Transport Association of America and others v Secretary of State for Energy and Climate Change* ECLI:EU:C:2011:864. For the literature, see, for instance, Damm (n 183) 186; Koutrakos (n 209) 228, holding that "the status of customary international law does not differ from that of international agreements binding on the Union"; Alessandra Gianelli, "Customary International Law in the European Union" in Enzo Cannizzaro, Paolo Palchetti and Ramses A Wessel (eds) *International Law as Law of the European Union* (Martinus Nijhoff 2012) 93–110 (105–106); Allan Rosas, "The European Court of Justice and Public International Law" in Jan Wouters, André Nollkaemper and Erika de Wet (eds) *The Europeanisation of International Law* (TMC Asser Press 2008) 71–85 (80); Peters (n 226) 37–38.

from the case *Hungary v Slovak Republic*, where the CJEU was ready to accept a constraint on the fundamental freedom of movement according to Article 21 TEU for Heads of States following "customary rules of general international law and those of multilateral agreements" giving Heads of States "a particular status in international relations."[533] From this follows, "[a]ccordingly, the fact that a Union citizen performs the duties of a Head of State is such as to justify a limitation, based on international law, on the exercise of the right of free movement conferred on that person by Article 21 TFEU."[534] However, the Court explicitly leaves open whether this follows from the CIL norm or the international agreement mentioned. Moreover, voices in the literature do not hesitate to capture this potentially groundbreaking finding by mentioning the autonomous EU legal order finally ranking CIL between primary and secondary EU law.[535]

8.2.7.4 Identification and Interpretation of CIL by the CJEU

The identification and interpretation of CIL is an arduous task.[536] Therefore, it is understandable that the CJEU is quite wary of conducting an analysis along the two-element approach in order to identify CIL norms.[537] Rather, the shortcut of a reference to ICJ case law or multilateral treaties is taken and sometimes also the analysis of the advocate general provides help.[538] Yet it seems that the CJEU limits the application of CIL norms to what it labeled "fundamental rules of customary international law."[539] This restriction, however, was not maintained in subsequent case law.

533 Case C-364/10 *Hungary v Slovak Republic* ECLI:EU:C:2012:630 para 46.

534 Case C-364/10 *Hungary v Slovak Republic* ECLI:EU:C:2012:630 para 51. This is particularly interesting as advocate general Bot has offered another way out when stating that "[t]he Treaties being silent on the question of access for Heads of State to the territory of Member States, I conclude that this is a competence reserved for the Member States." See opinion of advocate general Bot, C-364/10 *Hungary v Slovak Republic* ECLI:EU:C:2012:124 para 51. See Sonja Boelaert, "Minding the Gap: Reflections on the Relationship between EU Law and Public International Law in the Light of the Judgment in Case C-364/10 Hungary v Slovakia" in Jenő Czuczai and Frederik Naert (eds) *The EU as a Global Actor – Bridging Legal Theory and Practice: Liber Amicorum in Honour of Ricardo Gosalbo Bono* (Brill Nijhoff 2017) 217–240.

535 See only Damm (n 183) 189–191 with further references. For further discussion see Section 8.2.8.

536 This is a standard narrative, which can also be deduced from Section 8.2.7.

537 See Rosas (n 532) 85, on the reluctant attitude of the CJEU to "develop" or "advance" international law by identifying and interpreting CIL independently.

538 Damm (n 183) 206–207 with further references.

539 Case C-162/96 *Racke v Hauptzollamt Mainz* ECLI:EU:C:1998:293 para 48.

8.2.7.5 Changing CIL and Objecting to It

The very essence of CIL implies that changes to present norms of CIL can sometimes imply a violation of a CIL norm. According to the understanding described above this can also be captured by the logic of offer and acceptance. Depending on whether the suggested change is accepted by a relevant number of subjects of international law, a new CIL norm emerges. This, as much as persistent objection, is embraced by the general logic of CIL. Therefore, this also applies to the EU organs that carry out actions relevant for the formation of CIL. However, Article 21 (1) TEU asks that neither instrument is used in an abusive manner.[540]

8.2.8 *Interpretation and Critique of the Prevailing Doctrine*

Also concerning CIL and its relationship to the EU legal order, we meet positions that basically assume that theoretical choices do not make practical differences. For instance, it has been argued that whether we emphasize the autonomy of the EU legal order or whether we concede that the EU legal order is part of the international legal order, both perspectives would result in two "competing" legal orders.[541] This is simply untrue. If the autonomy of the EU legal order is upheld strictly, this is a straightforward dualist position. International law might only have an effect on and in EU law after its creation at the international level depending solely on the autonomous decision of the EU legal order, which might always be revoked unilaterally. This would obviously be different if the EU legal order were part of the international legal order as it would have to respect the rules of the international legal order to amend international law and its effect within the EU legal order.

Another major standard narrative is that international CIL norms also need to be perceived as an EU legal act in order to be valid within the EU legal order.[542] Public international law in general and CIL in particular would not demand bindingness within the EU legal order but only ask to be respected. In the case of a violation, state responsibility would apply.[543] According to this approach, it depends on the legal order concerned to determine how

[540] In this sense also Damm (n 183) 154–155.

[541] Damm (n 183) 171.

[542] Damm (n 183) 171 with further references; see also Schmalenbach (n 502) 70, speaking of the "Rechtssatzgemeinschaft" of CIL norms within the EU legal order.

[543] See eg Luzius Wildhaber and Stephan Breitenmoser, "The Relationship between Customary International Law and Municipal Law in Western European Countries" (1988) 48 Heidelberg Journal of International Law 163–207 (164); Peters (n 226) 20.

international law in general and CIL in particular is received in that legal order.[544] Apparently EU primary law does not provide for a particular regulation in this regard. Nevertheless, instead of using Article 3 (5) or Article 21 (1) TEU as a guiding standard, an appeal is made to Article 216 (2) TFEU and the narrative that has been described concerning the relation between international agreements and the EU legal order.[545] An unwritten rule that determines the incorporation of CIL is supposed to exist and do this job.[546] Even though the CJEU postulated none of this, the Court is supposed to have taken this approach too.[547] From this follows that if a CIL norm has been formed and is binding on the EU, which means that it has relevant content for the EU (and is not, for instance, a simple interstate norm), this CIL norm becomes an "integrated part" of the EU legal order.[548] Yet, to be fair, if this "integration" or "incorporation" of CIL into the EU legal order does not render international law EU law, and thereby subjugates it to a unilateral derogation by the EU (and not another CIL norm of international law), this is merely a formality. However, if this is not the case, such a submission clearly faces criticism. Beyond that, most scholars do emphasize that the EU as a subject of international law is obliged to comply with international law, and thus also CIL, in its external relations.[549] However, this is usually followed by the qualification that an international law would only demand state

544 Paradigmatically, Werner Schroeder, "Customary International Law in the European Union Legal System: Reception, Rank, Application and Interpretation" in Fernando Lusa Bordin, Andreas Th Müller and Francisco Pascual-Vives (eds) *The European Union and Customary International Law* (Cambridge University Press 2022) 177–209 (177): "Because international law does not regulate its own legal status in domestic legal orders, every subject of international law has the right to determine the classification of CIL in its own legal system" (despite not using the terms "incorporation" or "transformation" in order to avoid giving the misleading impression that EU law were monistic or dualistic (177–178)).

545 Damm (n 183) 173.

546 Peters (n 226) 21: "An unwritten Community rule which corresponds to article 228 (7) foresees the incorporation of customary international law into the Community legal order"; see also Damm (n 183) 181 with further references.

547 Damm (n 183) 181.

548 Damm (n 183) 184, 197, declaring that the universal CIL norms are incorporated into EU law on the basis of an unwritten order which constitutes them as a legal source of EU law including valid legal norms; Schmalenbach (n 502) 70; Gianelli (n 532) 94. However, see also Rosas (n 532) 80, who does not seem to imply that CIL norms become EU law when supposing that the "case-law appears to be based on the idea that customary international law, too, is directly applicable in the EU legal order (which is not to say that it would have direct effect), in accordance with a monistic approach."

549 Gianelli (n 532) 93; Astrid Epiney, "Zur Stellung des Völkerrechts in der EU. Zugleich Besprechung von EuGH, EuZW 1998, 572 – Hermès und EuGH, EuZW 1998, 964 – Racke" (1999) 9 Europäische Zeitschrift für Wirtschaftsrecht 5–11 (6).

responsibility as a consequence of a potential breach. Moreover, an internal effect of CIL would always be left to the legal order concerned.

From this incorporation follows the necessity of determining the rank of CIL within the norm hierarchy of the EU legal order. While the Court, like most of the literature, assumes a superior rank of CIL regarding secondary EU law, some voices even go so far as to declare CIL superior to EU primary law as well.[550] This does not, however, imply the option of referring questions to the CJEU pertaining only to an interpretation of CIL.[551] Other voices want to limit this approach in the sense that constitutional principles of EU primary law would prevail but other EU primary law would have to be balanced against the conflicting CIL norms.[552] Generally, it is of course a very welcome strategy if both legal orders seek a conciliatory solution when a norm conflict arises. Article 3 (5) TEU, for instance, is suggested as a driving factor for EU organs to influence CIL formation and the amendment process in case of conflict.[553] CIL, in turn, provides for this possibility as its unique nature and amendment procedure must allow for some potential violations of existing CIL norms in order to amend them. However, "[a]ffirming the transformation of international law commitments into EU law obligations does not confirm a dualist approach to international law. Monist or dualist concerns do not affect the receptive function of Article 216 TFEU, not addressed in Article 3 (5) TEU."[554]

[550] Epiney (n 504) 39 with reference to Christine Kaddous, "L'arrêt France c. Commission de 1994 (accord concurrence) et le contrôle de la 'légalité' des accords externes en vertu de l'art. 173 CE: la difficile réconciliation de l'orthodoxie communautaire avec l'orthodoxie internationale" (1996) Cahiers de droit européen 613–633 (620 ff). Epiney (n 504 39), however, rejects this approach, arguing with the support of Article 19 (1) TEU and with reference to Article 218 (11) TFEU. See Peters (n 226) 35–36, who, however, clearly distinguishes between an international law and an EU law perspective, which in her view is based on the premise that "no rule of international law tells the subjects of international law which hierarchical status they should attribute to international law *within* their internal legal system" [emphasis original].

[551] Epiney (n 549) 8–9.

[552] Gianelli (n 532) 105–106.

[553] Wessel (n 331) 31 ff. Qualifying this as a "neo-monist conception," Cannizzaro (n 331) 50–51.

[554] Neframi (n 506) 212, who continues her statement in the following: "That provision confirms by contrast the subordination of the Union to international law, including customary international law, which produces its effects as such, by regulating the exercise of the Union's competences without being the result of such an exercise. In that sense, customary international law is placed beyond conventional obligations. It is not a question of hierarchy, but of a difference in the nature of the interaction, the place of customary law expressing merely the interaction of legal orders, while conventional obligations are the result of an exercise of external competences."

8.2.9 *Interpretation According to Consent-Based Monism*

Similarly to the interpretation of international agreements in Section 8.2.7, CIL remains what it is on the EU or national level: international law and thereby a consensus of the larger, international circle. The prevailing doctrine regarding the relationship between international and EU law interprets relevant EU norms as so-called reception norms or incorporation norms of international law, which aim to integrate international law and thus also CIL in the EU legal order. This thinking is ingrained in most scholars writing on the relationship between international and Member State or national law. "Reception norms" are thought to be elementary for any relationship between international and EU or national law and, in the case of CIL and its effect within the EU legal order, they are genuinely missed; unwritten, invisible "reception norms" are invented or read into other provisions such as Articles 3 (5) and 21 (1) TEU, or analogies to Article 216 (2) TFEU are drawn. Consent-based monism provides relief from this painstaking process of identifying and interpreting adequate reception norms. Consent-based monism simply questions the need for the integration of CIL into the EU legal order and all the legal consequences that stem from the confrontation of international norms with the hierarchy of the EU or national legal order. In contrast to reception norms, consent-based monism only looks for norms of *authorization*, which equip EU organs with the competence to contribute to the formation of international law and, in this case, CIL. The validity and bindingness of CIL thus remains with the international circle.[555] Only with a dualistic thinking do we need an incorporation of the international norm. However, as we have seen, this is outdated.[556]

As a consequence, we must not associate a certain rank with the CIL norm within the EU legal order because according to consent-based monism we simply refer to the CIL norm as international law, which might, or might not, also have a direct effect within the EU legal order. What is important is to find out whether the CIL norm is simply applicable, directly applicable or individualizing.[557] While simply applicable rules, also called interstate laws,

[555] Apparently without referring to consent-based monism but with a similar conclusion already, Epiney (n 549) 6; Epiney (n 504) 31, speaking of CIL within the EU as a legal source as such maintaining its international law character.

[556] See Section 1.1.

[557] See Section 6.4 above. On the direct effect of CIL in particular, see eg Andreas Th Müller, "The Direct Effect of Customary International Law: The 'Treaty Analogy' and Its Limits" in Fernando Lusa Bordin, Andreas Th Müller and Francisco Pascual-Vives (eds) *The European Union and Customary International Law* (Cambridge University Press 2022) 210–239, pleading for a uniform application of testing the direct effect of CIL, treaties and EU law acts.

leave it up to the discretion of the national legal order – in our case the EU legal order – to decide how to implement these rules "domestically," directly applicable rules – in other words, self-executing rules – give no discretion to the EU legal order in deciding how to implement them. Directly applicable norms take effect within the EU legal order without any EU Act, except for ratification or CIL formation. Individualizing rules are those international rules that directly address individuals, without the need for an EU organ to enforce or apply them. They bind or grant rights to individuals directly without the EU intervening (again, except for the making of these international norms). Depending on the category, different legal conflicts and consequences might arise. This is not a question of the hierarchy of EU legal norms, however, because different norms from the international and the EU circle must not be blended.

Moreover, with regard to the contribution of EU organs to the formation of CIL within the realm of norms of authorization, it is important to define the limits of this authorization: One limit on the authorization to contribute to the formation of CIL is the external competences of the EU. Yet, concerning this limitation, it must again be borne in mind that the international legal order concerning CIL does not accept any subsequent protests once the CIL norm is established. The persistent objector rule allows for an intervention in the process of a new CIL norm emerging. However, once a CIL norm is established, a potential conflict with a norm from the EU legal order is no good justification for the violation of the CIL norm.

Conclusion

In this book I have argued that consent-based monism provides a theoretical foundation for finding a decisive source in a norm conflict situation. It is, however, important to emphasize that I do not intend to offer an absolute and invariable solution which fits any norm conflict arising between overlapping international, EU and national legal orders. In short, consent-based monism aims to give consideration to the complex and divergent structures of international, EU and national law. Consequently, it is important not to limit the scope of the theoretical background of the relationship between international and EU or domestic law by pressing international, EU and national law into the straitjacket of a certain, predetermined legal consequence. The relationship between international, EU and national law does not follow a uniform (political) order – for example, one legal order – yet, nowadays, international, EU and national law are not completely alien to each other.[1] This is in sharp contrast to old theories such as dualism and Kelsenian monism, which are considered to be incapable of coping with the major developments in international, EU and national legal orders since the inception of these grand but old theories. This important difference sets consent-based monism apart from still prevailing theories such as Kelsenian monism and dualism. While the predominant stream of global legal pluralism is also restricted when answering the question behind this book as it does not offer a satisfactory normative account, global constitutionalism suffers from major shortcomings too. Global constitutionalism presumes too many substantial values for the

[1] See Part II above. For criticism of the territoriality of both dualistic and monistic theory, see Catherine Brölmann, "Deterritorialization in International Law: Moving Away from the Divide between National and International Law" in Janne E Nijman and André Nollkaemper (eds) *New Perspectives on the Divide between National and International Law* (Oxford University Press 2007) 84–108.

envisaged common normative denominator to be a helpful concept for the relationship between international, EU and national law. While global constitutionalism cannot carry the "burden of universality," with constitutional pluralism we are likely to end up in a "constitutional stalemate." In contrast to global legal pluralism, which was said to provide for a descriptively but not prescriptively satisfying account, consent-based monism offers a theoretical explanation of the structural relationship between international, EU and national law.

Consent-based monism aims to reconceptualize the current debates that are based on Kelsenian monism, dualism, pluralism and constitutionalism. In the process, I also aim to avoid the pitfalls of global legal pluralism and global constitutionalism concerning their appropriateness for norm conflict solutions between international, EU and national legal orders. The goal is to answer the question of whether it is within the competence of EU (or Member State) law – or not – to determine the effect and validity of international or EU law within the domestic (constitutional) legal order and that of international law within the EU legal order. In a nutshell, the underlying understanding of law for the purpose of this book is defined as two or more individuals creating one single binding consensus. Consent-based monism is thus based on prelegal assumptions, namely the principles *pacta sunt servanda* and *pacta tertiis*. These prelegal principles are considered fundamental for all agreed consensuses. If a legal rule has been created by a consensus, unilateral abrogation is no longer possible. The rule of the larger circle always prevails over the rule of the smaller circle (A and B), if – and this is important – all members of the smaller circle are also members of the larger circle. In other words, the smaller circle is absorbed by the larger circle.

Thus, the approach advanced in this book offers a theory-based argument for why and how norm conflicts between different legal orders should be solved based on a common denominator that is found in the concept of consent-based monism. By most accounts of legal pluralism, such a norm conflict is either said to be solved by nonlegal means or to be lacking theoretical or ideological reasoning as to why and how it should be solved in a *common* way.[2] Consent-based monism, however, also starts from the debate on the constitutionalization of international or EU law, for example. This debate is concerned with substantial value questions at the international or European level. This book is not interested in such an endeavor. It simply focuses on the structural relationship between international, EU and Member

[2] See Chapter 2 above.

State law. Thus, consent-based monism is not interested in analyzing, criticizing or even changing the content of law or dealing with such daring ventures as ideologically based arguments on how international law or EU law should be. Consent-based monism offers a theory-based argument that if, for instance, an international (or EU) norm is directly applicable, it has to be applied by authorities applying EU (or national) law. While the constitutionalization debate is – along the lines of this example – about whether some norms or principles are so important that they are (or should be) directly applicable and thus self-executing in the EU or national legal orders, this book provides for a theoretical argument that, if they are directly applicable, they should be applied by organs applying EU and national law. It is important to point out that consent-based monism is not interested in value debates or how a society or international, EU or national law should be and therefore consent-based monism does not provide any arguments in this regard either.

Concerning the relationship between the EU and Member State law, consent-based monism does not hold – as a classic monistic perspective according to Hans Kelsen or Alfred Verdross has to assume – that Member State law is delegated from EU law. Nor does consent-based monism assume that in order to conceive of both EU law and Member State law as law, it is – again as Kelsenian monism advances – logically necessary to conceive of them as a unitary legal order. More importantly, consent-based monism does not share the doubtful epistemological basis of Kelsenian monism. Instead, this book's theory only states that once a consensus has been reached at the level of a larger circle (which, in our case here, is EU law), then it must not be derogated unilaterally by a smaller circle. Similarly, as consent-based monism does not say anything about the question of which political system or which specific norm might be just, nor does it say whether there should or should not be something like a core that is resistant to integration. This theory is neutral towards the content. It does, however, say that once a consensus has been agreed at the level of a larger circle, this consensus must not be violated unilaterally by a smaller circle. Therefore, it is crucial to analyze the norms of the smaller circle, which *authorized* and *authorizes* consensus formation in the larger circle. An "integration-resistant core," on the one hand, must not violate any consensus that has been obtained at the level of the larger EU circle. On the other hand, the larger circle must not autonomously add competences without the authorization of all the smaller circles. This also holds true for the interpretation of the scope of application of EU law, which, essentially, must be reflected in the consensus of the larger circle. Hence, this book does not provide a blanket solution finally answering the grand question as to who has the final say by simply giving the final say in any question to, for example, international law, the EU or the Member States. Rather, it aims at providing some guidance by indicating how we can know who has the final say. Answering this question might be a painstaking task in some cases. This is unavoidable for such dynamic processes as European integration, with its many constitution-like dynamics. Clearly revealing where we have to look does, arguably, inform the solution of norm conflicts with EU law significantly.

The theory advanced in this book does not claim to be a magical solution to all imaginable situations. Concerning the relationship between international and EU law, consent-based monism understands EU or national constitutional provisions to be rules of *authorization* for competent EU or national authorities to consent to an international norm (instead of the common understanding of reception, integration or incorporation norms). Once consent is given and the international norm has become binding, the norm is valid and effective in the EU or national legal order as well. To understand the effect of the international norm within the EU or national legal order, it is important to analyze the aim and content of the international (or EU) norm. An incontrovertible aspect of the theory is that a consensus agreed by the larger, international circle may not be infringed on or subsequently disrespected by any state or other subject of international law involved in the creation of such consensus (the smaller, EU or national circle). This means, as illustrated above, that the larger circle prevails over the consensus of the smaller circle. However, how this "primacy" is enforced – or even whether it is given its full effect – depends solely on the norms of international (or EU) law and their aims and content.

What I have done in this book might be disappointing, given the grand question of who has the final say. However, I am convinced that the slight turn proposed by asking the complex and enormously important question (how can we know who has the final say – international, EU or national law?) a little bit differently represents significant progress. This comes with the insight that we cannot answer the "final say" question in an easy and uniform way across the world and across jurisdictions. The vast array of massively diverging theories and doctrines on the table is proof of that. Yet I believe that it is important at least to attempt a sort of reconciliation between all these different approaches. Giving up on providing a normative framework for solving norm conflicts with EU law – at either international or national level – is not a convincing option. Consent-based monism is one such attempt to reconcile the various approaches out there in order to provide a normative framework for a norm conflict solution with the focus on a structural analysis.

Bibliography

Abi-Saab, Georges, "The Newly Independent States and International Law: An Outline" (1962) 8 (2) Howard Law Journal 97–121.

Ackermann, Thomas E A, "Editorial Comments: Clear and Present Danger: Poland, the Rule of Law & Primacy" (2021) 58 (6) Common Market Law Review 1635–1648.

Akehurst, Michael, "Custom as a Source of International Law" (1974–1975) 47 British Yearbook of International Law 1–53.

Albert, Hans, *Konstruktion und Kritik. Aufsätze zur Philosophie des kritischen Rationalismus* (Hoffmann und Campe 2nd ed 1975).

Traktat über rationale Praxis (Mohr Siebeck 1978).

Kritik der reinen Erkenntnislehre (Mohr Siebeck 1987).

Alexy, Robert, "Diskurstheorie und Menschenrechte" in Robert Alexy (ed) *Recht, Vernunft, Diskurs: Studien zur Rechtsphilosophie* (Suhrkamp 1995) 127–164.

"Hans Kelsens Begriff des relativen Apriori" in Robert Alexy et al (eds) *Neukantianismus und Rechtsphilosophie* (Nomos 2002) 179–202.

Alfano, Mark and Loeb, Don, "Experimental Moral Philosophy" in Edward N Zalta (ed) *Stanford Encyclopedia of Philosophy* (August 9, 2018), available at http://plato.stanford.edu/entries/experimental-moral/ [last accessed February 1, 2023].

Allen, Meredith, Perry, Conrad and Kaufman, Jordy, "Toddlers Prefer to Help Familiar People" (2018) 174 Psychology 90–102.

Als, Heidelise, "Social Interaction: Dynamic Matrix for Developing Behavioral Organization" in Ina Č Užgiris (ed) *Social Interaction during Infancy: New Directions for Child Development Vol 4* (Jossey-Bass 1979) 21–39.

Alvarez-Jiménez, Alberto, "Methods for the Identification of Customary International Law in the International Court of Justice's New Millennium Jurisprudence: 2000–2009" (2011) 60 (3) International & Comparative Law Quarterly 681–712.

Ameriks, Karl and Höffe, Otfried (eds), *Kant's Moral and Legal Philosophy* (Cambridge University Press 2009).

Amrhein-Hofmann, Christine, *Monismus und Dualismus in den Völkerrechtslehren* (Duncker & Humblot 2003).

Andersen, Hans Christian, "Des Kaisers neue Kleider" in Hans Christian Andersen (ed) *Gesammelte Märchen I* (Carl B Lorck 1847) 37–44.

Anderson, Benedict, *Imagined Communities: Reflections on the Origins and Spread of Nationalism* (Verso 6th ed 2006).

Anzilotti, Dionisio, *Corso di diritto internazionale* (Athenaeum 2nd ed 1912).

Lehrbuch des Völkerrechts (German translation by Cornelia Bruns and Karl Schmid W de Gruyter 1929).

Apel, Karl-Otto, "Das Apriori der Kommunikationsgemeinschaft und die Grundlagen der Ethik: Zum Problem einer rationalen Begründung der Ethik im Zeitalter der Wissenschaft" in Karl-Otto Apel (ed) *Transformation der Philosophie Vol 2* (Suhrkamp 1973) 358–435.

Understanding and Explanation: A Transcendental-Pragmatic Perspective (translated by Georgia Warnke MIT Press 1984 [*Die Erklären-Verstehen-Kontroverse in Transzendental-Pragmatischer Sicht* Suhrkamp 1979]).

Apperly, Ian and Butterfill, Stephen, "Do Humans Have Two Systems to Track Beliefs and Belief-Like States?" (2009) 116 Psychological Review 953–970.

Aquinas, Thomas, *Truth* (translated and edited by R W Schmidt, Robert W Mulligan and James V McGlynn Hackett 1994 [*Quaestiones disputatae de Veritate* 1256–1259]).

Arangio-Ruiz, Gaetano, "International Law and Interindividual Law" in Janne Nijman and André Nollkaemper (eds) *New Perspectives on the Divide between National and International Law* (Oxford University Press 2007) 15–51.

Ashford, Elizabeth and Mulgan, Tim, "Contractualism" in Edward N Zalta (ed) *Stanford Encyclopedia of Philosophy* (April 20, 2018), available at https://plato.stanford.edu/entries/contractualism/ [last accessed February 1, 2023].

Atwood, George E and Stolorow, Robert D, *Structures of Subjectivity: Explorations in Psychoanalytic Phenomenology and Contextualism* (Routledge 2nd ed 2014).

Auby, Jean-Bernard, "Globalisation et droit public" in *Gouverner, administrer, juger. Mélanges en l'honneur de Jean Waline* (Dalloz 2002) 135–157.

Audit, Robert, *Epistemology. A Contemporary Introduction to the Theory of Knowledge* (Routledge 3rd ed 2011).

Aust, Anthony, *Modern Treaty Law and Practice* (Cambridge University Press 3rd ed 2013).

Avbelj, Matej, "Supremacy or Primacy of EU Law: (Why) Does It Matter?" (2011) 17 (6) European Law Journal 744–763.

Avbelj, Matej, Fontanelli, Filippo and Martinico, Giuseppe (eds), *Kadi on Trial: A Multifaceted Analysis of the Kadi Trial* (Routledge 2014).

Awad, Edmond et al, "The Moral Machine Experiment" (2018) 563 (7729) Nature 59–64.

et al, "Universals and Variations in Moral Decisions Made in 42 Countries by 70,000 Participants" (2020) 117 (5) Proceedings of the National Academy of Sciences 2332–2337.

Baquero Cruz, Julio, "The Legacy of the Maastricht-Urteil and the Pluralist Movement" (2008) 14 (4) European Law Journal 389–422.

Barents, René, *The Autonomy of Community Law* (Kluwer 2004).

Basdevant, Jules, "Règles générales du droit de la paix" (1936) 58 Recueil des Cours IV 471–715.

Bast, Jürgen, "Autonomy in Decline? A Commentary on Rimšēvičs and ECB v Latvia" (May 13, 2019) Verfassungsblog, available at https://verfassungsblog.de/

autonomy-in-decline-a-commentary-on-rimsevics-and-ecb-v-latvia/ [last accessed February 1, 2023].

Bateson, Mary C, "The Epigenesis of Conversational Interaction: A Personal Account of Research Development" in Margaret Bullowa (ed) *Before Speech: The Beginning of Human Communication* (Cambridge University Press 1979) 63–77.

Batson, C Daniel et al, "Immorality from Empathy-Induced Altruism: When Compassion and Justice Conflict" (1995) 68 Journal of Personality and Social Psychology 1042–1054.

Bauerschmidt, Jonathan, *Die Rechtsperson der Europäischen Union im Wandel. Auswirkungen differenzierter Integration durch Völkerrecht auf die Europäische Union* (Mohr Siebeck 2019).

Baumann, Peter, *Erkenntnistheorie* (J B Metzler 3rd ed 2015).

Baumgartner, Gerhard, "Der Rang des Gemeinschaftsrechts im Stufenbau der Rechtsordnung" (2000) 8 Journal für Rechtspolitik 84–99.

Bäumler, Jelena, "Vom Vertragstext zum Inkrafttreten: Das Vertragsschlussverfahren im Mehrebenensystem am Beispiel CETA" (2016) 51 (6) Europarecht 607–631.

Bazalgette, Peter, *The Empathy Instinct: How to Create a More Civil Society* (John Murray 2017).

Beckermann, Ansgar, "Die realistischen Voraussetzungen der Konsenstheorie von J. Habermas" (1972) 3 (1) Zeitschrift für allgemeine Wissenschaftstheorie 63–80.

Bederman, David J, *Globalization and International Law* (Palgrave 2008).

Benhabib, Seyla, "In the Shadow of Aristotle and Hegel: Communicative Ethics and Current Controversies in Practical Philosophy" (1989) 21 (1) Philosophical Forum 1–31.

"Another Universalism: On the Unity and Diversity of Human Rights" (2007) 81 Proceedings and Addresses of the American Philosophical Association 7–32.

Benson, Peter, "François Gény's Doctrine of Customary Law" (1982) 20 Canadian Yearbook of International Law 267–281.

Bergmann, Andreas, *Zur Souveränitätskonzeption des Europäischen Gerichtshofs* (Mohr Siebeck 2018).

Bergmann, Gustav, "Strawson's Ontology" (1960) 57 (19) Journal of Philosophy 601–622.

Logic and Reality (University of Wisconsin Press 1964).

Berka, Walter, *Verfassungsrecht* (Verlag Österreich 6th ed 2016).

Berman, Paul S, "Global Legal Pluralism" (2007) 80 Southern California Law Review 1155–1238.

Global Legal Pluralism: A Jurisprudence of Law beyond Borders (Oxford University Press 2012).

"How Legal Pluralism Is and Is Not Distinct from Liberalism: A Response to Alexis Galán and Dennis Patterson" (2013) 11 (3) International Journal of Constitutional Law 801–808.

"Jurisgenerative Constitutionalism: Procedural Principles for Managing Global Legal Pluralism" (2013) 20 (2) Indiana Journal of Global Legal Studies 665–695.

"From Legal Pluralism to Global Legal Pluralism" in Richard Nobles and David Schiff (eds) *Law, Society and Community Socio-Legal Essays in Honour of Roger Cotterrell* (Ashgate 2014) 255–271.

"The Evolution of Global Legal Pluralism" in Roger Cotterrell and Maksymilian Del Mar (eds) *Authority in Transnational Legal Theory: Theorising across Disciplines* (Edward Elgar 2016) 151–188.

Besson, Samantha, "Whose Constitution(s)? International Law, Constitutionalism, and Democracy" in Jeffrey L Dunhoff and Joel P Trachtman (eds) *Ruling the World? Constitutionalism, International Law, and Global Governance* (Cambridge University Press 2009) 381–408.

Betlem, Gerrit and Nollkaemper, André, "Giving Effect to Public International Law and European Community Law before Domestic Courts. A Comparative Analysis of the Practice of Consistent Interpretation" (2003) 14 (3) European Journal of International Law 569–589.

Bianchi, Andrea, "Assessing the Effectiveness of the UN Security Council's Anti-Terrorism Measures: The Quest for Legitimacy and Cohesion" (2017) 17 (5) European Journal of International Law 881–919.

Biernat, Stanisław et al, "Statement of Retired Judges of the Polish Constitutional Tribunal" (October 11, 2021) Verfassungsblog, available at https://verfassungsblog.de/statement-of-retired-judges-of-the-polish-constitutional-tribunal [last accessed February 1, 2023].

Bigman, Yochanan E and Gray, Kurt, "Life and Death Decisions of Autonomous Vehicles" (2020) 549 (7797) Nature E1–E2.

Binder, Christina, *Die Grenzen der Vertragstreue im Völkerrecht* (Springer 2012).

Bird-Pollan, Stefan, "Rawls: Construction and Justification" (2009) 1 (2) Public Reason 12–30.

Bix, Brian, *Jurisprudence: Theory and Context* (Sweet & Maxwell 5th ed 2009).

Blaffer Hrdy, Sarah, *Mothers and Others* (Harvard University Press 2009).

Blecha, Jörg, "Mit Anstand auf die Welt" (December 16, 2006) Spiegel, available at www.spiegel.de/spiegel/print/d-49929836.html [last accessed February 1, 2023].

Blecha, Jörg and von Bredow, Rafaela, "Die Grammatik des Guten" (July 30, 2007) Spiegel, available at www.spiegel.de/spiegel/print/d-52417856.html [last accessed February 1, 2023].

Bleckmann, Albert, "Die Position des Völkerrechts im inneren Rechtsraum der EG. Monismus oder Dualismus der Rechtsordnungen?" (1975) 18 German Yearbook of International Law 300–319.

Blokker, Paul, "Populist Counter-Constitutionalism, Conservatism, and Legal Fundamentalism" (2019) 15 (3) European Constitutional Law Review 519–543.

Bloom, Paul and Jarudi, Izzat, "The Chomsky of Morality? A View of Morality as the Product of an Innate Mental Faculty – Rather Like Language" (2006) 443 Nature 909–910.

Bloom, Paul, *Against Empathy: The Case for Rational Compassion* (Ecco 2016).

Bobić, Ana, *The Jurisprudence of Constitutional Conflict in the European Union* (Oxford University Press 2022).

Boelaert, Sonja, "Minding the Gap: Reflections on the Relationship between EU Law and Public International Law in the Light of the Judgment in Case C-364/10 Hungary v Slovakia" in Jenő Czuczai and Frederik Naert (eds) *The EU as a Global Actor – Bridging Legal Theory and Practice: Liber Amicorum in Honour of Ricardo Gosalbo Bono* (Brill Nijhoff 2017) 217–240.

Bogdanowicz, Piotr and Taborowski, Maciej, "How to Save a Supreme Court in a Rule of Law Crisis: The Polish Experience" (2020) 16 (2) European Constitutional Law Review 306–327.

Bohman, James and Rehg, William, "Jürgen Habermas" in Edward N Zalta (ed) *Stanford Encyclopedia of Philosophy* (August 4, 2014), available at https://plato.stanford.edu/entries/habermas/ [last accessed February 1, 2023].

Bonelli, Matteo, "The Taricco Saga and the Consolidation of Judicial Dialogue in the European Union: CJEU, C-105/14 Ivo Taricco and Others, ECLI:EU:C:2015:555; and C-42/17 M.A.S., M.B., ECLI:EU:C:2017:936 Italian Constitutional Court, Order no. 24/2017" (2018) 25 (3) Maastricht Journal of European and Comparative Law 357–373.

Bonnefon, Jean-François, Rahwan, Iyad and Shariff, Azim, "The Social Dilemma of Autonomous Vehicles" (2016) 352 (6293) Science 1573–1576.

Bostrom, Nick, "Are You Living in a Computer Simulation?" (2003) 53 (211) Philosophical Quarterly 243–255.

Bradley, Kieran, "Investor–State Dispute Tribunals Established under EU International Agreements: Opinion 1/17 (EU-Canada CETA)" in Graham Butler and Ramses A Wessel (eds) *EU External Relations Law. The Cases in Context* (Hart 2022) 959–969.

Bråten, Stein and Trevarthen, Colwyn, "Prologue. From Infant Intersubjectivity and Participant Movements to Simulation and Conversation in Cultural Common Sense" in Stein Bråten (ed) *On Being Moved: From Mirror Neurons to Empathy* (John Benjamins North America 2007) 21–34.

Brazelton, T Berry, "Evidence of Communication During Neonatal Behavioural Assessment" in Margaret Bullowa (ed) *Before Speech: The Beginning of Human Communication* (Cambridge University Press 1979) 79–88.

Brazelton, T Berry and Nuget, J Kevin, *The Neonatal Behavioral Assessment Scale* (Mac Keith Press 1995).

Breuer, Hubertus, "Das Moral-Gen: Ist das Gute im Menschen angeboren? Wissenschafter meinen: ja" (March 31, 2007) Profil, available at www.profil.at/home/das-moral-gen-ist-gute-menschen-wissenschafter-169043 [last accessed February 1, 2023].

Breuer, Marten, "Wider das Recht auf Vergessen … des Bundesverfassungsgerichts!" (December 2, 2019) Verfassungsblog, available at https://verfassungsblog.de/wider-das-recht-auf-vergessen-des-bundesverfassungsgerichts/ [last accessed February 1, 2023].

Brierly, John L, *The Law of Nations* (Oxford University Press 1963).

Broad, Kevin D, Curley, James P and Keverne, Eric B, "Mother–Infant Bonding and the Evolution of Mammalian Social Relationships" (2006) 361 (1476) Philosophical Transactions of the Royal Society B 2199–2214.

Brockmöller, Annette, Kirste, Stephan and Neumann, Ulfrid (eds), *Wert und Wahrheit in der Rechtswissenschaft ARSP Beiheft* 145 (Franz Steiner 2015).

Brodherr, Anke, *Alfred Verdross' Theorie des gemäßigten Monismus* (Herbert Utz 2004).

Brölmann, Catherine, "Deterritorialization in International Law: Moving Away from the Divide between National and International Law" in Janne E. Nijman and André Nollkaemper (eds) *New Perspectives on the Divide between National and International Law* (Oxford University Press 2007) 84–108.

Buckle, Stephen, *Natural Law and the Theory of Property* (Oxford Clarendon Press 1991).
Budras, Corinna, "EZB hätte kooperativer sein müssen" *Frankfurter Allgemeine Zeitung* June 29, 2020.
Buergenthal, Thomas, "Self-Executing and Non-Self-Executing Treaties in National and International Law" (1992) 235 Recueil des Cours Vol IV 303–400.
Bulygin, Eugenio, "Das Problem der Geltung bei Kelsen" in Stanley L Paulson and Michael Stolleis (eds) *Hans Kelsen – Staatsrechtslehrer und Rechtstheoretiker des 20. Jahrhunderts* (Mohr Siebeck 2004) 80–95.
Burchardt, Dana, *Die Rangfrage im europäischen Normenverbund. Theoretische Grundlagen und dogmatische Grundzüge des Verhältnisses von Unionsrecht und nationalem Recht* (Mohr Siebeck 2015).
"Die Ausübung der Identitätskontrolle durch das Bundesverfassungsgericht – Zugleich Besprechung des Beschlusses 2 BvR 2735/14 des BVerfG vom 15.12.2015 (‚Solange III'/'Europäischer Haftbefehl II')" (2016) 76 Heidelberg Journal of International Law 527–551.
"Belittling the Primacy of EU Law in Taricco II" (December 7, 2017) Verfassungsblog, available at https://verfassungsblog.de/belittling-the-primacy-of-eu-law-in-taricco-ii/ [last accessed February 1, 2023].
"The Relationship between the Law of the European Union and the Law of Its Member States – A Norm-Based Conceptual Framework" (2019) 15 (1) European Constitutional Law Review 73–103.
Burgorgue-Larsen, Laurence, "La mobilisation de la Charte des droits fondamentaux de l'Union européenne par les juridictions constitutionnelles" (2019) Titre VII (2) De l'intégration des ordres juridiques: droit constitutionnel et droit de l'Union européenne 31–40.
Burke-White, William W, "International Legal Pluralism" (2005) 25 (4) Michigan Journal of International Law 963–979.
Bußjäger, Peter, *Homogenität und Differenz: Zur Theorie der Aufgabenverteilung zwischen Bund und Ländern in Österreich* (Braumüller 2006).
Bußjäger, Peter and Heißl, Gregor, "Nationaler Souveränitätsanspruch versus autonome Rechtsordnung? Integrationsschranken im Spannungsverhältnis zur Vorrangjudikatur" (2008) 34 (8) Österreichische Juristenzeitung 307–315.
"Folgerungen aus dem Lissabonurteil des Bundesverfassungsgerichts" (2010) 132 (5) Juristische Blätter 273–283.
Butler, Graham, *Constitutional Law of the EU's Common Foreign and Security Policy: Competence and Institutions in External Relations* (Hart 2019).
Buttelmann, David, Carpenter, Malinda and Tomasello, Michael, "Eighteen-Month-Old Infants Show False Belief Understanding in an Active Helping Paradigm" (2009) 112 (2) Cognition 337–342.
Buttelmann, David et al, "Eighteen-Month-Olds Understand False Beliefs in an Unexpected-Contents Task" (2014) 119 Journal of Experimental Child Psychology 120–126.
et al, "Great Apes Distinguish True from False Beliefs in an Interactive Helping Task" (2017) 12 (4) PLoS ONE.
Byers, Michael, *Custom, Power and the Power of Rules: International Relations and Customary International Law* (Cambridge University Press 1999).

Çalı, Başak, *The Authority of International Law: Obedience, Respect, and Rebuttal* (Oxford University Press 2015).

Calliess, Christian and van der Schyff, Gerhard, *Constitutional Identity in a Europe of Multilevel Constitutionalism* (Cambridge University Press 2019).

Cannizzaro, Enzo, "The Neo-Monism of the European Legal Order" in Enzo Cannizzaro, Paolo Palchetti and Ramses A Wessel (eds) *International Law as Law of the European Union* (Martinus Nijhoff 2012) 35–58.

Capps, John, "The Pragmatic Theory of Truth" in Edward N Zalta (ed) *Stanford Encyclopedia of Philosophy* (March 21, 2019), available at https://plato.stanford.edu/entries/truth-pragmatic/ [last accessed February 1, 2023].

Carpenter, Malinda and Liebal, Kristin, "Joint Attention, Communication, and Knowing Together in Infancy" in Axel Seemann (ed) *Joint Attention: New Developments in Psychology, Philosophy of Mind, and Social Neuroscience* (MIT Press 2011) 159–181.

Cartabia, Marta, "The Italian Constitutional Court and the Relationship between the Italian Legal System and the European Community" (1990) 12 Michigan International Law Journal 173–203.

Cassese, Antonio, *International Law* (Oxford University Press 2nd ed 2005).

Castoriadis, Cornelius, "The Logic of Magmas and the Question of Autonomy" in Cornelius Castoriadis, *The Castoriadis Reader* (translated and edited by David A Curtis Oxford University Press 1997) 290–318.

Charney, Jonathan Ian, "The Persistent Objector Rule and the Development of Customary International Law" (1985) 56 British Yearbook of International Law 1–24.

"Universal International Law" (1993) 87 (4) American Journal of International Law 529–551.

Cheng, Bin, "United Nations Resolutions on Outer Space: 'Instant' Customary International Law?" (1965) 5 Indian Journal of International Law 23–48.

Cheng, Yawei et al, "Love Hurts: An fMRI Study" (2010) 51 (2) Neuro Image 923–929.

Chomsky, Noam, *Syntactic Structures* (Mouton 1957).

Aspects of the Theory of Syntax (MIT Press 1965).

Christoph Krenn, "Warum Unionsrecht Vorrang hat: Zur aktualisierten Begründung des Vorrangprinzips in den Urteilen *Euro Box Promotion* und *R.S.*"

Churchland, Patricia S, *Braintrust: What Neuroscience Tells Us about Morality* (Princeton University Press 2011) 18–19.

"The Neurobiological Platform for Moral Values" (2014) 151 Behaviour 283–296.

Claes, Monica, *The National Courts' Mandate in the European Constitution* (Hart 2006).

"National Identity: Trump Card or Up for Negotiation?" in Alejandro Saiz Arnaiz and Carina Alcoberro Llivina (eds) *National Constitutional Identity and European Integration* (Intersentia 2013) 109–139.

"The Primacy of EU Law in European and National Law" in Damian Chalmers and Anthony Arnull (eds) *The Oxford Handbook of European Union Law* (Oxford University Press 2015) 178–211.

Cloots, Elke, *National Identity in EU Law* (Oxford University Press 2015).

Cohen, Hermann, *Das Prinzip der Infinitesimal-Methode und seine Geschichte* (Dümmler 1883 [partially translated by Hermann Cohen, "'Introduction' to The Principle of the Infinitesimal Method and its History (1883)" in Sebastian

Luft (ed) *The Neo-Kantian Reader* (partially translated by David Hyder and Lydia Patton Routledge 2015)]).

Kants Theorie der Erfahrung (Dümmler 2nd ed 1885 [partially translated by David Hyder as "'The Synthetic Principles' from Kant's Theory of Experience (1885)" in Sebastian Luft (ed) *The Neo-Kantian Reader* (Routledge 2015) 107–116]).

"Biographisches Vorwort und Einleitung mit kritischem Nachtrag" in Friedrich Lange (ed) *Geschichte des Materialismus und Kritik seiner Bedeutung in der Gegenwart* (Baedeker 6th ed 1898) xv–lxxvi.

Logik der reinen Erkenntnis (Cassirer 3rd ed 1922).

Logik der reinen Erkenntnis (Georg Olms Hermann Cohen Werke Vol 6 I 4th ed 1977 [Bruno Cassirer 2nd ed 1914]).

System der Philosophie, Zweiter Teil: Ethik des reinen Willens (Georg Olms Hermann Cohen Werke Vol 7 II 5th ed 1981 [Bruno Cassirer 2nd ed 1907]).

Kants Theorie der Erfahrung (Georg Olms 1987 *Hermann Cohen Werke Vol 1 I.3* [Dümmler 1st ed 1871]).

Cohen, Jean L, *Globalization and Sovereignty. Rethinking Legality, Legitimacy, and Constitutionalism* (Cambridge University Press 2012).

Cohon, Rachel, "Hume's Moral Philosophy" in Edward N Zalta (ed) *Stanford Encyclopedia of Philosophy* (August 20, 2018), available at https://plato.stanford.edu/entries/hume-moral/ [last accessed February 1, 2023].

Constantinesco, Vlad and Simon, Denys, "Quelques problèmes des relations extérieures des Communautés Européennes" (1975) 11 Revue trimestrielle de droit européen 432–469.

Conway, Gerard, "Conflicts of Competence Norms in EU Law and the Legal Reasoning of the ECJ" (2010) 11 (9) German Law Journal 966–1005.

Correa-Chávez, Maricela and Roberts, Amy L D, "A Cultural Analysis Is Necessary in Understanding Intersubjectivity" (2012) 18 (1) Culture & Psychology 99–108.

Corten, Olivier and Klein, Pierre, "Are Agreements between States and Non-State Entities Rooted in the International Legal Order?" in Enzo Cannizzaro (ed) *The Law of Treaties beyond the Vienna Convention* (Oxford University Press 2011) 3–24.

Costa, Albert et al, "Your Morals Depend on Language" (2014) 9 (4) Public Library of Science ONE 1–7.

Cotterrell, Roger, *Law, Culture and Society: Legal Ideas in the Mirror of Social Theory* (Ashgate 2006).

"Does Global Legal Pluralism Need a Concept of Law?" in Upendra Baxi, Christopher McCrudden and Abdul Paliwala (eds) *Law's Ethical, Global and Theoretical Contexts – Essays in Honour of William Twining* (Cambridge University Press 2015) 303–319.

Cover, Robert M, "The Supreme Court, 1982 Term-Foreword: Nomos and Narrative" (1983) 97 (4) Harvard Law Review 4–68.

"Violence and the Word" (1986) 95 (8) Yale Law Journal 1601–1629.

Cowie, Fiona, "Innateness and Language" in Edward N Zalta (ed) *Stanford Encyclopedia of Philosophy* (January 16, 2008), available at http://plato.stanford.edu/entries/innateness-language/ [last accessed February 1, 2023].

Craig, Paul, *The Lisbon Treaty. Law, Politics and Treaty Reform* (Oxford University Press 2010).

"The ECJ and Ultra Vires Action: A Conceptual Analysis" (2011) 48 (2) Common Market Law Review 395–437.

"Constitutional Identity in the United Kingdom. An Evolving Concept" in Christian Calliess and Gerhard van der Schyff (eds) *Constitutional Identity in a Europe of Multilevel Constitutionalism* (Cambridge University Press 2019) 284–302.

Craig, Paul and de Búrca, Gráinne, *EU Law. Text, Cases, and Materials* (Oxford University Press 7th ed 2020).

Crawford, James, *Brownlie's Principles of Public International Law* (Oxford University Press 8th ed 2012).

Cremer, Wolfram, "Artikel 21 EUV" in Christian Calliess and Matthias Ruffert (eds) *EUV/AEUV* (CH Beck 6th ed 2022) 351–356.

Cremona, Marise, "External Relations and External Competence of the European Union" in Paul Craig and Graínne de Búrca (eds) *The Evolution of EU Law* (Oxford University Press 2nd ed 2011) 217–268.

(ed), *Structural Principles in EU External Relations Law* (Hart 2018).

Croquet, Nicolas AJ, "The Import of International Customary Law into the EU Legal Order: The Adequacy of a Direct Effect Analysis" (2013) 15 Cambridge Yearbook of European Legal Studies 47–81.

Csibra, Gergely, "Recognizing Communicative Intentions" (2010) 25 (2) Infancy, Mind and Language 141–168.

Csibra, Gergely and Gergely, György, "Natural Pedagogy" (2009) 13 (4) Trends in Cognitive Sciences 148–153.

Cudd, Ann and Eftekhari, Seena, "Contractarianism" in Edward N Zalta (ed) *Stanford Encyclopedia of Philosophy* (March 15, 2017), available at https://plato.stanford.edu/entries/contractarianism/ [last accessed February 1, 2023].

Curtin, Deirdre, "Official Secrets and the Negotiation of International Agreements: Is the EU Executive Unbound?" (2013) 50 (2) Common Market Law Review 423–457.

D'Amato, Anthony, *The Concept of Custom in International Law* (Cornell University Press 1971).

D'Aspremont, Jean, *Formalism and the Sources of International Law: A Theory of the Ascertainment of Legal Rules* (Oxford University Press 2011).

Dahm, Georg, *Völkerrecht Vol I* (De Gruyter 1958).

Damestoy, Manon and Levrat, Nicolas, "The Mixed Nature of the EU-Canada FTA. Between Competences Distribution and Democratic Legitimacy" in Nicolas Levrat et al (eds) *The EU and Its Member States' Joint Participation in International Agreements* (Hart 2022) 77–95.

Damm, Carolin, Die Europäische Union im universellen Völkergewohnheitsrecht (Mohr Siebeck 2016).

Damon, William, "Fair Distribution and Sharing: The Development of Positive Justice" in Bill Puka (ed) *Fundamental Research in Moral Development* (Garland Publishing 1994) 189–254.

Danilenko, Gennady M, "Application of Customary International Law to Municipal Law" in Grigory I Tunkin and Rüdiger Wolfrum (eds) *International and Municipal Law* (Duncker & Humblot 1988) 13–23.

"The Theory of Customary International Law" (1988) 31 German Yearbook of International Law 9–47.

Law-Making in the International Community (Brill 1993).
Dashwood, Alan, "EU Acts and Member State Acts in the Negotiation, Conclusion, and Implementation of International Agreements" in Marise Cremona and Claire Kilpatrick (eds) *EU Legal Acts. Challenges and Transformations* (Oxford University Press 2018) 189–249.
David, Marian, "The Correspondence Theory of Truth" in Edward N Zalta (ed) *Stanford Encyclopedia of Philosophy* (May 28, 2015), available at https://plato.stanford.edu/entries/truth-correspondence/ [last accessed February 1, 2023].
Davidson, Donald, *Inquiries into Truth and Interpretation* (Oxford University Press 1984).
"The Centrality of Truth" in Jaroslav Peregrin (ed) *Truth and Its Nature (If Any)* (Springer 1999) 105–115.
"The Folly of Trying to Define Truth" in Michael P Lynch (ed) *The Nature of Truth. Classic and Contemporary Perspectives* (MIT Press 2001) 623–640.
De Baere, Geert, *Constitutional Principles of EU External Relations* (Oxford University Press 2008).
De Baere, Geert and Koutrakos, Panos, "The Interactions between the Legislature and the Judiciary in EU External Relations" in Phil Syrpis (ed) *The Judiciary, the Legislature and the EU Internal Market* (Cambridge University Press 2012) 243–273.
De Baere, Geert and Ryngaert, Cedric, "The ECJ's Judgment in Air Transport Association of America and the International Legal Context" (2013) 18 (3) European Foreign Affairs Review 389–409.
De Baere, Geert and Van den Sanden, Tina, "Interinstitutional Gravity and Pirates of the Parliament on Stranger Tides: The Continued Constitutional Significance of the Choice of Legal Basis in Post-Lisbon External Action" (2016) 12 (1) European Constitutional Law Review 85–113.
De Búrca Gráinne, "The European Court of Justice and the International Legal Order after Kadi" (2010) 51 (1) Harvard International Law Journal 1–48.
"The Road Not Taken. The European Union as a Global Human Rights Actor" (2011) 105 (4) American Journal of International Law 649–693.
"The ECJ and the International Legal Order: A Re-Evaluation" in Graínne de Búrca and Joseph H H Weiler (eds) *The Worlds of European Constitutionalism* (Cambridge University Press 2012) 105–149.
"International Law before the Courts. The EU and the US Compared" (2015) 55 (3) Virginia Journal of International Law 685–728.
De Sousa Santos, Boaventura, *Toward a New Common Sense: Law, Science and Politics in the Paradigmatic Transition* (Routledge 1995).
De Waal, Frans, *The Age of Empathy: Nature's Lessons for a Kinder Society* (Crown/Archetype 2010).
De Witte, Bruno, "European Union Law: How Autonomous Is Its Legal Order?" (2010) 65 Zeitschrift für Öffentliches Recht 141–155.
"Direct Effect, Primacy and the Nature of the Legal Order" in Gráinne de Búrca and Paul Craig (eds) *The Evolution of EU Law* (Oxford University Press 2011) 323–362.
De Witte, Bruno and Martinelli, Thibault, "Treaties between EU Member States as Quasi-Instruments of EU Law" in Marise Cremona and Claire Kilpatrick (eds)

EU Legal Acts. Challenges and Transformations (Oxford University Press 2018) 157–188.

Debiec, Jacek and Sullivan, Regina Marie, "Intergenerational Transmission of Emotional Trauma through Amygdala-Dependent Mother-to-Infant Transfer of Specific Fear" (2014) 111 (33) Proceedings of the National Academy of Sciences of the United States of America 12222–12227.

Décencière-Ferrandière, André, "Considérations sur le Droit International dans ses Rapports avec le Droit de l'État" (1933) 40 (1) Revue Générale de Droit International Public 45–70.

Decety, Jean and Cowell, Jason M, "Friends or Foes: Is Empathy Necessary for Moral Behavior?" (2014) 9 (4) Perspectives on Psychological Science 525–537.

Deckert, Martina, "Recht und Wahrheit. Zum gegenwärtigen Stand der Diskussion" (1996) 82 (1) Archiv für Rechts- und Sozialphilosophie 43–54.

Dederer, Hans-Georg, "Die Grenzen des Vorrangs des Unionsrechts – zur Vereinheitlichung von Grundrechts-, Ultra-vires- und Identitätskontrolle" (2014) 69 (7) JuristenZeitung 313–322.

Delafield-Butt, Jonathan and Trevarthen, Colwyn, "Theories of the Development of Human Communication" in Paul Cobley and Peter J Schultz (eds) *Theories and Models of Communication* (Mouton De Gruyter 2013) 199–222.

Delbrück, Jost, "Begriff, Geltung u. Erscheinungsformen des Völkerrechts" in Georg Dahm et al (eds) *Völkerrecht Vol I/1* (De Gruyter 2nd ed 1989) 27.

"Das Individuum im Völkerrecht" in Georg Dahm et al (eds) *Völkerrecht Vol. I/2* (De Gruyter 2nd ed 2002) 259.

"Verbindlichkeit und Geltungsbereich der Verträge" in Georg Dahm et al (eds) *Völkerrecht Vol I/3* (De Gruyter 2nd ed 2002) 600.

Delgado Casteleiro, Andrés, *The International Responsibility of the European Union. From Competence to Normative Control* (Cambridge University Press 2018) 32–33.

Delhomme, Vincent and Larripa, Lucie, "C-416/17 Commission v France: Failure of a Member State to Fulfil its Obligations Article 267(3) TFEU" (November 22, 2018) European Law Blog, available at https://europeanlawblog.eu/2018/11/22/c-416-17-commission-v-france-failure-of-a-member-state-to-fulfil-its-obligations-under-article-2673-tfeu/ [last accessed February 1, 2023].

Delmas-Marty, Mireille, *Les forces imaginantes du droit (II) : Le pluralisme ordonné* (Seuil 2006).

Ordering Pluralism: A Conceptual Framework for Understanding the Transnational Legal World (translated by Naomi Norberg Hart 2009).

Denza, Eileen, "International Aviation and the EU Carbon Trading Scheme: Comment on the Air Transport Association of America Case" (2012) 37 (3) European Law Review 314–326.

"Placing the European Union in International Context: Legitimacy of the Case Law" in Maurice Adams et al (eds) *Judging Europe's Judges: The Legitimacy of the Case Law of the European Court of Justice* (Hart 2013) 175–196.

Descartes, René, *The Philosophical Writings of Descartes* (edited by John Cottingham, Robert Stoothoff and Dugald Murdoch Cambridge University Press 1984).

Dewey, John and Bentley, Arthur, *Knowing and the Known* (Beacon Press 1949).

Di Giovanni, George and Livieri, Paolo, "Friedrich Heinrich Jacobi" in Edward N Zalta (ed) *Stanford Encyclopedia of Philosophy* (December 6, 2018), available at https://plato.stanford.edu/entries/friedrich-jacobi/ [last accessed February 1, 2023].

Dias, Brian G and Ressler, Kerry J, "Parental Olfactory Experience Influences Behavior and Neural Structure in Subsequent Generations" (2014) 17 (1) Nature Neuroscience 89–98.

Dickson, Julie, "Towards a Theory of European Union Legal Systems" in Julie Dickson and Pavlos Eleftheriadis (eds) *Philosophical Foundations of European Union Law* (Oxford University Press 2012) 25–53.

Dietze, Jan et al, "Europa – Quo Vadis? Ein kritischer Kommentar zum EZB-Urteil des BverfG" (2020) 31 (12) Europäische Zeitschrift für Wirtschaftsrecht 525–530.

Diggelmann, Oliver and Altwicker, Tilmann, "Is There Something Like a Constitution of International Law? A Critical Analysis of the Debate on World Constitutionalism" (2008) 68 Heidelberg Journal of International Law 623–650.

Doore, Isaak I, *The Epistemological Foundations of Law* (Carolina Academic Press 2007).

Dörr, Oliver, "Art 31 and 32" in Oliver Dörr and Kirsten Schmalenbach (eds) *Vienna Convention on the Law of Treaties – A Commentary* (Springer 2nd ed 2018).

Dougan, Michael, "The Primacy of Union Law over Incompatible National Measures: Beyond Disapplication and towards a Remedy of Nullity" (2022) 59 (5) Common Market Law Review 1301–1332.

Dreier, Horst, *Rechtslehre, Staatssoziologie und Demokratietheorie bei Hans Kelsen* (Nomos 2nd ed 1990).

Dreier, Ralf, "Bemerkungen zur Theorie der Grundnorm" in Hans Kelsen-Institut (ed) *Die Reine Rechtslehre in wissenschaftlicher Diskussion* (Manz 1982) 38–46.

Drinóczi, Tímea, "Hungarian Constitutional Court: The Limits of EU Law in the Hungarian Legal System: Judgment of 5 December 2016, No 22/2016" (2017) 11 (1) Vienna Journal on International Constitutional Law 139–151.

Duguit, Léon, *Souveraineté et liberté* (Éditions La Mémoire du Droit 1922).

Duhigg, Charles, *The Power of Habit: Why We Do What We Do in Life and Business* (Random House 2012).

Dummett, Michael, *Frege: Philosophy of Language* (Harper & Row 1973).

Origins of Analytical Philosophy (Harvard University Press 1993).

Dunoff, Jeffrey L and Trachtman, Joel P, "A Functional Approach to International Constitutionalization" in Jeffrey L Dunoff and Joel P Trachtman (eds) *Ruling the World: Constitutionalism, International Law, and Global Governance* (Cambridge University Press 2009) 3–35.

Dupoux, Emmanuel and Jacob, Pierre, "Universal Moral Grammar: A Critical Appraisal" (2007) 11 (9) Trends in Cognitive Sciences 373–378.

Dupré, John, "Making Hay with Straw Men. Book Review of Pinker, Steven. The Blank Slate" (2003) American Scientist, available at www.researchgate.net/profile/John-Dupre-2/publication/272353765_Making_Hay_with_Straw_Men_Review_of_Steven_Pinker_The_Blank_Slate_The_Modern_Denial_of_Human_Nature/links/54e2883b0cf296663796aabc/Making-Hay-with-Straw-Men-Review-of-Steven-Pinker-The-Blank-Slate-The-Modern-Denial-of-Human-Nature?_tp=eyJjb250ZXh0Ijp7ImZpcnN0UGFnZSI6InB1YmxpY2F0aW9uIiwicGFnZSI6InB1YmxpY2F0aW9uIn19 [last accessed February 1, 2023].

Eagleman, David, *Incognito: The Secret Lives of the Brain* (Pantheon 2011).

Eckes, Christina, *EU Powers Under External Pressure. How the EU's External Actions Alter its Internal Structures* (Oxford University Press 2019).

"The Autonomy of the EU Legal Order" (2020) 4 (1) Europe and the World: A Law Review 1–19.

Eeckhout, Piet, "Case C-308/06 The Queen, on the Application of International Association of Independent Tanker Owners (Intertanko) and Others v Secretary of State for Transport, judgment of the Court of Justice, (Grand Chamber) of 3 June 2008" (2009) 46 (6) Common Market Law Review 2041–2057.

EU External Relations Law (Oxford University Press 2nd ed 2012).

"Human Rights and the Autonomy of EU Law: Pluralism or Integration?" (2013) 66 (1) Current Legal Problems 169–202.

"The Integration of Public International Law in EU Law: Analytical and Normative Questions" in Piet Eeckhout and Manuel López-Escudero (eds) *The European Union's External Action in Times of Crisis* (Hart 2016) 189–204.

Ehrlich, Eugen, *Fundamental Principles of Sociology of Law* (translated by Walter Lewis Moll Harvard University Press 1936 [*Grundlegung der Soziologie des Rechts* Duncker & Humblot 1913]).

Eleftheriadis, Pavlos, "Cosmopolitan Legitimacy" paper presented at the "Philosophical Foundations of Global Law" conference at the University of Cartagena, Colombia on August 25, 2016 (on file with the author).

Elias, Olufemi, "The Nature of the Subjective Element in Customary International Law" (1995) 44 (3) International and Comparative Law Quarterly 501–520.

Emde, Robert N et al, "The Moral Self of Infancy: Affective Core and Procedural Knowledge" (1991) 11 (3) Developmental Review 251–270.

Engisch, Karl, *Die Einheit der Rechtsordnung* (Winter 1935).

Einführung in das juristische Denken (Kohlhammer 7th ed 1977).

Epiney, Astrid, "Zur Stellung des Völkerrechts in der EU. Zugleich Besprechung von EuGH, EuZW 1998, 572 – Hermès und EuGH, EuZW 1998, 964 – Racke" (1999) 9 Europäische Zeitschrift für Wirtschaftsrecht 5–11.

"Die Bindung der EU an das allgemeine Völkerrecht" in Walter Obwexer (ed) *Die Europäische Union im Völkerrecht* (Nomos 2012) 25–48.

Fabbrini, Federico, "After the OMT Case: The Supremacy of EU Law as the Guarantee of the Equality of the Member States" (2015) 16 (4) German Law Journal 1003–1023.

Falk, Richard A, "The New States and International Legal Order" (1966) 118 Recueil des Cours 1–103.

Falk Moore, Sally, "Certainties Undone. Fifty Turbulent Years of Legal Anthropology, 1949–1999" (2001) 7 (1) Journal of the Royal Anthropological Institute 95–116.

Faraguna, Pietro, "The Italian Constitutional Court in re Taricco: 'Gauweiler in the Roman Campagna'" (January 31, 2017) Verfassungsblog, available at https://verfassungsblog.de/the-italian-constitutional-court-in-re-taricco-gauweiler-in-the-roman-campagna/ [last accessed February 1, 2023].

Fassbender, Bardo, "Triepel in Luxemburg: Die dualistische Sicht des Verhältnisses zwischen Europa- und Völkerrecht in der 'Kadi-Rechtssprechung' des EuGH als Problem des Selbstverständnisses der Europäischen Union" (2010) 63 (8) Die öffentliche Verwaltung 333–341.

Fastenrath, Ulrich, *Kompetenzverteilung im Bereich der auswärtigen Gewalt* (CH Beck 1986).

Lücken im Völkerrecht – Zu Rechtscharakter, Quellen, Systemzusammenhang, Methodenlehre und Funktionen des Völkerrechts (Duncker & Humblot 1991).

"Anmerkung" (2016) 71 (12) JuristenZeitung 636–640.

Fastenrath, Ulrich and Groh, Thomas, "Art 59 GG" in Karl Heinrich Friauf and Wolfram Höfling (eds) *Berliner Kommentar zum Grundgesetz* (Erich Schmidt 22 sup 2007).

Feinäugle, Clemens, "Kadi Case" in Rüdiger Wolfrum (ed) *Max Planck Encyclopedia of Public International Law* (Oxford University Press 2014).

Fénelon, François, *Lives of the Ancient Philosophers* (Knight and Lacey 1825 [translated from *Abrégé des vies des anciens philosophes*, Paris 1726, 314]).

Fichte, Johann Gottlieb, "Über den Begriff der Wissenschaftslehre" in Immanuel Hermann Fichte (ed) *FichtesWerke Vol 1* (Walter de Gruyter 1971 [1834–1846]) 27–81.

Finnis, John, *Natural Law and Natural Rights* (Oxford Clarendon Press 2nd ed 2011).

Fischer-Lescano, Andreas and Teubner, Gunther, "Regime-Collision: The Vain Search for Legal Unity in the Fragmentation of Global Law" (2004) 25 (4) Michigan Journal of International Law 999–1046.

Fitzmaurice, Gerald G, "The Law and Procedure of the International Court of Justice 1951–54: General Principles and Sources of Law" (1953) 30 British Yearbook of International Law 1–70.

"The General Principles of International Law Considered from the Standpoint of the Rule of Law" (1957) 92 Recueil des Cours de l'Académie de Droit International 1–227.

"Some Problems Regarding the Formal Sources of International Law" in Frederik Mari van Asbeck et al (eds) *Symbolae Verzijl* (Martinus Nijhoff 1958) 153–176.

Flynn, Tom, *The Triangular Constitution. Constitutional Pluralism in Ireland, the EU and the ECHR* (Hart 2020).

Foot, Philippa, *The Problem of Abortion and the Doctrine of the Double Effect in Virtues and Vices* (Basil Blackwell 1978), originally appearing as Foot, Philippa, "The Problem of Abortion and the Doctrine of Double Effect" (1967) 5 Oxford Review 5–15.

Freeman, Colin L et al, "Structural Control of Crystal Nuclei by an Eggshell Protein" (2010) 49 (30) Angewandte Chemie International Edition 5135–5137.

Freeman, Walter J, "Nonlinear Brain Dynamics and Intention According to Aquinas" (2008) 6 (2) Mind and Matter 207–234.

Frege, Gottlob, *Die Grundlagen der Arithmetik. Eine logische mathematische Untersuchung* (Wilhelm Koebner 2nd ed 1884).

The Foundations of Arithmetic. A Logico-Mathematical Enquiry into the Concept of Number (translated by J L Austin Harper 2nd ed 1953 [*Die Grundlagen der Arithmetik. Eine logisch mathematische Untersuchung über den Begriff der Zahl* Wilhelm Koebner 1884]).

Fuller, Chris, "Legal Anthropology: Legal Pluralism and Legal Thought" (1994) 10 (3) Anthropology Today 9–12.

Gabriel, Gottfried, *Grundprobleme der Erkenntnistheorie. Von Descartes zu Wittgenstein* (utb 3rd ed 2008).

Gabriel, Markus, *An den Grenzen der Erkenntnistheorie. Die notwendige Endlichkeit des objektiven Wissens als Lektion des Skeptizismus* (Karl Alber 2nd ed 2014).

Die Erkenntnis der Welt – Eine Einführung in die Erkenntnistheorie (Karl Alber 5th ed 2016).

Galán, Alexis and Patterson, Dennis, "The Limits of Normative Legal Pluralism: Review of Paul Schiff Berman, Global Legal Pluralism: A Jurisprudence of Law beyond Borders" (2013) 11 (3) International Journal of Constitutional Law 783–800.

Garben, Sacha and Govaere, Inge (eds), *The Division of Competences between the EU and the Member States. Reflections on the Past, the Present and the Future* (Hart 2017).

Gärdenfors, Peter, "Slicing the Theory of Mind" (2001) 36 Danish Yearbook of Philosophy 7–34.

How Homo Became Sapiens: On the Evolution of Thinking (Oxford University Press 2003).

"Evolutionary and Developmental Aspects of Intersubjectivity" in Hans Liljenström and Peter Århem (eds) *Consciousness Transitions: Phylogenetic, Ontogenetic and Physiological Aspects* (Elsevier 2007) 281–305.

"The Role of Intersubjectivity in Animal and Human Cooperation" (2008) 3 (1) Biological Theory 1–12.

Gatti, Mauro and Manzini, Pietro, "External Representation of the European Union in the Conclusion of International Agreements" (2012) 49 (5) Common Market Law Review 1703–1734.

Geiger, Rudolf, "Article 216 TFEU" in Rudolf Geiger, Daniel-Erasmus Khan and Markus Kotzur (eds) *European Union Treaties. A Commentary. Treaty on European Union. Treaty on the Functioning of the European Union* (CH Beck and Hart 2015).

Gény, François, *Methode d'interpretation et sources en droit prive positif* (Librairie Générale de Droit et de Jurisprudence 2nd ed 1919).

Gianelli, Alessandra, "Customary International Law in the European Union" in Enzo Cannizzaro, Paolo Palchetti and Ramses A Wessel (eds) *International Law as Law of the European Union* (Martinus Nijhoff 2012) 93–110.

Gihl, Torsten, "The Legal Character of Sources of International Law" (1957) 1 Scandinavian Studies in Law 51–92.

Giner Torréns, Marta, Dreizler, Kristin and Kärtner, Joscha, "Insight into Toddlers' Motivation to Help: From Social Participants to Prosocial Contributors" (2021) 64 Infant Behavior and Development 101603.

Giudice, Michael, "Global Legal Pluralism: What's Law Got to Do with It?" (2014) 34 (3) Oxford Journal of Legal Studies 589–608.

Grabenwarter, Christoph, "Änderungen der österreichischen Bundesverfassung aus Anlaß des Beitritts zur Europäischen Union" (1995) 55 Heidelberg Journal of International Law 166–190.

"Offene Staatlichkeit: Österreich" in Armin von Bogdandy, Cruz Villalón and Peter M Huber (eds) *Handbuch Ius Publicum Europaeum. Vol 2 Offene Staatlichkeit – Wissenschaft vom Verfassungsrecht* (C F Müller 2008) 211–241.

"National Constitutional Law Relating to the European Union" in Armin von Bogdandy and Jürgen Bast (eds) *Principles of European Constitutional Law* (Hart et al 2nd ed 2011) 95–144.

Gragl, Paul, *The Accession of the European Union to the European Convention on Human Rights* (Hart 2013).

"The Silence of the Treaties: General International Law and the European Union" (2014) 47 German Yearbook of International Law 375–410.

"The Pure Theory of Law and Legal Monism – Epistemological Truth and Empirical Plausibility" (2015) 70 (4) Zeitschrift für Öffentliches Recht 665–736.

"In Defence of Kelsenian Monism: Countering Hart and Raz" (2017) 8 (2) Jurisprudence 287–318.

Legal Monism: Law, Philosophy, and Politics (Oxford University Press 2018).

Granat, Katarzyna, "Kontrolle des EU-Sekundärrechts durch den polnischen Verfassungsgerichtshof. Anmerkung zum Beschluss des polnischen Verfassungsgerichtshofs vom 16. November 2011, SK 45/09" (2013) 48 (2) Europarecht 205–214.

Green, James A, *The Persistent Objector Rule in International Law* (Oxford University Press 2016).

Green, Leslie, "Law and Obligations" in Jules Coleman and Scott Shapiro (eds) *The Oxford Handbook of Jurisprudence & Philosophy of Law* (Oxford University Press 2002 reprinted in 2011) 514–547.

Green, Michael S, "Hans Kelsen and the Logic of Legal Systems" (2003) 54 (2) Alabama Law Review 365–413.

"Marmor's Kelsen" in D A Jeremy Telman (ed) *Hans Kelsen in America* (Springer 2016) 31–55.

Greene, Joshua D, "Beyond Point-and-Shoot Morality: Why Cognitive (Neuro) Science Matters for Ethics" (2014) 124 (4) Ethics 695–726.

"The Rise of Moral Cognition" (2015) 135 Cognition 39–42.

Greene, Joshua D and Haidt, Jonathan, "How (and Where) Does Moral Judgment Work?" (2002) 6 (12) Trends in Cognitive Sciences 517–523.

Greenspan, Stanley and Shanker, Stuart, *The First Idea* (Da Capo Press 2004).

Grewe, Constance, "Methods of Identification of National Constitutional Identity" in Alejandro Saiz Arnaiz and Carina Alcoberro Llivina (eds) *National Constitutional Identity and European Integration* (Intersentia 2013) 37–48.

Griffiths, John, "What Is Legal Pluralism?" (1986) 18 (24) Journal of Legal Pluralism 1–47.

"The Idea of Sociology of Law and Its Relation to Law and to Sociology" in Michael Freeman (ed) *Law and Sociology: Current Legal Issues Vol 8* (Oxford University Press 2006) 49–68.

Griller, Stefan, *Die Übertragung von Hoheitsrechten auf zwischenstaatliche Einrichtungen* (Springer 1989).

"Verfassungsfragen der österreichischen EU-Mitgliedschaft" (1995) 9 Zeitschrift für Europarecht, internationales Privatrecht & Rechtsvergleichung 98–115.

"Blockademöglichkeiten gegen die Einführung des Euro" (1997) 4 Journal für Rechtspolitik 221–233.

"Der Stufenbau der österreichischen Rechtsordnung nach dem EU-Beitritt" (2000) 8 (4) Journal für Rechtspolitik 273–288.

"Völkerrecht und Landesrecht – unter Berücksichtigung des Europarechts" in Robert Walter, Clemens Jabloner and Karl Zeleny (eds) *Hans Kelsen und das*

Völkerrecht: Ergebnisse eines internationalen Symposiums in Wien (Manz 2004) 83–120.

"Executive Summary" in European Parliament and Directorate-General for International Policies (ed) *National Constitutional Law and European Integration* (European Parliament 2011) 11–31.

"Fragmentierungen im Öffentlichen Recht: Diskursvergleich im internationalen und nationalen Recht" (2018) 77 Veröffentlichungen der Vereinigung der Deutschen Staatsrechtslehrer 237–283.

Grimm, Dieter, "The Constitution in the Process of Denationalization" (2005) 12 (4) Constellations 447–463.

"The Democratic Costs of Constitutionalization: The European Case" in Dieter Grimm, *Constitutionalism. Past, Present, and Future* (Oxford University Press 2015) 295–313.

"The Role of National Constitutions in a United Europe" in Dieter Grimm, *Constitutionalism. Past, Present, and Future* (Oxford University Press 2015) 271–294.

Groce, Mariano and Goldoni, Marco, "A Sense of Self-Suspicion: Global Legal Pluralism and the Claim to Legal Authority" (2015) 8 (1) Ethics & Global Politics 1–20.

Groh, Kathrin, *Demokratische Staatsrechtslehrer in der Weimarer Republik. Von der konstitutionellen Staatslehre zur Theorie des modernen demokratischen Verfassungsstaats* (Mohr Siebeck 2010).

Grussmann, Wolf-Dietrich, "Grundnorm und Supranationalität – Rechtsstrukturelle Sichtweisen der europäischen Integration" in Thomas von Danwitz et al (ed) *Auf dem Wege zu einer europäischen Staatlichkeit* (Boorberg 1993) 47–64.

Guggenheim, Paul, "Les deux éléments de la coutume en droit international" in Librairie générale de droit et de jurisprudence (ed) *La technique et les principes du droit public: Études en l'honneur de Georges Scelle I* (Librairie générale de droit et de jurisprudence 1950) 275–284.

Traité de droit international public (Librairie de l'Université 1953).

Traité de droit international public I (Librairie de l'Université 2nd ed 1967).

Günther, Klaus, "Legal Pluralism or Uniform Concept of Law? Globalisation as a Problem of Legal Theory" (2008) 5 No Foundations – Journal of Extreme Legal Positivism 5–21.

"Normativer Rechtspluralismus: Eine Kritik" in Thorsten Moos, Magnus Schlette and Hans Diefenbacher (eds) *Das Recht im Blick der Anderen: Zu Ehren von Eberhard Schmidt-Aßmann* (Mohr Siebeck 2016) 43–62.

"Normative Legal Pluralism – A Critique" in Jorge Luis Fabra Zamora (ed) *Jurisprudence in a Globalised World* (Edward Elgar 2020) 85–99.

Guyer, Paul and Wood, Allen W, "Introduction" in Immanuel Kant, *Critique of Pure Reason* (Cambridge edition of the works of Immanuel Kant translated and edited by Paul Guyer and Allen W Wood Cambridge University Press 1998 [*Kritik der reinen Vernunft* Johann Friedrich Hartknoch 1781/1787]) 1–80.

Guzman, Andrew T, "Against Consent" (2012) 52 (4) Virginia Journal of International Law 747–790.

Guzman, Andrew T and Hsiang, Jerome, "Reinvigorating Customary International Law" in Curtis A Bradley (ed) *Custom's Future: International Law in a Changing World* (Cambridge University Press 2016) 275–304.

Haack, Susan, "The Legitimacy of Metaphysics: Kant's Legacy to Peirce, and Peirce's to Philosophy Today" (2008) 36 (1) Philosophical Topics 97–100.

Habermas, Jürgen, "Wahrheitstheorien" in Helmut Fahrenbach (ed) *Wirklichkeit und Reflexion. Walter Schulz zum 60. Geburtstag* (Neske 1973) 211–265.

"What Is Universal Pragmatics?" in Jürgen Habermas, *On the Pragmatics of Communication* (edited by Maeve Cooke MIT Press 1976 ["Was heißt Universalpragmatik?" in Karl-Otto Apel (ed) *Sprachpragmatik und Philosophie* Suhrkamp (1976) 174–272]) 21–103.

Communication and the Evolution of Society (Beacon Press 1979).

The Theory of Communicative Action. Lifeworld and System: A Critique of Functionalist Reason Vol 2 (translated by Thomas McCarthy Polity Press 1987 [*Theorie des kommunikativen Handelns Band 2: Zur Kritik der funktionalistischen Vernunft* Suhrkamp 3rd ed 1985]).

"Discourse Ethics: Notes on Philosophical Justification" in Jürgen Habermas, *Moral Consciousness and Communicative Action* (MIT Press 1990) 43–115.

Die postnationale Konstellation (Suhrkamp 1998).

Truth and Justification (translated by Barbara Fultner MIT Press 2003 [*Wahrheit und Rechtfertigung. Philosophische Aufsätze* Suhrkamp 1999]).

Legitimationsprobleme im Spätkapitalismus (Suhrkamp 2004).

"Die Krise der Europäischen Union im Lichte einer Konstitutionalisierung des Völkerrechts – Ein Essay zur Verfassung Europas" (2012) 72 Heidelberg Journal of International Law 1–44.

"Interview with Jürgen Habermas" in Andre Bächtiger et al (eds) *The Oxford Handbook of Deliberative Democracy* (Oxford University Press 2018) 871–882.

Hacker, Peter M S, "The Linguistic Turn in Analytical Philosophy" in Michael Beaney (ed) *The Oxford Handbook of the History of Analytic Philosophy* (Oxford University Press 2013) 926–947.

Halberstam, Daniel, "Local, Global and Plural Constitutionalism: Europe Meets the World" in Graínne de Búrca and Joseph H H Weiler (eds) *The Worlds of European Constitutionalism* (Cambridge University Press 2012) 150–202.

Halmai, Gábor, "The Hungarian Constitutional Court and Constitutional Identity" (January 10, 2017) Verfassungsblog, available at https://verfassungsblog.de/the-hungarian-constitutional-court-and-constitutional-identity/ [last accessed February 1, 2023].

"A Coup against Constitutional Democracy. The Case of Hungary" in Mark A Graber, Sanford Levinson and Mark Tushnet (eds) *Constitutional Democracy in Crisis?* (Oxford University Press 2018) 243–256.

Halper, Edward, *Aristotle's Metaphysics: A Reader's Guide* (Continuum 2012).

Hamlin, J Kiley, "The Case for Social Evaluation in Preverbal Infants: Gazing Toward One's Goal Drives Infants' Preferences for Helpers over Hinderers in the Hill Paradigm" (2015) 5 (1563) Frontiers in Psychology 1–9.

Hamlin, J Kiley, Wynn, Karen and Bloom, Paul, "3-Month-Olds Show a Negativity Bias in Their Social Evaluations" (2010) 13 (6) Developmental Science 923–929.

Hanley, Seán and Vachudová, Milada Anna, "Understanding the Illiberal Turn: Democratic Backsliding in the Czech Republic" (2018) 34 (3) East European Politics 276–296.

Hanna, Robert, "Kant's Theory of Judgment" in Edward N Zalta (ed) *Stanford Encyclopedia of Philosophy* (October 23, 2017), available at https://plato.stanford.edu/entries/kant-judgment/ [last accessed February 1, 2023].

Harman, Gilbert, "Does Marc Hauser's Moral Minds Plagiarize John Mikhail's Earlier Work?," formerly available at www.princeton.edu/~harman/Mikhail%20and%20Hauser.pdf [last accessed February 1, 2023].

Harris, J W, *Legal Philosophies* (Butterworths 1997).

Hart, Herbert L A, "Are There Any Natural Rights?" (1955) 64 (2) Philosophical Review 175–191.

Hartley, Trevor C, "National Law, International Law and EU Law – How Do They Relate?" in Patrick Capps, Malcolm Evans and Stratos Konstadinidis (eds) *Asserting Jurisdiction. International and European Legal Approaches* (Hart 2003) 65–81.

Hartmann, Moritz, "Review Essay: 'Lost in Disordered Clouds: Transnational Legal Pluralism and the Regulation of Global Asymmetries' – Mireille Delmas-Marty's Ordering Pluralism" (2009) 11 (9) German Law Journal 1025–1037.

Hatje, Armin and Mankowski, Peter, "Nationale Unionsrechte. Sprachgrenzen, Traditionsgrenzen, Systemgrenzen, Denkgrenzen" (2014) 49 (2) Europarecht 155–169.

Hauser, Marc D, *Moral Minds: How Nature Designed Our Universal Sense of Right and Wrong* (Ecco 2006).

"Response to Gil Harman's 'Did Marc Hauser's Moral Minds Plagiarize John Mikhail's Earlier Work?'," formerly available at www.princeton.edu/~harman/HauserResponse_Harman%20essay.pdf [last accessed February 1, 2023].

Hauser, Oliver P et al, "Cooperating with the Future" (2014) 511 (7508) Nature 220–223.

Hegel, Georg Wilhelm Friedrich, *Die Differenz des Fichteschen und Schellingschen Systems der Philosophie* (Jena (Akademische Buchhandlung) 1801).

Glauben und Wissen oder Reflexionsphilosophie der Subjektivität in der Vollständigkeit ihrer Formen als Kantische, Jacobische und Fichtesche Philosophie (Cotta 1802).

Grundlinien der Philosophie des Rechts (Nicolai 1821).

Encyclopedia of the Philosophical Sciences in Basic Outline Part I Science of Logic (translated and edited by Klaus Brinkmann and Daniel O Dahlstrom Cambridge University Press 2010 [*Enzyklopädie der philosophischen Wissenschaften* I 1830]).

The Science of Logic (translated by George di Giovanni Cambridge University Press 2010 [*Wissenschaft der Logik* 1832]).

The Phenomenology of Spirit (translated by Terry Pinkard Cambridge University Press 2018 from *Phenomenologie des Geistes* 1807].

Heidemann, Carsten, *Die Norm als Tatsache: Zur Normentheorie Hans Kelsens* (Nomos 1997).

Heis, Jeremy, "Neo-Kantianism" in Edward N Zalta (ed) *Stanford Encyclopedia of Philosophy* (May 18, 2018), available at https://plato.stanford.edu/entries/neo-kantianism/ [last accessed February 1, 2023].

Henkin, Louis, *International Law, Politics and Values* (Brill 1995).

"Elements of Constitutionalism" (1998) 60 (11) Special Issue of International Commission of Jurists. The Review 11–22.

Hilpold, Peter, "EU Law and UN Law in Conflict: The Kadi Case" (2009) 13 Max Planck Yearbook of United Nations Law 141–182.

Hobbes, Thomas, *Leviathan* (Three-Text Edition of *Thomas Hobbes's Political Theory. The Elements of Law, De Cive and Leviathan* edited by Deborah Baumgold Cambridge University Press 2017 [1651]).

Hobson, Jessica A and Hobson, R Peter, "Identification: The Missing Link between Joint Attention and Imitation?" (2007) 19 (2) Development and Psychopathology 411–431.

Hobson, R Peter and Hobson, Jessica, "Joint Attention or Joint Engagement? Insights from Autism" in Alex Seemann (ed) *Joint Attention: New Developments in Psychology, Philosophy of Mind, and Social Neuroscience* (MIT Press 2011) 115–136.

Hoerster, Norbert, *Was ist Recht? Grundfragen der Rechtsphilosophie* (CH Beck 2006).

Hoffmann, Tamás, "The Gentle Humanizer of Humanitarian Law: Antonio Cassese and the Creation of the Customary Law of Non-International Armed Conflicts" in Carsten Stahn and Larissa van den Herik (eds) *Future Perspectives on International Criminal Justice* (Asser Press 2010) 58–80.

Hoffmeister, Frank, "The Contribution of EU Practice to International Law" in Marise Cremona (ed) *Developments in EU External Relations Law* (Oxford University Press 2008) 37–127.

"Article 14" in Oliver Dörr and Kirsten Schmalenbach (eds) *Vienna Convention on the Law of Treaties – A Commentary* (Springer 2nd ed 2018).

Horsley, Thomas, *The Court of Justice of the European Union as an Institutional Actor. Judicial Lawmaking and Its Limits* (Cambridge University Press 2018).

Horton, John, *Political Obligation* (Macmillan 1992).

Horwich, Paul, "A Defense of Minimalism" in Michael P Lynch (ed) *The Nature of Truth. Classic and Contemporary Perspectives* (MIT Press 2001) 559–578.

Hösle, Vittorio, *Hegels System. Der Idealismus der Subjektivität und das Problem der Intersubjektivität Vol 1: Systementwicklung und Logik* (Felix Meiner 1st ed 1987).

Die Krise der Gegenwart und die Verantwortung der Philosophie. Transzendentalpragmatik, Letztbegründung, Ethik (CH Beck 3rd ed 1997).

Hrdy, Sarah Blaffer, *Mothers and Others* (Harvard University Press 2009).

Huber, Peter M, "Interview Das EZB-Urteil war zwingend" *Frankfurter Allgemeine Zeitung* May 12, 2020.

Huber, Peter M and Paulus, Andreas L, "Cooperation of Constitutional Courts in Europe: The Openness of the German Constitution to International, European, and Comparative Constitutional Law" in Mads Andenas and Duncan Fairgrieve (eds) *Courts and Comparative Law* (Oxford University Press 2015) 281–299.

Hübl, Philipp, *Die aufgeregte Gesellschaft. Wie Emotionen unsere Moral prägen und die Polarisierung verstärken* (C Bertelsmann 2019).

Hubley, Penelope and Trevarthen, Colwyn, "Sharing a Task in Infancy" (1979) 4 Social Interaction during Infancy: New Directions for Child Development 57–80.

Hudson, William D (ed), *The Is–Ought Problem. A Collection of Papers on the Central Problem in Moral Philosophy* (Penguin 1969).

Hume, David, *A Treatise of Human Nature. A Critical Edition Vol 1* (edited by David Fate Norton and Mary J Norton Oxford University Press 2007 [1739–1740]).

An Enquiry Concerning Human Understanding (edited with an introduction and notes by Peter Millican Oxford University Press 2007 [1748]).
Hummer, Waldemar, "Art 218" in Christoph Vedder and Wolff Heintschel von Heinegg (eds) *Europäisches Unionsrecht. Handkommentar* (Nomos et al 2nd ed 2018).
Husa, Jaako, "Global Constitutionalism – Some Critical Remarks" (2017) 47 (1) Hong Kong Law Journal 73–88.
Husserl, Edmund, *Cartesian Meditations: An Introduction to Phenomenology* (Martinus Nijhoff 1960 [originally published as *Méditations cartésiennes: Introduction à la phénoménologie* 1931]).
Isak, Hubert, "Kompetenzüberschreitende Akte von Organen der Europäischen Union – Die Sicht des österreichischen Verfassungsrechts" in Bruno Simma and Constanze Schulte (eds) *Völker- und Europarecht in der aktuellen Diskussion* (Linde 1999) 33–58.
Isensee, Josef, "Ethische Grundwerte im freiheitlichen Staat" in Ansgar Paus (ed) *Werte – Rechte – Normen* (Kevelaer et al 1979) 132.
Isiksel, Turkuler, "Global Legal Pluralism as Fact and Norm" (2013) 2 (2) Global Constitutionalism 160–195.
Itzcovich, Giulio, "The Interpretation of Community Law by the European Court of Justice" (2009) 10 (5) German Law Journal 537–560.
Iwasawa, Yuji, "The Doctrine of Self-Executing Treaties in the United States: A Critical Analysis" (1986) 26 Virginia Journal of International Law 627–692.
Jacobi, Friedrich Heinrich, "Ueber den transscendentalen Idealismus" in Friedrich Heinrich Jacobi, *Werke Vol 2* (edited by F Roth and F Köppen 1976 [1787]) 291–310.
"David Hume on Faith or Idealism and Realism: A Dialogue" in George di Giovanni (ed) *The Main Philosophical Writings and the Novel Allwill. Friedrich Heinrich Jacobi* (translated with an introductory study, notes and bibliography by George di Giovanni McGill-Queen's University Press 1994 [1787]) 253–338.
Jacot-Guillarmod, Olivier, *Droit communautaire et droit international public. Etude des sources internationales de l'ordre juridique des Communautés européennes* (Librairie de l'Université Genève 1979).
Jakab, András, "Kelsens Völkerrechtslehre zwischen Erkenntnistheorie und Politik" (2004) 64 Heidelberg Journal of International Law 1045–1057.
"Problems of the Stufenbaulehre: Kelsen's Failure to Derive the Validity of a Norm from Another Norm" (2007) 20 (1) Canadian Journal of Law and Jurisprudence 35–67.
European Constitutional Language (Cambridge University Press 2016).
"Informal Institutional Elements as Both Preconditions and Consequences of Effective Formal Legal Rules: The Failure of Constitutional Institution Building in Hungary" (2020) 68 (4) American Journal of Comparative Law 760–800.
Jakab, András and Sonnevend, Pal, "The Bundesbank Is under a Legal Obligation to Ignore the PSPP Judgment of the Bundesverfassungsgericht" (May 25, 2020) Verfassungsblog, available at https://verfassungsblog.de/the-bundesbank-is-under-a-legal-obligation-to-ignore-the-pspp-judgment-of-the-bundesverfassungsgericht/ [last accessed February 1, 2023].

Jaklic, Klemen, *Constitutional Pluralism in the EU* (Oxford University Press 2013).

James, William, "Pragmatism's Conception of Truth" in Michael P Lynch (ed) *The Nature of Truth. Classic and Contemporary Perspectives* (MIT Press 2001 [1907]) 211–228.

The Meaning of Truth: A Sequel to "Pragmatism" in William James, *Pragmatism and the Meaning of Truth* (edited with an introduction by Alfred J Ayer Harvard University Press 1978 [1909]).

Janko, Andreas, *Gesamtänderung der Bundesverfassung* (Verlag Österreich 2004).

Jellinek, Georg, *Die rechtliche Natur der Staatenverträge* (A Hölder 1880).

Jenks, Wilfried C, "The Conflict of Law-Making Treaties" (1953) 30 British Yearbook of International Law 401–453.

Jennings, Robert Y, "What Is International Law and How Do We Tell It When We See It?" (1981) 37 Annuaire Suisse de Droit International 59–88.

Jennings, Robert Y and Watts, Arthur, *Oppenheim's International Law* (Oxford University Press 9th ed 1992).

Jestaedt, Matthias, "Der Europäische Verfassungsverbund – Verfassungstheoretischer Charme und rechtstheoretische Insuffizienz einer Unschärferelation" in Rüdiger Krause, Winfried Veelken and Klaus Vieweg (eds) *Recht der Wirtschaft und der Arbeit in Europa: Gedächtnisschrift für Wolfgang Blomeyer* (Duncker & Humblot 2004) 637–674, reprinted in Christian Calliess (ed) *Verfassungswandel im europäischen Staaten- und Verfassungsverbund. Beiträge der Ersten Göttinger Gespräche zum deutschen und europäischen Verfassungsrecht vom 15. bis 17. Juni 2006* (Mohr Siebeck 2007) 93–128.

Jeutner, Valentin, *Irresolvable Norm Conflicts in International Law – The Concept of a Legal Dilemma* (Oxford University Press 2017).

Jovanović, Miodrag A, *The Nature of International Law* (Cambridge University Press 2019).

Jung, Florian, "Reben, Wein und der EuGH: Zur Auslegung von Art. 218 Abs. 9 AEUV – Anmerkungen zum Urteil des EuGH vom 07.10.2014, Rs. C-399/12 – Deutschland/Rat" (2015) 50 (6) Europarecht 735–745.

Kaddous, Christine, "L'arrêt France c. Commission de 1994 (accord concurrence) et le contrôle de la 'légalité' des accords externes en vertu de l'art. 173 CE: la difficile réconciliation de l'orthodoxie communautaire avec l'orthodoxie internationale" (1996) 32 Cahiers de droit européen 613–633.

Kadelbach, Stefan, "Konstitutionalisierung und Rechtspluralismus – Über die Konkurrenz zweier Ordnungsentwürfe" in Jochen Bung and Armin Engländer (eds) *Souveränität, Transstaatlichkeit und Weltverfassung ARSP-Beiheft 153* (Franz Steiner 2017) 97–108.

Kadens, Emily and Young, Ernest A, "How Customary Is Customary International Law?" (2013) 54 (3) William & Mary Law Review 885–920.

Kahneman, Daniel, *Thinking, Fast and Slow* (Penguin 2012).

Kaiser, Karen, "Treaties, Direct Applicability" in Rüdiger Wolfrum (ed) *Max Planck Encyclopedia of Public International Law* (Oxford University Press 2011).

Kammerhofer, Jörg, "Uncertainty in the Formal Sources of International Law: Customary International Law and Some of Its Problems" (2004) 15 (3) European Journal of International Law 523–553.

"Kelsen – Which Kelsen? A Reapplication of the Pure Theory to International Law" (2009) 22 (2) Leiden Journal of International Law 225–249.

Uncertainty in International Law: A Kelsenian Perspective (Routledge 2011).
Kant, Immanuel, *Prolegomena to Any Future Metaphysics. That Will Be Able to Come Forward as Science* (edited and translated by Gary Hatfield Cambridge University Press 2nd ed 2004 [*Prolegomena zu einer jeden künftigen Metaphysik, die als Wissenschaft wird auftreten können* 1783]).
Critique of Pure Reason (Cambridge edition of the works of Immanuel Kant translated and edited by Paul Guyer and Allen W Wood Cambridge University Press 1998 [*Kritik der reinen Vernunft* (Johann Friedrich Hartknoch 1781/1787)]).
Über den Gemeinspruch: "Das mag in der Theorie richtig sein, taugt aber nicht für die Praxis" (Berlinische Monatsschrift 1793).
Metaphysics of Morals: Doctrine of Virtue Vol I and Doctrine of Right Vol II (edited and translated by Mary J Gregor Cambridge University Press 1997 [*Die Metaphysik der Sitten: Tugendlehre und Rechtslehre* 1797]).
Metaphysische Anfangsgründe der Rechtslehre (1797).
Kantorowicz, Hermann, *The Definition of Law* (Cambridge University Press 1958).
Karl, Wolfram, "Conflicts between Treaties" in Rudolf Bernhardt (ed) *Encyclopedia of Public International Law* Vol VII (North-Holland 1984) 467–473.
Keleman, R Daniel, "On the Unsustainability of Constitutional Pluralism: European Supremacy and the Survival of the Eurozone" (2016) 23 (1) Maastricht Journal of European and Comparative Law 136–150.
Kelemen, R Daniel and Pech, Laurent, "Why Autocrats Love Constitutional Identity and Constitutional Pluralism. Lessons from Hungary and Poland" (2018) 2 RECONNECT working paper.
"The Uses and Abuses of Constitutional Pluralism: Undermining the Rule of Law in the Name of Constitutional Identity in Hungary and Poland" (2019) 21 Cambridge Yearbook of European Legal Studies 59–74.
Kelsen, Hans, *Das Problem der Souveränität und die Theorie des Völkerrechts* (Mohr Siebeck 1920).
Hauptprobleme der Staatsrechtslehre (Scientia 2nd ed 1923).
Allgemeine Staatslehre (Springer 1925).
"Les rapports de système entre le droit interne et le droit international public" (1926) 14 Recueil des Cours de l'Académie de Droit International, 227–331.
"Die Bundesexekution – Ein Beitrag zur Theorie und Praxis des Bundesstaates, unter besonderer Berücksichtigung der deutschen Reichs- und der österreichischen Bundes-Verfassung" in Zaccaria Giacometti and Dietrich Schindler (eds) *Festgabe für Fritz Fleiner zum 60. Geburtstag* (J C B Mohr 1927) 127–187.
Das Problem der Souveränität und die Theorie des Völkerrechts: Beitrag zu einer Reinen Rechtslehre (J C B Mohr 2nd ed 1928).
Reine Rechtslehre (Franz Deuticke 1934).
"Théorie du Droit International Coutumier" (1939) 1 (NS) Revue International de la Théorie du Droit 253–274.
Law and Peace in International Relations. The Oliver Wendell Holmes Lectures 1940–41 (Harvard University Press 1942).
General Theory of Law and State (translated by Anders Wedberg Harvard University Press 1945 [1928]).

Natural Law Doctrine and Legal Positivism (translated by Wolfgang Herbert Kraus as an appendix to Kelsen, *General Theory of Law and State* Harvard University Press 1945) 389–446.

Philosophical Foundations of Natural Law Theory and Legal Positivism (translated by Wolfgang H Kraus as an appendix to Kelsen, *General Theory of Law and State* Harvard University Press 1945 [1928]) 389–445.

Principles of International Law (Rinehart 1952).

"Der Begriff der Rechtsordnung" (1958) 1 (3) Logique et Analyse 150–167.

"Die Einheit von Völkerrecht und staatlichem Recht" (1958) 19 Heidelberg Journal of International Law 234–248.

Reine Rechtslehre (Franz Deuticke 2nd ed 1960).

Principles of International Law (Rinehart 2nd ed 1966).

Pure Theory of Law (University of California Press 2nd ed 1967).

Allgemeine Theorie der Normen (Manz 1979).

Introduction to the Problems of Legal Theory (translated by Bonnie Litschewski Paulson and Stanley L Paulson Oxford Clarendon Press 1992 [*Reine Rechtslehre* 1934]).

"The Pure Theory of Law, 'Labandism', and Neo-Kantianism: A Letter to Renato Treves" in Stanley L Paulson and Bonnie Litschewski Paulson (eds) *Normativity and Norms: Critical Perspectives on Kelsenian Themes* (Clarendon Press 1998) 169–175.

Keverne, Eric B, "Genomic Imprinting and the Evolution of Sex Differences in Mammalian Reproductive Strategies" (2007) 59 Advances in Genetics 217–243.

Keverne, Eric B and Curley, James P, "Vasopressin, Oxytocin and Social Behaviour" (2004) 14 (6) Current Opinion in Neurobiology 777–783.

Keynes, John Maynard, *The General Theory of Employment, Interest and Money* (Palgrave Macmillan 1936).

Khan, Daniel-Erasmus, *Die deutschen Staatsgrenzen. Rechtshistorische Grundlagen und offene Rechtsfragen* (Mohr Siebeck 2004).

Das Rote Kreuz: Geschichte einer humanitären Weltbewegung (CH Beck 2013).

"Territory Taking Centre Stage in International Law. Some Preliminary Thoughts on the Rise of Territoriality to the Bedrock of Modern Statehood" in Société Française pour le droit international (ed) *Droit des Frontières internationals / The Law of International Borders* (Pedone 2016) 53–64.

"Art 216" in Rudolf Geiger, Daniel-Erasmus Khan and Markus Kotzur (eds) *EUV/AEUV* (CH Beck 6th ed 2017) 795–801.

"Das Staatsgebiet und die Grenzen der Bundesrepublik Deutschland" in Wolfgang Kahl, Christian Waldhoff and Christian Walter (eds) *Bonner Kommentar zum Grundgesetz* (C F Müller 2022) 1–228.

Khan, Daniel-Erasmus and Kirchmair, Lando, "Art 216" in Rudolf Geiger et al (eds) *EUV/AEUV* (CH Beck 7th ed 2023) 868–875.

Kieber, Stefan and Klaushofer, Reinhard, "The Austrian Constitutional Court Post Case-Law after the Landmark Decision on Charter of Fundamental Rights of the European Union" (2017) 23 (2) European Public Law 221–236.

Kingsbury, Benedict, "Confronting Difference: The Puzzling Durability of Gentili's Combination of Pragmatic Pluralism and Normative Judgment" (1998) 92 American Journal of International Law 713–723.

Kirchmair, Lando, "The 'Janus Face' of the Court of Justice of the European Union: A Theoretical Appraisal of the EU Legal Order's Relationship with International and Member State Law" (2012) 4 (3) Goettingen Journal of International Law 677–691.

"Die autonome Rechtsordnung der EU und die Grenzen von Monismus und Dualismus" in Matthias C Kettemann (ed) *Grenzen im Völkerrecht – Grenzen des Völkerrechts* (Jan Sramek 2013) 275–291.

Die Theorie des Rechtserzeugerkreises. Eine rechtstheoretische Untersuchung des Verhältnisses von Völkerrecht zu Staatsrecht am Beispiel der österreichischen Rechtsordnung (Duncker & Humblot 2013).

"Is the EU Legal Order the Tombstone of the Dualistic and the Monistic Doctrine?" in Michael Thaler and Michel Verpeaux (eds) *La recherche en droit constitutionnel comparé* (L'Harmattan 2014) 71–86.

"The Theory of the Law Creators' Circle: Re-Conceptualizing the Monism–Dualism–Pluralism Debate" (2016) 17 (2) German Law Journal 179–214.

"Ist Art. 59 Abs. 2 GG tatsächlich dualistisch? Ein Beitrag zur Stärkung der innerstaatlichen Wirkung völkerrechtlicher Verträge und gleichzeitig einer stärkeren Einbindung der Legislative auf völkerrechtlicher Ebene" (2017) 72 (3) Zeitschrift für öffentliches Recht 515–547.

"Morality between Nativism and Behaviorism. (Innate) Intersubjectivity as a Response to John Mikhail's 'Universal Moral Grammar'" (2017) 37 (4) Journal of Theoretical and Philosophical Psychology 230–260.

"What Came First: The Obligation or the Belief? A Renaissance of Consensus Theory to Make the Normative Foundations of Customary International Law More Tangible" (2017) 59 German Yearbook of International Law 289–319.

"Who Has the Final Say? The Relationship between International, EU and National Law" (2018) 10 European Journal of Legal Studies 47–100.

"Descriptive vs Prescriptive (Global) Legal Pluralism: A Gentle Reminder of David Hume's Is–Ought Divide" (2019) 51 (1) Journal of Global Legal Pluralism and Unofficial Law 48–71.

"How (Not) to Argue for the Relation between Natural Sciences and Law: Why the Thesis of an Innate 'Universal Moral Grammar' and Its Relevance for Law as Argued by John Mikhail Fails" (2019) 105 (4) Archiv für Rechts- und Sozialphilosophie 523–535.

"Europäische Souveränität? Zur Autonomie des Unionsrechts im Verhältnis zum Völkerrecht sowie den Mitgliedstaaten am Beispiel der Corona Krise" (2021) 56 (1) Europarecht 28–39.

"Nationale Souveränität als Verfassungsidentität. Warum der EuGH Letztentscheider über den Gehalt nationaler Identität sein sollte" (2021) 73 (8) Die Öffentliche Verwaltung 321–326.

Kirgis, Frederick L, "Custom on a Sliding Scale" (1987) 81 (1) American Journal of International Law 146–151.

Klabbers, Jan, *The Constitutionalization of International Law* (Oxford University Press 2009).

The European Union in International Law (Editions A Pedone 2012).

"Straddling the Fence: The EU and International Law" in Anthony Arnull and Damian Chalmers (eds) *The Oxford Handbook of European Union Law* (Oxford University Press 2017) 52–71.

Klamert, Marcus, *The Principle of Loyalty in EU Law* (Oxford University Press 2014).

Klaushofer, Reinhard and Palmstorfer, Rainer, "Austrian Constitutional Court Uses Charter of Fundamental Rights of the European Union as Standard of Review: Effects on Union Law" (2013) 19 (1) European Public Law 1–11.

Kleinlein, Thomas, *Konstitutionalisierung im Völkerrecht* (Springer 2012).

"Neue starke Stimme in der europäischen Grundrechts-Polyphonie" (December 1, 2019) Verfassungsblog, available at https://verfassungsblog.de/neue-starke-stimme-in-der-europaeischen-grundrechts-polyphonie/ [last accessed February 1, 2023].

Knauff, Matthias, *Der Regelungsverbund: Recht und Soft Law im Mehrebenensystem* (Mohr Siebeck 2010).

Köck, Heribert-Franz, "Der erste Staatszweck in einer pluralistischen Gesellschaft" in Herbert Miehsler et al (eds) *Ius Humanitas. Festschrift zum 90. Geburtstag von Alfred Verdross* (Duncker & Humblot 1980) 87.

Koffka, Kurt, *Principles of Gestalt Psychology* (Harcourt-Brace 1935).

Köhnke, Klaus Christian, *Entstehung und Aufstieg des Neukantianismus. Die deutsche Universitätsphilosophie zwischen Idealismus und Positivismus* (Suhrkamp 1993).

Kokott, Juliane and Sobotta, Christoph, "The Kadi Case – Constitutional Core Values and International Law – Finding the Balance?" (2012) 23 (4) European Journal of International Law 1015–1024.

Kolb, Robert, "Selected Problems in the Theory of Customary International Law" (2003) 50 (2) Netherlands International Law Review 119–150.

Koller, Peter, *Neue Theorien des Sozialkontrakts* (Duncker & Humblot 1987).

"Meilensteine des Rechtspositivismus im 20. Jahrhundert: Hans Kelsens Reine Rechtslehre und H. L. A. Harts 'Concept of Law'" in Ota Weinberger and Werner Krawietz (eds) *Reine Rechtslehre im Spiegel ihrer Fortsetzer und Kritiker* (Springer 1988) 129–178.

Komárek, Jan, "Playing with Matches: The Czech Constitutional Court Declares a Judgment of the Court of Justice of the EU Ultra Vires; Judgment of 31 January 2012, Pl. ÚS 5/12, Slovak Pensions XVII" (2012) 8 (1) European Constitutional Law Review 323–337.

Konstadinides, Theodore, "When in Europe: Customary International Law and EU Competences in the Sphere of External Action" (2012) 13 (11) German Law Journal 1177–1201.

Kopelmans, Lazare, "Custom as a Means of the Creation of International Law" (1937) 18 British Yearbook of International Law 127–151.

Kosař, David, Baroš, Jiří and Dufek, Pavel, "The Twin Challenges to Separation of Powers in Central Europe: Technocratic Governance and Populism" (2019) 15 (3) European Constitutional Law Review 427–461.

Koskenniemi, Martti, "The Pull of the Mainstream" (1990) 88 (6) Michigan Law Review 1946–1962.

The Gentle Civilizer of Nations (Cambridge University Press 2001).

From Apology to Utopia: The Structure of International Legal Argument (Cambridge University Press 2005).

"Chairman of the Study Group of the ILC on Fragmentation of International Law: Difficulties Arising from the Diversification and Expansion of International Law" (2006) Report of the Study Group of the International Law Commission, UN Doc A/CN.4/L.682.

Köster, Moritz et al, "Cultural Influences on Toddlers' Prosocial Behavior: How Maternal Task Assignment Relates to Helping Others" (2016) 87 (6) Child Development 1727–1738.

Koutrakos, Panos, *EU International Relations Law* (Hart 2nd ed 2015).

"Institutional Balance and the Duty of Cooperation in Treaty-Making under EU Law" (2018) 68 (1) International and Comparative Law Quarterly 1–33.

"The European Union" in Michael J Bowman and Dino Kritsiotis (eds) *Conceptual and Contextual Perspectives on the Modern Law of Treaties* (Cambridge University Press 2018) 933–965.

Krabbe, Hugo, *Die moderne Staatsidee* (Nijhoff 2nd ed 1919).

Kraft, Victor, *Erkenntnislehre* (Springer 1960).

Kramer, Matthew H, "Legal and Moral Obligation" in Martin P Golding and William A Edmundson (eds) *The Blackwell Guide to the Philosophy of Law and Legal Theory* (Blackwell 2005) 179–190.

Krijnen, Christian, "'Back to Kant': Neo-Kantianism" in Gary Banham, Dennis Schulting and Nigel Hems (eds) *The Bloomsbury Companion to Kant* (Bloomsbury 2nd ed 2015) 318–324.

Krisch, Nico, *Beyond Constitutionalism: The Pluralist Structure of Postnational Law* (Oxford University Press 2010).

"Who Is Afraid of Radical Pluralism? Legal Order and Political Stability in the Postnational Space" (2011) 24 (4) Ratio Juris 386–412.

Kristoferitsch, Gisela, "The Charter of Fundamental Rights of the European Union to Be Treated like Constitutional Law. Austrian Constitutional Court Judgment of 14 March 2012, U 466/11 et al" (2013) 7 (1) Vienna Journal on International Constitutional Law 88–92.

Krönke, Christoph, *Die Verfahrensautonomie der Mitgliedstaaten der Europäischen Union* (Mohr Siebeck 2013).

Krunke, Helle, "The Danish Lisbon Judgment: Danish Supreme Court, Case 199/2012, Judgment of 20 February 2013" (2014) 10 (3) European Constitutional Law Review 542–570.

"Impact of the EU/EEA on the Nordic Constitutional Systems" in Helle Krunke and Björg Thorarensen (eds) *The Nordic Constitutions. A Comparative and Contextual Study* (Hart 2018) 167–202.

Krunke, Helle and Klinge, Sune, "The Danish *Ajos* Case: The Missing Case from *Maastricht* and *Lisbon*" (2018) 3 (1) European Papers 157–182.

Krygier, Martin, "Institutionalisation and Its Trials. (Anti-)Constitutional Populism in Post-Communist Europe" (2019) 15 (3) European Constitutional Law Review 544–573.

Kuijper, Pieter Jan, "Customary International Law, Decisions of International Organisations and Other Techniques for Ensuring Respect for International Legal Rules in European Community Law" in Jan Wouters, André Nollkaemper and Erika de Wet (eds) *The Europeanisation of International Law* (T M C Asser Press 2008) 87–106.

"The European Courts and the Law of Treaties: The Continuing Story" in Enzo Cannizzaro (ed) *The Law of Treaties beyond the Vienna Convention* (Oxford University Press 2011) 256–278.

"The Case Law of the Court of Justice and the Allocation of External Relations Powers: Whither the Traditional Role of the Executive in EU Foreign Relations?" in Marise Cremona and Anne Thies (eds) *The European Court of Justice and External Relations Law – Constitutional Challenges* (Hart 2016) 95–114.

"The Court and the New EU Foreign Relations Law: Institutional Balance?" in Jenő Czuczai and Frederik Naert (eds) *The EU as a Global Actor – Bridging Legal Theory and Practice: Liber Amicorum in Honour of Ricardo Gosalbo Bono* (Brill Nijhoff 2017) 48–64.

Kuisma, Mirka and Larik, Joris, "The Continuing Contestation of ERTA. Conferral, Effectiveness and the Member States' Participation in Mixed Agreements" in Nicolas Levrat et al (eds) *The EU and Its Member States' Joint Participation in International Agreements* (Hart 2022) 43–58.

Kumm, Mattias, "Who Is the Final Arbiter of Constitutionality in Europe? Three Conceptions of the Relationship between the German Federal Constitutional Court and the European Court of Justice" (1999) 36 (2) Common Market Law Review 351–386.

"The Legitimacy of International Law: A Constitutionalist Framework of Analysis" (2004) 15 (5) European Journal of International Law 907–931.

"The Jurisprudence of Constitutional Conflict: Constitutional Supremacy in Europe before and after the Constitutional Treaty" (2005) 11 (3) European Law Journal 262–307.

"The Cosmopolitan Turn in Constitutionalism: On the Relationship between National Constitutional Law and Constitutionalism beyond the State" in Jeffrey L Dunoff and Joel P Trachtman (eds) *Ruling the World: Constitutionalism, International Law, and Global Governance* (Cambridge University Press 2009) 258–325.

"The Moral Point of Constitutional Pluralism" in Julie Dickson and Pavlos Eleftheriadis (eds) *Philosophical Foundations of European Union Law* (Oxford University Press 2012) 216–246.

"Rebel Without a Good Cause: Karlsruhe's Misguided Attempt to Draw the CJEU into a Game of 'Chicken' and What the CJEU Might Do about It" (2014) 15 (2) German Law Journal 203–215.

Kunz, Josef L, *Völkerrechtswissenschaft und Reine Rechtslehre* (Deuticke 1923).

"La primauté de droit des gens" (1925) 6 Revue de droit international et de législation comparé 556–598.

"On the Theoretical Basis of the Law of Nations" (1925) 10 Transactions of the Grotius Society 115–142.

Lachmayer, Konrad, "The Constitution of Austria in International Constitutional Networks: Pluralism, Dialogues and Diversity" in Anneli Albi and Samo Bardutzky (eds) *National Constitutions in European and Global Governance: Democracy, Rights, the Rule of Law. National Reports* (Springer 2019) 1271–1322.

Langan, Christopher M, *The Art of Knowing: Expositions on Free Will and Selected Essays* (Mega Press 2002).

Larik, Joris, *Foreign Policy Objectives in European Constitution* (Oxford University Press 2016).

Lask, Emil, *Rechtsphilosophie* in Emil Lask, *Gesammelte Schriften Vol 1* (Paul Siebeck 1923).

Laurence, Stephen and Margolis, Eric, "The Poverty of the Stimulus Argument" (2001) 52 (2) British Journal for the Philosophy of Science 217–276.

Laurer, Hans René, "Europarecht und österreichische Rechtsordnung – Rechsnormen in einem einheitlichen Stufenbau? – Ein 'Vorwort'" (1997) 52 (21) Österreichische Juristenzeitung 801–810.

Lefkowitz, David, "(Dis)solving the Chronological Paradox in Customary International Law: A Hartian Approach" (2008) 21 (1) Canadian Journal of Law and Jurisprudence 128–148.

Legrain, Leon, Cleeremans, Axel and Destrebecqz, Arnaud, "Distinguishing Three Levels in Explicit Self-Awareness" (2011) 20 (3) Consciousness and Cognition 578–585.

Lenaerts, Koen, "Kooperation und Spannung im Verhältnis von EuGH und Verfassungsgerichten" (2015) 50 (1) Europarecht 3–27.

"The Rule of Law and the Constitutional Identity of the European Union" (March 5, 2023) part of the speech delivered by the president of the CJUE Koen Lenaerts on February 17, 2023 at the conference organized by the Bulgarian Association for European Law in Sofia, available at https://evropeiskipravenpregled.eu/the-rule-of-law-and-the-constitutional-identity-of-the-european-union/#_ftnref49 [last accessed February 1, 2023].

Lenaerts, Koen and Gutiérrez-Fons, José A, "To Say What the Law of the EU Is: Methods of Interpretation and the European Court of Justice" EUI Working Paper AEL 2013/9, available at http://cadmus.eui.eu/bitstream/handle/1814/28339/AEL_2013_09_DL.pdf?sequence=1&isAllowed=y [last accessed February 1, 2023].

Lenaerts, Koen, Gutiérrez-Fons, José A and Adam, Stanislas, "Exploring the Autonomy of the European Union Legal Order" (2021) 81 Heidelberg Journal of International Law 47–87.

Lepard, Brian D, *Customary International Law: A New Theory with Practical Implications* (Cambridge University Press 2010).

"Customary International Law as a Dynamic Process" in Curtis A Bradley (ed) *Custom's Future: International Law in a Changing World* (Cambridge University Press 2016) 62–94.

Lepper, Mark R, Greene, David and Nisbett, Richard E, "Undermining Children's Intrinsic Interest with Extrinsic Rewards: A Test of the 'Overjustification' Hypothesis" (1973) 28 (1) Journal of Personality & Social Psychology 129–137.

Lessnoff, Michael (ed), *Social Contract Theory* (New York University Press 1990).

Levrat, Nicolas et al (eds), *The EU and Its Member States' Joint Participation in International Agreements* (Hart 2022).

Liebmann, Otto, *Kant und die Epigonen* (Carl Schober 1865).

Lindahl, Lars and Reidhav, David, "Conflict of Legal Norms: Definition and Varieties" in Michał Araszkiewicz and Krzysztof Płeszka (eds) *Logic in the Theory and Practice of Lawmaking* (Springer 2015) 49–96.

Linderfalk, Ulf, "The Creation of Jus Cogens: Making Sense of Article 53 of the Vienna Convention" (2011) 71 Heidelberg Journal of International Law 359–378.

Lock, Tobias, *The European Court of Justice and International Courts* (Oxford University Press 2015).

Locke, John, *Two Treatises of Government* (*Two Treatises of Government and A Letter Concerning Toleration* edited by Ian Shapiro Yale University Press 2003 [1690]).

Lodge, Milton and Taber, Charles, *The Rationalizing Voter* (Cambridge University Press 2013).

Lohmann, Friedrich, *Karl Barth und der Neukantianismus. Die Rezeption des Neukantianismus im "Römerbrief" und ihre Bedeutung für die weitere Ausarbeitung der Theologie Karl Barths* (De Gruyter 1995).

"'Ethische Unruhe'. Die Funktion von Ethik bei der gesellschaftlichen Ordnungsbildung" in Helga Pelizäus and Ludwig Nieder (eds) *Das Risiko – Gedanken übers und ins Ungewisse. Interdisziplinäre Aushandlungen des Risikophänomens im Lichte der Reflexiven Moderne. Eine Festschrift für Wolgang Bonß* (Springer 2019) 95–125.

Loughlin, Martin, "Constitutional Pluralism: An Oxymoron?" (2014) 3 (1) Global Constitutionalism 9–30.

Low, Jason and Perner, Josef, "Implicit and Explicit Theory of Mind: State of the Art" (2012) 30 (1) British Journal of Developmental Psychology 1–13.

Lüddecke, Dirk, "Erstlingswerk: Der Konservatismus eines Radikalen. David Hume als Anatom politischer Loyalität" in Dirk Lüddecke and Felicia Englmann (eds) *Zur Geschichte des politischen Denkens. Denkweisen von der Antike bis zur Gegenwart* (J B Metzler 2014) 168–190.

Luf, Gerhard, "Zur Problematik des Wertbegriffes in der Rechtsphilosophie" in Herbert Miehsler et al (eds) *Ius Humanitas. Festschrift zum 90. Geburtstag von Alfred Verdross* (Duncker & Humblot 1980) 127–146.

"On the Transcendental Import of Kelsen's Basic Norm" in Stanley L Paulson and Bonnie Litschewski-Paulson (eds) *Normativity and Norms: Critical Perspectives on Kelsenian Themes* (Oxford Clarendon Press 1998) 221–234.

Luft, Sebastian, "Introduction: Hermann Cohen (1842–1918)" in Sebastian Luft (ed) *The Neo-Kantian Reader* (Routledge 2015) 93–100.

(ed), *The Neo-Kantian Reader* (Routledge 2015).

Luhmann, Niklas, *Soziale Systeme. Grundriß einer allgemeinen Theorie* (Suhrkamp 1984).

Rechtssoziologie (Westdeutscher Verlag 3rd ed 1987).

Das Recht der Gesellschaft (Suhrkamp 1993).

Macarthur, David, "Naturalism and Skepticism" in Mario De Caro and David Macarthur (eds) *Naturalism in Question* (Harvard University Press 2004) 106–124.

MacCormick, Neil, "Beyond the Sovereign State" (1993) 56 (1) Modern Law Review 1–18.

"The Maastricht-Urteil: Sovereignty Now" (1995) 1 (3) European Law Journal 259–266.

"Risking Constitutional Collision in Europe?" (1998) 18 (3) Oxford Journal of Legal Studies 517–532.

Questioning Sovereignty. Law State and Nation in the European Commonwealth (Oxford University Press 1999).

MacGibbon, Ian C, "Customary International Law and Acquiescence" (1958) 33 British Yearbook of International Law 115–145.

Maduro, Miguel Poiares, "The Heteronyms of European Law" (1999) 5 (2) European Law Journal 160–168.

"Contrapunctual Law: Europe's Constitutional Pluralism in Action" in Neil Walker (ed) *Sovereignty in Transition* (Hart 2003) 502–537.

"European Constitution: What if This Is as Good as It Gets?" in Joseph H H Weiler and Marlene Wind (eds) *European Constitutionalism beyond the State* (Cambridge University Press 2003) 74–102.

"Three Claims of Constitutional Pluralism" in Matej Avbelj and Jan Komárek (eds) *Constitutional Pluralism in the European Union and Beyond* (Hart 2012) 67–84.

Maher, Imelda, "The CILFIT Criteria Clarified and Extended for National Courts of Last Resort under Art. 267 TFEU" (2021) 7 (1) European Papers 265–274.

Mahlmann, Matthias, *Rationalismus in der praktischen Theorie: Normentheorie und praktische Kompetenz* (Nomos 2nd ed 2008).

"Mind and Rights: Neuroscience, Philosophy, and the Foundations of Legal Justice" in Mortimer N Sellers (ed) *Law, Reason, and Emotion* (Cambridge University Press 2017) 80–137.

Malinowski, Bronislaw, *Crime and Custom in Savage Society* (Kegan Paul 1926).

Mangoldt, Anna Katharina, *Gemeinschaftsrecht und deutsches Recht. Die Europäisierung der deutschen Rechtsordnung in historisch-empirischer Sicht* (Mohr Siebeck 2011).

Manin, Philippe, "The European Communities and the Vienna Convention on the Law of Treaties between States and International Organizations or between International Organizations" (1987) 24 (3) Common Market Law Review 457–481.

Marceau, Gabrielle, "Conflicts of Norms and Conflicts of Jurisdictions: The Relationship between the WTO Agreement and MEAs and Other Treaties" (2001) 35 (6) Journal of World Trade 1081–1131.

Marmor, Andrei, "The Pure Theory of Law" in Edward N Zalta (ed) *Stanford Encyclopedia of Philosophy* (January 4, 2016), available at https://plato.stanford.edu/entries/lawphil-theory/ [last accessed February 1, 2023].

Martines, Francesca, "Direct Effect of International Agreements of the European Union" (2014) 25 (1) European Journal of International Law 129–147.

Matthews, H E, "Strawson on Transcendental Idealism" (1969) 19 (76) Philosophical Quarterly 204–220.

Mayer, Franz C, *Kompetenzüberschreitung und Letztentscheidung. Das Maastricht-Urteil des Bundesverfassungsgerichts und die Letztentscheidung über Ultra vires-Akte in Mehrebenensystemen. Eine rechtsvergleichende Betrachtung von Konflikten zwischen Gerichten am Beispiel der EU und der USA* (CH Beck 2000).

"Verfassung im Nationalstaat: Von der Gesamtordnung zur europäischen Teilordnung?" (2016) 75 Veröffentlichungen der Vereinigung der Deutschen Staatsrechtslehrer 7–63.

"Auf dem Weg zum Richterfaustrecht? Zum PSPP-Urteil des BVerfG" (May 7, 2020) Verfassungsblog, available at https://verfassungsblog.de/auf-dem-weg-zum-richterfaustrecht/ [last accessed February 1, 2023].

Mayer, Heinz, "Rechtstheorie und Rechtspraxis" in Clemens Jabloner and Friedrich Stadler (eds) *Logischer Empirismus und Reine Rechtslehre: Beziehungen zwischen dem Wiener Kreis und der Hans Kelsen Schule* (Springer 2002) 319–331.

Mazzeschi, Riccardo P, "The Marginal Role of the Individual in the ILC's Articles on State Responsibility" (2004) 14 Italian Yearbook of International Law 39–51.

McCarthy, Thomas, *The Critical Theory of Juergen Habermas* (MIT Press 1978).

McDowell, John Henry, *Having the World in View. Essays on Kant, Hegel, and Sellars* (Harvard University Press 2009).

McKee, Derek, "Review Essay – Emmanuel Melissaris's Ubiquitous Law: Legal Theory and the Space for Legal Pluralism" (2010) 11 (5) German Law Journal 573–584.

Meadwell, Hudson, "The Foundations of Habermas's Universal Pragmatics" (1994) 23 (5) Theory and Society 711–727.

Melissaris, Emmanuel, "The More the Merrier? A New Take on Legal Pluralism" (2004) 13 (1) Social & Legal Studies 57–79.

Ubiquitous Law: Legal Theory and the Space for Legal Pluralism (Ashgate 2009).

Mendelson, Maurice H, "The Subjective Element in Customary International Law" (1996) 66 British Yearbook of International Law 177–208.

Mendez, Mario, *The Legal Effects of EU Agreements. Maximalist Treaty Enforcement and Judicial Avoidance Techniques* (Oxford University Press 2013).

Merkl, Adolf J, "Hans Kelsens System einer reinen Rechtslehre" (1921) 41 Archiv des öffentlichen Rechts 171–202.

Merry, Sally Engle, "Legal Pluralism" (1988) 22 (5) Law & Society Review 869–896.

Mesquita Ceia, Eleonora, *Die verfassungsgerichtliche Kontrolle völkerrechtlicher Verträge. Eine rechtsvergleichende Untersuchung zwischen Brasilien und Europa* (Nomos 2011).

Miasik, Dawid and Szwarc, Monika, "Primacy and Direct Effect – Still Together: Poplawski II" (2021) 58 (2) Common Market Law Review 571–590.

Michaels, Ralf, "Global Legal Pluralism" (2009) 5 Annual Review of Law and Social Science 243–262.

"On Liberalism and Legal Pluralism" in Miguel Maduro, Kaarlo Tuori and Suvi Sankari (eds) *Transnational Law: Rethinking European Law and Legal Thinking* (Cambridge University Press 2014) 122–142.

"Law and Recognition – Towards a Relational Concept of Law" in Nicole Roughan and Andrew Halpin (eds) *In Pursuit of Pluralist Jurisprudence* (Cambridge University Press 2017) 90–115.

Michel, Nicolas, "L'imprégnation du droit étatique par l'ordre juridique international" in Daniel Thürer, Jean-François Aubert and Jörg Paul Müller (eds) *Verfassungsrecht der Schweiz* (Schulthess 2001) 63–69.

Mikhail, John, "Universal Moral Grammar: Theory, Evidence and the Future" (2007) 11 (4) Trends in Cognitive Sciences 143–152.

Elements of Moral Cognition: Rawls' Linguistic Analogy and the Cognitive Science of Moral and Legal Judgment (Cambridge University Press 2011).

"Moral Grammar and Human Rights – Some Reflections on Cognitive Science and Enlightenment Rationalism" in Ryan Goodman, Derek Jinks and Andrew K Woods (eds) *Understanding Social Action, Promoting Human Rights* (Oxford University Press 2012) 160–202.

Mikhail, John and Mahlmann, Matthias, "Cognitive Science, Ethics and Law" in Zenon Bankowski (ed) *Epistemology & Ontology: IVR-Symposium Lund 2003* (Franz Steiner 2005) 95–102.

Mikulincer, Mario and Shaver, Phillip R, "Attachment Theory and Research: Resurrection of the Psychodynamic Approach to Personality" (2005) 39 (1) Journal of Research in Personality 22–45.

Miller, Greg, "The Roots of Morality: Neurobiologists, Philosophers, Psychologists, and Legal Scholars Are Probing the Nature of Human Morality Using a Variety of

Experimental Techniques and Moral Challenges" (2008) 320 (5877) Science 734–737.

Milward, Sophie J, Kita, Sotaro and Apperly, Ian A, "The Development of Co-Representation Effects in a Joint Task: Do Children Represent a Co-Actor?" (2014) 132 (3) Cognition 269–279.

"Individual Differences in Children's Corepresentation of Self and Other in Joint Action" (2017) 88 (3) Child Development 964–978.

Mögele, Rudolf, "Art 216" in Rudolf Streinz (ed) *EUV/AEUV* (CH Beck 3rd ed 2018).

Moore, George E, *Some Main Problems of Philosophy* (Macmillan 1953).

Moreno-Lax, Violeta and Ziegler, Katja S, "Autonomy of the EU Legal Order – A General Principle? On the Risks of Normative Functionalism and Selective Constitutionalism" in Katja S Ziegler, Päivi J Neuvonen and Violeta Moreno-Lax (eds) *General Principles in EU Law. Constructing Legal Orders in Europe* (Edward Elgar 2022) 227–252.

Morris, William Edward, "David Hume" in Edward N Zalta (ed) *Stanford Encyclopedia of Philosophy* (April 17, 2019), available at https://plato.stanford.edu/entries/hume/ [last accessed February 1, 2023].

Morscher, Edgar, "The Descriptive-Normative Dichotomy and the So Called Naturalistic Fallacy" (2016) 38 (2) Analyse und Kritik 317–337.

Müller, Andreas Th, "The Direct Effect of Customary International Law: The 'Treaty Analogy' and Its Limits" in Fernando Lusa Bordin, Andreas Th Müller and Francisco Pascual-Vives (eds) *The European Union and Customary International Law* (Cambridge University Press 2022) 210–239.

Müller, Claudius, *Die Rechtsphilosophie des Marburger Neukantianismus: Naturrecht und Rechtspositivismus in der Auseinandersetzung zwischen Hermann Cohen, Rudolf Stammler und Paul Natorp* (Mohr Siebeck 1994).

Müller, Jan-Werner, "Protecting the Rule of Law (and Democracy!) in the EU. The Idea of a Copenhagen Commission" in Carlos Closa and Dimitry Kochenov (eds) *Reinforcing Rule of Law Oversight in the European Union* (Cambridge University Press 2016) 206–224.

Müller, Matthias, *Das Rechtsprechungsmonopol des EuGH im Kontext völkerrechtlicher Verträge. Untersucht anhand der Rechtsprechung des Gerichtshofs der Europäischen Union* (Nomos 2012).

Murray, Lynne and Trevarthen, Colwyn, "Emotional Regulation of Interactions between Two-Month-Olds and Their Mothers" in Tiffany M Field and Nathan A Fox (eds) *Social Perception in Infants* (Ablex 1985) 177–197.

Nader, Laura, "The Anthropological Study of Law" (1965) 67 (6) Ethnography of Law. American Anthropologist. New Series. Part 2 3–32.

Nagel, Thomas, *The View from Nowhere* (Oxford University Press 1989).

Nagy, Emese, "Innate Intersubjectivity: Newborns' Sensitivity to Communication Disturbance" (2008) 44 (6) Developmental Psychology 1779–1784.

"The Newborn Infant: A Missing Stage in Developmental Psychology" (2011) 20 (1) Infant and Child Development 3–19.

Nagy, Emese and Molnár, Peter, "Homo Imitans or Homo Provocans? Human Imprinting Model of Neonatal Imitation" (2004) 27 (1) Infant Behavior and Development 54–63.

Narvaez, Darcia, *Neurobiology and the Development of Human Morality. Evolution, Culture, and Wisdom* (W W Norton & Company 2014).
Natorp, Paul, "'On the Objective and Subjective Grounding of Knowledge' (1887)" in Sebastian Luft (ed) *The Neo-Kantian Reader* (translated by Lois Phillips and David Kolb Routledge 2015 ["Über objective und subjective Begründung der Erkenntniss" (1887) 23 Philosophische Monatshefte 257–286]) 164–179.
"'Kant and the Marburg School' (1912)" in Sebastian Luft (ed) *The Neo-Kantian Reader* (translated by Frances Bottenberg Routledge 2015) ["Kant und die Marburger Schule" (1912) 17 Kant-Studien 193–221] 180–197.
Neframi, Eleftheria, "Customary International Law and the European Union from the Perspective of Article 3(5) TEU" in Piet Eeckhout and Manuel López–Escudero (eds) *The European Union's External Action in Times of Crisis* (Hart 2016) 205–222.
Neframi, Eleftheria and Gatti, Mauro (eds), *Constitutional Issues of EU External Relations Law* (Nomos 2018).
Newman, Lex, "Descartes' Epistemology" in Edward N Zalta (ed) *Stanford Encyclopedia of Philosophy* (February 15, 2019), available at https://plato.stanford.edu/entries/descartes-epistemology/ [last accessed February 1, 2023].
Nijman, Janne E and Nollkaemper, André, "Introduction" in Janne E Nijman and André Nollkaemper (eds) *New Perspectives on the Divide between National and International Law* (Oxford University Press 2007) 1–14.
Nollkaemper, André, *National Courts and the International Rule of Law* (Oxford University Press 2011).
"Inside or Out: Two Types of International Legal Pluralism" in Jan Klabbers and Touko Piiparinen (eds) *Normative Pluralism and International Law: Exploring Global Governance* (Cambridge University Press 2013) 94–139.
"The Duality of Direct Effect of International Law" (2014) 25 (1) European Journal of International Law 105–125.
Nollkaemper, André and Reinisch, August, *International Law in Domestic Courts. A Casebook* (Oxford University Press 2018).
Nollkaemper, André and van Alebeek, Rosanne, "Netherlands" in Fulvio Maria Palombino (ed) *Duelling for Supremacy: International Law vs. National Fundamental Principles* (Cambridge University Press 2019) 255–276.
O'Neill, Seamus, "Book Review: Nicholas Rescher, Pluralism against the Demand for Consensus" (1995) 7 (2) Utilitas 340–343.
Odermatt, Jed, *International Law and the European Union* (Cambridge University Press 2021).
"The European Union's Role in the Making and Confirmation of Customary International Law" in Fernando Lusa Bordin, Andreas Th Müller and Francisco Pascual-Vives (eds) *The European Union and Customary International Law* (Cambridge University Press 2022) 66–94.
Öhlinger, Theo, *Der Völkerrechtliche Vertrag im Staatlichen Recht – Eine Theoretische, Dogmatische und Vergleichende Untersuchung am Beispiel Österreichs* (Springer 1973).
Der Bundesstaat zwischen Reiner Rechtslehre und Verfassungsrealität (Braumüller 1976).
"Unmittelbare Geltung und Vorrang des Gemeinschaftsrechts und die Auswirkungen auf das verfassungsrechtliche Rechtsschutzsystem" in Stefan

Griller, Karl Korinek and Michael Potacs (eds) *Grundfragen und aktuelle Probleme des öffentlichen Rechts. Festschrift für Heinz Peter Rill zum 60. Geburtstag* (LexisNexis 1995) 359–379.

"Verfassungsrechtliche Aspekte der Übernahme von Gemeinschaftsrecht und Unionsrecht in die österreichische Rechtsordnung" in Waldemar Hummer and Michael Schweitzer (eds) *Österreich und das Recht der Europäischen Union* (Manz 1996) 169–197.

"Die Auswirkungen der Europäischen Integration auf die Rechtssysteme der Mitgliedstaaten" in Fritz Breuss, Gerhard Fink and Stefan Griller (eds) *Vom Schumann-Plan zum Vertrag von Amsterdam* Vol 2 (Springer 2000) 51–68.

"Die Transformation der Verfassung. Die staatliche Verfassung und die europäische Integration" (2002) 124 (1) Juristische Blätter 2–11.

"Die österreichische Verfassung und die europäische Integration" in Waldemar Hummer (ed) *Paradigmenwechsel im Europarecht zur Jahrtausendwende* (Springer 2004) 67–85.

"Die Einheit des Rechts: Völkerrecht, Europarecht und staatliches Recht als einheitliches Rechtssystem?" in Stanley L Paulson and Michael Stolleis (eds) *Hans Kelsen: Staatsrechtslehrer und Rechtstheoretiker des 20. Jahrhunderts* (Mohr Siebeck 2005) 160–175.

"Übernahme des Vertrages von Lissabon in die österreichische Rechtsordnung" in Waldemar Hummer and Walter Obwexer (eds) Der Vertrag von Lissabon (Nomos 2009) 411–425.

"EU-Beitritts-BVG" in Karl Korinek et al (eds) *Österreichisches Bundesverfassungsrecht* (Verlag Österreich 12sup 2016).

Öhlinger, Theo and Eberhard, Harald, *Verfassungsrecht* (facultas 11th ed 2016).

Öhlinger, Theo and Müller, Andreas, "Artikel 50 B-VG" in Karl Korinek et al (eds) *Österreichisches Bundesverfassungsrecht* (Verlag Österreich 14sup 2018).

Öhlinger, Theo and Potacs, Michael, *EU-Recht und staatliches Recht. Die Anwendung des Europarechts im innerstaatlichen Recht* (Linde 6th ed 2017).

Onishi, Kristine H and Baillargeon, Renée, "Do 15-Month-Old Infants Understand False Beliefs?" (2005) 308 (5719) Science 255–258.

Ottmann, Henning, *Geschichte des politischen Denkens: Das 20. Jahrhundert – Von der kritischen Theorie bis zur Globalisierung* (J B Metzler 2012).

Palmer Olsen, Henrik, "The Danish Supreme Court's Decision on the Constitutionality of Denmark's Ratification of the Lisbon Treaty" (2013) 50 (5) Common Market Law Review 1489–1503.

Palmstorfer, Rainer, "Bundesverfassungsrechtliche Integrationsschranken und Unionsrecht" in Clemens Jabloner et al (eds) *Scharfsinn im Recht. Liber Amicorum für Michael Thaler* (Jan Sramek 2019) 417–428.

Panksepp, Jaap, "At the Interface between the Affective, Behavioral and Cognitive Neurosciences: Decoding the Emotional Feelings of the Brain" (2003) 52 (1) Brain and Cognition 4–14.

Panksepp, Jaap and Trevarthen, Colwyn, "The Neuroscience of Emotion in Music" in Stephen Malloch and Colwyn Trevarthen (eds) *Communicative Musicality: Exploring the Basis of Human Companionship* (Oxford University Press 2009) 105–146.

Pardo, Michael S and Patterson, Dennis, *Minds, Brains, and Law: The Conceptual Foundations of Law and Neuroscience* (Oxford University Press 2013).

Patterson, Dennis, *Law and Truth* (Oxford University Press 1996).
"On the Conceptual and the Empirical – A Critique of John Mikhail's Cognitivism" (2008) 73 (2) Brooklyn Law Review 611–623.
Paulo, Norbert, Möck, Leonie and Kirchmair, Lando, "The Use and Abuse of Moral Preferences in the Ethics of Self-Driving Cars" in Fernando Aguiar, Antonio Gaitán and Hugo Viciana (eds) *Experiments in Moral and Political Philosophy* (Routledge 2024) 290–309.
Paulson, Stanley L, "Zur neukantianischen Dimension der Reinen Rechtslehre. Vorwort zur Kelsen-Sander-Auseinandersetzung" in Stanley L Paulson (ed) *Die Rolle des Neukantianismus in der Reinen Rechtslehre. Eine Debatte zwischen Sander und Kelsen* (Scientia 1988) 7–26.
"Kelsen's Legal Theory: The Final Round" (1992) 12 (2) Oxford Journal of Legal Studies 265–274.
"The Neo-Kantian Dimension of Kelsen's Pure Theory of Law" (1992) 12 (3) Oxford Journal of Legal Studies 311–332.
"On the Kelsen–Kant Problematic" in Ernesto Garzón Valdés et al (eds) *Normative Systems in Legal and Moral Theory. Festschrift für Carlos E Alchourrón and Eugenio Bulygin* (Duncker & Humblot 1997) 197–213.
"The Great Puzzle: Kelsen's Basic Norm" in Luís Duarte d'Almeida, John Gardner and Leslie Green (eds) *Kelsen Revisited: New Essays on the Pure Theory of Law* (Hart Publishing 2013) 43–62.
Paulus, Andreas L, "Kompetenzüberschreitende Akte von Organen der Europäischen Union – Die Sicht des Völkerrechts" in Bruno Simma and Constanze Schulte (eds) *Völker- und Europarecht in der aktuellen Diskussion* (Linde 1999) 49–58.
Die internationale Gemeinschaft im Völkerrecht. Eine Untersuchung zur Entwicklung des Völkerrechts im Zeitalter der Globalisierung (CH Beck 2001).
"Commentary to Andreas Fischer-Lescano & Gunther Teubner. The Legitimacy of International Law and the Role of the State" (2004) 25 (4) Michigan Journal of International Law 1047–1058.
"Jus Cogens in a Time of Hegemony and Fragmentation. An Attempt at a Re-appraisal" (2005) 74 Nordic Journal of International Law 297–334.
"The Emergence of the International Community and the Divide between International and Domestic Law" in Janne E Nijman and André Nollkaemper (eds) *New Perspectives on the Divide between National and International Law* (Oxford University Press 2007) 216–250.
"Zur Zukunft der Völkerrechtswissenschaft in Deutschland: Zwischen Konstitutionalisierung und Fragmentierung des Völkerrechts" (2007) 67 Heidelberg Journal of International Law 695–719.
"From Dualism to Pluralism: The Relationship between International Law, European Law, and Domestic Law" in Pieter H F Bekker, Rudolf Dolzer and Michael Waibel (ed) *Making Transnational Law Work in the Global Economy. Essays in Honour of Detlev Vagts* (Cambridge University Press 2010) 132–153.
"Human Rights Protection in a European Network of Courts" (2013) 107 Proceedings of the American Society of International Law 174–182.
"Internationales, nationales und privates Recht. Hybridisierung der Rechtsordnungen" (2014) 46 Berichte der Deutschen Gesellschaft für Internationales Recht 7–46.

"Engaging in Judicial Dialogue" in Amrei Müller (ed) *Judicial Dialogue and Human Rights* (Cambridge University Press 2017) 258–266.

Paulus, Andreas, "Horizontale und vertikale Aufgabenteilung beim Grundrechtsschutz in Europa" in Thomas Groh et al (eds) *Verfassungsrecht, Völkerrecht, Menschenrechte – Vom Recht im Zentrum der Internationalen Beziehungen. Festschrift für Ulrich Fastenrath* (C F Müller 2019) 79–88.

Paulus, Andreas L and Leiss, Johann Ruben, "Constitutionalism and the Mechanics of Global Law Transfers" (2018) 9 Goettingen Journal of International Law – 1 Special Issue: The Law behind Rule of Law Transfers 35–69.

Paulus, Andreas L and Lippold, Matthias, "Customary Law in the Postmodern World (Dis)Order" (2018) 112 American Journal of International Law Unbound 308–312.

Paulus, Markus, "The Emergence of Prosocial Behavior: Why Do Infants and Toddlers Help, Comfort, and Share" (2014) 8 (2) Child Development Perspectives 77–81.

Pawlowski, Hans-Martin, *Methodenlehre für Juristen. Theorie der Norm und des Gesetzes* (C F Müller 3rd ed 1999).

Peirce, Charles Sanders, "Truth and Falsity and Error" in James Mark Baldwin (ed) *Dictionary of Philosophy and Psychology Vol 2* (Macmillan 1901) 716–720.

"Science Immortality" in Charles Hartshorne and Paul Weiss (eds) *Charles Sanders Peirce. Collected Papers Vol VI: Scientific Metaphysics* (Harvard University Press 1935).

Collected Papers Vol VII (Harvard University Press 1958).

Pellet, Alain and Müller, Daniel, "Article 38" in Andreas Zimmermann et al (eds) *The Statute of the International Court of Justice: A Commentary* (Oxford University Press 3rd ed 2018).

Perner, Josef, *Understanding the Representational Mind* (MIT Press 1991).

Pernice, Ingolf, "Die Dritte Gewalt im europäischen Verfassungsverbund" (1996) 31 (1) Europarecht 27–43.

"Multilevel Constitutionalism and the Treaty of Amsterdam: European Constitution-Making Revisited?" (1999) 36 (4) Common Market Law Review 703–750.

"Europäisches und nationales Verfassungsrecht" (2001) 60 Veröffentlichungen der Vereinigung der Deutschen Staatsrechtslehrer 148–193.

"The Treaty of Lisbon: Multilevel Constitutionalism in Action" (2009) 15 (3) Columbia Journal of European Law 349–407.

"Der Schutz nationaler Identität in der Europäischen Union" (2011) 136 (2) Archiv des öffentlichen Rechts 185–221.

"The Autonomy of the EU Legal Order – Fifty Years after Van Gend" in Antonio Tizzano, Juliane Kokott and Sacha Prechal (eds) *50th Anniversary of the Judgment in van Gend en Loos* (EU Publications Office 2013) 55–80.

"Multilevel Constitutionalism and the Crisis of Democracy in Europe" (2015) 11 (3) European Constitutional Law Review 541–562.

Pernthaler, Peter, "Der österreichische Bundesstaat im Spannungsfeld von Föderalismus und formalem Rechtspositivismus" (1969) 19 Zeitschrift für öffentliches Recht 361–379.

Die Staatsgründungsakte der österreichischen Bundesländer: Eine staatsrechtliche Untersuchung über die Entstehung des Bundesstaates (Braumüller 1979).

Allgemeine Staatslehre und Verfassungslehre (Springer 1984).
Allgemeine Staatslehre und Verfassungslehre (Springer 2nd ed 1996).
"Die neue Doppelverfassung Österreichs" in Herbert Haller et al (eds) *Staat und Recht. Festschrift für Günther Winkler* (Springer 1997) 773–796.
Der Verfassungskern. Gesamtänderung und Durchbrechung der Verfassung im Lichte der Theorie, Rechtsprechung und europäischen Verfassungskultur (Manz 1998).
Pernthaler, Peter and Weber, Karl, "Bundesverfassung und Föderalismus" (1982) 21 (4) Der Staat 576–590.
Perry, Michael J, *A Global Political Morality: Human Rights, Democracy, and Constitutionalism* (Cambridge University Press 2017).
Pescatore, Pierre, *L'ordre juridique des Communautés Européennes: Étude des sources du droit communautaire* (Liège 2nd ed 1975).
Peters, Anne, "The Position of International Law within the European Community Legal Order" (1997) 40 German Yearbook of International Law 9–77.
Elemente einer Theorie der Verfassung Europas (Duncker & Humblot 2001).
"Compensatory Constitutionalism: The Function and Potential of Fundamental International Norms and Structures" (2006) 19 (3) Leiden Journal of International Law 579–610.
"The Globalization of State Constitutions" in Janne Nijman and Andre Nollkaemper (eds) *New Perspectives on the Divide between National and International Law* (Oxford University Press 2007) 251–308.
"Rechtsordnungen und Konstitutionalisierung: Zur Neubestimmung der Verhältnisse" (2010) 65 (1) Zeitschrift für Öffentliches Recht 3–63.
Beyond Human Rights. The Legal Status of the Individual in International Law (Cambridge University Press 2016).
"Constitutionalisation" in Jean d'Aspremont and Sahib Singh (eds) *Concepts for International Law – Contributions to Disciplinary Thought* (Edward Elgar 2019) 141–153.
Petersen, Nils, "Customary Law without Custom? Rules, Principles, and the Role of State Practice in International Norm Creation" (2007–2008) 23 (2) American University International Law Review 275–310.
"The Role of Consent and Uncertainty in the Formation of Customary International Law" in Brian D Lepard (ed) *Reexamining Customary International Law* (Cambridge University Press 2018) 111–130.
Pfersmann, Otto, "La production des normes: production normative et hiérarchie des normes" in Michel Troper and Dominique Chagnollaud (eds) *Traité international de droit constitutionnel. Distribution des pouvoirs, Vol 2* (Dalloz 2012) 483–528.
Piccirilli, Giovanni, "The 'Taricco Saga': The Italian Constitutional Court Continues Its European Journey" (2018) 14 (4) European Constitutional Law Review 814–833.
Pinkard, Terry, *Hegel's Phenomenology. The Sociality of Reason* (Cambridge University Press 1994).
Pinker, Steven, *The Blank Slate: The Modern Denial of Human Nature* (Viking 2002).
Pirker, Benedikt, *Grundrechtsschutz im Unionsrecht zwischen Subsidiarität und Integration. Zur Anwendung der Unionsgrundrechte auf die Mitgliedstaaten* (Nomos 2018).

Plutarch, *Quaestiones Convivales, Morals* (corrected and revised by William W. Goodwin, 1874), available at www.perseus.tufts.edu/hopper/text?doc=Perseus%3Atext%3A2008.01.0312%3Abook%3D2%3Achapter%3D3%3Asection%3D2 [last accessed February 1, 2023].

Podszun, Rupprecht, "Corporate Social Responsibility – Standards: Rechtstheoretische Aspekte und die Frage, was den 'Markenkern' der Rechtswissenschaft ausmacht" in Reto M Hilty and Frauke Henning-Bodewig (eds) *Corporate Social Responsibility: Verbindliche Standards des Wettbewerbsrechts?* (Springer 2014) 51–80.

Polakiewicz, Jörg, "International Law and Domestic (Municipal) Law, Law and Decisions of International Organizations and Courts" in Rüdiger Wolfrum (ed) *Max Planck Encyclopedia of Public International Law* (Oxford University Press 2012).

Pollicino, Oreste and Repetto, Giorgio, "Not to Be Pushed Aside: The Italian Constitutional Court and the European Court of Justice" (February 27, 2019) Verfassungsblog, available at https://verfassungsblog.de/not-to-be-pushed-aside-the-italian-constitutional-court-and-the-european-court-of-justice/ [last accessed February 1, 2023].

Polzin, Monika, *Verfassungsidentität: Ein normatives Konzept des Grundgesetzes?* (Mohr Siebeck 2018).

Popper, Karl, "Philosophical Comments on Tarski's Theory of Truth" in Karl Popper, *Objective Knowledge: An Evolutionary Approach* (Oxford Clarendon Press 2nd ed 1972) 319–340.

Logik der Forschung (Mohr Siebeck 8th ed 1984).

Porges, Stephen W and Carter, Carol Sue, "Neurobiology and Evolution: Mechanisms, Mediators, and Adaptive Consequences of Caregiving" in Stephanie L Brown, R Michael Brown and Louis A Penner (eds) *Self-Interest and Beyond: Toward a New Understanding of Human Caregiving* (Oxford University Press 2007) 53–71.

Poscher, Ralf, "Wahrheit und Recht. Die Wahrheitsfragen des Rechts im Lichte der deflationären Wahrheitstheorie" (2003) 89 (2) Archiv für Rechts- und Sozialphilosophie 200–215.

Pöschl, Magdalena, "Verfassungsgerichtsbarkeit nach Lissabon Anmerkungen zum Charta-Erkenntnis des VfGH" (2012) 67 (3) Zeitschrift für Öffentliches Recht 587–609.

Pospisil, Leopold, *Anthropology of Law: A Comparative Perspective* (Harper & Row 1971).

Potacs, Michael, "Zum Rang des Gemeinschaftsrechts gegenüber staatlichem Recht" in Clemens Jabloner, Otto Lucius and Alfred Schramm (eds) *Theorie und Praxis des Wirtschaftsrechts. Festschrift für H. René Laurer* (Springer 2009) 185–198.

"Das Verhältnis zwischen der EU und ihren Mitgliedstaaten im Lichte traditioneller Modelle" (2010) 65 (1) Zeitschrift für Öffentliches Recht 117–139.

Prinz, Jesse J, "Is Morality Innate?" in Walter Sinnot-Armstrong (ed) *Moral Psychology. Evolution of Morality: Adaptations and Innateness Vol I* (MIT Press 2007) 367–406.

The Emotional Construction of Morals (Oxford University Press 2008).

"Resisting the Linguistic Analogy: A Commentary on Hauser, Young, and Cushman" in Walter Sinnott-Armstrong (ed) *Moral Psychology. The Cognitive Science of Morality: Intuition and Diversity Vol. II* (MIT Press 2008) 157–170.

"Is Empathy Necessary for Morality?" in Amy Coplan and Peter Goldie (eds) *Empathy: Philosophical and Psychological Perspectives* (Oxford University Press 2011) 211–229.

Putnam, Hilary, "Why Reason Cannot Be Naturalized" (1982) 52 (1) Synthese 3–23.

Rand, David G, Greene, Joshua D and Nowak, Martin A, "Spontaneous Giving and Calculated Greed" (2012) 489 Nature 427–430.

Rask Madsen, Mikael, Palmer Olsen, Henrik and Šadl, Urška, "Legal Disintegration? The Ruling of the Danish Supreme Court in AJOS" (January 30, 2017) Verfassungsblog, available at https://verfassungsblog.de/legal-disintegration-the-ruling-of-the-danish-supreme-court-in-ajos/ [last accessed February 1, 2023].

Rasmussen, Morten, "Revolutionizing European law: A History of the *Van Gend en Loos* Judgment" (2014) 12 (1) International Journal of Constitutional Law 136–163.

Rauchegger, Clara, "Four Functions of the Principle of Primacy in the Post-Lisbon Case Law of the European Court of Justice" in Katja S Ziegler, Päivi J Neuvonen and Violeta Moreno-Lax (eds) *General Principles in EU Law. Constructing Legal Orders in Europe* (Edward Elgar 2022) 157–172.

Rauter, Thomas, *Judicial Practice, Customary International Criminal Law and Nullum Crimen Sine Lege* (Springer 2017).

Rawls, John, *A Theory of Justice* (Harvard University Press 1971).

"The Independence of Moral Theory" (1975) 48 Proceedings and Addresses of the American Philosophical Association 5–22.

The Law of Peoples (Harvard University Press 1999).

Political Liberalism (Columbia University Press expanded ed 2005).

Raz, Joseph, *The Concept of a Legal System: An Introduction to the Theory of Legal System* (Oxford University Press 2nd ed 1980).

"Why the State?" in Nichole Roughan and Andrew Halpin (eds) *In Pursuit of Pluralist Jurisprudence* (Cambridge University Press 2017) 136–162.

Reddy, Vasu, *How Infants Know Minds* (Harvard University Press 2008).

"Joining Intentions in Infancy" (2015) 22 (1–2) Journal of Consciousness Studies 24–44.

Rehbinder, Manfred, *Die Begründung der deutschen Rechtssoziologie durch Eugen Ehrlich* (Duncker & Humblot 2nd ed 1986).

Reid, Vincent M and Striano, Tricia, "The Directed Attention Model of Infant Social Cognition" (2007) 4 (1) European Journal of Developmental Psychology 100–110.

Reinisch, August, "Zur unmittelbaren Anwendbarkeit von EWR–Recht" (1993) 34 Zeitschrift für Europarecht, Internationales Privatrecht und Rechtsvergleichung 11–30.

International Organizations before National Courts (Cambridge University Press 2000).

"The Division of Powers between the EU and Its Member States 'After Lisbon'" in Marc Bungenberg, Joern Griebel and Steffen Hindelang (eds) *International Investment Law and EU Law – Special Issue of European Yearbook of International Economic Law* (Springer 2011) 43–54.

Rensmann, Thilo, "Article 46" in Oliver Dörr and Kirsten Schmalenbach (eds) *Vienna Convention on the Law of Treaties – A Commentary* (Springer 2nd ed 2018).

Rescher, Nicholas, *The Coherence Theory of Truth* (Oxford University Press 1973).
Pluralism: Against the Demand for Consensus (Oxford Clarendon Press 1993).
Epistemology. An Introduction to the Theory of Knowledge (State University of New York Press 2003).

Ress, Georg, "Wechselwirkungen zwischen Völkerrecht und Verfassung bei der Auslegung völkerrechtlicher Verträge" in Georg Ress and Christoph Schreuer (eds) *Wechselwirkungen zwischen Völkerrecht und Verfassung bei der Auslegung völkerrechtlicher Verträge* (C F Müller 1982).

Richardson, Alan, "'The Fact of Science' and Critique of Knowledge: Exact Science as Problem and Resource in Marburg Neo-Kantianism" in Michael Friedman and Alfred Nordmann (eds) *The Kantian Legacy in Nineteenth-Century Science* (MIT Press 2006) 211–226.

Richmond, Catherine, "Preserving the Identity Crisis: Autonomy, System and Sovereignty in European Law" (1997) 16 (4) Law and Philosophy 377–420.

Rifkin, Jeremy, *The Empathic Civilization. The Race to Global Consciousness in a World in Crisis* (Penguin 2009).

Riley, Patrick, *Will and Political Legitimacy* (Harvard University Press 1982).

Roberts, Anthea E, "Traditional and Modern Approaches to Customary International Law: A Reconciliation" (2001) 95 (4) American Journal of International Law 757–791.
Is International Law International? (Oxford University Press 2017).

Rochat, Philippe, "Five Levels of Self-Awareness as They Unfold Early in Life" (2003) 12 Consciousness and Cognition 717–731.
Others in Mind. Social Origins of Self-Consciousness (Cambridge University Press 2009).

Rochat, Philippe and Passos-Ferreira, Cláudia, "From Imitation to Reciprocation and Mutual Recognition" in Jaime A Pineda (ed) *Mirror Neuron Systems: The Role of Mirroring Processes in Social Cognition* (Humana Press Springer 2008) 191–212.

Rochat, Philippe, Passos-Ferreira, Cláudia and Salem, Pedro, "Three Levels of Intersubjectivity in Early Development" in Antonella Carassa, Francesca Morganti and Giuseppe Riva (eds) *Enacting Intersubjectivity. Paving the Way for a Dialogue between Cognitive Science, Social Cognition and Neuroscience* (Da Larioprint 2009) 173–190.

Rochat, Phillipe and Striano, Tricia, "Social-Cognitive Development in the First Year" in Philippe Rochat (ed) *Early Social Cognition: Understanding Others in the First Months of Life* (Lawrence Erlbaum 1999) 3–34.

Rodríguez Iglesias, Gil C, "Zu den Grenzen der verfahrensrechtlichen Autonomie der Mitgliedstaaten bei der Anwendung des Gemeinschaftsrechts" (1997) 24 (14–16) Europäische Grundrechtezeitschrift 289–295.

Rohlf, Michael, "Immanuel Kant" in Edward N Zalta (ed) *Stanford Encyclopedia of Philosophy* (January 25, 2016), available at https://plato.stanford.edu/entries/kant/ [last accessed February 1, 2023].

Rorty, Richard, "Introduction" in Richard Rorty (ed) *The Linguistic Turn: Essays in Philosophical Method. With Two Retrospective Essays* (University of Chicago Press 1967 reprinted in 1992) 1–39.
Philosophy and the Mirror of Nature (Princeton University Press 1979).
"Born to Be Good" (August 27, 2006) *New York Times*, available at at www.nytimes.com/2006/08/27/books/review/Rorty.t.html?pagewanted=all&_r=0 [last accessed February 1, 2023].

Rosas, Allan, "The European Court of Justice and Public International Law" in Jan Wouters, André Nollkaemper and Erika de Wet (eds) *The Europeanisation of International Law* (TMC Asser Press 2008) 71–85.

"When Is the Charter of Fundamental Rights Applicable at National Level?" (2012) 19 (4) Jurisprudence 1269–1288.

"International Responsibility of the EU and the European Court of Justice" in Malcolm Evans and Panos Koutrakos (eds) *The International Responsibility of the European Union. European and International Perspectives* (Hart 2013) 139–159.

"Recent Case Law of the European Court of Justice Relating to Article 218 TFEU" in Jenő Czuczai and Frederik Naert (eds) *The EU as a Global Actor – Bridging Legal Theory and Practice: Liber Amicorum in Honour of Ricardo Gosalbo Bono* (Brill Nijhoff 2017) 365–379.

Roughan, Nicole, "The Relative Authority of Law: A Contribution to 'Pluralist Jurisprudence'" in Maksymilian Del Mar (ed) *New Waves in Philosophy of Law* (Palgrave Macmillan 2011) 254–273.

Authorities. Conflicts, Cooperation, and Transnational Legal Theory (Oxford University Press 2013).

Rousseau, Jean-Jacques, *The Social Contract* (*The Social Contract and The First and The Second Discourses*, translated and edited by Susan Dunn Yale University Press 2002 [*Du Contract Social; Ou Principes du Droit Politique* 1762]).

Ruffert, Matthias, "Artikel 3 EUV" in Christian Calliess and Matthias Ruffert (eds) *EUV/AEUV* (CH Beck 6th ed 2022) 48–60.

"Artikel 47 EUV" in Christian Calliess and Matthias Ruffert (eds) *EUV/AEUV* (CH Beck 6th ed 2022) 450–453.

Russell, Bertrand, "On the Nature of Truth and Falsehood" (1906–1907) 7 Proceedings of the Aristotelian Society 28–49.

The Philosophy of Logical Atomism (Routledge 2010 [Fontana 1972]).

Sadurski, Wojciech, *Poland's Constitutional Breakdown* (Oxford University Press 2019).

Sahakian, Barbara J and Gottwald, Julia, *Sex, Lies, and Brain Scans. How fMRI Reveals What Really Goes on in Our Minds* (Oxford University Press 2017).

Saiz Arnaiz, Alejandro and Alcoberro Llivina, Carina (eds), *National Constitutional Identity and European Integration* (Intersentia 2013).

Salvadori, Eliala et al, "Probing the Strength of Infants' Preference for Helpers over Hinderers: Two Replication Attempts of Hamlin and Wynn (2011)" (2015) 10 (11) PLOS ONE 1–10.

Sarmiento, Daniel, "Crossing the Baltic Rubicon" (March 4, 2019) Verfassungsblog, available at https://verfassungsblog.de/crossing-the-baltic-rubicon/ [last accessed February 1, 2023].

Sauer, Hanno, "The End of History" (2022) Inquiry, available at https://doi.org/10.1080/0020174X.2022.2124542 [last accessed February 1, 2023].

Scanlon, Thomas M, "Contractualism and Utilitarianism" in Amartya Sen and Bernard Williams (eds) *Utilitarianism and Beyond* (Cambridge University Press 1982) 103–128, reprinted in Thomas M Scanlon, *The Difficulty of Tolerance: Essays in Political Philosophy* (2003 Cambridge University Press) 124–150.

What We Owe to Each Other (Harvard University Press 1999).
Scattola, Merio, "Alberico Gentili (1552–1608)" in Bardo Fassbender and Anne Peters (eds) *The Oxford Handbook of the History of International Law* (Oxford University Press 2012) 1092–1097.
Scelle, Georges, *Précis de droit des gens: Principes et systématique Vol I* (Librairie du Recueil Sirey 1932).
Schachter, Oskar, "Entangling Treaty and Custom" in Yoram Dinstein and Mala Tabory (ed) *International Law at a Time of Perplexity: Essay in Honour of Shabtai Rosenne* (Martinus Nijhoff 1989) 717–738.
Schaffer, Gregory, "A Transnational Take on Krisch's Pluralist Postnational Law" (2012) 23 (2) European Journal of International Law 565–582.
Schäffer, Heinz, "Österreich und die Europäische Union – Erfahrungen und Leistungen des österreichischen VfGH" (2005) 60 Zeitschrift für Öffentliches Recht 345–388.
Scheinin, Martin, "Is the ECJ Ruling in Kadi Incompatible with International Law?" (2009) 28 (1) Yearbook of European Law 637–653.
Schermers, Henry G and Blokker, Niels M, *International Institutional Law* (Brill 6th ed 2018).
Schilling, Theodor, "The Autonomy of the Community Legal Order: An Analysis of Possible Foundations" (1996) 37 (2) Harvard International Law Journal 389–409.
"Das Verhältnis zwischen Völkerrecht, Gemeinschaftsrecht und staatlichem Recht" in Stefan Griller and Heinz Peter Rill (eds) Rechtstheorie: Rechtsbegriff – Dynamik – Auslegung (Springer 2011) 153–194.
Schmalenbach, Kirsten, *Der neue Europaartikel 23 des Grundgesetzes im Lichte der Arbeit der Gemeinsamen Verfassungskommission* (Duncker & Humblot 1996).
"Normentheorie vs. Terrorismus: Der Vorrang des UN-Rechts vor EU-Recht" (2006) 61 (7) JuristenZeitung 349–353.
"Die Europäische Union und das universelle Völkerrecht" in Werner Schroeder (ed) *Europarecht als Mehrebenensystem* (Nomos/facultas 2008) 67–88.
"Struggle for Exclusiveness: The ECJ and Competing International Tribunals" in Isabelle Buffard et al (eds) *International Law between Universalism and Fragmentation: Festschrift in Honour of Gerhard Hafner* (Martinus Nijhoff 2008) 1045–1068.
"Art 2" in Oliver Dörr and Kirsten Schmalenbach (eds) *Vienna Convention on the Law of Treaties – A Commentary* (Springer 2nd ed 2018).
"Article 26" in Oliver Dörr and Kirsten Schmalenbach (eds) *Vienna Convention on the Law of Treaties – A Commentary* (Springer 2nd ed 2018).
"Article 27" in Oliver Dörr and Kirsten Schmalenbach (eds) *Vienna Convention on the Law of Treaties – A Commentary* (Springer 2nd ed 2018) 493–504.
"Art. 216 AEUV" in Christian Calliess and Matthias Ruffert (eds) *EUV/AEUV* (CH Beck 6th ed 2022) 2063–2083.
"Art. 218 AEUV" in Christian Calliess and Matthias Ruffert (eds) *EUV/AEUV* (CH Beck 6th ed 2022) 2096–2107.
Schöneberger, Christoph, "Identitäterä – Verfassungsidentität zwischen Widerstandsformel und Musealisierung des Grundgesetzes" (2015) 63 Jahrbuch des öffentlichen Rechts der Gegenwart 41–62.

Schopenhauer, Arthur, "Further Psychological Observations" in Arthur Schopenhauer, *Suffering, Suicide and Immortality. Eight Essays from The Parerga* (selected and translated by T Bailey Saunders Dover 2006 [*Parerga und Paralipomena. Kleine Philosophische Schriften* 1851]) 39–62.

The World as Will and Representation Vol I (translated by Judith Norman and Alistair Welchman and edited by Christopher Janaway Cambridge University Press 2010 [*Die Welt als Wille und Vorstellung* 1818]).

The World as Will and Representation Vol II (translated by Judith Norman and Alistair Welchman and edited by Christopher Janaway Cambridge University Press 2018 [*Die Welt als Wille und Vorstellung* 1848]).

Schroeder, Renée, *Die Henne und das Ei: Auf der Suche nach dem Ursprung des Lebens* (Residenz 2011).

Schroeder, Werner, *Das Gemeinschaftsrechtssystem: Eine Untersuchung zu den rechtsdogmatischen, rechtstheoretischen und verfassungsrechtlichen Grundlagen des Systemdenkens im Europäischen Gemeinschaftsrecht* (Mohr Siebeck 2002).

"Die Europäische Union als Völkerrechtssubjekt" in Walter Obwexer (ed) *Die Europäische Union im Völkerrecht* 2 (2012) Europarecht-Beiheft 9–24.

"Customary International Law in the European Union Legal System: Reception, Rank, Application and Interpretation" in Fernando Lusa Bordin, Andreas Th Müller and Francisco Pascual-Vives (eds) *The European Union and Customary International Law* (Cambridge University Press 2022) 177–209.

Schulte, Joachim, *Wittgenstein. Eine Einführung* (Reclam 2nd ed 2016).

Schuppert, Gunnar Folke, "Europa im Verfassungsfieber – Bemerkungen zu Sinn und Unsinn der europäischen Verfassungsdebatte" in Ines Katenhusen and Wolfram Lamping (eds) *Demokratien in Europa: Der Einfluss der europäischen Integration auf Institutionenwandel und neue Konturen des demokratischen Verfassungsstaates* (Springer 2003) 91–116.

Schweitzer, Michael, *Das Völkergewohnheitsrecht und seine Geltung für neuentstehende Staaten* (Gehlen 1969).

Schwöbel, Christine E J, *Global Constitutionalism in International Legal Perspective* (Martinus Nijhoff Publishers 2011).

Seinecke, Ralf, "Recht und Rechtspluralismus: Forschungsperspektiven der 'Rechts'-Wissenschaften und 'Rechts'-Philosophie" in Carsten Bäcker and Sascha Ziemann (eds) *Junge Rechtsphilosophie* (Franz Steiner 2012)143–158.

Selby, Jane M and Bradley, Ben S, "Infants in Groups: A Paradigm for the Study of Early Social Experience" (2003) 46 (4) Human Development 197–221.

Sellars, Wilfrid, *Empiricism and the Philosophy of Mind* (Harvard University Press 2nd ed 1997).

Sellers, Mortimer and Tomaszewski, Tadeusz (eds), *The Rule of Law in Comparative Perspective* (Springer 2010).

Shakespeare, William, *Romeo and Juliet* (John Danter 1597).

Shaw, Malcolm N, *International Law* (Cambridge University Press 7th ed 2014).

Sibley, William M, "The Rational versus the Reasonable" (1953) 62 (4) Philosophical Review 554–560.

Siegel, Daniel J, *The Developing Mind: How Relationships and the Brain Interact to Shape Who We Are* (Guilford 1999).

Simma, Bruno and Alston, Philip G, "The Sources of Human Rights Law: Custom, Jus Cogens, and General Principles" (1988–1989) 12 Australian Yearbook of International Law 82–108.

Simmons, A John, "Justification and Legitimacy" (1999) 109 (4) Ethics 739–771, reprinted in Simmons, A John, *Justification and Legitimacy – Essays on Rights and Obligations* (Cambridge University Press 2001) 122–157.

Solomon, Robert C, *From Rationalism to Existentialism: The Existentialists and Their Nineteenth-Century Backgrounds* (Rowman & Littlefield 2001).

Somek, Alexander, "Monism: A Tale of the Undead" in Matej Avbelj and Jan Komárek (eds) *Constitutional Pluralism in the European Union* (Hart 2012) 343–379.

The Cosmopolitan Constitution (Oxford University Press 2014).

Sørensen, Max, "Principes de droit international public" (1960) 101 Recueil des Cours III 1–254.

"Theory and Reality in International Law" (1981) 75 Proceedings of the American Society of International Law 140–149.

Spieker, Luke Dimitrios, *EU Values before the Court of Justice. Foundations, Potential, Risks* (Oxford University Press 2023).

Stammler, Rudolf, *Die Lehre vom richtigen Rechte* (De Gruyter 1902).

Starke, Joseph G, "Monism and Dualism in the Theory of International Law" (1936) 17 British Yearbook of International Law 66–81.

Stein, Ted L, "The Approach of the Different Drummer: The Principle of the Persistent Objector in International Law" (1985) 26 (2) Harvard International Law Journal 457–482.

Stern, Daniel N, *The Interpersonal World of the Infant. A View from Psychoanalysis and Development Psychology* (Basic Books 1985).

The Interpersonal World of the Infant. A View from Psychoanalysis and Development Psychology (Basic Books 1st paperback ed 2000).

Forms of Vitality. Exploring Dynamic Experience in Psychology and the Arts (Oxford University Press 2010).

Stettner, Rupert, "Europäisches Gemeinschaftsrecht als Quelle der Rechtsfindung deutscher Gerichte 1974–1984" (1986) 111 (3–4) Archiv des öffentlichen Rechts 359–413 and 537–594.

Stollmann, Rainer, *Groteske Aufklärung. Studien zu Natur und Kultur des Lachens* (M & P 1997).

Streinz, Rudolf, "Artikel 23" in Michae Sachs (ed) *Grundgesetz* (CH Beck 7th ed 2014).

Strupp, Karl, "Les règles générales du droit international de la paix" (1934) 47 Recueil des Cours I 259–595.

Suhler, L Christopher and Churchland, Patricia S, "Can Innate, Modular 'Foundations' Explain Morality? Challenges for Haidt's Moral Foundations Theory" (2011) 23 (9) Journal of Cognitive Neuroscience 2103–2116.

Suteu, Silvia, "The Populist Turn in Central and Eastern Europe: Is Deliberative Democracy Part of the Solution?" (2019) 15 (3) European Constitutional Law Review 488–518.

Taki, Hiroshi, "*Opinio Juris* and the Formation of Customary International Law: A Theoretical Analysis" (2008) 51 German Yearbook of International Law 447–466.

Talmon, Stefan, "Determining Customary International Law: The ICJ's Methodology between Induction, Deduction and Assertion" (2015) 26 (2) European Journal of International Law 417–443.

Tamanaha, Brian Z, "Understanding Legal Pluralism: Past to Present, Local to Global" (2008) 30 (3) Sydney Law Review 375–411.

Tarski, Alfred, "The Concept of Truth in Formalized Languages" in Alfred Tarski, *Logic, Semantics, Metamathematics* (Hackett 2nd ed 1983 [1935]) 152–278.

Tasioulas, John, "*Opinio Juris* and the Genesis of Custom: A Solution to the 'Paradox'" (2007) 26 Australian Yearbook of International Law 199–205.

"Custom, Jus Cogens, and Human Rights" in Curtis A Bradley (ed) *Custom's Future: International Law in a Changing World* (Cambridge University Press 2016) 95–116.

Terhechte, Philipp, "Article 216 TFEU" in Jürgen Schwarze (ed) *EU-Kommentar* (Nomos 4th ed 2018).

"Article 218 TFEU" in Jürgen Schwarze (ed) *EU-Kommentar* (Nomos 4th ed 2018).

Teubner, Gunther, "Globale Bukowina" (1996) 15 Rechtshistorisches Journal 255–290.

"Global Bukowina: Legal Pluralism in World Society" in Gunther Teubner (ed) *Global Law without a State* (Dartmouth 1997) 3–28.

"Globale Zivilverfassungen: Alternativen zur staatszentrierten Verfassungstheorie" (2003) 63 Heidelberg Journal of International Law 1–28.

Constitutional Fragments: Societal Constitutionalism and Globalization (translated by Gareth Norbury Oxford University Press 2012).

Thaler, Michael, "Rechtsphilosophie und das Verhältnis zwischen Gemeinschaftsrecht und nationalem Recht" (2000) 8 Journal für Rechtspolitik 75–84.

Theosophy, "Ancient Landmarks: Plato and Aristotle" (1939) 27 (11) Theosophy 483–491.

Thienel, Rudolf, "Ein 'komplexer' oder ein normativer Bundesstaatsbegriff?" (1991) 42 Österreichische Zeitschrift für öffentliches Recht und Völkerrecht (ZÖR) 215–252.

Thomas, Frederik, "Das Maastricht-Judgment des dänischen Obersten Gerichtshofs vom 6. April 1998" (1998) 58 Heidelberg Journal of International Law 879–906.

Thomson, Judith Jarvis, "Killing, Letting Die, and the Trolley Problem" (1976) 59 (2) The Monist 204–217.

"The Trolley Problem" (1985) 94 (6) Yale Law Journal 1395–1415.

Thym, Daniel, "In the Name of Sovereign Statehood: A Critical Introduction to the Lisbon Judgment of the German Constitutional Court" (2009) 46 (6) Common Market Law Review 1795–1822.

Tomasello, Michael, *The Cultural Origins of Human Cognition* (Harvard University Press 1999).

Tomasello, Michael and Vaish, Amrisha, "Origins of Human Cooperation and Morality" (2013) 64 Annual Review of Psychology 231–255.

et al, "Understanding and Sharing Intentions: The Origins of Cultural Cognition" (2005) 28 (5) Behavioral & Brain Sciences 1–61.

Trejo-Mathys, Jonathan, "Neo-Kantianism in the Philosophy of Law: Its Value and Actuality" in Nicolas de Warren and Andrea Staiti (eds) *New Approaches to Neo-Kantianism* (Cambridge University Press 2015) 147–170.

Trevarthen, Colwyn, "Communication and Cooperation in Early Infancy. A Description of Primary Intersubjectivity" in Margaret Bullowa (ed) *Before Speech: The Beginning of Human Communication* (Cambridge University Press 1979) 321–347.

"How Control of Movements Develops" in H T A Whiting (ed) *Human Motor Actions: Bernstein Reassessed* (Elsevier 1984) 223–261.

"Development of Intersubjective Motor Control in Infants" in Michael G Wade and H T A Whiting (eds) *Motor Development in Children: Aspects of Coordination and Control* (Martinus Nijhof 1986) 209–261.

"Form, Significance and Psychological Potential of Hand Gestures of Infants" in Jean-Luc Nespoulous, Paul Perron and André Roch Lecours (eds) *The Biological Foundation of Gestures: Motor and Semiotic Aspects* (Erlbaum 1986) 149–202.

"An Infant's Motives for Speaking and Thinking in the Culture" in Astrid H Wold (ed) *The Dialogical Alternative: Towards a Theory of Language and Mind. Festschrift für Ragnar Rommetveit* (Scandinavian University Press/Oxford University Press 1992) 99–137.

"The Concept and Foundations of Infant Intersubjectivity" in Stein Bråten (ed) *Intersubjective Communication and Emotion in Early Ontogeny* (Cambridge University Press 1998) 15–46.

"The Neurobiology of Early Communication: Intersubjective Regulations in Human Brain Development" in Alex Fedde Kalverboer and Albert Gramsbergen (eds) *Handbook on Brain and Behavior in Human Development* (Kluwer 2001) 841–882.

"First Things First: Infants Make Good Use of the Sympathetic Rhythm of Imitation, without Reason or Language" (2005) 31 (1) Journal of Child Psychotherapy 91–113.

"The Intersubjective Psychobiology of Human Meaning: Learning of Culture Depends on Interest for Co-operative Practical Work and Affection for the Joyful Art of Good Company" (2009) 19 Psychoanalytic Dialogues 507–518.

"The Generation of Human Meaning: How Shared Experience Grows in Infancy" in Alex Seemann (ed) *Joint Attention: New Developments in Philosophy, Psychology, and Neuroscience* (MIT Press 2011) 73–135.

"What Is It Like to Be a Person Who Knows Nothing? Defining the Active Intersubjective Mind of a Newborn Human Being" (2011) 20 (1) Infant and Child Development 119–135.

"Embodied Human Intersubjectivity: Imaginative Agency, to Share Meaning" (2012) 4 (1) Cognitive Semiotics 6–56.

Trevarthen, Colwyn and Aitken, Ken, "Infant Intersubjectivity: Research, Theory, and Clinical Applications" (2001) 42 (1) Journal of Child Psychology and Psychiatry 3–48.

Trevarthen, Colwyn and Bjørkvold, Jon-Roar, "Life for Learning. How a Young Child Seeks Joy with Companions in a Meaningful World" in Darcia Narvaez et al (eds) *Contexts for Young Child Flourishing: Evolution, Family, and Society* (Oxford University Press 2016) 28–60.

Trevarthen, Colwyn and Delafield-Butt, Jonathan, "Biology of Shared Meaning and Language Development: Regulating the Life of Narratives" in Maria Legerstee, David W Haley and Marc H Bornstein (eds) *The Infant Mind: Origins of the Social Brain* (Guilford Press 2013) 167–199.

"Intersubjectivity in the Imagination and Feelings of the Infant: Implications for Education in the Early Years" in E Jayne White and Carmen Dalli (eds) *Under-Three Year Olds in Policy and Practice* (Springer 2017) 17–39.

Trevarthen, Colwyn, Delafield-Butt, Jonathan and Schögler, Benjamin, "Psychobiology of Musical Gesture: Innate Rhythm, Harmony and Melody in Movements of Narration" in Anthony Gritten and Elaine King (eds) *Music and Gesture II* (Ashgate 2011) 11–43.

Trevarthen, Colwyn, Gratier, Maya and Osborne, Nigel, "The Human Nature of Culture and Education" (2014) 5 (2) Cognitive Science 173–192.

Trevarthen, Colwyn and Hubley, Penelope, "Secondary Intersubjectivity: Confidence, Confiding and Acts of Meaning in the First Year" in Andrew Lock (ed) *Action, Gesture and Symbol* (Academic Press 1978) 183–229.

Triepel, Heinrich, *Völkerrecht und Landesrecht* (C L Hirschfeld 1899).

Tunkin, Grigory I, "Remarks on the Juridical Nature of Customary Norms of International Law" (1961) 49 (3) California Law Review 419–430.

Theory of International Law (translated by W E Butler George Allen & Unwin 1974).

Tuori, Kaarlo, *European Constitutionalism* (Cambridge University Press 2015).

Twining, William, "A Post-Westphalian Conception of Law" (2003) 37 (1) Law and Society Review 199–258.

Tzevelekos, Vassilis, "Juris Dicere: Custom as a Matrix, Custom as a Norm, and the Role of Judges and (Their) Ideology in Custom Making" in Nikolas M Rajkovic et al (eds) *Power of Legality: Practices of International Law and Their Politics* (Cambridge University Press 2016) 188–208.

Tzu, Chuang, *The Complete Works of Chuang Tzu* (translated by Burton Watson Columbia University Press 1968).

Uerpmann-Wittzack, Robert, "The Constitutional Role of International Law" in Armin von Bogdandy and Jürgen Bast (eds) *Principles of European Constitutional Law* (Hart et al 2nd ed 2011) 131–167.

Uitz, Renata, "National Constitutional Identity in the European Constitutional Project: A Recipe for Exposing Cover Ups and Masquerades" (November 11, 2016) Verfassungsblog, available at https://verfassungsblog.de/national-constitutional-identity-in-the-european-constitutional-project-a-recipe-for-exposing-cover-ups-and-masquerades/ [last accessed February 1, 2023].

Van der Schyff, Gerhard, "EU Member State Constitutional Identity: A Comparison of Germany and the Netherlands as Polar Opposites" (2016) 76 Heidelberg Journal of International Law 167–191.

Van Elsuwege, Peter, "The Potential for Inter-Institutional Conflicts before the Court of Justice: Impact of the Lisbon Treaty" in Marise Cremona and Anne Thies (eds) *The European Court of Justice and External Relations Law – Constitutional Challenges* (Hart 2016) 115–136.

Van Roermund, Bert, "Norm-Claims, Validity, and Self-Reference" in Luís Duarte d'Almeida, John Gardner and Leslie Green (eds) *Kelsen Revisited: New Essays on the Pure Theory of Law* (Hart Publishing 2013) 11–42.

Van Sliedregt, Elies, *Individual Criminal Responsibility in International Law* (Oxford University Press 2012).

Vanderlinden, Jacques, "Le pluralisme juridique: essai de synthèse" in John Gilissen (ed) *Le Pluralisme juridique* (Université Libre de Bruxelles 1971) 19–56.

"Return to Legal Pluralism: Twenty Years Later" (1989) 21 (28) Journal of Legal Pluralism 149–157.

Vasak, Karel, "Was bedeutet die Aussage, ein Staatsvertrag sei 'self-executing'? – Zum Erkenntnis des Verfassungsgerichtshofs vom 27.6. 1960, B 469/59" (1961) 24 Juristische Blätter 352.

Verdross, Alfred, *Die völkerrechtswidrige Kriegshandlung und der Strafanspruch der Staaten* (Engelmann 1920).

"Grundlagen und Grundlegungen des Völkerrechts – ein Beitrag zu den Hypothesen des Völkerrechtspositivismus" (1921) 29 Niemeyers Zeitschrift für internationales Recht 65–91.

Die Einheit des rechtlichen Weltbildes auf Grundlage der Völkerrechtsverfassung (J C B Mohr 1923).

Die Verfassung der Völkerrechtsgemeinschaft (Springer 1926).

"Le fondement du droit international" (1927) 16 Recueil des cours I 247–323.

"Droit international public et droit interne" (1954) 32 Revue de Droit International, de Sciences Diplomatiques et Politiques 219.

"Das völkerrechtliche Gewohnheitsrecht" (1963) 7 Japanese Annual of International Law 1–7.

"Entstehungsweisen und Geltungsgrund des universellen völkerrechtlichen Gewohnheitsrechts" (1969) 29 Heidelberg Journal of International Law 635–653.

"Die normative Verknüpfung von Völkerrecht und staatlichem Recht" in Max Imboden et al (eds) *Festschrift für Adolf Julius Merkl zum 80. Geburtstag* (Wilhelm Fink 1970) 425–441.

Verdross, Alfred and Simma, Bruno, *Universelles Völkerrecht – Theorie und Praxis* (Duncker & Humblot 3rd ed 1984).

Verhoeven, Maartje, *The Costanzo Obligation. The Obligations of National Administrative Authorities in the Case of Incompatibility between National Law and European Law* (Intersentia 2011).

Villiger, Mark E, *Customary International Law and Treaties: A Study of Their Interactions and Interrelations with Special Consideration of the 1969 Vienna Convention on the Law of Treaties* (Martinus Nijhoff 1985).

"Article 46" in Mark E Villiger (ed) *Commentary on the 1969 Vienna Convention on the Law of Treaties* (Brill 2009) 583–594.

Vincze, Attila, "Das tschechische Verfassungsgericht stoppt den EuGH. Zum Urteil des tschechischen Verfassungsgerichts Pl. ÚS 5/12 vom 14.2.2012" (2013) 48 (2) Europarecht 194–204.

"Unsere Gedanken sind Sprengstoff – Zum Vorrang des Europarechts in der Rechtsprechung des ungarischen Verfassungsgerichts" (2022) 49 Europäische Grundrechte Zeitschrift 13–21.

Voegelin, Erich, "Kelsen's Pure Theory of Law" (1927) 42 (2) Political Science Quarterly 268–276.

Der autoritäre Staat. Ein Versuch über das österreichische Staatsproblem (Springer 1997 [1936]).

Von Benda-Beckmann, Franz, "Anthropology and Comparative Law" in Keebet von Benda-Beckmann and Fons Strijbosch (eds) *Anthropology of Law in the Netherlands* (Foris 1966) 90–109.

"Who's Afraid of Legal Pluralism?" (2002) 34 (47) Journal of Legal Pluralism and Unofficial Law 37–83.
Von Benda-Beckmann, Franz and von Benda-Beckmann, Keebet, "The Dynamics of Change and Continuity in Plural Legal Orders" (2006) 53–54 Special double issue of the Journal of Legal Pluralism and Unofficial Law 1–44.
Von Bernstorff, Jochen, *The Public International Law Theory of Hans Kelsen: Believing in Universal Law* (Cambridge University Press 2010).
Von Bogdandy, Armin, "Konstitutionalisierung des europäischen öffentlichen Rechts in der europäischen Republik" (2005) 60 (11) JuristenZeitung 529–540.
"Pluralism, Direct Effect, and the Ultimate Say: On the Relationship between International and Domestic Constitutional Law" (2008) 6 (3–4) International Journal of Constitutional Law 397–413.
"Common Principles for a Plurality of Orders: A Study on Public Authority in the European Legal Area" (2014) 12 (4) International Journal of Constitutional Law 980–1007.
Von Bogdandy, Armin and Schill, Stephan, "Overcoming Absolute Primacy: Respect for National Identity under the Lisbon Treaty" (2011) 48 (5) Common Market Law Review 1417–1454.
Von Bogdandy, Armin and Sonnevend, Pál (eds) *Constitutional Crisis in the European Union. Theory, Law and Politics in Hungary and Romania* (Hart/Beck 2015).
Von Danwitz, Thomas, "Einheitliche Auslegung und Vorrang des Unionsrechts im Dialog der Gerichte" Verfassunbslog (October 27, 2022), available at https://verfassungsblog.de/einheitliche-auslegung-und-vorrang-des-unionsrechts-im-dialog-der-gerichte/ [last accessed February 1, 2023].
Von der Pfordten, Dietmar, *Rechtsphilosophie. Eine Einführung* (CH Beck 2013).
Von Kleist, Heinrich, "An Wilhelmine von Zenge, Berlin, d. 22t März, 1801" [letter to Wilhelmine von Zenge] in Dieter Heimböckel (ed) *Heinrich von Kleist. Sämtliche Briefe* (Reclam 1991) 209–215.
Von Rintelen, Fritz-Joachim, "Philosophical Idealism in Germany: The Way from Kant to Hegel and the Present" (1977) 38 Philosophy and Phenomenological Research 1–32.
Voßkuhle, Andreas, "Multilevel Cooperation of the European Constitutional Courts: Der Europäische Verfassungsgerichtsverbund" (2010) 6 (2) European Constitutional Law Review 175–198.
"'European Integration through Law.' The Contribution of the Federal Constitutional Court" (2017) 58 (1) European Journal of Sociology 145–168.
"Interview Erfolg ist eher kalt" Die Zeit May 14, 2020.
Vranes, Erich, "Lex superior, lex specialis, lex posterior – Rechtsnatur der 'Konfliktlösungsregeln'" (2005) 65 Heidelberg Journal of International Law 391–405.
"The Definition of 'Norm Conflict' in International Law and Legal Theory" (2006) 17 (2) European Journal of International Law 395–418.
Wagner, Andreas, "Francisco de Vitoria and Alberico Gentili on the Legal Character of the Global Commonwealth" (2011) 31 (3) Oxford Journal of Legal Studies 565–582.
"Alberico Gentili: Sovereignty, Natural Law, and the System of Roman Civil Law" in Stefan Kadelbach, Thomas Kleinlein and David Roth–Isigkeit (eds) *System,*

Order, and International Law: The Early History of International Legal Thought from Machiavelli to Hegel (Oxford University Press 2017) 92–114.

Walden, Raphael M, "The Subjective Element in the Formation of Customary International Law" (1977) 12 (3) Israel Law Review 344–364.

Waldock, Humphrey, "The Legal Basis of the Continental Shelf" (1950) 36 Transactions of the Grotius Society 115–148.

Waldron, Jeremy, *Law and Disagreement* (Oxford University Press 1999).

Walker, Neil, "The Idea of Constitutional Pluralism" (2002) 65 (3) Modern Law Review 317–359.

"Late Sovereignty in the European Union" in Neil Walker (ed) *Sovereignty in Transition* (Hart 2003) 3–32.

Intimations of Global Law (Cambridge University Press 2014).

"Constitutional Pluralism Revisited" (2016) 22 (3) European Law Journal 333–355.

Walter, Christian and Vordermayer, Markus, "Verfassungsidentität als Instrument richterlicher Selbstbeschränkung in transnaitonalen Integrationsprozessen. Vergleichende Überlegungen anhand der Rechtsprechung von EuGH und EGMR" (2015) 63 Jahrbuch des öffentlichen Rechts der Gegenwart 129–166.

Walter, Maja, "Integrationsgrenze Verfassungsidentität – Konzept und Kontrolle aus europäischer, deutscher und französischer Perspektive" (2012) 72 Heidelberg Journal of International Law 177–200.

Walter, Robert, "Entstehung und Entwicklung des Gedankens der Grundnorm" in Robert Walter (ed) *Schwerpunkte der Reinen Rechtslehre* (Manz 1992) 47–59.

"Die Grundnorm im System der Reinen Rechtslehre" in Aulis Aarnio et al (eds) *Rechtsnorm und Rechtswirklichkeit: Festschrift für Werner Krawietz* (Duncker & Humblot 1993) 53–74.

Waluchow, Wil, "Constitutionalism" in Edward N Zalta (ed) *Stanford Encyclopedia of Philosophy* (December 20, 2017), available at https://plato.stanford.edu/entries/constitutionalism/ [last accessed February 1, 2023].

Walz, Gustav A, *Völkerrecht und staatliches Recht: Untersuchung über die Einwirkungen des Völkerrechts auf das innerstaatliche Recht* (W Kohlhammer 1933).

Warneken, Felix and Tomasello, Michael, "Varieties of Altruism in Children and Chimpanzees" (2009) 13 Trends in Cognitive Sciences 397–402.

Weber, Karl, *Kriterien des Bundesstaates: Eine systematische, historische und rechtsvergleichende Untersuchung der Bundesstaatlichkeit der Schweiz, der Bundesrepublik Deutschland und Österreichs* (Braumüller 1980).

Weber, Teresa, "Die völkerrechtskonforme Auslegung von Unionsrecht – primär nur bei Sekundärrecht, nur sekundär bei Primärrecht?" (2013) 68 Zeitschrift für Öffentliches Recht 389–416.

Wehberg, Hans, "Pacta Sunt Servanda" (1959) 53 (4) American Journal of International Law 775–786.

Wetz, Kassandra, *Funktionen von Verfassungsidentität als gerichtliches Konzept in der Europäischen Union* (Mohr Siebeck 2021).

Weiler, Joseph H H, "Epilogue. The European Courts of Justice: Beyond "Beyond Doctrine" or the Legitimacy Crisis of European Constitutionalism" in Anne-Marie Slaughter, Alex Stone Sweet and Joseph H H Weiler (eds) *The European Court and National Courts – Doctrine and Jurisprudence: Legal Change in its Social Context* (Hart 1998) 365–391.

"Europe: The Case against the Case of Statehood" (1998) 4 (1) European Law Journal 43–62.
"Prologue: Global and Pluralist Constitutionalism – Some Doubts" in Gráinne de Búrca and Joseph H H Weiler (eds) *The Worlds of European Constitutionalism* (Cambridge University Press 2012) 8–18.
Weiler, Joseph H H and Haltern, Ulrich R, "The Autonomy of the Community Legal Order – Through the Looking Glass" (1996) 37 (2) Harvard International Law Journal 411–448.
Weinberger, Ota, *Norm und Institution – Eine Einführung in die Theorie des Rechts* (Manz 1988).
Weiner, Joan, "Frege and the Linguistic Turn" (1997) 25 (2) Philosophical Topics 265–288.
Weiß, Wolfgang, "Verfassungsanforderungen und Integrationsverantwortung beibeschließenden Vertragsorganen in Freihandelsabkommen" (2016) 27 Europäische Zeitschrift für Wirtschaftsrecht 286–291.
Wendel, Mattias, *Permeabilität im europäischen Verfassungsrecht: verfassungsrechtliche Integrationsnormen auf Staats- und Unionsebene im Vergleich* (Mohr Siebeck 2011).
Wessel, Ramses A, "Reconsidering the Relationship between International and EU Law" in Enzo Cannizzaro, Paolo Palchetti and Ramses A Wessel (eds) *International Law as Law of the European Union* (Martinus Nijhoff 2012) 7–33.
"The EU and International Law" in Ramses A Wessel and Joris Larik (eds) *EU External Relations Law. Text, Cases and Materials* (Hart 2nd ed 2020) 139–174.
Wiederin, Ewald, "Was ist und welche Konsequenzen hat ein Normkonflikt" (1990) 22 Rechtstheorie 311–333.
Bundesrecht und Landesrecht. Zugleich ein Beitrag zu Strukturproblemen der bundesstaatlichen Kompetenzverteilung in Österreich und in Deutschland (Springer 1995).
"Deutschland über alles: Das Lissabon-Urteil des Bundesverfassungsgerichts" (2010) 48 (9) Österreichische Juristenzeitung 398–406.
"Der österreichische Verfassungsgerichtshof als Schöpfung Hans Kelsens und sein Modellcharakter als eigenständiges Verfassungsgericht" in Thomas Simon and Johannes Kalowada (eds) *Schutz der Verfassung: Normen, Institutionen, Höchst- und Verfassungsgerichte* (Duncker & Humblot 2013) 283–315.
Wildhaber, Luzius, *Treaty-Making Power and Constitution – An International and Comparative Study* (Helbing and Lichtenhahn 1971).
Wildhaber, Luzius and Breitenmoser, Stephan, "The Relationship between Customary International Law and Municipal Law in Western European Countries" (1988) 48 Heidelberg Journal of International Law 163–207.
Willey, Thomas A, *Back to Kant. The Revival of Kantianism in German Social and Historical Thought 1860–1914* (Wayne State University Press 1978).
Wimmer, Heinz and Perner, Josef, "Beliefs about Beliefs: Representation and Constraining Function of Wrong Beliefs in Young Children's Understanding of Deception" (1983) 13 (1) Cognition 103–128.
Windelband, Wilhelm, *Präludien: Aufsätze und Reden zur Philosophie und ihrer Geschichte Vol I* (Mohr 5th ed 1915).
"'Philosophy of Culture and Transcendental Idealism' (1910)" in Sebastian Luft (ed) *The Neo-Kantian Reader* (translated by Alan Duncan Routledge 2015

["Kulturphilosophie und transzendentaler Idealismus" in Wilhelm Windelband, *Präludien. Aufsätze und Reden zur Philosophie und ihrer Geschichte* Vol II (Mohr 5th ed 1915) 279–294]) 317–324.

Winkler, Roland, *Integrationsverfassungsrecht: Das österreichische Verfassungsrecht und das Recht der Europäischen Union – Koordination, Kooperation, Konflikt* (Springer 2003).

Wittgenstein, Ludwig, *Philosophical Investigations* (translated by G E M Anscombe Basil Blackwell 2nd ed 1958 reprinted 1986 [*Philosophische Untersuchungen* 1953]).

On Certainty (translated by G E M Anscombe and Denis Paul and edited by G E M Anscombe and G H von Wright Harper 1972 [*Über Gewißheit* 1969]).

Tractatus Logico-Philosophicus (translated by Kevin C Klement alongside both the Ogden/Ramsey and Pears/McGuinness English translations 2015 [original German Kegan Paul 1922]), available at http://people.umass.edu/klement/tlp/tlp.pdf [last accessed February 1, 2023].

Woleński, Jan, "The History of Epistemology" in Ilkka Niiniluoto, Matti Sintonen and Jan Woleński (eds) *Handbook of Epistemology* (Springer 2004) 3–54.

Wolff, Jonathan, *An Introduction to Political Philosophy* (Oxford University Press 1996).

Wolfke, Karol, *Custom in Present International Law* (Tow Nauk 1964).

Custom in Present International Law (Springer 2nd ed 1993).

Wolfrum, Rüdiger and Pichon, Jakob, "Consensus" in Rüdiger Wolfrum (ed) *Max Planck Encyclopedia of Public International Law* (Oxford University Press 2010).

Woodman, Gordon R, "Ideological Combat and Social Observation: Recent Debate about Legal Pluralism" (1998) 30 (42) Journal of Legal Pluralism 21–59.

Worster, William T, "The Inductive and Deductive Methods in Customary International Law Analysis: Traditional and Modern Approaches" (2014) 45 (2) Georgetown Journal of International Law 445–521.

Wouters, Dirk, "The External Relations of the European Union Since Lisbon: A Practitioner's Perspective" in Jenő Czuczai and Frederik Naert (eds) *The EU as a Global Actor - Bridging Legal Theory and Practice: Liber Amicorum in Honour of Ricardo Gosalbo Bono* (Brill Nijhoff 2017) 65–86.

Wouters, Jan, Odermatt, Jed and Ramopoulos, Thomas, "Worlds Apart? Comparing the Approaches of the European Court of Justice and the EU Legislature to International Law" in Marise Cremona and Anne Thies (eds) *The European Court of Justice and External Relations Law – Constitutional Challenges* (Hart 2016) 249–279.

Wouters, Jan A et al (eds) *The Law of EU External Relations: Cases, Materials, and Commentary on the EU as an International Legal Actor* (Oxford University Press 3rd ed 2021).

Young, James O, "The Coherence Theory of Truth" in Edward N Zalta (ed) *Stanford Encyclopedia of Philosophy* (June 26, 2018), available at https://plato.stanford.edu/entries/truth-coherence/ [last accessed February 1, 2023].

Zahavi, Dan, *Self and Other: Exploring Subjectivity, Empathy, and Shame* (Oxford University Press 2014).

Zoglauer, Thomas, *Normenkonflikte – zur Logik und Rationalität ethischen Argumentierens* (Frommann-Holzboog 1998).

Zolo, Danilo, "Hans Kelsen: International Peace through International Law" (1998) 9 (2) European Journal of International Law 306–324.

Index

For EU product safety concerns, contact us at Calle de José Abascal, 56–1°, 28003 Madrid, Spain or eugpsr@cambridge.org.

www.ingramcontent.com/pod-product-compliance
Lightning Source LLC
LaVergne TN
LVHW011700200926
848484LV00004B/1010
9781009380201